SECURED FINANCE LAW IN CHINA AND HONG KONG

This book examines systematically the current systems of secured lending in China and Hong Kong, where companies or individuals offer personal property as security for credit advanced by a lender. Valid and enforceable security reduces the risk to the lender and so lowers the cost of credit to the borrower. However, the Hong Kong system, being largely derived from English law, is highly complex and in need of root-and-branch reform. The forces of inaction have triumphed and valuable opportunities to create a modern, rational and efficient system have been squandered. In China, on the other hand, a completely new system has been created in the last twenty years which, whilst it has various problems and defects, has some notable advantages over the common law equivalent found in Hong Kong.

MARK WILLIAMS is Professor of Law at the School of Accounting and Finance, Hong Kong Polytechnic University.

LU HAITIAN is Assistant Professor of Law at the School of Accounting and Finance, Hong Kong Polytechnic University.

ONG CHIN-AUN served as Associate Professor of Law at the School of Accounting and Finance, Hong Kong Polytechnic University.

SECURED FINANCE LAW IN CHINA AND HONG KONG

MARK WILLIAMS,
LU HAITIAN
AND
ONG CHIN-AUN

CAMBRIDGE
UNIVERSITY PRESS

CAMBRIDGE UNIVERSITY PRESS
Cambridge, New York, Melbourne, Madrid, Cape Town, Singapore,
São Paulo, Delhi, Dubai, Tokyo, Mexico City

Cambridge University Press
The Edinburgh Building, Cambridge CB2 8RU, UK

Published in the United States of America by Cambridge University Press, New York

www.cambridge.org
Information on this title: www.cambridge.org/9780521519342

First published 2010

Printed in the United Kingdom at the University Press, Cambridge

A catalogue record for this publication is available from the British Library

Library of Congress Cataloguing in Publication data
Williams, Mark, LL.B.
Secured finance law in China and Hong Kong / Mark Williams,
Haitian Lu, Chin Aun Ong.
p. cm.
Includes bibliographical references and index.
ISBN 978-0-521-51934-2
1. Security (Law)–China. 2. Security (Law)–China–Hong Kong.
I. Lu, Haitian. II. Ong, C. A. III. Title.
KNQ859.W554 2010
346.5107′4–dc22
2010021899

ISBN 978-0-521-51934-2 Hardback

CONTENTS

PREFACE

This book owes its genesis to a tragedy. Some six years ago, my dear friend, Ong Chin-aun, died quite unexpectedly. He had just completed a PhD thesis which had been submitted to Bond University, Australia. The dissertation compared the law of Hong Kong and the Philippines in relation to credit advances that were secured against personal property rights. Sadly, he did not live to celebrate the award of his degree and his doctorate was bestowed posthumously.

As a result of this chain of events, and with the enthusiastic agreement of his widow, Rebecca, I conceived the notion to have a modified version of his manuscript published. The result is this book. Lu Haitian and I have worked together to rewrite the original text and to alter its focus, but not its analytical structure, to compare the common law-based provisions relating to personal property credit security lending in Hong Kong with the new chinese law which is largely (though exclusively based on civilian concepts.

This book attempts to create a comprehensive analytical framework to assess whether either system of credit security law can be assessed as being 'efficient'. As the reader will discover, we come to the conclusion that neither of them pass muster, though for different reasons. The current state of the law in Hong Kong is in the same deplorable state as it is in England, largely as a result of the plethora of security devices and the highly technical, complex and (often) confusing legal rules that govern their creation and perfection.

The English Law Commission has recommended substantial change in relation to security devices over personal property but there seems little evidence of support from the United Kingdom Parliament. The Companies Act 2006 made no substantial change to corporate security structures over personal property and there seems little prospect that a new regime for secured interests over personal property granted by individual or corporate borrowers will be introduced in the foreseeable future, despite the manifold weaknesses that have been identified in existing arrangements.

Unfortunately, the same reluctance to countenance change is evident in Hong Kong. As regards corporate security, the Hong Kong authorities appear unlikely to adopt substantial change to the existing system in the long overdue rewrite of the Hong Kong Companies Ordinance. The new legislation is due to be published in draft in 2010 and is likely to mirror the English statute and will probably only make cosmetic changes to the company security regime. More generally, the Law Reform Commission of Hong Kong has not yet investigated this subject and so it is also unlikely that a comprehensive overhaul of the law of personal property security will be attempted in the foreseeable future.

However, in China, a wholly new system of granting security interests by individual and corporate borrowers over personal property has been created in the last decade. As China has striven to develop a coherent and comprehensive system of commercial law, the grant of security by corporate and individual borrowers to providers of credit has been accorded significant priority. The enactment of the first comprehensive modern Property Law in China in 2007 included substantial and significant clarification of the types of property rights that exist in Chinese law as well as amplifying and expanding the types of security interests that can be created. This book attempts to examine these developments and submit them to critical analysis.

As a result of our analysis, we reach the somewhat surprising conclusion that whilst both the Hong Kong and the Chinese systems are inefficient, within the analytical framework we adopt the deficiencies are more manifold and serious in Hong Kong as the substantive law is the root of the problem. The new Chinese law certainly lacks detail and the publicity and registration arrangements are obviously unsatisfactory, but the system does have the benefit of simplicity and lacks the crucial distinction between the security that can be offered by personal borrowers and that which can be offered by corporate borrowers that bedevils the common law regime. However, the effective enforcement of security interests is superior in Hong Kong and China suffers notably in this respect.

We hope that this work will be a fitting tribute to Ong's scholarship and his fascination with this technical but vital aspect of commercial law.

We take responsibility for all errors and omissions in this text but we have attempted to state the law as at 1 March 2009.

Mark Williams
Lu Haitian
School of Accounting and Finance
Li Ka Shing Building
Hong Kong Polytechnic University
June 2009

TABLE OF CASES

TABLE OF LEGISLATION

UK

Agricultural Credits Act 1928: 317
Bills of Sale Acts: 39, 41, 54, 89, 197, 226, 280, 283, 296, 304, 398
Bills of Sale (Amendment) Act 1882: 42
Bills of Sale Act 1852: 38
Bills of Sale Act 1878: 38, 197
Bills of Sale Act 1882: 40
Bills of Sale Act 1890: 38
Companies Act 1948
  §95(1): 240, 259
Companies Act 1985
  §395 : 131, 197
  §397: 191, 201
  §405(1): 189
  §417(3)(e): 289
  §419: 183
Companies Act 1989
  §410(3): 182
  §415(1): 288
  §416 (1): 289
Companies Act 2006: 1, 90, 178, 206, 265, 284, 289, 293, 299, 301, 305
  §860: 131, 197
  §860(7)(b): 68, 192
  §861(2): 190
  §863: 191
  §869(5): 201
  §874: 131
  §877: 183
  §888: 189
  §1044: 202, 203
  §1052: 203
  §1282: 170

United States

New Zealand

Canada

EU Legislation

Australia

International Agreement

Hong Kong Self-Administrative Region

People's Republic of China (PRC)

Chapter 1

Introduction

Over many years, commentators have observed that the law governing credit security over personal property in common law jurisdictions (such as Australia, England, Malaysia and Singapore) is generally complex, cumbersome and inadequate, and have called for radical reform of the law.[1] The same is true of the Hong Kong Special Administrative Region

[1] For example, in Australia, the Australian Law Reform Commission Report No 64, Personal Property Securities (1993), para. 1.11, opined that there were serious inadequacies in the existing law governing secured lending over personal property, and recommended reform. Currently, the Australian Personal Property Security Law Reform Committee has produced a new bill based on a notice-filing system to replace the existing law. The English Law Commission Consultation Paper No 164, *Registration of Security Interest: Company Charges and Property Other than Land* (July 2002), as modified by the Consultation Paper No 176, Company Security Interests: A Consultative Report (August 2004), proposed radical reform of the present legal framework governing the creation and perfection of security of personal property of companies, and of corporate and non-corporate businesses. The English Law Commission Report No 296 (August 2005), based on the views elicited in response to Consultation Papers Nos 164 and 176, was limited only to reform of corporate security in a narrow sense and certain sales of receivables by companies; changes to this aspect of the law have been included in the Companies Act 2006. The original Law Commission paper recommended that a new notice-filing system along the lines of Article 9 of the Uniform Commercial Code (Revised) of the United States of America should be seriously considered for adoption in the UK. This conclusion followed a series of company law reviews carried out by the UK Department of Trade and Industry (DTI), notably Final Report, Modern Company Law for a Competitive Economy (URN 01/942, 26/7/2001) and the recent DTI consultation document, The Registration of Companies' Security Interests (Company Charges) – The Economic Impact of the Law Commissions' Proposals (July 2005). Earlier reports that criticised the existing legal framework and called for reform included the Crowther Report, Consumer Credit, Cmnd 4596; and A.L. Diamond, *A Review of Security Interests in Personal Property* (London: HMSO, 1989), particularly para. 17.17, p. 1. In New Zealand, the New Zealand Law Commission Report No. 8, A Personal Property Securities Act for New Zealand, Wellington Law Commission, April 1989, p. 1, commented that its legal framework was a 'quagmire' and badly in need of reform. The New Zealand Law Commission's earlier Preliminary Paper No. 6, Reform of Personal Property Security Law (1989) (J.H. Farrar and M.A. O'Regan), stated (p. 10), 'The law relating to security over personal chattels and intangibles in New Zealand is in a mess'. In 1999, New Zealand, in pursuance of the recommendations, enacted the Personal Property Securities Act 1999 (No. 126) ('PPSA').

('Hong Kong').[2] Being a former British colony, Hong Kong's legal system has a common origin with and exhibits similar features to these jurisdictions.[3] However, the Hong Kong Law Reform Commission has yet to turn its attention to this topic and call for a comprehensive review of the existing structure of credit security law affecting personal property.

China's legal system largely follows the continental civilian model and has not yet enacted a comprehensive civil code despite almost thirty years of transition from a classical socialist model to one that more closely resembles capitalism. Although the influence of common law systems has become more noticeable in Chinese law in recent years, the fundamental concepts and principles of Chinese civil law originate from the German paradigm.[4] Intensive legislative effort in the last twenty years has begun to create a unified and systematic legal framework. However, its credit security legal framework over personal property has been generally recognised as being both inadequate and ineffective.[5] Despite this state of

This basically adopted the notice-filing system, and it came into force on 1 May 2002 (Commencement Order 2002/60). In respect of Malaysia and Singapore, see D.E. Allan, M.E. Hiscock and D. Roebuck, *Credit and Security – The Legal Problems of Development Financing* (St Lucia: University of Queensland Press, 1974), pp. 31–40, where the authors commented that the credit security laws of these jurisdictions were generally cumbersome and inadequate.

[2] Hong Kong comprises the island of Hong Kong, the Kowloon Peninsula, the New Territories and a number of outlying islands (see Schedule 2 of the Interpretation and General Clauses Ordinance (Cap. 1)). All came under British rule at different times in the nineteenth century (see G.B. Endacott, *Government and People in Hong Kong 1841–1962 (A Constitutional History)* (Hong Kong: Oxford University Press, 1983), pp. 124–5). The British colonisation of Hong Kong officially began on 26 June 1843. The People's Republic of China resumed sovereignty over Hong Kong on 1 July 1997.

[3] By virtue of a series of colonial ordinances, namely Ordinance No 6 of 1845, §4, Ordinance No 2 of 1846, §3 (repealed), the Supreme Court Ordinance 1873 (repealed), and the Application of English Law Ordinance (Cap. 88) of 1966 (repealed) ('AELO'), English law comprising English legislation and common law and equity were, subject to limitations, applicable to the colony of Hong Kong. The limitations were: (a) where the English law was inapplicable to the circumstances of Hong Kong or its inhabitants: §3(1)(a) AELO; (b) where it was applicable but subject to such modifications as such circumstances may require: §3(1)(b) AELO; and (c) where its application was annulled by any order in Council, any English Act which applied to Hong Kong, or any Ordinance: §3(1)(c) AELO. The AELO was repealed by Annex 1, para. 2 of the Decision of the National People's Congress Standing Committee made on 23 February 1997. However, English common law and equity as a source of Hong Kong law was preserved by the Basic Law, Article 8.

[4] Bing Ling, 'Civil Law', in Chenguang Wang and Xianchu Zhang (eds.), *Introduction to Chinese Law* (Hong Kong: Sweet & Maxwell Asia, 1997).

[5] Chi Zhang, 'Some Thoughts on Security over Movables', *Law Science* 4 (2003), 64; Nengbi Yu and Xianglei Hou, 'Drawbacks and Perfection of Registration Rules of Security over Movables in China', *Law Science* 5 (2001), 33; Jinguang Xiong, 'Drawbacks and Perfection

affairs, no comprehensive review of the credit security legal framework has been undertaken in China. As part of the process of drafting a new comprehensive Civil Code, the method of improving the current credit security provisions has attracted the attention of many Chinese civil law scholars and caused a fierce debate amongst them.[6] The standalone provisions of the Security Law (1995) relating to this topic will be examined, as will the new provisions in the Property Law (2007) which form a major part of the legislation that will eventually be incorporated into the new Civil Code.[7]

1.1 Objective, hypothesis and significance

In view of the inaction noted in Hong Kong and the recent legislative activity in China, the objective of this book is to answer the following questions:

- Does the credit security legal framework governing security over personal property in Hong Kong and China function efficiently?
- Is there a need to reform the existing legal framework in Hong Kong and is the new Chinese law appropriate?
- What particular form and direction should the new legal framework take in Hong Kong and what revisions are needed to the Chinese system?

To help answer these questions and thus achieve this objective, the following hypothesis is postulated: the credit security legal frameworks governing security over personal property in domestic credit security arrangements in Hong Kong and China are not efficient if they fail to promote effectively the functions of (i) reducing the financial risk of the secured creditor, (ii) asset utilisation, (iii) fraud prevention and (iv) cost

of Chattel Mortgage Registering Institution in our Country', *Hebei Law Science* 22(5) (2004); Fumin Jiao, 'Legal Reflections on Perfection of Pledge Rules in China', *Law Science Magazine* 23(5) (2002), 36.

6 Shengping Gao, *Studies on Chattel Mortgage* (Beijing: China Industry and Commerce Press, 2004); Benhan Chen, *A Comparative Study of Security Law* (Wuhan: Wuhan University Press, 2003).

7 The official English translation of the Security Law (1995) can be found on the website of the National People's Congress, the People's Republic of China. See www.npc.gov.cn/zgrdw/english/news/newsDetail.jsp?id=2204&articleId=345071 (English). The Chinese version can be found at www.npc.gov.cn/zgrdw/common/zw.jsp?label=WXZLK&id=339451&pdmc=1502 (Chinese); another unofficial translation can be found at www.lawinfochina.com/law/display.asp?db=1&id=6642&keyword=propertylaw.

minimisation through four functional mechanisms, namely (a) creation, (b) perfection, (c) publicity and (d) enforcement of such security.

This book is thought to be the first detailed critical analysis of this subject as regards the law in Hong Kong and China.

The book will, we hope, provide new insights as to how these two substantially different legal systems function, both in theory and in practice, as regards the taking of security over personal assets. The book will also discuss issues concerning the relevance of law in relation to the contemporary commercial environment in Hong Kong and China. Finally, it will offer suggestions for reform of the credit security laws of other Asian jurisdictions to promote greater economic efficiency and legal certainty.

1.2 Methodology

In the social sciences, two types of research methodology can be discerned. The first is the 'verification-of-hypothesis method' or 'theory-methodological' approach (the 'verification approach').[8] The second is the grounded theory methodological approach ('grounded theory approach'), which was originally developed by the sociologists Glasser and Strauss.[9]

The verification approach involves two stages. The first is the construction of a hypothesis. The second is the testing of this hypothesis in a defined environment using a qualitative or quantitative method.[10] The qualitative method focuses on the collection and examination of data from personal observations, interviews, documents, journals, books and videotapes.[11] In contrast, the quantitative method focuses on the examination of statistical data collected, usually by means of empirical surveys.[12]

[8] See B.G. Glasser and A.L. Strauss, *The Discovery of Grounded Theory: Strategies for Qualitative Research* (New York: Aldine De Gruyter, 1967), pp. 10–15.

[9] Ibid.

[10] Whether one or the other should be used depends on the circumstances; see Glasser and Strauss, above, note 8, p. 17. See also M.B. Miles and A.M. Huberman, *Qualitative Data Analysis – A Sourcebook of New Methods*, 3rd printing (Beverley Hills, CA: Sage Publications Inc., 1985), p. 215; and K.M. Eisenhardt, 'Building Theories from Case Study Research', *Academy of Management Review* 14 (1989), 532 at p. 535.

[11] See Glasser and Strauss, above, note 8, p. 18. The other method is called the quantitative method. Here the findings of the research are arrived at by means of statistical procedure or other means of quantification: see A. Strauss and J. Corbin, *Basics of Qualitative Research* (London: Sage Publications Inc., 1990), p. 17.

[12] See Glasser and Strauss, above, note 8, p. 18.

Grounded theory, as defined by Glasser, is a general methodology of analysis linked with data collection that uses a systematically applied set of methods to generate an inductive theory about a substantive area.[13] The end result is the development of theories or hypotheses, without testing such theories or hypotheses. The testing or verification is left to others interested in these areas of research. This approach is particularly useful in areas in which there is an absence of theory or hypotheses.

The present book adopts the verification approach and the qualitative method of verifying hypotheses. This approach and method fit very well with the type of work undertaken here, because the existing credit security legal framework of Hong Kong is constant and well settled, and has a rich source of case law and statute with well-developed systems of law reporting. However, in China the system is, in many ways, much more rudimentary and lacks many of the attributes of a well-settled jurisprudence as might be found in established civilian jurisdictions such as Germany, Japan or France. Despite this problem, the ongoing process of creating a Civil Code, and the enactment of the Security Law and the Property Law, together with a significant Supreme Court Interpretation of the Security Law in 2000, does provide a sufficient basis for proper analysis. Further, the existing provisions in the Security Law have been well tested, and have been re-enacted in the new Property Law, thus providing some legislative stability in this area.

1.3 Key constructs of the hypothesis

The key constructs of the hypothesis are:

- the functions of financial risk reduction, asset utilisation, fraud prevention and cost minimisation in any security device;
- the creation, perfection, publicity and enforcement of such security devices; and
- the efficiency of such measures.

The functions of credit security, and the form of an efficient credit security legal framework to realise these functions, are matters of debate. Theories on the subject range from broad economic concepts, such as the promotion and development of a country's commerce and functioning

[13] B.G. Glasser, *Basics of Grounded Theory Analysis* (Mill Valley, CA: Sociology Press, 1992), p. 16.

financial markets,[14] leading to an expansion of a country's gross domestic product (GDP),[15] to narrow concepts, such as the reduction of the cost of borrowing,[16] the encouragement of creditors to lend to risky businesses (which they would otherwise refuse),[17] reduction of creditors' administrative costs in monitoring the loan, and the financial performance of the debtor.[18] Although it is generally recognised that the grant of security to creditors has a positive effect on economic activity, there are conflicting views as to the extent to which it does;[19] but it is not within the ambit of this book to verify which of these is correct. In addition, as Duggan has commented, it is not easy to determine precisely what constitutes an

[14] See F.S. Mishkin and S.G. Eakins, *Financial Markets and Institutions*, 2nd ed. (Reading, MA: Addison-Wesley, 1998), pp. 14–15; and R. Eyre, 'Collateral Security Damages', in 'Legal and Judicial Reform in Asia: Agenda for the New Millennium', Roundtable Meeting of Chief Justices and Ministers of Justice, Asian Development Bank (25 August 1997); available at www.adb.org/Documents/Conference/Seminar_Roundtable/round070.asp.

[15] See Eyre, above, note 14. The author noted that without such a legal framework no capital would be available and estimated that there would be a loss of between 5 and 10 per cent of GDP. A similar view was adopted by D. Fairgrieve, 'Reforming Secured Transaction Laws in Central and Eastern Europe', *EBLR* 9(7/8) (1998), 254.

[16] The argument is that the higher the risk, as in unsecured lending, the higher the interest; see S. Levmore, 'Monitor and Freeriders in Commercial and Corporate Setting', *Yale LJ* 92 (1982), 49–51.

[17] A. Schwartz, 'Security Interests and Bankruptcy Priorities: A Review of Current Theories', *JLS* 10 (1981), 1–37.

[18] See ibid., pp. 9–11; P. Jackson and A.T. Kronman, 'Secured Financing and Priorities among Creditors', *Yale LJ* 88 (1979), 1143 at p. 1147; R. Posner, *Economic Analysis of Law*, 3rd ed. (Boston: Little, Brown, 1986), p. 373: and see M. Gillooly (ed.), *Securities over Personalty* (Annandale, NSW: Federation Press, 1994), p. 241. They effectively suggested that 'the advantage of taking security is that it enables the creditor to focus its monitoring efforts more narrowly on a particular asset, whereas an unsecured creditor must monitor dealings in all the debtor's assets'. Note, however, that literature on the management of problem loans and loan losses by banks did not suggest that there was any difference in demands on managing secured loans and unsecured loans: see T.W. Koch, *Bank Management*, 3rd ed. (Fort Worth, TX: Dryden Press, 1995), Chapter 23, pp. 733–61.

[19] For example, the theory that an efficient credit security legal framework promotes the development of a country's commerce and a fully functioning market economy (see Mishkin and Eakins, above, note 14; and Eyre, above, note 14) is doubted by the views of Allan, Hiscock and Roebuck, above, note 1, pp. 3–4. See also J.J. Norton and M. Andenas (eds.), *Emerging Financial Markets and Secured Transactions* (London: Kluwer Law International, 1998) for discussion of the criticisms of the theories, in particular Chapter 3, H.W. Fleisig, 'Economic Functions of Security in a Market', pp. 21–25; also R.J. Mann, 'Explaining the Pattern of Credit', *Harv LR* 10 (1996–7) 625 at p. 633, where the author states, 'no single factor can capture the multiple and interrelated considerations that motivate borrowers and lenders as they structure their various transactions'.

efficient credit security framework and what direction law reform should take from an economic perspective.[20]

This book therefore emphasises the functions of a credit security legal framework from the perspective of creditors, debtors and third parties who might deal with the debtor in respect of the same secured asset as a subsequent purchaser or creditor.[21] This approach is adopted because these players are participants in real businesses with direct economic interests in the security arrangement.[22] They are not abstract economic actors. Their perceptions of what might be the appropriate function of a credit security legal framework are real and substantial.

What are their perceptions? The most serious concern of the creditor is the risk of being unable to recover the amount due if the debtor becomes insolvent,[23] because after the debtor's property has been distributed amongst secured creditors and preferential creditors, nothing may be left for unsecured creditors.[24]

Thus, from the point of view of the creditor, security reduces the creditor's financial risk associated with advances[25] by allowing the creditor to

[20] A.J. Duggan, 'Personal Property Security Interests and Third Party Disputes: Economic Considerations in Reforming the Law', Chapter 9 of Gillooly, *Securities over Personalty*, above, note 18.

[21] According to the Asian Development Bank (*Law and Policy Reform at the Asian Development Bank* (2000 ed.), vol. 2, para. 11, p. 3), the persons who might be interested in a secured transaction comprise a broad spectrum of persons, including the producers and suppliers of goods and services; the consumers; and the banks, savers and other financial intermediaries. This concept is too broad to provide a working definition for the present book. This book adopts the position that the creditor, debtor and third party are interested parties, as presented by J.L. Simpson and J.H.M. Rover, 'An Introduction to the European Bank's Model Law on Secured Transactions', in J.J. Norton and M. Andenas (eds.), *Emerging Financial Markets and the Role of International Financial Organizations* (London: Kluwer Law International, 1996), Chapter 10, p. 169. The authors opined that these three persons have direct legitimate interest in a credit security legal framework that fairly balances their competing interests.

[22] See Mann, above, note 19, pp. 630–1, 682, where the author postulates that abstract theory, however elegant, is not useful in studying the costs and benefits of secured and unsecured transactions, unless the analysis is focused on the actual decision makers.

[23] See Norton and Andenas, above, note 19, in particular Chapter 7, J.L. Simpson and J.H.M. Rover, 'General Principles of a Modern Secured Transactions Law', at pp. 144–6. See also Eyre, above, note 14, para. 11.

[24] See *Borden (UK) Ltd v Scottish Timber Products Ltd and Another* [1979] 3 All ER 961, 971, *per* Templeman LJ. See also *Law and Policy Reform at the Asian Development Bank*, above, note 21, para. 9, p. 3, where it was stated, 'Without a security interest, a creditor only has a general claim against a debtor's property.'

[25] See Eyre, above, note 14, section II: 'Taking security reduces risk and the cost of lending and contributes to sound banking practices.' See also the Australian Law Reform Commission Report No 64, above, note 1, para. 1.9, where it states, 'Securities ... reduce

have priority recourse to the secured property.[26] In this regard the function of a credit security legal framework is that it must promote the creation of effective security that is capable of reducing the creditor's financial risk.[27]

For a commercial debtor,[28] the smooth functioning of its business depends on being able to pursue its operations without restriction and, subject to the security interests of the creditor, being allowed to use the secured asset productively in the ordinary course of business.[29] As Gough has observed, one of the expectations of a borrower is to 'avoid the need for detailed and intrusive supervision and control of its business operations, whether by a bank or any other credit supplier'.[30] Simpson and Rover have made a similar observation.[31] They postulated that, without this freedom, financing would often be useless to the debtor because the debtor's business and trade would be seriously impeded.[32] Thus, from the perspective of a debtor, the function of a credit security legal framework is to promote the debtor's utilisation of the secured asset in the widest possible range of situations.[33]

A third party who wishes to deal with the debtor in respect of the same secured assets as a potential subsequent creditor is concerned with two factors – (i) the status of the debtor's assets offered as security;[34] and (ii) the creditworthiness of the debtor.[35]

In the absence of an independent and reliable mechanism that allows the third party easy access to the required information, the third party

the risk that the money advanced will not be repaid by enabling the creditor to have recourse to the property secured'; and Simpson and Rover, above, note 21, p. 144.

26 See the Australian Law Reform Commission Report No 64, above, note 1, para. 1.9; Mann, above, note 19, p. 639; and C.C. Wappett and D.E. Allan, *Securities over Personal Property* (Sydney: Butterworths, 1999), p. 4.

27 See Simpson and Rover, above, note 23.

28 The book is not concerned with consumer debtors.

29 See R.W. Turner, *The Equity of Redemption*, reprint (Holmes Beach, FL: W.M.W. Gaunt & Sons Inc., 1986) pp. ix and 1; and see also R.L. Jordan and W.D. Warren, *Commercial Law*, 4th ed. (New York: Westbury, 1928), p. 13, where the authors expressed the view that the major disadvantage of the pledge was that it paralysed the debtor's business operation.

30 W.J. Gough, *Company Charges*, 2nd ed. (London: Butterworths, 1996), p. 441.

31 Simpson and Rover, above, note 23, p. 153, and also *idem*, above, note 21, at p. 169, where the authors say, 'the lender must obtain real benefit from holding security but not at the expense of depriving the borrower of the use of the assets given as security of the flexibility needed to operate an efficient business'.

32 Simpson and Rover, above, note 23. 33 Ibid.

34 This was one factor identified in the Australian Law Reform Commission Report No 64, above, note 1, para. 2.17.

35 As postulated in Diamond, above, note 1, para. 11.1.5.

must rely on the goodwill and honesty of the debtor. However, in many cases, this is worthless. Furthermore, the absence of such a mechanism might subject the third party to the risk of loss of priority.[36] Thus, unsurprisingly, commentators on this issue have recommended that an efficient credit security legal framework must have an accurate and cost-effective publicity system.[37] Therefore, from the perspective of a third party, a credit security legal framework must contain an effective mechanism that protects the third party against the fraud of the debtor.

The creditor, debtor and third party are also concerned with the costs of creation, perfection, publicity and enforcement of security. As these costs are ultimately borne by the debtor,[38] high costs in any of these aspects mean that only large borrowers (who can bear such expense) can obtain credit.[39] This is not in the best economic interests of society as a whole or of the interested parties. Thus, to ensure that secured transactions are economically practical, the legal framework has to minimise the cost of creation, perfection, publicity and enforcement.[40]

A good credit security legal framework must therefore ensure that:

- the financial risk of the secured creditor is reduced in the event of default by the debtor ('reduction of risk' function);
- the debtor, as far as practicable, is able to continue to utilise the secured assets in the ordinary course of business ('asset utilisation' function);
- a third party is effectively protected against the fraud of the debtor in relation to the secured asset ('fraud prevention' function); and

[36] See *Law and Policy Reform at the Asian Development Bank*, above, note 21, at para. 267, p. 69.

[37] For example, the English Law Commission Report No 296, above, note 1; and the Australian Law Commission Report No 64, above, note 1, both advocated that the existing registration system be replaced with a notice-filing system. See also note 21 above, *Law and Policy Reform at the Asian Development Bank*, Part VII, 'Problems in Publicizing Security Interests', and Part VIII, 'Problems in Enforcing Security Interests'. See also Article 33 of the European Model Law on Secured Transactions at www.ebrd.com/sectrans/modelllaw5.htm, which sets out a purportedly efficient registration and information system.

[38] Fairgrieve, above, note 15, at p. 256. See also Gough, above, note 30, at p. 441, for a similar view on cost.

[39] See *Law and Policy Reform at the Asian Development Bank*, above, note 21, at para. 101, p. 19, and para. 10, p. xiv, where it was observed that if the process of creating secured transactions is expensive, only the largest borrowers can bear the cost. Further, in the event that the cost is borne by the creditor, the creditor will inevitably seek to recover the cost from the debtor: see Fairgrieve, above, note 15; and Gough, above, note 30.

[40] See Simpson and Rover, above, note 21, at pp. 145, 148.

- the costs of credit security arrangements are minimised ('costs minimisation' function).

This book contends that these functions are practical, substantive and conceptually sound. Accordingly, they form the central constructs of the hypothesis.

However, these functions are, in themselves, insufficient to provide clear direction on a number of critical issues – in particular, the formulation of the criteria to test the hypothesis, and the collection and analysis of data to substantiate the criteria. Two further steps are therefore necessary: (i) the identification and incorporation in the hypothesis of the essential functional mechanisms of creation, perfection, publicity and enforcement, and (ii) the identification and incorporation in the hypothesis of a mechanism that can confirm whether the legal framework has fully achieved its functions and has thus met the benchmark of efficiency.

1.3.1 Creation, perfection, publicity and enforcement of security

Four basic functional mechanisms can be identified in the security laws of Hong Kong and China, although they are not explicitly mentioned. However, Article 9 of the American Uniform Commercial Code describes three of the four mechanisms as being creation, perfection and enforcement.[41] Article 9 treats the fourth mechanism, publicity, as an aspect of perfection; however, for the purposes of this book, it is treated separately. Enforcement arises when the debtor defaults in the repayment of the credit. Each of mechanisms is linked to the objectives of the creditor, debtor and third party as discussed above. Indeed, the English Law Commission, in its Consultation Paper No 164 (2002), commented that these processes are inherent in the English credit security law, although they have not been explicitly stated as such.[42] The Consultation Paper No 176 (2004), on the other hand, has provided general explanations of the terms of attachment and perfection. Attachment is described as the point at which the secured party acquires a proprietary right in the collateral, and is a necessary step for perfection to occur. Perfection applies when a security interest has attached and it means completing the steps to secure,

[41] The first is called the 'attachment stage' (Article 9, §§201–10), the second 'perfection' (Article 9, §§308–16, sub-part 2, revised) and the third 'enforcement' (Article 9, §§601–24, Part 6, Revised).

[42] English Law Commission Consultation Paper No 164, above, note 1, para. 2.5.

so far as legally permissible and necessary, the effectiveness and priority of a security interest as against third persons.[43] For the purpose of this book, a precise functional definition is assigned as follows. 'Creation' is defined as the process by which the secured creditor and the debtor create the security interest and thereby confer on the secured party special rights, such as enforcement of the collateral against the debtor.[44] Thus, according to Davidson, Knowles and Forsythe, this process is primarily concerned with the relationship between the creditor and the debtor.[45] They do not necessarily confer on the creditor superior rights vis-à-vis other creditors of the debtor.[46] To acquire superior rights to the secured asset of the debtor, the secured creditor has to 'perfect' its security. In summary:

Perfection means the process by which the secured creditor protects its security from the claim of subsequent creditors, secured or general.[47] It might, for example, require the security to be registered with the relevant authority because failure to do so will render the security ineffective against the other creditors of the debtor.

Publicity is the means by which the security interest of the creditor is made known to the public.[48] The primary purpose of publicising secured transactions is to protect third parties who wish to deal with the debtor against any misleading representation on the part of the debtor that the secured assets are free from encumbrances or that the debtor is creditworthy.[49]

Enforcement is often regarded as relating to the 'rights' of the secured creditor to enforce the security.[50] However, more accurately, it deals with

[43] English Law Commission Consultation Paper No 176, above, note 1, at paras. 2.14–2.15, 3.72–3.73, 3.86–3.91. For the conditions to be fulfilled as 'attachment', see draft reg. 15(1). For the methods and steps required for 'perfection', see also draft reg. 19 attached at the end of the Consultation Paper. However, in the English Law Commission Report No 296, para. 3.6, the employment of the word 'attachment' was regarded as unnecessary, while the word 'perfection' was to be used only on the occasion 'when it is desirable to have a single word to refer to any steps necessary to render a type of security effective in the debtor's insolvency'. This was because the concepts 'attachment' and 'perfection' were found to be unfamiliar to most consultees of the report.

[44] This concept is modelled on the exposition of D.V. Davidson, B.E. Knowles and L.M. Forsythe regarding the meaning of 'attachment' and creation of security interest under the American Uniform Commercial Code; see their text, *Business Law*, 6th ed. (New York: West Educational Publishing Company, 1998), p. 652.

[45] Ibid., p. 659. [46] Ibid., p. 659. [47] Ibid., p. 659.

[48] See *Law and Policy Reform at the Asian Development Bank*, above, note 21, Part VII, p. 56.

[49] See Diamond, above, note 1, para. 11.1.3., p. 54.

[50] See note 44, above.

the types of remedy that the creditor is entitled to exercise in respect of the secured property if the debtor defaults in payment,[51] including the creditor's right to possession, sale and foreclosure.[52]

Because creation, perfection, publicity and enforcement are facilitating mechanisms of an efficient credit security legal framework, they are incorporated in the hypothesis.

1.3.2 The efficiency of security

The expression 'efficient' or 'efficiency' appear frequently in any discussion of the essentials of a credit security legal framework.[53] However, this term often lacks precise definition, and bears different meanings in different contexts. For the purposes of this book, the expression is construed in a functional legal sense. In this regard, Lord Dunedin defined 'efficient' in its general sense as indicating whether a 'thing is fit for the purposes for which it is intended'.[54] In the context of the credit security legal frameworks of Hong Kong and China, 'efficient' thus refers to whether the existing credit security legal framework governing personal property has realised the functions of risk reduction, asset utilisation, fraud prevention and cost minimisation. The hypothesis of this book thus postulates that a credit security legal framework is 'efficient' if its functions are realised through the effective operation of the four functional mechanisms.

1.4 Criteria for testing validity of hypothesis

To test the external validity of the hypothesis, the book establishes a set of criteria to measure the performance of the credit security laws of Hong Kong and China in respect of the four functional mechanisms of creation,

[51] For an example of this meaning, see J. Ziegel, 'Canadian Perspectives on the New Zealand Chattel Securities Act', *NZBLR* 7 (2001), 118 at pp. 123–4.

[52] For example, see Article 9-601 of the United States Uniform Commercial Code entitled 'Default and Enforcement of Security Interest', which specified the remedies of foreclosure, possession and sale of the secured property; and also R.M. Goode, *Legal Problems of Credit and Security*, 3rd ed. (London: Sweet & Maxwell, 2003), pp. 151–2, where the author discusses enforcement of security in the context of floating charge remedies.

[53] See Fairgrieve, above, note 15, generally; and Wappett and Allan, above, note 26, pp. 4–5.

[54] *Kennedy v Glasgow and South-Western Railway*, 43 SLR 321.

perfection, publicity and enforcement. These criteria will prove or disprove the effectiveness of the four functional mechanisms and, in turn, establish the validity or otherwise of the hypothesis.

The relevant criteria for assessing creation are as follows:

(1) the process of creating secured transactions must be simple, comprehensible, expeditious, and inexpensive;
(2) the process must enable security to be created over clearly defined and identifiable assets with a minimum of formality.[55]

Once created, the security device must:

(1) leave the debtor in possession of the asset;[56]
(2) be capable of identifying and protecting the legitimate interests of all parties to the transaction;[57]
(3) allow the debtor to deal freely with the secured assets, subject to the interest of the creditor;[58]
(4) be able to secure future advances made to the debtor by the creditor; and[59]
(5) be applicable to after-acquired or future assets.[60]

The relevant criteria for assessing perfection are as follows:

(1) the perfection process must be simple, comprehensible, expeditious and inexpensive;
(2) the rule regulating the priority of competing claims against the secured asset must be perfected in a manner that provides a fair and just ordering of such claims.

The relevant criteria for assessing publicity are as follows:

(1) there must be publicity given to security transactions, and it must be inexpensive to file and easy to search for particulars;
(2) the publicity process must be simple, comprehensible, expeditious and inexpensive;
(3) the information provided must be accurate as to the nature of the security, its status and exposure of the affected assets to priority claims; and
(4) accessibility to the information must be inexpensive and expeditious.

[55] Wappett and Allan, above, note 26, pp. 4–5, para. 1.5.
[56] Ibid. [57] Ibid. [58] Ibid. [59] Ibid. [60] Ibid.

The relevant criteria for assessing enforcement are as follows:

(1) the creditor's remedies must be certain;
(2) enforcement of the creditor's remedies must be expeditious;
(3) the cost of enforcing the remedies must be inexpensive; and[61]
(4) the quantum of money which the creditor is entitled to recover under the security arrangement must be certain.

These criteria were developed after a review of the relevant literature. This included the work of Turner,[62] Diamond,[63] Goode,[64] Ellinger,[65] Rudden and Moseley,[66] Fairgrieve[67] and Allan;[68] reports of various Commonwealth Law Commissions;[69] and reports of the European Bank for Reconstruction and Development[70] and the Asian Development Bank. Surprisingly, except for Fairgrieve, Allan and the Asian Development Bank, none of the above has established any substantial criteria for assessing an efficient credit security legal framework.[71] There is little literature in China discussing the criteria of an efficient credit security legal mechanism. The available literature indicates that Chinese scholars seem to be more concerned about borrowing concrete provisions from established Western practices rather than about reflecting the criteria of an efficient credit security legal framework.[72] Other Chinese authors only mention

[61] See *Law and Policy Reform at the Asian Development Bank*, above, note 21, in general.
[62] Turner, above, note 26, at p. 118.
[63] See Diamond, above, note 1, generally. Note that although Diamond made it in the context of security over goods, his observation would generally apply.
[64] See Goode, above, note 52, and R.M. Goode, *Commercial Law* (London: Penguin, 1982), particularly pp. 774–7.
[65] E.P. Ellinger, E. Lomnicka and R.J.A. Hooley, *Modern Banking Law*, 3rd ed. (Oxford: Oxford University Press, 2002) Chapter 18, particularly pp. 721–8.
[66] B. Rudden and H. Moseley, *An Outline of the Law of Mortgages* (London: The Estates Gazette Ltd, 1967), p. 2.
[67] See Fairgrieve, above, note 15, generally.
[68] See Wappett and Allan, above, note 26.
[69] For example, the English Law Commission Consultation Papers Nos 164 and 176 (and the resulting 2005 Report No 296) and the Australian Law Reform Commission Report No 46.
[70] The EBRD was established in 1991 to help economic reform in the former communist states in central and eastern Europe; see www.ebrd.com/about/main.htm. In 1994 a model law for secured transactions was published as a catalyst for reform in these states.
[71] For example, the English Law Commission Consultation Papers Nos 164 and 176 (and the resulting 2005 Report No 296) were, at best, sketchy on the criteria for an efficient credit security legal framework.
[72] See Mingyue Xu, *On Mortgage* (Beijing: Law Press, 1998); and Huabin Chen, *Studies on Property Law* (Beijing: Law Press, 2000).

the general values of an efficient framework but fail to establish testable criteria.[73] One scholar, Shengping Gao, does consider what might constitute an optimal mortgage system. After quoting the work of Goode and Fairgrieve, he argues that mortgages over movable property should possess the following characteristics:[74]

(1) security over movable property should be capable of creation over all kinds of such property, between all types of parties and to secure all kinds of obligations;
(2) publicity of security rights should be simple, efficient and inexpensive;
(3) enforcement of the security should be quick, efficient and inexpensive; and
(4) the priority sequence between the different creditors who hold security over the property should be explicit and fair.

Other authors have concentrated mainly on the role of credit security law in the wider economic development of the country. For instance, the work of Allan, Hiscock and Roebuck focused on the impact of the credit security legal framework on development finance.[75]

The Asian Development Bank developed a baseline model to evaluate the efficiency of the credit security framework of five Asian countries – the People's Republic of China, India, Indonesia, Pakistan and Thailand.[76] The baseline model included the following criteria:

- the creation and perfection of secured transactions must be inexpensive,[77] simple and comprehensive;
- there must be publicity of security transactions and this publicity must be inexpensive to file and easy to search;
- priority of secured transactions must be based on simple and unambiguous rules;
- the enforcement of secured transactions must be fast and inexpensive;[78] and
- the rules governing the creation, perfection, publicity and enforcement should be readily accessible and understandable to debtors and creditors.[79]

[73] See Benhan Chen, above, note 6; Kaizhong Hu, *Pledge on Rights* (Beijing: China Politics and Law University Press, 2004).
[74] Shengping Gao, *Studies on Mortgage over Movable Property* (Beijing: Industry and Commerce Press of China, 2004), pp. 17–18.
[75] See Allan, Hiscock and Roebuck, above, note 1.
[76] *Law and Policy Reform at the Asian Development Bank*, above, note 21, pp. 19–20, para. 101.
[77] Ibid. [78] Ibid. [79] Ibid., p. 19, para. 98.

Fairgrieve proposed similar criteria in his proposals for an effective credit security legal framework for central and eastern European countries:[80]

- the right to security must adhere to the essential qualities of a right *in rem*;
- the law should provide for the granting of security in the widest possible range of circumstances;
- the existence of security must be effectively publicised;
- there should be a rapid and cost-effective means of recovering the debt from the secured asset; and
- the costs of creating, maintaining and exercising the right should be kept to a reasonable level.

According to Fairgrieve, if these criteria are not met the resulting credit security legal framework will be inefficient and impede commercial lending.

Allan has proposed several elaborate and expansive criteria for an efficient credit security legal framework, namely:[81]

- the framework should enable security to be obtained over clearly defined and identifiable assets with a minimum of formality and expense;[82]
- the security must leave possession of the asset with the debtor;[83]
- any registration of the security interest of the creditor required to protect the general public should be simple and inexpensive to establish, maintain and access;[84]
- any such registration should be effective even if the secured asset is moved to another jurisdiction;[85]
- the security should be able to secure future advances made to the debtor by the creditor;[86]
- the security should be applicable to after-acquired or future assets;[87]
- the security should be capable of identifying and protecting the legitimate interests of all parties to the transaction;[88]
- in the event of default by the debtor the secured creditor should be able to realise the security and repay the debt quickly, inexpensively[89] and

[80] See Fairgrieve, above, note 15, generally.

[81] Wappett and Allan, above, note 26, pp. 4–5.

[82] Ibid., para. 1.5. [83] Ibid. [84] Ibid. [85] Ibid. [86] Ibid. [87] Ibid. [88] Ibid.

[89] *Law and Policy Reform at the Asian Development Bank*, above, note 21, para. 15, p. xv. See also Part 4 of the European Bank's Model Law on Secured Transactions, above, note 37, which aims to achieve this by allowing the secured creditor to enforce the security immediately without the aid of the court, such as taking possession at the outset. See Simpson

with priority over other subsequent claims against the debtor and the secured asset;[90]

- the debtor should be able to deal freely with the secured assets (subject to the interest of the creditor);[91]
- the law regulating the priority of competing claims against the secured asset should be clear and provide a fair and just ordering of those claims,[92] including provisions that the creditor has a right to (i) take payment from the proceeds of sale of the secured assets ahead of other creditors, (ii) trace any secured assets that have passed to third parties and (iii) request separation of the secured assets in the event of insolvency of the debtor;[93] and
- the legal, administrative and taxation costs of establishing, maintaining and realising the security should be kept as low as possible.[94]

Allan's criteria were formulated after careful consideration of the function of credit security and the strengths and weaknesses of traditional common law security devices. The criteria took into account the objectives of the credit security legal framework established in the United States by Article 9 of the Uniform Commercial Code, which is generally

and Rover, above, note 21, p. 147, where the authors offer an economic of scale rationale for this criterion, i.e. if the creditor is able to recover a high value from the secured assets in a short space of time, the security will be more valuable to the creditor than if the creditor could only enable it recover a low value in a long time.

90 This view was supported by Mann, above, note 19, p. 639; see also Wappett and Allan, above, note 26.

91 Also postulated by Gough, above, note 30, pp. 441–3; see also the statement of Simpson and Rover, above, note 31.

92 See Simpson and Rover, above, note 21, where the authors argue that all three parties, namely the debtor, creditor and the third party, have direct legitimate interests in competing claims against the secured asset.

93 Other authors' description of the advantage of secured credit is too narrow. They tend to see the advantage in terms of affording protection to the secured creditor against competing claims; see e.g. H.J. Thomas and T.K. Anthony, 'Secured Financing and Priorities among Creditors', *Yale Law Journal* 88 (1979), 1143 at p. 1143, where it is stated that 'one of the principal advantages of a secured transaction is the protection it provides against the claims of competing creditors'. H.G. Hanbury and C.H.M. Waldock, *The Law of Mortgage*, 1st ed. (London: Stevens & Sons Ltd and Sweet & Maxwell, 1938), p. 2, expressed the same function of credit security, i.e. that it gives the secured creditor a prior claim on specific property and the assurance of payment in the event of the debtor's insolvency; see also R.M. Goode, *Principles of Corporate Insolvency Law*, 3rd ed. (London: Sweet & Maxwell, 2005), p. 3: 'security [is taken] in order to ensure that if by mischance the borrower company does become insolvent they will be able to jump ahead of the creditors'. Similar terms, though more elaborate, are found in §2.4, Part II of the English Law Commission Consultation Paper No 164, above, note 1.

94 English Law Commission Consultation Paper No 164, Part III, §3.7.

thought to be simple, efficient and comprehensive. The Article 9 model was introduced in the United States in 1952 to remedy the problems and weaknesses then inherent in the American credit security legal framework, which had an origin in common law.[95] This system has been adopted in some Commonwealth countries, including all ten Canadian provinces and three territories,[96] as well as in New Zealand.[97] Allan's criteria are consistent with, and add detail to, the baseline policy model of the Asian Development Bank and that of Fairgrieve.

Another virtue of Allan's criteria is that they address the two major characteristics of a credit security framework discussed above – the functions of the legal framework and the four functional mechanisms of that legal framework. Viewed as a whole, Allan's criteria strike a balance between the various interests of persons who are directly or indirectly interested in a credit security arrangement. This balance is an important factor in the smooth development of commerce.[98]

That said, for the purposes of this book, some of Allan's criteria are unsuitable in their present form. One criterion that has been excluded is that of dealing with effective registration in the context of a secured asset being moved to another jurisdiction. Such complex cross-border issues and matters of international law are beyond the scope of the present book. Criteria that have to be modified for use here are those relating to professional and administrative costs of creating, perfecting and enforcing credit security. The empirical research required to collect reliable data on cost and economic benefits in Hong Kong and China is also beyond the scope of the book. Apart from these unsuitable criteria, Allan's other criteria are useful in testing the hypothesis.

In addition to Allan's proposals, a criterion developed by the Asian Development Bank is included here. This deals with the rules governing

[95] See R.L. Jordan and W.D. Warren, *Commercial Law*, 4th ed. (New York: Foundation Press, 1997), p. 13.

[96] The ten provinces are Alberta, British Columbia, Manitoba, New Brunswick, Newfoundland and Labrador, Nova Scotia, Prince Edward Island, Saskatchewan, Québec, Ontario. The territories are Northwest Territories, Nunavut and Yukon Territory. Note that Goode and Gower suggested that Article 9 of the Uniform Commercial Code was worthy of consideration for future reforms in common law jurisdictions; see R.M. Goode and L.C.B. Gower, 'Is Article 9 of the Uniform Commercial Code Exportable?', *Commonwealth Reactions* (September 1968), cited by A.L. Diamond in his *Instalment Credit* (London: Stevens & Sons, 1970), p. 23.

[97] The Personal Property Securities Act 1999.

[98] See F.O. Adeoye, 'The Anglo-American Law of Mortgages: A Quagmire for Creditors', *JBL* (November 1993), 544 at p. 544.

the substantive and procedural aspects of a credit security legal framework, and states that these must be readily accessible and understandable for all creditors, debtors and the general public. This was set out in the fifth criterion of the Asian Development Bank baseline model.

In summary, the criteria adopted in this book are therefore primarily Allan's criteria, with some deletions, modifications and additions. Taken together, they constitute a useful frame of reference to evaluate an efficient credit security legal framework governing security over personal property.

1.5 Hong Kong and China as the locus of this study

Hong Kong and China's credit security laws form the main focus of the hypothesis of this book for a number of reasons. Firstly, the credit security law of modern Hong Kong, both statute law and common law, is deeply infused with the legal concepts of Victorian England. Since 1843, when the British colonised the territory, English common law and equity have formed the foundation of Hong Kong commercial law,[99] including that relating to credit security over personal property. After 1 July 1997, when the People's Republic of China resumed sovereignty,

[99] On the basis of the review conducted by the authors on official law reports since 1910 (i.e. Hong Kong Law Reports) and the *China Mail* since 1854, it appears that neither Chinese law nor Chinese or foreign custom formed any part of the commercial law of Hong Kong. This situation was due to the following reasons: (1) to achieve the British objective of turning Hong Kong into a 'commercial centre in the Far East' (see G.B. Endacott, *A History of Hong Kong*, 2nd ed. (Hong Kong: Oxford University Press, 1962), p. 62) a functional and reliable British commercial legal framework that was familiar to the court and to British traders was the only necessary legal apparatus. This was ordained by the various applications of English law provisions (see note 3 above) which provided that as a general rule the courts should apply English common law and equity; (2) save in domestic matters, it was extremely difficult to prove an alleged Chinese commercial custom because the criteria based on English practice were strict (see *Kan-tat alias Kan Fat v Kan Yin Tat* [1987] HKLR 516) and (3) there were no reliable sources from which the courts could discover any Chinese commercial law or customs (see G. Jamieson, *Chinese Family Law and Commercial Law*, reprint (Hong Kong: Vetch and Lee, 1970), p. 1, who comments, 'details of crime and punishment were abundant in every possible variety, but of commercial law not a word was said'). Similar views have also been expressed by other Chinese studies scholars, such as F.T. Cheng, 'Law Codification in China', *JCLIL* 6 (1924), 284 at p. 285; T.T. Meadows, 'Land Tenure in China', *China Mail*, 14 September 1848, p. 3; S.V.D. Spreinkel, *Legal Institutions in Manchu China: A Sociological Analysis* (London: University of London, 1962), p. 95; and J.S. Burgess, *The Guilds of Peking* (Hong Kong: Cheng Wen Publisher Co., 1966), p. 201.

Article 8 of the Basic Law retained these important sources of commercial law.[100]

However, the preservation of English common law and equity does not mean that new decisions of the Privy Council and the House of Lords carry the same weight after 1997 as they did before.[101] Hong Kong courts now have a broad discretion with respect to these matters. The Privy Council has been abolished as the final forum of appeal for Hong Kong,[102] and has been replaced by the Hong Kong Court of Final Appeal.[103] In addition, the Basic Law expressly gives freedom to the courts to consider the judicial decisions of other common law jurisdictions where relevant.[104] Despite these changes in Hong Kong since 1997, the experience of other former British colonies suggests that, in the interests of maintaining consistency in the common law and certainty in commercial practices, decisions of the Privy Council and the House of Lords are likely to be followed in Hong Kong.[105]

Secondly, as noted above, the call for radical reform of credit security laws in the United Kingdom and other Commonwealth countries justifies a detailed examination of the strengths and weaknesses of the corresponding laws in Hong Kong.

Thirdly, because Hong Kong is one of the most successful commercial and financial centres in Asia, its credit security law is worthy of study.[106]

[100] The Basic Law is the mini-constitution of the Hong Kong Special Administrative Region. It came into force on 1 July 1997. Article 8 provides that laws previously in force in Hong Kong – i.e. the common law, rules of equity, ordinances, subordinate legislation and customary law – are maintained. Section 7(1) of the Hong Kong Reunification Ordinance No 110, 1997, reinforces Article 8.

[101] In *Tai Hing Cotton Mill Ltd v Liu Chong Hing Bank Ltd and Others* [1986] HKLR 1041, a Hong Kong appeal case, the Privy Council held that the courts in Hong Kong were bound by a decision of the Privy Council and the House of Lords on common legislation and general law.

[102] Articles 81 and 82, Basic Law.

[103] The Court of Final Appeal Ordinance established the Court of Final Appeal in 1997.

[104] Article 84, Basic Law.

[105] For example, see the Malaysian Supreme Court case of *United Asian Bank Bhd v Tai Soon Heng Construction Sdn Bhd* [1993] 1 MLJ 182, where in deciding to follow the Privy Council decision in *Tai Hing Cotton Mill v Liu Chong Hing Bank Ltd* [1986] HKLR 1041 that a customer, at common law, only owes the bank two limited duties (i.e. to avoid facilitating fraud or forgery when drawing a cheque and to inform the bank of any forgery of a cheque), Annuar J stated, 'In our judgment, it is important generally speaking, and more so in matters of commercial law, that there should be uniformity in the common law of the Commonwealth. We are of the view that this is good judicial policy and provides for consistency.'

[106] R.Y.K. Ho, R.H. Scott and K.A. Wong, *The Hong Kong Financial System* (Hong Kong: Oxford University Press, 1991), pp. 381–405.

In making this observation, it is nonetheless acknowledged that there appears to be little, or at best only doubtful, linkage between the economic development of a country and the efficiency of its credit and security legal framework.[107]

Fourthly, a study of Hong Kong might provide impetus for other Asian common law jurisdictions (including Malaysia and Singapore) to consider the future direction of their credit and security legal frameworks.

In contrast, China has had a very short history of substantial consideration of the complex issues discussed in this book. But given China's ever-increasing prominence in world trade, the very large quantities of foreign direct investment that have flowed into China in the last thirty years and the rapid transformation of her state-owned financial system, the subject of security interests in personal property is of increasing importance.

There are a number of other reasons for choosing China as a comparator with Hong Kong.

Firstly, the People's Republic of China resumed sovereignty over Hong Kong on 1 July 1997. In the last decade mainland China and the Hong Kong Special Autonomous Region (HKSAR) have been operating under the principle of 'one country, two systems'. The geographical adjacency and close economic relations between these two parts of the same state obviously justify a thorough understanding of the commercial laws in both jurisdictions. This is particularly important as the central government and HKSAR authorities signed the Closer Economic Partnership Arrangement (CEPA),[108] a regional trade agreement within the meaning of Article XXIV of the General Agreement on Tariffs and Trade (GATT)[109] and Article V of General Agreement on Trade in Services (GATS),[110] which provides early enhancement of economic opportunities for Hong Kong-based producers of goods and services in the mainland market. CEPA supposedly assists in more closely integrating the two separate economic

[107] As noted by Allan, Hiscock and Roebuck, above, note 1, pp. 3–4. The observation was made in the context of countries in Asia other than Hong Kong. But the varied economic backgrounds of these countries make the application of their observation to Hong Kong plausible.

[108] The mainland and Hong Kong Closer Economic Partnership Arrangement (CEPA) was signed on 29 June 2003 and 29 September 2003, with ongoing supplementary signatures. See www.tid.gov.hk/english/cepa/index.html for details.

[109] Hong Kong has become a separate contracting party to GATT (1947) since 1986, and was one of the original members of the World Trade Organization (WTO) when it was established on 1 January 1995. See www.wto.org/english/docs_e/legal_e/gatt47_e.pdf.

[110] For details, see www.wto.org/English/docs_e/legal_e/26-gats.pdf.

markets. This closer economic relationship between the two sides makes a mutual understanding of each other's economic laws even more important. Hong Kong-based banks, especially, began to take advantage of the liberalised market access in services granted by China under its World Trade Organization (WTO) accession concessions earlier than banks from other WTO member jurisdictions. Thus comparing legal security arrangements as regards the Hong Kong and Chinese systems is important to these new lenders in the mainland market.

Secondly, China has been one of the fastest-developing economies in the world for over two decades. Both the absolute and the relative size of the economy justifies a detailed review of its personal property security laws. China's entry into the WTO in 2001 further paved the way for foreign participation in this vast new market, especially in sectors such as financial services. It is therefore essential for both foreign entrants and domestic players to understand China's current credit security regulations and be aware of the many potential pitfalls.

Thirdly, China is in the process of overhauling its civil law system and aspires to enact a comprehensive Civil Law Code. In the meantime, security rights over property are a key issue in the new Property Law (2007) that will eventually form part of the completed Civil Code. In view of the general sentiment that the current legal regime for security over personal property remains suboptimal, it has never been more appropriate to conduct a thorough review of the re-enacted security mechanisms in the new Property Law.

Finally, as Hong Kong is considering reform of credit security laws governing security of personal property at least where companies are concerned, it is appropriate to conduct a detailed examination of the corresponding laws in the two jurisdictions and to compare their strengths and weaknesses.[111] This comparison will hopefully shed light on our understanding of security mechanisms over personal property and contribute to the debate on the ongoing reform efforts in both jurisdictions.

Before concluding this brief overview of the Hong Kong and Chinese jurisdictions, it should be noted that the expression 'civil law' is used in this book in the loose sense of distinguishing the credit security laws of China from the common law of Hong Kong.

[111] The Hong Kong SAR authorities are currently conducting a wholesale reform of company law including the regime for company charges and other security devices. For an explanation of progress made to date, see V. Stott, *Hong Kong Company Law* (Hong Kong: Pearson/Longman, 2008).

1.6 The scope of the book, and characteristics of security arrangements examined

The hypothesis is tested only in respect of security arrangements that satisfy the following conditions:

- the secured assets comprise *personal property*,
- the secured monetary obligations constitute *credit*,
- the arrangement confers upon the creditor a *security* over personal property,
- the security arrangement is constituted by *agreement* and not implied by law,
- the security arrangement is a *non-consumer* transaction and
- the credit provided is of *domestic* origin.

Each of these is discussed below.

1.6.1 Personal property

In Hong Kong, property is classified as *real property*[112] or *personal property*. There is no legal definition of 'personal property' in either statutory law or case law. The concept of 'personal property' is one of a range of 'rights' that exist over various kinds of property that can generally be reduced to a question of physical possession. This derives from the English medieval procedural forms of enforcing property rights.[113] Personal property in this sense, like its counterpart in England, can be classified into chattels personal and chattels real (leaseholds). For all practical purposes,

[112] Basically, real property means land and interests created over it, such as leases and easements, see §2, Conveyancing and Property Ordinance (Cap. 219).

[113] See R.J. Walker, *Walker and Walker, The English Legal System*, 5th ed. (London: Butterworths, 1985), pp. 3–4. If the remedies for wrongs committed against the property of the true owner could only be commenced by 'personal actions', the property would be classified as 'personal property'. Examples of historical personal actions include action of trespass, action of replevin and action of detinue: see *Potter's Historical Introduction to English Law*, 4th ed. (London: Sweet & Maxwell, 1958), p. 409. If the remedies for wrongs committed against the property of the true owner could only be commenced by 'real action', the property would be classified as real property. This action became associated with actions for the recovery of freehold land: see R.E. Megarry and H.W.R. Wade, *The Law of Real Property*, 4th ed. (London: Stevens & Sons, 1974), pp. 1167–74. A central feature of personal actions was that the wrongdoer had a choice; they could either restore the property or pay compensation to the true owner. In contrast, in the case of real actions involving real property, the wrongdoer had no choice but to return possession of the land to the true owner. These historical procedural forms are no longer important today.

chattels real are regarded as real property in Hong Kong.[114] They therefore fall outside the ambit of this book. Chattels personal are further divided into choses in possession and choses in action. Choses in action are, in turn, divided into legal choses in action and equitable choses in action. The modern trend is to describe choses in possession and choses in action as 'tangible property' and 'intangible property' respectively.[115] This is necessary because new technology and trade practices can create new forms of property that do not easily fit into any of the traditional classes of personal property.[116] For example, in the Hong Kong case of *AG v Chan Nai Keung*, the Judicial Committee of the Privy Council had to consider whether a textile export quota in Hong Kong was a chose in action.[117] The Privy Council, in a relatively short advice, held that, although an export quota was a valuable form of intangible property that could be stolen, sold, or mortgaged, it was not a chose in action.[118] The decision seems to have been based on the ground that no analogy could be drawn from the established categories of choses in action. The decision was not generally well received by the inferior local courts, but they accepted that they were bound by it.[119]

[114] In Hong Kong, except for the site of St John's Cathedral on Hong Kong Island, all land is leased.

[115] See *Halsbury's Laws of England*, 4th ed. (London: Butterworths, reissue, 1995), vol. 6, para. 8. Here no less than eighty types of choses in action are described and categorised into five classes. They are diverse in nature and character. Some of them embody the original concept of a chose in action – i.e. there must a debtor against whom the right is immediately enforceable such as a debt – but others do not. See also J.D. Lipton, *Security over Intangible Property* (Sydney: LBC Information Services, 2000), Chapter 1.

[116] See Lipton, above, note 115, Chapters 1 and 6, where the author observed that with the advent of innovative technologies, new intangible rights are continuously being created for example, words, phrases, names, marks and associated goodwill.

[117] [1987] 1 WLR 1339. [118] Ibid., *per* Lord Bridge of Harwich, at p. 1342.

[119] In the subsequent case of *Hong Kong and Shanghai Banking Corporation v Star Trans International Ltd* [1988] 2 HKLR 549, Hunter JA in the single judgment of the Court of Appeal, while accepting that he was bound by *Chan Nai Keung*, cast doubt on the Privy Council's decision. He expressed the view that Zimmern J's earlier decision in *Re Golden Wall Shirts Factory Ltd v The Director of Trade, Industry and Customs* [1981] 1 HKLR 144, that textile export quota was a chose in action was probably correct and had it been referred to by counsel at the Privy Council the conclusion might have been different. However, when the judgment of Zimmern J is closely analysed, save for a single sentence that stated 'the quota certificates are *valuable choses in action*' (emphasis added), his judgment was no better than the decision of the Privy Council. There was little analysis of the juridical characteristics of the export quota certificate and its relationship with the characteristics of the various established classes of choses in action. A serious attempt to clarify the basis of the Judicial Committee's decision was made by Godfrey J in *State Bank of India and Another v Lisbellow and Others* [1989] 2 HKLR 604.

In Chinese law, the starting point of understanding 'personal property' should be determined by considering the Security Law (1995), its Judicial Interpretation of the Supreme People's Court (2000) and the recently enacted Property Law (2007). Article 178 of the Property Law stipulates that in case of any inconsistency with the Security Law, the Property Law shall prevail. Therefore in relation to this book, the proper view is that as regards issues on security interests over personal property, they are now mainly governed by the Property Law. The previous Security Law and its corresponding judicial interpretations serve to complement the provisions of the Property Law.

In Chinese law, 'personal property' is an unknown concept. This is because the term 'personal property' derives from common law. Even the term 'property' is not used when discussing credit security, and the nomenclature utilised in this context can be translated as 'things' (known in Chinese as *wu*). 'Things' in the Chinese legal sense means movable or immovable material objects that have value to human beings and can be controlled by people.[120] 'Property rights' can be more accurately designated as 'the rights over things', including ownership, usufructuary and security interests in property rights.[121] Furthermore, 'things' must be tangible.[122] However, intangible things, such as heat or electricity, exist physically and are 'things' in this sense. Other intangible things that have a purely conceptual existence – such as intellectual property rights, trade secrets, know-how and information – are not 'things' in Chinese civil law.[123] Nevertheless, intellectual property rights can be pledged to secure a pledgor's obligations, being a departure from legal principle as a result of specific statutory provision.[124]

'Things' in Chinese law are generally classified into 'immovable things' and 'movable things'.[125] Immovable things include land, houses, trees and

He explained that an export quota could not be regarded as a chose in action as it was a property right that was not enforceable by action in private law but in public law – i.e. the quota holder's remedy, in the event that his right to export the stated amount was denied, was against the Hong Kong Department of Trade, which granted the export quota.

120 Faxin Lin, 'Thought on Concept of Property Right', *Journal of Fujian Institute of Political Science and Law* 2 (2004); see also Article 2 of the Property Law (2007) which provides that the term 'property' includes movable and real property.

121 Article 2 of the Property Law provides that 'property rights' as a term refers to exclusive rights enjoyed by the obligagee to directly control specific properties including ownership, usufructuary and security interests in property rights.

122 Huixing Liang, *Introduction to Civil Law* (Beijing: Law Press, 1996), p. 81; Zhenying Wei, *Civil Law* (Beijing University Press, 2000), p. 119.

123 Ibid. 124 Article 223 of the Property Law.

125 Article 92 of the Security Law, though the notion of 'movable things', in the context of security interest, is not defined in the Property Law.

other things firmly fixed to the land. Immovable things usually cannot be moved without some transformation in their nature or decrease in their economic value.[126] Things other than immovables are called 'movable things'. Movables can be moved without substantial diminution in their economic value. In this regard, money and negotiable securities are generally regarded as special movable property.[127]

Property, strictly speaking, is not a legal concept in Chinese law. When it is used, it covers a much wider meaning than 'things'. It may include anything, tangible or intangible, that possesses economic value.[128] Obviously, the Chinese use of 'things' rather than 'property' causes much confusion and is the subject of fierce debate amongst scholars.[129] Many argue that intangible things, such as intellectual property rights, are of increasing economic significance and should be recognised as 'things', since they can be pledged to secure obligations. Some venture to suggest that intangible property should be considered as a 'movable thing'.[130] Opponents argue that to recognise intangible intellectual property as a 'thing' will disrupt the whole civil law system and, in any event, intellectual property rights are governed by a separate law and should not be part of a property law scheme in China.

In general, China's concept of 'immovable things' and 'movable things' is largely synonymous with the concept of 'real property' and 'personal property' in Hong Kong law. However, they do not always coincide. For example, intangible property, such as intellectual property rights is regarded as 'personal property' in Hong Kong but is not considered to be 'movable things' in China. Bearing in mind the differences, we adopt the term 'property' rather than 'things' when discussing the Chinese credit security system over personal property for the sake of consistency. That is, the term 'personal property' is used in its common law sense, including both movable things and intangible property in China.

Thus, for the purpose of this book, the expression 'personal property' includes, in the Hong Kong context, choses in possession and choses in

126 Junhao Zhang, *Theories of Civil Law*, 3rd ed. (Beijing: Chinese University of Politics and Law Press, 2000), p. 371.

127 Huixing Liang, above, note 122; Junju Ma, *Civil Law* (Beijing: Law Press, 1998), p. 93.

128 Liming Wang, *On Property Law* (Beijing: Chinese University of Politics and Law Press, 1988), p. 13.

129 Liming Wang, Mingrui Guo and Liufang Fang, *Civil Law* (Beijing: Chinese University of Politics and Law Press, 2003), p. 18.

130 Shibing Cao, *Solutions and Prospects on Questions Related to Chinese Security Mechanism: Based on Security Law and its Judicial Interpretations* (Beijing: China Fa Zhi Press, 2001), p. 199.

action (as traditionally described above) and all forms of tangible and intangible property. In China, 'personal property' includes all forms of movable property and intangible property. It should be emphasised that intangible property is generally not regulated by the Property Law but subject to separate laws.[131]

Ships and aircraft, which are chattels,[132] fall outside the scope of this book because the laws governing them are very specialised, wide and highly complex.[133]

1.6.2 Credit

The word 'credit', in the commercial sense, has a narrow meaning. According to the Crowther Report,[134] it means either the deferment of payment for goods or services rendered at once or the straight lending of money. This narrow meaning has been accepted in the courts in several common law jurisdictions.[135] If the same view was adopted in this book, many arrangements that are 'credit' in substance, if not in form, would be excluded. Such arrangements include hire-purchase, conditional sale, leasing, discounting of receivables, factoring and consignment of goods ('quasi-security arrangements').[136] This would go against the tide

131 Liming Wang, 'Some Thoughts on the Legislation of Property Law in China' (speech), Sino-US Property Law Forum, Beijing, 2002.

132 See N. Palmer and E. McKendrick (eds.), *Interests in Goods* (London: LLP, 1998), especially Chapter 26, A. Clarke, 'Ship Mortgages', at pp. 663–95; and also Chapter 28, P. Thorne, 'Interests in Goods – Aircraft Mortgages', at pp. 697–726.

133 D.E. Allan, 'Personal Property Security – Rip Van Winkle Awakes in the Antipodes', *JIBL* 13(1) (1998), 1, where the author states, 'Ships and aircraft? Well, they might need special legislation which would be a matter for international agreement.'

134 Cmnd 4596, Part 1, Chapter 1, 1.2, p. 1.

135 For example, in the English case of *R v Miller* [1977] 3 All ER 986, the Court of Appeal held that the word 'credit' in the old Bankruptcy Act 1914, §155(a) (the equivalent of §131(a) of the Hong Kong Bankruptcy Ordinance (Cap. 6)), meant obtaining some benefit from another under an agreement which postponed payment of the consideration for the benefit. Thus obtaining goods under a hire-purchase agreement did not constitute obtaining the goods on credit. See also the Australian case of *Herbert v The King* [1941] 64 CLR 461, where McTiernan J said, 'In commercial and financial affairs the word "credit" may signify the financial arrangement in a transaction or reputation for insolvency and honesty which entitles a person desirous of incurring a debt or liability to do so on the terms that payment is to be deferred. In its former meaning it includes the delivery of goods or the advancing of money with the trust that the debtor will have the means to pay and will pay at the future date.'

136 See English Law Commission Consultation Paper No 164, above, note 1, Part VI, para. 6.16.

of opinion that the word 'credit' should be given a broad meaning, thus including arrangements of this type.[137] Accordingly, in this book the word 'credit' is given that extended meaning. However, we are not specifically concerned with the nature of the credit under these arrangements. Rather the emphasis is on the devices used to secure the repayment of the credit.

In China, the expression 'credit' has not received the sort of sophisticated discussion, either judicially or academically, that has occurred in common law jurisdictions. According to Article 173 of the Property Law, credit, or the scope of security interest, includes the principal debt and the interest thereon, default penalty, liquidated damages and the expenses for storage of pledged assets and enforcement of security interests, unless otherwise provided in the security contract.

1.6.3 Security

As Allan has noted, the expression 'security' is not easy to define in the common law.[138] In different contexts, it means different things. For instance, shares or debentures are also described as 'securities', but they are not credit security arrangements. For the purpose of this book, the hypothesis does not apply to these entities.

The hypothesis applies only to security transactions, which, according to Allan, confer on the secured creditor certain rights in specified property that can be asserted against strangers to the transaction.[139] These rights are rights of preference and pursuit in respect of the secured assets.[140] Preference not only means that the security holder has priority, but also includes:

- a right to pay his claim out of the secured assets or their proceeds in priority to both the general creditors and other secured creditors against

[137] See Crowther Report, Cmnd 4596, Part 1, Chapter 1, 1.2.1, p. 1; and E.I. Sykes and S. Walker, *Law of Securities*, 5th ed. (Sydney: Law Book Company Ltd, 1993), pp. 20–1, where the authors described the hire-purchase agreement as a legal fiction and took the view that it is in reality a chattel mortgage securing a loan. See also *Bridge v Campbell Discount Co. Ltd* [1962] 1 ALL ER 385, 397, HL, where Lord Denning, referring to Maitland, said that the hire-purchase agreement 'is the worst of our mortgage deed … it is one long *suppressio veri* and *suggestio falsi*'. For a similar view see the Australian case of *Esanda Finance Corporation Ltd v Plessnig and Another* [1989] 63 ALJR 238, (1989) 166 CLR 131, where Brennan J thought a hire-purchase agreement was a chattel mortgage.

[138] D.E. Allan, 'Some Mysteries, Myths, and Monstrosities', *Monash LR* 15 (1989), 337, particularly pp. 344–50.

[139] Ibid. at p. 345. [140] Ibid. at p. 346.

whom he has a prior claim under the rules of priority, whether statutory, legal or equitable;[141]
- the right of the secured party to follow the asset into the hands of third parties and to satisfy his claim out of the asset.[142]

The second right is a reinforcement and expansion of the first. A transaction that does not give the creditor these rights is not a security.

The extended definition also includes the interests of the supplier under hire-purchase, conditional sale, or leasing agreements. For example, the principles of 'a right to pay his claim out of the secured assets' and 'the right of the secured party to follow the asset into the hands of third parties' are also fundamental substantive rights of such a supplier.[143]

The definitions of other commentators have also been considered,[144] but they appear narrow and inadequate for the purpose of the hypothesis, as they do not include the rights involved in a hire-purchase, conditional sale and leasing, and are incapable of being extended to include them. The inclusion of hire-purchase, conditional sale and leasing as creating security interests, as adopted here, is in accord with contemporary views.[145]

However, in *Armour and Another v Thyssen Edelstahlwerke AG*,[146] the House of Lords unanimously held that a conditional sale that effectively retained title in goods sold to the buyer did not, in favour of the

141 Ibid. 142 Ibid. 143 See Chapters 5 and 7 below.

144 For example, Sykes and Walker, above, note 137, p. 12. See also Goode, above, note 64, at p. 733; Ellinger, Lomnicka and Hooley, above, note 65, particularly pp. 721–8; Diamond, above, note 1, p. 10; and Eyre, above, note 14, para. 4.

145 For example, see *Borden (UK) Ltd v Scottish Timber Products and Another* [1979] 3 All ER 961, at 971, where Templeman LJ said that a retention of title created a new super-equitable security; *John Snow & Co. Ltd v DGB Woodcroft* [1985] BCLC 54, at 63, *per* Boreham J; Crowther Committee Report on Consumer Credit, Cmnd 4596, para. 1.3.8; and S. Cowan, A. Clark and G. Goldberg, 'Will English Romalpa Clauses Become Registrable Securities?', *CLJ* (1995), 43, where the view was that a retention-of-title clause was in reality a chattel mortgage; and the English Law Commission Consultation Paper No 164, Part VI, 'Functional Equivalents to Security.' For modern legislation which adopts this broad definition, see Article 1, para. 201 of the US Uniform Commercial Code which defines a 'security interest' in goods to include leases if the following are satisfied: (a) the consideration consists of the lessee's obligation to pay the lessor for the right to possession and use of the goods, (b) the lease is not subject to termination by the lessor and (c) the lessee has an option to become the owner of the goods for no additional consideration or nominal additional consideration upon compliance with the lease agreement. See also §17 of the New Zealand Personal Property Act 1999, which provides that the term 'security interest' includes conditional sale agreement, hire-purchase and lease.

146 [1991] 2 AC 339.

buyer, create any security interests in the goods, but merely confirmed the seller's ownership interests in the goods sold. Their Lordships took an orthodox view, which in strict terms was correct. However, *Armour* has to be reconsidered in light of the more recent decision in *On Demand Information plc (in administrative receivership) and Another v Michael Gerson (Finance) plc and Another*,[147] where it was held by Their Lordships that a finance lease was, in substance, a security transaction that gave the lessee a proprietary interest. These matters are discussed further in Chapter 5 below.[148]

It is therefore possible to differ from the orthodox view in *Armour* and, instead, adopt the prevailing and more expansive majority view.

In China, the expression 'security' is not specifically defined in the Property Law or Security Law, nor has it received academic or judicial consideration in any depth. However, on the basis of the Property Law and judicial definitions of the function of various security devices in China, it appears that 'security' means a right to secure or guarantee the repayment of credit granted by a lender to a borrower. For instance, Article 208 of the Property Law states that a pledge of movable property gives the pledgee the right to retain possession of the thing pledged until the creditor is satisfied. Additionally, the pledgee is entitled to sell the property by public auction if repayment of the credit has not been made. In relation to the non-possessory security device of mortgage, Article 179 provides that the creation of the mortgage directly and immediately subjects the property over which it is imposed to an obligation to fulfil repayment of credit. Thus the substantive meaning of 'security' is consonant with the traditional meaning of 'security' at common law discussed earlier. As in Hong Kong, Chinese law does not regard a lease, hire-purchase or conditional sale as 'security'.[149] However, they are, for the purpose of this book, broadly treated in the same way as in Hong Kong – that is, they are regarded as credit 'security'.

1.6.4 Constituted by agreement

The ambit of this book is confined to consensual credit security arrangements over personal property. In the common law context,

[147] [2002] 2 All ER 949, UKHL 13. [148] See Chapter 5 below.

[149] In China, lease, hire-purchase and conditional sale are stipulated in the Contract Law (1999) rather than in the Property Law or the Security Law. Further, these devices are not mentioned in legal treatises in China which are concerned with the Property Law or the Security Law. In fact, no scholar advocates that these arrangements should form part of the scheme under the Property Law or the Security Law.

such forms of security arrangements mean all mortgages, charges and other security interests voluntarily created or granted by the mortgagor/chargor, including equitable mortgages and charges created accidentally or deliberately.[150] It does not include any security arising by operation of law.[151]

However, because the book includes China, where many of the security devices, such as the legal mortgage *strictu sensu*, are alien to Chinese law, a neutral but hopefully accurate meaning is given to the expression 'consensual credit security'. This is an arrangement arising from an express agreement between a person called 'the creditor' and another person called 'the debtor' or 'a third party' under which a security interest in the personal property of the debtor or third party is vested in the creditor. The security interest gives the creditor the security rights discussed above in relation to the meaning of 'security'. In the context of Chinese law, such forms of security arrangements include all mortgages, pledges, deposits and other voluntarily agreed security interests. Liens which arise by operation of law rather than consensual agreement are not discussed because of this definition. However, they do exist under the Security Law.[152] Under Article 82, a creditor shall be entitled to have the right to have a lien (a right to 'detain') the said property if the debtor does not perform the debt obligation by the time agreed in the contract. Examples include contracts of safekeeping, contracts of carriage or contracts for processing as stipulated in Article 84. This stipulation further provides that the right of lien can be explicitly excluded by agreement. Therefore it seems that liens described in the Security Law generally follow the definition of common law liens (as a general lien by way of contract – a contractual lien), which are non-consensual and non-possessory security interests that arise by the operation of law. However, Article 230 of the new Property Law seems to have enlarged the scope of liens to the extent that (1) in the absence of the specific contracts stipulated in Article 84 of the Security Law, contractual liens now seem to arise in any type of contract; and (2) in the absence of the express wording 'according to the agreement of the contract' in Article 230 (which was present in Article 82 of the Security Law), possessory liens (that is, liens arising by way of possession) may now be permitted.

[150] See the English Law Commission Report on Transfer of Land – Land Mortgages (London: HMSO, 1991), Law Cmnd. No 204, p. 1.

[151] Ibid. [152] Articles 82 and 84 of the Security Law.

In light of the expansion of the terms 'credit' and 'security', the term 'consensual security arrangement' includes hire-purchase, conditional sale and leasing.

1.6.5 *Non-consumer transaction*

The hypothesis applies only to non-consumer credit security arrangements.[153] This is to avoid both deviation from the focus of the hypothesis, and an unacceptable extension of the book's objectives that might result from any examination of this highly complex area of the policy relating to consumer transactions. However, consumer credit security arrangements will be referred to if they directly concern the fundamental operation and effect of credit security law.

1.6.6 *Domestic origin*

This limitation is necessary because Hong Kong is an international financial centre.[154] Large banks and financial institutions grant both international and domestic credit.[155] Domestic credit is defined as credit whereby (i) the creditor and the debtor are both situated in Hong Kong, (ii) the credit is denominated in Hong Kong dollars and (iii) the loans are for commercial use in Hong Kong. In these circumstances, the domestic legal framework and its machinery governing personal property are commonly used.[156] In contrast, international credit is credit whereby

[153] According to §4(1) of the Control of Exemption Clause Ordinance (Cap. 71) a consumer transaction is one where one party to the contract neither makes the contract in the course of a business nor holds himself out as doing so and the other party does make the contract in the course of a business. §3(1) of the Unconscionable Contracts Ordinance (Cap. 458) adopts the same definition of a consumer. China does not have such a clear definition. In China, although the Consumer Rights Protection Law (1993) uses the term 'consumer' in several sections of the Law, there is no definition of the term. It would not be inaccurate to postulate that the term 'consumer' in the Hong Kong Ordinances and China Act generally have the same meaning.

[154] See J. Yam, 'Hong Kong as an International Financial Centre to 2010', 22 February 2001, available at www.info.gov.hk/hkma.

[155] Ibid. See also J. Yam, 'Domestic Lending', 22 February 2001; see www.info.gov.hk/hkma.

[156] See P. Bourke and B. Shamugam (eds.), *An Introduction to Bank Lending – Risk Management in International Lending* (Sydney: Addison-Wesley Publishing Company Inc., 1990), Chapter 12, pp. 150–7. The Hong Kong Monetary Authority statistics (June 2002) on domestic lending identified the following area of commercial domestic borrowings of Hong Kong: manufacturing (textiles, footwear, etc.); agriculture and fisheries (fisheries, livestock, etc.); transport and transport equipment; building, construction,

(i) the credit is denominated in foreign currency, (ii) the credit is for overseas use and (iii) either the creditor or debtor is situated overseas.[157] There are two reasons for excluding international lending. Firstly, the credit and security arrangements are highly complex, multifactorial, and strategic.[158] Secondly, the domestic credit security legal framework over personal property is usually not an issue.[159] Similar considerations apply as regards China. For these reasons, international lending is beyond the scope of this work.

1.7 Structure of the book

Including this chapter, this book has eight chapters. The objectives of the subsequent seven chapters are as follows.

In Chapter 2 we build on the foundation established in Chapter 1. We examine the rules governing the creation, perfection and publicity of traditional credit security devices (other than quasi-security) over tangible personal property in Hong Kong and China, and the costs involved. The examination determines whether the criteria established in section 1.4 above have been satisfied.

Chapter 3 basically follows the same format as Chapter 2, except that the subject matter is intangible personal property. Again, the examination of the relevant rules determines whether the criteria relating to the creation, perfection, publicity and cost of the traditional security devices commonly used to secure intangible personal property in Hong Kong and China have been satisfied.

Chapter 4 examines the specific issues relating to companies granting security over personal property. In Hong Kong, the expression 'company' means any organisation registered under the Companies Ordinance (Cap. 32).[160] In China, however, classifying the types of business entity that have separate legal status is a complex exercise. 'Independent legal person'

property development and investment; wholesale retail trade; and others, such as hotels, boarding houses and catering; see www.info.gov.hk/hkma.

157 Bourke and Shamugam, above, note 156, p. 156.

158 The following factors usually concern the creditor: stability of currency in question, exchange control regulation, jurisdiction, sovereign risk and country risk. See Bourke and Shamugam, above, note 156.

159 See also Yam, above, note 155. Yam suggested that this would increasingly be the case for Hong Kong businesses in mainland PRC. They increasingly raise loans in renminbi (RMB) and the loans are secured by 'pledges' of factory premises on the mainland.

160 It includes overseas companies registered under §333 of the Companies Ordinance.

status conferred on a 'company' refers either to a limited liability company or a joint-stock limited company.[161] It can be seen that these organisations have similarities to those in Hong Kong and they have the same basic legal attributes, namely: (i) they are artificial legal persons having perpetual succession (except that the Company Law in China does not specifically mention the right of perpetual succession, though shares are transferable), (ii) they have the ability to own property and (iii) they bear the liabilities for their own debts and the right to own.[162] In view of the complexity and peculiarity of the rules governing the creation of securities by such organisations, particularly in Hong Kong, examination of company-granted security justifies a separate chapter.

In Chapter 5 we examine the rules governing the creation, perfection, publicity and cost of securing tangible personal property by way of hire-purchase, leasing and conditional sale. We consider whether the criteria relating to efficiency have been satisfied. These arrangements justify a separate discussion because their characteristics are different from the traditional security devices discussed in the earlier chapters.

Chapter 6 discusses the right of priority which is linked to the issue of perfection, but it justifies a separate chapter because the rules governing priority of competing claims in Hong Kong are highly complex and technical. Some of the rules are judge-made and some are statutory. In contrast, the rules of priority in China are primarily statutory. We therefore examine the nature of and differences between the rules of priority in Hong Kong and China, and determine whether they have satisfied the enunciated criteria on priority.

Chapter 7 examines the various types of remedy conferred by traditional and quasi-security devices in Hong Kong and China, and the process of enforcing such remedies. We then discuss whether the criteria on enforcement have been satisfied.

In conclusion, Chapter 8 addresses the question whether the hypothesis proffered here has been established in relation to either Hong Kong or China or both. We collate all the findings generated by the application of the criteria in each of the preceding chapters on the functional aspects of creation, perfection, publicity, enforcement and cost of security over

161 Articles 2 and 3 of the Company Law 2006.

162 In Hong Kong the following cases established these attributes of the company: *Salomon v A Salomon & Co. Ltd* [1897] AC 22; *Good Profit Development Ltd v Leung Hoi* [1993] 2 HKLR176; and *China Ocean Shipping Co. v Mitrans Shipping Co. Ltd* [1995] 3 HKC 720. In China the attributes are defined in Article 3 of the Company Law 2006.

personal property in Hong Kong and China. We also suggest reform of the credit security legal frameworks in Hong Kong and China.

1.8 A note on the status of the law

This book attempts to state the law as at 1 March 2009.

Chapter 2

Security over tangible personal property

2.1 Introduction

In Hong Kong, the types of consensual security device that can be created over tangible personal property are the legal mortgage *strictu sensu*, equitable mortgage, charge, pledge and trust receipt. The creation and perfection of these security devices are governed by the rules of common law, equity and legislation. Publicity, on the other hand, is mainly governed by legislation, namely the Bills of Sale Ordinance (Cap. 20)[1] and the Companies Ordinance (Cap. 32); both are very specific in their application. The former applies to security over certain types of tangible personal property created by non-corporate debtors.[2] It indirectly applies to companies via §80(2) of the Companies Ordinance, which strictly applies only to companies. Section 80(2) provides that where a security in writing granted by a company (that is, if executed by a non-corporate debtor) requires registration to constitute a bill of sale, the security is registrable with the Companies Registry.[3] This chapter concentrates on security over tangible personal property granted by non-corporate debtors.

In contrast, at present China has five types of consensual security device over tangible personal property, all clearly stipulated in legislation, namely mortgage, pledge, deposit, lien, charge and trust receipt.[4] The creation, perfection and publicity of these security devices are

[1] The origin of the Bills of Sale Ordinance is traced to Ordinance No 5 of 1856, which extended the whole of the United Kingdom Secret Bills of Sale Act, *17 & 18 Vict c 36*, except §8, to the colony. See A.J. Leach, *The Ordinances of the Legislative Council of the Colony of Hong Kong* (Hong Kong: Noronha & Co., 1890), vol. 1. The provisions of Ordinance No 5 were repealed by Ordinance No 10, which created separate 'Bills of Sale' provisions, but it was modelled on the United Kingdom Secret Bills of Sale Act.

[2] It does not apply to companies: see *Re Standard Manufacturing Co.* [1891–4] All ER Rep 1245, 1246–7, *per* Bowen LJ; also W.J. Gough, *Company Charges*, 2nd ed. (London: Butterworths, 1996), p. 36.

[3] The companies registration system will be discussed further below in Chapter 4.

[4] See Chapters III, IV, V and VI of the Security Law (1995) and the Trust Law (2001).

governed by legislation, related judicial interpretations, administrative regulations and government circulars. The most important amongst them is the Security Law enacted in 1995, and its related judicial interpretations issued by the Supreme Court in 2000; however, as previously mentioned, the relevant provisions of the recently enacted 2007 Property Law take priority.[5]

2.1.1 *Historical development of security interests in China*

Before the enactment of the Security Law in 1995, the major governing legislation on security was the General Principles of Civil Law (GPCL) of the PRC enacted in 1986 and its Judicial Interpretation issued in 1988. Legally speaking, both GPCL and the Security Law are applicable to security interests in China. But the Security Law greatly modified and expanded the provisions governing security found in the GPCL. Consequently the Security Law is the most comprehensive statement governing security matters in China. In sharp contrast to the Bills of Sale Ordinance and the Companies Ordinance, both the GPCL and the Security Law, together with their judicial interpretations in 2000, apply to securities granted by both corporate and non-corporate debtors.

However, in the late 1990s, the Chinese government issued proposals for a new property law to protect state-owned, collectively owned and private property. Real property, personal property and rights over property were all to be settled comprehensively. The Property Law was finally adopted at the fifth Session of the tenth National People's Congress of the People's Republic of China on 16 March 2007. The Property Law was then promulgated and came into effect on 1 October 2007. The bill had gone through seven drafts and various revisions. The first draft of the Property Law was submitted to the National People of China's Standing Committee (NPCSC) in December 2002. Amendments to the Constitution legalising private property ownership for the first time in China occurred in March 2004, and this helped the adoption of the seventh draft in March 2007. It was anticipated that the Property Law would be a fundamental law in the Chinese legal system with a far-reaching impact on China's legal and economic development. The new law was intended to provide equality and the same level of protection between state interests and private property rights. For example, where state-owned properties are concerned, the law

[5] By making some amendments to the Security Law (1995), the Property Law (2007) focuses on selected security devices, namely mortgage, pledge, charge and lien.

stipulates that anyone causing loss due to unlawful activities will bear legal responsibility.[6] Correspondingly, individual rights relating to private property such as dwellings, income, savings and investments were also explicitly protected. The rules governing tangible property rights may also affect ongoing development in the security interests created over them. However, for the purpose of this book, our primary focus is the security devices (e.g. mortgage, pledge, deposit, lien) currently being used in China to protect claims against personal property, rather than the underlying rights themselves.

Whilst acknowledged as a fifth security device, trust receipt is not mentioned as a form of security in the Security Law, the Property Law or their related judicial interpretations. Nevertheless, it is frequently accepted as a form of security by Chinese banks and is generally regarded as a customary banking practice. Thus the status of a trust receipt in law was quite ambiguous. However, the enactment of the Trust Law in 2001 served to clarify the situation and now provides the trust receipt with a solid legal basis.

2.1.2 Objective of this chapter

The objective of this chapter is to determine whether or not the rules governing the creation, perfection and publicity of the above-mentioned security devices in Hong Kong and China have fully satisfied the criteria established in Chapter 1 and can therefore be said to be efficient.

2.2 Objectives of the Bills of Sale Ordinance in Hong Kong

The Bills of Sale Ordinance has two objectives. The first is to prevent the fraudulent conveyance of certain types of tangible property, as defined by the Ordinance. The second is to protect debtors in difficult financial circumstances from oppression by creditors. To understand the background of these statutory objectives and their relevance to Hong Kong today, it is necessary to consider their origin in the bills of sale legislation in the United Kingdom.[7]

[6] Article 57 of the Property Law.

[7] The first being the Bills of Sale Act 1852. It was subsequently repealed. Today in the United Kingdom, bills of sale are regulated by the Bills of Sale Act 1878, the Bills of Sale (Amendment) Act 1882, and the Bills of Sale Act 1890 (as amended by the Bills of Sale Act 1891).

The prevention of 'fraudulent conveyances' had nothing to do with commercial practice in the old colonial Hong Kong. Rather, it related to a serious mischief that was widespread in Victorian England. At that time, debtors, after creating non-possessory security interests over tangible personal property, often created further security interests over the same property to different creditors, without disclosing the earlier security and without obtaining the prior consent of that original creditor.[8] This was possible because the debtor had physical possession of the property, which represented to the whole world that the debtor was creditworthy, and that the property was free from encumbrances. Creditors could therefore be entrapped by the fraud of the debtor. More importantly, creditors could not effectively protect themselves against such fraud because there was no publicity mechanism through which they could conveniently and accurately determine the status of the property offered as security.

To remedy this mischief, the United Kingdom Parliament enacted the Bills of Sale Acts (hereafter 'the Acts').[9] This legislation introduced, inter alia, a system of registration for certain types of security affecting specific classes of tangible personal property called 'personal chattels'. If a registrable security was not registered, the security was rendered void against the grantor of the security and any third party who might be interested in the relevant personal chattel. Registration therefore served two purposes: the perfection and publicity of the security. Thus the registration system enabled a creditor who wished to make an advance to a debtor on the security of a personal chattel to verify the status of the property by making a search of the register before entering into a credit arrangement.[10]

Another objective can be traced to the Bills of Sale (Amendment) Act 1882. This was designed to relieve debtors from being entrapped into signing instruments containing harsh and unreasonable terms, another

[8] See *Cookson v Swire* [1884] 9 AC 653, 664, *per* Lord Blackburn; *Manchester, Sheffield and Lincolnshire Railway Co. v North Central Wagon Co.* (1888) 13 App Cas 554, 560, *per* Lord Herschell; *Charlesworth v Mills* [1892] AC 231, 238, *per* Lord Halsbury; and see also W. Holdsworth, *A History of English Law*, reprint (London: Methuen & Co. Ltd, Sweet & Maxwell, 1971), vol. 15, p. 197; and H.G. Hanbury and C.H.M. Waldock, *The Law of Mortgages*, 1st ed. (London: Sweet & Maxwell, 1938), p. 364. Note, the hostility against secret bills of sale went as far back as Lord Coke's period. The English Act of 13 Eliz c 5 (1571) was enacted to prevent fraudulent conveyances. See J. Ziegel, 'Canadian Perspectives on the New Zealand Chattel Securities Act', *NZBLQ* 7 (2001), 118 at p. 121.

[9] Bills of Sale Acts, above, note 8.

[10] *Davis v Burton* (1883) 11 QBD 537, 539, *per* Brett MR.

widespread mischief at the time.[11] This Act imposed stringent duties on the creditor to comply with various statutory provisions, such as the form of the security and the circumstances in which the creditor could exercise certain remedies against the secured goods.[12]

It is clear that the combined effect of these Acts was not to abolish the consensual non-possessory credit security devices of legal mortgage *strictu sensu*, equitable mortgage, charge and trust receipt in relation to tangible personal property – they merely regulated the creation, perfection and publicity of the devices which fell within the scope of the Acts.

In Hong Kong,[13] there is little evidence that fraudulent and oppressive practices constituted a significant problem.[14] In spite of this, the provisions of the first Bill of Sale Act were extended to Hong Kong in 1856,[15] and later transplanted into the Hong Kong domestic legal corpus in 1864 in the Bills of Sale Ordinance (No 10). The Ordinance was subsequently repealed and replaced by the Bills of Sale Ordinance of 1886 (Cap. 20). The Ordinance basically has the same objectives, preamble and provisions as the Acts. The Ordinance's practicality and relevance to the colony at the material time appeared to be of little concern to the legislature.[16]

Over the years, there has been a precipitous decline in the popularity of bills of sale in Hong Kong. A review of the records at the Registry of the High Court showed that on average ninety bills of sale per year

[11] See the Bills of Sale Act 1882 and dictum of Lord Herschell LC in *Manchester, Sheffield and Lincolnshire Railway Co. v North Central Wagon Co.* (1888) 13 App Cas 554, 560; see also *Thomas v Kelly* (1888) 13 App Cas 506, 514, *per* Lord FitzGerald.

[12] See the Bills of Sale Ordinance (Cap. 20), §14.

[13] The *China Mail* (the main newspaper of the colony and kept in microfilm at the University of Hong Kong Main Library and the Chinese University of Hong Kong since the 1850s) and the Hong Kong Law Reports since 1915 (when official law reporting began), made no mention of reported cases of public concern on this issue. Unreported cases (since 1950s and kept at the then Supreme Court Library, Hong Kong) and the major text of J.W. Norton-Kyshe, *The History of the Laws and Courts of Hong Kong*, reprint (Hong Kong: Vetch and Lee, 1971), vols. 1 and 2, were also reviewed but did not reveal any such problem.

[14] The only early unreported cases of mortgages over personal chattels and held to be void under the Bills of Sale Ordinance No 12 of 1886 were: *Jamieson v Croker* (*China Mail*, 8 March 1887, p. 3), and *Chan Kim Chune v J.F. Webber* (*China Mail*, 29 July 1890, p. 3). There was, however, no evidence to defraud creditors in either of these two cases. Note that the pawn or pledge seemed to be the security device commonly used by the Chinese to secure personal chattels in the early colonial era. See J.H. Gray, *A History of the Laws, Manners, and Customs of the Chinese People* (London: Macmillan & Co., 1878), vol. 2, pp. 78–86; and also Norton-Kyshe, above, note 14, vol. 1, pp. 328, 465, 495.

[15] Bill of Sale Act, above, note 1.

[16] The common form of credit and security over personal chattels among the Chinese population in Hong Kong was the pledge or pawn; see Gray, above, note 14.

were registered with the High Court between the years 1981 and 1990. However, in 1991, there were only twenty-one bills of sale registered, in 1996 there were only sixteen,[17] and in 2001 there were only four.[18]

2.3 Scope of the Bills of Sale Ordinance

When a creditor wishes to obtain a security over tangible personal property in Hong Kong, the first factor the lender has to consider is whether or not the security falls within the scope of the Bills of Sale Ordinance. If it does, the creditor has to comply with the method of creation and perfection of the security as defined by the Ordinance. If the creditor fails to follow the relevant provisions the validity of the security can be seriously impaired as concerns the debtor and any third party who has become interested in the property. In Hong Kong, if the debtor is a company, the creditor has to comply with the method of creation and perfection stipulated in the Companies Ordinance.[19]

Some of the requirements of the Bills of Sale Ordinance do not generally create difficulties for the creditor. Firstly, the formalities imposed by the Ordinance in respect of creation, perfection and publicity apply only to non-corporate debtors. In the case of corporate debtors, the general law and the Companies Ordinance apply. Secondly, the legislation applies only to non-possessory types of security device. The Ordinance does not apply to pledges,[20] because actual possession by the creditor is regarded as publicity of the encumbrance and avoids the risk of 'false wealth'.[21] Thirdly, the Ordinance does not apply to hire-purchase, leasing and conditional sale arrangements. Fourthly, it does not apply to security created by oral agreement.[22]

[17] The High Court Registry was visited at the end of 1996 and the register book was easily located. But in 2002 serious problems were encountered. See note 18 below.

[18] One lender was a bank and three were finance companies. Interestingly, one borrower was a registered company. The security should have been registered with the Registrar of Companies under §80(2) of the Companies Ordinance. On 9 March 2002, court officials could not find the register for the years between 1997 and 2000. The next day, on further enquiry, they could still not find the book.

[19] This is discussed further in Chapter 4 below.

[20] See English Law Commission Consultation Paper No 164, para. 4.15.

[21] Ibid.

[22] *Re Hemingway, ex parte Hauxwell* (1883) 23 Ch D 626; *Newlove and Others v Shrewsbury* [1888] 21 QBD 41 and *Ramsay v Margrett* [1894] 2 QB 18, [1891–4] All ER Rep 453. In *Ramsay* the court held that an earlier independent oral absolute sale agreement was not registrable under the equivalent of the Bills of Sale Act.

However, it is necessary to examine two conditions for application of the Ordinance in some detail. Firstly, the tangible personal property offered as security must constitute 'personal chattels'. Secondly, the document creating the security must constitute 'a bill of sale'.

2.3.1 *Definition of personal chattels*

Section 2 of the Ordinance defines personal chattels in an extremely complex manner. Three methods can be utilised in determining whether an object falls within the definition of 'personal chattels', namely (i) whether it satisfies a basic criterion, (ii) whether it comes within one of the three categories of 'personal chattels' and (iii) whether it belongs to the category of property that falls outside §2.

Basic criterion

The basic criterion for designation as a 'personal chattel' is that the object must be capable of being removed completely and physically delivered to the creditor at the time the bill of sale was executed.[23] The time factor is derived from the statutory Form 2[24] to which a bill of sale must conform.[25] It requires the parties to describe the 'personal chattel' in the bill of sale at the time of execution of the document. This requirement, therefore, excludes after-acquired and future property from the definition of 'personal chattels'.

The courts have strictly interpreted this exclusion to mean that no written security can be granted by a non-corporate debtor over such property, even if the property could constitute 'personal chattels' when the property subsequently comes into the possession of the debtor. If the creditor mistakenly includes any after-acquired and future property in the bill of sale, §12 of the Ordinance will render the bill of sale void, except as against the debtor–grantor, in respect of the relevant property.[26]

This strict interpretation has two shortcomings. Firstly, it denies a large number of non-corporate businesses[27] the ability to create equitable

[23] See Bills of Sale Ordinance, §2, Appendix A; and see also *Thomas v Kelly* (1888) 13 App Cas 506, 518–19, *per* Lord Macnaghten.

[24] For further discussion of Form 2, see below in this chapter.

[25] See §11 of the Bills of Sale Ordinance. [26] Ibid.

[27] In Hong Kong there were approximately 239,298 examples of active unincorporated businesses in Hong Kong as of 31 March 2008 according to statistics kept by the Inland Revenue Department. See www.info.gov.hk/ird. Note that until the introduction of the statutory form in 1882 by the Bills of Sale Amendment Act 1882, and the enactment of

security, including floating charges,[28] over future property. Consequently, as the English Law Commission commented, this 'is an additional handicap to the raising of finance' by non-corporate traders.[29] This appears to be confirmed by the small number of bills of sale registered at the Registry of the High Court, as mentioned earlier.[30] It is contended that this limitation is unjustifiable in principle. It is contrary to the proactive commercial policy of the general law, particularly equity, which, in the Victorian era, extended equitable security by the creation of the floating charge that allowed corporate businesses in manufacturing and trade to raise additional loan capital.[31] The situation becomes even more untenable as the after-acquired and future property of the corporate businesses and non-corporate businesses may be the same.[32]

Secondly, §12 does not prohibit a debtor from orally creating security over after-acquired and future property.[33] If such security is created, it poses a potential risk to subsequent third parties dealing with the debtor in respect of 'personal chattels' that may have come into possession of the debtor. The third party cannot discover, in advance, whether or not

§4 in the same Act (equivalent to §11 of the Hong Kong Bills of Sale Ordinance), floating charges were commonly created by individuals. See *National Mercantile Bank v Hampson* (1880) 5 QBD 177 and *Walker v Clay* (1880) 42 LT 369.

[28] The orthodox view is that a floating charge is not capable of being created by a non-corporate debtor; see Gough, above, note 2, p. 54, and see also V. Stott, *Hong Kong Company Law*, 11th ed. (Hong Kong: Longman, 2005), p. 254. The orthodox view is based on the argument that §11 requires the schedule of every bill of sale to specifically describe all the affected personal chattels. Because a floating charge is ambulatory in nature (see *Re Yorkshire Woolcombers Association Ltd* [1903] 2 Ch 284, 295, *per* Romer LJ and on appeal *Illingworth v Holdsworth* [1904] AC 355, 358, *per* Lord Macnaghten) it gives the chargor the freedom to deal with its assets in the ordinary course of its business; a typical floating charge provision could not comply with this requirement. Consequently, any floating charge created by a non-corporate debtor would not be a valid bill of sale. But see the minority view of C.A. Ong, 'The Registration of Credit Securities over Personal Chattels in Hong Kong: A Case for Reform', *JCCL* 3 (1997), 93, particularly pp. 103–5, where the author argued that a floating charge could be created by virtue of the exclusionary provision of §2 of the Bills of Sale Ordinance.

[29] English Law Commission Consultation Paper No 164, para. 9.7. See also No 176, para. 2.78, where the Law Commission maintained that consumers should be prevented from charging their after-acquired property.

[30] Above, note 18.

[31] *Re Keenan Bros Ltd* [1986] BCLC 242, *per* Keane J; *Re Lin Securities (Pte) Ltd* [1988] 2 *MLJ* 137, 141, *per* Chao Hick Tin and see also R.R. Pennington, 'The Genesis of the Floating Charge', [1960] 23 *MLR* 630, 630–8. See also equity's recognition of assignment of choses in action by way of security, discussed below in Chapter 3.

[32] These rules are discussed below in Chapter 4.

[33] See English Law Commission Consultation Paper No 164, para. 8.7.

it is after-acquired property or future property subject to an earlier oral security. The earlier and subsequent creditors would have to turn to the complex rules of priority to determine the order of their securities.[34]

Categories of 'personal chattels'

The types of tangible personal property constituting 'personal chattels' can be classified into three categories.

The first category comprises 'goods and furniture'. The Ordinance, however, does not provide a definition of 'goods and furniture'. To understand the meaning of 'goods', the creditor must apply the definition in §26 of the Sale of Goods Ordinance, which provides that 'goods' include all chattels personal other than things in action and money. It further states that the term includes emblements, industrial growing crops, and things attached to or forming part of the land which are agreed to be severed before sale or under a contract of sale. The creditor is subject to a complex and circuitous definition of 'goods'.

The word 'furniture' should convey an ordinary or popular meaning.[35] In most cases, whether an object constitutes 'furniture' is pretty clear. However, in instances where the articles in question, such as movable wardrobes, tables or chairs, do not take the usual form of 'furniture', the creditor cannot describe the objects as 'furniture' with confidence. Two English cases illustrate the difficulty. In *Wilkes v Goodwin*,[36] the court held that linoleum fitted to the floor was furniture for the purpose of the old Increase of Rent Act 1920 after a tortuous analysis of the term. In *Gray v Fidler*[37] the objects in question were fitted wardrobes, cupboards, beds and a fitted dressing table, all of which could not be removed without first destroying the nature of the article or fitment. The court held that they were furniture according to the literal, ordinary meaning. Lord Greene thought, however, according to settled principles of land law, that they had become fixtures. The disagreement shows the difficulty the word 'furniture' can pose to creditors.

It is submitted that it is unnecessary for §2 to contain the words 'goods and furniture' when the criterion of objects 'capable of physical delivery', mentioned earlier, is sufficiently wide to cover these items, so rendering the term otiose.

The second category comprises 'fixtures' if the bill of sale expressly assigns or charges fixtures attached to land separately from the land. The

[34] Rules of priority are discussed in Chapter 6. [35] *Wilkes v Goodwin* [1923] 2 KB 86.
[36] Ibid. [37] *Gray v Fidler* [1943] 2 All ER 289, CA.

fact that the fixtures are not physically deliverable at the time of execution of the bill of sale is not relevant. This rule contradicts a settled principle of Hong Kong land law. According to the law fixtures are not personal chattels,[38] and unless there is an express intention to the contrary between the mortgagee and mortgagor of the land, a mortgage of land includes, by implication, all fixtures affixed to the mortgaged land at the time of execution of the mortgage, and at any time afterwards during the continuance of the security.[39]

This inconsistency between the Bills of Sale Ordinance and land law thus creates uncertainty and provides a potential source of conflict between a mortgagee of land with fixtures and a mortgagee of the fixtures alone. A subsequent mortgagee of the land may reasonably think that it includes the fixtures, which it sees as permanently attached to the land, but it may later discover that they have been earlier mortgaged separately as personal chattels. The earlier bill of sale will have priority.[40]

The third category comprises 'trade machinery' provided it is used or attached to a factory or workshop used for the purpose of manufacturing articles or part of any article; or for altering, repairing or finishing any article; or for adapting any article for sale.[41] A mortgage of any such 'trade machinery' is a bill of sale. Again, there is a contradiction between this category of 'personal chattel' and land law.

In practice, when the court regards trade machinery affixed to the land as a fixture,[42] the property passes with the mortgage of the land to the mortgagee, if such a mortgage is created.[43] Hanbury and Waldock have criticised this approach. They suggest that the court ignored the objective of the Bills of Sale Ordinance, which was to take this category of property

[38] *Irene Loong v Pun Tsun Hang and American Engineering Corp., Fed. Inc. and Far East Import & Export Ltd* [1959] HKDCLR 192; *Penta Continental Land Investment Co., Ltd v Chung Kwok Restaurant Ltd and Tai Shing Company Ltd* [1967] HKDCLR 192; and *Orient Leasing (Hong Kong) Ltd v NP Etches and Others* [1985] HKLR 292. The Hong Kong cases derived the principle from English land law established in *Meux v Jacobs* [1874–75] LR 7 HL 481; *Melluish (Inspector of Taxes) v BMI (No 3) Ltd* [1996] AC 454; and *Elitestone Ltd v Morris and Another* [1997] 2 All ER 513.

[39] *Reynolds v Ashby & Son* [1904] AC 466. This principle is discussed in further detail below in Chapter 6.

[40] See Chapter 6 below.

[41] Section 4(4) of the Bills of Sale Ordinance.

[42] Air-conditioners in restaurants have been regarded as fixtures. See *Irene Loong v Pun Tsun Hang and American Engineering Corp., Fed. Inc. and Far East Import & Export Ltd* [1959] HKDCLR 192; *Penta Continental Land Investment Co., Ltd v Chung Kwok Restaurant Ltd and Tai Shing Company Ltd* [1967] HKDCLR 192.

[43] *Reynolds v Ashby & Son* [1904] AC 466.

out of the general rule in land law governing fixtures.[44] On the other hand, the courts might be forgiven for this lapse as the Ordinance is not clear as to the ambit of this exclusion.

Categories of non-personal chattels

This category comprises property which is specifically excluded from the definition of 'personal chattels'. This includes interests in real property, fixtures when assigned together with a freehold or leasehold interest in any land or building to which they are affixed, growing crops when assigned together with any interest in the land on which they are grown, shares or interests in the stocks, funds or securities of any government or in the capital or property of incorporated or joint-stock companies, and choses in action.[45]

As can be readily appreciated, §2 is extremely complex. This is a result of 'a mass of words thrown together without any very logical distinction between them', and accordingly the words cannot possibly be taken to be an accurate definition of 'personal chattels'.[46] The complexity is further exacerbated as §2 attempts to include property which is not generally regarded as personal property under the general law. The definition of 'personal chattels' has therefore made it difficult for a creditor to determine whether a property offered as security is a personal chattel simply by reference to the section.

Another shortcoming is that the section excludes a range of intangible personal property, such as shares or interests in stock, funds or securities of any government, interests in the capital of companies, and receivables, which are increasingly valuable property today.[47] As a result, security created over them by non-corporate debtors is not registrable under the Bills of Sale Ordinance, or, for that matter, under any other ordinance. This is a huge legislative lacuna in Hong Kong, and presents a number of difficult problems.

2.3.2 Definition of bills of sale

If the property offered as security constitutes 'personal chattels' as defined, the creditor then has to consider whether the security

[44] See Hanbury and Waldock, above, note 8, p. 364.

[45] For details of §2, see Appendix B of the Ordinance.

[46] *Stephenson v Thompson* [1924] 2 KB 240, [1924] All ER Rep 736, 743, *per* Sargant LJ.

[47] English Law Commission Consultation Paper No 164, para. 8.14. See also D.E. Allan, 'Personal Property – Rip Van Winkle Awakes in the Antipodes', *JIBL* 13(1) (1997), 1–3, where it was observed that intangible personal property, which was once regarded as worthless assets, is now regarded as valuable.

constitutes a bill of sale. Again, the Ordinance's definition of what security documents are capable of constituting a bill of sale is highly complex and technical.

In Hong Kong, a creditor has once again to look at §2, which has both inclusionary and exclusionary definitions. Under the inclusionary definition, a bill of sale includes a wide spectrum of arrangements.[48] The exclusionary definition enumerates eight categories of documents which would otherwise have been regarded as bills of sale.[49] The exceptions were enacted because it was thought that the wide inclusionary definition might fetter commerce to an oppressive degree.[50]

Neither the included nor the excluded arrangements are discussed in detail here, because a review of the case law,[51] unreported cases,[52] and other legal literature[53] in Hong Kong demonstrates that these arrangements are not used in Hong Kong. Their use elsewhere is already adequately discussed in major texts.[54]

But, given the academic criticism of the definitions – 'a demon of clumsiness and ambiguity',[55] 'remarkable for its clumsiness'[56] and 'long and verbose'[57] – it is doubtful whether an ordinary commercial creditor could understand them without legal assistance.

These definitions are even more unjustifiable when a careful examination of the authorities[58] in other common law jurisdictions shows that the characteristics of a bill of sale can be reduced to four attributes:

- the document creates a security over personal chattels;
- the security gives the creditor a legal or equitable right, or a personal right, to seize the personal chattels;[59]

48 For details of arrangements, see §2 set out in Appendix A of the Ordinance.

49 For details of eight categories of documents, see §2 set out in Appendix A of the Ordinance.

50 *Re Willis* (1888) 21 QBD 384, 396, *per* Lindley LJ.

51 Namely Hong Kong Law Reports, Hong Kong Law Report and Digest and Hong Kong Cases.

52 Kept at the High Court Library since the 1950s.

53 *Butterworths Annotated Ordinances of Hong Kong – Bills of Sale* (Cap. 20).

54 For example, Hanbury and Waldock, above, note 8, pp. 366–9; and K. Anandarajah, *Bills of Sale in Singapore and Malaysia* (Singapore: Butterworths Asia, 1995), pp. 5–21.

55 Hanbury and Waldock, above, note 8, p. 366.

56 E.I. Sykes and S. Walker, *Law of Securities*, 4th ed. (Sydney: Law Book Company, 1993), p. 545.

57 A.L. Diamond, 'Hire-Purchase Agreements as Bills of Sale', *MLR* 23 (1960), 399 at p. 401.

58 For example, see *Charlesworth v Mills* [1892] AC 231; *Ramsey v Margrett* [1894] 2 QB 18, CA, [1891–4] All ER Rep 453; and *Youngs v Youngs* [1940] 1 KB 760, CA.

59 The right to seize includes the right of a receiver under equitable charges and equitable mortgages. Thus equitable charges and equitable mortgages are bills of sale.

- it is necessary to look at the document to establish the creditor's security interest in the personal chattels; and
- the document does not fall within the exclusionary provision of the Ordinance.[60]

When a document satisfies these characteristics, it is a bill of sale.

Special banking documents and bills of sale

What is important in Hong Kong, in relation to the Bills of Sale Ordinance, is whether or not certain commercial banking security documents that are commonly used constitute bills of sale. These documents are called 'letters of hypothecation' and 'trust receipts'. These instruments, together with the pledge,[61] usually form a chain of sequential security arrangements to secure banking facilities in the form of letters of credit granted by the banks to finance their customers' imported purchases of goods from overseas.

To determine whether they are bills of sale, it is first necessary to examine their legal nature and then to decide whether they are bills of sale within the meaning of §2.

Legal nature of letters of hypothecation and trust receipts

The expression 'hypothecation' generally denotes a security document which gives the creditor–grantee of the document a security over the debtor–grantor's goods without transferring either the ownership or possession of the goods to the creditor–grantee. It corresponds to an equitable charge.[62] In Hong Kong, letters of hypothecation issued by commercial banks can be classified into the traditional or the modern type.

The traditional type is usually specifically identified by the use of the heading 'Hypothecation'. It usually contains one of the following expressions: 'trust and trustee', 'lien', or 'to hold goods or documents of title on behalf of the bank'.[63] The modern type is described as a 'General agreement for commercial business' and it does not contain the word

[60] *Charlesworth v Mills* [1892] AC 231; *Ramsey v Margarett* [1894] 2 QB 18, CA, [1891–4] All ER Rep 453; and *Youngs v Youngs* [1940] 1 KB 760, CA.

[61] See below in this chapter.

[62] See J.M. Holden, *The Law and Practice of Banking – Securities for Banker's Advances*, 8th ed. (London: Pitman, 1993), vol. 2, p. 273, para. 22-11.

[63] This is the common form in Hong Kong bankers' letters of hypothecation, based on samples obtained from Jiang Sing Bank Ltd, Hong Kong.

'hypothecation' or any of the traditional expressions.[64] The modern type seems to be gaining popularity in Hong Kong.[65]

It is submitted that the modern type is only a change in form. The effect and substance basically remain the same; namely, it is intended to create a security in favour of the bank. Insofar as goods are concerned, it immediately creates a pledge or constitutes an agreement to create a pledge.[66] Until the pledge is created, it is likely to be regarded as a charge.[67]

Traditional letters of hypothecation received significant judicial attention in England in the nineteenth and the early twentieth centuries in an attempt to accurately classify them according to whether they constituted registrable bills of sale under legislation. But they have received little authoritative consideration in Hong Kong and virtually none has been undertaken of the more modern type of document.

Hypothecation with trust expression Both the courts[68] and commentators[69] often regarded the early English case of *Re Slee, ex parte North Western Bank*[70] as authority for the proposition that a letter of hypothecation, expressed in terms of a trust, created an equitable charge. In that case, the letter of hypothecation provided that the debtor was to hold the goods as trustee for the bank as security. Bacon CJ held that it created an

64 According to the credit officer of Jiang Sing Bank Ltd, Hong Kong, that bank and some other banks use this form.

65 Information obtained from the Bills Department of Jiang Sing Bank Ltd, Hong Kong; see also S.H. Ko, *Law and Practice of Banking Services in Hong Kong* (Hong Kong: City University of Hong Kong Press, 1998), p. 205. Note that some banks continue to use the traditional form; see also B.C.S. Chan, *Hong Kong Banking Law and Practice* (Hong Kong: The Hong Kong Institute of Bankers, 2001), vol. 2, pp. 184–8, who appears to share the same view; and see also Ko, p. 205.

66 See Ko, above, note 65, p. 205, where the author called it a 'letter of pledge cum letter of hypothecation'. It is submitted that this description is dubious and incorrect. The document is either a 'pledge' in the strict sense or a 'charge', and not both. See *Re Cosslett (Contractors) Ltd* [1997] 4 All ER 115, 126, CA, where Millett LJ said, 'There are only four kinds of consensual security known to English Law: (i) pledge; (ii) contractual lien; (iii) equitable charge and (iv) mortgage.'

67 See the English case of *Re Hamilton, Young & Co., ex parte Carter* [1905] 2 KB 772; and the Malaysian case of *Re Bonds Ltd* (1922) 1 FMSLR 263.

68 See *Re Steele, ex parte Conning* (1873) 16 Eq Cas 414; *Re Hamilton, Young & Co., ex parte Carter* [1905] 2 KB 772, 787, *per* Vaughan Williams LJ; and *Mercantile Bank of India Ltd v Chartered Bank of India, Australia and China and Another* (1937) 43 Com Cas 80, 85, *per* Porter J.

69 See Holden, above, note 62, pp. 309–10; E.P. Ellinger, E. Lomnicka and R.J.A. Hooley, *Modern Banking Law*, 3rd ed. (Oxford: Oxford University Press, 2002), p. 753; and M. Hapgood, *Paget's Law of Banking*, 12th ed. (London: Butterworths, 2002), para. 31.10.

70 *Re Slee, ex parte North Western Bank* (1872) LR 15 Eq 69.

equitable charge. However, Bacon CJ's judgment is not free from difficulty as the greater part of it points to a trust relationship, not that of a charge. He constantly referred to the bank as the 'true owner' and the customer as the 'trustee' or used expressions to that effect.[71]

It is submitted that the use of these words by Bacon CJ is contrary to the nature of an equitable charge. This is because no transfer of ownership or possession of the goods is involved but only an appropriation of the personal chattels by the creditor.[72]

Although, in a subsequent case dealing with the word 'owner' in §4(1) of the Factors Act 1889,[73] the Court of Appeal held that the word included a security holder,[74] it is arguable that the clear and the unequivocal use of the expressions 'true owner' and particularly 'trustee' by Bacon CJ rejects any such broad possibility.

In the subsequent case of *R v Townshend*,[75] a letter of hypothecation contained words similar to those in *Re Slee*. Day J held that the document constituted a declaration of trust without transfer. *Re Slee* was mentioned by counsel for the prosecution, who sought to distinguish it on the grounds that the earlier case was a commercial case and *Townshend* was a criminal one. But it was not referred to in the decision of Day J.

Thus there are two lines of authority for consideration. It is submitted that although *Townshend* has not been overruled in England,[76] it should be treated with caution because the criminal nature of the case might have influenced the strict approach of Day J. It should not be regarded as laying down a general rule in commercial law. The decision in *Re Slee* is preferred on commercial principles, although on strict analysis Bacon CJ's reasoning may not convincingly support his ultimate decision.

In any event, there is subsequent judicial support for *Re Slee*. In *Mercantile Bank of India Ltd v Chartered Bank of India, Australia and*

71 Ibid., Bacon CJ's judgment at p. 74.

72 See E.L.G. Tyler, *Fisher and Lightwood's Law of Mortgage*, 10th ed. (London: Butterworths, 1988), p. 4.

73 Equivalent of §3(1) of the Hong Kong Factors Ordinance (Cap. 48).

74 In *Lloyds Bank Ltd v Bank of America National Trust and Savings Association* [1938] 2 KB 147, the Court of Appeal held that the word 'owner' in §3(1) of the Factors Act, 1889, (equivalent of §3(1) of the Factors Ordinance (Cap. 48)) included the security holder. In any event it is arguable that the use of the words 'true owner' and 'trustee' by Bacon CJ was not intended to have the broad meaning given to 'owner' in §3(1).

75 *R v Townshend* (1884) 15 Cox CC 466.

76 See *Halsbury's Statutes of England and Wales*, 4th ed., reissue (London: Butterworths, 1993), vol. 5, p. 404.

China, and Another,[77] the court held that a trust receipt was an equitable charge of goods. Porter J took a realistic approach and held that in determining whether a document created a trust or an equitable mortgage the courts had to give the document a broad construction and look at its legal effect.[78] If the document was a business document and it was intended to give the bank a security over the goods, the word 'trust' used in the document should not be given the general equitable meaning but must be taken to create an equitable charge and not a trust.[79]

Notwithstanding the realistic approach in *Re Slee*, the Hong Kong court in *UDI (HK) Limited v Fantana Limited*[80] appeared to favour the narrower trust concept. UDI and Fantana had executed a loan agreement under which Fantana agreed, as security for a loan from UDI, to execute a trust receipt of jewellery, which it had earlier pledged to a bank, in favour of UDI. According to the terms of the trust receipts, the jewellery was held on trust for UDI by Fantana and the former could call for it, dispose of it or get the proceeds of sale if it were sold. When Fantana subsequently went into liquidation, Li J opined, though not directly, that the documents were a declaration of trust.[81]

The English case of *Re David Allester Limited*,[82] which is discussed below, appeared to have influenced the trust conclusion reached by Li J, though the exposition in that case on the possible different juridical nature of a trust receipt in other circumstances was not mentioned by him.

It is, however, possible that had *Mercantile Bank of India Ltd* been considered, Li J's view of the nature of the trust receipt might have been different.

Li J's decision may have to be reconsidered in view of the subsequent English case of *Re Bond Worth Ltd*,[83] where the court held that a retention-of-title clause, drafted in the nature of a trust covering the goods, the proceeds of any resale of the goods supplied on credit, or any final product which the goods may become part of or converted into, created a floating charge. Slade J unequivocally reaffirmed the charge concept and placed strong emphasis on the need to look at the commercial reality of

[77] *Mercantile Bank of India Ltd v Chartered Bank of India, Australia and China, and Another* (1937) Com Cas 80.

[78] Ibid. p. 85. [79] Ibid. pp. 85–6.

[80] *UDI (HK) Limited v Fantana Limited* (1978) High Court CWU No 19/76, unreported.

[81] See also the Hong Kong case of *CIC-Européenne International et Cie v Wing Sun and Company (a firm) and Another* [1985] 1 HKC 568, where the trust concept was preferred.

[82] [1922] 2 Ch 211. [83] [1980] Ch 228.

the transaction. He said that the court was bound to look at the substance of the transactions and if, indeed, the transaction was a security for the payment of a debt, or appropriated such property for the discharge of the debt, it must be regarded as a mortgage or charge.[84] The fact that it was called by another label was not important. Slade J's approach is similar to that of Porter J in *Mercantile Bank of India Ltd*. However, since then, *Re Bond Worth Ltd* appears to have been overtaken by a more recent development in the Australian High Court case of *Associated Alloys Pty Limited v ACN 001 452 106 Pty Limited (in liquidation) and Another.*[85] There the court held that the express intention of the parties to create a trust over the proceeds from the goods supplied in the retention-of-title clause should be given full effect. The court rejected the argument that the 'trust' was a charge. The details of the case and the decision will be further discussed in Chapter 5.[86] These two decisions may influence future Hong Kong courts when the matter arises again.

It is submitted that although Slade J's characterisation of such hypothecation as a charge is progressive and realistic, it does not necessarily mean that the debtor's position would be better. Firstly, it may not go to improve the borrowing capability of a trading individual who does not possess fixed assets, because an individual cannot create a floating charge. Secondly, the creditor would in most cases have failed to register the charge with the Companies Registry.[87] *Associated Alloys* is good for commerce as it ensures certainty. In this regard, *Associated Alloys* is preferred.

Hypothecation with 'lien' expressions In relation to the letters of hypothecation containing the expression 'lien', the law is settled. In the often-cited English case of *Re Young, Hamilton & Co., ex parte Carter,*[88]

[84] Ibid., p. 248. [85] [2000] 202 CLR 588. [86] See below, Chapter 5.

[87] This will be fully discussed in Chapter 5, in relation to retention-of-title clauses taking effect as a charge.

[88] [1905] 2 KB 772, CA. Note that although the term 'hypothecation' was not mentioned in the judgments at the Court of Appeal, it was treated as a hypothecation by Bigham J [1905] 2 KB 381, 389, at first instance, and also considered by major texts, namely Ellinger, Lomnicka and Hooley, above, note 69, pp. 753–6; and also R. Chorley and P.E. Smart, *Leading Cases in the Law of Banking*, 6th ed. (London; Sweet & Maxwell, 1990), pp. 287–9. See also the Malaysian case of *Re Bonds Ltd* (1922) 1 FMSLR 263. Note that *Paget's Law of Banking*, above, note 69, paras. 31.9 to 31.12, treats hypothecation, liens and trust receipts separately, but at para. 31.11 is of the view that the term 'lien' connotes hypothecation. It is submitted that the distinction is too fine to draw where it is given before the goods are actually pledged to the creditor. Note that the case of *Re Hamilton, Young & Co., ex parte Carter* was followed in the Straits Settlement (Singapore) case of *Re Winklemann & Lubking Limited* (1915) SSLR 19.

the borrower, an individual, executed a document which stated that in consideration of the advances, the borrower held certain goods specified in the document on the bank's account and under 'lien' to the bank. The debtor further enclosed receipts for the goods. As the receipts were not documents of title, the letter of hypothecation amounted to an agreement to create a pledge over the goods only. The Court of Appeal, on this basis, regarded the document as constituting an equitable charge.[89]

Hypothecation with other expressions In relation to letters of hypothecation which contain the words 'to hold goods or documents of title on behalf of the bank', the law appears to point in other directions and depends on the status of the goods.

First, if the debtor were unable to deliver possession of the goods at the time the documents were executed, the documents would be regarded as agreements to create pledges. On the basis of *Re Young, Hamilton & Co., ex parte Carter* and *Re Bond Worth Ltd*, they are either equitable fixed charges or floating charges.

In general, even if the security is created over a class of assets of the debtor which may include present and future assets, which might change from time to time in the ordinary course of business of the debtor, until it is converted into a fixed charge, the security is a floating charge.[90] On the other hand, if the security specifically identifies the personal chattels, it would be regarded as a fixed charge. Although these criteria are derived from company law, it is submitted that, with modification, they can be made applicable to non-corporate debtors.[91] However, if the document is regarded as a floating charge and the debtor–grantor is a non-corporate debtor, such a floating charge would be invalid by reason of §11 of the Bills of Sale Ordinance.[92]

Further, as the debtor could give actual or constructive possession of the goods, the court in *National Provincial and Union Bank of England v Lindsell*[93] held that the document created a legal mortgage of the goods by way of an assignment. *Lindsell* appears to be consistent with the earlier case of *Re Steele, ex parte Conning*,[94] where a similar view was expressed. However, the underlying prerequisites for the conclusions were not discussed in the brief judgments of Lord Coleridge and Bacon CJ in *Lindsell*

89 The same view was taken in the Malaysian case of *Re Bonds Ltd* (1922) 1 FMSLR 263.

90 See Chapter 4 below.

91 For recognition of this possibility, see the views of Vaughan Williams LJ and counsel in *Re Hamilton, Young & Co., ex parte Carter* [1905] 2 KB 772, 780.

92 See above, note 27. 93 [1922] 1 KB 21. 94 (1873) LR 16 Eq 414.

and *Re Steele* respectively. It is, however, submitted that much will depend on the intention of the parties.

Trust receipts The function of a trust receipt[95] and its effectiveness as a security device are discussed further below.[96]

In Hong Kong, the terms of trust receipts vary in length.[97] However, the objectives are similar; that is, they impose an undertaking on the debtor, that in consideration of the bank redelivering possession of the goods to the debtor, the debtor holds them – or, if sold, the proceeds – on trust for the bank.[98]

The precise nature of the trust receipt is far from settled. In the English case of *Re David Allester Ltd*,[99] Astbury J held that a trust receipt subsequently executed by the pledgor of goods in favour of the bank was not independent of the pledge and did not, therefore, constitute a declaration of trust within the inclusionary definition of a bill of sale mentioned earlier.[100]

Astbury J based his decision on the grounds that the trust receipt was no more than an acknowledgement by the pledgor that it was exercising the power of sale as agent for the pledgee and the goods had been delivered to him in pursuance of the agency. Consequently, the trust receipt did not terminate the pledge, which continued to subsist, nor did it create any new security.[101] According to Astbury J's view, trust receipts create two securities, namely the extension of the pledge over the goods and a trust agency over the proceeds of the goods.

95 Banks in England started to accept the concept of trust receipt in the late nineteenth century. See *Re David Allester Ltd* [1922] 2 Ch 211, p. 213, which originated in the United States in the last quarter of the nineteenth century; see also G. Gilmore, *Security Interests in Personal Property* (Boston: Little, Brown and Company, 1965), vol. 1, pp. 87–8.

96 See below in this chapter.

97 On the basis of documents provided by Jiang Sing Bank Ltd, Hong Kong, the trust receipts used by banks in Hong Kong are basically similar.

98 *North Western Bank Ltd v John Poynter Son and Macdonalds* [1895] AC 56; *Re David Allester Ltd* [1922] 2 Ch 211, *Lloyds Bank Ltd v Bank of America National Trust International* [1938] 2 KB 147 and *CIC-Union Européenne International et Cie v Wing Sun & Co. (A Firm) and Another* [1985] 1 HKC 568.

99 Ibid.

100 Astbury J was then referring to §4 of the UK Bills of Sale Act, the equivalent of §2 of the Hong Kong Bills of Sale Ordinance. See also R.M. Goode, *Commercial Law*, 2nd ed. (London: Penguin, 1995), p. 1029, who opined that a trust receipt issued after a pledge is not an independent security device but it secures the continuance of the pledge. The English Law Commission Report No 296, para. 3.22, supported this opinion.

101 Ibid., at pp. 216 and 218.

At first sight, the rationale in *Re David Allester Ltd* appears easy to understand. The decision gave judicial recognition to a banking practice and it established that 'trust receipts' had a technical meaning different from the concept of trust as understood in equity. But Astbury J's observation, *obiter*, that a trust receipt, given in the absence of a pre-existing pledge, would constitute a declaration of trust in respect of the goods, is doubtful. The weakness of this point has already been discussed above in the context of letters of hypothecation.

Thus far it can be readily appreciated that the attitude of the courts is, at best, confusing and, at worst, arbitrary. This state of affairs is unsatisfactory. It should be remembered that one of the objectives of the Bills of Sale Ordinance was that a debtor should understand the nature of the security given.[102] In light of the juridical confusion surrounding the nature of the above documents, a debtor cannot know in advance precisely what form of security it has given to the creditor.

In the event of a dispute, it can be disastrous for a debtor to discover subsequently that the security it has given the creditor is more substantial than it had bargained for. The debtor may find that it is not only subject to the financial obligation to repay but also that it has been completely deprived of the legal ownership of the charged property and, worse, it may be subject to potential criminal prosecution.[103] Under §2(1) of the Theft Ordinance (Cap. 210) a person commits theft if they dishonestly appropriate property belonging to another with the intention of permanently depriving the other of it. Under §6(2) of the Ordinance, property held under a trust is regarded as belonging to any person who has the right to enforce the trust and any intention of the trustee to defeat the trust will be regarded as an intention to deprive the person having the right of enforcement of that property. Hence, where a letter of hypothecation is regarded as a trust, the bank could use the criminal process to punish the debtor/trustee who was in breach of the trust and had dissipated the proceeds realised from the sale of the goods.

The real threat of criminal proceedings may constitute an incentive to the debtor to comply with the trust, and it has been noted that creditors in Hong Kong often use criminal process to recover civil debts.[104] However, the banks have not shown the same enthusiasm in relation to breaches of trust receipts by debtors. This can perhaps be attributable to the imprecise

[102] *Davis v Burton* (1883) 11 QBD 537 CA, 539, *per* Brett MR.

[103] See *R v Townshend* (1884) 15 Cox CC 466.

[104] *The Queen v Wong Wing-ho* [1982] HKDCLR 69, 70–1, *per* Cruden J.

juridical nature of letters of hypothecation and trust receipts, or an understandable reluctance to involve the police in a commercial matter in the absence of obvious fraud or deception.

Are letters of hypothecation and trust receipts bills of sale? Prima facie, letters of hypothecation and trust receipts are bills of sale. But in practice this is not entirely clear. This is because of the inconsistency of the courts' application of one of the exclusionary provisions in §2. According to §2, a bill of sale does not include 'any other documents used in the ordinary course of business as proof of the possession or control of goods'.[105]

In the English case of *Re Slee*,[106] discussed earlier, the court held that the equitable charge created by a letter of hypothecation was not a bill of sale, because it fell within this exclusionary provision. In *Townshend*,[107] the court regarded a letter of hypothecation as a declaration of trust, thus it did not come within the exclusionary provision. Accordingly, the court held that it was a bill of sale. In *National Provincial and Union Bank of England v Lindsell*,[108] the court regarded a letter of hypothecation with the expression 'to hold goods or documents of title on behalf of the bank' as a legal mortgage of the goods by way of an assignment and constituted a bill of sale but void for default of registration. In *Re Young, Hamilton & Co., ex parte Carter*, after considering that the letter of hypothecation was an equitable charge, the court held that it was not a bill of sale as it was a 'document used in the ordinary course of business as proof of the possession or control of goods' within the exclusionary provision.

In the Hong Kong case of *Fantana*, when it became obvious to Li J that his treatment of the trust receipts as declarations of trust would be tantamount to recognising them as bills of sale and that they would be void for lack of registration, he quickly solved the creditor's predicament by holding that the trust receipts were documents used in the ordinary course of business as proof of possession or control of the goods under the exclusionary provisions of §2 of the Bills of Sale Ordinance,[109] therefore the trust receipts were not bills of sale and not registrable. Thus they were not invalid for want of registration.

These cases illustrate that the court's treatment of letters of hypothecation and trust receipts as being within or without the exclusionary

105 For details of §2, see its Appendix A. 106 Above, note 70.

107 Above, note 75. 108 [1922] 1 KB 21.

109 For the purpose of this article, the pertinent part of §2 of the Bills of Sale Ordinance (Cap. 20) provides, 'Bills of Sale ... do not include ... any other documents used in the ordinary course of business as proof of the possession or control of goods'.

provision of the Bills of Sale Ordinance has been wholly unsatisfactory for two reasons. Firstly, decisions have been arbitrary. Secondly, the courts have looked at the nature of the business of the debtor, rather than the security transaction itself. Consequently, the court has artificially and misleadingly assumed that a third party dealing with a trading debtor was less likely to be prejudiced by a non-registrable security transaction than by a non-trading debtor.

Hong Kong law determining the rules concerning whether the Bills of Sale Ordinance governs a security arrangement over tangible personal property is outdated, uncertain, restrictive, anomalous and cumbersome. It is submitted that this in turn creates uncertainty for the creditor when selecting the right process to create security. This uncertainty, it appears, is one reason[110] why some major banks[111] in Hong Kong avoid the use of hypothecation to secure banking facilities to finance import transactions in relation to goods. They have resorted to more substantial security, such as charges over fixed deposits of the debtors/customers with the banks.

2.4 Creation, perfection and publicity of bills of sale, and cost

2.4.1 Creation of bills of sale

After being satisfied that the Bills of Sale Ordinance governs the creation of the security, the creditor has to ensure that the bill of sale document conforms with the statutory Form 2 in the schedule of the Ordinance.[112] If the security fails to conform, the security is void against the debtor–grantor and third party interested in the personal chattel.

Form 2 requires the bill of sale to contain no less than nine particulars:

- the date of the bill;
- particulars of the parties;
- the nature of the consideration;
- an express assignment of the goods;
- the rate of interest payable;
- method and date of repayment of the principal sum and interest;
- any other costs to be met by the grantee;

[110] The other reason is that it is a weak security; see Ellinger, Lomnicka and Hooley, above, note 69, p. 754; and also Ko, above, note 65, p. 205.

[111] For example, the Hong and Shanghai Banking Corporation Limited and the Standard Chartered Bank.

[112] See §15 of the Bills of Sale Ordinance.

- a statement that the goods assigned are not liable to seizure or to be taken into the possession of the grantee for any cause other than those specified in §14 of the Ordinance, such as default in payment of the sum secured by the bill of sale; and
- signature of the debtor–grantor, who seals the form, in the presence of a witness whose name, address and description must be specified in the bill of sale.

Failure to comply with any of these requirements renders the bill void.[113]

Brett MR in *Davis v Burton*[114] stated that Form 2 had two objectives. Firstly, to enable the debtor to understand the nature of the security which it was about to grant for the debt due to the creditor. Secondly, to enable a potential creditor, upon merely searching the register, to understand the position of the debtor without being compelled to obtain expensive advice from a lawyer. Form 2 was therefore intended to be simple and user-friendly in terms of creation, perfection and publicity.

However, an examination of English cases has shown that this aim has not been entirely realised. This is because the courts have been ambivalent about the degree of conformity required in completing Form 2. In respect of some requirements, the courts have demanded strict conformity,[115] and in others the courts have been more relaxed. The following have been held not to conform: the creditor's right to claim the entire interest due on the loan upon the debtor's failure to pay the first instalment,[116] the creditor's power to seize the goods under circumstances not permitted by the Ordinance,[117] and the creditor's right to take immediate possession of the goods as security for the debt even in the absence of default.[118] In Hong Kong, this strict approach was adopted in *Far East Bank Ltd v Donna Maria Knitters and Another.*[119] There the court held that the creditor's bill of sale did not conform with Form 2 because it failed accurately to reproduce the statutory formula, 'Provided always that chattels hereby assigned shall not be liable to seizure or to be taken possession by the said creditor for any cause other than those specified in §14 of the Bills of Sale Ordinance (Cap. 20).' Accordingly, the bill of sale was void.

[113] The Bills of Sale Ordinance, §15. [114] (1883) 11 QBD 537.

[115] For example, see *Re Townsend, ex parte Parsons* (1886) 16 QBD 532, 545. Lord Esher said the provisions must be strictly complied with. A far stricter view was adopted in *Re Morris, ex parte Official Receiver* (1882) 22 Ch D 136, 140, *per* Cotton LJ.

[116] *Davis v Burton* (1883) 537, 539. [117] Ibid.

[118] *Re Townsend, ex parte Parsons* (1886) 16 QBD 532. [119] [1963] HKLR 390.

It is submitted that this strict approach is unduly harsh, for the error was bona fide and it did not confer on the creditor any rights over and above those specified in §14 of the Ordinance. The decision, therefore, is one of policy, which seems to weigh heavily against the creditor.[120] Besides, the decision appears outmoded as the modern trend is not to regard nonconformity with a statutory formula as being fatal to a cause of action, provided the mistake does not prejudice the interest of an innocent party.[121]

The strict approach also has two important weaknesses. Firstly, it is questionable whether or not it is fair in cases where the debtor and the creditor, whether first or subsequent, are businesspeople,[122] who can be presumed to know the law and the transactions are purely commercial transactions. Secondly, the strict approach seems harsh when the Ordinance does not allow any rectification of defective words after the bill of sale is registered, except omissions or a misstatement pertaining to the name, residence or occupation of any relevant person.[123]

The circumstances where the courts have adopted a relaxed conformity requirement include variation and minor errors relating to the rate of interest, insurance, and the conditions for the maintenance and defeasance of the security. The rationale for this approach is that neither §15 nor Form 2 adequately addressed these issues and both are recognised secured lending practices.[124]

On the other hand, as Hanbury and Waldock recognised,[125] there is a serious disadvantage to this flexibility – the creditor cannot safely predetermine what variations from precise compliance are acceptable or not. They identified a number of cases which have and have not fallen

[120] See the comment of Blair-Kerr J in *Far East Bank Ltd v Meng Yung* [1963] HKLR 391, 395.

[121] See *Re Leung Hoi* [2000] HKEC 1404, where the court held that a Statutory Demand issued under the Bankruptcy Ordinance (Cap. 6) could not be set aside on the grounds that it did not contain the statutorily prescribed words 'before the expiration of 18 days after the service', because the debtor could not prove that it was prejudiced by the omission.

[122] On the basis of the information contained in the Bills of Sale Register at the High Court for the period 1991–6, the grantors were mainly businessmen.

[123] The Bills of Sale Ordinance, §20.

[124] The court has generally been flexible on most of the statutory requirements. See e.g. *Blackwell v England* (1857) 8 E & B 541; *Simmons v Woodward* [1892] AC 100; *Credit Co. v Pott* (1880) 6 QBD 295, CA; *Kemble v Addison* [1900] 1 QB 430. The same flexible attitude was displayed in the Hong Kong case of *Wong Shau Kee v Leung Hin Huen* (1930) 25 HKLR 7.

[125] Hanbury and Waldock, above, note 8, p. 373.

foul of the court's definition of 'not substantial or misleading'.[126] But Anandarajah has commented that this exercise simply showed that 'it is not a simple task to determine whether a deviation from the statutory form is or is not substantial'.[127] Thus a prudent and careful creditor who wishes to deviate from the statutory form in order to incorporate terms which have been agreed may be required to review authorities and draft the terms according to what has been approved by the courts. This is a tedious and expensive process and would appear to defeat the presumed user-friendly approach of the Bills of Sale Ordinance.

However, it should be mentioned that, in the context of Hong Kong, the difficulties posed by the Bills of Sale Ordinance discussed here are not as serious as might first have been thought. Since the beginning of the twentieth century, no cases have successfully supported a challenge on the grounds of nonconformity with the statutory Form 2.[128] Nonetheless, the continued existence of the Bills of Sale Ordinance means that the potential difficulties and risks to creditors in the actual creation process are ever-present.

2.4.2 *Perfection of bills of sale*

In Hong Kong, a bill of sale is void against the personal chattels comprised in the inventory not only against third parties, but also against the

[126] The line of cases in which the court held the bills of sale to be void for non-conformity are: *Davis v Burton* (1883) 11 QBD 537 (the offending terms were a rate of interest of 60 per cent and the creditor's right to seize the personal chattels for failure to produce rent after verbal demand); *Re Williams* (1883) 25 Ch D 656 (the grounds for seizure were considered too broad); *Melville v Stringer* (1884) 13 QBD 392 (the terms of the bills of sale were too complex and complicated) and *Bianchi v Offord* (1886) 17 QBD 484 (where the bill of sale imposed unfair and onerous financial obligation on the debtor in the event of the debtor's default in paying outgoings of the business premises). The other line, where the bills of sale were upheld, notwithstanding errors in the bill of sale, includes *Roberts v Roberts* (1884) 13 QBD 794 (omission of the words 'by way of security' did not invalidate the bill of sale); *Re Cleaver* (1887) 18 QBD 489 (the use of words 'by unequal payments' instead of the prescribed words 'equal instalment payments' did not render the bill of sale void).

[127] Anandarajah, above, note 54, p. 50.

[128] Between 1900 and 1997, there were only four reported cases, namely *Wong Shau Kee v Leung Hin Huen* [1930] 25 HKLR 7; *Yau Yung and Others v Tse Hap Man* [1958] HKDCLR 129; *Far East Bank Limited v Donna Maria Knitters and Another* [1963] HKLR 390; and *Ngan Chung-ching and Others v Yeung Yuk Sang Trading as Cheung Yuen Dyeing Factory* [1968] HKDCLR 319. Only in the cases of *Wong Shau Kee* and *Far East Bank Limited* were the bills of sale held to be invalid. The sizeable number of bills of sale in the past and the small number of reported cases appears to reinforce the uncertainty.

debtor–grantor of the bill of sale, unless the bill of sale is registered with the Registry of the High Court. However, the debtor is still personally liable to repay the loan to the creditor. Registration is therefore a crucial part of the perfection process of bills of sale.

According to the Bills of Sale Ordinance, the creditor has to register the bill of sale within seven days of its execution.[129] If the bill of sale was executed abroad, it must be registered within seven days after the time at which it would, in the ordinary course of the post, arrive in Hong Kong, if posted immediately after the execution of the bill.[130] Since 1990 the records of the Registry of the High Court have shown that no overseas bills of sale have been registered.[131] This could mean that either no overseas bill of sale was created or that such creditors have not been aware of the requirement.

If a creditor fails to register within time, it can apply to the court, which may grant an extension of time if the court is satisfied that the omission was accidental or due to inadvertence. Any extension may be on such terms and conditions as the court thinks fit.[132]

To effect the registration of the bill of sale, the creditor has to

- deliver to the Registrar of the High Court the original and a copy of the bill of sale and schedule attached therewith, and a verifying affidavit, to the Registrar of the High Court for registration, and
- pay the High Court the registration fee, currently HK$440.

When the registrar receives the documents and fee, the following details are recorded: the name, residence and occupation of the grantor; the name of the grantee; the nature of the instrument; the date of the execution; and the date of registration and the number.[133] In the case of satisfaction of the loan, the date of satisfaction would be recorded. When the bill of sale is duly registered, the original copy is endorsed by the registrar and returned to the creditor–grantee.

When a bill of sale is registered, it has three consequences. Firstly, it is legally valid and enforceable against the debtor–grantor. Secondly, it becomes an effective security against third parties who have acquired a registrable interest in the personal chattels, except subsequent superior interests, such as the interests of a pledgee and the purchaser of the goods in the ordinary course of the debtor's business without actual notice of the

[129] Section 7 of the Bills of Sale Ordinance. [130] Ibid.

[131] See above, notes 17 and 18 for the author's search at the High Court Registry.

[132] Section 20 of the Bills of Sale Ordinance. [133] Ibid., §19(1).

earlier bills of sale ('subsequent superior interests').[134] Registration does not impose constructive notice of the bill of sale on the whole world. The exclusion of constructive notice appears to rest on two notions. Firstly, personal chattels, unlike land, generally do not have formal documents of title,[135] therefore equity could not justifiably impose a duty on a subsequent acquirer of a superior interest to examine the status of the debtor's interest in the relevant personal chattels. Secondly, the demands of commercial convenience and the free flow of trade dictate this restriction on the doctrine of constructive notice.[136] Trade in goods could not be effected efficiently if every subsequent purchaser of goods were subject to the constructive-notice rule, as it would involve lengthy, tedious and expansive inquiries about them.[137]

However, it is contended that, although the restriction of the doctrine of constructive notice may have been advantageous, it does, nevertheless, create difficulties. In particular, it gives an original creditor, who has registered a bill of sale, a false sense of security, especially when the security is equitable, as a subsequent superior interest can defeat the priority.[138] It would thus seem to be a paradox that whilst the Ordinance imposes stringent requirements on the creditor to perfect its security so as not to mislead the general public, at the same time the law allows such security to be undermined by the subsequent dishonest dealing of the debtor.

The solution to this problem can be found in the English Law Commission's recommendation.[139] The Law Commission recommended, firstly, that the legislation on bills of sale be replaced with a notice-filing system. Under that system a purchaser (other than a creditor) who subsequently buys goods, subject to a duly registered security, takes free from the creditor's security interests, except where the charge is over uniquely identifiable goods[140] or the purchaser has actual knowledge of the charge.[141] Secondly, priority of all duly registered bills of sale

[134] *Joseph v Lyons* (1884) 15 QBD 280, where the Court of Appeal refused to extend the doctrine of constructive notice.

[135] The only exception under the general law is the bill of lading.

[136] See Goode, above, note 100, p. 52.

[137] Ibid.

[138] *Payne v Fern* (1881) 6 QBD 620 and *Joseph v Lyons* [1884] 15 QBD 280, and see also *National Mercantile Bank Limited v Hampson* (1880) 5 QBD 177 and *Walker v Clay* (1880) 42 LT 369.

[139] English Law Commission Consultation Paper No 164, para. 10.21 and 10.61.

[140] For example, motor vehicles and goods which have a serial number are easily identifiable; see English Law Commission Consultation Paper No 164, para. 4.186 and No 176, para. 3.263.

[141] Ibid.

over the same personal chattels is determined by the order of their date of registration.[142] These recommendations, it is submitted, would strike a balance between the security interests of creditors and demands of commercial convenience.

2.4.3 *Publicity of bills of sale*

The register of bills of sale is a public register. According to the Bill of Sale Ordinance, any person is entitled at all reasonable times to search the register[143] at the High Court on payment of a minimal fee.[144]

From the point of view of a creditor dealing with a potential borrower, certain information contained in Form 2 – such as the inventory[145] and the affidavit[146] pertaining to such matters as the nature of the security, the amount of the loan and the period of the loan – are very important. They help the creditor to ascertain the financial exposure of the debtor and the level of risk involved in lending. This information cannot, however, be easily obtained by inquiry at the High Court Registry. There are two reasons. Firstly, the information contained in the register is not as complete as the legislation envisages. Secondly, examination of the register has shown that not all of the particulars are accurate. For example, the column headed 'occupation' of the grantor of the bill of sale has often been described as 'mortgagor', 'borrower' or 'company'; the lender has been described in the column for borrower and vice versa; the column headed the 'nature of the instrument' has been constantly and mistakenly described as 'chattels', 'debt' or 'the lender' or left blank; the column for date of creation and registration is left blank. The errors indicated that the officials are either careless or did not understand the registration requirements prescribed by the Bills of Sale Ordinance.

Thus to obtain the full information the creditor has to take a further step of formally applying to the registrar for copies of the documents filed. The creditor has to wait for at least three days for this information.[147]

Thus, in practice, the publicity mechanism of the Bills of Sale Ordinance is slow and ineffective in providing the necessary information to third parties, though the search fee is minimal.

142 Section 9(3) of the Bills of Sale Ordinance.

143 Form 3 of the Schedule of the Bills of Sale Ordinance.

144 See below in this chapter.

145 Section 9(1)(b) of the Bills of Sale Ordinance.

146 Ibid.

147 According to an official at the High Court Registry.

2.4.4 Cost of creation, perfection and publicity of bills of sale

The cost of creating, perfecting and publicising bills of sale in Hong Kong is generally inexpensive.

Except for legal fees, where a lawyer is engaged, there is no tax or stamp duty involved in the creation of non-possessory securities over tangible personal property. They are exempt from stamp duty, as they are not instruments that are subject to duty under the Schedule 1 of the Stamp Duty Ordinance (Cap. 117).

The registration fee for bills of sale is currently HK$440. This appears to be on the high side when compared to the HK$340 registration fee for company charges by the Companies Registry.[148] Nevertheless, the fee of HK$440 can still be regarded as low.

The High Court Registry currently charges a search fee of HK$18,[149] and HK$210[150] for any copies or extracts of any registered bill of sale and affidavit of execution filed with the High Court.[151]

2.5 Creation, perfection and publicity of security outside the scope of the Bills of Sale Ordinance in Hong Kong

2.5.1 Creation of hypothecation, pledge and trust receipt

Hypothecation

Here the expression 'hypothecation' is used broadly to include both the traditional and modern type of hypothecation,[152] and it is assumed that these arrangements are exempted from the Bills of Sale Ordinance on the basis of the majority decision discussed earlier.[153]

Creating a security by hypothecation is simple as it is usually created in the form of a letter-of-credit facility granted by the creditor bank to the debtor.[154] The letter of hypothecation is usually in the bank's standard form of not more than two pages. The debtor executes the letter of hypothecation and deposits it with the creditor bank.

Letters of hypothecation are not by themselves effective security. They are bolstered by the pledge, which is anticipated by the parties in the instrument.

[148] See Chapter 4 below. [149] Para. 2 of the Bills of Sale (Fees) Regulations.
[150] Ibid. [151] Ibid., §22(1). [152] See above in this chapter. [153] Ibid.
[154] The practice in Hong Kong does not differ from the practice in Malaysia. The latter is based on the personal experience of author as a solicitor in the common law jurisdiction of Malaysia, 1982–90. The practice has not changed since then.

Pledge

Banks in Hong Kong commonly use a pledge[155] to secure goods for commercial lending. The process of creating a pledge in Hong Kong is simple. All that is required is that the goods offered as security must be actually or constructively delivered to the bank–pledgee.[156] The latter is more prevalent in commercial bank lending because the goods are usually overseas. Here, the pledge is commonly effected constructively by delivery of document title; that is, a bill of lading relating to the relevant goods.

When the goods arrive in Hong Kong, they are actually and physically delivered into the custody of the bank. Another special feature of commercial banks' lending is that the debtor executes a one-page pledge document in the bank's standard form, although this is not essential to create an effective pledge. It is, however, practically useful, as it clearly sets out the terms and purpose of the pledge.

155 For a traditional definition of 'pledge', see *Coggs v Bernard* (1703) 2 Ld Raym 909, p. 913, 92 ER 107, *per* Holt CJ. For broader definition, see J. Story, *Bailments*, 9th ed. (Boston: Little, Brown and Company, 1878), §290, p. 256: a pledge is 'a bailment of personal property as a security for some debt or engagement'; applied in the Hong Kong case of *Fat Kee Firm and Another v The Po On Marine Insurance Co. Ltd and Chan Wai Chi* [1905–10] 2 HKLR 64. For China, the identical nature of a pledge is described in Article 63 of the Security Law (1995) and Article 208 of the Property Law (2007). The interest of the pledgee is one of 'special property' in the goods. The 'special property' does not confer on the creditor any proprietary interest, but a right of possession of the property and a right to sell the property upon default by the pledgor. See *The Odessa* (1916) 1 AC 145, PC, where the Judicial Committee criticised *Donald v Suckling* (1866) LR 1 QB 585 on the ground that it suggested that the pledge acquired a proprietary interest. It is unfortunate that the JC should opine that the expression 'proprietary interest' was a useful term to describe the different types of security interest. If the expression is applicable only to a charge or a mortgage, legal or equitable, certainly the pledge also confers upon the creditor a 'proprietary interest'. In *Re Bank of Credit and Commerce International SA (No 8)* [1997] 4 All ER 568, HL, Lord Hoffmann said, 'A proprietary interest provided by way of security entitles the holder to resort to the property right only for the purpose of satisfying some liability due to him (whether from the person providing the security or a third party) and, whatever the form of transaction, the owner of the property retains an equity of redemption to have the property restored to him when the liability has been discharged.' His Lordship went on to say that proprietary interests confer a right *in rem* which is binding on third parties and unaffected by the insolvency of the debtor (p. 576). A pledge is a right *in rem*, as we have seen above; it is binding on an equitable mortgagee of goods, even one earlier in time. It should be noted that the label 'proprietary interest' seems to be outdated. As Lord Hoffmann commented (p. 578), '"proprietary interest" and "charge" are no more than labels given to clusters of related and self-consistent rules of law. Such concepts do not have a life of their own from which the rules are inexorably derived.'

156 *Fat Kee Firm and Another v The Po On Marine Insurance Co. Ltd and Chan Wai Chi* [1905–10] 2 HKLR 64.

Trust receipt

Trust receipt is the last stage in the chain of the process of granting security over goods to secure the same advances granted by a bank to the debtor to finance the purchase of the goods from overseas. It is used when the debtor has to sell the goods in order to repay the advance. It is, therefore, a security device that is designed to give the bank a security interest of relatively short duration.[157] Creation and perfection is simple. The debtor executes for the bank a one-page standard trust receipt document and deposits it with the bank. The trust receipt basically states that the goods are held in trust for the bank, that the debtor are authorised to sell the goods on behalf of the bank and that the debtor has to account to the bank in respect of the proceeds of the sale.

The trust receipt is popular in Hong Kong, because it avoids the complexities and technicalities of registration associated with the traditional security devices, such as the legal mortgage *strictu sensu*, that may be caught by the Bills of Sale Ordinance.[158] However, this advantage has forced banks to take the risk that the security might not adequately protect the bank against the fraud of the debtor. This occurs when a dishonest debtor sells the goods and absconds with the money. The bank cannot recover the goods from the subsequent bona fide purchaser for value without notice of the trust receipt.

This loss to the bank and the converse benefit to the subsequent purchaser can be illustrated in the Hong Kong case of *CIC-Union Européenne International et Cie v Wing Sun and Co. (A Firm) and Another*.[159] There, a French bank in Singapore (hereafter the French Bank) released a large quantity of polyethylene on a trust receipt executed by its customer. Subsequently, the customer sold the polyethylene to a Hong Kong purchaser (hereafter the Hong Kong Purchaser). A bank in Hong Kong (hereafter the Hong Kong Bank) financed the purchase price and issued letters of credit in favour of the customer. Later, the customer drew a bill of exchange drawn for an amount of money stated in the letter of credit in favour of the Hong Kong and Shanghai Banking Corporation (HSBC), to settle a loan owing by the customer. Soon after, but before the Hong Kong Bank paid the money to HSBC, a provisional liquidator was appointed in respect of the customer. The French Bank

[157] D.K. Malcolm, 'Uniform Commercial Code as Enacted in Massachusetts', *Bus Law* 13 (1958), 490, pp. 502–6; referred to by J.W. Wyatt and M.B. Wyatt, *Business Law – Principles and Cases*, 6th ed. (New York: Graw-Hill Book Company, 1963), Chapter 3, p. 17.

[158] Gilmore, above, note 95, p. 88.

[159] [1985] 1 HKC 568.

applied to the High Court in Hong Kong for an order directing the Hong Kong Purchaser to pay the purchase price to the French Bank. The court dismissed the application of the French Bank on the grounds that as the bank was not the legal owner of the goods, it had no locus standi without joining the customer, who had the legal title as owner. The court further observed, *obiter*, that the French Bank could not prevent the Hong Kong Purchaser from paying HSBC because HSBC had no knowledge of the pledge or trust receipt arrangement between the customer and the French Bank.

An English case which reinforces the inherent danger of the trust receipt is *Lloyds Bank Ltd v Bank of America National Trust and Savings Association*.[160] In this case, a bank released a bill of lading to a customer on a trust receipt so that the customer could sell the goods and the proceeds could be used to settle a debt owed to the bank. Instead of selling the goods, the customer pledged them to another bank. The court held that the subsequent pledgee bank acquired a good title to the goods free from the claim of the first bank.

No attempt has been made in Hong Kong to solve the problem. This could be because the honesty and good faith of the debtor on which the trust receipt rests is very rarely betrayed. This is probably true, as the *CIC-Union Européenne International et Cie* case appears to be the only reported case in Hong Kong on this issue, and even then the debtor was resident in Singapore and the fraud was committed in Singapore.

2.5.2 *Perfection of hypothecation, pledge and trust receipt*

There is no special external process for perfecting hypothecation, pledge or trust receipt. Perfection is dependent on internal rules. In the case of hypothecation and trust receipt, perfection is linked to priority.[161] Basically, they are not enforceable against a subsequent bona fide purchaser for value without notice.[162] In the case of the pledge, it is always binding on a subsequent purchaser. This is because the pledgee has a superior title which constitutes notice to the whole world of the pledge through perfection by possession of the collateral by the pledgee or its agent.[163] However, the situation is different where the goods are in the hands of

[160] [1938] 2 KB 147. [161] Rules of priority are discussed further in Chapter 6.

[162] For its full effect, see *Lloyds Bank Ltd v Bank of America National Trust & Savings Association* [1938] 2 KB 147 discussed earlier.

[163] See English Law Commission Report No 296, para. 3.18; and No 176, draft reg. 24.

the debtor and the debtor attorns to the creditor. A third party will find it difficult to discover that the debtor's apparent possession is subject to the creditor's security. Currently, in England, an attornment by the debtor (if in writing) would require registration as a bill of sale or under §860(7)(b) of the Companies Act 2006. The English Law Commission Report No 296 further recommended that a pledge, under which the debtor has possession of collateral and attorns to the pledgee, should have to be registered as if it were a charge.[164]

2.5.3 *Publicity of hypothecation, pledge and trust receipt*

The hypothecation, pledge and trust receipt are not registrable in Hong Kong under any legislation. There is therefore no publicity of the hypothecation and trust receipt. In respect of the pledge, publicity is achieved through the creditor's possession of the goods.[165] However, the lack of publicity of hypothecation and trust receipt seems to work in favour of a third party.[166]

The English Law Commission's Report No 296 appears to be reluctant to recommend any reform to make trust receipts registrable as company charges or to adopt the Canadian practice of rendering all trust receipts imperfect if the debtor has possession of the goods for more than fifteen days.[167]

The English Law Commission's position seems to be influenced by the fact that innocent third parties dealing with the debtor in respect of the affected property are not disadvantaged and trusts receipts are usually very short-term security instruments. However, surely the creditor's interests should also be borne in mind. In this regard, the Canadian practice should be seriously considered for adoption.

2.5.4 *Cost of creation, perfection and publicity of hypothecation, pledge and trust receipt*

The hypothecation, pledge and trust receipt are not subject to tax or stamp duty. The costs of creation and perfection are therefore inexpensive.

[164] See English Law Commission Report No 296, paras. 3.20–3.21.

[165] See English Law Commission Report No 296, para. 3.17.

[166] See *CIC-Union Européenne International et Cie v Wing Sun and Co. (a firm) and Another* [1985] 1 HKC 568, and *Lloyds Bank Ltd v Bank of America National Trust and Savings Association* [1938] 2 KB 147.

[167] Para. 3.22; see also R. Goode, *Commercial Law*, 3rd ed. (London: Penguin, 2004) p. 1015.

2.6 Types of security device in China

As mentioned at the beginning of this chapter, there are currently only four types of security device over tangible personal property expressly defined in the Security Law. These are mortgage, pledge, deposit and lien. The limited number of available security devices over personal property had been criticised as a serious weakness of the prior Security Law.[168] However, the Property Law now implies that a device similar to the common law fixed or floating charge may be created over specific tangible personal property, although no express declaration to this effect is made. An analysis of the position will be given later in the text.

2.6.1 *Mortgage* – DiYa (抵押)

In China, the most widely used security device in commercial transactions is the *DiYa*, commonly referred to as a mortgage, which can be granted over real[169] or personal property.[170] In contrast to other Asian jurisdictions that follow the civilian tradition, China does not have a separate mortgage statute. Instead, the Security Law and the Property Law contain the relevant provisions.

The *DiYa* mortgage, unlike the common law mortgage, does not involve a transfer of title from mortgagor to mortgagee. For this reason, and in order to prevent confusion, we will use the term *DiYa* mortgage to distinguish this Chinese security device from the traditional common law mortgage. In fact, the *DiYa* mortgage is in substance similar to a common law legal fixed charge, whereby a mortgagor grants a security that attaches to the secured property but does not require and transference of title or possession of the asset. However, the term 'charge' is unknown in China in connection with security interests. Should the mortgagor default in repayment of the secured sum, the mortgagee is entitled to convert the secured property into money to satisfy the debt. Further, a properly registered mortgagee will have priority over any other creditor in the event of the mortgagor's insolvency.[171] A *DiYa* mortgage must be contained in a written document and contain certain required particulars.[172] The essential characteristics of the *DiYa* mortgage – no transfer of title and

[168] See Benhan Chen, *A Comparative Study on Secured Property Law* (Wuhan: Wuhan University Press, 2003); Kaizhong Hu, *Pledge on Rights* (Beijing: China Politics and Law University Press, 2004).

[169] Article 180(i)–(iii) of the Property Law.

[170] Ibid., Article 180(iv)–(vii).

[171] Ibid., Article 179.

[172] Ibid., Article 185.

possession of the charged asset remaining with the debtor – ensure the popularity of this device and its widespread use in commerce.[173]

Again, in distinction to the common law mortgage, and pursuant to Article 179 and Article 186 of the Property Law, when a *DiYa* mortgagor defaults no automatic transfer of title to the mortgagee occurs and title of the secured asset remains with the mortgagor.[174] However, a consensual transfer of title is possible to satisfy the secured debt before the contractual repayment date is possible or alternatively a mandatory transfer of title occurs when a third party buyer satisfies the secured debt as agent of the mortgagee; both possibilities are contemplated by Article 191.[175] The position at common law is that the creation of common law mortgages, however, is based on the general principle of transferring title[176] of the mortgaged property to the mortgagee, subject to an equity of redemption[177] which has the effect of transferring the title back to the mortgagor upon satisfaction of the debt. Thus there is a fundamental distinction between the *DiYa* mortgage and the common law mortgage. Another practical distinction lies in the transferability of the mortgagee's right in the mortgaged asset. According to Article 192 of the Property Law, the right over the mortgaged asset cannot be transferred independently or used to secure other obligagee's rights. The rights over the mortgaged asset shall be transferred together with the mortgagee's principal rights in the loan to the mortgagor. However, this is subject to any agreement between the mortgagee and mortgagor to the contrary, and so in effect they can be transferred independently if both parties agree. This general statutory

[173] Mingyue Xu, *Studies on the Mortgage Law* (Law Press, 2000), p. 3.

[174] Formerly in Article 57 of the Judicial Interpretation of the Security Law.

[175] Except the only two cases listed as a valid transfer; other transfers could be challenged as invalid as an 'unauthorized disposal of property through contract' pursuant to Article 51 of the Contract Law (1999).

[176] In the case of a legal mortgage, the creditor obtains the legal title to the secured asset whilst the debtor retains an equitable interest in it. In the case of an equitable mortgage, the creditor obtains an equitable interest in the secured asset, whilst the debtor retains legal title to it.

[177] The concept of the equity of redemption has now extended from legal mortgages of land to all legal mortgages. At common law, if the debtor did not repay the secured liabilities on the due date for payment, the creditor became the unencumbered owner of the property, although he was still entitled to pursue the debtor for the unpaid debt. However, if the debtor applied to the Lord Chancellor, equity recognised his ability to recover the land on his repayment of the loan, even if that occurred after the due date for payment. This right now arises as a proprietary right because the Lord Chancellor allows the debtor to redeem not only against the original creditor, but also against anyone else who acquires the property, unless that party acquired the property for value without notice (of the debtor's right). See also *Kreglinger v New Patagonia Meat and Cold Storage Company* [1914] AC 25 at 35, per Viscount Haldane LC.

presumption of the non-transferability of mortgage rights is contrary to the position in common law mortgages where the mortgagee's rights are generally transferable.

2.6.2 *Pledge*

A pledge is a security device whereby a debtor or a third party uses movables to secure an obligation with the transfer of the possession of such property to the creditor. When the debtor fails to perform his obligation, the creditor is entitled to priority in receiving payment by converting the property into money or from proceeds of an auction or sale of such movables in accordance with provisions of the Property Law.[178] The pledged property can be either movables or rights.[179] A question arises as to the meaning of 'possession'. For the creation of a pledge over tangible movables,[180] the pledge shall be effective upon physical delivery of the pledged property.[181] But in relation to a pledge over rights, the pledge shall be effective upon delivery of the relevant document of title[182] to the pledgee or upon registration with the competent authority.[183]

2.6.3 *Lien*

The concept of a lien is defined in Chapter V of the Security Law and Chapter XVIII of the Property Law. Strictly speaking, the parties do not need to intentionally create such a security device over property. Creation occurs when a creditor, pursuant to a contract (e.g. storage contract, transport contract or processing contract),[184] already has possession of the relevant movable property. In cases of an obligor (debtor) failing to pay its due debts, the obligee (creditor) may exercise a lien over the obligor's movable property lawfully in his possession, and is entitled to seek preferential satisfaction from the proceeds of sale of the movable property.[185]

[178] Article 208 of the Property Law. [179] Ibid., Article 208 and Article 223.

[180] Ibid., Article 209, forbids the creation of pledges over some movables according to relevant laws and administrative regulations.

[181] Ibid., Article 212.

[182] Ibid., Article 223, allows intangible rights to be pledged, such as bills of exchange, cheques, promissory notes, bonds, certificates of deposit, warehouse receipts or bills of lading.

[183] See also the registration requirement to give effect to a pledge on intangible rights in Article 226 (units of fund and shares), Article 227 (intellectual property rights) and Article 228 (right to collect receivables) of the Property Law.

[184] Article 84 of the Security Law. [185] Article 230 of the Property Law.

2.6.4 *Deposit*

A debtor may also agree to offer a monetary deposit as a security for an obligation. After the debtor has performed his obligation, the deposit shall either be retained as a partial payment or returned. If the party paying the deposit defaults, he shall have no right to demand a return of the deposit. Where the party who receives a deposit defaults, he shall refund twice the amount of the deposit.[186]

2.6.5 *'Floating'* Diya *Mortgages*

As discussed above in 2.6.1, China's predominant security device, the *Diya* mortgage, is the equivalent of the common law fixed legal charge. Upon creation of the security, the mortgagee's rights attach to the charged property, which renders dealing with the property problematic in the ordinary course of business as a discharge or specific permission to alienate the encumbered property would be required in each case. Consequently, the *Diya* mortgage can be too cumbersome to be of practical use in many commercial settings, particularly where circulating assets are involved, as satisfaction and release of the security by the mortgagee would be required to allow transfer of title to an acquirer of the affected property.

This deficiency in Chinese law required the creation of a 'floating' security that does not attach to the charged asset on creation, so facilitating dealing with a pool of assets in the ordinary course of business including the alienation of individual assets by way of sale. Additionally, the ability to grant security over future property or over rotating assets or commodities that are physically changed during processing or in relation to components incorporated into new products as a result of a manufacturing process was required to complete an appropriate range of security devices. Such a security would facilitate commercial secured lending and promote the increase of trade; this is the same rationale that justified the invention of the floating charge in England in the 19th century.

These *lacunae* have now been partially addressed by Article 181 of the Property Law which provides that:

> 'enterprises, individual industrial and commercial household and agricultural producers may mortgage their existing and future equipment, raw materials, semi-finished and finished products'.[187]

[186] Article 89 of the Security Law.

[187] According to the meaning of 'mortgage' in Articles 179 and 186.

This new provision opens the door to the creation of a security interest over a wide range of circulating and future tangible commercial property by individuals, partnerships and limited liability companies.[188] However, the scope of the provision is limited as existing or future intangible assets are not included.

There is also a debate as to whether this new provisions effectively extends the 'fixed charge' *Diya* mortgage or creates a security analogous to the common law 'floating' charge as the statutory language is unclear as to whether this new security attaches to the specific asset on creation of the security or not.

The arguments in favour of such an interpretation are that Article 181 mentions 'existing and future property' and has a close resemblance to 'a class of assets of a company present and future' bearing the first characteristic of a floating charge mentioned in *Re Yorkshire Woolcombers*.[189] Secondly, the property mentioned in Article 180(4) as being capable of being offered as security is likely to be revolving in nature. This is equivalent to 'that class of assets … which, in the ordinary course of business of the company, would be changing from time to time', as in the second characteristic from the *Yorkshire* case. A further persuasive argument can be derived in Article 196, which provides that if the right of mortgage is in accordance with Article 181, the mortgaged property can be 'determined' in four circumstances. Whether the meaning of 'determination' is akin to 'crystallisation' in the common law sense is unclear, but those circumstances are very similar to common crystallisation events stipulated in a debenture.[190] It appears that this 'mortgage' under the Property Law relates to the moment in time at which the mortgaged property is determined, or, in common law terms, the time when the charge attaches to the asset. In relation to the third and most

[188] 'Enterprise' is not defined under PRC law. But when the law refers to 'enterprise', it means any legal-person or non-legal-person business entity. Article 67 of the Property Law provides, 'The State, any collective or individual may, according to law, make contributions to establish a limited liability company, a company limited by shares or any other enterprises.' For example, a partnership is an enterprise, but not a legal person (see Article 2 of the Partnership Enterprise Law of PRC, promulgated by the Standing Committee of the NPC on 27 August 2006, effective on 1 July 2007). Therefore 'enterprise' is a concept broader than 'company', which must be a separate legal person.

[189] *Re Yorkshire Woolcombers Association Limited* [1903] 2 Ch 284, 295. For details of the three characteristics see Chapter 4 below.

[190] Article 196 mentions the following the events: (1) the debtor's failure to perform any of its obligations, (2) insolvency or dissolution of the debtor, (3) other circumstances which may seriously affect the enforcement of the right of mortgage, (4) other circumstances which may seriously affect enforcement of the claim.

distinctive characteristic of the floating charge set forth in Re Yorkshire Woolcombers,[191] namely that 'the company may carry on its business in the ordinary way', the chargor so allowing liberty to deal with the secured property, Article 189 provides that a mortgagee who has taken a mortgage created under Article 181 and who has been protected by registration is unable to claim against a third-party purchaser who has paid a reasonable price in the ordinary course of business. It is generally believed that the mortgagor can freely deal with the mortgaged asset in the ordinary course of business on the condition that a reasonable price for the assets has been obtained.

However, Article 191 potentially casts some doubt as to the extent of the 'mortgagor's liberty' to deal with charged assets. The Article provides two situations where the mortgagor may exercise transfer of the mortgaged property during the mortgage period: either with the consent of the mortgagee, or without. If consent is obtained, the mortgagor can freely transfer the mortgaged property subject to the statutory obligation that he must satisfy his debts with the proceeds obtained from the transfer. If consent is not obtained, the validity of the transfer depends on the third-party transferee, who must pay off the secured debt on behalf of the mortgagor. In other words, the mortgagor's transfer of property is either dependent on the mortgagee's consent followed by an obligation of repayment, or is secured by debt satisfaction by the purchaser/transferee. Since Article 191 is a general provision applying to all Diya mortgages, to what extent this provision will affect the mortgagor's liberty to deal with the charged asset: under Article 181 is not entirely clear.[192]

We should also consider the possibility that Articles 181 and 191 create a fixed charge. According to Millet LJ in *Re Cosslett (Contractors) Limited*,[193] the essence of a fixed charge is that the charge is on a particular asset or class of assets which the chargor cannot deal with freely without the consent of the chargee. The question is not whether the chargor has complete freedom to carry on his business as he chooses, but whether the chargee

191 It is the third characteristic which is the hallmark of a floating charge and serves to distinguish it from a fixed charge, as explained by Lord Millet in *Agnew v Commissioner of Inland Revenue* [2001] UKPC 28, [2001] 3 WLR. 454.

192 See also Article 67 of the Judicial Interpretations of the Security Law, under which a mortgagor, without notifying the mortgagee, who makes the transfer of a registered mortgaged property during the mortgage period will be subject to the mortgagee's right against the third-party purchaser. The third party may be obliged to pay the debt to extinguish the mortgagee's right and then is entitled to have recourse against the mortgagor, the transferor.

193 [1997] 4 All ER 115, CA, [1998] Ch 495.

or chargor has control of the charged assets.[194] The issue raised by Article 191 seems to be whether the obligation to seek the mortgagee's consent to transferring the mortgaged property followed by the mortgagor's obligation to satisfy his debt with the proceeds from the transfer means that the mortgagee has an implied and sufficient control of the mortgaged assets. There is currently no case law or statutory interpretation to explain the Property Law. Assuming that control is implied by Article 191, it is also likely to be equivalent to a common law fixed charge created by companies over the tangible property specified in Article 181. At present, the position is unclear.

2.6.6 Trust receipt

In China, the trust receipt is essentially a confirmation document from the debtor to transfer ownership rights of goods to a bank. Holding a trust receipt means that the bank enjoys ownership rights over the goods.[195] A trust receipt expressly provides that the debtor holds the goods in storage and acknowledges the bank's security interest in goods. However, the debtor has the right to sell the goods for cash, but the debtor must hand the proceeds of sale to the bank. Until the goods are sold and the proceeds handed over, the debtor holds the goods or the proceeds, as the case may be, on trust for the bank.[196]

2.7 Mortgages

2.7.1 Scope of mortgages over personal property

A mortgage under Chinese law is significantly different from a mortgage under Hong Kong law in several regards. Firstly, the provisions governing mortgage in relevant laws apply to both corporate and non-corporate debtors. Secondly, the provisions apply to all forms of tangible personal property,[197] as well as real property.[198] Thirdly, a mortgage, until recently,

[194] The same approach was also adopted by the Privy Council in *Agnew* (see note 191 above), which was followed by the House of Lords in *Smith (Administrator of Cosslett (Contractors) Limited v Bridgend County Borough Council* [2002] 1 AC 336, 352, [41].

[195] Basic Provisions of International Accounts-Settling Business of Bank of China.

[196] Jinze Li, 'Some Legal Problems on Trust Receipt of Banks under Chinese Law', *Finance Forum* 7 (2001), 32–8.

[197] Article 180(4) and (6), and "ships and aircrafts under construction" provided in Article 180(5) of the Property Law.

[198] Article 180(1)–(3), and "buildings under construction" provided in Article 180(5) of the Property Law.

could not be created over after-acquired and future property, as the Security Law and its affiliated judicial interpretations did not deal with this issue. Further, under Article 113 of the Judicial Interpretation of the GPCL, it was provided that 'a mortgage is void where the mortgagor does not enjoy the ownership or management rights in respect of the mortgaged property'.[199] Upon registration of a mortgage, the interested parties have to provide specific details of the property to be mortgaged as a condition for registration,[200] and so it may be safely concluded that previously a mortgage could not be created over future or after-acquired property.[201] However, Article 47 of the Judicial Interpretation of the Security Law provided that

> if a mortgage is created over a building or other structure for which construction approval has been received but the building has not yet been constructed or it is currently under construction, and the parties have carried out the procedures for registering the mortgaged property, the People's Court may determine the mortgage to be valid.

This provision is only applicable to real estate. Nevertheless, it reflects China's efforts and willingness to reconcile the rigidity of the Security Law and a willingness to borrow practices from common law. Despite the reluctance of Chinese scholars and the legislature to recognise the validity of mortgage upon future or after-acquired movable property, Article 47 may be seen as example where a step to create mortgage over future property has been taken. Article 181 of the Property Law (2007) further provides that a mortgage can be created by enterprises, small industrial and commercial businesses and rural contractors over a limited class of existing and future property,[202] namely production equipment, raw materials, semi-finished products and finished products, according to the mortgage agreement.

2.7.2 Personal property that can be mortgaged

The nature of tangible personal property that can be mortgaged is governed by both inclusive and exclusive provisions. Article 34 of the Security Law specifies the personal property which can be mortgaged. The categories include:

199 Article 113 of the Judicial Interpretations of the GPCL.

200 Article 39 of the Security Law.

201 Yong Wang and Jianwei Fang, 'A Preliminary Research into Chattel Mortgage and Perfection of Legislation', *Administration and Law* 1 (2002), 50.

202 Article 181 of the Property Law.

- 'machinery, means of transport and other property owned by the mortgagor; ...
- state-owned machinery, means of transport and other property which the mortgagor is entitled to dispose of according to law; ...
- other property that may be mortgaged according to law.'

Article 180 of the Property Law extends the scope of tangible property which can be mortgaged, to include:

- production equipment, raw materials, semi-finished and finished products;
- buildings, ships and aircraft under construction;
- vehicles;
- other property that is not prohibited to be mortgaged according to law and administrative rules.

By virtue of Article 178[203] and Article 180(7) of the Property Law, additional classes of property capable of being mortgaged may be determined by the promulgation of new 'administrative rules'. A key question is the definition of 'other property' that could be rendered mortgageable by such new rules and the open-textured nature of Article 180 (7), which constitutes a non-exhaustive list but does not provide guidance on the potential scope of this category. However, some examples of 'other property' in this context do exist, for example, Article 3 of the Notary Depart Mortgage Registration Rules issued by the Department of Justice in 2002 define 'other personal property'[204] to include: (1) machinery, animals and other means of production owned by individuals, institutions, social organisations and other non-enterprise organisations; (2) furniture, electrical household appliances, gold and silver jewellery and other means of livelihood owned by individuals; and (3) other personal property except those mentioned in Articles 37[205] and 42[206] of the Security

[203] One should note that Article 178 provides that in case of any inconsistency or discrepancy arising between the Security Law and the Property Law, the latter shall prevail.

[204] Although Article 3 specifically provides the definition of 'other property' for the purpose of Article 43 (registration of other property to be mortgaged) of the Security Law, taking a contextual approach in the interpretation of the Security Law, this definition should apply to the 'other property to be mortgaged' under Article 34(6) of the Security Law and will likely apply to Article 180(7) of the Property Law when it comes into force.

[205] The same as in Article 184 of the Property Law listing property which cannot be mortgaged.

[206] Article 42 specifies the relevant department where some specific properties are registered. Tangible property includes: standing timber, aircraft, vessels, vehicles, equipment and movables of an enterprise. There is no corresponding article in the Property Law which lists the registration department of mortgaged property.

Law.[207] From these provisions we can see that, except for property explicitly prohibited by law as ineligible to be used as security, any other kind of tangible personal property can be mortgaged.

Thus Article 184 of the Property Law prevents the following personal property from being used as mortgage collateral:

- educational facilities, medical and health facilities of schools, kindergartens, hospitals and other institutions or public organizations established in the interest of the public and other facilities in the service of public welfare.
- property in relation to which the ownership or the right of use is unknown or disputed;
- property that is legally confiscated, seized or controlled; or
- other property which may not be mortgaged as prescribed by law.[208]

However, the Judicial Interpretation of the Security Law provides that where a social welfare organization such as a school or hospital owns personal property not connected to its core functions, such property may be given as collateral for a mortgage.[209]

The Interpretation reiterates the prohibitions in Article 184(3)[210] and (6)[211], violation of which renders the security void.

With regard to property such as gold, silver and cultural relics, sale of such property is restricted by specific laws and regulations.[212] Where such property is provided as security, the mortgage contract is not necessarily void.

The People's Court shall dispose of the property to realise the creditors' right in accordance with the relevant laws and regulations.[213] For example, the government is entitled to purchase cultural relics.

2.8 Creation, perfection and publicity of mortgages over tangible personal property, and cost

2.8.1 Creation of mortgages over tangible personal property

To create a mortgage over this type of property, the mortgagor and mortgagee are required to conclude a contract in writing.[214] The mortgage

[207] Article 3 of Rules for Notary Department Mortgage Registration Rules.

[208] Article 184(3) to (6).

[209] Article 53 of the Judicial Interpretation of the Security Law.

[210] Ibid., Article 3. [211] Ibid., Article 5.

[212] Ibid., Article 5(2). [213] Ibid.

[214] Article 185 of the Property Law, formerly Article 38 of the Security Law. They slightly differ in that Article 39(5), 'other items the parties consider necessary to agree', is now omitted. The practical effect of such omission does not appear to be significant.

contract may be separately concluded or be evidenced by letters, facsimiles and so on. The document should state the nature of the security, or there may be security clauses contained in the principal contract.[215] The mortgage contract must contain the following details:[216]

(1) the nature and amount of the principal obligation secured;
(2) the term under which the debt or obligation should be satisfied;
(3) the name, quantity, quality, condition, location, ownership utilisation rights of the property subject to the mortgage; and
(4) the scope of security granted.

If the mortgage contract does not include all the particulars specified in the preceding paragraph, the omission may be remedied by amendment. A grey area remains as to whether the above-mentioned contents of the mortgage contract are permissive or mandatory. Some scholars believe that they are purely exhortatory, thus the omission of some of the information has no effect on the validity of the mortgage contract.[217] A literal interpretation of the provisions may, however, indicate that the legislators intended otherwise. The Judicial Interpretation of the Security Law further stipulates,

> No mortgage is created if the nature of the principal obligation secured or the mortgaged property is unspecified or is specified in ambiguous terms in the mortgage contract, and the same cannot be supplemented on the basis of, or be inferred from, the principal contract and the mortgage contract.[218]

Therefore creditors must at least specify the type of the principal obligation secured and the mortgaged property should be unequivocally identified in the mortgage contract to avoid later disputes as to the validity of the mortgage contract itself.

In concluding a mortgage contract, the mortgagor and the mortgagee may not stipulate that the ownership of the mortgaged property shall be transferred to the creditor in case of the mortgagee's debt not being satisfied after maturity of the debt.[219] This prohibition does not, however, affect the validity of the other stipulations of the mortgage contract.[220]

215 Article 93 of the Security Law. 216 Article 185 of the Property Law.

217 Lihai Sun, *Annotations of the Chinese Security Law* (Beijing: Law Press, 1995), p. 59; Yamin Mao, *Security Law* (Beijing: China Fa Zhi Press, 1997), p. 152.

218 Article 56 of the Judical Interpretation of the Security Law.

219 Article 186 of the Property Law, formerly Article 40 of the Security Law.

220 Article 57 of the Judical Interpretation of the Security Law.

2.8.2 Perfection of mortgages over tangible personal property

China has a dual system for perfection of a mortgage. For some types of tangible personal property, such as vehicles, equipment and other movables owned by enterprises, the Security Law expressly provides that the creditor must register the mortgage with the relevant registration departments responsible for registration of that particular type of asset.[221] The mortgage will be effective at the date of registration.[222] Article 43 of the Security Law stipulates that for 'other tangible personal properties', registration is voluntary. Failure to register does not render the mortgage itself void. Once the mortgagee's rights are created, they become effective at the date of execution of the document.[223] Failure to register prevents the mortgagee claiming priority against a third party in case of a dispute over the secured property. In a situation where a third party acquires property that he knows to be mortgaged, unless the mortgage has been properly registered the third party will take the property free of the encumbrance. This means that even with actual knowledge of the mortgage, the third party is not bound by the security.

Article 180 of the Property Law further provides for a number of new types of mortgageable tangible property, notably 'manufacturing facilities, raw materials, semi-manufactured goods and products' and 'ships and aircraft under construction'.[224] For these types of personal property, failure to register prevents the mortgagee from claiming priority against a third party who obtains rights over such property in 'good faith'. In other words, there exists a 'good-faith' requirement which is, in some respects, similar to the common law concept of a bona fide purchaser for value without notice.[225] In particular, if the mortgage was created by an enterprise, a small industrial and commercial business, or a rural contractor over any of the specific classes of tangible property listed in Article 181, the effect of registration against a third party is subject to the exception rule of bona fide third-party purchaser for value in the ordinary course of business.[226]

[221] Article 42 of the Security Law. [222] Ibid., Article 41.

[223] Ibid., Article 43. [224] Article 180(4)–(5).

[225] Article 188 of the Property Law. Ping Jiang, *Property Law of the People's Republic of China: Explained* (Beijing: China University of Political Science and Law Press, 2007), p. 245, suggested that the meaning of 'good faith' in this article is the third party's lack of knowledge of the fact that (1) the mortgage contract has been formed, and (2) the property concerned has been mortgaged, and the third party has legally obtained the mortgaged property.

[226] Ibid., Article 189.

In both types of mortgage, the rights are created and are thus effective on the date of agreement between the mortgagor and mortgagee.[227] However, from the mortgagee's perspective, it is submitted that registration of a mortgage over tangible personal property is always necessary to ensure protection against claims by third parties.

To effect registration, the mortgagee must deliver to the appropriate registry all the necessary documents specified by the relevant registration agency. Article 44 of the Security Law provides that the following documents or copies shall be produced to the registration department: (1) the master contract and the mortgage contract, and (2) the certificate of ownership or right to the use of the property. The agency will record the mortgage, all the relevant particulars, and the date the mortgage particulars were received by the registry. The information registered by the registration department shall be available upon inquiry in the form of a handwritten copy or photocopy.[228]

Several issues arise from this mortgage registration process. Firstly, neither the Security Law nor the Property Law specifies the period during which a mortgage must be registered with the relevant agencies. As a result, there is no provision for extension of time. Clearly it is advisable for the creditor to register the mortgage as quickly as possible, for the date of registration determines the priority of competing claims.

Secondly, China operates a multiple registration system for different types of personal property. Therefore different classes of property are registered by their corresponding registration agencies. For example, the forestry administration departments at or above the county level are the relevant registration agency if growing trees are mortgaged. Vehicle mortgages are registered at the vehicle registration department.

[227] One should carefully distinguish between the effect of mortgage registration and the creation of mortgage rights. Articles 188 and 189 of the Property Law provide that the rights of mortgage over the prescribed personal property come into existence on the day of the mortgage agreement (the day the contract has binding force). One should also note the inconsistency where the mortgage contract has been effective at the date of registration provided in Article 41 of the Security Law (as far as the same property prescribed under Article 42 of the Security Law and Article 187 of the Property Law is concerned), and this is now resolved by Article 178 of the Property Law which prevails over the Security Law in case of inconsistency. Therefore the existence of the mortgage rights between the parties to the mortgage does not depend on registration of the mortgage. But without registration, such rights are not valid against bona fide third parties. This is contrary to the position of the rights of mortgage over real property (Article 180(1)–(3) and (5), 'buildings under construction') where the rights come into existence as of the date of registration.

[228] Article 45 of the Security Law.

For general property such as equipment, the mortgage must be registered in the local office of the State Administration of Industry and Commerce (SAIC) in which the property is located.[229] If such property is situated in two or more locations, the relevant agency is the one where 'the majority of the charged assets' are located. It is unclear whether the term 'majority of … assets' refers to the value of the property or its mere physical bulk. Upon registration, the principal registration department must forward a copy of the registration document to other registration departments where the residue of the affected property is located.[230]

For the 'new classes of mortgageable tangible property' under Article 180(4)–(5) of the Property Law, except for buildings under construction, including production equipment, raw materials, semi-finished and finished products of an enterprise, small business or rural contractors,[231] it is likely that the appropriate registration agency of these these types of property will be the relevant local SAIC office in which the property is located. As for ships and aircraft, registration should be at the local transport registration agency in which the property is located. Mortgages of properties which are outside the ambit of Article 42 are subject to voluntary registration at the notary department where the mortgagor resides.[232]

Thirdly, registration of a mortgage operates as constructive notice of the mortgage to the whole world. If the mortgagor sells or assigns the mortgaged property during the existence of the mortgage without notifying the mortgagee or informing the assignee, the mortgagee may still exercise his mortgage rights against an innocent third party if the mortgaged property has been registered.[233] In this regard, China's registration system is far more effective than the registration system under the Bills of Sale Ordinance in protecting the interests of the creditor and third parties. The fear expressed by Goode that the doctrine of constructive notice may impede the smooth flow of trade does not appear to be true in China.[234] One major reason is that the mortgage is like

[229] Ibid., Article 42.

[230] Article 2 of Registration and Administration Rules for Mortgaged Movable Property of Enterprise (2000).

[231] Read in line with Article 181 of the Property Law.

[232] Article 43 of the Security Law.

[233] Article 67 of the Judical Interpretation of the Security Law.

[234] Goode, above, note 100, p. 52.

a 'floating lien'. It allows a mortgagee–trader to pursue and obtain the mortgaged property wherever it is located.

2.8.3 *Publicity of mortgages over personal property*

According to the Security Law, the details of a registered mortgage can be consulted, transcribed or duplicated.[235] The administrative regulations issued by the responsible registration agencies confirm that the information registered is available for inspection by any person producing a proper identity document.[236] The registration department may charge a fee for this service.[237] The quantum is not specified in the regulations.

China's search procedure appears simple, in theory. The registration agencies are required to keep a mortgaged property register open to public inspection. In practice, it can be a slow and difficult process to access information. According to the registration rules, when the mortgaged property of an enterprise and a secured lender are in different places, the appropriate registration agency is where the mortgaged property is located. This creates a great risk for lenders since the secured property may be moved to another place after registration is completed. When a new potential lender or purchaser consults the register of mortgaged property at the new location of the property, he may be misled into believing that it is free from encumbrances, whilst in fact the property mortgage has actually been registered elsewhere. Logically the system should require registration in the place of registration of enterprises, not at the location of the property.[238] But China has no central enterprise registry. Each local authority has its own business registration office. Furthermore, unless the searcher knows the complete mortgage file number, it is a difficult and lengthy process to locate the mortgage file. This is made worse as the data at some registration offices is not computerised. The officials have to manually search thousands of files that are kept in alphabetical order of the name of the mortgagor. Worse still, some prescribed registration departments may refuse to register some

[235] Article 45 of the Security Law.

[236] Article 17 of Rules for Notary Department to Handle Mortgage Registration; Article 16 of Registration and Administration Rules for Mortgaged Movable Property of Enterprise.

[237] Ibid.

[238] Shengping Gao, *Studies on Chattel Mortgage* (Beijing: Chinese Press of Industry and Commerce, 2003), p. 274.

types of personal property[239] or charge arbitrary fees before allowing consultation of the registry.[240]

Hence information at the registration agencies is not easily accessible and creditors who wish to take tangible personal property as security are exposed to a serious risk that the property may be encumbered by a prior security. The Property Law envisages a more rational registration system but this may take years to implement.

2.8.4 Cost of creation, perfection and publicity of mortgages over personal property

The SAIC charges fees on an *ad valorem* scale based on the value of the loan. The issue of who shall be liable to pay the registration fee is negotiated between the mortgagor and the mortgagee; but if an agreement cannot be reached, the cost is split equally.[241] No national registration fee scale exists. Each local agency sets its own scale in accordance with local regulations or arbitrarily. For example, the SAIC Bureau of Ningbo city charges on an *ad valorem* scale, ranging from 1 per cent to 0.1 per cent of the principal loan with a minimum of 50 RMB and a maximum of 5,000 RMB.[242] The SAIC Bureau of Harbin, however, charges 0.1 per cent of the principal loan, up to a maximum of 5,000 RMB.[243] However, the forestry administration departments do not impose registration fees when trees are mortgaged.[244] When motor vehicles are mortgaged, the registration fee is the fixed amount of 100 RMB.[245] Mortgage registration fees for other personal property are not clearly stipulated since the Department of Justice has not issued any guidelines on the issue. The decision is left to the discretion of different local notarisation agencies. Needless to say, the issue of registration fees is unsatisfactory.

239 Ibid., p. 181. 240 Jie Xu, *On Mortgage* (Beijing: Law Press, 2003), p. 132.

241 Article 15 of Registration and Administration Rules for Mortgaged Movable Property of Enterprise.

242 For the Chinese version of the official website, see www.yfzs.gov.cn/gb/info/LawData/difang/ZheJiang/2003-03/14/1719385714.html; accessed 6 May 2009.

243 See www.hrbgs.gov.cn/newshrbgsj/2006-4-29/2006429164613.htm; accessed 6 May 2009.

244 Article 7 of Mortgage Registration of Forest Resources (for Trail Implementation), effective on 5 July 2004.

245 'Notice on the fee Standard for the Registration Certificate Cost Fee and Mortgage Registration fee of Motor Vehicles', Department of Development and Reform and Department of Finance, 2001.

2.9 Scope of pledge and trust receipt

2.9.1 Creation of pledge and trust receipt

Pledge of tangible personal property

The pledge is commonly used in China to secure goods for commercial lending. It shares the same substantive features as the pledge in Hong Kong – possession of the goods must be actually or constructively delivered to the pledgee. Article 208 of the Property Law provides the definition of a pledge of movable property: the pledgor transfers the possession of his movables to the pledgee as a security for debt. If the pledgor defaults, the pledgee is entitled to enjoy priority in having his claims satisfied with the proceeds of auction or sale of the pledged property.[246] When the pledgor performs his obligation at or prior to its maturity, the pledgee must return the pledged property. Upon the default of the pledgor, the pledgee is entitled to conclude an agreement with the pledgor to convert the pledged property into money from the proceeds of sale or auction. Market prices are now used as a reference in such conversion.[247] Where the proceeds exceed the debt (i.e. pledgor's obligation), the difference shall be paid to the pledgor. Where the proceeds do not discharge the whole debt, the pledgor remains under an obligation to pay the residual amount to the pledgee. Furthermore, since the Property Law has been promulgated, the pledgor and pledgee can now set a maximum value of the pledged debt by mutual agreement,[248] but it is unclear as to whether this provision should apply after maturity or upon the pledgor's default.

The creation of pledges depends upon whether relate to movables (tangible) or rights (intangible). Where movables are pledged, physical possession by the pledgee is required in order to make the pledge effective; that is, the pledgee's rights are created upon actual delivery of the pledged property,[249] not the date of the agreement.[250] In relation to a pledge of

[246] Article 208 of the Property Law (formerly Article 63 of the Security Law).

[247] Article 219 of the Property Law, similarly to Article 71 of the Security Law.

[248] Ibid., Article 222. See also Article 203 of the Property Law.

[249] Ibid., Article 212. See also Article 87 of the Judicial Interpretation of the Security Law, which provides that a pledge contract will not be effective if the pledgor holds the pledged property in his possession or on behalf of the pledgee. It further provides that the pledgee's rights against a third party could evaporate if he returns the pledged property to the pledgor. However, if the pledgee loses possession of the pledged property without any fault, he may require the unjust possessor to cease infringement, restore the original position of the pledgee or return the property.

[250] One should differentiate the effective time of the pledge agreement (i.e. the contract becomes effective at the time of its formation pursuant to Article 44 of the Contract

intangible rights, these are classified into different types. Some are created upon delivery of the document of title and others upon registration with the relevant agency.[251] However, in both cases, the pledgor and pledgee are required to execute a formal pledge document in writing. The pledge contract shall include the following particulars:[252]

- the kind and amount of the principal debt secured;
- the time for the debtor to perform his obligations;
- the name, quantity, quality and condition of the pledged property;
- the scope of the pledge; and
- the time of delivery of the pledged property.

Another interesting issue arises as to whether a pledge can be created where the pledgor is not in possession of the pledged assets at the time of the pledge agreement. Article 88 of the Judicial Interpretation of the Security Law provides that where the pledgor pledges an indirectly possessed property, the receipt of written notice of pledge contract shall be regarded as a valid transfer of possession. Any form of disposal by a person in actual possession, even if instructed by the pledgor after receipt of such a notice, shall be regarded as invalid. Thus 'deemed possession' of the pledged property by way of pledge contract is permissible.

The Property Law has clarified the pledgor–pledgee position as regards new rights, obligations and liabilities. For example, a pledgee has an obligation to maintain the pledged property in good condition and is liable

Law (1999), usually by way of signature) from the effective time of pledge rights under the agreement (i.e. delivery). A further implication is that the non-delivery of pledged property (i.e. pledge rights have not been created) does not invalidate the pledge contract.

[251] Article 224 of the Property Law provides that if the property pledged is in the following list: bills of exchange, cheques, promissory notes, bonds, certificates of deposit, warehouse receipts or bills of lading, then the pledgee's rights are created upon delivery of the document of title (formerly Article 76 of the Security Law), in the absence of which the creation of the pledgee's rights is upon registration of the pledge with the relevant department. Where the property pledged is not within the above-mentioned list – namely intangible properties such as shares, portions of funds (Article 226); intellectual property rights including trademarks, patents and copyrights (Article 227); and rights of collecting receivables (Article 228) – the pledgee's rights are created upon registration of the pledge with the relevant department.

[252] Ibid., Article 210, formerly Articles 64 and 65 of the Security Law. They differ in the omission of Article 64(6), which provides 'other matters that the parties deem necessary to include in the pledge contract. If a pledge contract has the contents incompletely prescribed in the preceding paragraph, it may be supplemented'. This does not appear to produce significant effect in the pledgee's rights, but it is unclear as to whether Article 210 has now provided a 'closed' requirement in the pledge's creation.

for loss, destruction or damage to the pledged property. A breach of the obligation entitles the pledgor to demand the deposit of pledged property, or to demand an earlier discharge of the obligation with return of the property.[253] A pledgee is also responsible for the use or disposal of the pledged property without the consent of the pledgor.[254] However, a pledgee, by consent of the pledgor, may transfer his rights by pledging the property in his possession to a third party in order to secure his own debt. Without such consent, such re-pledge is invalid. The pledgee is likely to be liable for loss, destruction or damage to property arising from the re-pledge (in such cases it is reasonable to presume that the pledgee still retains an obligation to maintain the re-pledged property in good condition).[255] Further, a pledgee is entitled to additional security from the pledgor if the pledged property is perishable or becomes devalued.[256] A pledgee can also abandon his rights of pledge.[257]

Trust receipt

The trust receipt in China generally resembles the Hong Kong trust receipt in form and substance. A trust receipt is a security device that creates a 'security interest' in the goods offered as security. Under a trust receipt, the bank holds title in the goods and the debtor has possession of the goods or documents of title to the goods. The debtor has the right to sell the goods for cash, but the debtor must hand over the proceeds of sale to the bank. Until the goods are sold and the proceeds handed over, the debtor holds the goods or the proceeds, as the case may be, on trust for the bank. Trust receipt is not specified in the Security Law as a security device. However, as a customary bank practice, it is governed at present by the Trust Law of the People's Republic of China and associated administrative regulations of the People's Bank of China.

2.9.2 *Perfection of pledge and trust receipt*

Unlike perfection of a mortgage, there is no special external requirement for perfection with regard to a pledge in China. The pledge contract

[253] Article 215 of the Property Law.

[254] Ibid., Article 214. One possible meaning of 'use' can be referred to Article 94 of the Judicial Interpretation of the Security Law, which provides that a pledgee shall not use the pledged property to secure his own debt without the consent of the pledgor.

[255] This view has been taken by reading Article 94 of the Judicial Interpretation of the Security Law in line with Article 217 of the Property Law.

[256] Property Law, Article 216.

[257] Ibid., Article 218.

becomes effective upon delivery of the pledged property, or deemed delivery, into the possession of the pledgee and thereafter becomes binding on both parties.[258]

The same situation applies to trust receipts as there exists no requirement for its perfection. Whether a trust receipt is binding on the party would depend on the existence of a mutual agreement between the bank and its clients.

2.9.3 Publicity of pledge and trust receipt

Since the pledge of tangible personal property is not registrable in China, the creditor's physical possession of the property by way of actual or deemed delivery is considered adequate publicity that the property is encumbered. As in Hong Kong, there is no registration system in China for a trust receipt.

2.9.4 Cost of creation, perfection and publicity of pledge and trust receipt

The costs of creating pledges in China are minimal since they do not involve any third parties. No tax or duty is imposed upon pledges in China. The same applies to trust receipts.

2.10 Conclusion

The foregoing discussion reveals the strengths and weaknesses of the laws governing the system of creating, perfecting and publicising security over tangible personal property in Hong Kong and China.

With regard to Hong Kong, there are three strengths in the creation process. Firstly, there is no tax or stamp duty cost on any of the security devices. Secondly, the security devices of hypothecation (both traditional and modern types), trust receipt and pledge are simple and quick to create. Thirdly, except for the pledge, the debtor has possession the and freedom to deal with the secured assets.

However, these strengths are outweighed by two serious weaknesses. They are discussed below.

There are no less than six security devices, although they serve the same purpose: to provide the creditor with security. They are the legal

[258] Article 210 of the Property Law, formerly Article 64 of the Security Law.

mortgage *strictu sensu*, equitable mortgage, charge, hypothecation, trust receipt and pledge.

To the ordinary commercial creditor, debtor or third party this superfluity can be baffling. In addition, some of the security documents, such as the trust receipt and the hypothecation with trust expression, not only fail accurately to describe the true relationship of the parties (i.e. one of creditor and debtor), but also are suggestive of other dubious relationships, such as trustee and beneficiary.

The Bills of Sale Ordinance underpins the creation of a wide spectrum of security devices in writing, yet it is fraught with difficulties for both creditors and debtors. As the Crowther Report critically commented, 'It is difficult to imagine any legislation possessing more technical pitfalls than the Bills of Sale Acts, particularly in relation to security bills of sale.'[259]

The English Law Commission in Consultation Paper No 176 held the same view. It commented that the corresponding Bills of Sale Act imposes 'highly complex and draconian registration requirements on mortgages and charges created by unincorporated debtors'.[260] The difficulties include the following. Firstly, there is lack of legal clarity and consistency on which security instruments are capable of constituting bills of sale of personal property; as a result it is difficult to ascertain whether or not a given security is governed by the Ordinance. Secondly, the statutory form with which the bill of sale must comply is complex and highly technical. In view of this, the invalidity of a bill for failure to comply with the requirement of the form is harsh on the creditor. This unfairness on creditors has particularly been mentioned in the English Law Commission's Consultation Paper No 164, which stated,

> To have strict, detailed requirements as to form, and a registration system needing the presentation of attestations and affidavits, all upon pain of the avoidance of the bill in the case of error not only as between grantor and third parties but also grantor and grantee is, in our view, far too complicated an approach to be compatible with a modern economy.[261]

[259] Crowther Committee Report on Consumer Credit, Cmnd 4596, para. 4.2.12. Also English Law Commission Consultation Paper No 164, para. 9.2, where the English Law Commission shared the same view that it contained a complex mass of technical rules and requirements. See also the critical comments of Lord Macnaghten in *Thomas v Kelly* (1888) 13 App Cas 506, 517, where he stated, 'For my own part, the more I have the occasion to study the Act the more convinced I am that it is beset with difficulties which can only be removed by legislation.'

[260] English Law Commission Consultation Paper No 176, para. 2.70.

[261] English Law Commission Consultation Paper No 164, para. 9.4.

It is likely that this complexity is one of the reasons for the extremely small number of bills of sale created in relation to the large number of active business transactions carried by non-incorporated businesses.[262] Therefore the English Law Commission recommended that the notice-filing scheme for companies should be extended to security interests created by other business debtors as soon as possible, but subject to the additional cost for such extension.[263]

The rules governing the creation of non-possessory security over tangible personal property by non-corporate debtors have satisfied the creation criteria of being inexpensive, being capable of securing future advances, giving the debtor possession of the asset, and freedom to deal with the asset.[264] However, they have failed to satisfy the other creation criteria relating to simplicity, comprehensibility, clarity of definition and identification of assets, and securing after-acquired or future assets.[265] However, hypothecation, that is not within the scope of the Bills of Sale Ordinance, can secure after-acquired or future assets. The pledge has satisfied all the creation criteria, except those relating to the debtor's possession of the asset and freedom to deal with it. Accordingly, the rules relating to creation of security, both non-possessory and possessory, over tangible personal property by non-corporate debtors in Hong Kong have not, as a whole, satisfied the creation criteria established in Chapter 1.[266]

With regard to the rules governing the perfection of security of tangible personal property, all security devices are subject to external perfection rules. Only securities constituting bills of sale have to be registered with the Registry of the High Court. The weakness of the perfection process is linked to the complexities and technicality of the creation process discussed above. The actual registration itself does not appear to be difficult. The cost of perfecting security devices is also inexpensive.

For those security devices, such as hypothecation, trust receipt and pledge, perfection coexists with the creation process. Perfection is therefore expeditious and inexpensive.

Thus the rules governing the perfection process have, as a whole, satisfied one of the two perfection criteria established in Chapter 1;[267] that is,

262 See above in this chapter.

263 English Law Commission Consultation Paper No 176, para. 2.75–2.79. However, these recommendations were not incorporated into the Companies Act 2006. For further detail, see H. Beale, M. Bridge et al., *The Law of Personal Property Security* (New York: Oxford University Press, 2007), Chapter 21, para. 21.82, 'Notice-filing'.

264 See Chapter 1 above.

265 See Chapter 1 above.

266 See Chapter 1 above.

267 See Chapter 1 above.

the perfection process must be simple, comprehensible, expeditious and inexpensive. The other criterion – that the rules regulating the priority of competing claims against the secured asset should provide a fair and just order of those claims – cannot be determined at this stage; this is further considered in Chapter 6 below.

With regard to publicity, there is a major strength in the rules governing the publicity of security in Hong Kong; that is, the cost of facilitating the publication of bills of sale is low and, in respect of pledges, nil.

But a number of security devices are not required to be publicised at all, even though this would constitute important information to third parties. Hire-purchase, leasing, conditional sale, hypothecation and trust receipt fall into this category. The exclusion of hypothecation and trust receipt, as discussed above, seems to favour the bona fide third party without notice of them. This is one plausible explanation for their exclusion from the existing registration system. In respect of bills of sale there is poor administrative support and access to the Registry of the High Court. Consequently, the benefits of publicity envisaged by the Bills of Sale Ordinance cannot be fully realised. This leads to weak publicity process, as publicity is linked to a weak creation and perfection processes. The exclusion of the doctrine of constructive notice has weakened the efficiency of the publicity system in protecting creditors against subsequent dealing by the grantor of a bill of sale. A subsequent superior pledge of the same goods takes free from an earlier security bill of sale which may be duly registered. Presently, the weaknesses have not had a serious impact on Hong Kong's commercial community . This does not necessarily mean that the debtors/grantors have been honest but, rather, that few bills of sale are created in Hong Kong today.

Consequently, the rules governing the publicity of security over tangible personal property have satisfied only the criterion relating to cost. The rules have not satisfied the other publicity criteria previously established – ease of search, expedience, simplicity and comprehensibility – in giving accurate information about the nature of the security, the status of the affected assets, and the extent of financial exposure of the asset.

The credit security legal framework of China, like that of Hong Kong, also has strengths and weaknesses.

With regard to creation, in comparison to Hong Kong, China appears to have a superior system. Firstly, the cost of creation is minimal. Secondly, the rules governing the creation of the Diya mortgage (possibly likewise with floating charges), pledge and trust receipt are, generally, simple and straightforward, although there is some formality involved in respect of the first and second security devices. However, this formality does not appear to create serious problems. Simplicity is achieved through the application of a common set of rules applicable both to individuals and to companies based on the provisions of the Property Law and the Security Law and its Judicial Interpretation, as opposed to the complex interwoven rules of common law and equity which make up the law of security in Hong Kong. The basic and consistent terminology in China, except for trust receipt, is that the non-possessory 'mortgage' security provides a generic security device similar in concept to the fixed charge, floating charge, legal mortgage *strictu sensu*, equitable mortgage and so on which were developed over a long period of time in common law jurisdictions. The consistent use of the terminology avoids complexity and uncertainty in the law. It further ensures certainty to third parties who wish to deal with the debtor, namely that the security is what the document represents it to be and nothing else.

The major weakness of the creation mechanism is that Chinese security devices cannot secure future advances. The only exception is Article 181 of the Property Law, which is modelled on the common law floating charge. Under Article 181, enterprises, individual industrial and commercial businesses or agricultural production operators can create Diya mortgage over their present and future raw materials, manufacturing equipment, and semi-finished and finished products. However, given that this Article has only been recently introduced into Chinese law, its effectiveness remains to be tested.

In light of the above, it is submitted that the rules governing the creation of security over tangible personal property in China have, as a whole, satisfied all the creation criteria established in Chapter 1, except for the criteria relating to future advances and after-acquired and future property.

With regard to perfection, the rules governing the perfection of security over tangible personal property in China are generally simple and comprehensible. The actual process of perfecting the mortgage by registration is also expeditious. The cost of perfecting security devices in China is minimal. However, one weakness is the various administrative departments responsible for the registration of different types of security, in contrast to the situation in Hong Kong where the Registry of the High Court and the Companies Registry are the only two agencies involved. The situation in China has increased the complexity of the registration process, as well as the cost for those who wish to check the status of secured personal property in China.

Thus the rules governing the perfection of chattel mortgage credit security over personal property in China have not satisfied all the perfection criteria established in Chapter 1.

With regard to publicity, there are three strengths in the Chinese publicity rules. The first is that the cost of publicity is minimal. This gives credibility and reliability to the system of registration. In addition, it encourages creditors to make inquiries at the registration agencies and take appropriate steps to protect their security interests. The second is the rule that the date of registration determines priority. This encourages diligence by the creditor and gives information to the public expeditiously. The third is the strong administrative support to record accurate information and to process enquiries.

However, there are four weaknesses in the publicity regime. First and foremost, the registration filing system is weak and seriously undermines the objectives of registration. Records are not easily accessible as files are poorly kept and not computerised. Secondly, the courts' flexible treatment of the chattel mortgage law form may not provide credibility and certainty in the creation and perfection of security over movable property. Lastly, the regime does not publicise leases with an option to purchase (equivalent to the Hong Kong hire-purchase), leasing, conditional sale or trust receipt.

Based on this analysis, the rules governing the publicity of security over tangible personal property in China have generally satisfied the publicity criteria established in Chapter 1, namely that the system is inexpensive and easy to file, and provides accurate information relating to the nature of the security, the status of the affected assets, and the financial exposure of the assets. However, it has not satisfied the criterion on the accessibility of information by the public.

In light of the above findings, this chapter concludes that the rules governing security over tangible personal property in Hong Kong and China have not, as a whole, fully satisfied all the criteria of creation, perfection and publicity established in Chapter 1. Accordingly, the legal frameworks of Hong Kong and China are inefficient in respect of the reduction of risk to the creditor and the protection of third parties who wish to deal with the debtor in relation to its tangible personal property. However, in relation to the debtor, because the debtor generally has possession of the secured assets, except for the pledge, the legal framework can be regarded as satisfactorily efficient.

Chapter 3

Security over intangible personal property

3.1 Introduction

In Hong Kong, there are basically four forms of consensual security device available to secure intangible personal property, namely the legal mortgage, equitable mortgage, equitable charge and pledge. In contrast, China has only one form of security device over intangible property, namely the pledge.

In Hong Kong, the creation, perfection and publicity of the security devices are in some cases governed by general law, in others by legislation, and in yet others by a combination of both. The applicable law is determined by a number of factors, such as the nature of the security device and the type of intangible personal property concerned. In contrast, in China, the creation, perfection and publicity of the security devices are primarily governed by the Property Law and the Security Law, the Supreme Court's Judicial Interpretation and various administrative regulations.

The objectives of this chapter are to examine:

- the diametrically opposed substantive and procedural rules governing the creation, perfection and publicity of the above-mentioned security devices over intangible personal property in Hong Kong and China, and the cost involved;
- whether the rules relating to the creation, perfection and publicity of the security devices have satisfied the criteria established in Chapter 1[1] in respect of these functional mechanisms.

[1] See Chapter 1 above.

3.2 Creation, perfection and publicity of security over choses in action in Hong Kong, and cost

3.2.1 Creation, perfection and publicity of pledges over choses in action in the form of negotiable instruments

Creation of pledges

In Hong Kong, a pledge can be created only over choses in action in the form of negotiable instruments.[2] The pledge cannot be created over other types of choses in action because they do not possess any physical form that is capable of delivery, a fundamental requirement of a pledge.[3] A fairly recent Hong Kong case which applied this rule is *Keller v Ying Wah Tak Holdings Ltd and Another*.[4] There the court held that a pledge over a numbered account at a bank in Hong Kong was ineffective. Accordingly, a subsequent legal transfer of the credit balances in the account by the pledgor to its trustee in bankruptcy in the United States had priority.

The court appeared to take a strict view. The possibility that the 'pledge' might take effect as a charge or an equitable mortgage was not considered. In contrast, in the more recent case of *Bank of China (Hong Kong) Ltd v Kanishi (Far East) Ltd and Another*[5] the court held that a security described as a 'pledge' of certain shares created an equitable mortgage. The facts of

[2] See M. Hapgood, *Paget's Law of Banking*, 12th ed. (London: Butterworths, 2002), para. 31.18. This exception was not common law in origin, but a rule of the merchant law, which was absorbed by the common law in the sixteenth century. See R.J. Walker, *Walker and Walker – The English Legal System*, 6th ed. (London: Butterworths, 1985), pp. 67–8. This exception has been criticised as creating an artificial distinction in the sphere of intangible personal property, i.e. a chose in action is given the physical attributes of goods which it does not possess: see Hapgood, *Paget's Law of Banking*, para. 31.18; and see also N. Palmer, 'Pledge', Chapter 5 of M. Gillooly (ed.), *Securities over Personality* (The Federation Press, 1994), p. 138, where it is stated, 'modern judges are beginning to look benignly on the prospect of a custodial bailment of intangible property (for example, confidential information) so it is not inconceivable that future authority will recognise a pledge of intangibles'. 'Negotiable instrument' has a wide meaning; see J.S. James (ed.), *Stroud's Judicial Dictionary* (London: Sweet and Maxwell, 1986), vol. 3, p. 1673, citing *Miller v Race* (1978) 1 Burr 452, 97 ER 398, *Crouch v Credit Foncier of England Ltd* (1873) LR 8 QB 374. Typical examples of negotiable instruments include bills of exchange, cheques, promissory notes and bearer securities. Note that bearer securities are not common in Hong Kong; see B.C.S. Chan, *Hong Kong Banking Law and Practice* (Hong Kong: Hong Kong Institute of Bankers, 2000), vol. 1, para. 20.1.3(5). See Palmer, 'Pledge', p. 138. A pledge can also be created over bills of lading, but as part of a broader security arrangement in respect of goods; see Chapter 2 above.

[3] *Harold v Plenty* [1901] 2 Ch 314, and also the Singapore case of *Re Lin Securities (Pte)* [1988] 2 MLJ 137.

[4] [1997] 3 HKC 301. [5] [2002] 2 HKLRD 52.

the transaction, which involved the deposit of the share certificate and instrument of transfer duly executed by the borrower, clearly indicated the intention to create an equitable mortgage. This decision followed the precedent of English authorities which stated that where there is sufficient evidence that the parties intended to create a security, the security device may be treated as a charge or a mortgage (legal or equitable) even where a pledge has been used by mistake.[6]

A pledge over negotiable instruments can be created by the holder of the negotiable instrument delivering, or by endorsing[7] and delivering, the negotiable instrument to the creditor for value.[8]

The pledge satisfies nearly all the creation criteria established in Chapter 1,[9] namely simplicity, comprehensibility, expedience, identifiability of assets, ability to secure future advances, and capability to protect the legitimate interests of the creditor and debtor. However, the pledge does not satisfy three criteria; namely, it does not leave possession of the negotiable instruments with the debtor, it cannot secure after-acquired and future negotiable instruments, and the debtor has no freedom to deal with the negotiable instruments.

Perfection of pledges

There is no separate mechanism for perfecting pledges of negotiable instruments in Hong Kong; it co-exists with the process of creation. A valid pledge has priority over other subsequent encumbrances because it confers upon the pledgee a superior security interest immediately when it is created. This has been discussed in Chapter 2.

In respect of perfection, the pledge satisfies all the perfection criteria established in Chapter 1.[10] The rules are simple and comprehensible and confer upon the pledgee a superior priority.

Publicity of pledges

Publicity of the security is achieved by the creditor's possession of the negotiable instrument itself, which is notice to the world that it is encumbered and, therefore, the rule against 'apparent ownership' and 'false wealth' does not apply to the pledge.[11] Accordingly, the view is that the

[6] *Halliday v Holgate* (1868) LR 3 Ex 299, and also *Harold v Plenty* [1901] 2 Ch 314.

[7] Endorsement is necessary if the negotiable instrument such as a cheque is payable to order; see Chan, above, note 2, para. 8.5(1).

[8] Hapgood, above, note 2, para. 31.18; also Chan, above, note 2, para. 20.1.3(5).

[9] See Chapter 1 above. [10] See Chapter 1 above.

[11] See English Law Commission Consultation Paper No 164, para. 4.15.

pledge of negotiable instruments should continue to be non-registrable.[12] However, it was proposed that if the negotiable instruments continued to be in the possession of the debtor after the pledge was purportedly created and the debtor attorned to the creditor after the pledge, the attornment should be registrable.[13] However, in this situation it is likely that the security will be regarded as a charge.

The rules governing the publicity of the pledge over negotiable instruments would satisfy the publicity criteria established in Chapter 1[14] relating to simplicity, comprehensibility and expedience, with the status of the negotiable instruments easily determined.

Cost of creation, perfection and publicity of pledges

The cost of creating, perfecting and publicising the pledge over negotiable instruments is inexpensive. There is no tax or stamp duty payable on it, and the pledge is not subject to any registration requirement. The pledge therefore fully satisfies the criterion of low cost in the creation, perfection and publicity of credit security over negotiable instruments.[15]

3.2.2 Creation, perfection and publicity of legal mortgages and equitable mortgages over choses in action in the form of debts and monetary obligations, and cost

In Hong Kong, both legal and equitable mortgages over choses in action are effected by a conveyancing mechanism called 'assignment'. This involves an immediate transfer of an existing proprietary right, vested or contingent, from the debtor (the 'assignor') to the creditor (the 'assignee') as security.[16] A legal mortgage is created when the assignor (i.e. the legal mortgagor) absolutely assigns a legal interest to the assignee (i.e. the legal mortgagee) with a proviso for a reassignment of the interest from the assignee to the assignor.[17] In contrast, an equitable mortgage is created when the chose in action assigned is equitable or there is an equitable

[12] See English Law Commission Report No 296, para. 3.17.
[13] Ibid., para. 3.20. [14] Above, note 9, para. 3, 'Criteria for publicity'.
[15] See Chapter 1 above.
[16] *Norman v Federal Commissioner of Taxation* [1962–3] 109 CLR 9, 26, *per* Windeyer J.
[17] See Mallesons, Stephen and Jacques, *Australian Finance Law*, 5th ed. (Sydney: Law Book Company, 2002), p. 409.

assignment of a legal interest.[18] The processes of creating legal mortgages and equitable mortgages are discussed below.

The mechanism of assignment is also used in situations where the debtor sells outright trade debts at discount to a factor in exchange for cash.[19] This is called a 'factoring arrangement'. This book is not concerned with factoring arrangements per se because they usually constitute an outright sale of the book debts to the factor, though there may be recourse against the factor's client[20] in the event of the default of the client's trade customer.[21] The book focuses on the underlying assignment process that effects the sale of the book debts.[22]

Because the law governing the creation of legal and equitable mortgages over choses in action in Hong Kong is complex, it is necessary to first review the history to facilitate a better understanding of the present position of the rules governing the creation of legal and equitable mortgages of choses in action.

Historical overview of legal assignment and equitable assignment

At common law, subject to very narrow exceptions,[23] legal choses in action could not be assigned,[24] because of the fundamental rule[25] that a party who was not privy could not enforce an obligation against any

[18] Ibid.

[19] See T.K. Ghose, *The Banking System of Hong Kong*, 2nd ed. (Hong Kong: Butterworths Asia, 1995), p. 223. The author notes (p. 226) that factoring is still underdeveloped in Hong Kong; much of the factoring business is domestic.

[20] That is, the assignor of the debt. In a factoring arrangement, the assignor is referred to as the factor's client. See Chan, above, note 2, p. 364.

[21] That is, the account debtor of the client (assignor). See ibid., p. 364.

[22] See Ghose, above, note 19, p. 223; and also Chan, above, note 2, pp. 364–8, where it is observed that factoring in Hong Kong is effected by the mechanism of assignment.

[23] The only types of chose in action that could be assigned at law were debts due to and by the Crown and negotiable instruments (e.g. bills of exchange) by custom of merchants. See W. Ashburner, *Principles of Equity*, 2nd ed. (London: Butterworths, 1933), p. 236.

[24] W.W. Cook, in his article 'The Alienability of Choses in Action', *Harv LR* 26 (1816), 816–37, strenuously argued that choses in action were alienable at common law. But the weight of authorities is against him: see G.J. Tolhurst, 'Equitable Assignment of Legal Rights: A Resolution to a Conundrum', *LQR* 118 (2002), 98 particularly pp. 112–13.

[25] There were other justifications, namely choses in action have no physical delivery, so the common law legal mortgage requirement of physical delivery could not be satisfied; a debt was too personal to assign; assignment constituted maintenance; and choses in action could not be assigned because they were too uncertain. See P.M. Biscoe, *Law and Practice of Credit Factoring* (London: Butterworths, 1975), pp. 96–7.

other party.[26] However, towards the end of the eighteenth century, the common law courts relaxed their practice for economic reasons,[27] allowing an assignee to sue the debtor at law if the debtor refused to pay the assignee, subject to the caveat that the action was in the name of the assignor.[28]

In contrast to common law, equity from the seventeenth century onward adopted a commercially realistic approach. It permitted assignment of equitable and legal choses in action. It regarded choses in action as property which 'ought, in the interest of commercial convenience, to be transferable, such as to provide security for a loan'.[29]

However, to prevent any potential prejudice that might be caused to the interests of the assignor or third party in two special situations – namely where the assignment was only an assignment of a partial interest in the chose in action,[30] and where the legal title continued to be vested in the assignor[31] – equity introduced a procedural rule that required the assignee plaintiff to join the assignor as a co-plaintiff or co-defendant.[32] This ensured that all interested parties were brought before the court for full determination of their rights, and bound the assignor to the decision of the Court of Chancery.[33] The procedural rule was not absolute as it could be dispensed with if it could be shown that the assignor was simply a bare trustee of the chose in action.[34] Recent cases have raised the

[26] See J. Beatson QC, *Anson's Law of Contract*, 27th ed. (Oxford: Oxford University Press, 1998), p. 407.

[27] Fees collected from actions filed in the court met the administrative costs of the Common Law Courts. As no assignments could be enforced in the Common Law Courts, except in the Chancery Court, the Common Law Courts were losing to the latter fees they could have earned. See Cook, above, note 24.

[28] *Winch v Keely* (1787) 1 TR 619, 99 ER 1284; and also *Potter v Turner*, Winch. 8, 124 ER 1657.

[29] Ibid.

[30] See Beatson, above, note 26, p. 448, citing the cases of *Goodson v Ellison* (1827) 3 Russ 583, 38 ER 694; *Cator v Croydon Canal Co.* (1841) 4 Y&C Ex 593, 160 ER 1149; and *Donaldson v Donaldson* (1854) Kay 711; 69 ER 303. See also J. McGhee, *Snell's Equity*, 13th ed. (London: Sweet and Maxwell, 2000), p. 93, para. 5-21.

[31] Here, the assignor, as legal owner, could bring an action in the common law courts against the debtor, notwithstanding the equitable assignment.

[32] See *Three Rivers District Council and Others v Bank of England* [1995] 4 All ER 312, CA, *per* Gibson LJ.

[33] Ibid.

[34] *William Brandt's Sons & Co. v Dunlop Rubber Company* [1905] AC 454; *Three Rivers District Council and Others v Bank of England* [1995] 4 All ER 312, CA; and *Thomas v NAB Ltd and Others* [1999] 2 Qd R 448, followed in *Jennings v Credit Corp Australia Pty Ltd* [2000] 48 NSWLR 709.

question whether or not the procedural rule could co-exist with the substantive rule, which is whether notice is necessary to the debtor before the assignee has a right of action against the debtor.[35]

The effect of assignment at law and in equity on the substantive ownership of the chose in action was thus settled.[36] If the chose in action were legal, the legal ownership in the chose in action remained vested in the assignor. In equity the assignee was the beneficial owner of the chose in action after the assignment. If the chose in action were equitable, the equitable ownership would vest in the assignee in equity. This, then, was the position before the enactment of §25(6) of the Judicature Act 1873, which, inter alia, made choses in action assignable at law provided the statutory requirements were satisfied.[37]

The position was the same in Hong Kong, by virtue of early colonial ordinances dealing with the application of English law to Hong Kong.[38] Before the Ordinance, as Gompertz J in *WH Coole Trading as JT Shaw v B. Pasco*[39] (*Pasco*) stated, 'an ordinary debt or chose in action was not assignable so as to pass the right of action at law'.[40]

As in England, but much later, Hong Kong's local legislature enacted the Law Amendment Ordinance No 2 in 1901,[41] which made legal choses in action assignable at law in the same way as contained in §25(6) of the Judicature Act 1873. Like the Judicature Act, the 1901 Ordinance did not abolish assignment in equity. The Ordinance was subsequently replaced by the Law Amendment Reform (Consolidation) Ordinance ('LARCO'), §9. The section provides:

> Any absolute assignment, by writing under the hand of the assignor (not purporting to be by way of charge only), of any debt or other legal chose in action, of which express notice in writing has been given to the debtor, trustee or other person from whom the assignor would have been entitled to receive or claim such debt or chose in action, shall be and be deemed to have been effectual in law ... to pass and transfer the legal right to such debt or chose in action from the date of such notice, and all legal and

[35] This is discussed below in this chapter.

[36] By virtue of a series of colonial ordinances relating to the application of English Law, namely Ordinance No 6 of 1845, §4, Ordinance No 2 of 1846, §3 (repealed), the Supreme Court Ordinance 1873 (repealed), and the Application of English Law Ordinance (Cap. 88) of 1966 (repealed). The Basic Law of Hong Kong now governs the application of common law and equity.

[37] This is further discussed below in this chapter.

[38] See Chapter 1, note 3.

[39] (1925) 23 HKLR 62, 63.

[40] That is, the Law Amendment Ordinance No 2, 1901.

[41] The Law Amendment Ordinance No 2, 1901, allowed debts and choses in action to be assigned at law. It was modelled on §25(6) of the English Judicature Act 1873.

> other remedies for the same, and the power to give a good discharge for the same, without concurrence of the assignor.[42]

There are no officially reported cases in Hong Kong on assignment in equity before 1901. But this does not mean that assignments in equity had not taken place during this period. For the post-1901 period, there are only two reported cases, namely *Pasco* and *UTG Investment (Far East) Ltd v Petra Bank and Another*,[43] a fairly recent case. *Pasco* was concerned with a statutory assignment under the Law Amendment Ordinance No 2. *Petra Bank* was concerned with an equitable assignment. In both cases the courts were not required to discuss in detail the elements of a statutory assignment under §9 of LARCO and equitable assignment. In *Pasco*, Gompertz J, in a very short judgment, held that a purported assignment of a chose in action was invalid because no notice was served on the debtor. The possibility of its taking effect as an equitable assignment was not considered. In *Petra Bank*, it was accepted without any dispute that an irrevocable assignment of future book debts was an equitable assignment. The central issue was whether the assignee was obliged to reassign the book debt to the assignor when the debt owing to the assignee by the assignor was fully settled. The court held that the assignee had to do so, for the assignor had a right of redemption under equity's maxim: 'once a mortgage always a mortgage'.

Creation, perfection and publicity of equitable mortgages, and cost

Creation of equitable mortgages The prerequisites of a valid equitable assignment are that the assignor and assignee have a clear intention to assign,[44] and there is no express prohibition against assignment.[45] The

[42] The full meaning of the provisions of this section will be discussed below in this chapter.

[43] [1995] 2 HKC 157.

[44] See H.G. Hanbury and C.H.M. Waldock, *The Law of Mortgages*, 1st ed. (London: Sweet and Maxwell, 1938), pp. 403–5.

[45] In *Helstan Securities Ltd v Hertfordshire County Council* [1978] 3 All ER 262, the court held that a purported assignment by the assignor without the required consent was invalid against the original debtor, approved in the House of Lords case of *Linden Gardens Trust v Lenesta Sludge Disposals* [1993] 3 All ER 417, 430, *per* Lord Browne-Wilkinson, who held that such prohibition was not against public policy. His Lordship further noted that commercial reality did not require a free market in choses in action. E.P. Ellinger, E. Lomnicka and R.J.A. Hooley, in *Modern Banking Law*, 3rd ed. (Oxford: Oxford University Press, 2002), p. 791, supported the decision on two grounds, namely (1) the original debtor may wish to avoid the risk of making the error of paying the assignor due to oversight of notice of assignment; (2) the original debtor may wish to retain up to the

assignment can be made in writing, orally or inferred from the conduct of the parties.[46] The intention to assign is satisfied if the terms of the agreement show that the assignor completely 'relinquishes control' over the fund to the assignee.[47] If the assignor retains control over the fund, such as the power to collect the fund on its own account or to revoke the disposition, there is no effective equitable assignment.[48]

The equitable assignment may also secure after-acquired and future choses in action.[49]

Therefore, theoretically, equitable mortgages by way of equitable assignments are simple and flexible. However, examination of cases in other common law jurisdictions identifies three major problems in relation to equitable assignments, namely the relevance of consideration in equitable assignment, the function of notice in equitable assignment, and the content and nature of notice. The first is a creation prerequisite as it affects the validity of the contract of the assignment itself. Many textbooks and cases have devoted substantial discussion to the need for consideration in assignments of future choses in action.[50] However, these

very date of the discharge of the debt his right of set-off and the right of raising counterclaims based on different liabilities. R. Goode expresses a contrary view in his *Legal Problems of Credit and Security*, 3rd ed. (London: Sweet and Maxwell, 2003), p. 107. He thought such prohibition wrong, for 'the debtor can have no legitimate interest in controlling the application of his payment after it has reached the hands of the assignor, and reason rebels against the proposition that the assignor, having received from the assignee the price of sale of the debt, is then entitled to keep the debtor's payment for himself'. Goode's view is better, for to hold otherwise would be tantamount to interfering with the terms of a contract freely and validly contracted by the original parties. However, the prohibition can be circumvented by the debtors declaring that he holds the chose in action on trust for the creditor: see *Re Turcan Trust* (1888) 40 Ch D 5, and *Don King Productions Inc. v Warren* [1998] affirmed [1999] 2 All ER 218.

46 S. Williston, *Williston on Contract*, 3rd ed. (New York: Barker Voorhis, 1957–78), vol. 3, pp. 168–70, §430.

47 See *Re Gibraltar Resources Inc. and Others* (United States Bankruptcy Court for the Northern District of Texas, Dallas Division) (1997) 211BR 216; 1997 Bankr Lexis 1193. Similar requirements can be found in the English House of Lords case of *William Brandt's Sons & Co. v Dunlop Rubber Company Limited* [1905] AC 454, 462, where Lord Macnaghten stated that 'All that is necessary [for an equitable assignment] is that the debtor should be given to understand that the debt has been made over by the creditor to some third person.'

48 In *Re Stiger*, District Court, D. New Jersey, 202 F. 791; 1913 US Dist. Lexis 1819, p. 3, *per* Rellstab, DJ.

49 See *UTG Investment (Far East) Ltd v Petra Bank and Another* [1995] 1 HKC 157; E.F. Cousins and I. Clarke, *The Law of Mortgages*, 2nd ed. (Sweet and Maxwell, 2001), pp. 173–9; and E.I. Sykes and S. Walker, *The Law of Securities*, 5th ed. (Sydney: The Law Book Company, 1993), pp. 765, 769–71.

50 For example, see Cousins and Clarke, above, note 49; and Sykes and Walker, above, note 49.

discussions were concerned with gifts of future choses in action, which are not relevant in the context of commercial credit and security, where the requirement of consideration is not, as commented by Williston,[51] a problem. He said that consideration – that is, the credit – is expressed or implied. Accordingly, this issue has not been pursued further. In relation to notice, on close analysis, the problems are perfection and publicity issues; they are discussed below.

In conclusion, it is submitted that the creation aspect of equitable assignment by way of equitable mortgage has satisfied all the creation criteria established in Chapter 1,[52] except two – namely, the debtor should have possession of the asset and the freedom to deal with it.

Perfection of equitable mortgages The process of perfecting equitable assignment of choses in action is governed by general law and, in some cases, by general law and statute. This part will first consider the position under general law.

General law As between the assignee and the assignor, notice on the debtor serves no further purpose for the assignment is complete and binding on the assignor. Notice to the debtor is not necessary to perfect the assignee's title as against the assignor.[53]

In equity, the perfecting effect of notice arises in two types of relationship, namely between the assignee and debtor, and subsequent assignees of the same chose in action. Both relationships require full examination, particularly the former.

Assignee and debtor In respect of the assignee and the debtor, the perfecting functions of notice can be separated into two main steps, namely the *substantive perfection function* and the *practical perfection function.*

[51] *Williston on Contract*, above, note 47. [52] See Chapter 1 above.

[53] In *Dearle v Hall* (1828) 3 Russ 21, 38 ER 475, p. 483, Thomas Plumer MR stated that 'notice does not form part of the necessary conveyance of an equitable interest ... if you mean to rely on contract with the individual, you do not need to give notice; from the moment of the contract, he, with whom you are dealing is personally bound'; *Gorringe v Irwell India Rubber and Gutta Percha Works* (1885) 34 Ch D 128, 135, *per* Bowen LJ, 'there is no necessity for such notice as between the assignor and the assignee'; and *William Brandt's Sons & Co. v Dunlop Rubber Company Limited* [1905] AC 454, 462, *per* Lord Macnaghten, on the point of whether the documents in question constituted a 'good equitable assignment' or a notice, his Lordship decided on the former, stating, 'As between [the parties] the assignment was ... perfect without them [the notice]'.

The issue with the substantive perfection function is whether notice to the debtor is necessary in order to confer on the assignee a right of action against the debtor, in the event the debtor refuses to pay or honour the chose in action.

There is no clear answer to this question in Hong Kong. The very short, half-page judgment in *Pasco*, discussed earlier, is not helpful. Decisions in other common law jurisdictions are not wholly in agreement.[54] This is because there are two distinct lines of authority on this matter. The first is that notice to the debtor is not necessary to confer on the assignee a right of action against the debtor because notice only affects priority (the 'liberal' approach). This is the situation whether or not the chose in action is legal or equitable. The second is that notice to the debtor is necessary to pass the title to the debt to the assignee as against the debtor if the chose in action is legal (the 'orthodox' approach). Two recent Commonwealth cases, namely *Mountain Road (No 9) Ltd v Michael Edgley Corp Pty Ltd*[55] and *Thomas v NAB Ltd*[56] have further complicated the distinction between these two positions. As the case law in this area is complex, the following discussion begins by examining the state of law before *Mountain Road (No 9)* and *Thomas v NAB Ltd.*

The cause of divergence between the authorities in the common law jurisdictions can be traced to the dictum of Sir Thomas Plumer MR in the early nineteenth-century English case of *Dearle v Hall*,[57] a landmark case on equitable assignment. At that time it was common among heirs in straitened financial circumstances habitually to assign their beneficial interests repeatedly by way of security without the consent or knowledge of successive assignor creditors.

To alleviate this mischief, Plumer MR introduced a doctrine of notice and gave it a proprietary function. As he explained,

[54] The cases are: *William Brandt's Sons & Co. v Dunlop Rubber Company Limited* [1905] AC 454; *Re City Life Assurance Company Limited* [1926] Ch 191; *Comptroller of Stamps (Vict) v Howard-Smith* (1936) 54 CLR, 622 *per* Dixon J; *Walter & Sullivan Ltd v J. Murphy & Sons Ltd* [1955] 1 All ER 843, 845, CA, *per* Parker LJ; *Weddell and Another v J.A. Pearce & Major (a firm) and Another* [1987] 3 All ER 624; and *Thomas v NAB Ltd and Others* [2000] 2 Qd R 448, where the courts decided that notice on the debtor was not necessary to perfect the assignee's title. On the other hand, *Warner Bros Records Inc. v Rollgreen Ltd and Others* [1975] 2 All ER 105; and *Mountain Road (No 9) Ltd v Michael Edgley Corporation Pty Ltd* [1999] 1 NZLR 335 decided the opposite.

[55] [1999] 1 NZLR 335.

[56] [1999] QCA 525. Note, in *Showa Shoji Australia Pty Ltd v Oceanic Life Ltd* (1994) 34 NSWLR 548, the court adopted the orthodox approach.

[57] *Dearle v Hall*, above, note 54.

> to make your right attach upon the thing which is the subject of the contract, it is necessary to give notice … and unless notice is given, you do not do that which is essential in all cases of transfer of personal property.[58]

On the basis of his formulation it was held that all the assignments of the choses in action in that case were invalid against a Commissioner in Bankruptcy (as the trustee in bankruptcy was then known) because no notice of the assignment was duly served on the original debtor. Providing notice was therefore regarded as performing a proprietary function of vesting possession and ownership of the chose in action in the assignee, thereby taking the chose in action out of the reputed ownership of the assignor. It was clear that Plumer MR drew authority from the earlier case of *Ryall v Rowles*,[59] a bankruptcy case, to substantiate his proprietary function principle. Subsequently, he was criticised on the ground that he had wrongly extended the statutory doctrine of reputed ownership in bankruptcy to a non-bankruptcy case.[60]

For present purposes, it is necessary to concentrate on the meaning of the dictum of Plumer MR and the two approaches mentioned above.

The first important judgment that marked the beginning of the liberal approach was the speech of Lord Macnaghten in the House of Lords case of *Ward v Duncombe*.[61] He thought that notice was irrelevant to the perfection of the assignee's title.[62] An assignee of an equitable interest from a person capable of disposing of it has a perfect equitable title, whether or not the debtor knows of the assignment.[63]

In the subsequent case of *William Brandt's Sons & Co. v Dunlop Rubber Company Limited*,[64] Lord Macnaghten not only reiterated this view, but also explained that notice was not essential if the assignment were an equitable assignment of a legal chose in action. He stated, 'At law it was considered necessary that the debtor should enter into some engagement with the assignee. That was never the rule in equity.' He further stated that

58 Ibid., at p. 483. 59 (1749) 1 Ves Sen 349, 27 ER 1074.

60 The flaw and its impact on the efficiency of the credit security law of Hong Kong will be discussed further below in Chapter 6.

61 (1893) AC 369.

62 Ibid., at p. 393. A similar view was expressed in the earlier case of *Donaldson v Donaldson* (1854) Kay 711, 69 ER 303.

63 *Ward v Duncombe* (1893) AC 369, 394, *per* Lord Macnaghten. 64 [1905] AC 454.

in the event there was a conflict between the rules of common law and rules of equity, the latter should prevail.[65]

The Australian High Court case of *Anning v Anning*[66] appears to support Lord Macnaghten's proposition. There, default in serving the statutory notice of voluntary assignment of bank deposits and book debts on the bank rendered the assignment incomplete and equitable. The assignment could not therefore ordinarily transfer the title of the choses in action to the assignee. Questions therefore arose regarding what had to be done and by whom in order to render the imperfect voluntary equitable assignment valid and effective.[67] A majority of the court, Griffith CJ and Isaacs J, by separate tortuous routes, which need not be discussed further for the present purposes, concluded that the assignees did obtain the benefit of the gift. On the issue of notice Isaacs J stated,[68]

> The trustee of a fund which has been equitably assigned holds it for the person equitably entitled whoever it may be, as he did before, and notice is only necessary to inform him of the change of identity of the person entitled and to warn him against parting with the fund to the person who has in fact parted with it, but whom the trustee already reasonably and justifiably believes to be the equitable owner.[69]

The other judges, Griffith CJ and Higgins J, were not as emphatic as Isaacs J, but the terms of their speeches were consistent with Isaacs J's basic view that two separate modes of assignment existed.

Despite the decisions in *Brandts* and *Anning*, the English Court of Appeal in *Warner Bros Records v Rollgreen Ltd and Others*[70] held that the grantor of a legal option was not bound by the assignee's exercise of the option since the assignee had not previously served notice of the

[65] *Re City Life Assurance Co. Ltd* [1926] 1 Ch 191, where the court held that the trustee of an insurance company could enforce the assignment against the policy holder though no notice was served on the policy holder.

[66] [1907] 4 CLR 1049.

[67] According to *Milroy v Lord* (1862) 4 De G F & J 264, 45 ER 1185, in order for the court of equity to compel a donor to complete an imperfect gift 'the donor must have done everything which, according to the nature of the property comprised in the settlement, was necessary in order to transfer the property and render the settlement binding upon him'. For discussion of the meaning of 'necessary', see Sykes and Walker, above, note 49, pp. 765–7; and also R.P. Meagher, W.M.C. Gummow and J.F.R. Lehane, *Equity: Doctrines and Remedies*, 3rd ed. (Sydney: Butterworths, 1992), paras. 617–35.

[68] *Anning v Anning* [1907] 4 CLR 1049, at pp. 1068–9.

[69] Isaacs J derived this paragraph from Lord Macnaghten's dictum in *Ward v Duncombe* (1893) AC 369, p. 392.

[70] [1975] 2 All ER 105.

assignment of the grantor. The decision in *Warner* is generally taken to represent the orthodox approach.[71] However, the reasoning in *Warner* has been criticised by academics[72] and by the courts.[73] For instance, in the fairly recent English Court of Appeal case of *Three Rivers District Council and others v Bank of England*,[74] the court thought that *Warner* was wrong. It regarded *Brandts* as authority for the proposition that notice was not necessary to render the debtor liable to the assignee. The Court of Appeal's observation was, however, *obiter* as it was concerned with whether or not the assignor had a right to sue after the chose in action had been already effectively assigned to the assignee.

Turning now to the authorities of *Thomas v NAB Ltd*, in *Mountain Road* the New Zealand Court of Appeal adopted the orthodox approach. There the court had to consider two main issues: firstly, whether a deed executed by a purported assignor and assignee created a valid assignment of the former's rights, interest, ownership and benefits in tents supplied by the supplier; secondly, if there was indeed a valid assignment, whether or not the assignee (who had not served notice of the assignment on the supplier) had a cause of action for damages against the supplier as a result of faults in the fabric and the manufacturing process. On the first issue, the court held that there was no effective assignment, as the purported assignee had not signed the deed, which, according to an express term of the deed, was a condition precedent to the effectiveness of the assignment. That could have easily disposed of the case, but the court went on to consider the second issue. Consequently, the observation on the second issue was *obiter*. Tipping J, delivering the single judgment of the court, held that the purported assignee had no cause of action against the supplier, as it had not served notice on the supplier. His Honour's decision is radical. He observed that as the chose in action was a legal chose in action, equity had to follow the law[75] – that is, §130 of the New Zealand Law of Property Act (equivalent to §9 of Hong Kong

[71] *Compania Colombiana de Seguros v Pacific Steam Navigation Co.* [1964] 1 All ER 216. There Roskill, *obiter*, observed that an insurance company, the assignee, had no cause of action against the tortfeasor as no notice of the assignment was given to it.

[72] See D.M. Kloss, 'Notice of the Equitable Assignment of a Chose in Action', *Conv* 39 (1975), 261 particularly pp. 263–7, where the commentator debunked the reasoning in the case. See also A.G. Guest (gen. ed.), *Chitty on Contracts*, 27th ed. (London: Sweet and Maxwell, 1994), para. 19-002, and G.H. Treitel, *The Law of Contract*, 10th ed. (London: Sweet and Maxwell, 1999), p. 628, note 90.

[73] See *Three Rivers District Council and Others v Bank of England* [1995] 4 All ER 312, 332, CA, *per* Gibson LJ.

[74] [1995] 4 All ER 312, CA.

[75] [1999] 1 NZLR 335, 340.

LARCO) – which required notice to be served on the debtor in order to constitute an effective legal assignment.

Undeniably, Tipping J avoided the difficulties of *Warner*, which he discussed at some length. But he retrogressively anchored the law of assignments in a realm of artificiality and illogicality. Equitable assignments of equitable choses in action are subject to less stringent rules of notice, but equitable assignments of legal choses in action are not. Equitable assignments of legal choses in action for valuable consideration can be struck down for a technical fault in the notice, but a voluntary equitable assignment of a legal chose in action is enforceable without notice if the necessity test is satisfied by the assignee.[76]

In contrast, the Queensland Court of Appeal in *Thomas v NAB* rejected the approach of *Mountain Road* and adopted the liberal approach. There, an assignee brought an action to enforce rights of action assigned to him by deed, by a trustee in bankruptcy. At the time the action was brought the assignee had not given the debtor notice of the assignment. The court in the first instance held that the assignee, not having been given notice of the assignment prior to the commencement of the action, had no right to bring and maintain the action. The court followed *Mountain Road*. On appeal, the Court of Appeal unanimously disagreed and declined to follow *Mountain Road*, saying that it was not necessary for the equitable assignee to serve notice on the original debtor in order to bind him to the assignment. Consequently, the assignee, as owner of the debt, could sue the debtor without joining the assignor as a plaintiff or defendant. All three judges, McMurdo P and Pincus and Thomas JJA, agreed but gave different reasons. McMurdo P relied on Lord Denning MR's criterion of 'surprise' between the assignee and the debtor. Her Honour reasoned that the grantor in *Warner* was not bound by the exercise of the option because the grantor had no previous dealings with the grantee and the letter exercising the option was therefore a surprise to the grantor. In contrast, in this case there was no element of surprise, for the assignee previously had direct dealing with the debtor before he was made bankrupt.

Her Honour's reasoning is not compelling for both practical and substantive reasons. Firstly, it may create practical difficulties for many commercial transactions, such as factoring transactions; the debtors are unlikely to have any commercial or domestic dealings with the factor. Every assignment of the debt by the creditor to the factor would be a 'surprise' to the debtor and therefore unenforceable. Secondly, where

[76] See note 67, above.

agreements, such as in *Warner*, confer on the opposing party the right to assign, arguably it cannot be said that the debtor is 'surprised'. The debtor may not know or even be satisfied with the character of the assignee, but it certainly cannot claim that it is not aware of the full effect of the agreement.[77] Besides, if the debtor wishes to protect itself against 'surprises', it could include a clause to prohibit assignment of the chose in action without its consent.[78] Lastly, the 'surprise' element seems to introduce an unsatisfactory inconsistency in the law of assignment. When the chose in action is assigned, the debtor is converted into a 'registrar' and subject to a number of obligations and liabilities.[79] It has to keep records of various assignments which it has received notice of and the amount involved. It is liable if it makes any error in its records and pays the wrong amount, or wrong party, or negligently misrepresents to a subsequent assignee as to the status of an earlier assignment.[80] The debtor has never been allowed to disclaim its obligations or liabilities on the ground that it was 'surprised' to find that it was converted into a 'registrar' without its consent.[81] This is considered a reasonable commercial hazard.

Pincus JA took a cautious approach. His Honour considered a number of cases, both English and Australian, and concluded that on balance the authorities favoured the equitable assignee; that is, his title to the chose in action is complete, not only against the assignor, but also against the debtor, without notice to the latter.[82]

Thomas JA's reasoning, which was very much along the lines of that of Pincus JA, held that after the assignment the assignor was only a bare trustee of the benefit.

It now appears that there is convergence between the Australian and the English courts to the effect that notice is not essential to vest an equitable right in the assignee as against the debtor, but the reasons are not

[77] By analogy with the doctrine of *non est factum*; the doctrine cannot be relied on to avoid obligation under a written document if the complainant does not make a mistake as to the nature of the document but only as to identity. See Treitel, above, note 72, pp. 301–4.

[78] At the time *Warner* was decided it was uncertain whether a debtor could prohibit assignment of the chose in action without its consent. It is now settled that such prohibition is valid and not against public policy. See *Linden Gardens Trust v Lenesta Sludge Disposals* [1993] 3 All ER 417.

[79] See *Ward v Duncombe* (1893) AC 369, where the point of the debtor as registrar was raised, but did not impress Lord Macnaghten.

[80] For example, see *William Brandt's Sons & Co. v Dunlop Rubber Company Limited* [1905] AC 454, where poor record-keeping was one reason that contributed to the liability of the debtor.

[81] For this proposition see *Ward v Duncombe* (1893) AC 369, 393.

[82] See *Thomas v NAB Ltd and Others* [1999] QCA 525, *per* Pincus JA at para. 25.

completely congruent. This rule makes no distinction between legal and equitable choses in action and between different types of chose in action, such as a debt or an option. Section 25(6) of the Judicature Act, as re-enacted in the various common law jurisdictions, has not abolished the special rules governing equitable assignments. The decision of the Queensland Court of Appeal is to be preferred as it reinforces the broader argument that the Judicature Acts 1873–5 did not fuse the substantive rules of common law and equity but preserved the supplementary role of equity.[83] On the other hand the decision of the New Zealand Court of Appeal in *Mountain Road* is not only far from having a fusing or harmonising effect, it actually destroys the very jurisprudential theory; that is, that rules of equity and common law co-exist and, in the event of conflict, the former should prevail. On this basis and on the preponderance of the authorities considered above, the decision of the New Zealand Court of Appeal should not be followed.

Therefore it appears that the Hong Kong case of *Pasco*, which seems to take a similar approach to the New Zealand case of *Mountain Road*, may not be correct. However, Tolhurst recently in the *Law Quarterly Review* took the view that there is difficulty in *Thomas v NAB Ltd*,[84] as it proceeds on the basis of the fusion concept, which Tolhurst opined is not the case.[85] It is submitted that Tolhurst's view is conservative and that it rigidly divides the two branches of the law without considering that since 1873 the dividing line between the two has been disappearing for most practical purposes.[86]

The natural effect of *Thomas v NAB Ltd* is that equity's procedural rule on the joinder of parties and the substantive requirement of notice co-exist. However, they could not if the orthodox approach was adopted and applied strictly, as in the case of *Mountain Road*.[87] Tolhurst appears

[83] For detailed discussion of Australian views on the fallacy of the fusion theory, see G. Pont and D.R.C. Chalmers, *Equity and Trusts in Australia and New Zealand*, 2nd ed. (Pyrmont, NSW: LBC Information Services, 2000), pp. 10–11, and Meagher, Gummow and Lehane, above, note 67, pp. 46–7, where they criticised the fusion theory, calling it a 'fusion fallacy' which lacks statutory basis.

[84] Tolhurst, above, note 24. [85] Ibid.

[86] His view also seems to go against the judicial trend in Australia. For example, in *Associated Alloys Pty Limited v ACN 452 106 Pty Limited (in liquidation) and Another* [2000] 202 CLR 588, the High Court favoured the co-existing role of common law and equity when it held that a retention-of-title clause created a trust.

[87] See *Jennings v Credit Corp Australia Pty Ltd* (2000) 48 NSWLR 709, *per* Santow J; and also the earlier case of *Long Leys Co. Pty Ltd v Silkdale Pty Ltd* (1991) BPR 11, 512, *per* Shellar JA.

to prefer the orthodox approach in this regard but thought that it had difficulties, in that if the chose in action was equitable the substantive requirement of notice was not an issue.[88]

In respect of the practical perfection function, it is clear that, in order to bind the debtor to the assignment effectively, the creditor–assignee should serve notice on the debtor expeditiously. If the assignee fails to serve notice of the assignment or delays in giving notice, and the debtor disposes of the chose in action to a third party, the assignee loses his security.[89] The debtor is not liable to pay the assignee.[90] But if, after notice, the debtor disposes of the chose in action the debtor is liable to the assignee.[91] In addition, expeditious notice to the debtor is also important in that it prevents the debtor from setting up against the assignee any new equities that may arise between the assignor and the debtor after service of the notice.[92]

Despite the obvious importance of notice for both types of perfection, the courts, except for some vague remarks, have not attempted to define any special formula for an effective notice. For instance, in the House of Lords case of *Brandt's*, Lord Macnaghten observed that the words in the notice

> may be couched in the language of command. It may be a courteous request. It may assume the form of mere permission. All that is necessary is that the debtor should be given to understand that the debt has been made over by the creditor to some third person.[93]

On the other hand, the court seems to have laid down an objective test for determining whether a notice is sufficient. In the early case of *Lloyd v Banks*,[94] Lord Cairns LC said that notice is sufficient if the notice could bring home to a reasonable person, or an ordinary person of business, that the chose in action is encumbered, so that the person would act upon

[88] Tolhurst, above, note 24, at pp. 108–9.

[89] *William Brandt's Sons & Co. v Dunlop Rubber Company Limited* [1905] AC 454; and *Walter & Sullivan Ltd v J. Murphy & Sons Ltd* [1955] 1 All ER 843.

[90] See *Stocks v Dobson* (1853) 4 De G M & G 15; 43 ER 411, where the court held that the original debtor was not liable to the assignee (mortgagee) because the debtor without notice of the assignment had entered into a bona fide arrangement with the assignor whereby the debtor was fully released from the debt.

[91] *William Brandt's Sons & Co. v Dunlop Rubber Company Limited* [1905] AC 454. Here the original debtor, Dunlop, was held liable to pay the bank, Brandt's Sons & Co., when Dunlop ignored the notice and paid the debt to a third party, Kleinwort.

[92] *Roxburghe v Cox* (1881) 17 Ch D 520.

[93] [1905] AC 454, 462.

[94] (1868) LR 3 Ch App 488, 491.

the information and would regulate their conduct in such a way as not to prejudice the security. The objective test was endorsed in the House of Lords case *Mannai Investment Co. Ltd v Eagle Star Life Assurance Co. Ltd*.[95] Two principles can be discerned from the court's decision. Firstly, the test considers how a reasonable recipient would have understood the notice. Secondly, when considering this question, the notice must be construed in the relevant objective contextual scene. There the court held that a notice by a tenant on the landlord, which contained a minor discrepancy in relation to the date on which the lease was to be determined and did not comply strictly with the lease agreement, was effective to terminate the lease. This is because the lessee as a reasonable recipient, like the landlord, would clearly understand it was a bona fide mistake.

This objective test creates problems for both the assignee and the debtor. From the perspective of the assignee it may mistakenly be believed that the notice served by it is effective, but this may not be the case when an objective test is applied. Consequently, the debtor is not liable if it pays funds to the assignor or a third party. From the perspective of the debtor, if it pays a third party because it did not understand the contents of the document, but the court considers the notice reasonably sufficient, it is liable to pay the assignee again. This problem is illustrated in the earlier case of *Denney, Gasquet and Metcalfe v Conklin*.[96] There, solicitors for the trustees of a deed of arrangement executed by an assignor wrote to the debtor of the assignor, informing the debtor that they were instructed by the trustees of the deed, and seeking to know the amount owing by the debtor to the assignor. The letter did not mention any assignment and a deed of arrangement did not necessarily involve an assignment. Atkin J held that it was good notice of assignment. It was, however, doubted in the subsequent case of *Van Lynn Developments Ltd v Pelias Construction Co. Ltd*,[97] where Davies LJ thought the letter was not very clear.

The problem of notice is therefore risk to assignees and debtors who are not familiar with commercial law and practice.

[95] [1997] 3 All ER 352, 369, HL, *per* Lord Stein.

[96] [1913] 3 KB 177.

[97] [1969] 1 QB 607, 614. Followed in the case of *Grey v Australian Motorists & General Insurance Co. Pty Ltd* [1976] 1 NSWLR 669, where the court held that the omission of the date or signature did not render the notice inadequate. Some earlier cases had imposed strict conditions: see *Stanley v English Fibres Industries* (1889) 68 LJQB 839, and *W.F. Harrison & Co. Ltd v Burke* [1956] 1 WLR 419, where Lord Denning, MR, stated that notice must be strictly complied with because 'the notice in writing was a crucial part of the transfer of the title to the debt under the Act [Ordinance]'. There, a notice which misstated the date of the assignment was held to be ineffective.

There are other special rules which both assignees and debtors must fully understand in order to avoid the risk of losing the security or becoming liable a second time. Firstly, the assignee creditor should avoid serving notice in the course of a casual conversation with the debtor, for the court is less inclined to accept notice made in such casual conversation.[98] Secondly, the assignee should avoid serving oral notice, as in the event of dispute it can be difficult to establish that notice has been served. Thirdly, if there is more than one fund held by the debtor, the notice must sufficiently describe the amount secured and the type of fund involved. If the assignee intends to secure two or more funds in the hands of the debtor but the notice only describes one fund, the notice is ineffective against the other undescribed funds.[99] Fourthly, if a chose in action or other intangible personal property is held by several debtors, such as trustees of a trust fund or partners in a partnership,[100] notice on one is sufficient, for notice on one is deemed notice on all.[101] If a debtor, who has notice, ceases to be a debtor, the notice will continue to be binding on the others, even if they do not have notice of the security.[102] This rule subjects the other debtors to the risk of paying the funds to the wrong person.

Assignee and subsequent assignees The perfecting function of notice in this relationship is clear and settled; it determines priority between competing assignees over the same chose in action.[103] The assignee who first serves notice on the debtor has priority over other assignees and general creditors. Once again, problems of the form and content of notice as discussed above have impact on the priority.[104]

Statute If an equitable assignment is a general assignment[105] of book debts, either present or future, granted by an individual trader, §48 of the Bankruptcy Ordinance (Cap. 6) requires the general assignment to be registered with the High Court Registry. If the trader is subsequently

98 *Lloyd v Banks* [1868] LR 3 Ch App 488, 490.
99 *Re Bright's Trust* (1856) 21 Beav 430, 2 ER 784.
100 One partner is an agent of the other partner.
101 *Re Dallas* [1904] 2 Ch 385; *Smith v Smith* (1833) 2 Cl & M 231, 149 ER 745; *Browne v Savage* (1859) 4 Drewery 635, 62 ER 244; and *Ward v Duncombe* (1893) AC 369.
102 *Ward v Duncombe* (1893) AC 369.
103 *Dearle v Hall* (1828) 3 Russ 21, 38 ER 475; applied in *ABN Amro Bank NV v Chiyu Banking Corp Ltd and Others* [2000] 3 HKC 381, [2001] 2 HKLRD 175.
104 The full impact will be discussed further below in Chapter 6.
105 The term 'assignment' includes charges.

adjudicated bankrupt and the assignment is not registered, the assignment is void against the trustee in bankruptcy to the amount of such book debt that is not paid before the date of commencement of the bankruptcy.[106] As §48 is silent on the form of assignments, it appears that §48 covers both oral and written assignments.

The recent English case of *Hill v Alex Lawrie Factors*[107] showed how the creditor could easily overlook such a provision. There the partners of a firm ('assignors') had assigned generally their book debts to a factor. The factor had not given notice of the assignment to the original debtors, nor had the factor registered it with the English Supreme Court of Judicature. However, the assignors subsequently created specific assignments of the book debts. The assignors were later adjudicated bankrupt. The court held that the general assignment was void, but the specific assignments were valid, as they were not required to be registered.

However, in Hong Kong the High Court Registry has not, in the last ten years, registered any instruments under §48 of the Ordinance.[108] This could mean that either assignments and charges of general book debts are not popular in Hong Kong, or that the creditors are not aware of the registration requirement.

Section 48 is not intended to promote an efficient system of creating assignments and charges over general book debts, but simply to solve the difficulty of ascertaining whether a general assignment or charge has been given under value by an individual debtor who subsequently becomes bankrupt.[109] Thus it was commented that registration of a general assignment does not secure priority.[110]

In contrast, if a company granted the equitable assignment, general or specific, by way of security, the assignment must be registered with the Companies Registry. Failure to do so would render the assignment void against the company's creditors and liquidator.[111]

In view of the uncertainty surrounding the substantive and practical perfection functions of notice and the anomalous statutory perfection process between non-corporate and corporate assignors, it is submitted that the rules governing the perfection of equitable mortgages have not satisfied the criteria of simplicity and comprehensibility established in Chapter 1.[112]

[106] Section 48, Bankruptcy Ordinance (Cap. 6). [107] [2000] BPIR 1038.

[108] The author enquired with the High Court Registry Official on 28 May 2002.

[109] English Law Commission Consultation Paper No 164, para. 8.36.

[110] Ibid., para. 8.38. [111] This is discussed further below in Chapter 4.

[112] See Chapter 1 above.

Whether or not the rules have fully satisfied the criterion relating to just and fair ordering of priority is further discussed in Chapter 6.

Publicity of equitable mortgages Publicity of equitable mortgages of choses in action is governed by general law, and in some cases by general law and statute.

General law Under general law, publicity is not mandatory. It is indirectly promoted through the diligence of the assignee. This is not a disadvantage to the third party, who has duly served notice on the debtor, for it takes free from an earlier defaulting assignee.

Nonetheless, from the perspective of the third party, the publicity aspect of equitable assignment by way of mortgages suffers from the following difficulties:

- weak dissemination of information and
- poor bookkeeping

Weak dissemination of information function One immediate consequence of the rule in *Dearle v Hall* is that it converts the debtor into the role of 'public registrar'. Thus, theoretically, a subsequent creditor, by making inquiry of the debtor, should be able to clarify whether the property is encumbered.

However, in practice, the creditor may not necessarily be able to obtain the required information. This is because the debtor is not under any duty, legal or equitable, to reply to inquiries as to the status of the fund.[113] This is so whether the inquiry comes from the beneficial owner of the fund or a potential creditor. The rationale for this rule is well established in early English cases; it is that the debtor is not under any duty to assist the beneficial owner in selling or mortgaging its beneficial interest and in squandering or anticipating its fortune.[114] Thus a potential creditor who proposes to lend money on the security of the chose in action has no greater rights than the beneficial owner itself.[115]

At first sight, this rationale appears justifiable: the debtor is not a party to the transaction between the creditor and the beneficial owner of the intangible asset.

113 *Ward v Duncombe* (1893) AC 369, 392–393, *per* Lord Macnaghten.
114 *Low v Bouverie* [1891] 3 Ch 82, 99–100, *per* Lindley LJ; and see also *Ward v Duncombe* (1893) AC 369, 393-394, *per* Lord Macnaghten.
115 *Ward v Duncombe* (1893) AC 369, 393–394, *per* Lord Macnaghten.

However, this rationale is outdated when it is considered in a wider commercial context. This formulation may discourage lending and increase lending risk. For example, if the debtor decides not to reply, the creditor is faced with two difficult choices. If it chooses to lend, it takes the property at its own peril that there may be a prior competing claim or that the property may not be sufficient to meet the debt. If it chooses not to lend, it loses a commercial opportunity and the debtor may be unjustifiably deprived of finance.

Further, the rationale loses its credibility should the debtor reply. This is because the debtor is under a duty only to ensure that its reply is honest to the best of its knowledge. There is no guarantee of the accuracy of the content. Consequently, if, in good faith, the debtor's reply fails to disclose all the mortgages created by the assignor and as a result there are insufficient funds to meet all the claims, the debtor is not liable to the creditor for any losses the creditor may have suffered.[116] The potential creditor's position is not, therefore, significantly better even if the debtor does reply.

However, the tort of negligent misrepresentation has developed in the economic field since the rule was established at the end of the nineteenth century.[117] On the basis of this tortious concept, it is arguable that the debtor is liable if it is plain that the potential creditor seeking information trusted the debtor to exercise care and the debtor gave the information when it knew or ought to have known that the potential creditor was relying on it.[118] This argument per se gives some credibility to the reply of the debtor. But this potential can be demolished by the debtor's incorporating in its reply an effective exemption[119] clause that it accepts no responsibility for the reply.[120] Moreover, such reply may discourage a potential creditor from lending even if the fund appears sufficient to cover the loan.

Another point that should be noted is that there is no time limit during which the debtor is required to respond to an inquiry. As a result there can be delay in the reply, even if the debtor chooses to respond. The delay may cause the creditor to lose a potential borrower.

A problem which is often overlooked is that the creditor takes the assignment subject to all of the debtor's equities and other defences

[116] *Low v Bouverie* [1891] 3 Ch 82, CA.

[117] *Hedley Byrne & Co. Ltd v Heller and Partners Ltd* [1964] AC 465.

[118] Ibid., p. 486, *per* Lord Reid.

[119] Assuming that it satisfies the 'reasonableness test' in the Control of Exemption Clauses Ordinance (Cap. 71).

[120] In *Hedley Byrne & Co. Ltd* (see note 118 above) the bank was guilty of negligent misstatement but was not liable because of an exemption clause in the letter.

which may be available against the assignor at the time of creation of the security.[121] The problem posed by such equities is real. For instance, if a creditor inquires about encumbrances only, the debtor, if it chooses to reply, is not required to inform the creditor about any equities that may have arisen. Further, even if the debtor wishes to oblige the creditor, the debtor may not be able to do so unless the debtor has actual knowledge that the equities have arisen.

Poor bookkeeping If the debtor is not familiar with keeping records there is a high risk that the system of record-keeping is haphazard and inaccurate. This has two consequences. Firstly, a subsequent creditor making inquiry may be given inaccurate information on the nature of the asset, the status of the asset affected and/or the financial exposure of the asset. Secondly, the secured creditor may lose the security if the debtor mistakenly pays the wrong amount or pays out to the wrong person. This disastrous consequence is illustrated in the English House of Lords case of *William Brandt's Sons & Co. v Dunlop Rubber Company Limited*.[122] There, the debtor was a large business establishment, and notice of an equitable assignment received by its branch office was not communicated to its head office. The head office mistakenly paid the assigned sum of money to wrong person.

Of course, the debtor, as in *William Brandt's Sons & Co. v Dunlop Rubber Company Limited*, was liable to pay again to the correct assignee but it would be unhelpful if the debtor were insolvent. Besides, it is unfair that, owing to the error of the debtor, the status of the creditor is reduced to that of an unsecured creditor.

Statute It was explained earlier that if the assignment is a general assignment of book debts, the assignment has to be registered with the High Court Registry under §48 of the Bankruptcy Ordinance (Cap. 6). However, as discussed earlier, this registration system is not intended to promote publicity. If a company granted the assignment, general or specific, by way of security it has to be registered with the Companies Registry. As mentioned earlier, failure to do so would render the assignment void against the creditors and the liquidator.[123] In contrast to §48 of the Bankruptcy Ordinance, it will be seen in Chapter 6 that the Company Registry registration system promotes publicity.

[121] *Roxburghe v Cox* (1881) 17 Ch D 520, 526, *per* James LJ.
[122] [1905] AC 454. [123] See Chapter 6.

To solve the publicity problem, the English Law Commission recommended that all dispositions of receivables, whether by way of sale[124] or security, should be registered under its proposed notice-filing system,[125] subject to some exemptions from the registration scheme in the sale and assignment of receivables.[126] The Commission also recommended that the sale of a receivable by a company should not be effective against an administrator or liquidator unless it has been registered by the onset of insolvency.[127] For those existing arrangements for the sale of receivables, the registration is subject to a transitional period of two years, non-registration being ineffective in the event of the company's insolvency.[128] The priority of sales of receivables by companies should depend on the date of registration in the Company Security Register.[129]

On the basis of the above discussion, it is submitted that the rules relating to publicity are not simple, and do not ensure accurate information and/or accessibility of information. They have not, therefore, satisfied the perfection criteria established in Chapter 1[130] on this aspect.

Cost of creation, perfection and publicity of equitable mortgages The creation, perfection and publicity process of equitable assignment of choses in action is not subject to any tax, stamp duty or state administrative cost. It has therefore satisfied the criterion of low cost.

Creation, perfection and publicity of legal mortgages under §9 of LARCO, and cost

Creation of legal mortgages Section 9 applies to assignments by way of legal mortgage by corporate and non-corporate assignors.

It has both a substantive and a procedural impact on assignments of legal choses in action that have complied with its requirements.[131] If a legal

[124] English Law Commission Report No 296, para. 4.45, recommended that the provisions on sales of receivables should be limited to sales by companies registered in England and Wales.

[125] English Law Commission Report No 296, para. 4.12, supports this view on the registration of sale of receivables at least for the purpose of priority. Para. 4.26 confined 'receivables' which are involved in factoring or discounting agreements. It did not intend to extend registration to the receivables used in securitisations. See also the United States Uniform Commercial Code Article 9, §§9-102, which requires all sales of receivables.

[126] English Law Commission Report No 296, para. 4.31, listed four special classes of exemption.

[127] English Law Commission Report No 296, para. 4.25.

[128] English Law Commission Report No 296, paras. 4.46–4.48.

[129] English Law Commission Report No 296, para. 4.18.

[130] See Chapter 1 above.

[131] *Anning v Anning* [1907] 4 CLR 1049.

assignment is created and perfected according to §9, the assignee acquires the legal title to the chose in action, and the legal assignee/mortgagee may commence legal proceedings against the debtor in its own name, without having to join the assignor as plaintiff or co-defendant as a party to the action.

On the other hand, the impact of §9 on the assignment of an equitable chose in action is minimal. An equitable assignment in compliance with §9 does not alter the equitable nature of the chose in action or the rights of the equitable assignee.[132]

To create an effective legal assignment under §9, the assignment has to satisfy the following conditions:

(1) the subject matter must be a legal debt or legal chose in action,
(2) the assignment must be an absolute assignment and not by way of a charge,
(3) the assignment must be in writing and signed by the assignor or its authorised agent, and
(4) express notice in writing must be given to the debtor from whom the assignor would have been entitled to receive or claim such debt or chose in action.

If any of the above conditions are not met, the purported legal assignment will take effect as an equitable assignment.[133]

The conditions of §9 are well discussed in several textbooks[134] and in many cases, particularly English ones. Briefly, the subject matter of the assignment, the 'debt or other legal thing in action', includes legal and equitable choses in action, except those which can only be transferred by complying with some other legislation.[135] The requirement that the assignment should be absolute and not by way of charge means that the assignment, in the case of a legal mortgage, must transfer the entire legal interest of the assignor in the debt or chose in action to the assignee.

In practice, the creation process under §9 does not give rise to difficulty if the service of a lawyer is engaged.[136] A standard sample of banks'

[132] Guest, *Chitty on Contracts*, above, note 72, para. 20-039-040.

[133] *William Brandt's Sons & Co. v Dunlop Rubber Company Limited* [1905] AC 454, p. 461, *per* Lord Macnaghten.

[134] For example, see Guest, *Chitty on Contracts*, above, note 72, para. 20-001; Treitel, above, note 72, Chapter 16, pp. 622–30; and McGhee, above, note 30, pp. 83–7.

[135] See Treitel, above, note 72, pp. 624–5.

[136] It appears from the author's interview with Mr Patrick Ho, the general manager of Jiangsu Bank, who provided advice on the present authors' co-authored book *Law*

legal assignments by way of security in Hong Kong[137] showed that the conditions are complied with. In addition, the sample also contained other usual banking terms and conditions, such as that the loan is repayable on demand, that the security is to secure future advances, that the chose in action would be applied to settle the loan in the event of default and that an acknowledgement of notice of the assignment by the debtor be given.

However, in cases where the assignee is not familiar with the rules of assignment and does not engage a lawyer, it may have difficulty with the prerequisite of notice. Notice under §9 is complex. Firstly, under §9, the statutory notice must be in writing. Secondly, unlike notice in equity, which performs a priority function, the statutory notice performs two functions: it perfects the legal assignment by vesting the legal title in the assignee and it determines priority. Thirdly, the statutory notice shares the same problem with notice in equity, which is the question of what would effectively constitute notice. Once again, the objective test with its uncertainty, discussed earlier, would be applied. Despite the difficulties, §9 of LARCO has not attempted to address the problem; it has not prescribed the form notice should take to be deemed effective.

The notice under condition (4) above can be given even after the commencement of the action against the debtor.[138] But it would serve little purpose if the debtor had already paid the funds to the assignor or a third party.

In the Privy Council case *Agnew v Commissioner of Inland Revenue*,[139] Lord Millett thought that the creation process of §9 had inherent practical commercial problems, particularly where the assignor was a trader. Firstly, if the assignor has a large number of book debts and the creditor intends to create a legal assignment of all of them, it would be commercially impractical. The creditor, such as a bank or financial institution, is not in a position to maintain credit control over the debts from time to time owing to its debtor or to be able to collect the debt

and Practice of Banking in Hong Kong (Hong Kong: Chartered Institute of Bankers, 1993), that assignment of book debts and other debts is usually prepared by the bank's solicitors.

137 Deacons, Hong Kong, provided the sample. The asset was a time-fixed deposit with another bank. The sample further showed that the debtor had to 'acknowledge receipt' of the notice.

138 *Thomas v NAB Ltd and Others* [2000] 2 Qd R 448.

139 [2001] 2 BCLC 188, 195–6, PC.

itself. Secondly, giving notice to the debtors may seriously harm the credit of the assignor.[140]

In such a situation, Lord Millett observed that, at least in England, creditors usually took an equitable assignment of the book debts but refrained from giving notice to the debtor until the assignor defaulted. The security document would give authority to the creditor to collect the debts on behalf of the assignor. Until the creditor exercised the authority, the debtor was trustee of the proceeds for the assignee and it had to account to the creditor for them.[141] But this, it is submitted, is not a good solution for two reasons. Firstly, the creditor faces the risk of an intervening interest which may be superior, such as a legal assignment. Secondly, the assignment may constitute a general assignment of book debts and it would be void if the creditor overlooked registering it with the High Court Registry.[142]

In conclusion, it is submitted that the rules governing the creation of legal assignment satisfied only four of the seven creation criteria established in Chapter 1.[143] They have not satisfied the other three creation criteria; namely, that the debtor should have possession of the asset and freedom to deal with the asset, and that the rules should be simple and comprehensible.

Perfection of legal mortgages In contrast to equitable assignment, perfection of the legal assignment between the assignee and the debtor and other creditors of the assignor is governed by statute, though more than one statute may apply in some situations.

The basic statutory requirement is contained in §9 itself; that is, service of notice in writing of the assignment on the debtor is necessary, otherwise the assignee cannot enforce the assignment in its own name against the debtor and the other creditors. The difficulties relating to sufficiency of the notice have already been discussed in Chapter 2 above.

140 This disadvantage was also recognised in the United States of America; see *Miami National Bank, Appellant, S. Krudsen, Trustee for Ladman Corporation, Bankruptcy, Appellee* (No 19009) 26 February 1962, US App Lexis 5821, p. 3. Wisdom J stated, 'In the first place there appears to be a genuine apprehension among those concerned that their prestige and consequently their "goodwill" might be affected by any publicity given to the fact of their resorting to this method of credit accommodation.' Ghose, above, note 19, p. 223, noted that in Hong Kong in some factoring agreements, no notice of the assignment is served on the account debtor. This could be due to this reason.

141 *Agnew v Commissioner of Inland Revenue* [2001] UKPC 28, [2001] 3 WLR. 454, 721, *per* Lord Millet, para. F.

142 See above in this chapter.

143 See Chapter 1 above.

The other statutes that may additionally apply are §48 of the Bankruptcy Ordinance and the Companies Ordinance, which require registration of certain types of assignment of choses in action. The discussion on them in the context of equitable assignment above applies here equally.

As the difficulties experienced and discussed in the context of equitable assignments also apply here, particularly the perfecting function of notice and the anomalous statutory perfecting process between non-corporate and corporate assignors, the negative conclusion made therein applies here equally. Whether or not the rules have fully satisfied the criterion relating to just and fair ordering of priority is further discussed in Chapter 6.

Publicity of legal mortgages Publicity of legal assignment by way of legal mortgage is governed by one single statute, which is §9 of LARCO, and, where the assignor is a company, by the Companies Ordinance as well.[144] Under §9, publicity is achieved by requiring the assignee to serve notice in writing on the debtor. However, this mechanism has difficulties in practice, namely a weak dissemination of information function and poor book-keeping by the debtor. These have already been discussed in the context of equitable assignment and they apply equally here.

In relation to the Companies Ordinance, if a company granted the assignment, general or specific, by way of security it has to be registered with the Companies Registry. As mentioned earlier, failure to do so would render the assignment void against the creditors and the liquidator.[145]

On the basis of the above discussion, it is submitted that the rules governing publicity of legal mortgages have failed to satisfy all the publicity criteria established in Chapter 1.[146] The existing rules are not simple, do not ensure accurate information and do not ensure accessibility of information.

Cost of creation, perfection and publicity of legal mortgages The process of creation, perfection and publicity of legal assignment by way of legal mortgage is not subject to tax or stamp duty. There is also no state administrative cost involved in the publicity of legal assignments.

Therefore legal mortgages by way of legal assignments have satisfied the criterion of low cost established in Chapter 1.[147]

[144] See Chapter 4 below. [145] See Chapter 4 below.
[146] Chapter 1 above. [147] See Chapter 1 above.

3.2.3 Creation, perfection and publicity of charges over choses in action in the form of debts and monetary obligations in Hong Kong, and cost

Creation of charges over choses in action

In Hong Kong, the charge device is commonly used by commercial banks to create security over the debtor's choses in action, in the form of book debts and credit balances in their banks.[148] The latter comprises balances in the customer's current accounts, savings accounts and fixed deposits.

In the case of book debts, both corporate and non-corporate debtors may create a fixed charge or a floating charge over them. Theoretically, this is a simple process, but in practice there can be difficulty, particularly in ascertaining whether the charge is a fixed charge or a floating charge.[149]

In relation to savings accounts and fixed deposits, the banks in Hong Kong usually create a fixed charge over them. The process is simple. The debtor/customer executes a one-page charge document in favour of the bank, and in the case of fixed deposits the certificates are deposited with the bank. The charge documents contain the bank's usual terms, namely if the debtor defaults the bank can combine the debtor/customer credit balances with the account in debit,[150] if the debtor is formally declared insolvent[151] the account in credit will automatically be set off against the loan under §35 of the Bankruptcy Ordinance (Cap. 6)[152] and the bank can simply (as in the case of a third-party security) apply the credit balances to discharge the debt owing to the bank.[153] This type of charge is called a 'charge-back security arrangement'.

148 Credit balances and fixed deposits are not classified as 'book debts'. Although they are debts due and owing by the banks to the customer, they are regarded as cash in hand; see *Re Brightlife Ltd* [1986] 3 All ER 673, and *Permanent House (Holdings) Ltd* [1986] BCLC 563. R.A. Pearce, 'Fixed Charges over Book Debts', *JBL* (1987), 18–29, argues that current balances can constitute book debts if the customer carries on a business of lending and the balance arises from that business.

149 This is discussed further below in Chapter 4.

150 *Garnett v M'Kewan* [1872] LR 8 Ex 10.

151 Formally made bankrupt in the case of an individual and wound up in the case of a corporation.

152 Automatic set-off under §35 of the Bankruptcy Ordinance (Cap. 6) also applies to insolvent corporations by virtue of §264 of the Companies Ordinance (Cap. 32).

153 A typical charge sample can be found in the Hong Kong case of *Tam Wing Chuen and Another v Bank of Credit & Commerce Hong Kong Ltd (in liquidation)* [1996] 1 HKC 692, PC. The charge document provides, inter alia, 'If the customer has failed to pay any

In England and Australia, there are conflicting views whether such a charge-back security arrangement is valid.[154] In Hong Kong, the uncertainty was removed in 1993 when the legislature enacted §15A of LARCO, which essentially provides that such charge-back arrangements are valid.[155] The different position was recognised in *Tam Wing Chuen and Another v Bank of Credit & Commerce Hong Kong Ltd (in liquidation)*,[156] where the Privy Council held that a charge created by the depositor in favour of the bank as security for banking facilities granted was clearly valid under the section.

In conclusion, the rules governing the creation of charges over savings and fixed deposits with the banks have satisfied four of the seven creation

moneys hereby secured when due or if the depositor is in default … the bank may without notice on the depositor … apply the deposit towards payment and settlement of the moneys and liabilities referred to in clause 1.01.'

[154] In *Re Charge Card Services Ltd* [1986] 3 All ER 289, Millett J held that a creditor cannot create, in favour of a debtor, a charge over the debtor's own indebtedness to the chargor. Such a charge was said to be conceptually impossible. Dillon LJ in the Court of Appeal case of *Welsh Development Agency v Export Finance Co. Ltd* [1992] BCC 270 cast doubt on this. In the case of *Re Bank of Credit and Commerce International SA (No 8)* [1998] 1 BCLC 68, Lord Hoffmann also cast doubt on *Re Charge Card Services Ltd*, and thought that such charge-back security arrangements are valid. He further commented that the courts should be very slow to declare a practice of the commercial community to be conceptually impossible. However, the courts in Australia appear to be divided. Yet the majority support the doctrine of conceptual impossibility established in *Re Charge Card Services Ltd*; see *Broad v Commissioner of Stamp Duties* (1980) 2 NSWLR 40, 40, *per* Lee J; *Estate Planning Associates (Australia) Pty Ltd v Commissioner of Stamp Duties* (1985) 2 NSWLR 495, 499, *per* Yeldham J; and *Wily as Liquidator of AUR NL (in liquidation) and Another v Rothschild Australia* (1999) 47 NSWLR 555, 564–5, in which Windeyer J stated, 'The position … seems partly at least to have been brought about through a desire to make accord with the desires of commerce rather than through totally convincing reasoning.' For a minority view against the doctrine, see *Cinema Plus Ltd (Administrators Appointed) and Another v Australia and New Zealand Banking Group Ltd* (2000) 49 NSWLR 513, 521, where Spigelman CJ commented (*obiter*), 'In my opinion, there is no reason why, in an appropriate case, equity could not find that the intention of the parties to create a charge between a debtor and creditor, overrides what would be regarded, at common law, as a "conceptual impossibility".' See also R. Goode, 'Charge-Backs and Legal Fictions', *LQR* 114 (1998), 178, where he argued that Lord Hoffmann's proposition cannot withstand substantive examination.

[155] It provides, 'For the avoidance of doubt, it is hereby declared that a person ("the first person") is able to create, and has always been able to create, in favour of another person ("the second person") a legal or equitable charge or mortgage over all or any of the first person's interest in a chose in action enforceable by the first person against the second person, and any charge or mortgage so created shall operate neither to merge the interest thereby created with, nor to extinguish or release, that chose in action.'

[156] [1996] 1 HKC 692, PC.

criteria established in Chapter 1.[157] The other three creation criteria, which the rules have not satisfied, are that the security must be capable of attaching to after-acquired or future assets and that the debtor must continue to have possession of the assets and freedom to deal with the credit balances. However, discussion of the question whether the process of creating fixed and floating charges over book debts and credit balances has satisfied the criteria relating to just and fair ordering of priority is postponed to Chapter 6.[158]

Perfection of charges over choses in action

Perfection of charges over choses in action is governed by general law and, in some cases, by statute.

General law The rules under general law are complex. First, if the charge is a fixed charge over book debts and credit balances, and the charge is between the debtor–chargor and bank–chargee, such as customer and bank, the security is perfected when the charge is completed.[159] However, if the chargee is a different bank, the rule in *Dearle v Hall*[160] relating to service of notice on the debtor, discussed earlier in Chapter 2, and the uncertainty and complexities surrounding the function of notice, apply here equally.[161]

The recent case of *ABN Amro Bank NV v Chiyu Banking Corp Ltd and Others*[162] illustrates that this requirement of notice can be easily overlooked even by a professional institution, such as a bank, and the serious consequence of such an omission. Essentially the bank, a fixed chargee, had not served notice on the debtor, another bank, of its fixed charge over certain fixed deposits of the borrower. When the borrower was wound up, the court held that the fixed charge lost priority to the debtor who had subsequently created a fixed charge over the same deposits. The debtor is deemed to have served notice on itself. If the charge is only a floating charge, no notice is required to be served.[163]

157 See Chapter 1 above.

158 See *ABN Amro Bank NV v Chiyu Banking Corp Ltd and Others* [2000] 3 HKC 38, *Siebe Gorman v Barclays Bank* [1979] 2 Lloyd's Law Reports 142; *Re Brightlife Ltd* [1986] 3 All ER 673; and *Re Permanent Houses (Holdings) Ltd* [1988] BCLCC 563.

159 Based on *Dearle v Hall* (1828) 3 Russ 21, 38 ER 475.

160 Ibid.

161 *ABN Amro Bank NV v Chiyu Banking Corp Ltd and Others* [2000] 3 HKC 38, where it was held that the rule established in *Dearle v Hall* (1828) 3 Russ 21, 38 ER 475, applies to choses in action in the control of a third party. That case concerned fixed charges over fixed-time deposits. This will be discussed further in Chapter 6.

162 [2000] 3 HKC 38.

163 Ibid.

Statute Section 9 of LARCO does not apply to charges over book debts and other debts. However, if the chargor is a non-corporate body and the charge is a general fixed charge or floating charge[164] over its book debts, the charge has to be registered with the High Court Registry under §48 of the Bankruptcy Ordinance. The objective of the section and consequence of failure to comply have already been discussed above in this chapter.

If the chargor is a company, the position is slightly complicated. If the company creates a charge, fixed or floating, over book debts, it has to be registered with the Companies Registry, otherwise it is null and void against the chargor's other creditors and liquidator.[165] However, if the company creates a fixed charge over debts owing to it, other than book debts, such as credit balances with its bank, the charge is not registrable, because it is not within the list of registrable charges under the Companies Ordinance.[166] On the other hand, if the company creates a floating charge over the same credit balances, it is registrable under the list.[167] Therefore the crucial issue of charges over book debts lies in the nature of the difference between floating and fixed charges. In its recent judgment in the *Spectrum Plus* case,[168] the House of Lords has held that a charge over book debts will be a fixed charge only if the proceeds of the debts have to be paid into an account over which the chargor has no control. It is insufficient to become a fixed charge if the chargee prevents the chargor from drawing on the account without its consent; the account must actually be operated as a blocked account.[169] However, for the purpose of the distinction, the court will look into the substance of the transaction rather

[164] The Bills of Sale Ordinance which prohibits a non-corporate borrower from creating floating charges is restricted only to security over personal property. See Chapter 2 above.

[165] These are discussed further in Chapter 4 below.

[166] See Chapter 4. See also Consultation Paper No 164, para. 2.75, where it states, 'Charges over debts are normally registrable only if the debts are book debts or the charge is a floating charge.' See also *Re Bank of Credit and Commerce International SA (No 8)* [1998] 1 BCLC 68, 71, where Lord Hoffmann said that fixed charges over such debts are unlikely to be registrable.

[167] Section 80(2) of the Companies Ordinance provides a list of registrable charges created by companies. A floating charge created on the undertaking or property of the company is listed under subsection (f). For further discussion, see Chapter 4 below.

[168] *National Westminster Bank plc v Spectrum Plus Ltd* [2005] UKHL 41, [2005] 3 WLR 58, allowing the appeal from the decision of the CA in [2004] EWCA Civ 670; [2004] 4 All ER 995.

[169] The judgment refers to the speech of Lord Millet in *Agnew v Commissioner of Inland Revenue* [2001] UKPC 28, [2001] 3 WLR 454, at p. 48.

than its form.[170] Alternatively, book debts may be subjected only to a floating charge which is registrable, but the charge may include a prohibition on factoring or other disposition of the book debts (i.e. a negative pledge clause).

The position of charges over debts and monetary obligations is nearly identical to equitable assignment of choses in action. The rules are complex and highly technical. Accordingly, it is submitted that the rules governing the perfection of charges over these assets have not satisfied the perfection criteria of simplicity and comprehensibility established in Chapter 1.[171] Discussion of the question whether or not the rules have fully satisfied the criteria relating to just and fair ordering of priority is postponed to Chapter 6.

Publicity of charges over choses in action

The discussion of publicity in respect of equitable mortgages above in this chapter also applies here with similar force.

If the charge over choses in action is granted by a company and the charge is registrable under the Companies Ordinance, publicity is promoted through the registration system.[172]

Accordingly, it is submitted that except for cost-efficiency, the rules governing the publicity of equitable mortgages fail to satisfy all the publicity criteria established in Chapter 1.[173] The existing rules are not simple, do not ensure accurate information, and do not ensure accessibility of information, except where charge, if registrable, is registered with the Companies Registry.

Cost of creation, perfection and publicity of charges over choses in action

Generally, there is no cost involved in creating, perfecting and publicising charges over choses in action because charges are exempt from tax and stamp duty. However, if the charge has to be registered at the Companies Registry, the creditor has to pay registration fees, which are minimal.[174]

In conclusion, the costs of creation, perfection and publicity of charges over choses in action have satisfied the low-cost criterion established in Chapter 1.[175]

[170] The same approach was also adopted by the House of Lords in *Re Spectrum Plus Ltd* [2005] UKHL 41.

[171] See Chapter 1 above. [172] See Chapter 4 below. [173] See Chapter 1 above.

[174] See Chapter 4 below. [175] See Chapter 1 above, on cost.

3.2.4 Creation, perfection and publicity of security over company shares in Hong Kong, and cost

Creation of security over shares

In Hong Kong, a legal mortgage, equitable mortgage or charge can be created over the shares of companies. Where a pledge is used, the pledge may be regarded as an equitable mortgage or a charge, as evidenced by the intention of the parties.[176] As the legal title, equitable title, or control over the shares is vested in the debtor, notice in *Dearle v Hall* and §9 of LARCO are not relevant. Priority is generally determined by the general rule of first in time of creation of the security, but different views on priority have also been discussed on the basis of whether the shares are directly held or not.[177] The English Law Commission has proposed a notice-filing scheme to establish clear and harmonised rules of the priority of charges over shares.

However, in Hong Kong the most common types of security device over shares used by the creditor, usually a bank, are the legal mortgage and the equitable mortgage, the latter being more popular.

The process of creating a legal mortgage is cumbersome and expensive. It involves the following steps. Firstly, the mortgagee executes a loan agreement under which the mortgagor undertakes to re-transfer the shares back to the mortgagee when the loan is fully settled. Secondly, the mortgagee, if it is also the registered owner of the shares, executes the instrument of transfer of the shares. Thirdly, the mortgagee sends the duly executed instrument together with the share certificates to the issuing company for registration. Fourthly, the mortgagee is registered as shareholder in the register of members of the issuing company. Fifthly, the old share certificates are cancelled and new share certificates are issued to the mortgagee in its name. The whole process is reversed when the loan is fully satisfied.

In contrast, the process of creating equitable mortgages is quick and inexpensive. It usually takes the form of the debtor executing a memorandum of deposit, setting out the terms of the loan and the rights of the creditor over the security, and depositing the share certificates and blank

[176] See *Bank of China (Hong Kong) Ltd v Kanishi (Far East) Ltd and Another* [2002] 2 HKLRD 52, discussed above in this chapter.

[177] See *Société Général de Paris and Colladon v Walker* (1885) 11 App Cas 20, and also English Law Commission Consultation Paper No 164, para. 2.65, and No 176, para. 2.146, for different views on priority of charges over shares. See also Chapter 6 for discussion of this rule.

memorandum of transfer duly executed by the debtor with the creditor. When the loan is fully settled, the documents are returned to the debtor. From the perspective of securing the priority of the creditor against other competing claims, these forms of security device appear effective. It is only in the very rare situation of fraud, where the share certificate is a forgery,[178] that the security interests of the creditor might be defeated by the claim of the true owner.

However, with the introduction of the scripless share transfer system called the Central Clearing and Settlement System (CCASS) in Hong Kong in 1992,[179] traditional legal and equitable mortgages have declined in use. The only form of security over scripless shares is a varied form of equitable mortgage.

Briefly, under CCASS the buying and selling of listed shares is effected through debit or credit entries to CCASS participants' stock accounts with Hong Kong Securities Clearing Company Ltd (HKSCC), which is responsible for operating the system. The shares affected are registered not in the name of the true owner, but with a common nominee, HKSCC Nominees Ltd. When an investor acquires any listed shares, the intermediary (which is the stockbroker) merely issues it a contract note indicating the number of the shares it has acquired. The interest of the acquirer is an equitable interest. The interest therefore assumes the character of a chose in action discussed above in this chapter. But it differs in several aspects. Firstly, the trustee, HKSCC Nominees Ltd, has no power to dispose of the shares. Secondly, control of the equitable interest rests with the intermediary of the investor.[180] The intermediary alone could shift the equitable ownership of the shares to another intermediary.[181] Thirdly, the intermediary

[178] The only reported case where share certificates of a listed company were obtained by forgery is *Yeung Kai Yung v The Hong Kong and Shanghai Banking Corporation* [1980] 2 All ER, PC. The original shareholder, the victim of the forgery, was restored to the register of shareholders of the company.

[179] The Hong Kong Securities Clearing Company Ltd operates the system.

[180] See 'Tracking your Stocks in CCASS', SFC (June 2002), at www.hksfc.org.hk/.

[181] To reduce the risk of the intermediary disposing of the shares without the consent of the investor, HKSCC offers two types of service, namely a Stock Segregated Account with Statement Service and an Investor Account. Under the first type of account the investor will be informed daily of the status of its shares by HKSCC, but the intermediary account holder could still dispose of the shares without the investor's consent. Under the second type of account, the intermediary may not dispose of the investor's shares without its written consent. These types of account are not widely used probably because a fee has to be paid for the services. For further literature on these accounts, see www.hksfc.org.hk/.

acts according to the instruction of the equitable owner in relation to the shares.

On the basis of the above, an equitable mortgagor gives instructions to its intermediary to transfer its equitable interest into the account of the equitable mortgagee with the same intermediary or another intermediary. As the intermediary is not responsible for keeping records of the loan and security transaction, the equitable mortgagee and equitable mortgagor have to sign a separate security document. It appears that the CCASS system indeed offers a more efficient way of taking security over listed shares. When the equitable mortgagor defaults, the equitable mortgagee simply instructs the intermediary to dispose of the equitable interest. The instruction is unnecessary if the equitable mortgagee is a bank and it holds a broker's license.

There is an advantage in Hong Kong's method of creating security over shares, which is that the creation and perfection processes co-exist. A noteworthy advantage of rules governing the creation of security in Hong Kong is their flexibility. The change in physical evidence of the shareholders' interests from share certificates to scripless equitable interests has not left the creditor without any security device over scripless shares of companies. Equitable mortgages can be created over them.

In view of the above, it is submitted that the rules governing the creation of security over shares of companies have satisfied all seven creation criteria established in Chapter 1.[182]

Perfection of security over shares

If the security provider is an individual, there are no special rules governing perfection of the security. This is because creation and perfection co-exist.

If the security provider is a company, the security has to be perfected according to §80 of the Companies Ordinance. This section is discussed further in Chapter 4.[183] For present purposes, however, briefly, if a company creates a floating charge over shares, the floating charge has to be registered with the Companies Registry. If it is not registered, the floating charge is null and void against the company's creditors and liquidators. On the other hand, if the charge is a fixed charge, the charge does not require registration, because it is not registrable under §80 of the Companies Ordinance.[184] The situation of the registration of charges

[182] Chapter 1 above. [183] See Chapter 4 below.
[184] Ibid., where it is discussed further.

over shares in the United Kingdom, limited by European law,[185] is very different from that in Hong Kong. The European Directive on Financial Collateral Arrangements (hereafter the Financial Collateral Directive or FCD) provides that when financial collateral subject to a 'security financial collateral arrangement' (that is, a mortgage, charge or pledge) has been 'provided' in such a way as to be in the 'possession or control' of the 'collateral taker', formalities such as registration cannot be required in order to render the arrangement enforceable.[186] Registration under §860 and §874 of the Companies Act 2006[187] are explicitly excluded by the Financial Collateral Arrangement (No 2) Regulations 2003[188](FCAR), which apply particularly to security financial arrangements between non-natural persons.[189] Both FCD and FCAR particularly apply to property of an investment nature (termed 'financial instruments') and to 'cash'.[190] Therefore the perfection by registration of charges over shares is likely to be restricted, and though the perfection of security over shares by 'possession' or 'control by the secured party' is permitted, it is not clearly defined in FCD or FCAR.[191] The priority of competing security interests over financial collateral brought by FCD and FCAR are also critically examined by the English Law Commission Report No 296.[192]

The rules governing the perfection of security granted by non-corporate debtors are simple and they have satisfied all the perfection criteria established in Chapter 1.[193] In relation to companies, although registration is required in respect of floating charges, it is submitted that there is no compliance difficulties, as will be seen in Chapter 6. It is therefore submitted

[185] Directive 2002/47/EC of the European Parliament and Council of 6 June 2002, OJ L 168/43. Note that Financial Collateral Arrangement (No 2) Regulations 2003 (FCAR) has implemented the directive.

[186] Articles 2 and 3, the Financial Collateral Directive (FCD). The agreement or arrangement must also be evidenced in writing. See also Financial Collateral Arrangement (No 2) Regulations 2003 (FCAR), reg. 4(4).

[187] Formerly Companies Act 1985, §395.

[188] Financial Collateral Arrangement (No 2) Regulations 2003 (FCAR), reg. 4(4).

[189] Financial Collateral Arrangement (No 2) Regulations 2003 (FCAR), reg. 3.

[190] Ibid. See also H. Beale et al., *The Law of Personal Property Security* (New York: Oxford University Press, 2007), p. 390.

[191] Beale, above, note 190, at pp. 396–401. See also the English Law Commission Report No 296, paras. 5.12–5.13 and 5.42–5.74, for detailed discussions. However, in the draft titled 'The Company Security Regulations 2006' attached to the same report, the meanings of 'possession or control' are proposed, which are currently pending implementation.

[192] English Law Commission Report No 296, paras. 5.78–5.99, for detailed discussions.

[193] See Chapter 1 above.

that in respect of companies, the rules governing the perfection process have also satisfied all the perfection criteria.

Publicity of security over shares

As security over a non-corporate debtor's shares of a company is not registrable with any relevant authority, there is no publicity of the security. In the case of security over a company's shares in another company, publicity is limited to floating charges, which, as discussed earlier, are required to be registered with the Companies Registry. Thus the rules governing the publicity of security over shares of a company not only differ dramatically between individuals and companies, but also between different types of company charge. There is, therefore, a publicity vacuum insofar as individuals are concerned and in respect of fixed charges of companies.

It is submitted that the rules governing the publicity of security over shares of a company are weak and have not satisfied the publicity criteria set out in Chapter 1.[194]

Cost of creation, perfection and publicity of security over shares of companies

The cost of creating, perfecting and publicising security over shares of companies is inexpensive. The security is not subject to tax or stamp duty, and registration of floating charges is minimal. Therefore security over shares has satisfied the criterion of low cost.

3.2.5 Creation, perfection and publicity of security over copyright in Hong Kong, and cost

Basically, except for the pledge, any of the security devices discussed earlier can be created over copyright and the discussion therein in relation to creation, perfection and publicity will generally apply.

There is, however, a creation requirement imposed by §102(3) of the Copyright Ordinance (Cap. 528). This requires an assignment of copyright to be in writing and signed by the assignor or its agent. Unless this is complied with, the assignment is invalid. Whether the word 'assignment' includes charges is uncertain, as the Copyright Ordinance does not define the word 'assignment'. In relation to perfection, if the security provider is a company, the security, whether a fixed charge or a floating charge, has to be registered with the Companies Registry, otherwise it is

[194] Ibid.

null and void against the creditor and liquidator of the company.[195] An individual security provider is not subject to any registration requirement to perfect the security.

On the point of publicity, since there is no registration requirement for security provided by individuals, there is no publicity. However, in the case of a company security provider, the security is publicised through the registration system of the Companies Registry. Again, here there is inconsistency between the rules governing individuals and those governing companies.

In respect of cost, the creation, perfection and publicity of security of copyright is inexpensive.

It is therefore submitted that the rules governing the creation and perfection of security over copyright have satisfied the creation and perfection criteria set out in Chapter 1.[196] However, the rules governing publicity of the security have not satisfied the publicity criteria.[197]

3.3 Creation, perfection and publicity of security over other forms of intangible property in Hong Kong, and cost

In Hong Kong, three forms of valuable intangible property which are not regarded as choses in action are export quotas for textiles,[198] patents[199] and trademarks. However, this part will not discuss the process of creation, perfection and publicity in detail, as the security devices that can be created over them have already been discussed in this chapter.

Export quotas

In relation to creation, in *Hong Kong and Shanghai Banking Corporation v Star Trans International Ltd*,[200] the Court of Appeal held that security in

[195] Companies Ordinance §80(2)(i) (Chapter 32).

[196] See Chapter 1 above. [197] See Chapter 1 above.

[198] Textile quotas are now of historical significance only as the Multi-Fibre Agreement (MFA) ended in 1994, replaced by the WTO Agreement on Textiles and Clothing 1995–2004. The ultimate aim is complete removal of relevant export quotas applicable to textile goods. For further details see www.wto.org/english/tratop_e/texti_e/texintro_e.htm.

[199] Under general law, a patent constituted a chose in action: *Halsbury's Laws of England*, 4th ed., reissue (London: Butterworths, 1991), vol. 6, p. 8, para. 8, note 60, but this has been altered by the Hong Kong Patents Ordinance (Cap. 514), §50(1). It provides that a patent is personal property but not 'a thing in action'.

[200] [1988] 2 HKLR 549.

the form of a fixed charge and a floating charge can be effected over an export quota allocation. Theoretically, an equitable assignment can be effected over it, but in practice there is a limitation. Under the Textiles Export Control System of Hong Kong,[201] the transferee of the quota must be a textile exporter or manufacturer registered with the Department of Trade. Thus a bank lender is not eligible and could not obtain an equitable assignment from a borrower who is a holder of an export quota.

In relation to the perfection aspect, security created by non-corporate holders of export quotas is not subject to any registration. Thus creation and perfection co-exist. However, in relation to corporate holders of export quotas, all security created by them has to be registered with the Companies Registry, otherwise it is null and void against the creditors and liquidator.[202]

In relation to publicity, there is no publicity for security created by non-corporate holders of export quotas because the security is not required to be registered with any authority. However, in the case of security created by a company export quota holder, publicity is achieved through registration with the Companies Registry. There is, therefore, inconsistency between the rules governing non-corporate and corporate export quota holders.

In respect of cost, creation, perfection and publicity are inexpensive.

It is therefore submitted that the rules governing the creation and perfection of security over export quotas have satisfied the creation and perfection criteria established in Chapter 1.[203] However, the rules governing publicity of the security have not satisfied the publicity criteria.

3.3.2 Patents

Except for pledges, all forms of non-possessory security devices can be created over patents. However, the Patents Ordinance (Cap. 514) has an impact on the creation of security over patents. Under §50(6) of the Ordinance, security over a patent has to be in writing and signed by or on behalf of the owner of the patent and in the case of a company it is so

201 For detailed discussion see C.A. Ong, 'Taking a Judicious Look at Export Quota as Security', *ALP* (1993), 5–9.

202 *Hong Kong and Shanghai Banking Corporation v Star Trans International Ltd* [1988] 2 HKLR 549. The Court of Appeal held that a floating charge over an export quota was null and void because it was not duly registered with the Companies Registry.

203 See Chapter 1 above.

signed or is under the seal of that body.[204] In default, the security is void[205] against the mortgagor and third party.

In relation to perfection, the rules are complicated. Firstly, under the Patents Ordinance, security over patents has to be registered with the Registrar of Patents. No date is prescribed for registration. The date of registration determines priority. However, a duly registered security will have priority over an earlier unregistered security if the earlier security holder has not, at the time of creation of the subsequent security, applied to the registrar for registration of its security and the subsequent security has no actual knowledge of the earlier security.[206] Failure to register does not render the security void; thus registration has only a priority effect. Secondly, if a security, fixed or floating, over patents were granted by a company, the security must be registered with the Companies Registry, otherwise the security is null and void.[207] There is therefore a conflict between the registration system under the Patents Ordinance and that under the Companies Ordinance.

In relation to publicity, this is promoted through registration with the Patents Registry and, additionally, through the Companies Registry, if the patent owner is a company. Information, including mortgages, on patents registered with the Patents Registry is electronically recorded and can be accessed electronically by computers at the Registry.[208] However, search is only expeditious if the searcher has the registration number of the patent. Without it, the searcher will have to conduct a very slow and tedious process of searching the entire register. However, in practice, this is not a real problem, as the owner of the patent would have given the creditor the particulars.

The cost of creation, perfection and publicity is inexpensive. Security over patents is not subject to any tax or stamp duty. The Patents Registry charges a flat fee of HK$500 for registration and a search fee of HK$100. The Companies Registry charges a flat fee of HK$340 for registration and a search fee of HK$20.

It is therefore submitted that the rules governing creation, perfection and publicity have satisfied the creation, perfection and publicity criteria established in Chapter 1.[209] However, it is doubtful whether it is necessary in the case of companies that there should be double

[204] Patents Ordinance (Cap. 514), §50(6). [205] Ibid.

[206] Ibid., §52(1). [207] This is discussed in Chapter 4 below.

[208] The author visited the Intellectual Property Department, and Ms Eva Li explained how the registration system operates in Hong Kong.

[209] See Chapter 1 above.

registration in respect of perfection and publicity. This is discussed further in Chapter 6.

3.3.3 Trademarks

Except for pledges, any form of non-possessory security device can be created over trademarks.[210]

In relation to creation, the Trade Marks Ordinance (Cap. 43) does not state that the security has to be in writing, but in practice it would have to be in writing in order to satisfy the Registrar of Trade Marks that the security is registrable (see below).

In relation to perfection, security over trademarks has to be registered with the Registrar of Trade Marks.[211] As under the Patents Ordinance, an unregistered security is not void. But, in contrast to the Patents Ordinance, the Trade Marks Ordinance is silent on whether registration has an effect on priority. However, it appears that the general rules determining priority would apply to determine priority of all competing registered securities.[212] This is because §31 of the Ordinance provides that equities relating to a trademark may be enforced in like manner as in respect of any other personal property. The general rules of priority are discussed further in Chapter 6.

If a company grants security, fixed or floating, over trademarks, the security has to be registered with the Companies Registry, otherwise it is null and void.[213] Here again, there is, in the case of companies, a double registration requirement, and there is a conflict between the two registration systems in respect of the consequences of default in registration.

Publicity is promoted through registration with the Registrar of Trade Marks, and, additionally, through the Companies Registry, if the owner of the trademark is a company. Information about a duly registered trademark at the Trade Marks Registry is electronically recorded and accessible by computers at the Registry. A party searching would also need to know the specific trademark number. Again, as in the case of patents, this is not a real problem in practice.

In respect of cost, the cost of creation, perfection and publicity is minimal. The observation made in relation to security over patents in respect of fees discussed above also applies here.

[210] Trade Marks Ordinance (Cap. 43), §41(1). [211] Ibid., §43(1).
[212] The general rules of priority are discussed further in Chapter 6.
[213] This is discussed further in Chapter 4 below.

It is therefore submitted that the rules governing the creation, perfection and publicity of security over trademarks have satisfied the criteria of creation, perfection and publicity established in Chapter 1.[214] However, as in the case of patents, it is doubtful whether it is necessary that there should be double registration for perfection and publicity of company security over trademarks. This is discussed further in Chapter 6.

3.4 Creation, perfection and publicity of security over intangible property in China that corresponds with choses in action in Hong Kong, and cost

This section examines the creation, perfection and publicity of pledges over intangible property in China, and their cost. The nature of the pledge has already been fully discussed in Chapter 2.

3.4.1 Pledges

Creation of pledges

In contrast to Hong Kong, China takes a different approach to the creation of a pledge. Article 223 of the Property Law (with minor changes the former Article 75 of the Security Law) enables pledges to be created over intangible personal property, which largely corresponds to choses in action in Hong Kong. Thus company shares, bills of exchange, promissory notes, warehouse receipts, bills of lading, intellectual property rights and the right to collect receivables in China can be pledged.[215]

Taking a pledge over intangible personal property is similar to that over tangible property which has been discussed in Chapter 2, because Article 229 of the Property Law expressly provides that the pledge of rights is governed not only by current provisions of §2 (Pledge of Rights) but also by the provisions of §1 (Pledge of Movable Property) which were discussed in Chapter 2. The parties should conclude a pledge contract, specifying such particulars as the category and amount of the principal creditor's rights to be guaranteed, the time limit for the debtor to pay the debt and the scope of the guarantee.[216] In fact, except for provisions especially designed to apply to pledges over intangible property, the provisions

[214] See Chapter 1 above.

[215] The right to collect receivables is newly added as pledgeable intangible property in the Property Law. See Article 233(6) of the Property Law.

[216] Ibid., Article 210.

governing pledges over tangible personal property apply to pledges over intangible property.[217]

To create an effective pledge, two conditions have to be satisfied. Firstly, the document must evidence the pledgor's right to the intangible property. Secondly, the documents are generally required to be delivered to the pledgee. In case of intangible property such as bills of exchange, cheques, promissory notes, bonds, certificates of deposit, warehouse receipts and bills of lading where the documents of title are evident, the pledge contracts become effective (i.e. the rights of pledge between the parties are created) on the date of the delivery of the document of title to the pledgee.[218] However, for portions of funds, shares, intellectual property rights (trademarks, patents, copyrights) and rights to collect receivables where documents of title are generally not evident, the pledge contract becomes effective upon registration with the relevant public authorities.[219] For example, the pledge of the right to collect receivables must be registered with the credit information system (a national information system established by the People's Bank) in order to give effect to the pledge contracts created.[220] The Property Law now further provides that once these pledges are registered, they cannot be transferred or used by another unless otherwise agreed between the pledgor and the pledgee. The proceeds the pledgor obtains from a consensual transfer of these registered pledges shall be used to pay in advance the pledgee's claims secured or deposited.[221]

In China, it is not clear whether pledges can be created over future or after-acquired intangible property. It is generally thought that since the nature and extent of future property has not been determined, the pledge cannot be created over such property.[222] Some scholars consider that anticipatory rights such as creditor's rights attached with conditions or time limits are of economic value, and that therefore such future property can be pledged.[223]

According to Article 223 of the Property Law the type of intangible personal property which may be pledged includes:

(1) bills of exchange, cheques, promissory notes;

[217] Ibid., Article 229, formerly Article 81 of the Security Law.

[218] Article 224 of the Property Law.

[219] Ibid., Articles 226, 227 and 228.

[220] Ibid., Article 228.

[221] Ibid., Articles 226, 227 and 228.

[222] Kaizhong Hu, *Studies on Pledge over Rights* (Beijing: Chinese University of Politics and Law Press, 2004), p. 152.

[223] Yi Wang, 'Study on Anticipatory Rights', *Legal Science* 4 (1996).

(2) bonds, certificates of deposit;
(3) warehouse receipts, bills of lading;
(4) portions of funds, shares that are transferable according to law;
(5) trademarks, patents and copyrights among property rights that are transferable according to law;
(6) the right to collect receivables; and
(7) other rights that may be pledged according to laws and administrative regulations.

The right to collect receivables has now been added in the Property Law as a type of intangible property which can be pledged, which extends the class of intangible property mentioned in the old Article 75 of the Security Law. The meaning of 'shares' in Article 223(4), read in conjunction with Article 75, should include 'shares and share certificates'.

It is unclear what 'other rights' in subparagraph (7) means. Some believe that 'other rights', if not clearly specified by other legal provisions, can be pledged. The contrary view holds that any rights can be pledged so long as the rights are capable of transfer. The compromise proposal is that only those rights evidenced by documents or regulated by certain institutions can be pledged.[224]

It is submitted that the rules governing the creation of the pledge over intangible personal property in China have satisfied four of the seven creation criteria established in Chapter 1.[225] The three criteria which have not been satisfied are that the security must be capable of attaching after-acquired or future property, that the debtor has possession of the asset and that the debtor has the freedom to deal with the asset in the ordinary course of its business.

Perfection of pledges

There is a separate mechanism for the registration process of perfecting pledges in China. For example, for the pledge of fund units or shares, the parties concerned shall conclude a written contract. For fund units or shares registered in the securities depository and clearing institution, the right of pledge is only established after the securities depository and clearing institution has registered the pledge. As for the pledge of other shares, the right of pledge shall be established after the local office of the SAIC has

[224] Shibing Cao, *The Solutions and Prospects on Some Chinese Security Law Issues* (Beijing: China Fazhi Press, 2001), p. 298.

[225] See Chapter 1 above.

registered the pledge.[226] Intellectual property rights such as trademarks, patents or copyrights are perfected upon registration with their corresponding administrative agencies.[227] The right to collect receivables is perfected by registration with the 'credit information system' (a national information system established by the People's Bank). A valid pledge has priority over other subsequent encumbrances because it immediately, when it is created, confers upon the pledgee a superior security interest. This has been discussed in Chapter 2.

Publicity of pledges

There is no statutory requirement for publicity of a pledge over intangible property. The pledgee's possession of the document with proof of title constitutes sufficient publicity that the intangible property is encumbered. In case of intellectual property rights (Article 227), rights to collect receivables (Article 228), portions of funds, shares and share certificates (Article 226), registration with the relevant public agency is required to render the pledge effective and this constitutes sufficient publicity. Another issue relates to whether 'publicity' by way of the registration of the said pledge imposes a physical restraint on the pledgee's ability to deal with the property. By reading Articles 226, 227 and 228 in a contextual manner, it is likely that a statutory restriction is immediately imposed to prevent the pledgor from transferring the registered pledge rights unless the pledgee agrees. However, where consent has been obtained from the pledgee, the pledgor is obliged to repay the pledgee's claims obtained from the proceeds of the transfer.

In this regard it is submitted that the four publicity criteria established earlier in Chapter 1 are satisfied.[228]

Cost of creation, perfection and publicity of pledges

In Chapter 2, it was noted that the cost of creating, perfecting and publicising pledges is minimal.

Thus the minimal cost of creation, perfection and publicity of the pledge has satisfied the general low-cost criterion established in Chapter 1 on these aspects.[229]

[226] Article 226 of the Property Law. In China the shares of the joint-stock limited companies (similar to public companies in Hong Kong) are required to be registered at securities depository and clearing institutions. Here the 'other shares' refer to the shares of limited liability companies (similar to private companies in Hong Kong).

[227] Article 227 of the Property Law, similar to Articles 79, and 80 of the Security Law.

[228] See Chapter 1 above. [229] See Chapter 1 above.

3.4.2 Diya Mortgages

Creation of Diya mortgages over intangible property

The Property Law 2007 does not explicit recognise mortgages over intangible property. The scope of property that can be mortgaged is limited to tangible property (movable or real). The 'other property' in Article 180(7), as discussed in Chapter 2, does not include any form of intangible property. On the other hand, 'floating charges' may be permissible (as discussed in Chapter 2) in respect of tangible movables.[230]

3.5 Conclusion

3.5.1 Changes to reflect the position in Hong Kong and China

When the above compartmentalised discussion is combined, the overall picture that emerges is that the rules governing the creation, perfection and publicity of security over intangible personal property in Hong Kong cannot satisfy all the criteria established in Chapter 1.[231] The only criterion which the rules have consistently satisfied is cost. Generally there is no cost, but where there is cost involved, such as registration of the security with the relevant authority, the cost is minimal. The same picture also appears to be true in relation to China. Again, the rules of creation, perfection and publicity have satisfied only one criterion – cost, which is minimal. The discussion following summarises the causes of the strengths and weaknesses of the two jurisdictions in relation to the criteria of creation, perfection and publicity.

With regard to creation, the rules governing the creation of security devices in Hong Kong are complex, and often difficult. This stems from two causes.

The first is the multiplicity of security devices, namely pledge, legal mortgage, equitable mortgage and charge. Each of these is attended by its own peculiar rules. Whether a particular security should be used is in turn determined by two principles, namely the characteristics of the property and the jurisprudential classification of the property, legal or equitable. These principles are not always consistent. For instance, a pledge cannot be created over intangible property, but it can if the intangible property

[230] Article 181 of the Property Law. [231] See Chapter 1 above.

is represented by a negotiable instrument.[232] A legal mortgage cannot be created over equitable intangible property, but an equitable mortgage has no such restriction.[233] For an ordinary creditor who is unfamiliar with the nature of each security device, the task of selecting the appropriate device can be tortuous and baffling. Yet if a creditor selects the wrong security device, as shown in *Keller v Ying Wah Tak Holdings Ltd and Another*,[234] it may lose its security.

The second cause is, as mentioned above, the division of intangible personal property into legal property and equitable property. Each of these two types of property has its own peculiar sets of rules of creation and perfection of different types of security that fall within its domain. Logically, their historical uniqueness should not be permitted to hamper the full realisation of the creditors' and debtors' intentions. However, in practice the courts are locked in a debate as to whether the common law rules, including statute, should prevail over equity or vice versa. This debate is particularly heated in the assignment of legal and equitable mortgages of choses in action. In contrast, the rules on creation in China are generally simple, because China operates only one simple form of security device – the pledge. The rules are also simple and comprehensible. However, there are enforcement weaknesses in the pledge.[235]

With regard to perfection, the rules governing perfection of security over intangible personal property in Hong Kong are complex and difficult. The problem is traced to the same cause as in creation, namely a multiplicity of security devices and the underlying legal rules. Some of the rules relating to notice in legal and equitable assignments lack certainty. There are, however, some strengths in the system of Hong Kong security over intangible personal property. These are to be found in security over shares in companies. The equitable mortgage is a flexible, inexpensive and expeditious security device, as illustrated in the case of equitable security over shares in companies.

In contrast, China's rules on perfection are simple and straightforward. Once again this is due to its strict insistence on one form of security device, namely the pledge.

[232] It is possible to transfer a bill of exchange or other negotiable instrument at common law simply by delivering the instrument to the transferee and, if necessary, endorsing it. Similarly, bearer securities are transferable by delivery.

[233] The general rule is that common law does not recognise the transfer of most other types of intangible property; security over them is generally taken either by means of an equitable mortgage or charge or by means of a statutory form of security under §136 of the Law of Property Act 1925.

[234] [1997] 3 HKC 301.

[235] This is appropriately discussed in Chapter 7.

Another problem in Hong Kong is the conflict between specialist registers, namely the Patents Register, the Trade Marks Register and the Companies Register. A charge that is valid under the first two registers may be rendered invalid for default in registration in the last. In order to avoid this conflict, the English Law Commission recommended that registration with the specialist register is sufficient. For example, if a fixed charge over registered land is registered in the Land Registry, it will not need to be registered in the proposed notice-filing Computer Security Register.[236] A new proposal subsequently suggested forwarding the information from the Land Registry to the Computer Security Register to enable searches to be conducted. Furthermore, in relation to resolving priority conflicts arising from dual registration, the draft of the Company Security Regulations 2006 by the English Law Commission clarified the position and that the priority rules set out in the specialist legislation in relevant registers will apply.[237]

With regard to publicity of security over intangible personal property in Hong Kong, the weakness in this aspect is primarily due to the legal framework and to a lack of policy commitment to promote an effective publicity mechanism. There is either no publicity at all under general law or statute, or, if there is, publicity is restrictive[238] or heavily reliant on the actors' initiative in the security arrangement,[239] or there is duplicity.[240] The rules of publicity are therefore complex and technical. In view of this, the English Law Commission has provided some recommendations as to the centralisation of publicity of some types of intangible property. Consultation Paper No 164 recommended that all security over receivables be registrable under a proposed notice-filing system.[241] The recent Law Commission Report No 296 provided more detailed rules of publicity prior to and following the commencement of the proposed notice-filing

[236] The case is not the same as floating charges over registered land or charges over unregistered land where they are recommended to register on the Company Security Register whether or not they are registered on the Land Charges Register. See English Law Commission Report No 296, paras. 3.33–3.38.

[237] English Law Commission Report No 296, p. 12, and the draft Company Security Regulations 2006 proposed by the same report at p. 160, currently pending implementation. See also below, Chapter 8.

[238] For example, the registration system of the Companies Ordinance is restricted to company security providers.

[239] For example, notice on the debtor of *Dearle v Hall* (1828) 3 Russ 21, 38 ER 475.

[240] For example, fixed charges over book debts have to be registered with the Companies Registry and also comply with the notice rule in *Dearle v Hall* (1828) 3 Russ 21, 38 ER 475.

[241] English Law Commission Consultation Paper No 164, para. 7.35. The impact of such registration is discussed below in Chapter 6.

system. For example, charges over receivables (whether fixed or floating) which were not registrable prior to the new scheme should not have to be registered after the new scheme comes into effect. Pre-commencement registerable charges over receivables should be treated as registered under the new scheme.[242]

In contrast, in China, a pledge is effectively publicised by the pledgee's possession of the documents of title and so is effective in practice.

On the basis of the above findings, this chapter concludes that the credit security legal frameworks of Hong Kong and China governing the creation, perfection and publicity of security over intangible personal property are inefficient.

[242] English Law Commission Report No 296, paras. 3.285–3.290.

Chapter 4

Company security over personal property

4.1 Introduction

The processes of creating, perfecting and publicising company securities in Hong Kong and China differ significantly. In Hong Kong, general law and/or the Companies Ordinance govern these three processes. In China, two statutes, namely the Property Law (2007) and the Security Law (1995), supplemented by the Judicial Interpretation of the Security Law (2000) and various administrative regulations, regulate the creation, perfection and publicity of companies granting security over their assets.

In theory, companies in Hong Kong may grant their creditor a mortgage or a charge over personal property in the same way as individuals. However, in practice, it is common for company debtors to execute a special document known as a 'debenture'.[1] The expression 'debenture' is commonly used in two situations, namely when the company raises debt capital from the public (in the case of a public company) or privately from financial institutions. Discussion here is strictly confined to the latter situation.

Chitty J described a debenture as 'a document which either creates a debt or acknowledges it, and any document which fulfils either of these conditions is a debenture'.[2] Section 2(1) of the Companies Ordinance

[1] For historical development of debentures since the 1860s in England see R.R. Pennington, *Company Law*, 5th ed. (London: Butterworths, 1985), p. 475; *Palmer's Company Law*, 19th ed. (London: Stevens & Sons Ltd, 1949), p. 272. In Hong Kong the statutory balance-sheet form of Table A of the First Schedule of the first locally enacted Companies Ordinance (No 1 of 1865) specifically mentioned the term 'debenture bonds' but no definition was given in that Ordinance.

[2] *Levy v Abercorris Slate & Slab Co.* (1887), 37 Ch D 260, 264. See the earlier case of *British India Steam Navigation Co. v IRC* (1881) 7 QBD 165, at 169, *per* Grove J, and *Knightsbridge Estates Trust Ltd v Byrne* [1940] AC 613, at 622, *per* Viscount Maugham, where the same observation was made. Note that Chitty J's description has since been generally accepted as the meaning of the term 'debenture'; see *Gower's Principles of Modern Company Law*, 4th ed. (London: Stevens & Sons Ltd, 1979), p. 401, and also *Charlesworth's Company Law*, 13th ed. (London: Stevens & Sons Ltd, 1987), p. 611.

(Cap. 32) gives the term a much broader meaning. It provides that 'debenture' includes debenture stock, bonds and any other securities of a company, whether constituting a charge on the assets of the company or not. However, today, whether a document is a debenture rarely poses any serious 'juristic debate' in theory or in practice.[3]

In this book, the word 'debenture' strictly means a loan document issued by a company which creates securities described as fixed or floating charges.[4] There are a large number of such securities in Hong Kong. Between the years 1998 and 2002, the number of charges registered with the Companies Registry totalled 98,594.[5]

The expression 'charge' used in a debenture has a wider meaning than the traditional meaning in equity. Section 80(9) of the Companies Ordinance (Cap. 32) provides that a charge includes a mortgage.[6] As this is not an exclusionary definition, the term includes all forms of consensual security device contemplated in common law, equity or legislation,[7] including the statutory legal charge[8] and the statutory equitable mortgage[9] under the Conveyancing and Property Ordinance (Cap. 219).

[3] See Pennington, above, note 1, p. 528. Note that in Hong Kong the Standing Committee on Company Law Reform Eighth Report (1991), at p. 73, stated that it was notoriously difficult to define the term 'debenture' and decided there should not be any statutory definition of the term.

[4] Letters of request were officially sent to fifteen major solicitors' firms in Hong Kong requesting sample debentures creating fixed and floating charges. Unfortunately they were unwilling to provide them. Six samples were subsequently obtained from officers working at three banks and some solicitor friends from Baker & McKenzie, Clifford Chance, Deacons, Johnnie Yam, Jacky Lee & Co. and Linklaters, Hong Kong. A sample provided by Johnnie Yam, Jacky Lee & Co., Rm 502–5, 5th Floor, San Toi Building, 137–9 Connaught Road Central, Hong Kong, showed that only a floating charge was created.

[5] 1993: 32,657; 1994: 33,224; 1995: 29,046; 1996: 33,788; 1997: 47,705; 1998: 20,205: 1999: 20,139; 2000: 23,411; 2001: 22,579; July 2002: 12,263. Source: Hong Kong Registry – Key Statistics: www.info.gov.hk/cr/. This is in sharp contrast with the extremely low number of non-corporate securities (i.e. bills of sale) registered with the High Court Registry; see Chapter 2 above.

[6] The term 'mortgage' is given a restricted meaning in §2 of the Conveyancing and Property Ordinance (Cap. 219). It provides that a 'mortgage' means a security over land for securing money or money's worth. Although it covers both legal statutory charges and equitable mortgages and charges, the definition is restricted to real property only. In the UK, see also Part I, reg. 2 of the draft regulation 'Company Security Regulations 2006' to implement the recommendations of the UK Law Commission Report No 296.

[7] The English Law Commission Report No 296 did not appear to object to that view.

[8] A mortgage of a legal estate, including any second or subsequent mortgage of that legal estate, may be effected at law only by a charge by deed expressed to be a legal charge: §44(1), Conveyancing and Property Ordinance (Cap. 219).

[9] An equitable mortgage can be effected over an equitable interest in land: Form 3, Conveyancing and Property Ordinance (Cap. 219).

The broad definition, however, does not extend to contractual rights of a creditor to seize or apply the debtor's assets in the future to extinguish the debt upon the occurrence of a specified event,[10] such as the creditor's right of combination of accounts of the debtor with the creditor.[11]

Thus the question whether a fixed 'charge' in a debenture creates a legal mortgage *strictu sensu*, or an equitable mortgage, or an equitable charge has to be ascertained from the intention of the parties.

Further, it should be noted that the Hong Kong SAR government's Financial Services and Treasury Bureau has launched a comprehensive exercise to update and modernise the Companies Ordinance. During 2007 and 2008, several consultation exercises were undertaken to solicit views on proposed reforms to the Ordinance. The second consultation paper, issued on 2 April 2008, included consideration of changes to certain aspects of the company charge registration regime.[12] The government's conclusions were published on 10 December 2008, and incorporate current thinking on the changes to be made to the extant charge regime when the new Companies 'White' Bill is published towards the end of 2009. The current proposals will be referred to where relevant in the text.[13]

In relation to China, the expression 'debenture' has only one substantive meaning. It is a document that acknowledges a debt; but unlike the debenture in Hong Kong, it does not create any security. It is used to raise long-term finance from the public.[14] Thus, if a creditor wishes to obtain

[10] See *Cinema Plus Ltd (Adminstrators Appointed) and Another v Australia and New Zealand Banking Group Ltd* (2000) 49 NSWLR 513. The Court of Appeal of New South Wales held that the banker's contractual right to consolidate current and loan accounts was not a charge within the broad definition of a charge under §9 of the Australian Corporations Law. See also the English case of *National Provincial and Union Bank of England v Charnley* [1924] 1 KB 431, 449–450, *per* Atkin LJ: 'If, on the other hand, the parties do not intend that there should be a present right to have the security made available, but only that there should be a right in the future by agreement, such as a license, to seize the goods, there will be no charge.'

[11] For example, the banker's right of set-off or combination of accounts of the customer. See *Garnett v M'Kewan* [1872] LR 8 Ex 10.

[12] For details of the Second Consultation Paper, see www.fstb.gov.hk/fsb/co_rewrite/eng/pub-press/consult.htm.

[13] For full details of the Companies Ordinance reform exercise, see www.fstb.gov.hk/fsb/co_rewrite/eng/home/home.htm.

[14] For example, 'corporate bonds' in PRC companies refers to the securities issued by a company according to the statutory procedures with guaranteed payment of the principal plus interest by a specified future date. But the term 'securities' here does not contain any notion of security interest. It merely refers to a means of raising finance within a company. See also Article 154 of the Company Law (2006).

security from a company in China, the creditor and the company have to use the same credit security devices, namely the pledge and mortgage, and follow the same procedure to create, perfect and publicise the security devices as in the case of an individual.[15]

The 'floating charge', in the common law sense, was neither acknowledged nor defined in the Security Law (1995). As a result, the law does not recognise the floating charge as a valid security device for companies.[16] The closest analogue of the floating charge is the 'collective mortgage' available to companies under the Security Law.[17] The collective mortgage allows the company in question to create a mortgage over various assets of a company, including real property, in one single mortgage contract.[18] However, that is as far as the analogy goes. Unlike the floating charge, which can secure after-acquired and substituted movable property, the identity of the mortgaged property under a collective mortgage must be certain before a mortgage contract is concluded.[19] The concept of crystallisation, a crucial mechanism to convert the floating charge into a fixed security, is unknown to the collective mortgage.

In recognition of common law floating charges, professors Huixing Liang's and Liming Wang's drafts of a proposed Property Law of China introduced the concept of the 'floating charge' as a new type of security device for companies.[20] In academic circles, scholars had previously advocated the introduction of floating charges into the Chinese Security Law.[21] However, it was the enactment of the Property Law, which came into force in October 2007, that provided the possibility that 'floating

[15] The processes are discussed in Chapters 2 and 3 above.

[16] Guoguang Li, *Understanding and Application of the Interpretation of Some Issues in Application of the Security Law by the Supreme Court* (Jilin: Jilin People's Press, 2001), p. 196.

[17] Shibing Cao, *Solutions and Prospects on Questions Related to Chinese Security Mechanism: Based on Security Law and its Judicial Interpretations* (Beijing: China Fa Zhi Press, 2001), pp. 203–4.

[18] Article 34(1) of the Security Law and Article 50 of the Judicial Interpretations on the Security Law.

[19] Article 39 of the Security Law.

[20] See Professor Huixing Liang's draft of Article 351–7, and Professor Liming Wang's draft of Article 447–4 in the proposed version of Property Law. There were two working groups led separately by the two professors, which resulted in two drafts of the Property Law. Both drafts included the introduction to floating charges. See www.sinofile.net/saiweng/sip_blog.nsf/d6plinks/YZHI-6ZKAZJ.

[21] Liangang Chen, 'Introduction of Floating Charge into Chinese Law', *People's Justice* 3 (1999), 28–9; Benhan Chen, 'Collective Mortgage, Floating Charge and Perfection of Enterprise Security in China', *Modern Law Review* 4 (1998), 53–6.

charges' may now be created, although the term 'floating charge' is not used. This issue was discussed in Chapter 2 in relation to Articles 181 and 189 of the Property Law.

In Hong Kong and China, company credit securities, which are within the scope of the Companies Ordinance and the Property Law respectively, must be registered with the relevant authority.[22] The Ordinance and the Property Law generally invalidate all unregistered, but registrable, securities against other creditors of the company. This converts registration into a principle of perfection.[23]

The objectives of this chapter are to determine the following:

- whether or not the rules governing the creation, perfection and publicity of company credit security over personal property, both tangible and intangible, in Hong Kong and China have satisfied the criteria established in Chapter 1 in respect of these functional mechanisms;[24] and
- whether or not the cost of creation, perfection and publicity of company credit security is inexpensive.

4.2 Creation, perfection and publicity of company security in Hong Kong, and cost

4.2.1 Creation of company security

Creation of fixed and floating charges

Examination of debentures in Hong Kong has shown three common characteristics, namely that secured debentures are usually granted to commercial bank creditors, that there is usually a panel of solicitors nominated by the creditor banks to prepare the debenture, and that the provisions of debentures purporting to create fixed charges and floating charges are almost identical.[25]

22 For example, §80(2) of the Company Ordinance; Articles 188 and 189 of the Property Law. See also below in this chapter.

23 See the United Kingdom Department of Trade and Industry consultation paper, Modern Company Law – For a Competitive Economy: Registration of Company Charges, URN 00/1213 (October 2000), para. 3.5, p. 14: 'Registration is, in principle, merely a perfection requirement.'

24 See Chapter 1 above.

25 Based on the debentures provided by the solicitors' firms of Baker & McKenzie, Clifford Chance, Deacons, Johnnie Yam, Jacky Lee & Co. and Linklaters, Hong Kong.

In relation to a fixed charge over intangible personal property, such as book debts, the charge clause usually takes the following form (hereafter referred to as sample A):

> The Borrower as beneficial owner and as continuing security … hereby charges (and agrees to charge) to and in favour of the Lender by way of a **first fixed charge** all the book and other debts of, and sums of money owing to, the Borrower whatsoever both present and future, actual or contingent.

In relation to tangible personal property the expression usually takes the following form (hereafter referred to as sample B):

> The Borrower hereby charges by way of a **first fixed charge** over the machines, implements and chattels of the Borrower specified in the Second Schedule hereto.

Sometimes the words 'fixed charge' are not used. For example, the expression may take the following form (hereafter referred to as sample C):

> The Borrower hereby charges by way of a **first specific charge** all those movable property or properties specified in the Schedule hereto.

In contrast to fixed charges, the expression in respect of floating charges usually takes the following form (hereafter referred to as sample D):

> The Borrower hereby charges to and in favour of the Lender by way of **first floating charge** all the undertaking, stock, goodwill and all other property, assets and rights (both tangible and intangible) whatsoever both present and future of the Borrower, including its uncalled capital.

A more elaborate and extensive expression may take the following form (hereafter referred to as sample E):

> The Borrower hereby charges by way of a **first floating charge** all its undertaking, property, assets, goodwill, right and revenues whatsoever, both present and future, including all book and other debts now and from time to time due or owing to the Lender, the uncalled capital, goodwill and all patents, patent applications, trademarks, trade names, registered designs, copyrights, licences and ancillary and connected rights both present and future.

The intangible personal property mentioned in the sample E form of floating charge reflects the nature of the business of the debtor. It is likely to be involved in the creation of intellectual property. However, the sample D form of floating charge, though more general in expression, would be sufficient to cover the intangible personal property mentioned in the second form. Its use of more general forms of expression is not in anyway inferior to the second, for it is established that a subsequent floating charge does not obtain priority over an earlier general floating charge simply because the former specifically describes the debtor's assets.[26]

Do the above expressions effectively create fixed and floating charges?

Examination of English and other common law jurisdiction cases since the early twentieth century has shown that the approach taken by the courts in determining whether a charge created is fixed or floating is complex and confusing. In order to maintain a coherent examination of these cases, the discussion is divided into the following subheadings:

- the pre-*Re New Bullas Trading Ltd*[27] stage,
- the *Re New Bullas Trading Ltd* stage and
- the *Agnew and v Commissioner of Inland Revenue and Another*[28] and *Re Spectrum Plus Ltd*[29] stage (hereafter the *Agnew/Spectrum* stage).

The pre-*Re New Bullas Trading Ltd* stage Until *Re New Bullas Trading Ltd* it was a well-settled rule that whether a charge was fixed or floating was a matter of substance, not merely a matter of the drafting terminology used in the debenture. The label the parties placed on the security did not bind the court.[30] Thus in *Evans v Rival Granite Quarries Ltd*,[31] Fletcher Moulton LJ explained that whether a charge was fixed or floating 'did not depend upon the special language used in the particular document, but upon the essence and nature of a security'. In *Re Keenan Bros Ltd*,[32] McCarthy J said that one must not look at the narrow confines of the terminology or the declared intentions of the parties alone, but to the full effect of the instruments purporting to create the security. This approach is referred to as the 'basic substantive rule' of interpretation of the debenture. Thus the fact that the parties use

[26] *Benjamin Cope & Sons Limited* [1914] 1 Ch 800, 807, *per* Sargant J; and also *Re Automatic Bottle Makers Ltd* [1926] All ER 619. In the latter case the second floating charge had priority over the first floating charge not because the floating charge was created over specific property, namely commercial documents, but because the first floating charge expressly reserved power to the chargor to create subsequent floating charges that have priority over the first floating charge.

[27] [1994] BCLC 36. [28] [2001] 2 BCLC 188. [29] [2005] 2 AC 680.

[30] For example, see *Tailby v Official Receiver* (1888) 13 AC 523: a mortgage described to be by way of assignment was held to be a floating charge; and *Re Yorkshire Woolcomber's Association* [1903] 2 Ch 284: a floating charge was held to have been created though it was called a specific security.

[31] [1910] 2 KB 979. [32] [1986] BCLC 242, 247.

the words 'fixed charge' or 'floating charge', as illustrated by the expressions discussed above, was not conclusive as to the legal effect of those provisions.

Examination of Hong Kong's official law reports since 1915[33] shows that the courts in Hong Kong were not required to analyse the meaning and effect of the basic substantive rule in depth in the local context. But this does not mean that the rule was not applicable. The lack of discussion is likely to be a result of the fact that the cases that have come before the courts are straightforward on the facts.[34]

In contrast, there is a wealth of case law on the subject in the other common law jurisdictions, particularly in England. The authorities, however, show that the law has been in a state of flux. Despite this, three mechanisms appear to underpin the operation of the basic substantive rule. They are:

- Romer LJ's three characteristics of a floating charge (hereafter the three characteristics of a floating charge),
- the intrinsic rule of interpretation[35] of the document purporting to create the charge (hereafter the intrinsic rule of interpretation) and
- the combined intrinsic rule of interpretation and extrinsic rule of interpretation (hereafter the extrinsic rule of interpretation).[36]

[33] This was the date when official law reporting in the form of the Hong Kong Law Report began. Note that the authors also looked at unreported decisions kept at the High Court Library since 1965. The same picture appeared.

[34] Should the occasion arise, it is more likely than not that the basic substantive rule and the underlying English cases are seriously considered. This proposition is not unreasonable in view of the consistency in a number of Hong Kong company credit security law cases where the courts adopted *dicta* in English cases: for example, see *Hong Kong and Shanghai Banking Corporation v Star Trans International Ltd* [1998] 2 HKLR 549, where the Court of Appeal adopted the definition of a floating charge in *Re Yorkshire Woolcombers Association Ltd* [1903] 2 Ch 284; and also *ABN Amro Bank NV v Chiyu Banking Corp Ltd and Others* [2000] 3 HKC 381, where the Court of First Instance applied extensively the English rule that registration of a floating charge is not constructive notice of the contents of a floating charge. Note also the Basic Law, Article 84, which provides: 'The courts of the Hong Kong Special Administrative Region shall adjudicate cases in accordance with the laws applicable in the Region as prescribed in Article 18 of this Law and may refer to precedents of other common law jurisdictions.'

[35] This can be found in the decision of Staughton LJ in *Welsh Development Agency v Export Finance Co. Ltd* [1992] BCLC 148, 185–6. He used the expressions 'internal' and 'external' routes.

[36] In *Welsh Development* Staughton LJ discussed the two concepts as mutually exclusive. But in this book in many cases they are not. Both have to be considered to ascertain the true nature of the transaction.

The three characteristics of a floating charge can be traced to the seminal 1903 English case of *Re Yorkshire Woolcombers Association Ltd.*[37] There Romer LJ described a floating charge as follows:[38]

(1) it is a charge on a class of assets of a company, present and future;
(2) that class is one which, in the ordinary course of the business of the company, would be changing from time to time; and
(3) it is contemplated by the parties that, until some future step is taken by or on behalf of the chargee, the company may carry on its business in the usual way as far as it concerns the particular class of assets the company is dealing with.[39]

Until 1979, these three characteristics were treated like a judicial mantra; each of them was generally given the same weight by the courts. If a charge could not satisfy any one of them, the charge was usually regarded as a fixed charge.[40] This was the situation in Hong Kong, where the courts were not required to microscopically consider the elements of each of the three characteristics, but accepted and applied them with little difficulty.

[37] [1903] 2 Ch 284, applied in the recent case of *Re Cosslett (Contractors) Ltd* [1997] 4 All ER 115, CA, affirmed on appeal; see *Smith (Administrator of Cosslett (Contractors) Ltd) v Bridgend County Borough Council* [2002] 1 All ER 292, HL. Note that the landmark case of *Re Panama, New Zealand and Australian Royal Mail Co.* (1870) 5 Ch App 318, only gave an idea of what a floating charge was, there was no precise definition of a floating charge. Attempts to give it some juridical characteristics began only in the late nineteenth century and took some defined form only in the first decade of the twentieth century. See J.H. Farrar, 'Floating Charges and Priorities', *Con* 38 (1974), 315; J.H. Farrar and B.M. Hannigan, *Farrar's Company Law*, 4th ed. (London: Butterworths, 1998), p. 632. It began with the cases of *Government Stock and Other Securities Investment Co. Ltd v Manila Rly Co. Ltd* [1897] AC 81; *Re Yorkshire Woolcombers Association Ltd* [1903] 2 Ch 284; *Illingworth v Holdsworth* [1904] AC 355; and *Evans v Rival Granite Quarries Ltd* [1910] 2 QB 979. Subsequent attempts to define it have not been satisfactory.

[38] It was commented that Romer LJ was not attempting to give the floating charge a substantive definition, but merely laying down an evidentiary rule. See K.J. Naser, 'The Juridical Basis of the Floating Charge', *Co. Lawyer* 15 (1994), 11 at pp. 15–16. But for all practical purposes the courts have elevated it to a substantive definition. This practice is adopted in this book as a reality.

[39] When the case went up to the House of Lords and took the name of *Illingworth v Holdsworth* [1904] AC 355, Lord Macnaghten gave it a more elusive definition. He said that a floating charge was a charge which was 'ambulatory and shifting in nature, hovering and floating with the property which it was intended to affect until some event causes it to settle and fasten on the subject within its reach and grasp'. Lord Macnaghten's description of the floating charge is sometimes viewed as no more than an elaboration of Romer LJ's third characteristics. See *Siebe Gorman v Barclays Bank* [1979] 2 Lloyd's Law Reports 142, at pp. 158–9, *per* Slade J.

[40] As Gough commented, the fixed charge was a mere 'antithesis' of the floating charge. See W.J. Gough, *Company Charges*, 2nd ed. (London: Butterworths, 1996), p. 92.

This is mainly because generally the factual matrix of the cases, as mentioned earlier, was not complicated. For example, in the Hong Kong Court of Appeal case of *Hong Kong and Shanghai Banking Corporation v Star Trans International Ltd*,[41] the court accepted the three characteristics of a floating charge with little fanfare and held that the floating chargor, Star Trans International Ltd, was entitled to deal with the secured export quota until crystallisation of the floating charge.

However, the English courts appear to agree that characteristics (1) and (2) are today, generally, no longer as important as they used to be. For instance, in the recent Privy Council case of *Agnew*, Lord Millett commented that the two characteristics were typical of a floating charge but they were not distinctive of it, since they were not necessarily inconsistent with a fixed charge. It is submitted that this is a reinforcement of an earlier court of first instance decision in the 1979 English case of *Siebe Gorman v Barclays Bank*.[42] There the court held that present and future ambulatory assets, such as book debts, could form the subject matter of a fixed charge.[43] Prior to that case, it was generally thought that book debts could not be so subject for two reasons. The first, a commercial reason, was that because book debts were part of the circulating capital of the company's business and constituted an important source of the company's cash, any fixed charge created over them would paralyse the company's business. The second, a conceptual reason, was that a charge on fluctuating assets, which came within the meaning of characteristic (2) above, had to be a floating charge.[44]

The crux of characteristic (3) is 'freedom' of the chargor to deal with the assets purportedly covered by the charge in the ordinary course of its business, or, from the perspective of the creditor, is the 'control' of the chargee over the secured assets. The 'freedom' of the chargor and the 'control' of the chargee are opposite sides of the same coin. If the chargee deprives the chargor of this freedom and vests control of the assets in the chargee, the charge is a fixed charge. In *Re Cosslett (Contractors) Ltd*,[45] Millett LJ (as he then was), at the Court of Appeal stage, categorically stated that in

[41] [1998] 2 HKLR 549. [42] [1979] 2 Lloyd's Law Reports 142.

[43] For example, until *Siebe Gorman & Co. Ltd v Barclays Bank Ltd*, it was thought that book debts, being circulatory in nature, could not form the subject matter of a fixed charge. Since that case it is now settled that they can.

[44] *Agnew v Commissioner of Inland Revenue* [2001] UKPC 28, [2001] 3 WLR. 454, 194, *per* Lord Millett.

[45] [1998] Ch 495, p. 510.

contradistinction with the floating charge, the essence of a fixed charge is that the charge is on a particular asset or class of assets which the chargor cannot deal with freely without the consent of the chargee.[46] The details of *Cosslett* will be discussed below.

Today, characteristic (3) appears, on the basis of English and other common law jurisdiction authorities, to be given more weight,[47] especially in charges affecting intangible personal property, such as book debts. In the following discussion, characteristic (3) is referred to as the 'control' criterion.

In practice it is often difficult to ascertain whether or not the control criterion is satisfied.[48] Examination of the authorities in Hong Kong, England and other common law jurisdictions has shown that the courts, in their endeavours, begin with an exposition of Romer LJ's three characteristics of the floating charge, followed by an application of one of the remaining mechanisms of interpretation, the intrinsic rule or a combined intrinsic and extrinsic rule of interpretation.

The two rules of interpretation have a common aim, which is to determine whether the charge satisfies the control criterion. The operation of these rules will now be discussed.

Intrinsic rule of interpretation According to the intrinsic rule of interpretation the court has to strictly consider the whole text of the document creating the charge.[49] Every recital and every relevant term has to be read together to determine whether the creditor has control. If, on a proper construction of the document as a whole, the chargee has no control over the assets covered by the charge, the charge is a floating charge,

[46] On appeal, the House of Lords affirmed Millet LJ's proposition. See *Smith (Administrator of Cosslett (Contractors) Ltd) v Bridgend County Borough Council* [2002] 1 ALL ER 292, 306, *per* Lord Scott.

[47] See also ibid., p. 302. Lord Hoffmann applied both criteria (2) and (3), as he said, 'the property was a fluctuating body of assets which could be consumed or removed from the site in the ordinary course of the contractor's business, it was a floating charge'. There it was tangible personal property in issue.

[48] The difficulty is discussed in a number of articles, such as R.A. Pearce, 'Fixed Charges over Book Debt', *JBL* (1987), 18–29; R.M. Goode, 'Charges over Book Debts: A Missed Opportunity', *LQR* 110 (1994) 592; A. Berg, 'Charges over Book Debts: A Reply', *JBL* (1995) 443; and S. Worthington, 'Fixed Charges over Book Debts and Other Receivables', *LQR* 113 (1997), 562.

[49] *Re Yorkshire Woolcombers Association Ltd* [1903] 2 Ch 284, at 207, *per* Cozens-Hardy LJ, *Evans v Rival Granite Quarries Ltd* [1910] 2 KB 979, at 993, *per* Fletcher Moulton LJ, and *Stave Falls Lumber Co. v Westminster Trust Co.* (1940) 4 DLR 382, at pp. 385–6, *per* O'Halloran JA.

notwithstanding that the parties may have labelled the charge 'fixed' or 'specific'.[50]

The application of the intrinsic rule of interpretation can be discerned in a number of prominent English cases, namely *Re Yorkshire Woolcombers Association Ltd*, *Siebe Gorman v Barclays Bank*,[51] *Re Bond Worth Ltd*,[52] *Re Armagh Shoes Ltd*,[53] *Re Brightlife Ltd*[54] and *Re Keenan Bros Ltd*.[55] To understand how this mechanism operates, it is necessary to explain the essential facts of some of the cases.

In *Re Yorkshire Woolcombers Association Ltd*, the debenture purportedly created a fixed charge over the chargor's book debts. The Court of Appeal held that a floating charge was in fact created, because under the debenture the chargor had the freedom to receive the book debts into its own account and deal with the proceeds without any reference to the chargee. Vaughan LJ explained that the chargee had control only if the chargor could not at its will render the secured assets no longer a security, such that the chargor could dispose of it.[56] The fact that something else may be substituted more or less for it would not constitute control by the chargee.

In *Siebe Gorman*, the company gave the bank a debenture which expressly provided that the company charged to the bank by way of a 'first fixed' charge all its book debts and other debts then and from time to time due or owing to the company. The words and their effect were essentially the same as sample A of Hong Kong's fixed charge above. The debenture further provided the following: (a) the company was prohibited from disposing of the uncollected book debts; (b) the company was free to collect the book debts, but it had to pay all moneys received in respect of such debts into the company's account with the bank; and (c) the company could not thereafter assign or charge to any other person the book debts without the written consent of the bank (i.e. clause 5(c) of the debenture).

Among the debts charged by the debenture were some bills of exchange held by the bank. The bills of exchange were later assigned outright by the company to the plaintiff to discharge the company's indebtedness to them. The bank collected the bills and refused to pay the proceeds to the plaintiff.

[50] *Re Armagh Shoes Ltd* [1984] BCLC 405, *per* Hutton J; *Re Keenan Bros Ltd* [1986] BCLC 242, at 247, *per* McCarthy J; *Re Lin Securities (Pte) Ltd* [1988] 2 MLJ 137,142, *per* Chao Hick Tin J; and also *Re Brightlife Ltd* [1986] 3 All ER 673.

[51] [1979] 2 Lloyd's Law Reports 142. [52] [1980] 1 Ch 228. [53] [1984] BCLC 405.

[54] [1986] 3 All ER 673. [55] [1986] BCLC 242, particularly McCarthy J.

[56] [1903] 2 Ch D 284, 295.

One of the issues raised was whether the charge was a fixed charge or a floating charge. If it was a floating charge the bank had to pay the proceeds to the plaintiff but not otherwise. Slade J was not prepared to treat the charge as a fixed charge simply on the basis of the words 'fixed charge' in the debenture. He held that the charge was, on a proper interpretation of the debenture, a fixed charge. He arrived at his conclusion by the following means. Firstly, he observed that the charge on the book debts satisfied the first two characteristics set out by Romer LJ.[57] Secondly, it also satisfied the third characteristic, as clause 5(c) of the debenture required the chargor to collect and pay the proceeds into a designated account. This, he said, deprived the chargor of the freedom to deal with the book debts.

Although Slade J was correct in principle, his second reason was flawed, because the terms of the debenture did not in effect prohibit the chargor from drawing on the account. The flaw was noted in *Agnew*.[58] How Slade J arrived at the conclusion that there was control over the book debts by the bank remains a mystery.

The principle in *Siebe Gorman* was followed in the Irish case of *Re Keenan Bros Ltd*,[59] a case stronger on its facts. The company granted its bank 'fixed charges' over its present and future book debts. The terms of the debenture prohibited the company from disposing of the book debts or creating other charges over them without the consent of the bank. It allowed the company to collect the book debts, but required the company to pay the proceeds into a designated account with the bank. In contrast to *Siebe Gorman*, the terms of the debenture expressly provided that the company could not make any withdrawals from the account without the written consent of the bank. The court held that a fixed charge was created; the bank had absolute control over the proceeds. The dicta of McCarthy J and Henchy J emphasised the importance of control and the intrinsic evidence approach.[60]

The next case is *Re Bond Worth Ltd*, which, although not exactly a case of an express charge, brought home the importance of the intrinsic rule of interpretation. The case concerned a retention-of-title clause in a document concerning the supply of synthetic fibre. The pertinent terms of the document provided that (a) equitable and beneficial ownership was to remain with the seller until full payment had been received or until prior resale, in which case the seller's beneficial entitlement would attach to the

[57] Note 51 above, particularly at p. 158. [58] [2001] 188, 196, *per* Millett LJ.
[59] [1986] BCLC 242. [60] Ibid., p. 247.

proceeds; (b) should the goods become constituents of or be converted into other products while subject to the seller's equitable and beneficial ownership, the seller would have the equitable and beneficial ownership in such other products as if they were solely and simply the goods. Slade J held that the clauses clearly created a floating charge, because term (b) gave freedom to the buyer to use the goods in the ordinary course of business, as contemplated by the terms of the document.

Re Keenan Bros Ltd was followed in the English case of *Re Brightlife Ltd*.[61] There Hoffmann J held that, although the debenture expressly described the charge over book debts as a fixed charge, it was a floating charge, because the terms of the debenture permitted Brightlife Ltd to collect its debts and pay the proceeds into its bank account. Once in the account, Brightlife Ltd could dispose of the proceeds if it decided to do so. They were therefore outside the charge.[62]

However, in *Re Armagh Shoes Ltd*,[63] the court, when applying the intrinsic rule of interpretation, gave it an unusual twist. In that case the relevant term of the debenture read as follows: 'the mortgagor hereby charges in favour of the bank by way of fixed charge all receivables debts, plant machinery, fixtures, fittings and ancillary equipment now or at any time hereafter belonging to the mortgagor'. The preferential creditors claimed, despite the words 'fixed charge', that the debenture created a floating charge. Therefore they had priority over the bank's claim in respect of assets covered by the charge. Hutton J agreed. While this may be correct, for, as mentioned earlier, the label was not crucial, the way by which the learned judge arrived at the conclusion is questionable. Firstly, His Lordship disregarded the adjective 'fixed' in the words 'fixed charge' as irrelevant.[64] Secondly, as the term referred to all plant machinery, fixtures, fittings and ancillary equipment now or at any time hereafter belonging to the mortgagor, the parties, His Lordship observed, contemplated that the assets were constantly changing. This, he said, satisfied the second characteristic enunciated by Romer J. Thirdly, there was nothing in the document which prohibited the debtor from dealing with the assets freely.

The third ground is perhaps the only one that justifies the decision of Hutton J. The first and the second grounds are clearly untenable. In relation to the first, it appears he had acted beyond the basic principle that the courts do not bargain for the parties. By omitting the word 'fixed' His Lordship was rewriting the document in order to fit it into a preconceived

[61] [1986] 3 All ER 673. [62] Ibid., at p. 677. [63] Above, note 53. [64] Ibid., p. 408.

conclusion. Indeed, the approach contradicts the intrinsic rule of interpretation, which requires the court to consider each and every term as it is. Further, Hutton J's disregard of the declaratory words (i.e. 'fixed charge') breached a fundamental rule of construction. According to Chitty, save in very exceptional circumstances, a word or phrase in a document should not be rejected in order to bring it into line with what the court may think the parties really intended or ought to have intended.[65] In relation to the second reason, it was inconsistent with *Siebe Gorman*, where Slade J thought the constant changing nature of the property was not crucial.

Combination of intrinsic and extrinsic rules of interpretation This method does not directly determine whether or not the chargee has control, but gives an implication of the true meaning.

Examination of authorities shows that this mechanism is resorted to when the intrinsic rule of interpretation is unable to clearly identify whether the charge is fixed or floating. Extrinsic evidence, which the court may consider, includes the commercial purpose, the nature of the chargee's business, the chargor's business, and the factual background against which the security was given.[66] This approach can be discerned from Cozens-Hardy LJ's dictum in *Re Yorkshire Woolcombers Association Ltd*, where he stated:[67]

> In construing this deed, we are of course entitled and bound, to a certain extent, to look at the surrounding circumstances. The mortgagor – the association – is a company carrying on a very large business, and having a large number of book debts and stock-in-trade, and having bankers with whom there was an overdrawn account ...
>
> Now under these circumstances it seems to me impossible to doubt that it was in contemplation, and it was the intention of the parties, that the association were to have the right to receive the book debts and to deal with them for the purposes of the business, unless and until the mortgagees thought fit to intervene.

The extrinsic rule of interpretation supplements the intrinsic rule. In that case, the extrinsic facts pointed to a floating charge, as Cozens-Hardy LJ observed that if a fixed charge were created, the chargor's business would be paralysed.

The combined approach was applied in the Singapore case of *Re Lin Securities (Pte) Ltd*,[68] where the court followed the dictum of

[65] *Chitty on Contracts – General Principles*, 26th ed. (London: Sweet & Maxwell, 1989), vol. I, paras. 827–35.

[66] Ibid., at paras. 809 and 867. [67] [1903] 2 Ch 284, at pp. 297–8. [68] [1988] 2 MLJ 137.

Cozens-Hardy LJ. There a share-dealing company executed letters of hypothecation of shares in favour of several banks. One of the main questions which required the court's consideration was whether the letters of hypothecation, which did not mention the words 'fixed' or 'floating', created a floating charge or a fixed charge. Some of the terms of the letters of hypothecation pointed to a fixed charge, namely the expression 'pledge upon the said securities', 'the company must furnish daily certificates at the end of each day and hold them upon trust for the banks', and 'the banks may inspect the share certificates at the company's premises and take possession of them'. However, the other terms pointed to a floating charge, such as the company's ability to sell any of the shares in the ordinary course of its business. Further, there was no identification of the shares covered by the security. Chao Hick Tin JC decided that the letters of hypothecation created a floating charge. In coming to that conclusion he said,[69]

> It seems that one should not determine the effect of the LOH [letters of hypothecation] wholly within the four corners of the document. It must be viewed in the context of the surrounding circumstances of the transaction. First was of course the business of the company itself, the stockbroking business. I think this court is quite entitled to take judicial notice of what this line of business involved and how such business was transacted, that is the buying and selling of shares on behalf of clients.
>
> Secondly, at the time each LOH [letter of hypothecation] was executed, the relevant bank ... would have noticed that other banks also had similar charges over shares of the company.
>
> Thirdly, and this point is related to the second, each and every bank registered its charge or charges with the ROC [Registry of Charges]. A fixed charge does not require to be registered.
>
> The construction to be placed on the LOH must take into account these surrounding circumstances and the fact that the company was not required to identify in the daily certificate the precise share certificates that were being charged.

This approach was followed in *Re City Securities (Pte) Ltd*,[70] where the facts were identical.

It is also arguable that the combined approach had some influence on the outcome in *Re Brightlife Ltd*.[71] There the charge over the book debts was treated as a floating charge, because the chargor was a trading company. If a fixed charge were held, the chargor's business would be paralysed, because the book debts would be tied up.

[69] Ibid., p. 141. [70] [1990] 2 MLJ 257. [71] [1986] 3 All ER 673.

In *Agnew*, Millett LJ's examination of the two-stage process did not explicitly mention the combined approach. His explanation was strictly confined to the intrinsic language of the debenture. But on close analysis of his speech, there appear to be indications that extrinsic factors had some influence on the outcome. Towards the end of his speech, he commented, 'But their Lordships would wish to make clear that it is not enough to provide in the debenture that the account is a blocked account if it is not operated as one in fact.'[72]

This line of argument was reinforced by Lord Scott of Foscote in *Re Spectrum Plus Ltd*, where His Lordships opined,

> The expression 'floating charge' has never been a term of art but is an expression invented by equity lawyers and judges to describe the nature of a particular type of security arrangement between lenders and borrowers. The categorisation depends upon the commercial nature and substance of the arrangement, not upon a formalistic analysis of how the bank clearing system works.[73]

Under the intrinsic rule of interpretation and the combined rules of interpretation approaches, the court may not take into consideration the conduct of the parties subsequent to the execution of the document in order to ascertain the true nature of the security.[74] Thus, if the first or second approach showed that the charge, at the time of creation, was a fixed charge, the fact that the parties subsequently behaved as if it were a floating charge should not alter the true characteristics of the security as a fixed charge. But it has been suggested that as between the parties and a third party who has been misled by their conduct, the chargee can be estopped from denying that the chargor has the freedom to deal with the assets.[75] It is, however, submitted that this is purely an issue of estoppel by conduct; it does not alter the fundamental nature of the fixed charge.

***Re New Bullas Trading Ltd* stage** Thus far, the cases examined clearly illustrate that the label or declared intention of the parties is not crucial

[72] [2001] 2 BCLC 188, 204, PC, *per* Millett LJ. [73] [2005] 2 AC 680, 723.

[74] *Whitworth Street Estates Ltd v J. Miller and Partners Ltd* [1970] AC 583; *Schuler AG v Wickman Machine Tool Sales Ltd* [1974] 2 Ch 284; *Re Armagh Shoes Ltd* [1984] BCLC 405; *Re Keenan Bros Ltd* [1986] BCLC 242; and *Re Lin Securities (Pte) Ltd* [1988] 2 MLJ 137.

[75] See Pearce, above, note 48, particularly at p. 26, where the author suggested that the subsequent conduct may be tantamount to a variation of the original charge, and the chargee may be estopped from denying that the charge is a fixed charge or a floating charge as the case may be.

in determining the legal effect of the charge document. However, in the 1994 English Court of Appeal case of *Re New Bullas Trading Ltd*,[76] the Court of Appeal departed from what was thought to be the settled rule. In that case, the Court of Appeal emphasised the paramount importance of declaratory words. Nourse LJ stated that whether a charge is a fixed charge or a floating charge,

> it is agreed that the question depends on the intention of the parties, to be ascertained from the terms of the debenture; legal impossibility apart, that there are no considerations of public policy which prevented them from making whatever contracts they chose; that it was possible for them to create a fixed equitable charge over future as well as present book debts; that their declared intention was to create such a charge.[77]

In this case, New Bullas Trading Ltd first executed a debenture in favour of Lloyds Bank plc and later it gave a second debenture to 3i plc. The second debenture created a fixed charge over book debts due or owing to the company. The second debenture further provided the following:

- the company was required to pay all proceeds from the book debts into the company's current account or if 3i plc so required a separate designated account;
- the company could only deal with the proceeds paid into the account in accordance with any directions given by 3i plc; and
- in the absence of any such directions, moneys paid into the account were automatically released from the fixed charge and instead became the subject of a floating charge.

The objective of these stipulations was to avoid inconvenience to the bank. The bank did not want to monitor the account and be required to give its consent whenever New Bullas Trading Ltd wished to make a withdrawal.[78]

Subsequently, New Bullas Trading Ltd was put into receivership by the bank. After paying the bank, the receiver applied to the court for its determination on whether 3i plc's charge was a fixed charge or a floating charge over book debts that were uncollected. The receiver argued that the charge was a floating charge, because the company was free to withdraw the book debts from the security. It could do so simply by collecting them

[76] [1994] BCLC 36.

[77] Ibid., p. 40. The other appeal judges, Russell and Scott Baker LJJ, concurred.

[78] This was noted in *Agnew v Commissioner of Inland Revenue* [2001] UKPC 28, [2001] 3 WLR. 454, 195–6, PC, *per* Millett LJ.

and using them in the ordinary course of the business. Knox J agreed. On appeal, Nourse LJ reversed the decision. He held that unless and until the proceeds of the book debts were paid into the account they were not subject to a floating charge but rather a fixed charge. He reasoned that whether a charge was fixed or floating depended on what the parties had agreed in advance when they entered into the debenture. Here the parties had expressly declared that the book debts when uncollected were subject to a fixed charge; that was sufficient.

However, Goode has criticised this decision.[79] He was of the view that the Court of Appeal was wrong, because according to the terms of the debenture, so long as the book debts were not collected, 3i plc had no control. By ignoring this important fact, the Court of Appeal had effectively and incorrectly disregarded the real-control requirement of a fixed charge. As a result, Goode commented that the Court of Appeal had cast the law, in what is already a highly complex area, into further uncertainty.[80] In contrast, Berg[81] disagreed and supported Nourse LJ, on the grounds of the argument of freedom of contract.

However, the more recent House of Lords case of *Smith (Administrator of Cosslett (Contractors) Ltd v Bridgend County Borough Council*[82] appeared to settle the point and establish that the *Agnew* ratio would be followed in England. Thus Nourse LJ's declaratory approach appeared no longer good law. The matter has now been settled conclusively; both *Siebe Gorman* and *Re New Bullas Trading Ltd* were decisively overruled on the true characterisation of, and the distinction between, a floating and a fixed charge by the House of Lords in *Re Spectrum Plus Ltd*. In light of this, both *Cosslett* and *Agnew* are discussed below.

***Agnew* stage** The Privy Council in *Agnew* rejected Nourse LJ's approach. There, Brumark, which was in receivership, had previously granted a debenture to its bank. The debenture was closely modelled on the debenture in *Re New Bullas Trading Ltd*. The relevant provisions of the debenture stated that a fixed charge was created on the book debts of the company which arose in the ordinary course of trading present and

[79] Goode, above, note 48. See the subsequent case of *Re Pearl Maintenance Services Ltd* [1995] 1 BCLC 449, which distinguished *Re New Bullas Trading Ltd* as a case decid on its own facts. In *Re Pearl* a charge was held to be a floating charge notwithstanding the words 'specific charge'.

[80] J. Naccarato and P. Street, '*Re New Bullas Trading Ltd*: Fixed Charge over Book Debts – Two into One Won't Go', *JIBL&FL* 9(3) (1994), 109–16.

[81] Berg, above, note 48. [82] [2002] 1 All ER 292.

future, but only a floating charge was created over the proceeds collected by the chargor. Subject to this, the charge was expressed to be a floating charge as regards other assets of the company. The debenture prohibited the company from disposing of its uncollected book debts, but permitted it to deal freely with the proceeds in the ordinary course of its business, subject to the floating charge. Thus, essentially, the debenture purported to create a fixed charge over the book debts, which were outstanding at the time the receiver was appointed. Any proceeds of already collected debts in cash in the chargor's account were only subject to a floating security. Prior to the receiver's appointment, Brumark was free to collect the book debts and deal with the proceeds in the ordinary course of its business, though Brumark was unable to assign or factor them. The question was whether Brumark's right to collect the debts and deal with the proceeds free from the security meant that the charge on the uncollected debts, though described in the debenture as fixed, was nevertheless a floating charge.

At first instance, the judge held that the charge was a fixed charge. But on appeal, the New Zealand Court of Appeal reversed the decision and held that a floating charge was created. On further appeal to the Privy Council by the receivers, the Privy Council affirmed the decision of the New Zealand Court of Appeal and held that the charge was a floating charge. The Privy Council considered that Nourse LJ's approach in *Re New Bullas Trading Ltd* was 'fundamentally mistaken'. Lord Millett, delivering the advice of the Privy Council, reinforced the basic substantive rule of whether a charge so created was fixed or floating, the label or declaratory expression being insufficient to determine the true characteristics of the charge. Two conditions must be satisfied. First, the terms of the charge must deprive the chargor of the power of disposal of the charged assets, which must not be capable of being used in the chargor's business without the consent of the chargee. Secondly, it must be further shown that control was real and not merely hypothetical. Thus it was not sufficient to show that the proceeds from the book debts were paid into a blocked account. It must be shown that the blocked account was actually being operated and that the proceeds were actually paid into the account.

It is submitted that this point reinforces the view expressed here of the nature of the intrinsic and extrinsic rules of interpretation, and further confirms that the rules are not necessarily mutually exclusive.

Lord Millett also laid down a two-stage process for identifying whether a charge is fixed or floating, namely:

- The first stage is not to discover whether the parties intended to create a fixed or a floating charge, but rather to construe the charge document and to ascertain the nature of the rights and obligations which the parties intended to grant each other in respect of the charged assets.
- Once this has been ascertained, the court can then embark on the second stage, which is one of categorisation. This is a matter of law. It does not depend on the intention of the parties. If their intention, properly understood from the language of the instrument, is to grant the company rights in respect of the charged assets which are inconsistent with the nature of a fixed charge, then the charge cannot be a fixed charge however they may have chosen to describe it.[83]

Until *Cosslett*, there was some uncertainty whether or not *Re New Bullas Trading Ltd* was still good law in England. In *Cosslett*, the essentials were that a clause under the contract of employment gave the employer a right to remove a coal washing plant, goods or materials which belonged to its contractor though situated on the work site, and dispose of them to satisfy any sums due to the employer under the contract in various circumstances of default. The clause was held to create a floating charge even though express words of security, such as 'charge', were not used. The court accordingly held that it was void against the administrator as it was not registered with the Companies Registry. Although the House of Lords did not expressly overrule *Re New Bullas Trading Ltd*, the decision was regarded as having had that effect. *Agnew* was cited with approval by both Lord Hoffmann and Lord Scott, who was more emphatic. He stated,

> In my opinion, a contractual right enabling a creditor to sell his debtor's goods and apply the proceeds in or towards satisfaction of the debt is a right of a security character. The conclusion does not depend on the parties' intention to create a security. Their intention, objectively ascertained, is relevant to the construction of their contract. But once contractual rights have, by the process of construction, been ascertained, the question whether they constitute security rights is a question of law that is not dependent on their intentions (see *Agnew v Commissioner of Inland Revenue* [2001] 3 WLR 454, 465–466 per Lord Millett).[84]

It is submitted that Lord Millett's two-stage process is not only a reinstatement of the pre-*Re New Bullas Trading Ltd* approach,[85] but also

[83] *Agnew v Commissioner of Inland Revenue* [2001] UKPC 28, [2001] 3 WLR. 454, 195–6, PC.

[84] [2002] 1 All ER 292, 305.

[85] See the earlier House of Lords case *Helby v Matthews* [1895] AC 471, where *Agnew*'s approach of substance over form was applied at pp. 475–6, *per* Lord Herschell LC, who

has two implications. Firstly, it corrects the commonly held notion that whether a charge is fixed or floating is dependent on the intention of the parties.[86] Secondly, his Lordship was being candid, as in reality the decision of the court, one way or the other, may not always coincide with the true intention of the parties. A good illustration of this is *Smith (Administrator of Cosslett (Contractors) Ltd)* itself, as it is very likely that the decision that a charge was created must have come as a surprise to the industry. Indeed it was commented that the decision in *Agnew* made litigation in this area of the law more 'challenging and the results unpredictable'.[87]

The process of confirming the distinction between fixed and floating charges culminated in England with the House of Lords decision in *Re Spectrum Plus Ltd*.[88] In this case, Their Lordships unanimously endorsed the approach taken by Lord Millet in *Agnew*. The crucial issue was the requirement that the asset be permanently appropriated to the security for it to be characterised as a fixed charge and for the actual conduct of the parties after the execution of the debenture to reflect the reality of that permanent appropriation. Generally, this means that no dealing in the relevant asset or class of assets should take place without the prior specific consent of the chargee that the asset could be withdrawn from the security arrangement. In essence it must be demonstrated that the chargee had actual, and not merely theoretical, control of the charged asset.

Berg has argued convincingly that the inherent principle in play here is that substance over form is the crucial determinant of the legal status of a

stated, 'But the substance must, of course, be ascertained by a consideration of the whole of the agreement'; and also *Swiss Bank Corpn v Lloyds Bank Ltd* [1982] AC 584, at pp. 595–6, where Buckley LJ stated that if on proper construction of the document a charge was the consequence, 'the fact that they may not have realised this consequence will not mean that there is no charge'.

86 For example, see Gough, above, note 40, p. 88, where he stated that, traditionally, what the judges regarded as necessary to create a floating charge was not the use of any particular words but the expression of *contractual intention* to create a security (but at Chapter 21 the author expresses a different view); R. Tomasic and S. Bottomley, *Corporations Law in Australia* (Sydney: Federation Press, 1995), p. 531, where they state, 'The courts have acknowledged that the question of whether a charge is fixed or floating depends upon the intention of the parties'; and see also P. Lipton and A. Herzberg, *Understanding Company Law*, 6th ed. (Sydney: LBC Information Services, 1995), p. 277, where it is stated, 'whether a charge is a fixed charge or floating charge depends on the intention of the parties'.

87 See the paper of B. Collier entitled 'Trans Tasman Perspectives on Select Issues of Financing Stock and Debtors – Australian Perspectives', presented at the 19th Annual Banking and Financial Services Law Conference, Gold Coast, 6 June 2002, p. 15, where it is stated, 'Predicting the result in any particular litigation however will continue to be a challenge.'

88 [2005] 2 AC 680.

property right.[89] This is exemplified by the decision of the House of Lords in *Street v Mountford*,[90] where the occupation of residential premises was characterised as a tenancy rather than a mere occupational license despite the express statement in the document creating the legal relationship between the parties to the contrary. Lord Templeman admitted that whilst the parties had freedom to contract and used it in the instant case, this alone was not determinative of the legal relationship thereby created between them. As His Lordship stated,

> the consequences in law of the agreement, once concluded, can only be determined by consideration of the effect of the agreement. If the agreement satisfied all the requirements of a tenancy, then the agreement produced a tenancy and the parties cannot alter the effect of the agreement by insisting that they only created a licence.[91]

Berg also noted that the whole rationale of bankers and their equity draftsmen was to attempt to prevent the negative consequences to the value of a chargee's security of classifying such security devices – as in *Siebe Gorman*, *Re New Bullas Trading*, *Agnew* and *Re Spectrum Plus* – as floating charges. This is because of the effect of insolvency legislation that displaced floating charges in favour of preferential creditors (generally employees and the Crown). This was akin to the Rent Acts, which granted extensive protection to tenants which disadvantaged residential landlords who strove to characterise occupatory rights as those of a licensee rather than of a tenant, as the protective effect of the legislation did not apply to mere licensees.

Thus, in part, the *Spectrum* decision is an affirmation that parties are not permitted to 'contract out' of legislation that diminishes the value of floating charges as security.

A key issue is whether the three Mechanisms Promote certainty in the creation of company security.

On the basis of the above discussion, the answer has to be in the negative. The reasons can be summarised as follows:

- A change in the nature of commercial assets may render one or more of the characteristics redundant. For instance, until *Siebe Gorman*, it was thought that a book debt, owing to its ambulatory nature, could

[89] A. Berg, 'The Cuckoo in the Nest of Corporate Insolvency: Some Aspects of the Spectrum Case', *JBL* 22 (2006), 22.

[90] [1985] AC 809. [91] Ibid., at 819.

not form the subject matter of a fixed charge. This aspect of the *Siebe Gorman* decision has been reaffirmed.[92]

- A characteristic regarded as crucial in one case may not be so regarded by the court in another case. For instance, in *Re Atlantic Computer Systems plc*,[93] the court held that a fixed charge was created, though there were no words of restriction or prohibition, simply because the subleases and the rentals were present assets and not ambulatory.
- The intrinsic rule of interpretation approach, as expressed in *Agnew* and *Spectrum*, requires a meticulous examination of the terms of the debenture by subsequent potential lenders. Clauses in debentures are complex and legalistically drafted. A potential lay creditor may grant a further loan on the mistaken belief that the earlier debenture created a floating charge when on proper interpretation it created a fixed charge. Engaging a solicitor to examine the debenture may reduce the risk, but it does not guarantee the interpretation will be correct when tested in court. As illustrated by the cases of *Re New Bullas Trading Ltd* and *Agnew*, divergence can be discerned at different levels in the appealate process on what was essentially a similar clause.
- The combined intrinsic and extrinsic rules of interpretation approach also has weaknesses. The creditor and subsequent third party who wish to deal with the debtor have to take steps to ascertain the precise nature of the extrinsic factors. In particular, they would need to ascertain whether appropriate 'control' was exercised over the affected asset. This in itself is highly problematic as the House of Lords in *Spectrum* did not give precise or practical guidance as to what can constitute sufficient control by the chargee. This would not only increase costs, but what a judge deems an important constituent of control may not be given the same recognition by another court in a subsequent dispute.
- As the three-mechanisms approach embodies an objective test,[94] unless the document expressly evinces the intention of the parties and in many cases the result is likely to be unpredictable.
- Owing to the substantial emphasis placed on Romer LJ's floating charge criteria, one consequence is apparent. The fixed charge seems unable to develop its own independent identity. This is reflected in major textbooks' treatment of the subject. A significant proportion

[92] *Per* Lord Scott at 719. [93] [1992] 1 WLR 367.

[94] See *Smith (Administrator of Cosslett (Contractors) Ltd) v Bridgend County Borough Council* [2002] 1 All ER 292, 305, *per* Lord Scott, 'Their intention, objectively ascertained, is relevant to the construction of their contract.'

of their treatment of this topic is devoted to an analysis of the nature of a floating charge,[95] but they only give superficial treatment to fixed charges.[96] As a result, a creditor and a debtor who wish to create a fixed charge will invariably look at the features of a floating charge. The creditor may mistakenly believe that a security document that does not fit these features would create a fixed charge. As pointed out by Slade J, this can be disastrous, for a charge could still be a floating charge even though it did not contain each of the three characteristics mentioned.[97]

A fundamental dispute also exists as to the nature of the proprietary interest created in charged property prior to crystallisation. On the one hand, Goode argues that it is a present security in a fund of assets whereby the chargor is free to deal with them in the ordinary course of business including the right to alienate them and pass the title of the good to a third party. Before a crystallising event occurs, the chargee's proprietary interest lies in the fund of assets and the security interest attaches to particular assets only upon crystallisation.[98] On the other hand, Worthington has argued that a floating charge provides the chargee with the same type of proprietary interest as a fixed charge, except that 'defeasance' occurs when a third party acquires an interest in such a charged asset as a result of an act of the chargor that has been permitted by license of the chargee.[99]

The better view is that of Professor Goode, which is now supported by Lord Walker in *Spectrum*, where His Lordship stated, 'The chargee has a

[95] For example, see Farrar and Hannigan, above, note 37, pp. 632–5; *Gower's Modern Company Law*, 4th ed. (London: Stevens & Sons, 1979), pp. 472–4; *Charlesworth's Company Law*, 13th ed. (London: Stevens & Sons, 1987), pp. 625–32; and V. Stott, *Hong Kong Company Law*, 7th ed. (Hong Kong: Pitman, 1997), pp. 251–5.

[96] Berg, above, note 48, pp. 433–71, criticised the court's reliance on Romer J, but did not suggest any credible alternative criteria.

[97] [1979] 2 Lloyd's Law Reports 142. In *Re Keenan Bros Ltd* [1985] BCLC 302, at 307, Keane J said, 'In considering the first of these questions, I think it relevant to point out that Romer LJ nowhere says that a floating charge to be such must exhibit all three characteristics; indeed he expressly guards himself against such an inference being drawn from his remarks. What he did undoubtedly say was that where it had all three characteristics it was a floating charge.'

[98] R.M. Goode, *Legal Problems of Credit and Security*, 3rd ed. (London: Sweet & Maxwell, 2003), p. 116.

[99] S. Worthington, *Proprietary Interest in Commercial Transactions* (Oxford: Clarendon Press, 1996), pp. 74–77; see also S. Worthington, 'Floating Charges – An Alternative Theory', *CLJ* 53(1) (1994) 81.

proprietary interest but its interest is in a fund of circulating capital, and unless and until the charge intervenes (on crystallisation of the charge) it is for the trader, and not the bank, to decide how to run its business.'[100]

In a recent article, Sevenoaks argued that the floating charge, as an efficient security device in commercial transactions, may have to come to the end of its useful life.[101] She enumerated six significant deficiencies that impair the utility of floating charge as a security device in England:

(1) the duty to register floating charges – failure to do so renders the charge void against a liquidator, administrator or (post-insolvency) creditor whereas not all fixed charges are so constrained, so rendering some fixed charges more flexible than the floating charge;
(2) floating chargees rank behind statutory preferential creditors on liquidation or receivership and to subsequent fixed charges, which do not suffer diminution in value as a result of any prior claims;
(3) under a suspended provision of the old Insolvency Act 1986 (§176A), a fund of 10 per cent of the net realisation of assets subject to a floating charge must be reserved for unsecured creditors;
(4) the UK Companies Act 2006, §1282, subordinates floating charges to the costs of liquidation;
(5) the UK Insolvency Act 1986, §245, invalidates floating charges created without new value being given within the immediate period leading up to the insolvency, whereas fixed charges are not so disadvantaged;
(6) any floating charges created after 15 September 2003 cannot include a clause allowing the appointment of an administrative receiver. The Enterprise Act 2002 amended §72A of the Insolvency Act 1986 to this effect.

Despite these myriad disadvantages, some of which are mirrored in Hong Kong, and the restrictive definition as to what constitutes a floating charge in *Spectrum*, floating charges remain popular due to their inherent flexibility in allowing the chargor possession of charged assets and an unfettered ability to deal with them in the ordinary course of business. However, the state of the law relating to company security, especially that relating to floating charges, remains highly unsatisfactory. In 2004, the English Law Commission recommended in Consultation Paper No 176

[100] *Re Spectrum Plus Ltd* [2005] 2 AC 680, 729, para. 139.

[101] H. Sevenoaks, 'Financing Requirements in the 21st Century and the (In)Adequacy of the Floating Charge', *ICCLR* 17 (2009), 17.

('Company Security Interests') that the floating charge be replaced with a new type of security based on the US Commission's notice-filing system in Article 9. However, by 2005, the Law Commission's Final Report retreated from recommending substantial reform in the new Companies Bill due to lack of time to prepare new legislation and the limited remit the Commission had been given, which did not include a comprehensive consideration that such a major reform would have on the closely associated insolvency regime. As a result, substantive reform has been shelved indefinitely. Unfortunately, this dismal result may well be replicated in Hong Kong when the issue of corporate security is revisited the new Companies Bill in 2010 or 2011.[102]

Crystallisation of floating charges

In Hong Kong, crystallisation is a process by which a floating charge is converted into a fixed charge.[103] Farrar has stated that when this occurs, the fixed charge attaches or fastens to all those assets which the company owns at that date or subsequently acquires, provided the after-acquired assets are within the scope of the particular charge.[104] Crystallisation can therefore be regarded as an automatic creation of a fixed charge – no further execution of any security is required.

The creditor sees the crystallisation process as an important mechanism to protect its financial interests against events which the creditor perceives as threatening its financial interests. The protection is achieved by two consequences of crystallisation:

- it prohibits the chargor from dissipating the chargor's assets by virtue of the floating charge being converted to a fixed charge;
- it prevents other unsecured creditors from obtaining priority, which they could under the creditor's floating charge.[105]

[102] Further details may be found in the Crowther Report on Consumer Credit (Cmnd 4596), para. 5.7.77; see also A.L. Diamond, *A Review of Security Interests in Personal Property* (London: HMSO, 1989).

[103] Gough, above, note 40, p. 84, defined crystallisation as 'the process whereby the equitable charge attaches specifically and finally to all the items of the class of the mortgaged assets'. The Report of the Cork Committee on Insolvency Law and Practice (Cmnd 8558) at para. 1570, noted that crystallisation is simply the metaphorical term for the conversion of a floating security into a fixed security. Note that it was not until the 1890s that the term crystallisation was used in *Re Victoria Steamboats Ltd* [1897] 1 Ch 158, at 161, *per* Kekwich J, who said, 'It was a newly adopted term.'

[104] See Farrar and Hannigan, above, note 37, p. 635.

[105] How far this advantage has been eroded by legislation will be discussed in Chapter 6 below.

The conversion may, however, be an illusory security, because when the chargee, for the first time, ascertains the true value of the chargor's assets, as a fixed charge, they may be worthless.

Today it is clear that the events which may trigger the crystallisation of a floating charge can be divided into two categories. The first category covers those events implied by law as causing crystallisation. The second category covers those events agreed by the parties as constituting crystallising events.

Creditors in Hong Kong are continuously expanding the events under the second category. This is because the creditors see the first category events as unhelpful; they come too late for the creditor to preserve their priority against competing or third-party claims.

Events of both categories have substantive problems, may prejudice third parties dealing with the chargor and may not adequately protect the security interest of the chargee against competing claims. The last of these matters will be discussed further in Chapter 6.

Crystallising events implied by law The events under the first category are winding-up proceedings[106] which have commenced against the company (whether compulsorily[107] or voluntarily[108]) and when a holder of a debenture appoints a receiver out of court.[109] These events are both legally and commercially justifiable. The first event marks the beginning of the end of the chargor's business. In respect of the second, it terminates the chargor's licence[110] to deal with its assets freely – a fundamental characteristic of a floating charge. The receivership freezes all disposition of the chargor's property and stops the chargor carrying on business in its own name.[111]

[106] Including winding up is for the purposes of reconstruction: *Re Crompton & Co.* [1914] 1 Ch 954. L.S. Sealy expressed the view that it is because the licence to deal with the assets in the ordinary course of business will necessarily be terminated. See L.S. Sealey, *Cases and Materials in Company Law*, 5th ed. (London: Butterworths, 1992), pp. 395–6.

[107] *Re Colonial Trusts Corpn, ex parte Bradshaw* (1879) 15 Ch D 465, and *Wallace v Universal Automatic Machines* (1894) 2 Ch 547, CA.

[108] *Re Roundwood Colliery Co.* [1897] 1 Ch 373.

[109] *Evans v Rival Granite Quarries Ltd* [1910] 2 KB 979. However, to have this crystallisation effect, the receiver must be actually appointed; it is not sufficient if the holder of the debenture merely took steps to appoint a receiver. See *Re Colonial Trusts Corpn* (1879) 15 Ch D 465, *Re Roundwood Colliery Co.* [1897] 1 Ch 373, CA, and *Re Hubbard & Co. Ltd* [1898] 68 LJ Ch 54.

[110] Vaughan Williams LJ described the freedom of the floating chargor to deal with the assets as a licence. See *Evans v Rival Granite Quarries Ltd* [1910] 2 KB 979, pp. 988–9. See also Sealey, above, note 106, pp. 395–6, who used the same expression.

[111] *MG Charley Pty v FH Wells Pty Ltd* [1963] NSWR 22, 26, *per* Jacobs J.

Examination of standard debenture forms in Hong Kong shows that debentures commonly describe the events that entitle the creditor to appoint a receiver.[112] Some of the events are general, some specific. Examples of the general events include:

- the chargor's failure to perform any of its obligations under the debenture and
- any event which constitutes or would constitute a default under any other agreement to which the debtor is a party or which has an adverse effect on the ability of the debtor to perform its obligations under the debenture.

Examples of the specific events include:

- the chargor ceasing or threatening to cease carrying on of its business,
- a material adverse change in the financial position of the chargor that is likely to affect the chargor's ability to perform any of its obligations under the debenture and
- the chargor becoming or being declared insolvent.

Thus what appears, at first blush, to be narrow grounds of crystallisation implied by law can be widened by specifying broad circumstances under which a receiver can be appointed.

There was strong judicial[113] and academic[114] opinion, especially in the 1980s, that the first category (i.e. crystallisation events implied by law) should be expanded to include situations where the company voluntarily ceases to carry on business.[115] However, the Cork Committee's report on Insolvency Law and Practice[116] was against such a proposition on the

[112] On the basis of samples provided by the solicitors' firms of Baker & McKenzie, Clifford Chance, Deacons, Johnnie Yam, Jacky Lee & Co. and Linklaters, Hong Kong, there are no less than fifteen events that entitle the bank to appoint a receiver.

[113] For example, see *Re Woodroffes (Musical Instruments) Ltd* [1986] Ch 366, *per* Nourse J.

[114] For instance, H. Picarda, *The Law Relating to Receivers and Managers*, 1st ed. (London: Butterworths, 1984), at pp. 15–18. He cites several cases as authorities, such as *Hubbuck v Helms* (1887) 56 LJ Ch 536; *Robson v Smith* [1895] 2 Ch 118; *Re Victoria Steamboats Ltd* [1897] 1 Ch 158; *Government Stock and Other Securities Investment Co. Ltd v Manila Rly Co. Ltd* [1897] AC 81; and *Edward Nelson & Co. Ltd v Faber* [1903] 2 KB 367 at 376; Sealey, above, note 106, p. 398, Farrar and Hannigan, above, note 37, p. 634, and G.A. Penn, A.M. Shea and A. Arora, *The Law Relating to Domestic Banking* (London: Sweet & Maxwell, 1987); p. 360; and Goode, above, note 98, pp. 135–7.

[115] Nourse J, above, note 113.

[116] Cmnd 8558 paras. 1579–81. At para. 1580, the Committee recommended only the traditional mentioned grounds.

ground that its inclusion may cause practical difficulty to the chargee and to third parties dealing with the company. It would be difficult for them to ascertain at what moment the company has ceased to carry on business, and what acts or transactions will amount to the company ceasing to carry on business. Commercial logic and reality favour the Cork Committee's view.

However, the tide of law and practice appear to be against the Committee's view. In respect of the law, in the Australian case of *Fire Nymph Products Ltd v The Heating Centre Pty Ltd (in liq.) and Others*,[117] the court unanimously held that a chargor's subsequent disposal of its entire heating unit stocks automatically crystallised the floating charge, because the disposal was not in the ordinary course of business of the chargor, which was one of supplying and installing heating units.[118] Gleeson CJ appears to found his decision on the narrow ground that the disposal came within the expressly agreed automatic crystallisation event; that is, if 'the mortgagor shall deal with all or any of the mortgaged property other than in the course of its ordinary business then the floating charge' shall crystallise.[119] Sheller JA, on the other hand, appears to lay down a broader principle; that is, so long as the subsequent dealing was effected otherwise than with a view to carrying on the chargor's business, the floating charge automatically crystallises. In respect of practice, the chargor's ceasing to carry on business is commonly specified in the debenture as a crystallising event. Both law and practice thus heavily lean in favour of the protection of the creditor. Certainty of the law seems to be a marginal issue.

It is submitted that the first category of crystallising events, implied by law, do not, as a general rule, prejudice third parties dealing with the chargor after the crystallisation. This is because the event that causes the crystallisation is a 'public event'; that is, the public is deemed to have notice of the event. In the case of a compulsory winding-up, a winding-up petition is filed with the court.[120] In the case of a receiver being appointed, notice is given to the Registrar of Companies within seven days of appointment.[121] The notice is entered in the register of charges and the company has to notify the appointment of the receiver in all documents where the name of the company appears, such as invoices, orders for goods and business letters.[122]

[117] (1992) 10 ACLC 629. [118] Ibid., p. 641. [119] Ibid., p. 636.
[120] Companies Ordinance (Cap. 32), §184(2).
[121] Companies Ordinance (Cap. 32), §87(1).
[122] Companies Ordinance (Cap. 32), §299(1).

Examination of the English authorities, however, has shown that one form of crystallisation – that is, partial crystallisation – may create practical uncertainty.[123] This concept has not been adopted in Hong Kong. But there is no reason why it may not become operational there.

Partial crystallisation occurs when a receiver[124] takes possession of only part of the assets covered by the floating charge provisions of the debenture.[125] The charge continues merely to float over the other assets.[126] Gough describes it as a process of 'selective pouncing down'.[127] It is generally felt that the concept should be rejected as it could prejudice subsequent creditors where the charge is over personal property,[128] especially assets which are ambulatory in nature. This risk was recognised in earlier cases. For instance, in *Evans v Rival Granite Quarries Ltd*,[129] Fletcher Moulton LJ stated, *obiter*, that it was 'inconsistent with the nature of a floating security that the holder should be able to pounce down on particular assets and to interfere with the company's business while still keeping his security a floating security; he cannot at once give freedom and insist on servitude'. Gough expresses the same view that 'to preserve priority, the chargee must crystallise the charge as a whole'.[130]

However, the concept of freedom of contract seems to protect its legitimacy. If the parties clearly and expressly agree to a partial crystallisation provision, then there is no good reason why this should not be recognised.[131]

To balance the theory of freedom of contract with the protection of the interests of third parties, authorities showed that the courts will apply

[123] It has been generally regarded as a valid method of activating the charge; see *Re Griffin Hotel Co. Ltd* [1940] 4 All ER 324, a case regarded as authority for this proposition; see also Picarda, above, note 114, p. 24.

[124] The floating chargee may himself take possession of the assets of the company, but this is rare.

[125] Picarda, above, note 114, p. 24.

[126] One reason could be that these assets are less valuable to the chargee. See *Re Griffin Hotel Co. Ltd* [1940] 4 All ER 324, *per* Bennett J.

[127] Gough, above, note 40, p. 168.

[128] In *Re Griffin Hotel Co. Ltd* [1940] 4 All ER 324, the partial crystallisation was over land; Picarda, above, note 114.

[129] [1910] 2 KB 979, p. 998; Buckley LJ also expressed a similar view. An earlier case, which appears to support this view, is *Robson v Smith* [1895] 2 Ch 118, 126, *per* Romer J.

[130] Gough, above, note 40, p. 169; G. Lightman and G. Moss, *The Law of Receivers of Companies*, 1st ed. (London: Sweet & Maxwell, 1986), p. 28, n. 39; and also Goode, above, note 98, pp. 140–2.

[131] Gough, above, note 40, citing *R v Consolidated Churchill Copper Corpn Ltd* [1978] 5 WWR 652, 261.

the concept strictly, so that partial crystallisation cannot occur unless the terms of the floating charge are sufficiently clear. This can be discerned from the Singapore case of *Re City Securities (Pte) Ltd.*[132] There the High Court held that a court order, demanding the delivery of some share certificates of the company chargor to the chargee, did not crystallise the floating charge in respect of those shares as there was no express provision in the floating charge to this effect.

The second category of crystallisation events can be divided into two types:

- semi-automatic crystallisation events and[133]
- automatic crystallisation events.

The semi-automatic event refers to the situation where the chargee serves notice in writing on the chargor that the charge is now converted into a fixed charge. No reason is required to be given. In Hong Kong, this right of the chargee is commonly specified in debentures creating floating charges,[134] in what is called a 'semi-automatic crystallisation clause'.[135]

The automatic crystallisation event refers to the situation where the floating charge becomes a fixed charge immediately on the occurrence of certain events without any notice served on the chargor by the chargee. A clause in the debenture expressly defines the automatic crystallisation events and is commonly called the 'automatic crystallisation clause'.

The purpose of the automatic crystallisation clause is to overcome the problem created by the case of *Wilson v Kelland*,[136] where the court held that a subsequent fixed charge created without the consent of the earlier floating chargee has priority. The automatic crystallisation clause prevents this from happening by automatically converting the earlier floating charge into a fixed charge when that event occurs.[137]

132 [1990] 2 MLJ 257.

133 Goode, above, note 98, p. 145, and Lightman and Moss, above, note 130.

134 This clause was found in all the sample debentures of all the solicitors' firms of Hong Kong, namely Baker & McKenzie, Clifford Chance, Deacons, Johnnie Yam, Jacky Lee & Co., and Linklaters.

135 See Goode, above, note 98, p. 144.

136 [1910] 2 Ch 306.

137 However, it cannot be said that the crystallised charge should be treated in the same way as if it had been fixed from the outset. Professor Goode, above, note 98, at pp. 118 and 134, pointed out that 'all that happens is that the security interest brought into being by the floating charge ceases to float over a fund of assets and attaches *in specie*'. The reason is that crystallisation is not retrospective, and it does not give a new security interest.

In practice the automatic crystallisation events are more extensive. The events usually include the following:[138]

- the chargor's attempt to create or permit any other security or interest in such assets without the consent of the floating chargee,
- a creditor's taking possession of the assets,
- any distress or any execution being levied on any assets of the chargor and
- the chargor's failing to maintain the ratio of assets to liabilities as from time to time determined by the bank.[139]

In the context of the priority accorded to competing interests in insolvency, a crystallised charge is still regarded as a floating charge as created for the purpose of ranking behind some preferential debts, whether the debts arise before or after crystallisation.[140] Fixed charges and real rights held by third parties, on the other hand, are not subject to this 'battle of priorities'.[141] However, the effect of a crystallisation clause, assuming its validity, could convert a floating charge into a fixed one and so create priority issues with respect to a subsequent fixed charge created by the chargor company prior to crystallisation. The general rule in this situation is that except for preferential debts, since the floating charge has been crystallised to become fixed at the time of crystallisation, it generally has priority over subsequent interests,[142] in just the same way as if it had been fixed at the outset.

The practice of inserting an automatic crystallisation clause in debentures is relatively new in Hong Kong.[143] Its validity was only judicially

[138] The examples are extracted from debentures provided by John White of Cameron Markby Hewitt, London, UK, at a conference organised by the Chartered Institute of Bankers in Hong Kong in 1991 which the author attended; also found in the debenture of Clifford Chance, Hong Kong (see note 143 below) and see also Goode, above, note 98, at p. 145.

[139] This was found in one of the sample debentures of Cameron Markby Hewitt.

[140] Companies Ordinance (Cap. 32), §79. For the situation in the UK, see Insolvency Act 1986, §251. See also UK Law Commission Consultation Paper No 164, para. 2.44.

[141] It is because those assets, subject to fixed security or real rights by third parties (e.g. retention-of-title clause) do not constitute the property of the company at all and therefore do not compete in the priority stakes. See R.M. Goode, *Principles of Corporate Insolvency Law*, 3rd ed. (London: Sweet & Maxwell, 2005), pp. 211–12.

[142] See *Re Real Meat Co. Ltd* [1996] BCC 254.

[143] Such a clause was not found in the sample debentures of the solicitors' firms examined in 2003 of Baker & McKenzie, Deacons, Johnnie Yam, Jackie Lee & Co., and Linklaters, nor the examples of I.A. Tokley in his *Securities* (Hong Kong: Longman, 1994), p. 88. However, it was in the debenture of Clifford Chance (Hong Kong), clause 4.2, which provided that the floating charge would automatically crystallise on the occurrence of seven

recognised in the year 2000 in the case of *ABN Amro Bank NV v Chiyu Banking Corp Ltd and Others*.[144] There the pertinent part of the automatic crystallisation clause of ABN's debenture provided that the floating charge under a debenture will automatically operate as a fixed charge, without notice, if the company charges, pledges or otherwise encumbers (whether by way of fixed charge or floating charge) any of the charged undertaking, property and assets or the company attempts so to do without the prior consent in writing of ABN. The company subsequently created fixed charges of its deposits in favour of other banks to secure advances by those other banks. When the company was compulsorily wound up, ABN claimed that it had priority over the fixed deposits on the ground that it had a fixed charge over the deposits, for the floating charge automatically crystallised when the company created fixed charges over the fixed deposits in favour of the other banks. The Court of First Instance held that the automatic crystallisation clause was valid. However, the crystallised fixed charge had no priority over the subsequent fixed charges, for ABN had not served notice on the fundholder of the fixed deposit, but the subsequent chargee banks had done so. According to the rule of priority in *Dearle v Hall*[145] the subsequent chargee had priority.[146]

The decision in *ABN Amro* appears to suggest that the crystallised floating charge, if not for the rule in *Dearle v Hall*, would have priority over the subsequent fixed charge, even though the subsequent chargee had no actual knowledge. The English Law Commission, however, disagrees. It expressed the view that it was extremely unlikely that such a device would

specified events. But it is quite popular in England: see the United Kingdom Department of Trade and Industry consultation paper, Modern Company Law – For a Competitive Economy: Registration of Company Charges, URN 00/1213 (October 2000), p. 30. Note, one of the counsel in *ABN Amro Bank NV v Chiyu Banking Corp Ltd and Others* [2000] 3 HKC 381, 402, was correct when he submitted it was not a common practice in Hong Kong to insert such a clause in a floating charge.

[144] [2000] 3 HKC 381. The validity of automatic crystallisation was recognised much earlier in other common law jurisdictions, e.g. for Australia, see *Fire Nymph Products Ltd v Heating Centre Pty Ltd (in liq.) and Others* (1992) 10 ACLC 629 (NSW), and *Re Wrights Hardware Pty Ltd* (31 Oct 1988, unreported, cited in H.A.J. Ford, *Principles of Company Law*, 5th ed. (Sydney: Butterworths, 1990), at para. 1225); *Stein v Saywell* (1969) 121 CLR 526; *FCT v Lai Company Pty Ltd* [1987] WAR 15; and for New Zealand see *Re Manurewa Transport Ltd* (1971) NZLR 909.

[145] *Dearle v Hall* (1828) 3 Russ 1, 38 ER 475. Under the repealed section of Companies Act 1989, §410 and §411, the rule in *Dearle v Hall* was confirmed. However, this section was never implemented, and has been entirely repealed by the Companies Act 2006, Schedule 16.

[146] This rule of priority is discussed further in Chapter 6 below.

be effective unless the subsequent chargee had actual knowledge of the automatic crystallisation clause.[147] However, there is some authority in Australia, such as *Fire Nymph Products Ltd*,[148] discussed earlier, which supports the decision in *ABN Amro*. There is, however, a weakness in both cases. They create an anomaly in the law, which is that while a 'negative pledge'[149] in a floating charge has no effect on a subsequent fixed charge unless the subsequent chargee has actual knowledge, the same rule does not apply to automatic crystallisation clauses. On the basis of this, it is submitted that the Law Commission's view is more compelling. The Law Commission Report No 296 proposed a notice-filing system in which priority is simplified by the order of the date of filing, but given the debate on reform of floating charges in the UK, it is unlikely that substantive change will occur soon.[150]

Well before *ABN Amro* there were two schools of thought on the desirability of the automatic crystallisation concept. The first can be described as the public policy theory, which proposed that automatic crystallisation should be abolished. The second is the doctrine of freedom of contract, which adopts an opposite view. The strongest proponent of the first view is the Cork Committee. In its report the Cork Committee thought that automatic crystallisation was against public policy, because it puts at

147 UK Law Commission Consultation Paper No 164, para. 2.44 mentioned that 'it is extremely unlikely that such a device [an automatic crystallisation clause] will be effective unless the subsequent chargee has actual knowledge of the automatic crystallization clause'. UK Law Commission Report No 296 further confirmed such a view.

148 (1992) 10 ACLC 629.

149 For discussion on the effect and impact of a negative pledge, see Chapter 6 below.

150 UK Law Commission Report No 296; see, for example, paras. 1.22, 1.33(2), 2.3(7), 3.178, 3.201–3.204, etc. Under current law, an execution creditor may take goods that are subject to an uncrystallised floating charge, as the secured creditor is not regarded as having rights that have attached to any specific item. See *Evans v Rival Granite Quarries Ltd* [1910] 2 KB 979, CA (see in particular 999). When the floating charge crystallises, the priority position between the crystallised charge pursuant to an automatic crystallisation clause against the unsecured interests held by execution creditors has changed. The charge is likely to be effective in gaining a priority position unless the execution creditor has completed execution prior to crystallisation. However, under the proposed notice-filing scheme by the Law Commission in which priority between execution creditor and floating charge holder is characterised on the basis of date of filing (but not the time of crystallisation), a registered floating charge at the relevant time is very likely to strengthen its priority position over the interests of the execution creditor. A failure in registration, however, will still render the floating charge ineffective against the claims of an execution creditor (or liquidator or administrator) at the time when his interest arises. See in particular paras. 3.78 and 3.204. For further details on notice-filing schemes see also H. Beale et al., *The Law of Personal Property Security* (New York: Oxford University Press, 2007), para. 21.109, 'Priority by date of filing'.

risk anyone who deals with a company that has given a floating charge.[151] The Australian Law Reform Commission agreed with this view, and gave additional reasons. It thought that such clauses had practical difficulties and uncertainties.[152] For instance, the charge might crystallise without anyone, including the parties to the security, being aware of it. As a result both parties may continue to act as though the charge were floating. If there are competing claims or an insolvency of the debtor ensues it may be difficult or impossible to adjudicate the respective competing rights to particular property.[153]

However, the courts and other commentators support the doctrine of freedom of contract. For instance, in the Australian case of *Fire Nymph Products Ltd*,[154] Gleeson CJ, in upholding the validity of an automatic crystallisation clause, crisply commented, 'there is nothing in legal theory that prevents parties from making a contract that might produce results adverse to third parties'.[155] Hoffman J expressed a similar view in the earlier English case of *Re Brightlife Ltd*.[156] He thought that in the absence of any statutory prohibition, it was wholly inappropriate for the courts to restrict the contractual freedom of parties to insert an automatic crystallisation clause in a floating charge. Thus the parties are free to agree on any event they choose, however trivial or invisible to the outside world, which will cause the floating charge to crystallise.

Gough also supports the doctrine of freedom of contract.[157] He thought that the Cork Committee's argument of prejudice to third parties was greatly overstated.[158] McCormack agreed with Gough, but gave an economic justification for the argument of contractual freedom.[159] According to him, if automatic crystallisation clauses were cut down, it would make the floating charge less attractive, consequently the flow of credit to industry would be curtailed. It is, however, submitted that this argument has to

151 Paras. 1576–9.

152 See Australian Law Reform Commission Report No 45, General Insolvency Inquiry (1988) para. 191, where it also identified four additional problems that would cause significant inconvenience.

153 Australian Law Reform Commission, ibid. The Law Reform Commission in its subsequent Report No 64, Personal Property Securities (1993), para. 10.13, reaffirmed its previous criticisms and recommendations.

154 (1992) 10 ACLC 629. 155 Ibid., p. 639. 156 [1986] 3 All ER 673.

157 See Gough, above, note 40, pp. 239, 408–17. The author, in Chapter 16, 'Policy Issues', sets out the arguments for and against automatic crystallisation in considerable depth.

158 Ibid., p. 410.

159 G. McCormack, *Registration of Company Charges* (London: Sweet & Maxwell, 1994), pp. 148–9.

be treated with caution, as there is no empirical evidence to substantiate it. Perhaps for this reason the economic argument has not featured in judicial decisions that approve automatic crystallisation.

It is submitted that the fears expressed by the Cork Committee and the Australian Law Reform Commission cannot be simply brushed aside or treated lightly in Hong Kong. This is because, in Hong Kong, after registration of a charge, the original charge document is not deposited with the Registrar of Companies. As a result, a third party who makes a search at the Companies Registry cannot ascertain whether or not its proposed dealing would be subject to an automatic crystallisation clause contained in the prior security. The third party may obtain the floating charge document from the company chargor but it may have to obtain the services of solicitors to interpret the effect of the document. Besides, the solicitor's interpretation does not bind the court in the event of a dispute between competing claimants.

Examination of English and Australian authorities appears to suggest that the courts are aware of this danger, and they have attempted to balance the doctrine of freedom of contract with the interests of third parties by introducing certain caveats. Firstly, the courts will not treat an act as an automatic crystallising event unless it clearly falls within those acts expressly agreed by the parties. For instance, in *Re Woodroffes (Musical Instruments) Ltd*,[160] the court held that if there are two or more floating charges created over the same assets, the crystallisation of one will not automatically crystallise the others unless this was expressly stipulated in the floating charge.[161] Secondly, it is clear in Australia, and likely to be in England as well, that automatic crystallisation clauses are strictly construed.[162]

However, it is submitted that these caveats provide little comfort to third parties. It is only in cases where the debenture is poorly drafted that such caveats might allow a third party to successfully rely on these

[160] [1986] Ch 366. Other literature which favours its validity includes J.H. Farrar, 'The Crystallisation of a Floating Charge', *Conv* 40 (1976), 397; A.J. Boyle, 'The Validity of Automatic Crystallisation Clauses', *JBL* (1979), 231; and R.L. Dean, 'Crystallisation of a Floating Charge', *CSLJ* (1982–4) 185.

[161] But if the floating charge did so provide, crystallisation of one floating charge will simultaneously crystallise the other: *Stein v Saywell* (1969) 121 CLR 529. Note that before this case, it was already strongly argued by Picarda, above, note 114, pp. 21–3, that crystallisation of one floating charge will not automatically crystallise another floating charge, whether it is a subsequent or earlier floating charge.

[162] Ford, above, note 144, para. 12.25.

caveats. Despite these weaknesses, the caveats merit serious consideration in Hong Kong when the courts are confronted with the contractual effectiveness of automatic crystallisation clauses.

Thus far, the criticisms mentioned have focused on automatic crystallisation in the strict sense. Insofar as third parties are concerned, they also apply equally to semi-automatic crystallisation, as notice by the chargee upon the chargor is a private act between them. Unless a potential subsequent chargee makes inquiry with the chargor or chargee and is fully informed of the event, the potential subsequent chargee has no means of ascertaining whether the earlier chargee has exercised its right.

Attempts have been made in England to alleviate the commercial risk created by the semi-automatic and automatic crystallisation clauses. Section 410(3) of the UK Companies Act 1989 empowered the Secretary of State to make regulations requiring notice in the prescribed form to be given to the registrar of an event causing a floating charge to crystallise. Such event may be invalid unless registration is effected. However, it should be noted that these provisions were never implemented, as the relevant part of the Companies Act 1989 was never brought into force. Commentators are, however, divided as to whether or not the §410(3) solution is the optimal way to deal with the problem. In 2001, the United Kingdom Department of Trade and Industry Steering Group (hereafter 'the Steering Group')[163] proposed that a future reform should require the particulars to be registered and should indicate whether an automatic crystallisation clause was contained in the security.[164] However, the English Law Commission disagreed and proposed that it was sufficient to register the fact in the event that the floating charge had crystallised, for the purpose is one of providing third parties with the information as to the chargor's authority to dispose of its assets, which has already ceased.[165] This was also in line with the earlier recommendation of the Australian Law Reform Commission.[166] This would appear to be the best approach as it ensures certainty and, at the same time, would not do violence to the doctrine of freedom of contract. The Law Reform Commission of Hong Kong has yet to express its view on the matter. The issue here is relevant when deciding whether automatic crystallisation clauses should be abolished. The English Law Commission Report No 296 appears to suggest that they

[163] UK DTI Steering Group on Modern Company Law for a Competitive Economy (URN 01/942, 26 July 2001).

[164] Ibid., paras. 12.25 and 12.28.

[165] See UK Law Commission Consultation Paper No 164, para. 4.143.

[166] See Australian Law Reform Commission Report No 45, above, note 152, para. 196.

are no longer necessary because the proposed notice-filing scheme allows for prioritisation based on the date of filing rather than the time of crystallisation. Therefore for priority purposes under the proposed scheme, the authors take the view that automatic crystallisation clauses could be abolished subsequent to the introduction of the notice-filing scheme.[167] However, this reform was not introduced in the 2006 Companies Act and the current state of law remains largely unchanged.[168]

Consequently, the question arises as to whether do semi-automatic and automatic crystallisation clauses effectively protect the interests of the chargee.

There does not seem to be a clear answer, due to two factors. The first is the nature of the competing claims and the second is the conduct of the chargee after the debenture is executed. In relation to the first factor, the semi-automatic and automatic crystallisation clauses are not effective in two situations:

- against claims of preferential creditors, such as the wages of employees and various debts owed to the government, as a floating charge will remain a floating charge notwithstanding the fact that it has crystallised;[169]
- where the rules of priority defeat the charge, as in *ABN Amro*, where the crystallised equitable charge loses priority to a subsequent equitable fixed charge as the latter, but not the former, was perfected by notice on the fundholder.

In relation to the second factor, which is particularly relevant to automatic crystallisation clauses, the practical difficulties have already been mentioned in the Australian Law Reform Commission Report (see above). It may, however, be added that an expansively drafted automatic crystallisation clause may paralyse the business by the occurrence of trivial events, such as a minor delay in instalment or interest payments. The drastic effects of crystallisation occurring as a result of minor infractions of lending covenants may be unintended by the parties.[170]

[167] See Beale et al., above, at note 150, at para. 4.59.

[168] With regard to registration of floating charges, the Companies Act 2006, §877, retained most of its equivalent in the Companies Act 1985, §419, with minor changes made in §877(2). For further details see A. Alcock, J. Birds and S. Gale, *Companies Act 2006: The New Law* (Bristol: Jordan Publishing, 2007), at p. 846.

[169] Companies Ordinance (Cap. 32), §265(3B).

[170] See *Re Caroma Enterprises Ltd* (1979) 108 DLR (3d) 412, at 418, *per* Macdonald J; see also *Government Stock and Other Securities Investment Co. Ltd v Manila Rly Co. Ltd* [1897] AC 81, at 87, *per* Lord Macnaghten.

4.2.2 Perfection of company security

The discussion under this section is divided into the following subheadings, namely

(1) perfecting Hong Kong company security,
(2) perfecting overseas company security.

Perfecting Hong Kong company security

Owing to the complexity of this area of the law, this part is subdivided into four parts:

(1) the registration system under the Companies Ordinance, and objectives;
(2) registrability of company security;
(3) conclusiveness of registration and perfection; and
(4) substantive impact of registration on the priority of competing claims.

The registration system under the Companies Ordinance, and objectives Section 80(2) of the Companies Ordinance requires that particulars of a registrable charge (see below) must be properly delivered to the Registrar of Companies for registration within a period of five weeks after the date of creation of the charge.[171] If the charge is not registered, §80(1) of the Ordinance renders the charge void against creditors and the liquidator of the company. This serious consequence is illustrated in the Hong Kong case of *Chase Manhattan Asia v Official Receiver and Liquidator of First Bangkok City Finance*.[172] There the Privy Council held that a purported assignment of a company's book debts was a fixed charge and that it was void for want of registration. Accordingly, the Official Receiver was entitled to claim the book debts for the general creditors. The 'sanction of invalidity' thus provides a powerful incentive

[171] The HK SAR government has signalled that it will introduce a short period within which to require registration of a company charge. In the government's conclusions on the second public consultation issued on 10 December 2008, the government announced that the period would be reduced to twenty-one days. This change was incorporated into the 'White' Bill, Draft Companies Bill: First Phase Consultation, issued in December 2009; see p. 22, para. 3.13.

[172] [1990] 1 WLR 1181. Also the cases of *Esberger & Son Ltd v Capital and Counties* [1913] 2 Ch 366; *Re Bond Worth Ltd* [1979] 3 WLR 629; and *Re Pearchdart Ltd* [1983] 3 All ER 204.

for the secured creditors to ensure proper registration of their registrable security.[173]

The objectives of the registration system are:

- to protect the creditors of an insolvent company by giving them the opportunity to discover, by consulting the register, whether company assets are encumbered so as to reduce the amount available for unsecured creditors in liquidation;[174]
- to 'prevent markets being misled by the apparent ownership by companies of assets which were in fact already encumbered in favour of prior creditors'.[175]

To effect registration, the chargee has to deliver the following particulars to the Companies Registry:

- date and description of the instrument creating the charge;
- description of the amount secured;
- short particulars of the property mortgaged or charged; and
- the names, addresses and description of the mortgagees or persons entitled to the charge.[176]

The Registrar of Companies has to record the above particulars in the register.[177] The particulars are today kept on microfilm. The registration process is relatively simple and expeditious in Hong Kong.

An important feature of the registration requirements is that it is a registration of the particulars of the charge. The original charge documents or copies are not required to be deposited with the Registrar of Companies.[178] The impact of this practice on the protection of third parties will be discussed below.[179] However, the government has now proposed that in the reformed Companies Ordinance, a provision be included that will require

[173] See the United Kingdom Department of Trade and Industry consultation paper, Modern Company Law – For a Competitive Economy: Registration of Company Charges, URN 00/1213 (October 2000), para. 1.2.

[174] See *Smith (Administrator of Cosslett (Contractors) Ltd) v Bridgend County Borough Council* [2002] 1 All ER 292, HL, *per* Lord Hoffmann. Note that the present system for the registration of company charges in England and Wales dates back to 1900; see Companies Act 1900, §14. In Hong Kong, the registration system was introduced in 1911 via §95 of the Companies Ordinance of 1911.

[175] See UK DTI, above, note 163.

[176] Companies Ordinance (Cap. 32), §80(1A).

[177] Ibid., §83(1).

[178] This was also noted in *ABN Amro Bank NV v Chiyu Banking Corp Ltd and Others* [2000] 3 HKC 381.

[179] See below in this chapter.

registration of the charge instrument and prescribed particulars, both of which would be open to public inspection.[180]

The Companies Ordinance also requires the chargor company to keep a copy of the charge document[181] and a register of charges at its registered office ('private register').[182] The register of charges has to note all charges specifically affecting the property of the company and all floating charges over the undertaking or any property of the company, giving in each case a short description of the property charged, the amount of the charge, and, except in the case of securities to bearer, the names of the persons entitled thereto. According to the Companies Ordinance,[183] copies of instruments creating any charge requiring registration and the register of charges kept at the registered office have to be open during business hours for inspection by any existing creditor or member of the company without fee. However, registration at the private register has no perfecting effect.

Extension of time for registration If a secured creditor fails to register the charge it is not completely disastrous for two reasons. Firstly, if the chargor defaults, the chargee may still exercise all its rights and remedies, including sale, under the terms of the charge, against the chargor and the ordinary unsecured creditor, provided the company is not insolvent.[184] Secondly, which is a better solution, the chargee may apply to the court for an order to extend the time for registration.[185]

The Hong Kong courts usually grant the chargee an extension of time subject to three conditions being satisfied: (1) the default is due to inadvertence or to some other sufficient cause, (2) the grant of the order is not of a nature to prejudice the position of the creditors or shareholders, or (3) it is just and equitable to grant the order.[186]

In *Re Ashpurton Estates Ltd*,[187] one of the grounds for the court's refusal to grant an extension of time was that the chargee delayed application to the court for four months after it first discovered the default. In short, the chargee should act expeditiously. Another situation is where the chargor is not being compulsorily wound up, according to *Sun Hung Kai v Attorney General*.[188] There is no direct authority in cases of voluntary

[180] Consultation Conclusions, above, note 171, para. 55.

[181] Companies Ordinance (Cap. 32), §88. [182] Ibid., §89. [183] Ibid., §90(1).

[184] *Erhmann Bros Ltd* [1906] 2 Ch 697, 708, *per* Romer LJ.

[185] Companies Ordinance, §86(1). [186] Ibid. [187] [1983] 1 Ch 110.

[188] [1986] HKLR 587, at 601, *per* Huggins VP. On appeal to the Privy Council, it became known as *Sun Tai Cheung Credits Ltd v Attorney General* [1987] HKLR 1010, where the

winding up. However, according to the Court of Appeal's observation in *Sun Hung Kai*, the English case of *Re Ashpurton Estates Ltd*[189] should apply in Hong Kong. In *Re Ashpurton Estates Ltd*, it was held that extension of time would not be granted if notice of an extraordinary general meeting to pass a resolution to wind up the company had been sent out, but no liquidation had yet taken place.

These propositions were relaxed in subsequent English cases and in other common law jurisdictions. In *Re Braemar Investments Ltd*,[190] the court thought that even imminent liquidation was not an absolute bar to an order for extension.[191] There the court granted the extension subject to the proviso that the creditor might apply to have it set aside if the company went into liquidation. In the Australian case of *Vector Capital Ltd v SNS Software Network Systems Pty Ltd*,[192] the court held that the order could be made if a large part of the company's assets at the time of the liquidation represented advances given by the unregistered creditor. The court appeared to regard registration as simply a technicality. In the absence of fraud, the bona fide creditor should not be deprived of security.

However, *Braemar Investments Ltd* and *Vector Capital* are not free from difficulty. They cast doubt on the credibility of the registration system, the function of which is to provide expeditious and accurate information to the public. A subsequent creditor, whether secured or otherwise, who enquires at the Companies Registry is likely to be deceived as to the precise financial status of the company should the criteria for late registration become too relaxed.[193]

If the court grants the order to extend time, it will be on the general terms that it should not prejudice any other secured creditor.[194] The meaning of this caveat has been given a narrow interpretation. In Hong Kong there is the view that it would only protect those duly registered fixed charges created after the expiry of the five-week period of

Privy Council refused the extension on the ground that the forms submitted for registration were not in the proper statutory forms.

189 [1983] 1 Ch 110. 190 [1988] BCLC 556.

191 This is a departure from the strict view discussed by G. McCormack, 'Extension of Time for Registration of Company Charges', *JBL* (1986) 282.

192 (1988) 12 ACLR 723.

193 This difficulty was not recognised by the Hong Kong Standing Committee in its Eighth Report, when it recommended the retention of the existing provision.

194 The proviso protects only proprietary interest, legal or equitable, in the property. The court does not make provision to protect unsecured creditors who had given advances at the time when the charge should have been notified via registration. See *Re Cardiff Workmen's Cottage Co. Ltd* [1906] 2 Ch 627, *per* Buckley J.

a first unregistered charge.[195] Consequently, if the first and subsequent charges were created within the five-week period, and the subsequent fixed charge was duly registered within the same period but the earlier fixed charge was registered out of time with a court extension order, then the duly registered subsequent fixed charge will not gain priority over the earlier fixed charge.[196] The rationale of this view is that the second chargee could not, during the statutory period, claim that the first charge was void against it.[197] In other words, the order has a retrospective rather than a prospective effect.

It is submitted that this view is outdated. Recognising that the retrospective rule is clearly unfair to a subsequent unsuspecting creditor, who may have acted diligently and taken all the necessary precautions by making inquiries at the Companies Registry, yet its security would be postponed by reason of an extension of time, the courts in England remedied this mischief by changing the terms of the standard order in 1974. The practice, as illustrated in the English case of *Re Braemar Investments Ltd*,[198] is to state in the extension order that the order 'shall not prejudice any rights acquired in the charged property between the date of the creation of the charge and its actual registration'. The subsequent chargee who acquires its security during the five-week period and duly registered the charge is, therefore, protected under this new form of order. An analysis of a sample order provided by Deacons, a firm of solicitors in Hong Kong, shows that Hong Kong also adopts the practice.[199]

One final point to note is that the process involved in obtaining an extension-of-time order is tedious and expensive. This is because the chargee usually has to engage the services of a solicitor and barrister and a time has to be fixed for a hearing of the application before a judge in open court.

In light of the inconvenient extension-of-time process, the United Kingdom Parliament, in pursuance of Diamond's proposal,[200] enacted

[195] See the Hong Kong Standing Committee Eighth Report, at pp. 80–1.

[196] *Watson v Duff Morgan and Vermont (Holdings) Ltd* [1974] 1 WLR 450.

[197] Ibid. [198] [1988] BCLC 556.

[199] The current authors were provided with a sample Court of First Instance extension order by the solicitors' firm Deacons. The order states, 'AND IT IS FURTHER ORDERED that this Order is without prejudice to the rights of the parties acquired during the period between the date of creation of the said document and the date of its actual registration'.

[200] Diamond, above, note 102, para. 25.3.3.

the Companies Act 1989,[201] which provided, inter alia, that, if delivery of the particulars of the charge were made after the expiry of the period for filing, the charge would be valid, provided there is no evidence that the company was insolvent at the material time or that it had become insolvent as a result of the transaction.[202] However, under the notice-filing system proposed by the English Law Commission in 2004, the registration of charges was to be perfected by filing, and there would be generally no time limit for filing particulars of the security subject to the termination of the validity of the security.[203]

Despite these cogent criticisms of the current registration system, the Hong Kong government appears to have concluded that minimal change to the current system is required. In particular, there will be a mere shortening of the registration period to twenty-one days, as is the case in the UK. No change to the existing regime in relation to extension of time for registration will be made. Applications to the court will continue to be required notwithstanding the financial cost of employing lawyers to make the application and waste of management time involved.[204]

Registrability of company security The Companies Ordinance operates a limited registration system, where only specified charges are registrable. The rationale for this limitation is that 'to embrace all types of charges might impose impossible duties on creditors to register charges that might arise in the ordinary course of day-to-day business and which are impracticable to register'.[205]

201 That is, §99 of the Act, which inserted a new §405(1) into the Companies Act 1985, which was not implemented.

202 Section 400(1) of the 1985 Act, as inserted by §95 of the 1989 Act, but the provision was not implemented. Instead, §888 of the Companies Act 2006 retains the procedure for extension of the period of registration.

203 Reg. 11, 'Company Security Regulations 2006', drafted in the UK Law Commission Report No 296. Earlier papers had suggested other alternatives; e.g. the Crowther Report on Consumer Credit (Cmnd 4596), para. 5.755 suggested no time limit, but a security interest filed more than twenty-one days after its execution would be void against the liquidator in the event of the company being wound up within three months; also, the DTI Steering Committee recommended in its Final Report, para. 12.46, that the charge should be rendered void by insolvency proceedings which began before its registration.

204 Consultation Conclusions, above, note 171, para. 55.

205 See J. De Lacy, *The United Kingdom Company Law – Reflections on the Ambit and Reform of Part 12 of the Companies Act 1985 and the Doctrine of Constructive Notice* (London: Cavendish Publishing Limited, 2002), Chapter 15, p. 335. The author stated, 'this statement does represent an accurate statement' of the present registration system policy.

The Companies Ordinance thus defines the following types of company security that must be registered:[206]

(1) a charge for the purpose of securing any issue of debentures;
(2) a charge on uncalled share capital of the company;
(3) a charge created or evidenced by an instrument which, if executed by an individual, would require registration as a bill of sale;
(4) a charge on land, wherever situated, or any interest therein, but not including a charge for any rent or other periodical sum issuing out of land;
(5) a charge on book debts of the company;
(6) a floating charge on the undertaking or property of the company;
(7) a charge on calls made but not paid;
(8) a charge on a ship or any share in a ship; and
(9) a charge on goodwill, on a patent or a licence under a patent, on a trademark or on a copyright or a licence under a copyright.

These securities can be classified into two categories. The first comprises documents and the second comprises assets.

Thus the creditor has to first look at the nature of its security document and ascertain whether it falls within the first class of documents. If it does not, the creditor should next consider whether the nature of its secured assets falls within any of the second class of assets. If the security document does not fall within either class, the security is not a registrable security.

In the discussion following, each class will be separately considered.

The nature of the document According to Farrar and Gough,[207] category (1) is a catch-all category for charges not falling within the second class. It refers to the inherent nature of the documents; that is, the issue of a series of secured debentures. The nature of the charged asset is not relevant. Thus the debenture can include both tangible and intangible personal property. The only prerequisite is that it only applies to 'issues of debentures' and not to a single debenture.

There are no cases in Hong Kong or in England evidencing a problem with the meaning of category (1) in practice. However, the New Zealand

[206] Companies Ordinance, §80(2); see Appendix A of the Ordinance for details of this section.

[207] For example, see Farrar and Hannigan, above, note 37, p. 642; Pennington, above, note 1, p. 528; Gough, above, note 40, p. 656. The English equivalent was then §396(1)(d) of the Companies Act 1985, currently §861(2) of the Companies Act 2006.

case of *Automobile Association (Canterbury) Incorporated v Australasian Secured Deposits Ltd*[208] showed that there was difficulty in respect of the meaning of 'issued debentures'. The Court of Appeal thought that the words were not meant to cover the issue of a single debenture. They applied only to an aggregate number of debentures issued by the company at a particular time or they must be connected together so as to constitute a collective group.[209] Accordingly, the court held that as the three charges in question were distinct and separate, they were not registrable. Diamond agreed with the decision.[210] He recommended that the word 'issue' should be replaced with the word 'series'.[211] In any event, it is questionable whether category (1) is necessary, when secured single debentures would in any event be caught by the second class of registrable security. The Hong Kong government has recently proposed that this category of registrable security be deleted from the list of registrable charges.[212]

The most inappropriate definition is category (3) of registrable company charges. In determining whether or not a company charge over personal chattels is within the definition, a creditor is referred to the Bills of Sale Ordinance. As was discussed in Chapter 2, the provisions of the Ordinance are highly complex and cumbersome as to the definitions of the type of security documents that are registrable under that Ordinance.[213]

A creditor who has obtained a bill of sale security from a company may mistakenly think it is not registrable, because the Bills of Sale Ordinance is usually associated with individuals. For instance, in *Re Intex Garment Factory Ltd*,[214] the court held that a document expressed to be a bill of sale over a company's machines was a registrable charge under §80(2)(c) and that it was null and void against the liquidator, because the creditor had not registered it with the Companies Registry. In 1984 the Hong Kong Standing Committee on Company Law Reform[215] recommended that category (3) should be repealed and replaced with a simple independent provision, which required that all charges over personal chattels created or

208 [1973] 1 NZLR 417. 209 Ibid., p. 424, *per* Richmond J.

210 Diamond, above, note 102, at p. 119, para. 23.9.13.

211 The word 'series' was enacted in §397 of the Companies Act 1985 (equivalent of §80(7) of the Companies Ordinance), currently §863 of the Companies Act 2006.

212 Consultation Conclusions, above, note 171, paras. 38–40.

213 See Chapter 2 above. 214 [1977–9] HKC 579.

215 Hong Kong Standing Committee on Company Law Reform, Report on Company Law Reform (1984), pp. 18–19.

evidenced by an instrument be registered,[216] except where pledges were in the actual or constructive possession of creditors.[217] The English Law Commission recently addressed two cases in which some specific pledges in the possession of debtors should also be registrable under category (3).[218] Unfortunately, the Hong Kong government is not minded to delete or amend this category of registrable charge in the rewritten Companies Ordinance.[219]

Category (6) looks at the nature of the charge as the assets are described in generic terms of 'undertaking' and 'property'. The nature of a floating charge and the problem associated with this security have already been discussed above. Generally, assets which do not fall within any other categories may be covered by this category, such as shares[220] and export quotas of the company.[221]

Nature of charged assets The assets of the company, which subject a charge over them to registration, can be divided into real property, tangible personal property and intangible personal property.

Category (4) covers all forms of charge of interests over land, freehold or leasehold, and legal or equitable, in Hong Kong and overseas. They are outside the scope of this text.

A broad spectrum of intangible personal property is covered by categories (2), (5), (7) and (9). These have already been explained in Chapters 1 and 3 above.

[216] Diamond, above, note 102, at pp. 120–21, para. 23.9.19, suggested that all forms of possessory securities, such as pledge, possessory liens and trust receipt should continue to be non-registrable.

[217] See the United Kingdom Department of Trade and Industry consultation paper, Modern Company Law – For a Competitive Economy: Registration of Company Charges, URN 00/1213 (October 2000), para. 3.33, p. 23.

[218] These are registrable under §396(1)(c) in situation (1) where the debtor has attorned to the creditor and (2) where the pledge has released the goods to the debtor under a trust receipt or similar arrangement (the equivalent of which is §860(7)(b) of the Companies Act 2006). See UK Law Commission Report No 296, paras. 3.17–3.211.

[219] Consultation Conclusions, above, note 171, paras. 42–3.

[220] In *Re City Securities Pte* [1990] 2 MLJ 257, the High Court of Singapore held that a floating charge over shares of the company was registrable under Singapore's identical company legislation.

[221] In the *State Bank of India and Another v Lisbellow Ltd and Others* [1989] 2 HKLR 604, the Court of Appeal held that an export quota could be sold, assigned and charged. If a fixed charge is created it is not registrable, but a floating charge over it will fall within category (f) (§860(7)(h) of the Companies Act 2006).

The meaning of book debts – that is, category (5) – has been the subject of judicial and academic discussion and criticism. The first problem is that the term is ambiguous. The United Kingdom Department of Trade and Industry consultation report commented that the expression is ' a somewhat indeterminate concept and the courts have looked at a whole range of different types of legal transaction and classified them as book debt or not in a case by case basis'.[222] Consequently, what constitutes book debts and other debts is confusing.[223] The second is that it excludes from registration fixed charges over other types of debt, such as credit balances and time deposits.

In 1986 the Hong Kong Standing Committee on Company Law Reform[224] recommended that category (5) be repealed or provision made that expressly provided that the term 'book debts' should not apply to charges over credit balances held by any person carrying on banking business or the business of taking deposits, because they are not traditionally regarded as book debts.[225] The Standing Committee simply echoed the view of the English court expressed in *Re Brightlife* and is, strangely, against the trend calling for a broader definition to include credit balances. For instance, Diamond suggested that the term 'book debts' should be replaced with the term 'receivables'. This term is used in the United States. The United Kingdom Steering Group, however, opined that there would still be uncertainties over the precise meaning of 'receivables'.[226] It suggested that the alternative is to retain the word 'debt' and drop the word 'book'.[227]

[222] See the United Kingdom Department of Trade and Industry consultation paper, Modern Company Law – For a Competitive Economy: Registration of Company Charges, URN 00/1213 (October 2000), at p. 24.

[223] Gough (above, note 40, pp. 681–6) listed several examples of transactions that the courts have decided are or are not book debts.

[224] Hong Kong Standing Committee on Company Law Reform, Third Report (1986), pp. 19–20.

[225] In *Re Brightlife Ltd* [1986] 3 All ER 673, Hoffmann J, *obiter*, thought that the term 'book debts' did not include credit balances in a bank account, because business custom and accounting practice do not regard these as book debts. Diamond, above, note 102, paras. 23.4.7–23.4.12, p. 119, and the Hong Kong Standing Committee on Company Law Reform, Eighth Report, 1991, pp. 69–71, took the view that the term 'book debts' should not include bank accounts, and owing to the bank's duty of secrecy and to practical difficulties, charges over bank accounts should not be made registrable.

[226] UK Department of Trade and Industry (DTI) Consultation Document, Modern Company Law – For a Competitive Economy: Registration of Company Charges (URN 00/1213), paras. 3.34–3.35, noted that the meaning of 'book debts' has been the source of constant debate.

[227] Ibid.

However, the English Law Commission Report No 296 resolved the legal complexities in their distinction because under the proposed notice-filing system all charges created by a company would be registrable unless specifically exempted.[228] In Hong Kong, the government has now concluded not to reform the existing position and to leave the thorny definition of book debts to the courts.[229]

Category (8) introduces double registration in relation to charges over ships and shares in ships. The Merchant Shipping (Registration) Ordinance (Cap. 415) governs the creation of mortgages over ships and any shares in ships. All such mortgages are required to be registered with the Registrar of Ships in Hong Kong. The Hong Kong Standing Committee on Company Law Reform[230] thought that as a matter of principle and practice it was not necessary to register at both registries as it was a duplicitous and increased cost. The Committee recommended that registration at the Companies Registry be abolished and replaced with a notation system in the Companies Registry. It further recommended that failure to notify the Registrar of Companies should entail the same consequences as failure to register a registrable charge. Their views appear to suggest that one registration is sufficient to achieve the purpose of warning third parties who wish to deal with the company. The Hong Kong government has apparently decided not to make any change to this category of registrable charge. But they intend to clarify whether charges over aircraft should also be included within the definition.[231]

Apart from the weaknesses above, there are other criticisms of the present method of listing which type of security is registrable. Firstly, the list of registrable charges is arbitrary. Lawson has commented that there was no particular reason why some forms of property were included, and others not.[232] Secondly, the list is outdated as a number of company securities or transactions (see below), which should be registrable, are outside the ambit of §80(2) of the Companies Ordinance. Thus it was commented that the list of charges had effectively been determined by 1928 but the nature of commercial transactions has become considerably more complex since that

[228] English Law Commission Report No 296, paras. 3.16, 4.1–4.2.

[229] Consultation Conclusions, above, note 171, paras. 44–8.

[230] Hong Kong Standing Committee on Company Law Reform, Fifth Annual Report (1988), at pp. 11–13.

[231] Consultation Conclusions, above, note 171, paras. 35–7.

[232] As M. Lawson, 'The Reform of the Law Relating to Security Interests in Property', *JBL* 287 (1989), at p. 297.

time.[233] As a result, the registration system is outdated and does not give complete and accurate information regarding the financial status of the company. The Hong Kong Standing Committee of Company Law Reform[234] recognised this weakness, but did not comprehensively review the matter. However, Diamond, in a more in-depth review, identified several security transactions which he thought should be registrable. They are:[235]

- security documents which do not amount to bills of sale, such as pledge and trust receipts over goods, assignment of book debts not by way of a charge;
- accounts with a bank, a charge over insurance policies,[236] a fixed charge over shares;[237]
- a retention of title over goods supplied to the chargor, hire-purchase and conditional sale agreements in respect of goods supplied to the chargor;
- negotiable instruments given to secure the payment of any book debts of the company and deposited with the creditor to secure any advancement to the company; and
- securities which are implied by law, such as a charging order obtained by a judgment creditor or a vendor's lien for unpaid purchase money.[238]

McCormack critically commented that failure to make such securities registrable constituted a significant lacuna in the legislation.[239]

The English Law Commission regarded the current list of registrable charges as inadequate, out of date and uncertain as to what should be registered.[240] It proposed that the list be abolished and replaced with a

[233] See English Law Commission Consultation Paper No 164, para. 3.12, citing the work of De Lacy, above, note 205, pp. 336–7.

[234] Hong Kong Standing Committee on Company Law Reform, Eighth Report (1991), pp. 69–73.

[235] These were identified by Diamond, above, note 102, paras. 23.4–23.9.25.

[236] *Paul & Frank Ltd v Discount Bank (Overseas) Ltd and Board of Trade* [1967] Ch 348; the court held that charges of an insurance policy whether the claim has arisen or not are not registrable. The Hong Kong Standing Committee expressed no opinion.

[237] As noted above, floating charges, which affect shares owned by the company, are registrable. Diamond, above, note 102, at paras. 23.8.12–13, thought that charges over all kinds of shares should not be registrable; this view was echoed by the Standing Committee in its Eighth Report, at pp. 72–3. The Cork Committee, on Insolvency Law and Practice (Cmnd 8558, para. 1520, 1982), however, recommended that charges on stocks and shares and other marketable securities should be made registrable.

[238] *Capital Finance Co. Ltd v Stokes* [1969] 1 Ch 261; and *London and Cheshire Insurance Co. Ltd v Laplagrene Property Co. Ltd* [1971] Ch 499, [1971] 1 All ER 766.

[239] McCormack, above, note 159, p. 66.

[240] English Law Commission Consultation Paper No 164, para. 5.3.

new system that required all charges to be registrable unless specifically exempted.[241] The exceptions were listed in the draft Regulation 4 of Company Security Regulations included in the English Law Commission Report No 296 for possible adoption as part of the proposed notice-filing scheme.[242] This proposal was subject to security interests over certain types of asset to be registered in specialist registers (see draft Regulation 25). Draft Regulation 20 further provided that unless a charge is exempt from registration, it would not be effective against the company's administrator or liquidator or an execution creditor. However, this reform is now unlikely to be adopted in the UK. In Hong Kong, the government has not considered such a radical change but has recently decided not to include charges over insurance policies, fixed charges over shares or the assignment of rental income or proceeds of sale as registrable charges in the reformed Companies Ordinance.[243]

In relation to the issue whether 'quasi-securities' such as retention-of-title devices should be included for registration in the new notice-filing system, the earlier English Law Commission Consultation Paper No 164 considered at length the items identified by Diamond that should be made registrable,[244] and recommended that hire-purchase, financial lease and retention-of-title clauses[245] should be registrable under its proposed notice-filing system. However, the English Law Commission Report No 296 received adverse opinions and intended at that time to reconsider the issue in the context of a broader project on transfer of title by non-owners.[246]

On the other hand, the English Commission did propose that the following should not be registrable – pledges,[247] trust receipts,[248] contractual

[241] English Law Commission Report No 296, paras. 3.15–3.16.

[242] The exceptions include, for instance, fixed charges over registered land (with the introduction of electronic conveyancing the Land Registry has the power to forward information about the charges to Companies House), lien, and some particular scenarios in the assignment and sale of receivables, etc.

[243] Consultation Conclusions, above, note 171, paras. 33–4.

[244] English Law Commission Consultation Paper No 164, Part V.

[245] Ibid., para. 5.13.

[246] English Law Commission Report No 296, at p. 14.

[247] Except some pledges which will be treated as registrable charges if collateral is made available to the debtor. See draft reg. 22, 'Company Security Regulations 2006', in the English Law Commission Report No 296. The UK Law Commission Report No 296, paras. 3.23–3.25, recommended that if the debtor has possession of the goods for less than fifteen days, the pledge (and the pledgee's interest in the proceeds) should be treated as a charge over goods and their proceeds. The charge must be registered within fifteen days unless the collateral is returned to the creditor's possession before that time.

[248] This is because a trust receipt is regarded as securing the continuance of the pledge rather than as an independent security device; see English Law Commission Report

liens,[249] charges over shares and investment where the chargee has 'control or possession' and some securities which give the creditor control or possession over investment property.[250] Recently, the Hong Kong SAR government has made it clear that it, too, does not accept the case for registration of these securities in the context of the reformed Companies Ordinance.[251]

In relation to the question whether the proposed notice-filing system should be extended to non-corporate debtors, the English Law Commission noted that this might result in expanding the register[252] for no good purpose. The Commission did not recommend a definite solution, but thought that an option worth considering was to exclude consumer security interests from the need to register security.[253] The Law Commission Report No 296 was unable to produce detailed recommendations as to the question whether the new system should be extended to unincorporated businesses and individuals where the charges granted must comply with the Bills of Sale Acts 1878–91. However, it took the view that replacing the Bills of Sale Acts was desirable.[254] In Hong Kong, the government appears to have no appetite for any such radical action in the foreseeable future.[255]

Given this state of affairs the question arises as to whether the current definition of registrable charges too complex for a creditor to comprehend.

It is submitted that this is the case, particularly where the creditor is an ordinary businessperson unfamiliar with the technical legal terms. As the English Law Commission commented,[256] 'In some cases it is hard to

No 296, para. 3.22. But what happens if it is not? See discussion on this in Chapter 2 above. If it is an independent trust receipt it should be registrable.

[249] Notwithstanding *Re Welsh Irish Ferries (The Ugland Trailer)* [1986] Ch 471, which held that such liens were charges, the Law Commission thought that it should be made clear that liens over sub-freights were not charges. See also draft reg. 42, 'Company Security Regulations 2006', in the Law Commission Report No 296, which provided that pledges should include contractual liens.

[250] Financial Collateral Arrangement (No 2) Regulations 2003 (FCAR), regs. 3 and 4(4), explicitly excluded the formality requirement of registration of security financial collateral arrangements under §395 of the Companies Act 1985 (currently §860 of the Companies Act 2006) in order to render the arrangement enforceable. The agreement or arrangement must also be evidenced in writing. Note that the Hong Kong Standing Committee on Company Law Reform basically shared the same view; see the Eighth Report, pp. 73–4.

[251] Consultation Conclusions, above, note 171, para. 31.

[252] Ibid., para. 10.35. [253] Ibid., paras. 10.35–10.38.

[254] English Law Commission Report No 296, p. 14, notes 23–4.

[255] Consultation Conclusions, above, note 171, para. 31.

[256] English Law Commission Consultation Paper No 164, para. 3.14.

decide what falls within the type of charge listed. For a non-lawyer the list can be particularly hard to interpret.'

Therefore the registration system is far removed from the earlier observation that simplicity and comprehensibility are the hallmarks of an ideal registration system as envisaged by Brett MR.[257]

Conclusiveness of registration and perfection When a charge is registered, the Registrar of Companies has to issue the chargee with a certificate of registration. The certificate has serious implications for creditors of the company. According to §83(2) of the Companies Ordinance, the certificate issued by the Registrar of Companies is final and conclusive evidence that the requirements of the Companies Ordinance in relation to the charge have been complied with. The certificate of registration also states the amount secured by the charge.[258] The certificate serves two purposes:

- it protects the chargee, as it is evidence that the charge is perfected and the priority of the charge secured;[259]
- it creates certainty, which is vital to the smooth running of business.[260]

The Privy Council in *Sun Tai Cheung Credits Ltd v Attorney General* considered the extent to which the final and conclusive rule could or could not be challenged.[261] There Lord Templeman observed that the following could not constitute grounds for challenging the final and conclusive rule of the certificate:[262] (i) the purported date of creation did not represent the actual date, (ii) registration arose from *ultra vires* acts of the registrar[263] and (iii) proper procedure of registration was not followed by the registrar.[264]

[257] See Chapter 2 above.

[258] Companies Ordinance (Cap. 32), §81(2). Note that the Hong Kong Standing Committee on Company Law Reform recommended that the certificate of registration of charge should not in the future state the amount secured by a charge in the certificate. See the Seventeenth Report, para. 6.2(a).

[259] See the United Kingdom Department of Trade and Industry consultation paper, Modern Company Law – For a Competitive Economy: Registration of Company Charges, URN 00/1213 (October 2000), p. 17.

[260] Ibid., para. 3.15, p. 18. [261] [1987] HKLR 1010. [262] Ibid.

[263] *R v Registrar of Companies, ex parte Central Bank of India* [1986] 1 All ER 105, approved by the Privy Council in the Hong Kong case of *Sun Tai Cheung Credits Ltd v Attorney General* [1987] HKLR 1010, at 1015, *per* Lord Templeman.

[264] *Re Yolland, Husson and Birkett Ltd* [1908] 1 Ch 152.

However, the general rule could be challenged if the certificate were procured by fraud or duress, or there appeared to be an error on its face.[265] It should, however, be noted that Lord Templeman's observations were *obiter*, because no certificate of registration had been issued in that case.

In *Sun Tai Cheung Credits Ltd*,[266] several charges were created over the chargor's properties. The charges arose from several letters of exchange between the chargor and the chargee. To discover the precise nature of the charge and when the charges were created, it was necessary to read and interpret each of the letters. Further, the chargee had not accurately described the charges in the relevant column of statutory Form IV. When the registrar queried the sufficiency of the information, it was emphasised that the statutory time period for registration would expire very shortly. Two months after the expiry of the five-week period, the chargee replied and said that the security was an equitable mortgage arising from an oral agreement. However, the Registrar refused to register the charge, as a result of the insufficient information, and because, in any event, the five-week period had expired. The chargee could, however, register the charge if they obtained a court order for extension of time. The chargee decided to challenge the registrar's decision rather than apply for an extension of time. The High Court ordered the registrar to register the charge. The registrar appealed against the decision, and the Court of Appeal allowed the appeal. On appeal by the chargee to the Privy Council, the Privy Council dismissed the appeal on the grounds that the registrar had discretion to reject the application if he was not satisfied with the information provided by the applicant.

Sun Tai Cheung raises an interesting point: whether the situation in the earlier English Court of Appeal case of *CL Nye Ltd*, where the chargee had deliberately altered the actual date of creation of the charge, falls within (i) above, which does not allow the certificate to be challenged, or falls within the ambit of 'fraud', which does allow the certificate to be challenged. There a chargee, having discovered a failure to register a charge a few months after the charge was created, inserted in the charge instrument the date of its discovery and not the actual date of creation. The charge was registered by the registrar and a certificate of registration was issued. When the chargor was subsequently liquidated, the liquidator challenged the charge on the ground that it was registered out of time.

[265] *R v Registrar of Companies, ex parte Central Bank of India* [1986] 1 All ER 105, CA, approved in *Sun Tai Cheung Credits Ltd v Attorney General* [1987] HKLR 1010 (PC).

[266] [1987] HKLR 1010.

The court dismissed the challenge on the ground that the certificate when issued was final and conclusive and that there was compliance with all the statutory requirements.

The English case of *CL Nye Ltd* was not cited in Lord Templeman's speech. Notwithstanding this, it is submitted that in light of his observation, *CL Nye Ltd* should no longer be regarded as good law, at least in Hong Kong. This conclusion is clear from his speech, which states that:

- Owing to the serious consequence of the issue of a certificate of registration, it is incumbent on the chargee to prove his right to be registered by giving the date of the charge and thus demonstrating that the five-week time limit has not expired.
- If a charge was in fact created outside the five-week time limit set by §80 of the Companies Ordinance, the chargee should not be entitled to apply for registration.
- A chargee who knowingly applied for and obtained a certificate by falsely affirming or implying in column 1 of the statutory Form IV that his charge was created within the time limit would be liable to have his certificate set aside by the court on the grounds of fraud.[267]

In addition to these reasons, there are others that support this position. Firstly, *Sun Tai Cheung*, being a Hong Kong Privy Council decision, should carry greater weight than *CL Nye Ltd*, an English Court of Appeal's decision. Secondly, this position protects subsequent unsuspecting third parties from obtaining security from a chargor on the mistaken belief that it had priority, but is then at risk of being superseded by the 'fraud' of the earlier chargor. As between the two parties, the subsequent creditor being the innocent party has a better equity than the earlier chargee.

Though *Sun Tai Cheung* is a commendable attempt to protect third parties by limiting the impact of the conclusiveness effect, the fact remains that the certificate does not guarantee that all particulars required to be registered, in the absence of fraud, are accurate. In fact the certificate implies that the particulars supplied are true.

Owing to the legal complexities and the question of the reliability of such certificates, it is suggested that the two purposes mentioned earlier could be achieved without the issuance of a certificate but by the

[267] Ibid., at 1014.

adoption of a simpler mechanism.[268] In this regard, the United Kingdom enacted provisions in the Companies Act 1989 to abolish the issuance of such certificates.[269] When a charge is registered, the registrar merely gives the presentor a copy of the filed particulars and a note of the date on which they were delivered to him. There is a presumption that the particulars were delivered on that date, but the presumption can be rebutted by evidence that they were actually delivered earlier.[270] However, this new practice was not implemented and the certificate procedure has been retained.[271] More recently, the English Law Commission reinforced the call for abolition of the certification system.[272] Under its proposed notice-filing system, particulars of the financing statement can be challenged.[273]

In 1991, the Hong Kong Standing Committee on Company Law Reform[274] expressed the view that Hong Kong should likewise abolish the rule and adopt the new practice in England. However, the recommendation has yet to be adopted in Hong Kong. It is, however, submitted that the purported injustice and inaccuracies that may be created by the certificate may be overstated. In the long history of the certificate in Hong Kong, its potential problem was only raised in *Sun Tai Cheung*. Even then, the observation of Lord Templeman was *obiter*.

The current position is that the Hong Kong government has reviewed the registration process and has decided that in the reformed Companies Ordinance, as both the charge instrument and relevant particulars will be delivered for registration, the registrar will no longer be required to scrutinise the charge documents. A certificate will be issued but it will only be evidence of the fact of the delivery of the instrument and the required particulars, and the date upon which they were received. Further, on satisfaction or partial satisfaction of the charge, relevant details will also have to be filed at the Registry.[275]

[268] See the United Kingdom Department of Trade and Industry consultation paper, Modern Company Law – For a Competitive Economy: Registration of Company Charges, URN 00/1213 (October 2000), para. 3.38, p. 21, where it was stated, 'it actually serves no greater purpose than an acknowledgement of receipt'.

[269] Supposedly inserted under §398(3) of the Companies Act 1985 but never implemented.

[270] Under §397(5) of the Companies Act 1985.

[271] Section 869(5) of the Companies Act 2006.

[272] Above, note 7, para. 3.76.

[273] This is discussed further in Chapter 8 below.

[274] Hong Kong Standing Committee on Company Law Reform, Eighth Report (1991), pp. 76–8.

[275] Consultation Conclusions, above, note 171, paras. 55–7.

Substantive impact of registration on priority of competing claims
When a registrable charge is duly registered with the Companies Registry, registration serves as constructive notice of the charge to the whole world. A subsequent third party who deals with the company is bound by the charge. However, constructive notice does not extend to the contents of the charge in Hong Kong.[276] The impact of constructive notice on competing claims of subsequent third parties in respect of the same secured assets is discussed further in Chapter 6 below.

Perfecting overseas company security

Basically, the rules relating to the period of registration and registrable security discussed above apply equally to security granted by foreign companies in Hong Kong.[277] However, they are governed by an additional set of rules in §91, Part III and Part XI of the Companies Ordinance.[278]

Previously, by virtue of §91, if a foreign chargor company established a place of business in Hong Kong after a charge was created or acquired, the company had to register the charge with the Registrar of Companies within five weeks of the date on which it had established a place of business in Hong Kong.[279] This requirement recognised Hong Kong's place as an international commercial and financial centre and the need to protect the interests of creditors who may deal with such companies. This provision has been retained under §91(5) of the now amended Companies Ordinance.

However, Part XI of the Companies Ordinance does contain a practical operational difficulty in the foreign chargor company's registration system. Section 333 required an overseas company to register itself with the Registrar of Companies within one month of its 'establishment of business in Hong Kong'.[280] The Hong Kong Law Reform Commission

[276] *ABN Amro Bank NV v Chiyu Banking Corp Ltd and Others* [2000] 3 HKC 381.

[277] A foreign company is a company incorporated overseas; see §332 of the Companies Ordinance (Cap. 32).

[278] As amended in 2004 and implemented on 14 December 2007.

[279] Section 91(3) of the Companies Ordinance (Cap 32).

[280] The English equivalent is §1044 of the Companies Act 2006 (replacing §744 of the Companies Act 1985). The difficulty in defining the expression had been noted in the following cases: *Re Oriel Ltd* [1986] 1 WLR 180, at 184, where Oliver LJ said, 'the word "established" ... connotes not only the setting up of a place of business at a specific location but a degree of permanence or recognisability as being a location of the company's business', followed in *Cleveland Museum of Art v Capricorn International SA* [1990] BCLC 546. In *Lord Advocate v. Huron and Erie Loan and Savings Co.* (1911) SC 612, 616, Lord Dunedin stated, 'The expression [establishes a place of business] seems to me

Standing Committee expressed the view that it was common practice among the creditors, usually the banks, when taking charges over property located in Hong Kong from a foreign company chargor, to search the Companies Registry to discover whether the company had been duly registered with the Registrar of Companies.[281] If not, the bank generally concluded that the charge did not need to be registered. The Hong Kong Standing Committee considered this conclusion to be potentially erroneous. In the English case of *Slavenburg's Bank NV v Intercontinental Natural Resources Ltd and Others*,[282] the court held that there was no relationship between the English equivalent of §91[283] and §333.[284]

Accordingly, if a company had in fact a place of business in Hong Kong then any charge granted by it on property in Hong Kong must be registered even if the foreign company has not registered with the Registrar of Companies under Part XI. Although, strictly speaking, *Slavenburg's Bank NV* is not binding on the Hong Kong courts, there is nothing to prevent it from being followed.

The Standing Committee, on the basis of *Slavenburg's Bank NV*, identified the following potential problems:[285]

- Except by a search of the register, it is extremely difficult for a creditor to ascertain whether the company has an established place of business in Hong Kong, and if not, it can only be conclusively determined by a decision of the court.[286] Thus a chargee may mistakenly fail to register

clearly to point to this, that the company must have what I may call a local habitation of its own.' In the Hong Kong case of *Chingman Company v Popular Fabrics Inc.* [1963] HKLR 855, the defendant, an overseas company, was held to have an established place of business in Hong Kong, because it had appointed a person at a particular room at Mongkok to meet people and receive telephone messages and the room was regarded as a postal address; but in *Elsinct (Asia-Pacific) Ltd v Commercial Bank of Korea Ltd* [1994] 3 HKC 365, it was held that a foreign bank did not have a place of business in Hong Kong although it carried on the activities of promotion, interviews and persuasion for the purpose of promoting its banking activities. However, on almost similar facts, the court came to a different conclusion in *National Bank of Canada v Commercial Bank of Korea Ltd* (Comm L 23/92, unreported).

281 First Report (January 1985), pp. 1–7.

282 [1980] 1 All ER 955. There a charge over an asset of a foreign company subsequently brought into the UK was held to be void for non-registration.

283 Equivalent to §1052 of the Companies Act 2006 (§409 of the Companies Act 1985).

284 Equivalent to §1044 of the Companies Act 2006 (§744 of the Companies Act 1985).

285 This problem was also discussed at some length in the UK Law Commission Consultation Paper No 164, paras. 3.33–3.40.

286 Hong Kong Standing Committee on Company Law Reform, First Report (1985), pp. 1–7.

a charge on the grounds that the chargor has no registered place of business in Hong Kong, but in the event of dispute, the court may decide to the contrary.

- Even if the chargee wishes to register the charge, the Registrar of Companies will not accept a charge for registration unless the overseas company has already been registered with the registrar.
- The creditor may not know that an asset of the company has subsequently come into Hong Kong after the charge was created, for example when an aircraft or a ship comes into port.

There could also be a fourth problem.[287] This related to the statutory registration period of five weeks. If an overseas company, having a place of business in Hong Kong, created, say, a floating charge, but the chargor had no assets in Hong Kong, the charge will not be registrable. However, if, five weeks later, the chargor acquired assets in Hong Kong, the chargee would have to apply to the court for an extension of time, otherwise the application for registration might be rejected by the registrar.

To solve these difficulties, the Standing Committee made three recommendations. Firstly, §91 should only apply to a foreign company which had actually registered a place of business under Part XI. Secondly, aircraft and ships should be deemed to be situated where they are registered as vessels.[288] Thirdly, a registered foreign company should only be required to register a floating charge over assets which are situated in Hong Kong while the debt remains unpaid. These recommendations generally follow §105, Schedule 15, of the United Kingdom Companies Act 1989, which abrogated the rule of *Slavenberg's Bank NV* and inserted several provisions into Part XXIII of the Companies Act 1985, but was never implemented.[289]

Except for the recommendation on floating charges, the reforms were enacted by the Companies (Amendment) Ordinance (Ord. No 30 of

[287] See McCormack, above, note 159, p. 154.

[288] This is the same as recommended by the English Law Commission in its Report No 296, para. 3.272. See also draft reg. 3(2), 'Company Security Regulations 2006', attached to the same report.

[289] Briefly, under the new provisions charges given by an overseas company are not registrable unless the company has been registered with the UK Registrar of Companies; a registered overseas company is obliged to deliver details of any charges over any assets situated in the UK to the Registrar; and lastly, when assets are brought within the jurisdiction and are subject to a charge, the company has four months to register the charge from the date of the asset's presence in the jurisdiction and not from the date of creation of the charge. Failure to do so will not render the charges unenforceable but will subject the company to a fine.

2004). By virtue of Schedule 2, §91(1) now states that Part III (registration of charges) extends only to non-Hong Kong companies which are registered under Part XI, while §91(2) ensures that the charged property must be in Hong Kong. Read together with §91(5), a charge can only be registered in Hong Kong by a non-Hong Kong company when (i) the company is registered under Part XI, (ii) the property is physically situated in Hong Kong and (iii) registration of the charge is undertaken within five weeks of the registration of the non-Hong Kong company at the Hong Kong company registry, or if registered already, within five weeks of the creation of the charge.

In contrast to the charged property where physical location determines registration, aircraft and ships are treated by §91(7) as property based on their place of registration rather than physical location.[290] Section 91(4) further allows for three situations where non-Hong Kong companies may not need to register their charges despite being registered under Part XI.[291] However, as these three situations generally involve the company no longer being active in Hong Kong, the general position is that registered non-Hong Kong companies are required to register their charges granted over property located in Hong Kong.

The English Law Commission took a slightly different view on the first and third points. Report No 296 recommended that the proposed notice-filing scheme be not limited to registration of charges created by overseas companies which have registered a place of business.[292] The position recommended was that any charge created by an overseas company over its assets in England and Wales should be registrable. Those existing charges over goods brought in by an overseas company should also be subject to registration within sixty days of import.[293] It must be noted, however, that

[290] Section 91(7) reads, '(a) a ship or aircraft that is registered in Hong Kong shall be treated as property in Hong Kong notwithstanding that the ship or aircraft is physically located outside Hong Kong; and (b) a ship or aircraft that is registered in a place outside Hong Kong shall be treated as property outside Hong Kong notwithstanding that the ship or aircraft is physically located in Hong Kong'.

[291] These are, namely, where the company has ceased to have a 'place of business in Hong Kong', where it has been dissolved, and where it has been struck off the companies' register.

[292] While retracting its previous recommendation at this point, the Law Commission Report No 296, para. 3.264, had argued that a scheme that applied only to companies with places of business would not offer sufficient protection to buyers or potential secured parties.

[293] Law Commission Report No 296, paras. 3.265–3.268. See also draft regs. 3(1) and 21, 'Company Security Regulations 2006', attached to the report.

overseas companies under the Companies Act 2006 are governed under new provisions in Part 34. Section 1052 of the Act confers wide powers to the Secretary of State with regard to overseas companies who may promulgate regulations in respect of registration of charges, such regulations being subject to a negative Parliamentary resolution.[294]

4.2.3 *Publicity of company security*

Publicity of company security is linked to the rules governing perfection discussed above. Thus publicity is achieved through registration of the particulars of all registrable charges.

Any member of the public may inspect the microfilm on the payment of a fee of HK$20.[295]

Conducting a search at the Hong Kong Companies Registry is expeditious.[296] There are two reasons for this. Firstly, the information regarding the registered security is electronically recorded. Secondly, there are adequate computer terminals to meet demand for searches. The waiting time for a free computer terminal averages between ten and fifteen minutes. In the future, remote online searching may well become possible.

The Companies Registry plays a useful function for third parties who desire to deal with a company. The register of charges provides important information on the financial exposure and status of the company's assets. However, there are two major weaknesses in the current practice. These are discussed below.

Incomplete information

There is incomplete information in relation for three matters, namely total indebtedness of the company, secured assets of the company and pertinent terms of the registered security. Each of them can have a serious impact on third parties.

In respect of total indebtedness, the Companies Registry does not record any changes in the amount of the loan secured by the charge. The loan may decrease by reason of the chargor's repayment of part of the loan or it can increase by reason of further advances made under an 'all

[294] See Alcock, Birds and Gale, above, note 168, at para. 2.22.

[295] Current fee as of 6 May 2009. For a detailed fee structure, see www.cr.gov.hk/en/public/fees.htm#5.

[296] This is based on the personal observation of the current authors at the Companies Registry.

monies' clause.[297] This clause is also commonly found in charges in Hong Kong.[298] Consequently, as the English Law Commission commented, the Companies Register did not accurately reflect the amount secured at the time of searching.[299] Indeed, the Law Commission further commented, 'in the case of an "all monies" charge, it is inherently impossible to determine the current indebtedness from the Companies Register'.[300] One solution for a potential subsequent creditor is to check the actual amount with the chargor or chargee, but this itself defeats the purpose of a registration system.[301] Another recent recommendation made by the Law Commission was to confer power on the registrar to make rules that may require further information on the filing particulars.[302]

The Hong Kong Standing Committee in its Seventeenth Report notes the problem posed by the 'all monies' clause, but no detailed examination of the problem was made or significant suggestions for remedy proposed. Instead, the Committee recommended that the certificate of registration should not state the amount secured by a charge in the certificate at all. Perhaps the Standing Committee felt that this would be sufficient to warn the subsequent potential chargee that further inquiry with the prior chargee or chargor was necessary.[303]

In respect of the security granted over assets, several securities granted by the company over its assets are not registrable. Consequently there is no publicity of these securities, though they are important to a third party when judging the creditworthiness of the company.

In respect of the third issue, the pertinent terms of registered security, the registered information does not disclose particulars relating to semi-automatic and automatic crystallisation clauses contained in the charge. The prejudicial effect on a third party has already been discussed above. Its impact on the priority of competing claims is discussed further below.[304] However, this problem may be at least partially addressed by the recent decision to require registration of the charge instrument and specified particulars in the reformed Companies Ordinance.

[297] The doctrine of tacking on further advances is discussed further in Chapter 6 below.

[298] Some 95 per cent of charges registered with the Companies Registry had an 'all monies' clause. See the Hong Kong Standing Committee on Company Law Reform, Seventeenth Annual Report (2000/2001), para. 6.2 (a).

[299] English Law Commission Consultation Paper No 164, para. 3.17. [300] Ibid.

[301] The recommendations of Consultation Paper No 164 and the Eighth Report (1991) of the Hong Kong Standing Committee on Company Law Reform will be discussed in Chapter 8 below.

[302] Law Commission Report No 296, paras. 3.118–3.120.

[303] Above, note 298, at p. 21, para. 6.2(a). [304] See Chapter 6.

Publicity is not expeditious

As discussed above, the secured creditor has five weeks to register the charge. This period is commonly referred to as 'the five-week invisibility window'.[305] This extended period has two problematic consequences. Firstly, there is a long period of uncertainty for third parties who wish to deal with the company. Secondly, as Diamond commented, 'Inspection of the register showing that there is no charge means nothing, because there may already be in existence valid charges which may subsequently be registered.'[306] The impact of this delay will be fully appreciated when its implications on the priority of competing claims are discussed below.[307]

The Standing Committee suggested that the five weeks be reduced to twenty-one days.[308] This period is still unduly long, considering that Hong Kong is small geographically and registration is electronically effected. Indeed, the English Law Commission recently thought that the invisibility period was a serious weakness and should be completely removed and be replaced by a voluntary notice-filing system with no time limit for filing.[309] In contrast, the Hong Kong government does not consider the invisibility problem to be a serious one but it has proposed reducing the period to twenty-one days in the reformed Companies Ordinance.[310]

It should be mentioned that the public may search the private register of charges of the company, which is open to inspection by any person on payment of a fee of HK$2 for each inspection as the company may prescribe.[311] However, in Hong Kong the practice is that potential creditors do not conduct such searches.[312] This raises the question of whether it is necessary to continue this requirement as the public registry seems sufficient. The English Law Commission thought that if the Companies

[305] See the United Kingdom Department of Trade and Industry consultation paper, Modern Company Law – For a Competitive Economy: Registration of Company Charges, URN 00/1213 (October 2000), para. 3.79, p. 39. The consultation paper, however, thought that the invisibility problem period 'is greater in theory than in practice'; see para. 3.80, p. 39. It suggested that shortening the period to ten days could reduce the problem; ibid.

[306] Diamond, above, note 102, para. 26.1. [307] See Chapter 6.

[308] Hong Kong Standing Committee on Company Law Reform, Eighth Report (1991), p. 81.

[309] English Law Commission Report No 296, paras. 1.32 and 3.79–3.82.

[310] Consultation Conclusions, above, note 171, para. 55.

[311] See the recommendation of the English Law Commission Report No 296, p. 101, para. 3.298.

[312] The current authors conducted email interviews with a number of law firms in Hong Kong and all replied that no search is done at the private register of the borrower company. All of them only conducted searches at the Companies Registry. The law firms were: Linklaters; Paul Hastings & Co.; Koo & Partners; Herbert Smith; Deacons; and Johnnie Yam, Jacky Lee & Co.

Registry were reformed to widen the list of registrable charges, as suggested above, to include other security interests, the requirement for a company to record the charges on its private register should be abolished.[313] This change is not proposed for inclusion in the reformed Companies Ordinance in Hong Kong.

4.2.4 *Costs of creating, perfecting and publicising company security in Hong Kong*

Except for legal fees, there is no cost involved in the creation of company securities in Hong Kong. Company charges are exempt from stamp duty as they are not instruments liable to stamp duty under Schedule 1 of the Stamp Duty Ordinance (Cap. 117).

In relation to perfection, publicity and search, the cost is minimal. The Hong Kong Companies Registry charges a flat fee of HK$340 for registration and a search fee of HK$20.

4.3 Creation, perfection and publicity of company security over personal property in China, and cost

4.3.1 *Creation of company security*

In sharp contrast to Hong Kong, there are no special security devices for companies in China. As legal persons, they are able to use the same security devices – Diya mortgage, pledge and trust receipt – to secure personal property as are natural persons. Accordingly, the rules governing creation of these securities explained in Chapters 2 and 3 above apply here equally. On the other hand, some provisions in the Company Law 2006 and some administrative regulations have been enacted specifically to limit the creation of security interests by companies. For example, the Company Law (as amended in 2004) provides that the directors and managers are prohibited from providing the company's assets as security for personal obligations incurred by the company's shareholders or other individuals.[314] Violation of this provision will render the security contract void. The debtor and the security provider are jointly and severally liable for any loss incurred by the creditor, unless the creditor knew or ought to have known of the use of company assets.[315]

[313] English Law Commission Report No 296, paras. 3.298–3.300.

[314] Article 60(3) of the Company Law (2004 amendment).

[315] Article 4 of the Judicial Interpretations of the Security Law.

However, the latest amendment to the Company Law (in 2005), which came into force in January 2006, relaxed this prohibition. Article 16 now provides that where a company intends to invest in any other enterprise or provide security for other obligations, it shall, according to the provisions of its articles of association, be approved at a meeting of the board of directors or a shareholders' meeting. If a company intends to provide security interests to a shareholder, a resolution should be passed at a shareholder's meeting. In other words, the granting of security interests by companies to the third parties is now governed by procedural approval by the company's directors or shareholders, as appropriate, rather than there being an outright prohibition.

There is little difficulty in China in determining whether a security created by a company is a mortgage, a pledge or a trust receipt. This is because the demarcation between them is distinct and leaves little room for disagreement as to characterisation. For example, examination of standard company mortgage documents in China reveals that the terms are, generally, similar to those of a fixed charge in Hong Kong. They usually contain the following: a statement that the mortgage is granted to secure a loan from the mortgagee, a description of the secured property in a schedule, the amount of the loan, the rate of interest, and the remedies of the mortgagee in the event of default of the mortgagor or failure to pay any monies secured by the mortgage.[316] The creation aspect is therefore free from the difficulties surrounding the common law fixed charge and floating charge discussed above.

4.3.2 *Perfection of company security*

As in Hong Kong, all mortgages granted by companies must be registered with the relevant registration agency in China, depending on the nature of the mortgaged property, i.e. timber trees at the forestry bureau; aircraft, ships and vehicles at the transportation agency; equipment and other movable property of an enterprise at the local SAIC.[317] At the same time, the registration agency is responsible for forwarding a copy of the registration document to the mortgagor's home registration agency and the local SAIC office where other mortgaged

[316] Shengping Gao, *Studies on Chattel Mortgage* (Beijing: China Industry and Commerce Press, 2004), pp. 95–101.

[317] Article 42 of the Security Law; see also §2.8.2, 'Perfection of Mortgages over Tangible Personal Property'.

property is located.[318] Registration constitutes constructive notice of the mortgage to the whole world.[319] If a mortgage is not registered it is invalid against third parties.[320] Registration in China, as in Hong Kong, is a perfection requirement. The procedural rules relating to registration of the mortgage and discussed in Chapters 2 and 3 above apply here equally.

There are two distinct differences between the Property Law (together with the Security Law) and the Hong Kong Companies Ordinance registration systems. They are:

(1) In China no period is fixed for registration whereas in Hong Kong, as discussed above, the charge has to be registered within five weeks (to be reduced to twenty-one days in the reformed Ordinance).

Although the Property Law and Security Law do not specify a period during which the chattel mortgage has to be registered, a prudent secured creditor should, however, register it expeditiously as the Property Law and Security Law provide that priority between competing claims is determined by the date of registration. Thus it appears that the Chinese registration system encourages diligence on the part of creditors and provides more timely information to the public on the financial status of the company than does the Hong Kong system.

(2) The registration system in China is based on the nature of asset encumbered. This is in contrast to the Hong Kong registration system, where the distinction is based on ownership, namely ownership by companies or by individuals.

The Security Law mandates registration according to the nature of assets, and makes little mention of the nature of ownership.[321] Therefore companies and individuals need to register a particular mortgage with the relevant authority that administers that type of asset. The only

[318] Article 2 of Registration and Administration Rules for Mortgaged Movable Property of Enterprises (2000).

[319] Its impact will be discussed further in Chapter 6 below.

[320] See Articles 188 and 189 of the Property Law – a good-faith requirement imposed on third parties in relation to the general scope of the property to be mortgaged. Readers should also read Article 180 of the Property Law along with Article 43 of the Security Law relating to 'other property that may be mortgaged according to law and administrative rules' where no good-faith requirement is imposed.

[321] For example, where the properties are 'trees' under Article 42(3) of the Security Law, the Forestry Administration Department is the stipulated registration agency.

difference is that a company is supposed to follow the Registration and Administration Rules for Mortgaged Movable Property of Enterprises (2000).[322] Furthermore, a marked difference is where the personal property concerned constitutes 'other personal property' and not that administratively designated as the responsibility of any particular registration authority.[323] In this case voluntary registration at the notary department of the local justice bureau can be accomplished in accordance with the Rules for Notary Departments to Administer Mortgage Registration (2002) to effect registration in respect of such property.

As in Hong Kong, the registration departments issue conclusive evidence certificates. The registrar endorses on the original mortgage deed the date the mortgage was received by the agency, the volume number, the file number and the folio number, and the instrument is returned to the mortgagee.

4.3.3 *Publicity of company security*

All mortgages are publicised through the registration system. The rules on publicity are simple and they have already been discussed in Chapter 2.

A serious weakness is the poor public accessibility of information at the various registration agencies, which has already been discussed in Chapter 2.

The registration systems in Hong Kong and China differ significantly in respect to the particulars to be registered with the Companies Registry and the different registration authorities respectively. In China, the system of registration is a registration of particulars of the mortgage and the mortgage instrument. However, the proposed reforms in Hong Kong will, in the future, align with this particular aspect of the registration process.

4.3.4 *Cost of creation, perfection and publicity of company security*

In China, there are several costs in relation to the creation of company security devices. They are subject to stamp duty on a sliding scale. However, there is no nationally set criterion on how much the responsible

[322] As amended in 2009.

[323] Article 43 of the Security Law stipulates that individual owners may effect voluntary registration of such property with the notary department, and the mortgage agreement takes effect from the day of registration.

registration department should charge. As a result, registration fees charged vary considerably from place to place. Generally, the fee charged is a small fraction of the principal loan and with the maximum amount of 5,000 RMB.[324]

In relation to the cost of perfection and publicity, the registration fee at the relevant authority is not a flat fee. As discussed in Chapter 2, fees are charged on a sliding scale: the larger the loan, the greater the fee. Nonetheless, the fee is minimal.

4.4 Conclusion

The foregoing discussion shows that the rules governing the creation, perfection and publicity of company security over personal property in Hong Kong and China have both strengths and weaknesses in relation to the creation, perfection and publicity criteria established in Chapter 1.

With regard to creation, the rules governing the creation of company security over personal property in Hong Kong have satisfied nearly all the creation criteria.[325] The creation process is expeditious and inexpensive. The non-possessory security devices – which give the debtor possession of the secured assets – are capable of securing future advances, give the debtor (subject to the security) the freedom of dealing with secured assets, and are capable of securing after-acquired and future assets. However, there are three criteria which the rules of creation do not satisfy, namely simplicity, comprehensibility and protection of legitimate interests of interested parties. The last is a consequence of the first two.

The major causes of these weaknesses are the highly complex and uncertain substantive rules governing the creation of fixed and floating charges. Whilst it is conceptually easy to understand what constitutes the substantive characteristics of these charges, in practice, except in very straightforward cases, it is not always easy to state confidently in advance that a charge created is what the security document purportedly labels it as. This is illustrated above in this chapter,[326] where charges described as fixed charges have on a number of occasions turned out to be floating charges when tested in court. This is a result of the objective two-stage process criteria and the intrinsic and extrinsic rules of interpretation, which the courts use to ascertain the true nature of the security.

[324] See Chapter 2 above. [325] See above, Chapter 1.
[326] That is, 'Creation of company security'.

Another substantive doctrine which contributes to this failure to meet the criteria is the doctrine of crystallisation. Generally, the crystallising events implied by law do not pose significant difficulty, but the crystallising consensual events do. They have been expanded to give the floating charge creditor the widest possible protection against the security interests of other creditors, particularly against potential competing claims. One set of consensual events that appears to create uncertainty in law and practice are automatic crystallisation events. These were examined in this chapter and, owing to their automatic nature, creditors, debtors and third parties may not know that the floating charge has been transformed into a fixed charge and are therefore incapable of acting to safeguard their interests.

With regard to perfection, the rules governing the perfection of company security over personal property have satisfied the following perfection criteria: expedition and low cost. However, the rules do not appear to have satisfied the perfection criteria relating to simplicity and comprehensibility.

The weaknesses can be traced back to the complex method of identifying whether the general law or the Companies Ordinance applies to the perfection of a company security. If general law applies, perfection co-exists with the creation of the security device. If the Companies Ordinance applies, the creditor has to register the security with the Companies Registry within five weeks in order to perfect the security. The physical registration process is relatively simple. There is, however, some difficulty in the initial stage of determining whether or not the security is within the list of registrable charges. This is because the list is complex, and uses multiple criteria to determine whether the security should be registered or not. Some of the criteria even confuse lawyers, let alone lay creditors. For instance,

- floating charges over shares are registrable, but not fixed charges;
- the complex Bills of Sale Ordinance, usually associated with securities granted by individuals, determines whether a company security over personal chattels is registrable;
- fixed charges over books debts are registrable but not other debts, though a floating charge over them is registrable; and
- security over certain assets, which are similar in legal nature to an asset within the list, are not registrable, such as security over insurance policies and security over book debts. Both are choses in action.[327]

[327] See above, Chapter 3.

Other requirements, such as the five-week registration period and rules governing overseas company security, have also contributed to the complexity of the rules and adversely affect the smooth operation of the system. The five-week period has unnecessarily rendered the rules of perfection cumbersome and complicated: cumbersome as when a creditor inadvertently fails to register a charge and so requires an extension of time, which entails an application to the court; complexity occurs as the courts have devised safety measures to protect the interests of third parties, where, for example, the terms of the extension order contain caveats. Furthermore, the financial status of the company security provider cannot be easily ascertained at any given time as valid but unregistered charges may already exist, which creates opacity during the five-week window of invisibility. Interestingly these complexities are avoided in China as there is no perfection period under Chinese law.

In respect of overseas companies, the now amended Companies Ordinance has resolved the problem of determining 'place of business'. However, the inherent difficulty created by the five-week period remains, though it will soon be shortened to three weeks in line with the general shortening of the perfection period proposed for the rewritten Companies Ordinance. Shortening the period of registration does not in any way deal with the fundamental problems of the invisibility period, it merely reduces the risk of deception of the true financial status of a subsequent chargee by reducing the period of vulnerability. Furthermore, where a charge is registrable within the meaning of the Companies Ordinance and the creditor has not complied with the perfection period (whether the current five weeks or the shortened three weeks in the future), the creditor will still be subject to the complicated and expensive process of application for extension of time.

With regard to publicity, it is submitted that the rules governing publicity of company security over personal property in Hong Kong have failed all the publicity criteria. A cursory inspection would suggest that the rules have at least satisfied the criteria of easy access and inexpensive accessibility to relevant information. Upon further consideration, however, this is only correct in respect of registrable security under the Ordinance. There are many company charges that are outside the scope of the registration system. They are either not publicised or the process of publicity under general law is seriously inadequate.[328]

[328] For example, fixed charges over debts other than book debts; see Chapter 3 above.

The weaknesses of the publicity rules are attributable to the failure of the registration system to:

- contain full and accurate information in respect of charges that are registrable, particularly in relation to automatic crystallisation clauses, and the actual financial exposure of chargors and affected assets, which has a serious impact on the interests of third parties dealing with the company;
- register information relating to a number of security arrangements, such as fixed charges over shares of the company, security over insurance policies and all charges that are exempted from registration under the Bills of Sale Ordinance;
- contain information relating to other security arrangements, such as hire-purchase, leasing and conditional sale, which are in fact security transactions.

The only criterion which Hong Kong rules of creation, perfection and publicity of company security have fully satisfied is cost. Either no cost is incurred or it is minimal.

The ongoing reform process of the Companies Ordinance will not address most of these critical weaknesses. Hong Kong and the UK have both missed a golden opportunity to reform their illogical and incoherent law relating to the creation, perfection and publication of company-created security over personal property. In the UK, muddle over legislative procedures and timetabling as well as conservative objections to radical reform caused abandonment of the wider project of reform of the personal property security regime.

In Hong Kong, the government is of the opinion that the current system has few problems and works well, and thus the impetus for a thorough reform of the company security system is unjustified. The government has also taken note that the UK failed to substantially reform its own system in the 2006 Companies Act, which, it appears to suggest, justifies its own complacency. The Hong Kong government has blandly determined that, whilst other jurisdictions may have made substantial changes to their property security system, the Hong Kong system is substantially sound and workable. The Hong Kong government has 'rejected' significant reform as unnecessary and inappropriate in the Hong Kong context without providing a convincing rationale for this stance, given the major weaknesses identified in the analysis presented here.

To summarise, the reforms the government rejected on this basis include:

(1) comprehensive codification of the law on priorities where there is more than one charge over the same property created by the company,
(2) the creation of a provisional registration system,
(3) provision of legislative clarification of the kinds of retention-of-title clauses that constitute registrable charges,
(4) registration of sale or absolute assignment of book debts (or receivables),
(5) registration of pledges,
(6) registration of trust receipts,
(7) registration of insurance policies and
(8) registration of fixed charges on shares.[329]

The government's decision to make no substantive changes to the law or procedure appears to be informed by an absence of voices demanding change. The perceived inertia of the UK authorities and resistance to change by practitioners appear also to have been motivating factors against changes, so justifying the maintenance of the status quo.

This policy choice is very disappointing as the manifest deficiencies of the current system of granting security over personal property in Hong Kong are in need of a thorough overhaul, as was recommended by the English Law Commission in relation to that jurisdiction, whose system almost perfectly mirrors that of Hong Kong. However, both the UK and Hong Kong appear destined to retain their current highly unsatisfactory arrangements for the creation, perfection and publicity of corporate security.

In relation to China, as the same rules of creation, perfection and publicity of credit security discussed in Chapters 2 and 3 above apply to company security, the strengths and weaknesses discussed therein apply here equally.

By way of summary, in respect of creation, the rules have satisfied the criteria of simplicity, comprehensibility, expedition and affordability. Securitisable assets are well defined, and protect the interests of the creditor, debtor and third party. In particular, the rules governing floating charges by way of legal mortgage seem to have satisfied the following criteria: the security may be capable of securing after-acquired and future advances (Article 181 of the Property Law); the debtor, subject to the security, is generally able to 'deal' with the assets freely (subject to the obligation to repay the creditor arising from a consensual transfer, as

[329] See Chapter 5, 'Registration of charges'.

discussed in Chapter 2 above – Article 191 of the Property Law); and this security should be able to secure future advances made to the debtor by the creditor.

With regard to perfection, the rules governing the perfection of company security in China have satisfied all the perfection criteria. The rules are simple and comprehensible. The actual process of perfecting the security is also expeditious and inexpensive.

With regard to publicity, the rules governing publicity of company security in China have satisfied some of the publicity criteria – namely publicity of company security must be inexpensive, security information must be easy to file – and the recorded information relating to the nature of the security, status of the affected assets and financial exposure of the assets must be accurate. The publicity mechanism, however, does not satisfy the publicity criterion of easy access, because physical search is an extremely slow and wasteful process at the various relevant registration authorities.

In light of the above findings, this chapter concludes that the rules and practice of creating, perfecting and publicising company security over personal property, both tangible and intangible, in Hong Kong and China have not satisfied all the criteria defined in Chapter 1. Their legal frameworks in this regard cannot therefore be regarded as efficient.

Chapter 5

Hire-purchase, leasing and conditional sale of tangible personal property

5.1 Introduction

Previous chapters have explained how traditional security devices – such as legal mortgages *strictu sensu*, equitable mortgages, charges and pledges – are created, perfected and publicised, where relevant, over various types of tangible and intangible personal property. This chapter focuses on the quasi-security devices, namely the hire-purchase, lease and conditional sale agreements in Hong Kong and China.[1]

The nature of a hire-purchase agreement is well settled.[2] Chitty defines the hire-purchase agreement

> as an agreement under which an owner lets chattels of any description out on hire and further agrees that the hirer may either return the goods and terminate the hiring or elect to purchase the goods when the payments for hire have reached a sum equal to the amount of the purchase price stated in the agreement or upon payment of a stated sum.[3]

A less elaborate definition, but with the same meaning, is given by Goode: '[a] hire-purchase agreement as known to common law may be

[1] Unless otherwise stated, the term 'quasi-security' shall mean hire-purchase, leasing and conditional sale.

[2] *Helby v Matthews* [1895] AC 471 defined the five essentials of a hire-purchase agreement. Note that earlier cases had already recognised the distinction between a hire-purchase agreement and a purchase agreement, for example *Cramer v Giles* (1883) Cab & El 151 (affirmed on appeal as *Cramer v Carlton, The Times*, 9 May 1884); and *Lee v Butler* [1893] 2 QB 318. The first hire-purchase case officially reported in Hong Kong in 1933 was *Ty Chee & Company v The Sik Knitting Factory and Chan Sing Ming* [1933] 26 HKLR 25. There Wood J had no difficulty in holding that an agreement by a creditor to let on hire to a hirer a sewing machine was a hire-purchase agreement, and not a sale of goods with postponed payments. It was therefore not entitled to exemption from stamp duty under the old Stamp Ordinance 1921.

[3] *Chitty on Contracts – Specific Contracts*, 26th ed. (London: Sweet & Maxwell, 1986), vol. 2, para. 3603. Similar description is also found in *Halsbury's Laws of England* (London: Butterworths, 1908), vol. 1, para. 1124, and *Helby v Matthews and Others* [1895] AC 471.

defined as a contract for the delivery of goods under which the hirer is granted an option to purchase the goods'.[4] The Hong Kong Law Reform Commission's Report on Contracts for the Supply of Goods (2002)[5] adopted a refined version of Goode's definition and gave a concise description of hire-purchase as follows: 'a hire-purchase agreement is an agreement, or a combination of agreements, by which goods are supplied on hire and the hirer has the right but not the obligation to buy the goods'.[6] Thus the essence of a hire-purchase agreement is that the financier of the purchase price of the goods remains the owner until the option to purchase the goods is exercised by the hirer.

Today, the hire-purchase agreement is widely used in Hong Kong to finance the purchase of a variety of consumer[7] and non-consumer goods.[8]

In striking contrast, the expression 'hire-purchase' does not exist in China. However, a transaction with similar effect is found in Article 237 of the Contract Law (1999), which describes such a contract as 'lease-finance contract'. However, the similarity is largely superficial at best because, under Chinese law, the lessee does not automatically enjoy the right to buy the goods. Article 250 of the Contract Law provides,

> The lessor and the lessee may stipulate in which party ownership of the leased thing shall vest upon expiration of the lease. If they have not stipulated in which party ownership shall vest upon expiration or the same has not been stipulated explicitly, ownership of the leased thing shall vest in the lessor.

4 R.M. Goode, *Hire-Purchase Law and Practice*, 2nd ed. (London: Butterworths, 1970), p. 32.

5 This report recommended, inter alia, that the contract of hire-purchase should be governed by new legislation that implies into the contract terms relating to sample, quality, description and quiet possession.

6 The Hong Kong Law Reform Commission's Report on Contracts for the Supply of Goods (2002), para. 2.69. For wider definition of a hire-purchase agreement, see Order 84A r 1, para. (3)(a), High Court Rules, which appears to include a lease.

7 They include cars, computer products, electrical appliances and telecommunication equipment. See the Law Reform Commission of Hong Kong, Report on Contracts for the Supply of Goods (February 2002), para. 2.49, p. 281.

8 For example, plant and machinery. See ibid., para. 2.49, p. 281. See also T.K. Ghose, *The Banking System of Hong Kong*, 2nd ed. (Hong Kong: Butterworths Asia, 1995), p. 218, where the author said that in 1993 there were 36,193 agreements for hire-purchase of equipment and 36,958 for hire-purchase of vehicles. The current authors had a personal discussion with T.K. Ghose about the availability of subsequent figures. There were none; apparently the Hong Kong Equipment and Leasing Association, which provided the figures, had closed down.

If the lessee defaults, the lessor is entitled to demand payment of the entire amount of rent and, alternatively, the lessor may terminate the contract and repossess the leased goods.[9] On the other hand, if the parties have stipulated that ownership of the leased thing shall pass to the lessee upon expiration of the lease, and the lessee has already paid most of the rent but is unable to pay the balance, and if the lessor repossesses the leased goods on those grounds, the lessee may demand a partial refund if the value of the leased things repossessed exceeds the rent and any other expenses paid by the lessee.[10] The object is to protect the hirer, who is usually a consumer, against the economically more powerful supplier, and any potential abuse of the supplier's power of possession and sale. In contrast, in Hong Kong, the juridical nature of the hire-purchase is consistent throughout the life of the arrangement.

In Hong Kong, leasing[11] is a contract between the lessor and lessee whereby the lessee obtains a right to use the leased goods in return for the payment of the price of the lease to the lessor, the owner of the goods.[12] Such a lease is similar to a hire-purchase agreement except that the lessee

[9] Article 248 of the Contract Law (1999). [10] Ibid., Article 249.

[11] The origins of equipment leasing are traced to the 1664 English case of *Nurse v Barns* [1664] T Raym 77, 83 ER 43. There the jury awarded the lessee damages for the lessor's breach of contract to lease iron mills to the lessee for six months. However, the modern form of equipment leasing arose during the industrial revolution in England in the nineteenth century when owners of coal wagons would lease their wagons to coal owners to transport the coal on the railway: see D.R. Soper, R.M. Munro and E. Cameron, *The Leasing Handbook* (London: McGraw-Hill Book Company, 1993), pp. 13–14; and see also T. Clark, *Leasing Finance* (London: Euromoney Publications, 1985), p. 1. In the course of time, the wagon form of equipment leasing spread to boot and shoe manufacturing, textiles and telephone system equipment. In all these industries, leasing performed the same economic function as the hire-purchase, i.e. enabling the lessees to use assets without expending costly capital. See Clark, ibid.

[12] *Halsbury's Law of England*, 4th ed. (London: Butterworths, 1991), vol. 2, para. 1850. The common law contract of hire seems to have its origin in Roman law, where such an arrangement was defined as *locatio-conductio est contractus, quo de re fruenda pro certo pretio convenit* ('a contract whereby the use of a thing, or the services and labour of a person, are stipulated to be given for a reward'). See J. Story, *Law of Bailment*, 9th ed. (Boston: Little Brown & Co., 1878), §§368–9, pp. 323–4. Note, §39E(5) of the Inland Revenue Ordinance (Cap. 112) defines a lease to include (a) any arrangement under which a right to use machinery or plant is granted by the owner of the machinery or plant to another person; and (b) any arrangement under which a right to use machinery or plant, being a right derived directly or indirectly from a right referred to in paragraph (a) is granted by a person to another person. Under the same section a lease does not include a hire-purchase agreement or a conditional agreement unless, in the opinion of the commissioner, the right under the agreement to purchase or obtain the property in the goods would reasonably be expected not to be exercised.

is not given an option to purchase the goods. However, in practice, the lessee is expected to purchase the goods upon the expiry of the lease. In contrast to hire-purchase, leasing is not popular in Hong Kong.[13] For this reason, the legal literature and law reports in Hong Kong are almost silent on the subject. The Hong Kong Law Reform Commission in their recent report on Contracts for the Supply of Goods (2002) mentioned it only in one short sentence without further discussion.[14]

In Hong Kong, leasing agreements can be divided into two types, namely operating and finance leases. An authoritative description of the two was given in the English case of *On Demand Information plc (in administrative receivership) and Another v Michael Gerson (Finance) plc and Another*,[15] and they are consistent with usage in Hong Kong.[16] In that case an operating lease has been described as one where the lessee pays a rental for the hire of an asset for a period of time which is normally substantially less than its useful economic life. The lessor retains most of the risk and rewards of ownership of the asset. A finance lease, on the other hand, involves payment by a lessee to a lessor of the full cost of the asset, without transfer of legal title. The substantive distinction between the two is therefore not significant, and the economic distinction between them is essentially one of degree. It is not the objective here to consider the economic aspects of these leases.

In China, leasing of equipment appears to be a fairly frequent phenomenon. The Contract Law recognises two types of equipment leasing in China, namely the common lease and the finance lease (or full payout lease).[17]

[13] See Ghose, above, note 8, p. 214, where the author comments, 'Hong Kong's leasing market continues to be small, which does not allow any significant specialization'. At p. 218, he states that there were approximately 1,096 businesses operating leasing of equipment and vehicles in 1993; and 84,191 hire-purchases of equipment and vehicles. These figures were recorded by the Hong Kong Equipment and Leasing Association. Since 1993 no statistics are available.

[14] At para. 2.40, p. 24: 'This type of contract may be described as a "lease".' Also the other major text did not discuss it, though he did discuss the hire-purchase in considerable length; see I. Tokley, *Hong Kong Banking Law and Practice* (Hong Kong: Butterworths Asia, 1999).

[15] [1999] 2 All ER 811, 813–14, *per* Laurence QC. This description was affirmed on appeal; see [2000] 4 All ER 734, p. 737. On further appeal, the House of Lords did not dispute the description; see [2002] 2 All ER 949.

[16] See B.C.S. Chan, *Hong Kong Banking Law and Practice* (The Hong Kong Institute of Bankers, 2000), vol. 1, para. 14.3.1, at pp. 370–8.

[17] Chapters 13 and 14 of the Contract Law (1999) respectively.

According to Chapter 13 of the Contract Law, a common lease is regarded as a contract under which the asset is not wholly amortised during the primary period of the lease, and where the lessor does not rely solely on the rentals during the primary period for his profit, but looks for the recovery of the balance of his costs and for the rest of his profits from the sale or re-lease of the returned asset at the end of the primary lease period.[18] A finance lease, on the other hand, has been defined as a contract involving payment over an obligatory period (also called the primary or basic period) of specified rental amounts for the use of a lessor's property, sufficient in total to amortise the capital outlay of the lessor and to provide for the lessor's borrowing costs and profits. They, in substance, correspond to the operating and finance leases in Hong Kong.

In Hong Kong, Ho has defined the conditional sale of goods agreement as one 'under which possession of the goods is delivered to the buyer, but the ownership or property in the goods remains with the seller until full payment of the purchase price'.[19] The Hong Kong Law Reform Commission's Report on Contracts for the Supply of Goods adopts this definition.[20] The difference between a conditional sale and a hire-purchase is that a buyer under the former does not have a right to terminate the agreement or an option to buy.[21] The buyer is obliged to buy the goods. In practice, it is agreed that when the buyer defaults in repayment of the instalments, the seller is entitled to terminate the agreement and repossess the goods.

However, today, as the English Law Commission commented,[22] the concept of 'conditional sale' has been extended to commercial arrangements that do not involve the traditional seller–buyer relationship, such as consignment of goods to a dealer for subsequent dispositions.[23]

18 Ibid., Articles 225 and 226.

19 B. Ho, *Security for Credit – Law and Practice* (Hong Kong: Butterworths Asia, 1992), p. 176. A similar definition is found in the Crowther Report, para. 1.2.14. Although payment of the full purchase price is the underlying condition precedent to the transfer of ownership, the transfer may be subject to other conditions as well. However, this chapter is only concerned with the payment of the price of the goods as a condition.

20 Para. 2.55, p. 28.

21 In *Sun Hung Kai Credit Ltd v Szeto Yuk-Mei* [1985] 1 HKC 345, an agreement described as 'hire-purchase' was held to be a conditional sale because it did not possess either of these conditions.

22 English Law Commission Consultation Paper No 164, paras. 6.11–6.23.

23 Ibid., paras. 6.22–6.23, also describes another situation where the concept of conditional sale is being used; that is, a tripartite relationship where the buyer selects goods from the supplier, who sells the goods to a finance company, who then sells them to the buyer on conditional sale terms.

Nonetheless, the underlying mechanism that protects the supplier of the goods against default of the dealer is that title in the goods remains with the seller until the price is fully paid.

Although conditional sale agreements were already in existence at common law[24] before the enactment of the Hong Kong Sale of Goods Ordinance (Cap. 26) in 1896,[25] today the basis of the legal effect of the modern conditional sale with a retention-of-title clause is taken to rest on §21 of the Sale of Goods Ordinance,[26] especially in the case of a seller–buyer relationship. That section, consonant with the principle of freedom of contract, permits the seller of specific goods to retain ownership in the goods until the purchase price is fully paid, notwithstanding the fact that the goods are delivered to the buyer.[27] The 'retention'-of-title clause is commonly called the 'Romalpa' clause.[28]

Although many of the reported cases involving the retention-of-title clause are from England, Australia and New Zealand, there is sufficient evidence that sellers of goods on credit in Hong Kong also commonly use this device.[29]

[24] The Cork report on Insolvency Law and Practice, Cmnd 8558, June 1982, para. 1559; C. Blackburn, *A Treatise on the Effects of the Contract of Sale* (London: William Benning & Co., 1845), vol. 2, pp. 147–50, B. Collier, *Romalpa Clauses: Reservation of Title in Sale of Goods Transactions* (Sydney: The Law Book Company Ltd, 1989), p. 2. Examples of cases include *Bishop v Shillito* (1816) 2 B & Ald 329, 106 ER 387; *Walker v Clyde* (1861) 10 CBNS 381, 142 ER 500; *Bateman v Gren and King* [1868] IR 2 Ch 607, *McEntire v Crossley Brothers Ltd* [1985] 1 AC 457.

[25] Equivalent of the old English Sale of Goods Act 1893. Currently the Sale of Goods Act 1979. The Hong Kong equivalent is the Sale of Goods Ordinance (Cap. 26), which was enacted in 1896, then known as Ordinance No 4 1896.

[26] Equivalent of §19 of the English Sale of Goods Act. See also Order 84A r 1, para. (3)(a), which defined a 'conditional sale' according to the terms of §21 of the Sale of Goods Ordinance.

[27] The section permitted a laissez-faire approach to the intention as to when property is to pass between contracting parties. See J. Tribe, 'The Morality of *Romalpa* Clauses in Corporate Insolvency: A Case for Reform?', *TILP* 17 (2001), 166.

[28] The designation 'Romalpa' is derived from the eponomous English case *Aluminium Industrie Vaassen BV v Romalpa Aluminium Ltd* [1976] 1 WLR 676.

[29] See *Jebsen & Co. Ltd v Asia Furniture* [1982] HKC 218: a seller's invoice had the following notation, 'Goods mentioned in this voice will remain our property until full payment of them has been received in cash or, by cheque, until clearance of the cheque.' But the legal effect of the notation was not considered, as the court held that the notation was not a term of the contract of the sale and purchase. See also *Gilman & Co. Ltd v Yokohama Musen Industrial Co. (HK) Ltd* [1976] HKLR 821, where the court commented that a clause which provided that 'property in the goods described above shall not pass to the buyer until delivery to the buyer of the seller's debit note has been made' did not amount to a reservation of the right of the disposal of the goods within §21(1) of the Sale of Goods Ordinance. The Hong Kong Standing Committee's

The conditional sale contract also exists in China by virtue of Articles 45 and 134 of the Contract Law. Article 45 provides that 'the parties may agree to attach conditions to the effectiveness of the contract'. Article 134 provides that the 'parties may stipulate that ownership in the thing shall not pass to the purchaser until he has fully paid the price'. However, examination of official and unofficial law reports and legal literature[30] in China shows no reports or commentary on the operation of the articles in the strict context of sale of goods on commercial credit. This could be due to two reasons. Firstly, conditional sale and retention-of-ownership rights are not generally viewed as a security device in China, though they actually guarantee, to some extent, the full payment of the debt. Secondly, the mortgage affords a more effective set of remedies in the event that the debtor defaults.[31] But, evidently, conditional sale is very popular in the sale of real property in China. This is outside the scope of this book. In light of this situation, we will not further examine the conditional sale agreement in China.

Thus far an overview has been provided of the nature of the hire-purchase, leasing and conditional sale agreements as credit security devices in Hong Kong and China.

The objectives of this chapter are:

- to consider whether the rules governing the creation, perfection and publicity of hire-purchase, leasing and conditional sale have satisfied the criteria established in Chapter 1;[32] and
- to determine whether the cost involved in the process of creation, perfection and publicity of these quasi-securities is inexpensive.

Eighth Report on Company Law Reform (1991), pp. 84–5, also noted that the contracts used by some suppliers of goods in Hong Kong sometimes contain retention-of-title clauses. But it has not received any judicial pronouncement in Malaysia and Singapore. In recent years there were some reported cases in New Zealand, for example *Len Vidgen & Leisure Ltd v Timaru Marine Supplies (1982) Ltd* [1986] 1 NZLR 349, *New Zealand Forest Products Ltd v Pongakawa Sawmill Ltd* [1991] 3 NZLR 112, *Re Country Stores Pty Ltd, Re Tandrio Pty Ltd* [1987] 2 Qd R 318, *Puma Australia Ltd v Sportsman's Australia Ltd* (1990, unreported) 1991 Con 375. For a recent Australian High Court discussion on this, see *Associated Alloys Pty Limited v ACN 001 452 106 Pty Limited (in liquidation) and Another* [2000] 202 CLR 588. This is discussed further below in this chapter.

[30] The current authors reviewed the following major legal text books on commercial law: Jianyuan Cui, *Contract Law* (Beijing: Law Press, 2003); Liming Wang, *Research into Contract Law* (Beijing: Law Press, 2003); Hailin Zhu and Min Chang, *The Means and Application of Security Devices* (Beijing: Fazhi Press, 1998).

[31] This is discussed in Chapter 7 below. [32] See Chapter 1 above.

5.2 Theoretical rationale behind the development of hire-purchase, leasing and conditional sale

The rationale behind the emergence and popularity of hire-purchase, leasing and conditional sale today is linked to several advantages they confer both on the suppliers of goods on credit and on the debtor, although the advantages for the supplier are more pronounced.[33] The advantages include:

- Quasi-security reinforces the common law rule of *nemo dat quod non habet* against the subsequent purchaser of the goods, even if the goods were purchased in good faith and without notice of the true creditor–owner's interest.[34]
- Quasi-security provides better remedies against the original buyer, as the case may be, of the goods for in many cases a personal action against the buyer for default is usually worthless.
- Quasi-security avoids the rigidity and complexity of a number of special statutes enacted in the late nineteenth century – namely the Bills of Sale Acts (equivalent of the Hong Kong Bills of Sale Ordinance (Cap. 20), §9 of the Factors Act 1889 (equivalent of the Hong Kong Factors Ordinance (Cap. 48)), the Sale of Goods Act (equivalent of the Hong Kong Sale of Goods Ordinance (Cap. 26)), and, much later, the Money Lenders Act (equivalent of the Hong Kong Money Lenders Ordinance 1911, repealed and replaced with the Moneylenders Ordinance (Cap. 163)). The bills of sale legislate has already been discussed in Chapter 2. The quasi-security is not subject to that regime.

With regard to §9 of the Factors Act and §25(1) of the Sale of Goods Act (the equivalent of §27(2) of the Sale of Goods Ordinance (Cap. 26)), these provisions permit, as an exception to the *nemo dat* rule, a buyer in possession to pass a good title to a subsequent bona fide purchaser for value without notice.[35] The hire-purchase and leasing agreements overcame the risk in these provisions. Under such agreements, the hirer and lessee are

[33] According to Goode, above, note 4, p. 2, these arrangements were already well established by 1846 to finance the purchase of consumer goods on instalment payments.

[34] Ibid., at p. 3.

[35] *Lee v Butler* [1893] 2 QB 318, CA, where a purported hire-purchase agreement of furniture was held to be a pure sale and purchase and the buyer in possession could pass a good title under §9 of the Factors Act.

not persons who have 'agreed to buy the goods' under the Factors Act and the Sale of Goods Act.

However, conditional sale does not overcome §9 because the debtor is a buyer. Nonetheless, it gives the conditional sale seller three advantages in the event the debtor becomes insolvent. The first is that it enables the seller to 'escape from the doomed category of unsecured creditors',[36] who are 'usually left with the crumbs, if any, of the debtor'.[37] Under an effective retention-of-title clause, the seller has priority over unsecured creditors and secured creditors of the debtor–buyer who have registered their security.[38] The second is that it protects the seller against the prejudicial effect of 'hiving down'[39] in the event the debtor–buyer is a company and a receiver is appointed against the company.[40] The third is that the retention-of-title clause can be extended to secure performance of other obligations and liabilities owing by the buyer to the seller.[41] Indeed, the first and second advantages are also features of the hire-purchase and leasing arrangements.

[36] J. Spencer, 'The Commercial Realities of Reservation of Title Clauses', *JBL* 220 (1989), 220 at p. 220.

[37] In *Borden (UK) Ltd v Scottish Timber Products Ltd and Another* [1979] 3 All ER 961, 971, Lord Templeman commented, 'Unsecured creditors rank after preferential creditors, mortgagees and the holders of floating charges, and they receive a raw deal.' In Hong Kong, the proceeds from the sale of the debtor's assets are distributed in following order: costs of the insolvency proceedings, secured creditors, statutory preferential debts (see §38(1) of the Bankruptcy Ordinance (Cap. 6) and §265 of the Companies Ordinance (Cap. 32)), floating charges (in cases of company debtors), and unsecured creditors.

[38] A. Hicks, 'Reservation of Title: A Pious Hope', *MLR* 27 (1985), 63 at p. 63, referring to Davies's article 'Reservation of Title Clauses: A Legal Quagmire?', *LMCLQ* 1 (1984) 49; and see also R.J. Ahdar, 'Romalpa's Empire: The Reception of Reservation of Title Clauses in New Zealand', *LMCLQ* (1993), 382.

[39] See Chapter 7 below.

[40] *Re Bond Worth Ltd* [1979] 1 WLR 1198 is an illustration of a 'hiving down' operation.

[41] *Armour and Another v Thyssen Edelstahlwerkr AG* [1991] 2 AC 339, 353, *per* Lord Keith of Kinkel. Until the case of *Armour* it was uncertain whether retention-of-title clauses expressed to cover all debts and obligations owing by the buyer to the seller created a security interest. Such a provision is commonly found in standard mortgage instruments – it was found in the cases of *Aluminium Industrie Vaassen BV v Romalpa Aluminium Ltd* [1976] 1 All ER 552, *Borden (UK) Ltd v Scottish Timber Products and Another* [1979] 3 All ER 961, *E Pfeiffer Weinkellerei-Weineinkauf GmbH & Co. v Arbuthnot-Factors Ltd* [1988] 1 WLR 150; however, no comments were expressed by the judges. However, in *John Snow & Co. Ltd v DBG Woodcroft & Co. Ltd* [[1985] BCLC 54, 62, Boreham J explicitly said, *obiter*, that the retention-of-title clause does not create a charge even if property in the goods supplied remains with the seller until the buyer has discharged the whole of his indebtedness to the seller.

With regard to the Money Lenders Ordinance,[42] the financier–supplier of goods on credit finds the following three drawbacks troublesome:

- it sanctions any person who carries on a moneylending business without a moneylender's licence with a fine and imprisonment;[43]
- it allows the court in appropriate cases to reopen a moneylending transaction, if it is of the view that the transaction is extortionate;[44] and
- the conduct of a moneylending business is strictly regulated by the provisions of the Ordinance, such that the form of the moneylending advertisements, circulars and business letters are defined and restricted.

The financier–supplier of goods under hire-purchase agreement, conditional sale or leasing is not subject to any of these drawbacks. This is because they are not moneylending transactions.

However, in Hong Kong, hire-purchase and leasing agreements are subject to §24(1) of the Money Lenders Ordinance. It provides that a person, whether a moneylender or not, commits a criminal offence if they charge interest at a rate in excess of 60 per cent per annum. This, in practice, is not a serious problem to the finance company, for the rates of interest charged by them on the costs of financing are well below the maximum statutory rates of interest.

Thus, in Hong Kong, we can expect the following advantages of quasi-security over the traditional security devices:

- Quasi-security holder's remedies for default are expeditious and inexpensive.[45]
- The creation and perfection of these quasi-security devices are fast and inexpensive.[46] This is because a quasi-security is exempt from registration under the Bills of Sale Ordinance and the Companies Ordinance.[47] This advantage benefits to both creditor–supplier and debtor–acquirer.

[42] The Hong Kong Money Lenders Ordinance, 1911, which was patterned on the United Kingdom Moneylenders Act 1900, was repealed and replaced by the Money Lenders Ordinance (Cap. 163), 1980.

[43] Money Lenders Ordinance (Cap. 163), 1980.

[44] Examples of where the old Moneylenders Acts 1900–27 had been raised and rejected are *Automobile and General Finance Corporation Ltd v Morris and Another* (1929) 73 Sol J 451, *Olds Discount Co. Ltd v Cohen* [1938] 3 All ER 281, and *Trade Promotion Trust Ltd v Young* (1940) 84 Sol J 646.

[45] The remedies will be discussed further in Chapter 7 below.

[46] English Law Commission Consultation Paper No 164, para. 6.3.

[47] The operational framework of the Companies Ordinance registration system will be discussed further in Chapter 5.

- Quasi-security avoids the uncertainty of the law surrounding fixed and floating charges,[48] where the buyer is a corporation.[49]
- Quasi-security is not strictly traditional security. It is free from the burdensome obligation of the mortgagees, in that the creditor of the goods is not accountable to the buyer for any surplus arising from the sale of the assets in the event of the buyer's default. However, whether there will be closer assimilation of the two will be discussed and explored further.[50]
- The hire-purchase and the lease afford tax advantages. Where plant or machinery is acquired under a hire-purchase agreement, for tax purposes the hirer is regarded as an owner at the outset.[51] The hirer is entitled to claim an initial depreciation allowance of 60 per cent on the capital element of the initial allowance over the period during which the instalments are paid. The hirer is further entitled to claim the interest element as a revenue expense for the period in which it was incurred. It is not entitled to do so in the case of interest paid on a loan. In the case of a lease, the lessee is not entitled to claim capital depreciation allowance, but the revenue expense on the rentals. The lessor as owner is, generally, entitled to claim the capital depreciation allowance.[52]

Some of the advantages described above are less obvious in China, because it has no equivalent legislation to the cumbersome ordinances mentioned above. However, the expeditious, cost-efficient and priority-advantage factors may be good reasons for the creditor to enter into these arrangements in any event.

The advantages of the quasi-security are therefore obvious and substantial, especially in Hong Kong, at least in theory. Whether these advantages do exist or are illusory will become clear when the process of creating, perfecting and publicising them, and the costs involved, are examined below.

[48] The rules determining whether a charge is a fixed charge or a floating charge are highly volatile and the results unpredictable, due to shifts in judicial definitions as to what is and is not a registrable charge; see Chapter 4 above.

[49] This was noted in the English Law Commission Consultation Paper No 164, para. 6.5.

[50] See Chapter 7 below.

[51] Section 37A of the Inland Revenue Ordinance.

[52] To prevent the abuse of the tax allowances given to the lessor, the Inland Revenue Ordinance excludes certain kind of lessors from benefit, namely sale and leaseback, and leverage leases. Here the lessor is not entitled to initial depreciation allowance.

5.3 Creation, perfection and publicity of hire-purchase in Hong Kong, and cost

5.3.1 Creation of hire-purchase

In Hong Kong, the common way in which hire-purchase is effected is in the form of a triangular transaction.[53] Goods are first selected from the dealer by the customer. The dealer sells the goods to a finance company, which as owner hires out the goods to the customer. The hire-purchase agreement is made between the finance company and the customer.

Today the essentials of a hire-purchase agreement in Hong Kong are settled. Like any other contract, it can be made orally, in writing or under seal. To constitute a valid and binding contract, it must satisfy the usual requirements of a valid and binding contract, such as offer and acceptance, consideration, capacity of parties and legality.[54] The usual rules of construction of terms of contract also apply to hire-purchase agreements.[55] In practice, commercial hire-purchase agreements in Hong Kong are always in writing and entered into with a fair amount of documentation. The terms in the standard hire-purchase agreement of Hong Kong are lengthy. The pertinent terms can be summarised as follows:[56]

- the amount of the deposit paid by the hirer,
- the amount and number of instalment payments,
- the minimum-payment clause in the event of breach of the hire-purchase by the hirer,
- the due date for each instalment payment,
- the consequence of the hirer's default in payment on due date,

[53] The Hong Kong Law Reform Commission's Report on Contracts for the Supply of Goods (February 2002) para. 3.75, p. 68. The finance companies in Hong Kong have little direct contact with the hirers. Much of the processing of the 'loan' applications is conducted by the motor vehicles dealers themselves, and the amount that a finance company is willing to lend has more to do with the make and model of the vehicle and less to do with the financial position of the hirer; see Hong Kong Monetary Authority, Motor Vehicle Financing, Guideline 5.1.1, 1992, p. 1. The HKMA made a number of recommendations to promote prudent lending, including assessment of the creditworthiness of the potential hirer, the finance house to be directly involved in the processing and assessment of loan applications, and so on; see guideline 5.1.1, p. 2.

[54] *Mercantile Union Guarantee Corpn v Ball* [1937] 2 KB 498, *Yeoman Credit Ltd v Latter* [1961] 1 WLR 828, and *Stadium Finance Ltd v Helm* 109 Sol J 471.

[55] *Anson's Law of Contract*, 26th ed. (Oxford: Clarendon Press, 1984), pp. 135–7.

[56] Based on the samples of Belgian Bank (Hong Kong), Dah Sing Finance Ltd and Wing Lung Finance Ltd (Hong Kong). See also Tokley, above, note 14, para. 653, where summarised terms of current practice are set out.

- the right of the hirer to exercise the option to purchase the goods at the end of the contract or to terminate the contract of hire,
- the obligation of the hirer to keep the goods in good condition,
- the obligation of the hirer to insure the goods,
- the prohibition of the hirer's assigning the goods,
- the prohibition of the hirer's selling the goods,
- the prohibition of the hirer's parting with possession of the goods,
- a minimum-payment clause on termination of the hire-purchase,
- an accelerated-payment clause,
- the consequence of the hirer's breach of any terms of the agreement and
- the consequence of the hirer's premature termination of the agreement.

If the 'option' to purchase is not expressly stated, the option can be implied from the terms of the agreement, such as a term which gives the hirer the right to terminate the hire-purchase agreement at any time.[57]

In practice, the standard hire-purchase agreements in Hong Kong produce the desired result of an owner-and-hirer relationship. It is only in very exceptional situations, such as poor drafting of the agreement, that an unexpected relationship occurs. When this happens, the owner usually holds an inferior security. This occurred in the case of *Sun Hung Kai Credit Ltd v Szeto Yuk-Mei and Others*.[58] There a finance company supplied the acquirer with a light bus under an agreement which was expressed to be a hire-purchase agreement. The fourth defendant ('the guarantor') guaranteed all monies that might become due and owing to the acquirer. The acquirer subsequently repudiated the agreement. The bus was repossessed and after it was sold there was, according to the terms of the agreement, still a substantial sum of money owed by the acquirer. When the acquirer failed to pay, the finance company sued the guarantor. The guarantor raised several defences, which were all rejected by the court. Accordingly, the court held the guarantor liable. The interesting point was the court's consideration of the nature of the agreement. It held that it was not a hire-purchase agreement because the agreement did not give the acquirer the right to terminate the agreement or the option to purchase the bus after payment of the last instalment. It was a conditional sale agreement. Consequently, if the acquirer had sold or pledged the bus

[57] In *Helby v Matthews* there was no express option but it was implied from the right of the debtor to return the goods and terminate the hiring. Also in *United Merchants Finance Limited v Tang Woon-wing* [1980] DCLR 53.

[58] [1986] HKDCLR 1.

to a bona fide purchaser for value, the latter would have acquired the bus free from the claim of the finance company.

However, examination of standard hire-purchase agreements and the actual practice adopted by the finance companies in Hong Kong to protect their interests in the goods, especially vehicles, raises a question – what exactly is the interest of the finance company? Can they actually be regarded as legal owners? To answer this, the practice has to be explained at the outset.

In Hong Kong, after a hire-purchase agreement is executed, the finance company will register the motor vehicle in the name of the hirer with the Department of Transport.[59] To safeguard the interest of the finance company, the original registration book[60] is deposited with the finance company and is endorsed with the claim of the finance company. The endorsement states that the vehicle 'is currently under hire-purchase and the original registration book is held in the custody' of the finance company.[61] The hirer is given a photocopy of the registration book. This security process is to ensure that the hirer will not be able to dispose of the vehicle and the third party is put on notice that the vehicle is encumbered.

This process gives rise to three propositions. Firstly, if the ownership is transferred to the hirer, it is submitted that legally speaking the transaction is no longer a hire-purchase agreement but an absolute sale of the vehicle by instalment payment. Secondly, if ownership has already been transferred, all the finance company has is an equitable ownership. Thirdly, the equitable ownership could be regarded as tantamount to an equitable charge, since the transaction has ceased to be a hire-purchase agreement. An analogy in this respect can be drawn with *Re Bond Worth Ltd*.[62] There a purported retention-of-title clause in an agreement to supply goods was held to create a charge over goods after the legal ownership had passed to the buyer. The charge would be void if the 'hirer' was a company and the charge was not registered with the Companies Registry. If the 'hirer' were an individual, it would constitute a bill of

[59] Samples were obtained from colleagues who had acquired cars on hire-purchase. The vehicle registration document states the hirer as the registered owner.

[60] Commonly called the 'log book' in the United Kingdom. In Hong Kong it is issued by the Road Transport Department under the Road Transport (Registration & Licensing of Vehicles) Regulations (Cap. 374).

[61] In Hong Kong the registration document is not a document of title; see *Fanlin Investment Ltd v Hang Seng Finance Ltd and Another* [1994] 3 HKC 433.

[62] [1979] 3 ALL ER 919. See also *Clough Mill Ltd v Martin* [1984] 1 WLR 111, where the Court of Appeal, *obiter*, held that the reservation-of-title clause constituted an equitable charge.

sale and it would be void for default in registration with the High Court Registry.[63]

However, these propositions have not been raised or considered by the courts in Hong Kong. On the contrary, the courts have vigorously adhered to an orthodox approach that the practice has not altered the owner-and-hirer relationship. Consequently, it is the hire-purchase document that establishes title, and the hirer's possession of the document of title is not representation that the hirer is authorised to dispose of the vehicle free from the ownership claim of the owner. This was the view in the Hong Kong case of *WOC Finance Co. Ltd v Fullrate Enterprises Ltd*.[64] In this case, the finance company gave the hirer of the car the registration book which recorded the hirer as the owner. The hirer sold the car to another finance company. The court held that the subsequent buyer could not rely on estoppel to defeat the claim of the finance company because the giving of possession of the car to the hirer and the car registration book in its name did not amount to estoppel.[65] The decision also shows that hire-purchase practice in Hong Kong can be harsh on innocent third parties, who are not legally conversant with hire-purchase and the nature of a vehicle registration document. However, from the point of view of the finance company the orthodox approach gives it a strong and effective security.

5.3.2 *Perfection of hire-purchase*

Perfection of hire-purchase against third parties co-exists with creation. It is not governed by any special legislation. A third party can acquire no better title than the hirer.[66] If the hirer disposes of the goods without the consent of the finance company, it can recover the goods from the third party.[67] The exceptions to the *nemo dat* rule in the Factors Ordinance and the Sale of Goods Ordinance, which have already been briefly explained above in this chapter, generally do not apply.

However, this simple rule of perfection has a weakness. The owner's claim under the hire-purchase agreement can be defeated by a third party's claim, such as that of a mortgagee, to land to which the goods supplied are attached and have become fixture.[68]

63 See Chapter 2 above. 64 [1982] HKLR 476.

65 In England a similar strict approach was taken in *Mercantile Bank of India Ltd v Central Bank of India Ltd* [1938] AC 287.

66 See *WOC Finance Co. Ltd v Fullrate Enterprises Ltd* [1982] HKLR 476.

67 *Helby v Matthews* [1895] AC 471 and *Lee v Butler* [1893] 2 QB 318.

68 This circumstance is complex and will be appropriately discussed further in Chapter 6 below.

5.3.3 *Publicity of hire-purchase*

There is no publicity of Mechanism for hire purchase agreements as they are outside the scope of the registration systems of the Bills of Sale Ordinance[69] and the Companies Ordinance,[70] and there is no other statutory machinery to publicise them. Consequently, a third party who wishes to deal with the hirer is placed at a serious security disadvantage; it cannot determine the 'apparent wealth' of the hirer and status of the goods by examining any independent and reliable source.

To avoid the security risk, a diligent and prudent third party may make a personal inquiry of the hirer. This alone may be adequate, because hire-purchase and leasing involve a fair amount of formality and documentation, and because documents evidencing ownership in goods, such as registration books of vehicles, are kept with the finance company. If the hirer attempts to dispose of or deal with the goods without the documents, a third party would be warned that the goods may be encumbered. However, personal enquiry does not solve some outstanding problems. Firstly, in cases where there are no documents evidencing title or formality involved in the security arrangement, personal enquiry will not help. Secondly, personal enquiry can cause embarrassment for both the hirer and the third party or damage the goodwill between them, for the hirer may perceive the enquiry by the third party as a sign of mistrust or intrusion into the privacy of the hirer.

5.3.4 *Cost of creation, perfection and publicity of hire-purchase*

One of the advantages of a hire-purchase agreement is its cost-effectiveness. This is attributable to two factors:

- The cost of creation is minimal. Hire-purchase is not subject to stamp duty.[71] In addition, since the agreement is in a standard form and it is usually executed in the office of the finance company or dealer,[72] neither party has to engage the services of a solicitor.

[69] See Chapter 2 above. [70] See Chapter 4 above.

[71] It does not fall within any of the taxable heads in the Schedule of the Stamp Duty Ordinance.

[72] Above, note 23.

- The perfection process is expeditious and inexpensive. It is not required to be registered with any authority. It is perfected and binding on the hirer and third parties, generally, as soon as the agreement is signed by the hirer and the finance company.

5.4 Creation, perfection and publicity of leasing in Hong Kong, and cost

As the rules governing the creation, perfection and publicity of leasing in Hong Kong are generally similar to those in relation to hire-purchase, these issues will, therefore, only be discussed briefly.

In respect of creation, fundamentally, except for the absence of the option to purchase the leased chattel, the terms and conditions of the lease and hire-purchase are similar.[73]

In respect of perfection, it is expeditious and inexpensive, because leasing arrangements are not subject to the registration systems of the Bills of Sale Ordinance[74] and the Companies Ordinance.[75] The effects of a leasing agreement on third parties are similar to those of hire-purchase discussed earlier in this chapter.

In respect of publicity, as with the hire-purchase, there is no Publicity mechanism for leasing agreements. Thus the consequential problems and difficulties posed to third parties discussed earlier in this chapter apply here equally.

Like hire-purchase, the cost of creating, perfecting and publicising leasing arrangements is minimal.

5.5 Creation, perfection and publicity of conditional sale in Hong Kong, and cost

5.5.1 *Creation of conditional sale*

Because the rules governing the creation of conditional sale with retention-of-title clause are quite complex, this part is further divided into the following subheadings:

(1) process of creating an effective retention-of-title clause,

[73] *Halsbury's Laws of England*, 3rd ed. (London: Butterworths, 1953), vol. 2, paras. 237–8. The samples from Belgium Bank (Hong Kong) and Dah Sing Finance Ltd (Hong Kong) confirm this.

[74] See Chapter 2 above.

[75] See Chapter 4 above.

(2) retention-of-title and 'all debts' clause and
(3) alternative to retention-of-title clause.

Process of creating an effective retention-of-title clause

To create an effective retention-of-title contract, the creditor has to satisfy two conditions:

- the agreement is a valid and binding contract, and
- the clause in the contract purporting to retain the legal title in the goods has that effect in law.

The first condition is satisfied if the agreement possesses the basic elements of a valid contract, namely offer and acceptance, intention to create legal relations, consideration and legality. The contract can be made orally, in writing or under seal. Thus, in theory, it is relatively easy and expeditious to create a retention-of-title contract. For present purposes, we will not pursue these matters further. It is assumed that the elements have been satisfied. The examination will, however, focus on the second condition, the crux of this section – that is, the prerequisites of an effective retention-of-title clause.

This examination relies heavily on English authorities and cases from other common law jurisdictions,[76] because the retention-of-title contract has not received significant judicial consideration or commentary in Hong Kong, which is somewhat perplexing, as such clauses are commonly used in Hong Kong.

[76] Local textbooks on this subject also had to rely heavily on English authorities, for example V. Stott, *Hong Kong Company Law*, 12th ed. (Hong Kong: Financial Times/ Pitman Publishing, 2008), Chapter 13, a major text on company law, could only cite English authorities as illustrations; Tokley, above, note 14, paras. 253–401, cited only one local case, *Sun Hung Kai Credit Ltd v Szeto Yuk-Mei* (1986) HKDCLR 1, but more relevant in the context of hire-purchase; and see also J. Sihombing, *Goods: Sales and Securities* (Hong Kong University Press, 1989), pp. 69–73, where all the cases cited on the subject were English. The current authors also reviewed the official Hong Kong Law Reports, Hong Kong Cases and unreported cases, but could find only one reported case on the retention-of-title clause, namely *Jebsen & Co. v Asia Furniture* [1982] HKC 218. This was a straightforward case which did not require any in-depth judicial analysis of the nature of the retention-of-title clause. There the court held that the seller's invoice, which stated, 'Goods mentioned in the invoice will remain our property until full payment of them has been received in cash or by cheque, until clearance of the cheque', did not prevent title in the goods from passing to the buyer because the invoice was issued after the contract of supply was completed.

English cases show that the retention-of-title clause can take a variety of forms. McCormack identified four types of retention-of-title clause,[77] which range from the very simple to the very complex. A simple retention-of-title clause will seek to retain the legal ownership or property in the goods sold to the buyer in the seller until the price is fully paid by the buyer.[78] This type of clause is commonly used in Hong Kong, particularly where the buyer is not expected to resell the goods or use the goods in a manufacturing process[79] – but the buyer utilises it in its unaltered form.[80]

An extended retention-of-title clause will not only seek to retain the legal ownership in the seller but will also seek to claim ownership rights in the proceeds of the sub-sales and in any final product made as a result of the mixing of the goods supplied by the seller with other goods. This extended form of retention-of-title clause is used when the seller foresees at the outset that the buyer will subsequently sell the goods or use the goods to manufacture a particular product in the ordinary course of business.[81] Here the buyer is usually a commercial entity.

The typical extended retention-of-title clause discerned from English and other common law jurisdictions include the following attributes:

- the seller has legal ownership of any end product into which the goods are incorporated;[82]
- the buyer will hold the proceeds of sale of the relevant goods or the end product on trust or in a fiduciary capacity for the seller;[83]

[77] G. McCormack, *Registration of Company Charges* (London: Sweet & Maxwell, 1994), pp. 68–9; see also S. Jones, 'Retention of Title Clauses Ten Years from Romalpa', *Co. Lawyer* 7 (1986) 233, where the author identified four types of retention-of-title clause.

[78] See English Law Commission Consultation Paper No 164, para. 6.17, which uses this expression.

[79] For example, Hutchinson Paging Limited (HK) has a simple retention-of-title clause which states, 'Title in the CT2 product shall not pass to the subscriber until payment in full of the purchase price'. And in *Jebsen & Co. v Asia Furniture* [1982] HKC 218, the seller's invoice stated, 'Goods mentioned in the invoice will remain our property until full payment of them has been received in cash or by cheque, until clearance of the cheque'.

[80] J.R. Bradgate, in 'Reservation of Title Ten Years on', *Conv* (November 1987), 434–47, p. 438, called this type of clause 'domestic' retention-of-title arrangements.

[81] Bradgate, in ibid., called them 'commercial' retention-of-title clauses.

[82] *Borden (UK) Ltd v Scottish Timber Products Ltd* [1981] Ch 25, and *Re Peachdart Ltd* [1984] Ch 131.

[83] *Aluminium Industrie Vaassen BV v Romalpa Aluminium Ltd* [1976] 2 All ER 552.

- the seller has the right to resume possession and sell the goods in the event the buyer defaults in payment or on the occurrence of any other event, for example insolvency of the buyer;[84]
- the seller has the right to retain legal ownership in the relevant goods until all present and future indebtedness of the buyer to the seller is fully settled;[85]
- if any of the goods are incorporated in or used as materials for other products, then ownership of that proportion of the new products equal in value to the total sum owing to the seller shall on manufacture immediately vest in the seller.[86]

According to *Romalpa*, one common substantive prerequisite runs through all the simple and extended versions of retention-of-title clauses; that is, the clause must create a 'bailor-and-bailee' or 'principal-and-agent' relationship[87] between the seller and the buyer. That case further established that this requirement is satisfied if the clause effectively retains the general property of the goods in the seller. The essential facts of the case were as follows. The plaintiffs, a Dutch company, sold to the defendants, an English company, aluminium foil. The crucial terms of the agreement were: (a) ownership of the aluminium remained with the plaintiffs until full payment of the monies owing to the plaintiffs; (b) until full settlement, the defendants, if the plaintiffs so desired, had to store the aluminium foil separately as property of the plaintiffs; (c) the ownership in new objects manufactured from the aluminium foil was to be transferred to the plaintiffs as surety for full payment of what the defendants

[84] This express provision is necessary because a seller does not have a right of possession under general law. See *Chitty on Contracts – Specific Contracts*, 26th ed. (London: Sweet & Maxwell, 1987), vol. 2, para. 3720, citing *Hewison v Ricketts* (1894) 63 LJQB 711.

[85] *Aluminium Industrie Vaassen BV v Romalpa Aluminium Ltd* [1976] 2 All ER 552, *Borden (UK) Ltd v Scottish Timber Products Ltd* [1981] Ch 25, and *John Snow & Co. Ltd v DGB Woodcroft Co. Ltd* [1985] BCLC 54.

[86] *ICI New Zealand Ltd v Agnew* [1998] 2 NZLR 129.

[87] This relationship has been described as 'internal-sale agency' and is different from the classical type of principal-and-agent relationship because the 'internal-sale agency' does not possess the legal consequences of the latter. See J.D. Lacy, 'Romalpa Theory and Practice under Retention of Title in the Sale of Goods', *Anglo-Am LR* 24(3) (1995), 327 at p. 333. For example, under the internal-sale agency the buyer binds the seller to the sub-buyer. See also D. Everett, 'Romalpa Clauses: The Fundamental Flaw', *ALJ* 68 (1994), 404 at p. 407, where the author identified three other features of this special agency, namely that the buyer/agent (1) is not accountable for the profits, if any; (2) has unfettered discretion to determine the resale price of the goods; and (3) does not receive any commission.

owed the plaintiffs; (d) until full payment, the defendants had to keep the new objects for the plaintiffs in their capacity of fiduciary owner, and if required by the plaintiffs, the objects had to be separately stored as property of the plaintiffs, in such a way that they could be recognised as such; (e) the defendants were entitled to sell the new objects to a third party in the normal course of their business, but so long as the defendants had not fully discharged their debts to the plaintiffs, the defendants had to hand over the proceeds to the plaintiffs. Subsequently, their bank, under a power contained in a debenture, appointed a receiver in respect of the defendants. After the appointment, the receiver confirmed that it held a sum of £35,152.66, being the proceeds of sale of aluminium foil by the defendants to third parties, and that it also held aluminium foil to a value of £50,235. The plaintiffs claimed that by virtue of the retention-of-title clause they were entitled to the unsold aluminium foil and the sum of £35,152.66. The Court of Appeal decided in favour of the plaintiffs. The grounds of its decision were as follows: firstly, in respect of the unsold aluminium, the plaintiffs remained the legal owners of the unsold foil by virtue of term (a) above. Secondly, in respect of the £35,152.66, there was a fiduciary relationship arising from the relationship of principal–agent or bailor–bailee between the plaintiffs and the defendants by virtue of (e) above. Accordingly, the buyer had to account for the £35,152.66 to the plaintiffs. This relationship also extended to the proceeds from the sale of the goods. The court further held[88] that the plaintiffs were entitled to trace the proceeds of the sub-sales and to recover them in priority to the general body of creditors and the bank as floating chargee.[89]

In the subsequent case of *Clough Mill Ltd v Martin*,[90] a contract of supply stated that the ownership of yarn supplied by the seller on credit would remain with the sellers until payment in full for the yarn had been received, and if the yarn was incorporated in other goods, the seller's ownership would extend to those other goods. The buyer became insolvent and the sellers claimed the unused yarn. The court held that the seller was entitled to do so. The legal complexities relating to the other yarn which has lost its identity will be discussed later.

Thus far, theoretically, the underpinning element of an effective retention-of-title clause is relatively clear. However, the voluminous case law post-*Romalpa* suggests that, even in its simple form, this is not

[88] On the authority of *Re Hallett's Estate* [1880] 13 Ch D 696.
[89] *Clough Mill Ltd v Martin* [1985] 1 WLR 111. [90] [1985] 1 WLR 111.

completely true in practice. The following reasons can be discerned from the cases:

(1) the difficulty of drafting 'retention-of-title' clauses and
(2) changes in the characteristics of the goods supplied.

The difficulty of drafting of retention of title The creditor has to use words that effectively retain the general property, legal and equitable, in it. A slip in the right choice of vocabulary may render the terms ambiguous, without effectively creating the required bailor–bailee relationship or principal–agent relationship. Though legal skill and experience in drafting retention-of-title clauses are helpful, they do not always produce the desired result.

This seller's dilemma is illustrated in the English case of *Re Bond Worth Ltd*.[91] The essentials of the case were that the seller supplied synthetic fibre on credit terms to the buyer, whom the seller knew would use the materials to manufacture carpets. The pertinent terms of the contract of supply stated that until full payment for the fibre was received, 'the equitable and beneficial ownership' of the fibre was to 'remain' with the seller. Further, the equitable and beneficial ownership was to attach to any proceeds from the sale of the fibre and in the final product, in which the fibre became a constituent. Subsequently, the buyer became insolvent and a receiver was appointed. The question that came before the court was whether the seller had any ownership interest in the yarn and the carpets, which comprised the fibres and other materials. The court held that the seller did not, on two grounds. Firstly, the words 'the equitable and beneficial ownership' indicated that the legal ownership had passed to the buyer. Accordingly, there was no bailee–bailor relationship or principal–agent relationship. Secondly, the court held that, since the substance of the transaction was a security transaction, the words 'equitable and beneficial ownership' could not be treated as having created a trustee-and-beneficiary relationship, but a security in the form of a floating charge, because the property was ambulatory. However, since the floating charge was not registered under §95(1) of the then Companies Act 1948,[92] it was void. The orthodox basis of the second ground – that is, substance over form – is not, as will be seen later, consistently followed in common law jurisdictions.[93]

[91] [1979] 3 All ER 919.

[92] Equivalent of §80(1) of the Hong Kong Companies Ordinance.

[93] See *Armour and Another v Thyssen Edelstahwerke AG* [1991] 2 AC 339, where the court held that an effective retention-of-title clause does not create a security interest. See

Change in the characteristics of the goods supplied If the goods remain identifiable and the words of the retention-of-title clause are unambiguous, it can be safely said that the retention-of-title clause is effective to retain the legal ownership in the goods.[94] No further discussion is necessary.

Serious problems, however, arise when there is a change in the nature of the goods. In many of these situations, the seller, at the outset, usually contemplates that the goods sold to the buyer may change in character as a result of the buyer's ordinary course of business.

There are three situations in which the goods may change their character:

- change in physical characteristics through a manufacturing process,
- when a new product is created by mixing the goods supplied with other materials and
- where the goods have ceased to exist in their original form and are represented by cash.

Retention-of-title clauses are therefore drafted to protect the monetary interests of the seller against these eventualities.

We will now examine the impact of each of the above situations on the retention-of-title clause.

Change in physical characteristics through manufacturing process The change in the physical character of the goods can be the result of one of the following two types of manufacturing process:

- where the manufacturing process converts the goods supplied into a new product without mixing them with other raw materials and
- where the manufacturing process converts the goods supplied into a new product by mixing them with other raw materials.

In respect of the impact of the first type of manufacturing process, there are conflicting views.[95] In the New Zealand case of *Pongakawa Sawmill*

the Australian High Court case of *Associated Alloys Pty Limited v ACN 001 452 106 Pty Limited (in liquidation) and Another* [2000] 202 CLR 588, where form prevailed over substance. There the court upheld a security in the form of a trust.

[94] The cases on this point include *Len Vidgen Ski & Leisure Ltd v Timaru Marine Supplies (1982) Ltd* [1986] 1 NZLR 349; *Hendy Lennox (Industrial Engines) Ltd v Grahame Puttick Ltd* [1984] 2 All ER 152; and *Clough Mill Ltd v Martin* [1984] 1 WLR 111.

[95] A.G. Guest, in 'Accession and Confusion in the Law of Hire-Purchase', *MLR* 27 (1964), 505 at pp. 518–19, referred to this as a 'confusion' of goods situation. The change in

Ltd v NZ Forest Products Ltd,[96] the seller supplied timber logs to the buyer subject to a 'retention-of-title' clause, which extended the seller's title to the products and proceeds of sale of the logs and their products. The court held that the retention of title was effective in respect of the resulting timber, bark, chips and sawdust. The main reason was that there was no mixture of the logs with other goods – the logs were simply processed into another form.

The simple and straightforward approach of *Pongakawa* was followed in *Re Weddell New Zealand Ltd*,[97] another New Zealand case. There the court held that an extended retention clause did not only retain title in the animals supplied, but also the carcasses of the animals after slaughter and parts of the carcasses packed in boxes with similar parts from other carcasses.

However, in the more recent case of *ICI New Zealand Ltd v Agnew*,[98] the court came to a different conclusion, although the headnote of the report claimed that *Pongakawa* was applied. In *ICI*, the seller supplied the buyer with plastic pellets subject to retention-of-title terms. The buyer used the pellets to manufacture transparent plastic containers. The retention-of-title clause extended to the finished products and to proceeds from the sale of the finished products. The court, however, held that the retention-of-title clause was ineffective against the finished products and the proceeds, because the containers had an obvious identity of their own. The court rejected the seller's argument that the pellets had not been combined with other goods to manufacture the finished product containers and that neither had they changed their identity, that the containers were still plastic, chemically the same as the pellets supplied, and that they were simply a different physical manifestation of plastic.

ICI is not alone in this strict, but illogical, approach. Support can be discerned in English cases, such as *Re Peachdart Ltd*[99] and *Chaigley Farmers Ltd v Crawford, Kaye & Grayshire Ltd (t/a Leylands)*,[100] which adopted an approach which is at variance with *Re Weddell New Zealand Ltd*. In *Re Peachdart*, it was held that the conversion of raw leather materials into handbags destroyed the retention-of-title clause. In *Chaigley Farmers Ltd*, the court held that a retention-of-title clause, which was effective against animals supplied to an abattoir, ceased to have effect

commercial practice and the consequential complexities have rendered the solutions discussed in the article dated.

[96] [1992] 3 NZLR 481. [97] [1996] 5 NZBLC 104, 55. [98] [1998] 2 NZLR 129.

[99] [1984] Ch 131. [100] [1996] BCC 957.

when the animals were slaughtered. This is in conflict with *Re Weddell New Zealand Ltd*.

In respect of the second type of manufacturing process – that is, when the original goods become mixed with other goods to produce a new product – the law is clear: the retention-of-title clause is ineffective against the new product (the 'orthodox approach').[101] An early English case on this point is *Borden (UK) Ltd v Scottish Timber Products Ltd and Another*.[102] There the seller supplied resins to the purchaser who used them in the manufacture of chipboard. The court held that the retention-of-title clause in the supply agreement was ineffective against the chipboard. This was because the resin was mixed with other raw materials to produce a wholly new product; the original goods 'simply disappeared',[103] consequently there was 'nothing to trace'.[104] The same rule was applied in *Clough Mill Ltd v Martin*,[105] which has already been considered.

There have been attempts in New Zealand and in England to modify the orthodox approach. In New Zealand two positions were canvassed to support the modification. Firstly, where the process of mixing is reversible; secondly, where the value of the part of the final product that is attributable to the goods supplied can be ascertained. The second position is derived from the United States rule found in Article 9-336 of the Uniform Commercial Code. The article provides that if a collateral becomes commingled goods, the secured party's interest is transferred from the original collateral to the product or mass.[106] The security interests of the various suppliers in the final product will rank equally in proportion to the value of the collateral at the time it became commingled goods.[107] Both positions were put before the court in *ICI New Zealand Ltd*,[108] but they were rejected. In respect of the first position, the court held that the fact that the plastic containers could be reconverted to plastic pellets did not matter, the retention-of-title clause ceased to be effective when the plastic pellets had lost their identity as pellets. It has been suggested that the underpinning reason is that reversing the process is not economically

[101] *Coleman v Harvey* [1989] 1 NZLR 723. [102] [1979] 3 All ER 361.

[103] *Borden (UK) Ltd v Scottish Timber Products Ltd and Another* [1979] 3 All ER 961, 961(b), *per* Bridge LJ.

[104] Ibid., at 973(g), *per* Templeman LJ. [105] [1985] 1 WLR 111.

[106] Article 9-336(c) of the Uniform Commercial Code.

[107] See *Uniform Commercial Code (Official Text with Comments)*, 8th ed. (Florida: Gould Publication, 2000), pp. 583–65.

[108] [1998] 2 NZLR 129, 134.

realistic.[109] In respect of the second position, the court felt that there were too many uncertain practical difficulties to make the argument viable. The difficulties included identifying and ascertaining the value of each separate contribution to the mass of the product, that the value had to equal the current indebtedness and that the sellers of the other products might also have the same clause. Accordingly, in *ICI New Zealand Ltd*, the court held that the following clause created a charge:

> if any of the goods are incorporated in or used as material for other products so as to lose their separate identity, then ownership of that proportion of the new products equal in value to the total sum owing to ICI shall on manufacture immediately vest in ICI.

In England, an attempt to modify the orthodox approach was undertaken by Goff[110] and Oliver LJJ[111] in *Clough Mill Ltd*. They theorised that freedom of contract required the court to give full effect to the agreement of the parties that title in the new product should vest in the seller. Goff LJ, however, realised that this theory had two major difficulties.

Firstly, the buyer's default in the repayment of the purchase price is tantamount to a repudiation of the contract, and the seller is entitled to sell the goods as owner, and to keep the proceeds, including any windfall increase in the full value of the new product.[112] Goff LJ thought that this was unfair, because the seller would be deriving the windfall not merely from the labour of the buyer, but also from any other materials mixed with the goods. The parties, he continued, could not have intended this. Indeed, the English Law Commission thought this would be contrary to the principle of credit security, including quasi-security, where the creditor has to account for the surplus.[113]

To prevent injustice, Goff LJ suggested that it could be implied that the seller should account for the surplus to the buyer. However, this suggestion has the effect of treating the seller as a quasi-mortgagee. Perhaps for this reason, Oliver LJ chose to disagree. He thought that the seller did not owe the buyer any duty to account for the surplus.[114] Oliver LJ's suggestion would entitle the seller to prove a shortfall, if any, in the buyer's liquidation. It is submitted that this is much more complicated than it might

[109] See D. Webb, 'Title and Transformation: Who Owns Manufactures Goods?', *JBL* 513 (2000), 525.

[110] [1984] 3 All ER 982, 989.

[111] Ibid., p. 993.

[112] This appears to be the position at law; see Guest, above, note 95, particularly at pp. 518–19.

[113] This is discussed further in Chapter 7 below.

[114] [1984] 3 All ER 982, p. 992.

first appear. Surely, as seller–owner, the creditor's cause of action would be in contract for damages. The usual complex rules of damages should therefore apply accordingly to ascertain the loss and not simply a 'shortfall'. McInnes has suggested that to circumvent the problem of the quasi-mortgage theory,[115] it may be possible to make the seller accountable on the principle of unjust enrichment.[116] An alternative, as suggested by De Lacy, is to make the seller liable for the buyer's contribution via *quantum meruit*.[117] Both approaches seem plausible.

The second obstacle, a practical problem, which appears to be more serious, is that the other materials, which also constitute the final product, May well have been supplied by other sellers under similar retention-of-title clauses. In this situation, Goff LJ admitted that it would be difficult to work out the entitlement of each of the suppliers.[118] He conceded that in this situation, the extended retention-of-title clause had to be treated as a charge. This was so even if it is contrary to the express intention of the parties. Oliver LJ disagreed, but he held that in *Clough Mill Ltd* the purported retention-of-title clause created a charge. Sir John Donaldson MR, in a shorter judgment, thought the purported retention-of-title clause created a charge, as the seller was not the owner of the other materials.

It appears that Goff LJ's proposition is unlikely to receive further support in view of *ICI New Zealand Ltd*. The second proposition in that case, which was discussed above, was essentially identical to Goff LJ's proposition, but was rejected.

When a new product is manufactured by mixing the goods supplied with other materials If a new product is manufactured by mixing the goods supplied with other materials, the English case of *Hendy Lennox (Industrial Engines) Ltd v Grahame Puttick Ltd*[119] is authority for the

[115] Especially in view of the House of Lords decision in *Armour and Another v Thyssen Edelstahlwerke AG* [1991] 2 AC 339, that an effective retention-of-title clause does not create a security interest.

[116] See M. McInnes, *The Structure and Challenges of Unjust Enrichment* (Sydney: Law Book Company, 1996), Chapter 2, where the author proposed that in a particular contract it may be possible to infer such an obligation, and there was also the possibility of relief under the principle of unjust enrichment.

[117] Lacy, above, note 87, at p. 360.

[118] This difficulty was also recognised in *ICI New Zealand Ltd v Agnew* [1998] 2 NZLR 129, 135, *per* Henry J.

[119] [1984] 2 All ER 153.

proposition that the retention of title is effective, provided the goods supplied remain identifiable in their original form, and that they can be separated from the other materials by a simple process. In that case, the seller supplied several diesel engines to the buyers on credit on the terms that the 'goods shall be and remain the property of the seller until the full purchase price is paid' (term one) and that 'the seller has the right to retake possession of the goods in the event of default' (term two). Each of the diesel engines was incorporated in a diesel generating set and sold to sub-buyers. However, the process of incorporation did not alter or destroy the substance of the diesel engine. A simple process of disconnecting it from the generating set could detach the engine. Three diesel engines were in issue here. They were incorporated into three generating sets. One was sold to a sub-buyer after the credit period expired (X diesel engine). The other two were sold before the expiry of the credit period; the buyer subsequently went into receivership (Y diesel engines). The seller claimed from the receiver the proceeds from the sale of the generating sets representing the three diesel engines. The court held that the seller was entitled to reclaim the X diesel engine as the retention of title was still effective on two bases. Firstly, the seller's proprietary right in the diesel engines was not affected because after the incorporation they remained engines, albeit connected to other things. Secondly, payment for this engine had become overdue, so the seller was entitled to repossess the engine under term two above. In respect of the Y diesel engines, the court held that although the retention of title was effective, the seller was not entitled to the proceeds because the ownership of the engines had passed to the sub-buyers before the seller's right to retake possession arose.

However, if the goods, after undergoing the manufacturing process, are no longer identifiable, then, according to *Clough Mill Ltd* and *ICI New Zealand Ltd*, the rule is that title in the new product is vested in the buyer.

Where the goods have ceased to exist in their original form and are represented by cash When the buyer has sold the goods and cash represents them, the issue of whether or not the extended retention of title is effective against the proceeds is, at best, confusing.

The often-cited proposition is that if the cash is not mixed with any other monies, the seller could recover the money provided there was a bailor–bailee relationship or principal–agent relationship between the seller and the buyer in respect of the cash. When this is established, the cash is traceable in common law.[120] For present purposes this is referred to as the seller's right of legal tracing.

Examination of this proposition has, however, shown that it is mired in contradiction and confusion. The crux of the issue that appears to confront the courts and academics is whether the existence of a fiduciary relationship is essential to establish this legal right of tracing. One view is that it is not necessary as the fiduciary relationship is presumed when a bailor–bailee relationship or a principal–agent relationship is established[121] (the first view). This can be discerned from the English cases of *Re Bond Worth Ltd*,[122] *Borden (UK) Ltd v Scottish Timber Products Ltd and Another*[123] and *Re Peachdart Ltd*.[124]

However, there is an opposing view, which states that a fiduciary relationship between the seller and the buyer must actually be proved by the seller in respect of the cash (the second view). For instance, in *Hendy Lennox (Industrial Engines) Ltd*, one of the grounds for the court's rejection of the seller's claim in respect of the proceeds from the sale of the other two diesel engines was the absence of a fiduciary relationship between the seller and the buyer in respect of the proceeds. As Staughton J stated, 'I do not find it implied that the buyers were to occupy a fiduciary position in respect of the proceeds of sale.' He further commented that the fiduciary relationship did not arise simply on the ground that there was a bailee–bailor or principal–agent relationship over the proceeds. If this was the case, he continued, the '*Romalpa* case could have been decided very shortly indeed: the buyers were admitted to be bailees, and found to be agents: there was no need to consider any implied term as to their

120 The seller's right of tracing is a complex concept. It does not appear to have received any precise definition: see R. Goff and G. Jones, *The Law of Restitution*, 4th ed. (London: Sweet & Maxwell, 1993), Chapter 2; and R.M. Goode, 'The Right to Trace and its Impact in Commercial Transactions – Part I', *LQR* 92 (1976), 360, where they said that a definition was unnecessary. But see *Chitty on Contracts – General Principles*, 26th ed. (London: Sweet & Maxwell, 1989), para. 2089, where the right to trace has been defined as one where a 'true owner of the property may "follow" or "trace" it and claim its recovery' from a person in possession of it. The advantages of a tracing claim include: the assertor obtains priority over the unsecured creditors of the assertee, in the event he becomes insolvent; he may recover profits made by the assertee; and the limitation period governing proprietary claims may be longer. Goff and Jones, ibid., p. 73.

121 *Sinclair v Brougham* [1914] AC 398, 420, *per* Viscount Haldane LC. Also *Re Diplock* [1947] 1 Ch 716, at 744, *per* Wynn-Parry J.

122 [1979] 3 All ER 919. 123 [1979] 3 All ER 961.

124 [1984] Ch 130; and see also *Peerless Carpets Ltd v Moorhouse Carpet Market Ltd* (1992) 4 NZBLC 102, where the seller was allowed to recover the proceeds from the sale of the carpet because there was a fiduciary relationship between the buyer and the seller.

obligation: they were bound to account as a fiduciary.' However, on further analysis, Staughton J's observation is confusing, for he later admitted in his judgment that in bailor–bailee and principal–agent relationships the normal fiduciary relationship was presumed.[125]

The earlier part of Staughton J's proposition was followed in *Re Andrabell Ltd (in liquidation), Airborne Accessories Ltd v Goodman*,[126] where the facts were more straightforward. Gibson J thought that there was no such presumption; each individual case had to be examined to determine whether there was a fiduciary relationship.[127] There the issue was whether the seller was entitled to claim from the liquidator the buyer's proceeds from the sale of travel bags supplied by the seller. The pertinent terms of the contract of supply between the seller and the buyer expressly provided the following: (a) ownership in the bags was not to pass to the buyer until the buyer had paid the seller the total purchase price, including value added tax, and (b) the proceeds from sale should be deposited with a designated bank and the seller had a lien over them and the buyer should not remove them without the authority of the seller. Peter Gibson J held that the terms did not create any

[125] There are strong views that a fiduciary relationship is merely an ordinary incident of an agency. For example, see *Bowstead on Agency*, 15th ed. (London: Sweet & Maxwell, 1985), pp. 156–7; *Halsbury's Laws of England*, 4th ed., reissue (London: Butterworths, 1990), vol. 1(2), para. 87; L.S. Sealey, 'Fiduciary Relationships', *CLJ* (1962), 69 at pp. 79–81; J.C. Shepherd, *The Law of Fiduciaries* (Toronto: Carswell, 1981), at p. 25. R.P. Meagher, W.M.C. Gummow and J.R.F. Lehane, *Equity: Doctrines & Remedies*, 2nd ed. (Sydney: Butterworths, 1984), pp. 145–51, took the view that an agent generally owed fiduciary duties to the principal, and doubted whether cases commonly referred to could be regarded as authority for the contrary position. Note that the case of *Lister v Stubbs* (1890) 45 Ch D 1, which these authors regarded as the stumbling block to their view, has been disproved in the case of *Attorney General for Hong Kong v Reid* [1994] AC 324. It is submitted that this view is preferred, but whether an agent owes a particular fiduciary duty to the principal is a question of fact.

[126] [1984] 3 All ER 407, [1984] BCLC 522.

[127] Academics support this approach; for example, see Kimchai Chiah, 'Romalpa Revisited–Again' (1985) *JBL*, 160 at p. 162; N.E. Palmer, *Bailment*, 2nd ed. (Sydney: Law Book Company Ltd, 1991), Chapter 3; A. Hicks, 'Reservation of Title: A Pious Hope', *MLR* 27 (1985), 73; Collier, above, note 24, p. 90; P.S. Atiyah, *The Sale of Goods* (London: Pitman, 1990), pp. 459 and 450. Note I. Davies, *Effective Retention of Title* (London: Format Publishing, 1991), p. 63, which supports the old view. There are, however, decided cases and text writers dealing specifically with the matter of bailment and agency which support the recent view, for example *Boardman and Another v Phipps* [1966] 3 All ER 721 at 751, *per* Lord Upjohn. Note that Upjohn LJ's judgment was a dissenting judgment. The majority held that there was an agency relationship in that case, and Lord Cohen's judgment, one of the majority, was approved by the Privy Council in the case of *Attorney General for Hong Kong v Reid* [1994] 1 AC 324.

fiduciary relationship between the buyer and the seller. Accordingly, the claim of the seller must fail.

If the above confusion is not enough, further obfuscation is added when a third, extreme, view of fairly recent origin is considered. This view holds that it is unnecessary to consider whether there was a fiduciary, bailee–bailor or principal–agent relationship between the seller and the buyer (the third view). Accordingly, the parties' respective rights over the cash should be determined solely from the terms of the agreement.[128] In *Agip (Africa) Ltd v Jackson*,[129] Millett J (as he then was) appeared to agree with this third view. He stated that the requirement of fiduciary relationship was based on authority rather than on any logical established legal principles.[130] Several academics strongly support this position. For example, the authors Goff LJ and Jones[131] cast doubt on the often-cited House of Lords case of *Sinclair v Brougham*[132] as authority for the need of the existence of a fiduciary relationship.[133]

The third view appeared to receive support in the Australian High Court case of *Associated Alloys Pty Limited v ACN 001 452 106 Pty Limited*

[128] *Clough Mill Ltd v Martin* [1985] 1 WLR 111, *per* Goff LJ, *John Snow & Co. Ltd v DBG Woodcroft & Co. Ltd* [1985] BCLC 54, 58, *per* Boreham J. The strongest support for this approach is the *E Pfeiffer* case [1988] 1 WLR 150, 158, where Philip J said, 'It seems to me inappropriate to describe the relationship of a seller and a buyer in possession to whom title has not yet passed as that of bailor/bailee, for it will not normally have the same incidents as the classic bailment relationship. The relationship of a buyer and a seller is inevitably the creature of contract.' For the orthodox view see *Re Hallett's Estate* [1880] 13 Ch D 696, at pp. 710 and 708 *per* Sir George Jessel MR; *Re Diplock* [1948] 1 Ch 465 at pp. 520–1, *per* Lord Greene MR, *Chase Manhattan Bank v Israel-British Bank (London)* [1980] 2 WLR 202 at 209, *per* Goulding; and also G.A. Penn, A.M. Shea and A. Arora, *The Law Relating to Domestic Banking* (London: Sweet & Maxwell, 1987), para. 22.04.

[129] [1990] 1 Ch 265. [130] Ibid., at 285.

[131] See Goff and Jones, above, note 120, Chapter 2, where the authors are of the view that in *Sinclair v Brougham* Lord Dunedin did not mention the fiduciary relationship, and that Lord Haldane and Lord Parker seemed to mention it but wrongly held that the directors were in fiduciary relationships with the shareholders. A.J. Oakley, 'Proprietary Claims and their Priority in Insolvency', *CLJ* 54(2) (1995), 377 at p. 383, opined that *Sinclair v Brougham* did not impose such a requirement and suggested that the requirement of fiduciary relationship should be abolished.

[132] [1914] AC 398.

[133] The Privy Council cases of *Attorney General for Hong Kong v Reid* [1994] 1 AC 324 and *Re Goldcorp Exchange Limited* [1995] 1 AC 74 have not definitively clarified the matter. This is due to their special circumstances, namely that, in the first case, it involved a clear case of constructive trust, which was imposed in respect of the bribes received by the defendant. In the second case, the legal title in the gold bullion did not pass to the investors in law or in equity because of the pure investment nature of the scheme.

(in liquidation) and Another,[134] where the court held that express intention of the parties to create a trust over the proceeds from the goods supplied on a retention-of-title clause should be given full effect. The court rejected the argument that the 'trust' was a charge. The issue of fiduciary relationship was not considered. The details of the case and the decision will be discussed later.

In view of these conflicting positions, it appears that should the courts in Hong Kong be confronted with the issue they have the choice of following any of the three views. This situation does not bode well for sellers as the outcome is entirely uncertain.

The first and third views are attractive as they conclusively settle the matter. The second view would not end the uncertainty, and leads to another question – what constitutes a fiduciary relationship?

In this regard, it has been suggested that the *Romalpa* terms have to possess some resemblance of a trustee-and-beneficiary relationship,[135] such that the property in the goods must remain with the seller until the purchase price is fully paid;[136] the buyer must keep the goods separated from other goods;[137] the buyer is obliged to keep a separate record of sales of the goods;[138] and the buyer is obliged to pay the proceeds of sale of the goods into a separate account pending payment to the seller.[139] A declaration in the contract that the sale relationship between the parties is a fiduciary relationship is helpful,[140] but not conclusive, for equity looks at substance, not form. For instance, the presence of the expression 'fiduciary' did not prevent the court in *Re Peachdart Ltd* from concluding that there was no fiduciary relationship. These are only general guidelines. Each case turns on its own individual facts.

The seller's common law right to trace is lost when the proceeds from the sale of the goods become mixed with other monies. This strict rule has

[134] [2000] 202 CLR 588.

[135] See *Snell's Equity*, 29th ed. (London: Sweet & Maxwell, 1990), p. 298.

[136] As in the *Romalpa* case; see note 151 below.

[137] *Andrabell Ltd (in liquidation) Airborne Accessories Ltd v Goodman* [1984] 3 All ER 407.

[138] *Re Peachdart Ltd* [1983] 3 All ER 204, 210.

[139] This stipulation was not present in the *Romalpa* case. This was considered an important criterion in *Andrabell Ltd (in liquidation) Airborne Accessories Ltd v Goodman* [1984] 3 All ER 407.

[140] For example, in *Hendy Lennox Ltd v Grahame Puttick Ltd* [1984] 2 All ER 152, one of the reasons for Staughton J's conclusion that there was no fiduciary relationship was that 'there was no mention in any other part of the clause of the expression (derived from the Dutch) "fiduciary owner"'.

been criticised[141] as being illogical and unnecessarily incapacitating the common law from identifying 'specific coins when they are mixed with other coins'.[142] In this situation the seller has to trace the money in equity. If the seller succeeds in establishing its right to the proceeds at law or in equity, it acquires a proprietary interest in the property.[143] The proprietary interest is in the nature of ownership and not of security.[144]

To succeed in equitable tracing, it appears that the seller has to prove three conditions. The first is that there be no better intervening third-party claim to the proceeds, for example if the proceeds from the sale of the goods are paid into the buyer's personal account (which is often the case) and are later drawn out and paid to a third party. When this occurs the seller's right of tracing may be lost in three ways:

- if the third party can establish that it received the proceeds in good faith, without notice and for value, the right to trace is lost;[145]
- if the buyer has dissipated the property, such as where it is used to pay the business expenses of the buyer or it is used to alter or improve assets of the buyer, the right to trace is lost;[146]
- if the proceeds were used to pay off the buyer's debt, tracing is lost unless the buyer acquired something in exchange for the debt.[147]

The second condition is that the property has to be identifiable.[148] Equity adopts what has been described as the 'metaphysical' approach.[149]

[141] G. McCormack, *Retention of Title* (London: Sweet & Maxwell, 1990), p. 32.

[142] Ibid.

[143] There are also diverse views on the nature of the proprietary interests: see H.M. Hanbury and R.H. Maudsley, *Modern Equity*, 10th ed. (London: Stevens, 1976), p. 563, para. 2089, which states, 'A proprietary remedy is one which entitles a claimant to treat specific property or a portion thereof as his own'; Goff and Jones, above, note 120, Chapter 2. But in *Agip (Africa) Ltd v Jackson* [1990] 1 Ch 265, at 285, Millett J said, 'Tracing at common law, unlike its counterpart in equity, is neither a cause of action nor a remedy but serves an evidential purpose. The cause of action is for money had and received.' Millett J is correct: the cause of action is usually based on conversion or for money had and received, but the right of the assertor over the property is always proprietary.

[144] *Armour and Another v Thyssen Edelstahlwerke AG* [1991] 2 AC 339.

[145] *Banque Belge pour l'Etranger v Hambrouck* [1921] 1 KB 321. This is derived from equity's settled principle of the bona fide purchaser for value without notice.

[146] *Re Diplock* [1948] 1 Ch 465, at pp. 566–567.

[147] L.D. Smith, 'Tracing into the Payment of a Debt', *CLJ* 54(2) (1995), 290–305.

[148] G. McCormack, 'The Eye of Equity: Identification Principles and Equitable Tracing', *JBL* (May 1996), 225.

[149] *Re Diplock* [1948] Ch 465 at 516, CA. According to A.J. Oakley, 'The Prerequisites of an Equitable Tracing Claim', *CLP* (1975), 64 at pp. 66–9, in the beginning equity was as rigid as common law, and could not allow the beneficiary to trace into a mixed fund; see

Thus, if the buyer pays the proceeds from the sale of the seller's goods into its bank account and mixes them with its own monies, equity will hold that the buyer holds the appropriate amount on trust for the seller.[150] The seller has no interest whatsoever at law.

The third condition is that there was a fiduciary relationship between the seller and the buyer in respect of the cash.[151] However, on this point, the law is once again unclear as to whether a fiduciary relationship is essential. Goff LJ and Jones opined that a fiduciary relationship is not a prerequisite in tracing in equity and they would be surprised if the House of Lords were to hold otherwise.[152]

The Australian High Court case of *Associated Alloys*, mentioned above, appears to afford the seller a solution to the fiduciary relationship muddled in law and in equity. The relationship can be rendered irrelevant if an express declaration of trust[153] by the buyer over the proceeds can be incorporated into the conditional sale contract at the outset. In *Associated Alloys*, the seller sold steel, over a period of fifteen years, to a buyer on terms contained in invoices under which it retained ownership until the goods were fully paid for. The pertinent term of the invoices, for present purposes, provided that if the buyer used the steel in a manufacturing or construction process, or supplied the steel to a third party for such use, the buyer had to hold in trust for the seller such part of the 'proceeds' of such manufacture or construction as related to the goods supplied under the invoice. Such part was deemed equal in dollar terms to the amount owing to the seller on the invoice at the time of receipt of the proceeds. The goods were used in the manufacture of steel fabrication and sold to

the cases of *Ryall v Ryall* (1739) 1 Atk 59, 26 ER 39; *Lane v Dighton* (1841) Cr & Ph 126; *Lord Chedworth v Edwards* (1802) 8 Ves 46, 34 ER 1005. It was only in 1853, in *Pennel v Deffell* (1853) 4 DM & G 372, 43 ER 551, that equity allowed a beneficiary to trace the trust property to a mixed fund.

150 For authority on this see *Re Hallett's Estate, Knatchbull v Hallett* [1879] 13 Ch D 696: the court held that a client was entitled to trace his monies into the personal account of his dishonest solicitor though his monies had become mixed with the solicitor's personal funds. See also *Agip (Africa) Ltd v Jackson* [1990] Ch 265, [1992] 4 All ER 385. But in *Attorney General for Hong Kong v Reid* [1994] 1 AC 324, the Privy Council had allowed the beneficiary to claim the entire properties although the purchase price may have been from bribes and the dishonest fiduciary's personal and lawful earnings. *Reid* raised this point but was not considered by the Judicial Committee.

151 *Aluminium Industrie Vaassen v Romalpa Aluminium Ltd* [1976] 1 WLR 676, and also A.J. Oakley, 'Property Claims and their Priority in Insolvency', *CLJ* 54(2) (1995), 377 particularly at 406.

152 Goff and Jones, above, note 120, Chapter 2.

153 The use of trust as a security device is not known; see Chapter 2 above.

a third party. Before the full amount of the goods was paid, the buyer went into voluntary liquidation. The seller applied to the court for a declaration that the buyer held the proceeds from the sale of the steel fabrication on trust for the seller. The court at first instance, and the Court of Appeal, dismissed the seller's application on the grounds that the declaration of trust created a charge and, since it was not registered with the Companies Registry, it was void. The reasoning essentially followed the Law in England;[154] that is, the substance of the transaction was a security, and to hold otherwise would defeat the purpose of the transaction. This is the substance-over-form theory.[155] However, on further appeal, the High Court, by a majority,[156] rejected the security-substance argument. It held that since the declaration of trust was clear it should be given full effect. The joint decision of Gaudron, McHugh, Gummow and Hayne stated:

> The contracts, in respect of each of the invoices, spoke for the future and provided the attachment of a trust for 'the proceeds' received from time to time. There being value, and equity regarding that as done that which ought to be done, a completely constituted trust would arise in respect of those 'proceeds' ...[157]
>
> In the present case there is nothing to suggest, at this subjective level, that the parties in their written instrument did not mean what they said, or did not say what they meant. There is no suggestion of a sham. It must follow that the terms of the invoices embodied the intentions of the parties.[158]

The decision of the majority was influenced by a determination to maintain certainty in commercial transactions and in the law. As Their

[154] See the English cases of *Tatung (UK) Ltd v Galex Telesure Ltd* [1989] 5 BCC 325; and *Modelboard Ltd v Outer Box Ltd* [1992] BCC 945, where the English High Court held that the clause which required the buyer to hold the proceeds on 'trust' in a separate account created a registrable charge. See also the case of *Compaq Computer Ltd v Abercorn Group Ltd* [1991] BCC 484, where Mummery J held that a clause which required the buyer to keep the proceeds in a separate account created a registrable charge. In contrast, in the New Zealand case of *Peerless Carpets Ltd v Moorhouse Carpet Market Ltd* (1992) 4 NZBLC 102, it was held that that the buyer not only held the carpet as 'bailee and agent' but also held the proceeds on trust for the seller.

[155] Gough, in *Company Charges*, 2nd ed. (London: Butterworths, 1996), Chapter 21, 'Disguised Charges', gives a detailed exposition of the theory, and concludes that the approach of the English courts is one of substance over form in determining whether a transaction creates an absolute sale, retention of title or a charge.

[156] The majority were Gaudron, McHugh, Gummow and Hayne JJ, Kirby J dissenting.

[157] *Associated Alloys Pty Limited v ACN 001 452 106 Pty Limited (in liquidation) and Another* [2000] 202 CLR 588, p. 603, para. 28.

[158] Ibid., p. 606, para. 35.

Honours, after referring to the unsatisfactory state of the current law,[159] emphatically stated, 'It is of some importance that parties to sophisticated commercial transactions have structured, and will continue to structure, their affairs on the basis that a certain and predictable course can be charted through this terrain.'[160]

Unfortunately, the positive observation of the High Court did not assist the seller. The High Court held that no trust was created on the facts of the case because the seller was not able to establish which part of the proceeds in the general account of the buyer was derived from goods described in the invoices. This requirement appears to be flawed for several reasons:

- It imposes a near-impossible burden on the seller who seeks to rely on the clause because in practice the buyer does not operate such an accounting process.[161]
- It fails to recognise, as mentioned earlier, that equity adopts a 'metaphysical approach' in tracing. Even if the money is mixed, equity could hold that the buyer holds the appropriate amount on trust for the seller.
- By placing strong emphasis on the declared intention of the parties, the High Court seems to ignore the statutory direction of §22(2) of the Sale of Goods Act 1923.[162] The section requires the court to have regard to the terms of the contract, the conduct of the parties, and the circumstances of the case when determining the full effect of the terms of the contract of sale of goods.

Despite these flaws, three new developments can be discerned from the decision and merit further discussion. Firstly, the Highcourt appears to be determined to cut through the rigid line that seemed to separate the rules of common law from rules of equity in commerce. Counsel for the liquidator had strongly relied on this artificial line, which was prevalent in England, at least until *On Demand Information*,[163] to support its

159 They cited Staughton J's remark in *Hendy Lennox (Industrial Engines) Ltd v Grahame Puttick* [1984] 2 All ER 152, 159, i.e. 'a maze if not a minefield'.

160 *Associated Alloys Pty Limited v ACN 001 452 106 Pty Limited (in liquidation) and Another* [2000] 202 CLR 588, p. 592.

161 See T.M. Carlin, '*Associated Alloys Pty Ltd v ACN 001 452 106 Pty Ltd*: A Commentary and Analysis', *ABLR* 30 (2002), 106 at p. 113.

162 Equivalent of §19(2) of the Sale of Goods Ordinance.

163 *On Demand Information plc v Michael Gerson (Finance) plc* [2000] 4 All ER 734 (partly reversed in [2003] 1 AC 368).

argument that the trust term could not be construed to be anything other than a charge. The trust term must be examined against the contract of sale as a whole[164] and it was evident that the purpose of the term was to provide a security. The High Court, by a majority, rejected this argument on the grounds that though the origins and nature of contract and trust are quite different, there being no contradiction between the two.[165] The contractual relationship provides one of the most common bases for the establishment, implication or definition of a trust. This was the situation in *Associated Alloys*, where the contracts provided for the attachment of a trust when the goods are converted to 'proceeds'. Secondly, the High Court seems to take a different stance from the Privy Council[166] and the House of Lords[167] where they had held that in determining whether a security document created a fixed or floating charge the declared intention of the parties was not relevant.[168] *Re Bond Worth Ltd*, an earlier English case which was more problematic on the point and bears some similarity with *Associated Alloys*, was cited by counsel but ignored by the High Court. There Slade J unequivocally rejected the trust concept and held that the document created a charge, though he admitted that it was suggestive of a trust. He said that the court was bound to look at the commercial reality of the transaction and the substance of the transaction. If, indeed, the transaction was a security for the payment of a debt, or appropriated such property for the discharge of the debt, it must be regarded as a mortgage or charge.[169]

The Australian High Court's decision is inconsistent with several English cases, such as *Tatung (UK) Ltd v Galex Telesure Ltd*[170] and *Modelboard Ltd v Outer Box Ltd*,[171] where the English High Court held that the clause which required the buyer to hold the proceeds on 'trust' in a separate account created a registrable charge.[172]

Hong Kong courts, if confronted with the issue, have two options: they can either follow the concept of business efficacy as established in *Associated Alloys*, or follow the English approach of substance over form,

164 See *Tatung (UK) Ltd v Galex Telesure Ltd* [1989] 5 BCC 325.

165 They based it on the observation of Mason and Deane JJ in the earlier case of *Gosper v Sawyer* (1985) 160 CLR 548, at pp. 568–9.

166 See *Agnew v Commissioner of Inland Revenue* [2001] UKPC 28, [2001] 3 WLR 454, PC.

167 See *Smith (Administrator of Cosslett (Contractors) Ltd) v Bridgend County Borough Council* [2002] 1 All ER 292, UKHL 13.

168 These cases and their impact have already been discussed above in Chapter 4.

169 See *Re Bond Worth Ltd* [1980] 1 Ch 228, [1979] 3 All ER 919, 939, *per* Slade J.

170 [1989] 5 BCC 325.

171 [1992] BCC 945.

172 See also the case of *Compaq Computer Ltd v Abercorn Group Ltd* [1991] BCC 484.

a commercially less certain option. Given that this latter approach appears now to be favoured by the House of Lords and the Privy Council at least as regards the determination of charges (see *Agnew* and *Re Spectrum*),[173] the 'substance-over-form' view appears to have become the orthodox approach in construing commercial agreements relating to the creation of security devices.

A significant consequence that follows the trust concept for the buyer appears to have been overlooked. If the buyer receives the proceeds, the subject matter of the trust, and it does not pay them over to the seller but uses them for other purposes, such as to pay other debts, the buyer can be charged and convicted for criminal breach of trust.[174] This would seem rather draconian. Consequently, the better view is that the substance of the transaction is likely to be confirmed as the preferred approach in Hong Kong.

Retention-of-title clause and 'all debts' clause

It was already well recognised in the 1970s that sellers in England had developed the practice of including an 'all debts' stipulation into retention-of-title clause.[175] For example, a conditional sale contract may provide that 'all goods delivered by the seller will remain the property of the seller until "all debts" owing to the seller are settled'.[176] This issue received authoritative attention in the House of Lords case of *Armour and Another v Thyssen Edelstahlwerke AG*.[177] There the seller sold the buyer a

[173] *Agnew v Commissioner of Inland Revenue* [2001] UKPC 28, [2001] 3 WLR. 454; and *Re Spectrum Plus Ltd* [2005] 2 AC 680; for a detailed discussion, see Chapter 4 above.

[174] See the Theft Ordinance (Cap. 210), §§2(1), 6(2). Section 2(1) provides that a person commits theft if he dishonestly appropriates property belonging to another with the intention of permanently depriving the other of it. Section 6(2) provides that property held under a trust is regarded as belonging to any person who has the right to enforce the trust and any intention of the trustee to defeat the trust will be regarded as an intention to deprive the person having the right of enforcement of that property.

[175] For example, it was found in *Aluminium Industrie Vaassen BV v Romalpa Aluminium Ltd* [1976] 2 All ER 552, [1976] 1 WLR 676; *Borden (UK) Ltd v Scottish Timber Products Ltd and Another* [1979] 3 All ER 961; *John Snow & Co. Ltd v DBG Woodcroft & Co. Ltd* [1985] BCLC 54; and in the New Zealand cases of *Len Vidgen Ski & Leisure Ltd v Timaru Marine Supplies (1982) Ltd* [1986] 1 NZLR 349; and *Peerless Carpets Ltd v Moorhouse Carpet Market Ltd* (1992) 4 NZBLC 102.

[176] Extracted from *Armour and Another v Thyssen Edelstahwerke AG* [1991] 2 AC 339, HL. An almost similar term was also used in the earlier case of *John Snow & Co. Ltd v DBG Woodcroft & Co. Ltd* [1985] BCLC 54, p. 57. It was stated, 'The property of the goods agreed to be sold will only pass to the purchaser when the purchaser has met all indebtedness to the seller'.

[177] [1991] 2 AC 339, HL.

large quantity of steel strip under an 'all debts' retention-of-title clause. When the buyer was put into receivership, a dispute arose as to whether the steel strip was the property of the seller or the buyer and thus available to the general creditors. The House of Lords unanimously held that the retention-of-title clause effectively retained ownership in the steel strip. The receiver's argument that it created a charge was rejected. The House of Lords had no difficulty in coming to this conclusion because most of the steel strip had remained in the same state and in the possession of the buyer. The House also held that there was no objection to the parties incorporating an 'all debts' clause and subjecting the passing of the property to the settlement of all debts owing by the buyer and that such a clause did not create a charge.[178] This case illustrates how with a contractual clause the seller is able to extend the advantage normally enjoyed by the banks to an area of sale of goods. The effect of the 'all debts' clause is almost identical to the 'all monies and liabilities' clause commonly found in banking security documents.[179] Such expression permits the bank to secure not only the assets against the loans lent under the security but also other debts and future advances.[180]

Critics have, however, commented that the 'all debts' clause has generated a new theoretical and practical problem,[181] which the House of Lords was not required to address in *Armour*. The issue is whether 'all debts' clauses allow the seller to repossess goods supplied under separate contracts[182] which the buyer has settled because of non-payment of another debt.[183]

There are three views on this issue. The first is that the seller should be entitled to repossess the goods fully paid by the buyer, but the seller has to refund the buyer the price of the goods on the grounds of total failure of consideration.[184] The second view is that there is no total failure

[178] Ibid., p. 353, *per* Lord Keith.

[179] The impact of such clauses on priority is discussed further in Chapter 6 below.

[180] See also Chapter 6 below.

[181] See W. Goodhart and G. Jones, 'Infiltration of Equitable Doctrine into English Commercial Law', *MLR* 43 (1980), 486; W. Goodhart, '*Clough Mill Ltd v Martin* – A Comeback from *Romalpa*?', *MLR* 43 (1986), 96; J.R. Bradgate, 'Reservation of Title Ten Years on', *Conv* (1987), 434; and R. Bradgate, 'Retention of Title in the House of Lords: Unanswered Questions', *MLR* 54 (1991), 726.

[182] For example, in *John Snow & Co. Ltd v DBG Woodcroft & Co. Ltd* [1985] BCLC 54, there were nine separate contracts. It is generally agreed that if the goods are supplied under one single contract, there is no problem: see Goodhart and Jones, above, note 181, at p. 508.

[183] Bradgate, above, note 181, at p. 729.

[184] See Goodhart, above, note 181; R. Bradgate, above, note 181.

of consideration because the buyer had the use of the goods from the date of delivery of the goods to the date of repossession.[185] Accordingly, the seller has to refund the buyer the proceeds. However, the seller may set the sum off against the debt owing by the seller under the contract of sale.[186] The third view is that an 'all debts' clause creates a charge.[187] This, it is submitted, has a difficulty – namely, why should an 'all debts' clause be construed as creating a charge, when, by analogy with banking documents, such expression has no bearing on the nature of the security, except for the ambit of the security and the doctrine of tacking.[188] It is submitted that neither the first nor second are attractive because they create commercial uncertainty. As Master Hansen in *Rees Plastics Ltd v Ineson*[189] critically commented, in cases where the buyer was given a reasonable length of time to pay the purchase price in each contract, there are a number of questions that cannot be answered easily – namely, when should ownership pass? Was ownership never to pass as long as the relationship of seller and buyer was one of creditor and debtor? Should ownership pass only when each contractual order was paid?

In conclusion, the efficacy of 'all debts' clauses and the many questions that arise from them, remain to be determined. The seller who relies on such a clause sails into uncharted waters, and bears a substantial legal risk that it might not be fully effective.

Alternatives to retention-of-title clauses

If a purported retention-of-title clause fails, there is ample authority, such as *Re Bond Worth Ltd* and *Clough Mill Ltd*, for the proposition that the seller will not necessarily be denied security. Depending on the intention of the parties, the security may be a mortgage or charge in the form of a bill of sale in the case of an individual, or an equitable fixed charge or floating charge in the case of a company.[190]

185 See G. McCormack, '"All Liabilities" Reservation of Title Clauses and Company Charges', *Conv.* (March 1989), 92; also J. Mance, 'The Operation of an "All Debts" Reservation of Title Clause', *LMCLQ* (1992), 35.

186 See Goodhart, above, note 181.

187 Goodhart and Jones, above, note 181, p. 508; and also *Clough Mill Ltd v Martin* [1984] 3 All ER 982, where Goff and Oliver LJJ discussed the problem and favoured the charge concept.

188 See note 179, above.

189 Unreported, High Court, Christchurch CP 104/90, 5 July 1990. Master Hansen's dictum was sourced from the article of R.J. Ahdar entitled 'Romalpa's Empire: The Reception of Reservation of Title Clauses in New Zealand', *LMCLQ* 382 (1993), 391.

190 *Re Yorkshire Woolcombers Association* (1903) 2 Ch 284.

However, this consolation may be in practice cold comfort to the supplier. This is because in many cases the security will be invalid against third parties for default of registration. If the buyer is a company, the seller will often fail to register the security. This is not a deliberate failure. It is simply due to the fact that the seller does not know that the retention-of-title clause has created a registrable charge.[191] This disaster is illustrated in *Re Bond Worth Ltd*. There Slade J held that a clause which failed to take effect as a retention of title created a floating charge over the assets and book debts of the buyer company but it was void for want of registration with the Registrar of Companies.[192] Similarly, in *E Pfeiffer Weinkellerei-Weineinkauf GmbH & Co. v Arbuthnot Factors Ltd*,[193] the court held that an agreement to supply wine with a retention-of-title clause created an assignment of the proceeds by way of a fixed charge but was void against the subsequent assignee because the seller did not register the charge with the Companies Registry under §95(1) of the old English Companies Act 1948. In the New Zealand case of *ICI New Zealand Ltd v Agnew* a purported retention-of-title clause was held to have created a floating charge but was void against the receiver for want of registration.

5.5.2 *Perfection of conditional sale*

On the issue of perfection, the conditional sale with retention-of-title clause occupies the same position as hire-purchase and leasing. For reasons already explained above in this chapter, perfection coexists with the creation of the conditional sale contract. There are, however, limits to its effectiveness against third parties. It cannot be enforced against a subsequent bona fide purchaser of the goods for value without notice of the retention-of-title clause.[194] This is an exception afforded by §9 of the Factors Ordinance and §27(2) of the Sale of Goods Ordinance (Cap. 26). These are discussed above in this chapter.

[191] Section 80(2) of the Companies Ordinance (Cap. 32), in the case of a company, and §7 of the Bills of Sale Ordinance in the case of an individual.

[192] A similar conclusion was reached in the case of *Re Peachdart Ltd* [1983] 3 All ER 204.

[193] [1988] 1 WLR 150.

[194] *Lee v Butler* [1893] 2 QB 318, CA, where a purported hire-purchase agreement of furniture was held to be a pure sale and purchase and the buyer in possession could pass a good title under §9 of the Factors Act.

5.5.3 Publicity of conditional sale

As in hire-purchase and leasing, the conditional sale with retention-of-title clause is not subject to any publicity requirements. This is because it is outside the scope of the registration systems of the Bills of Sale Ordinance[195] and the Companies Ordinance,[196] and there is no other statutory machinery to publicise it. Consequently, third parties who wish to deal with the buyer are disadvantaged. Such third parties are in an even more serious position than that in respect of hire-purchase and leasing arrangements. This is because, unlike hire-purchase and leasing, there is no formal contractual document or documents evidencing title of the goods in retention-of-title arrangements. Thus the general consensus is that the retention-of-title clause is unfair and not transparent, and may shrink the estate of the buyer even further in the event of the buyer's insolvency.[197]

5.5.4 Cost of creation, perfection and publicity of conditional sale

The cost of creating, perfecting and publicising a conditional sale with retention-of-title clause in Hong Kong is nil. The agreement is not subject to any stamp duty. As there is no formal publicity involved, no cost is incurred.

5.6 Creation, perfection and publicity of lease with option to purchase in China

5.6.1 Creation of lease with option to purchase

In China, the way in which the lease with option to purchase is contracted is also similar to the practice of hire-purchase in Hong Kong. In the Contract Law (1999), a 'lease-finance contract' is defined as a contract whereby the lessee selects an item which the seller sells to the lessor, who then allows the lessee to use the property on payment of a rental charge.[198] The ownership rights of the leased item at the expiry of the term are specified in the agreement in the lease contract. Where

[195] See Chapter 2 above. [196] See Chapter 4 above.

[197] See the Cork Committee's Report on Insolvency Law and Practice, Cmnd 8558, para. 1600, p. 361.

[198] Article 237 of the Contract Law (1999).

there is no express agreement, the lessor is presumed to be the owner.[199] The rights, obligations and liabilities between lessor and lessee are also provided.[200] The agreement is fairly simple and does not require notarisation by a notary public. The standard agreement usually contains the following terms:[201]

- the name, quantity, specifications, technical performance and method of inspection of the leased item;
- the lease term;
- the rental charge and any other obligations;
- the time, method and currency of payment; and
- the ownership of the leased item at the end of the lease term.

5.6.2 *Perfection of lease with option to purchase*

Like quasi-security in Hong Kong, the perfection of the lease with an option to purchase co-exists with the creation. There are no external perfection requirements. The registration system of Chinese mortgages in the Security Law (1995) and Property Law (2007) does not apply to a lease with an option to purchase.[202] Generally, a third party who acquires the goods from the hirer acquires no better title than the hirer has.

5.6.3 *Publicity of lease with option to purchase*

There is no machinery in China for registration of the lease with an option to purchase the goods. It is outside the registration system created by the Security Law and the Property Law. Consequently, as in Hong Kong, third parties who wish to deal with the hirer cannot determine the financial status of the hirer and status of the goods by any independent and reliable means.

5.6.4 *Cost of creation, perfection and publicity of lease with option to purchase*

The creation and perfection of the lease with option to purchase is cost-effective. There is no cost of publicity as publicity is not required.

199 Ibid., Article 250; and see further Article 242.

200 See, for example, ibid., Articles 244–50.

201 Ibid., Article 238.

202 See Chapter 2 above.

5.7 Creation, perfection and publicity of leasing in China, and cost

As the process of creation, perfection and publicity of leasing is similar to leases with an option to purchase, this section discusses them only briefly.

In respect of creation, the Contract Law has flexibly recognised a 'leasing contract' as a contract whereby the lessor delivers to the lessee the lease item for it to use or accrue benefit from, and the lessee pays the rent.[203] Thus the definition includes the way in which equipment leasing is practised in both China and Hong Kong: the debtor selects the equipment from the dealer, who will then sell the equipment to the finance company. The finance company will then enter into a leasing agreement with the debtor. The terms are basically the same as the lease with an option to purchase, except the debtor does not have an option to purchase the goods and the debtor should return the goods at the end of the lease term.[204] The Contract Law also imposes obligations on the lessor, which include keeping the item fit for purpose and maintaining and repairing the item. The lessee's obligations include using the item in the agreed manner and keeping it with due care. The rights and obligations of the lessee and lessor are also listed. Examples include the lessee's right to make improvements to the item or to benefit from the use or possession of the item, the lessee's right to sublease and right to reduce the rent upon damage of the item by third parties, and the lessor's right to terminate the lease contract on default of payment. The standard agreement usually contains the following terms:[205]

- the name, quantity and purpose of the lease item;
- the lease term;
- the quantum of rent;
- the time and method of rent payment;
- the maintenance and repair of the lease item.

In respect of perfection, publicity and cost, the discussion in relation to the lease with an option to purchase applies here equally.

5.8 Conclusion

The above discussion shows that the law governing the creation, perfection and publicity of hire-purchase, leasing and conditional sale arrangements

[203] Article 212 of the Contract Law. [204] Ibid., Article 235. [205] Ibid., Article 238.

in Hong Kong and the corresponding arrangements have both strengths and weaknesses.

With regard to creation, there are three advantages in the rules governing the creation of the hire-purchase, lease and conditional sale. Firstly, the creation process is expeditious and inexpensive. Secondly, where they are effectively created, they generally constitute effective security. Thirdly, subject to the claim of the owner of the goods, the hirer, lessee and buyer are entitled to use and deal with the goods freely in the ordinary course of their business. In this regard, they are superior to the floating charge.

However, there are weaknesses in the creation rules. Firstly, there is a jurisprudential misrepresentation in all of them. Borrowing from Maitland's criticism of the legal mortgage – the hire-purchase, lease and conditional sale are 'one long *suppressio veri suggestio falsi*'.[206] The courts in Hong Kong treat them as a pure supply of goods unless there is clear evidence of moneylending arrangements. This simply exhibits an unrealistic approach by the courts. The law and reality do not therefore coincide.

Secondly, in relation to the conditional sale with retention-of-title clause, the rules for determining whether or not it is effective are complex and confusing. This is because the question is one of fact and depends on many varying factors, such as the nature of the goods, the fate of the goods, the nature of the acquirer's business, the expressions used in the document, and how the matter was presented to the court.[207] The complexity is further compounded by the retention-of-title clause encompassing numerous branches of the English law – namely agency, bailment, sale of goods, trusts and the principles of tracing, common law and equity. As Staughton J commented, 'this area of the law is presently a maze if not a minefield, and one has to proceed with caution every step of the way'.[208]

It is, therefore, quite beyond the comprehension of an ordinary commercial actor to understand fully how a retention-of-title clause that normally does not exceed four lines can have such a complex and confusing legal pedigree. The suggestion has also been made that the retention-of-title clause is morally unacceptable as between unsecured creditors who supply goods where a retention-of-title clause is available and unsecured

[206] Referring to the hire-purchase, Lord Denning MR in *Bridge v Campbell Discount Co. Ltd* [1962] 1 All ER 385, HL, 397, said the hire-purchase was in substance a moneylending transaction secured by a mortgage.

[207] *Clough Mill Ltd v Martin* [1984] 3 All ER 982, 985, *per* Goff LJ.

[208] *Hendy Lennox (Industrial Engines) Ltd v Grahame Puttick Ltd* [1984] 2 All ER 152.

creditors who supply services and utilities where such a mechanism is not available.[209] The latter cannot benefit from the retention-of-title clause and they stand to lose due to the use of such clauses by the suppliers of goods.[210]

Accordingly, the rules governing the creation of hire-purchase and leasing have satisfied the creation criteria established in Chapter 1 relating to simplicity and comprehensibility of the law, expedition, expense, a clear identification of the encumbered assets and the debtor remaining in possession of the goods with the freedom to deal with them in the ordinary course of business, whilst the legitimate interests of all parties to the transaction are protected. They do not, however, satisfy the creation criteria relating to securing future debts and after-acquired and future property.

Conditional sale satisfies most of the creation criteria established in Chapter 1, which hire-purchase and leasing also satisfy, except the criteria relating to simplicity and comprehensibility of the law and the clear identification of the affected assets. Other criteria are also not satisfied (as with hire-purchase and leasing), save security as to future indebtedness. This is because of the courts' recognition that a retention-of-title clause may secure 'all debts' of the buyer owed to the seller.

With regard to perfection, the rules governing the perfection of the hire-purchase, lease, and conditional sale in Hong Kong have satisfied one of the two sets of perfection criteria established in Chapter 1[211] – that is, the perfection process is simple, comprehensible, expeditious and inexpensive. Whether the rules have satisfied the other criterion relating to orderly priority is discussed in Chapter 6 below.

With regard to publicity, the rules governing the publicity of hire-purchase, leasing and conditional sale in Hong Kong are extremely weak. No publicity is required of them. Accordingly the rules fail to satisfy all the criteria established in Chapter 1 on publicity.

The consequences are serious.[212] Third parties who wish to deal with the hirer, lessee and conditional buyer are placed at a serious disadvantage. The route open to them to reduce the security risk is not attractive

[209] See J. Tribe, 'The Morality of Romalpa Clauses in Corporate Insolvency: A Case for Reform', *TILP* 17 (2001), 166 at p. 167.

[210] Ibid. [211] See Chapter 1 above.

[212] Lack of publicity of quasi-security is also a serious problem in England and Australia; see English Law Commission Consultation Paper No 164, para. 7.22; and also the Australian Law Reform Commission Report No 64, Personal Property Securities (1993), paras. 5.23–5.24. Both documents recommended that hire-purchase, leasing and conditional

and violates the fundamental principle of an efficient credit security legal framework, namely that inquiry should not go beyond the register of encumbrances affecting the goods. Further, the absurdity that the two current registration systems of the Bills of Sale Ordinance and the Companies Ordinance, which contain detailed systems of rules relating to registration of bills of sale and charges, can be wholly avoided by these simple devices.[213]

As the English Law Commission critically commented,

> One of the major difficulties resulting from the way the current law deals with quasi-securities is that they are not required to be registered under the Companies Act 1985,[214] their existence will not be apparent to a person searching the Company Charges Register. Potential creditors, investors and purchasers of a company's assets will therefore not know, in the absence of information from the company itself, that … [the assets] apparently free from registered charges are in fact not the absolute property of the company, and will thus not be alerted to the existence of what amounts to a security over such assets of the company.[215]

Although it is accepted that weaknesses of the hire-purchase, lease, and conditional sale are obvious, the United Kingdom Consultation Paper No 164 did not recommend their abolition. This, it appears, is for pragmatic reasons. They recommended that the devices should be made registrable under the proposed notice-filing system and that subsequent purchasers should generally take free from the ownership of the creditor.[216] However, due to this controversial proposal, the Law Commission Report No 296 thought that the whole regime of quasi-security, particularly its registration, should be reviewed.[217] However, as previously noted, no substantial change was enacted as regards company security in the Companies Act 2006. As regards Hong

sale should be publicised through registration. However, due to the controversies on whether quasi-security should be registrable in the proposed notice-filing scheme, the recent English Law Commission Report No 296, at p. 14, intended to reconsider this issue in the context of a broader project. This will be discussed further in Chapter 8 below.

213 See S. Jones, 'Retention of Title Clauses Ten Years from *Romalpa*', *Co. Lawyer* 7 (1986), 233 at p. 238.

214 Equivalent to the Hong Kong Companies Ordinance (Cap. 32).

215 English Law Commission Consultation Paper No 164, paras. 7.8–7.9.

216 English Law Commission Consultation Paper No 164, paras. 7.11–7.24. For further discussion see Chapter 8 below.

217 English Law Commission Report No 296, p. 14.

Kong, the same forces of inaction and complacency have been at work in respect of the rewrite of the Companies Ordinance and the government is very unlikely to propose any significant reforms in the new Companies Bill soon to be published.

In relation to China, the rules governing the creation, perfection and publicity of the lease with option to purchase and the lease enjoy the same strengths and suffer the same weaknesses as quasi-securities in Hong Kong.

With regard to creation, the rules governing the creation of the lease with option to purchase and the lease have satisfied the creation criteria of expedition, expense, the debtor's freedom to deal with the goods in the ordinary course of business, clear identification of the affected goods, simplicity and comprehensibility of the law. However, they have not satisfied the creation criteria relating to the security of future credits and after-acquired and future assets.

With regard to perfection, like the quasi-security in Hong Kong, the lease with option to purchase and the lease satisfy one of the two sets of criteria in this respect; that is, the perfection process is simple, comprehensible, expeditious and inexpensive. Similarly, whether the rules of perfection have satisfied the other criteria relating to orderly priority will be discussed in Chapter 6 below.

With regard to publicity, the lease with option to purchase and the lease do not require publicity. The rules therefore suffer from the same weaknesses as in Hong Kong. Accordingly, the rules in China have also not satisfied all the publicity criteria established in Chapter 1.

Returning to whether the rationale behind the development of these quasi-security devices still holds good today, the answer is both positive and negative. In respect of the positive, the advantages of speed, low cost, effective security, simplicity of rules and tax continue to prevail. However, these advantages are bought at significant cost:

- The anomaly is in the legal rules between traditional credit security and quasi-security, despite the fact that they serve the same security purpose; that is, to give security.
- In relation to the conditional sale with the retention-of-title clause, the law has become unduly complex and doubt has been cast on whether such a security device indeed protects the seller, as might have been initially imagined.
- Owing to the lack of publicity, there is little protection for third parties dealing with the hirer, lessee and buyer. Further, this attribute

undermines the broader rule against the 'false representation of wealth' of the debtor.

In light of the above findings, we conclude that the rules governing the creation, perfection and publicity of quasi-security devices in Hong Kong and China, as a whole, are inefficient.

Chapter 6

Priority of security interests over personal property

6.1 Introduction to Priority of Security Interests in Hong Kong

In Hong Kong, the mortgagor of property may create successive interests, by way of security or sale,[1] over the same property. In China, subject to the consent of the earlier mortgagee, the mortgagor may exercise the same rights as its counterpart in Hong Kong. In a property transfer, the mortgagor has the right to transfer the mortgaged property with the consent of the mortgagee during the mortgage period. If the mortgagor fails to obtain the mortgagee's consent and makes the transfer, the disposal can still be valid provided that the transferee repays the secured sum,[2] thereby obtaining unfettered ownership or possession rights.[3] On the other hand, subject to an earlier interest (for example a mortgage), the mortgagor can create further pledges or mortgages over the same property and subordinate interests of the later mortgagees or pledgees will arise. As a result, there will be competing interests over the secured personal property. Thus when one or more of the interested parties seeks to enforce their security interests, issues with regard to the priority of those competing interests are crucially important. It is in this situation that the efficiency of the credit security laws of both jurisdictions are tested to the fullest extent.

In Hong Kong, three rules underpin the legal framework for determining priority of competing interests in the same property: firstly, the first-in-time rule of creation of the interests, expressed in Latin as *qui prior est tempore, potior est jure*; secondly, the rule in *Dearle v Hall*;[4] thirdly, the rule of *nemo dat quod non habet*, which states that a person cannot pass any title to another person if the transferor has no title. Therefore the

1 That is, interest arising from the mortgagor's sale of the secured property.

2 Article 191 of the Property Law. Other transfers might be invalidated as 'unauthorised disposal of property through contract' pursuant to Article 51 of the Contract Law (1999).

3 Ping Jiang, *Property Law of the People's Republic of China: Explained* (Beijing: China University of Political Science and Law Press, 2007), p. 250.

4 (1828) 3 Russ 1, 38 ER 955, applied in the Hong Kong case of *ABN Amro Bank NV v Chiyu Banking Corp Ltd and Others* [2000] 3 HKC 381.

true owner's title in the goods prevails over subsequent claims in relation to the same goods. In Hong Kong, the *nemo dat* rule is restated in §23(1) of the Sale of Goods Ordinance. It provides that, subject to the provisions of the Ordinance, 'where goods are sold by a person who is not the owner, and who does not sell them under the authority or with the consent of the owner, the buyer acquires no better title than the seller'.

6.2 Introduction to Priority of Security Interests in China

6.2.1 First-in-time rule in China

In China, the original version of the Security Law (1995) did provide some basic rules for determining priority of competing interests over the same property. The Judicial Interpretation of the Security Law (2001) issued by the Supreme Court added further rules to determine the priority sequence. It is, however, noteworthy that the rules specified in the Security Law are in conflict with the Judicial Interpretation in many circumstances. In practice, the People's Courts follow the later Judicial Interpretation. The Property Law (2007) has confirmed the stance of the Judicial Interpretation by creating a comprehensive regime for determining the priority of mortgages in Article 199.

Firstly, the rule of first in time of creation of the security interests (other than quasi-security) basically has very little impact in China in determining priority, although there is a general recognition that the rule of first in time, being derived from Roman civil law,[5] has significance as China is fundamentally a civil law jurisdiction. However, in China, priority of interests is overwhelmingly determined by registration.

The original position was set out in Article 54 of the Security Law, which provided:

> Where the same property is mortgaged to two or more creditors, the proceeds from the auction or sale of the mortgaged property shall be used for payment in accordance with the following provisions:
>
> (1) where a mortgage contract becomes effective on the date of registration, payment shall be made according to the chronological order of registrations [Rule 1]; in case of same chronological order, payment shall be made according to the proportion of the obligations [Rule 2]

[5] The civilian source of this rule was confirmed in the English case of *Dearle v Hall* (1828) 3 Russ 1, 38 ER 475, *per* Thomas Plumer MR; and also W.A. Hunter, *Introduction to Roman Law*, 9th ed (London: Sweet & Maxwell Ltd, 1934), p. 80; and C.H.M. Waldock, *Law of Mortgages*, 2nd ed. (London: Sweet & Maxwell, 1950), p. 384.

> (2) where a mortgage contract becomes effective on the date of signature, and it has been registered, payment shall be made according to (1) [Rule 3]; if it has not been registered, payment shall be made according to the chronological order of execution of the mortgage; in case of same chronological order,[6] payment shall be made according to the proportion of the obligations [Old Rule 4].
>
> The registered mortgage has priority over an unregistered mortgage [Rule 5].

However, Old Rule 4 is contrary to Article 76 of the Judicial Interpretation of the Security Law (2001), which stipulated that 'if the same movable is mortgaged to two or more creditors and the parties did not register the mortgage, each mortgagee will receive payment in proportion to his obligations [but not the chronological order of signature] when the mortgage rights are realized' (Rule 4).

It is submitted that Article 76 is more reasonable because, as far as unregistered competing mortgages are concerned, the earlier mortgage rights should not be ineffective against any third party, including the later mortgagee where the mortgage was executed subsequently. Therefore resort to the encumbered property is justified in proportion to the respective obligations. Another practical reason to condone this interpretation is that the Judicial Interpretation was promulgated by the Supreme Court and therefore will be followed by the lower courts.[7]

Thus, Rule 1, Rule 2 and Rule 3 may be combined and considered as follows:

> Where a mortgage contract has been registered [whether it is effective on the date of registration or execution], the priority shall be accorded to the chronological order of registration. Where they are unregistered but were executed on the same date, the proceeds of the charged property are to be divided in proportion to the value of the obligations.

This rule is essentially the same as Article 199(1) of the Property Law. In other words, the creation rule of 'first in time' plays no part at all in the priority battle between registered mortgages.

Rule 5 and Rule 4 are essentially the same as Article 199(2) and Article 199(3) respectively. Therefore the whole Article 199 of the Property Law

[6] Article 58 of the Judicial Interpretation of the Security Law provides that where the two mortgages are registered on the same day, they shall be deemed to be the same.

[7] Guoguang Li and Shengping Gao, *New Interpretations of the Security Law and its Implementation Rules*, 2nd ed. (Beijing: The People's Court Press, 2006), p. 612.

has successfully amalgamated the previous priority rules for mortgages in the Security Law and its Judicial Interpretation.

Although the rule of first in time of creation has no place at all in the priority issue of security interests in China, it is essential to understand that different types of security interest have different times of effectiveness, namely the date of registration, signature and delivery. Accordingly, the effect of their registration can vary.

In relation to the legal effectiveness of mortgage contracts, Article 188 of the Property Law provides that where the contract involves mortgageable personal property such as ships and aircraft under construction,[8] as well as other means of transportation,[9] the contract becomes effective on the date of signature (and thus registration against bona fide third parties is voluntary). For other mortgageable personal property, under Article 34 of the Security Law,[10] including machines and other property owned by the mortgagor,[11] state-owned machinery and other property of which the mortgagor is entitled to dispose of pursuant to the law,[12] as well as other property which may be mortgaged according to other laws and administrative rules,[13] the mortgage contract is effective on execution and does not depend on registration.[14] However, if the mortgage is not duly registered, it does not bind a third party whether or not that person has actual knowledge of the encumbrance.

With regard to the legal effectiveness of floating Diya mortgages (as discussed in Chapter 2 above), Article 189 of the Property Law provides that where a mortgage contract involves mortgageable personal property such as production equipment, raw materials, semi-finished products and finished products,[15] it becomes effective on the date of execution. The position as regards the registration is the same as under Article 188. However, even if the contract is duly registered, protection of the mortgagee (or chargee) does not extend beyond third parties who are 'purchasers who pay a reasonable consideration and obtain possession of the mortgaged property in the ordinary course of business'.[16] Other types of acquirer of a transfer of company property, for example a person who receives a gift of

[8] Article 180(5) of the Property Law. [9] Ibid., Article 180(6).

[10] Ibid., Article 178, provides that the Property Law prevails over the Security Law in case of inconsistency.

[11] Article 34(2) of the Security Law. [12] Ibid., Article 34(4).

[13] Article 180(7) of the Property Law. This should have overruled Article 34(6) of the Security Law, which does not contain the words 'administrative rules'.

[14] Article 43 of the Security Law. [15] Ibid., Article 180(4),

[16] See Article 133 of the Contract Law (1999) for the details of title to pass in a sales contract transaction at the time of 'delivery'.

company property that is subject to Article 189, are not considered to be a party in good faith, and therefore take subject to the encumbrance.

The legal effectiveness of pledges over movable personal property and pledges of intangible rights can be different. In case of pledges over movables, physical possession by the pledgee is required in order to make the pledge effective; that is, the pledgee's rights are effective at the date of actual delivery of the pledged property,[17] not the date of execution of the agreement.[18] In case of pledges of intangible rights, validity depends on the type of the property concerned. Some rights are effective on the date of delivery of document of title and others are effective on the date of registration with the relevant department.[19] Once intangible rights under Article 223 of the Property Law are pledged, the pledgor cannot transfer or permit others to use such property unless there is agreement between the pledgor and pledgee. In addition, the money derived from the transfer or authorised use of such property shall be used to fulfil the obligee's rights in advance, or be deposited with a competent authority.[20]

6.2.2 Nemo dat *and bona fide purchaser rule in China*

In the past the application of the *nemo dat* rule was not very clear in China. The *nemo dat* rule essentially requires that 'where a person who is not the lawful owner sells goods, the buyer acquires no better title to

[17] Article 212 of the Property Law. See also Article 87 of the Judicial Interpretation of the Security Law, which provides that a pledge contract will not be effective if the pledgor holds the pledged property in his possession or on behalf of the pledgee. It further provides that the pledgee's rights against a third party could be lost if he returns the pledged property to the pledgor. However, if the pledgee loses possession of the pledged property without any fault, he may require the unjust possessor to cease infringement, restore the property to its original condition if damaged and return the property to the pledgee.

[18] One should differentiate the different effective times of the pledge agreement (i.e. the contract becomes effective at the time of its formation pursuant to Article 44 of the Contract Law 1999, usually by way of signature) with the effective time of pledge rights under the agreement (i.e. delivery). A further implication is that non-delivery of the pledged property (i.e. pledge rights have not been created) does not invalidate the pledge contract.

[19] Article 224 of the Property Law provides that if bills of exchange, cheques, promissory notes, bonds, certificates of deposit, warehouse receipts or bills of lading are pledged, the pledgee's rights are created upon delivery of the document of title (formerly Article 76 of the Security Law) or, in the absence of which, upon registration with the relevant department. For other intangible properties such as shares, portions of funds (Article 226), intellectual property rights including trademarks, patents, copyrights (Article 227) and rights to collect receivables (Article 228), the pledgee's rights are created upon registration with the relevant department.

[20] Articles 225–8 of the Property Law.

the goods than the seller had'. Article 51 of the Contract Law provides that 'where a person without the right to dispose of another's property does so upon ratification by the obligee or if the person without the right of disposal obtains the right of disposal after making the contract, the contract shall be valid'. The terms of this article are not as clear as to the position of the owner under §23(1) of the Sale of Goods Ordinance in Hong Kong. There is no mention of the owner's right to the title of the goods as against an unauthorised transferee, and thus the true owner's position is unclear.

Recently, the Property Law has strengthened the *nemo dat* rule. Under Article 106 of the Property Law, a rightful owner of property (real or movable) can generally recover his property when an unauthorised transferor has transferred the property to a third party (the transferee).[21] The transferee concerned does not obtain ownership of the property because the transfer is unauthorised. In other words, the existence of the *nemo dat* rule is apparently confirmed because where a transferor, without lawful authority, makes a transfer, he cannot pass any better title to the transferee than he himself possesses. However, this variant of the *nemo dat* rule is subject to the exception that the transferee can obtain ownership if he is a purchaser in good faith ('the rule of bona fide purchaser for value without notice'). This is clearly not the case under Hong Kong law. Article 106 provides that:

> Where the real or movable property is transferred to a transferee by a person without the power to do so,[22] the rightful owner shall have the right to recover such property.[23] Unless otherwise provided by law, the transferee shall obtain the ownership [or other property rights as in

[21] This refers to legal transfer by way of contract evidenced by the intention of the parties with the effect of changing the ownership (or other property rights). See Ping Jiang, above, note 3, p. 136. But note that the effective time of transfer is delivery for movable property and registration for real property, according to Articles 9 and 23 of the Property Law.

[22] This is known as 'unauthorised transfer through contract', similarly prescribed in Article 51 of the Contract Law. Under Article 51, the contract of transfer will still be valid either (1) by the ratification of the rightful transferor or (2) by subsequent acquisition of the right to transfer by the unauthorised transferor. Note that a contract of transfer without (1) or (2) is not invalid *ab initio*, but is a contract of transfer with pending effect until it is rendered valid if the act of transfer is subsequently authorised according to (1) or (2). However, one should note that according to Article 106 of the Property Law, a third party in good faith can obtain ownership of real or movable property even under a contract of transfer with pending effect.

[23] According to Article 34 of the Property Law, it should mean the right to request the return of the property from the people without right of possession.

> paragraph 3] respecting such real or movable property if the following events are satisfied:
>
> (1) The transferee accepts the transfer bona fide;
> (2) Such property is transferred with a reasonable price;
> (3) The transferred property has been registered in accordance with the laws requiring such registration, and those not requiring registration have been delivered to the transferee [paragraph 1].
>
> Where the transferee has obtained the ownership in respect of the real or movable property in accordance with the preceding paragraph, the original holder of the right may enjoy the right to claim damages from the unauthorised transferor [paragraph 2].
>
> Where the parties concerned have obtained the other property rights in good faith, the above two paragraphs shall apply [paragraph 3].

According to paragraph 1, where there is no provision in law governing the transfer, and if the transfer has satisfied the three conditions – namely (1) an unauthorised transferor to a bona fide purchaser,[24] (2) at a fair value and (3) the satisfaction of the relevant publicity requirement[25] – then the transferee will obtain ownership even though the transfer is unauthorised, and the title of the rightful 'owner' is extinguished.[26] According to paragraph 2, the rightful 'owner' is, in those circumstances, prohibited from recovering the property from the transferee, but does have a right to claim the damages from the unauthorised transferor though not from the bona fide transferee.[27] Thus the risk in such cases falls on the true owner and not on the innocent transferee. The rule appears to be a policy choice to prefer the innocent buyer rather than the 'true' owner.

According to paragraph 3, apart from obtaining ownership out of an unauthorised transfer, obtaining 'other property rights' (e.g. security interests) by a transferee is also possible. Accordingly, paragraphs 1 and 2 also apply to the transfer of a security interest by a transferor who has no power to transfer.

[24] If the act of transfer is authorised, the 'good-faith' requirement on a purchaser is meaningless. Therefore an unauthorised transferor is said to be a precondition of the good-faith requirement on the purchaser. In the context of transfer of movables, 'good faith' in Article 106 means that the transferee, without serious fault on his part, does not know or should not have known that the transferor is not the owner (or lacks the power to dispose of the property) at the time of transfer. See Ping Jiang, above, note 3, pp. 138–9.

[25] Unless otherwise provided by law, the publicity requirement shall take effect by registration in Article 9 (real) and by delivery in Article 23 (movable) of the Property Law. See also the meaning of 'delivery of movables' in Articles 25–7 of the Property Law.

[26] Ping Jiang, above, note 3, p. 139.

[27] See also Article 106 of the General Principles of the Civil Law of the PRC (1986).

6.2.3 *Pledge without ownership*

Where the pledgor has no ownership rights in a movable but has lawful possession of it, and the property is pledged ('pledge without ownership'), he has no power to create a security interest, and in such circumstances this constitutes an unauthorised transferor of that security interest.[28] According to the *bona fide* purchaser rule in paragraph 1, if the pledgee is in good faith,[29] he obtains the pledge rights effective from the delivery of the movable to him.[30] The legal effect is that the rightful owner, who has the power to create security interest over the pledged movable,[31] is now prohibited from recovering the movable from the pledgee in possession.[32] According to paragraph 2, the rightful owner only has the right to claim damages from the unauthorised pledgor.[33] On the other hand, if the pledgee is not in good faith, he does not obtain any rights but, as he is in possession, according to the *nemo dat* rule in paragraph 1, the rightful owner can recover the movable (i.e. request its return).[34]

6.2.4 *Re-pledge without consent*

The previous example must be distinguished from the case of unauthorised re-pledge ('re-pledge without consent'). That is, during the term of a pledge, the pledgee (not the owner), without the consent of the pledgor, pledges the property to a third party. Here, it does not matter whether the transferee is in good faith or not, because the *bona fide* purchaser rule in Article 106 is only applicable if there is no other provision in law governing the transfer. In this instance, Article 94 of the Judicial Interpretation of the Security Law and Article 217 of the Property Law govern unauthorised re-pledging. According to Article 94, re-pledging without the consent of the original pledgor is invalid.[35] Article 217 further provides that the unauthorised transferor shall bear any loss or damage caused to the pledged property.[36] Also, as a result of the *nemo dat* rule in Article 106,

[28] This example corresponds to Article 84 of the Judicial Interpretation of the Security Law.

[29] Similar to the good-faith requirement in paragraph 1 of Article 106.

[30] Article 212 of the Property Law.

[31] Ibid., Article 40, provides that the owner shall have the right to create security interests for real or movable property.

[32] Article 34 of the Property Law.

[33] See also Article 84 of the Judicial Interpretation of the Security Law.

[34] Article 34 of the Property Law.

[35] Article 94 of the Judicial Interpretation of the Security Law.

[36] See also Article 217 of the Property Law.

the rightful owner of the pledged property does have the right to recover the property from the transferee in possession.

6.2.5 Mortgagor's transfer of mortgaged movable without consent

Consider the situation of an unauthorised transfer of a mortgaged movable by a mortgagor during the term of a mortgage ('mortgagor's transfer of mortgaged movable without consent of mortgagee'). According to Article 191 of the Property Law, during the term of a mortgage, the mortgagor has no power to make such a transfer.[37] However, if he does transfer the mortgaged movable, the *bona fide* purchaser rule in Article 106 applies. If the transferee is in good faith, he will obtain ownership of the transferred movable which, according to Article 106(3), has been registered (if registrable) or delivered to the transferee (if not registrable). Article 67 of the Judicial Interpretation of the Security Law explains the effect following the transfer. If the mortgage has been registered, the mortgagee can still exercise his rights against the original mortgagor. The transferee (the subsequent owner) can discharge the obligation secured on behalf of the mortgagor to extinguish the mortgagee's rights. After payment, the transferee is entitled to recover against the mortgagor. On the other hand, if the security has not been registered, the mortgagee is not entitled to claim against the transferee. Therefore the mortgagee will only be able to claim against the original mortgagor. However, where a transferee is not in good faith, he will not obtain title to the property and ownership will remain with the mortgagor, and the mortgagee has the right to recover the property.[38]

6.2.6 Short conclusion

In conclusion, the use of the *nemo dat* rule and the *bona fide* purchaser rule have had some impact on security devices in China, especially where they involve a transfer in which the transferor has no power to transfer the secured property. Unless otherwise provided by law, the *bona fide* purchaser rule ensures that the transferee will obtain the security interest (or other property rights) in question. However, if the transferee is not in good

[37] Except if the mortgagor gets the consent of the mortgagee or has redemption from the transferee against his debts.

[38] Article 106 of the Judicial Interpretation of the Supreme People's Court on Some Issues Regarding Application of the Security Law (2000).

faith, the property (if in his possession) is subject to recovery by the rightful owner, pursuant to the *nemo dat* rule in Article 106 of the Property Law. In addition, the use of the *nemo dat* rule is also applicable to quasi-security devices – leases, leasing arrangements and conditional sales as stipulated in the Contract Law (1999). For example, a lessor can recover his property (real or movable) from a lessee who is not authorised to transfer the property but has in fact done so to a third party who is not in good faith.

6.2.7 *The* Dearle v Hall *rule in China*

The rule in *Dearle v Hall* has no place in the credit security law of China, because the civil law does not recognise security by way of assignment.[39]

Consequently, the object of the remainder of this chapter is to examine

- the rules of priority governing different types of traditional security interests and quasi-security interests in Hong Kong and China,
- the position of subsequent buyers of secured assets,
- the extent to which the rules of priority have satisfied the priority criteria established in Chapter 1.

6.3 Priority of Security Interests in Hong Kong

6.3.1 *Rule of first in time of creation in respect of security interests (other than quasi-security interests) in Hong Kong*

This part examines the first-in-time rule in relation to security interests over tangible and intangible personal property outside the ambit of *Dearle v Hall*.[40]

For the purpose of this part, unless otherwise stated, the expression

'legal creditor' means the legal mortgagee,
'equitable creditor' means the equitable mortgagee and
'personal property' means tangible and intangible personal property.

According to the first-in-time rule, the creditor who created a security first has a superior claim over the secured property free from other subsequent

[39] See Chapter 3 above.

[40] For example, the rule in *Dearle v Hall* only applies to competition between equitable interests and where the legal title to or control of the intangible property is vested in the debtor. See F. Oditah, *Legal Aspects of Receivables Financing* (London: Sweet & Maxwell, 1991), p. 129.

encumbrances. It is immaterial whether or not the subsequent creditor, at the time the later security was created, had notice of the first security.[41]

However, there are important exceptions to the rule. They can be classified into four categories, namely exceptions under general law and exceptions under legislation.

Exceptions to the first-in-time rule under general law

In Hong Kong, the two fundamental exceptions to the first-in-time rule are:

- where equities are equal, the legal interest prevails, and[42]
- the doctrine of tacking further advances.

Where equities are equal, the legal interest prevails The exception of 'where equities are equal, the legal interest prevails' ('basic exception') recognises the superiority of the legal security interest over the equitable interests. However, this exception is subject to two qualifications: firstly, where the first creditor's security interest is legal in nature and the creditor is guilty of inequitable conduct; secondly, where the legal security interest is subsequent to an earlier equitable security interest, and the legal creditor is not a bona fide purchaser for value without notice.

The operation of the basic exception and two qualifications can be classified into three situations of competing interests:

- legal interest and a subsequent equitable interest,
- equitable interest and a subsequent legal interest and
- equitable interest and a subsequent equitable interest.

Legal interest and subsequent equitable interest When there is a competition between an earlier legal security interest and a subsequent equitable security interest over the same personal property, the former has priority on the basis of the first-in-time rule and the superiority of the legal security interest.

However, the earlier legal security interest is not allowed to prevail over the subsequent equitable security interest if the earlier legal creditor is guilty of inequitable conduct.

[41] *Chu Kit Yuk and Another v County Wide Industrial Ltd and Others* [1995] 1 HKC, where the Court of Appeal ruled that the first purchaser's equitable interest arising from a sale and purchase of a flat prevailed over the second purchaser's interest.

[42] *Bailey v Barnes* [1894] 1 Ch 25, at 36, *per* Lindley LJ.

In Hong Kong, in the context of personal property, there have not been any judicial decisions on the meaning of inequitable conduct in this regard. However, examination of English authorities and texts shows that inequities include fraud and, arguably, the gross negligence of a prior legal creditor.[43]

According to Story,[44] the word 'fraud' has both a common law and an equitable definition. The meaning of common law fraud is narrower – it means 'actual intention to cheat'.[45] On the other hand, equitable fraud, according to Story,[46] means

> such acts as, although not originating in any actual evil design or contrivance to perpetuate a positive fraud or injury upon other persons, are yet, by their tendency to deceive or mislead other persons, or to violate

[43] Cases and major texts appear divided on whether 'gross negligence' of the earlier legal creditor may postpone the legal interest. English cases such as *Evans v Bicknell* (1801) 6 Ves 174, 189, 3 ER 988, 1003, *per* Lord Eldon; *Northern Counties of England Fire Insurance Company v Whipp* (1884) 26 Ch D 482, 495, CA, *per* Fry LJ; *Mercantile Bank of India Limited v Central Bank of India Limited* [1938] AC 287; *Moorgate Mercantile Co. Ltd v Twitchings* [1977] AC 890; and *Saltoon v Lake and Others* [1978] 1 NSWLR 52 suggest that gross negligence will not postpone a prior legal mortgage unless it amounts to fraud. See also R.P. Meagher, W.M.C. Gummow and J.R.F. Lehane, *Equity: Doctrines and Remedies*, 3rd ed. (Sydney: Butterworths, 1992), p. 248, where the authors state, 'But it is decidedly not the law that any act of carelessness or imprudence on behalf of the legal owner will (in the absence of fraud) suffice to postpone his interest and this is so even if that act of carelessness or imprudence could reasonably be described as "gross".' At the same page, however, they opine that 'failure to get in the deeds from the conveyor' may constitute inequity. On the other hand, there are cases where it was thought that 'gross negligence' alone was sufficient and constituted an independent ground for postponement. See *Colyer v Finch* (1856) 5 HLC 905; *Clarke v Palmer* (1882) 26 Ch D 482, CA; *Oliver v Hinton* (1899) 2 Ch 264; *Derry v Peek* (1889) 14 AC 337; and *Walker v Linom* [1907] 2 Ch 104. Leading texts, such as H.G. Hanbury and C.H.M. Waldock, *Law of Mortgages*, 1st ed. (London: Stevens & Sons Ltd / Sweet & Maxwell Ltd, 1938), p. 235; E.I. Sykes and S. Walker, *Law of Securities*, 5th ed. (Sydney: The Law Book Company Ltd, 1993), p. 398; E.F. Cousins and I. Clarke, *Law of Mortgages* (London: Sweet & Maxwell, 2001), pp. 408–11; E.L.G. Tyler, *Fisher & Lightwood's Law of Mortgage*, 10th ed. (London: Butterworths, 1988), p. 481; and *Snell's Equity*, 29th ed. (London: Sweet & Maxwell, 1990), at pp. 57–8, favour the latter as they hold that its more representative of the modern view. The current authors prefer the second view because the distinction between the legal creditor's failure to retain the title (as postulated in *Whipp*) and the legal creditor's failure to obtain the title (as postulated in *Linom*) is artificial. In addition, some of the cases, such as *Mercantile Bank of India* and *Moorgate Mercantile Co. Ltd*, were mainly concerned with agents' authority and the tort of negligence. The concept of 'gross negligence' is narrower; it is not concerned with the concept of duty of care but with the concept of 'inequities'.

[44] J. Story, *Commentaries on Equity Jurisprudence*, 13th ed., reprint (Littleton, CO: Fred B. Rothman & Co., 1987), §258.

[45] *Nocton v Lord Ashburton* [1914] AC 932, at pp. 952–7, *per* Viscount Haldane LC.

[46] Story, above, note 44.

> private or public confidence, or to injure the public interests, prohibited as within the same reason and mischief as acts and contracts done *malo animo.*

Story's equitable definition embraces the modern types of fraudulent misrepresentation established by the House of Lords in *Derry v Peek*.[47] On the basis of that case, if an earlier legal creditor knowingly, or without any belief in its truth, or recklessly misrepresented the true status of the property, and thereby allowed a subsequent equitable security to be created over that property, the legal creditor is guilty of fraudulent misrepresentation and its legal security is postponed.

However, no cases in Hong Kong or in any other common law jurisdiction have been found where fraudulent misrepresentation has been successfully invoked in the sphere of personal property to defeat the claim of the earlier legal creditor. The fact that the legal creditor continues to allow the debtor to have possession and use of the secured goods after the mortgage does not, of itself and without a further positive act, constitute fraudulent misrepresentation. This is so even if the possession of the goods by the debtor may have the effect of falsely representing to the general public that the debtor is creditworthy or that the goods were free from encumbrances. This proposition is supported by the objective of the Bills of Sale Ordinance.[48] To limit the effect, the Ordinance generally renders void all registrable security of goods which is not registered with the relevant authority.[49] Similarly, in relation to intangible personal property, there is little room for the possibility of fraudulent misrepresentation, except where the creditor is also guilty of some clear act of fraudulent misrepresentation. Thus Story's broad definition of fraud is difficult to apply in practice.

In relation to gross negligence, a legal creditor is guilty of gross negligence if the creditor displays a total 'mental indifference to obvious risks'[50] by not taking appropriate steps to safeguard its interest against those risks.[51] Many of the reported cases where the court had held that the conduct of the legal creditor constituted gross negligence related to competing claims over land. In these cases the legal creditor had a right to the title deeds, but failed to obtain any of them from the debtor without a reasonable excuse and thereby enabled a subsequent equitable security to be

47 (1889) 14 AC 337; and *Taylor v Russell* (1891) Ch D 8, 29.

48 Equivalent of the United Kingdom Bills of Sale Acts.

49 See Chapter 2 above.

50 *Hudston v Viney* [1921] 1 Ch 98, at 104, *per* Eve J.

51 Ibid.

created.[52] However, the same situation is unlikely to be found in personal property, particularly tangible personal property, where generally there are no documents of title.[53]

In the case of intangible personal property, some of it does have documents of title[54] or documents evidencing title,[55] but the risk of the legal creditor being grossly negligent is theoretical rather than real. In compliance with the requirements of a legal security, the creditor would either obtain possession of the relevant document[56] or register the intangible personal property in its name.[57]

The difficulty of establishing inequities on the part of the earlier legal creditor–holder leads to the conclusion that the degree of certainty of the creditor's priority over subsequent inferior security interests is high in practice.

Equitable interest and subsequent legal interest Where there is a competing claim between an earlier equitable security interest and a subsequent legal security interest, the subsequent legal interest has priority.

However, the earlier equitable creditor may defeat the claim of the subsequent legal creditor if the equitable creditor can establish that the subsequent legal creditor, at the time of acquiring the security, was not *bona fide*, or did not provide value, or had notice of the earlier equitable

[52] *Worthington v Morgan* (1849) 16 Sim 547, 60 ER 987; *Colyer v Finch* (1856) 5 HL Cas 905, 10 ER 1159; and *Clarke v Palmer* (1882) 21 Ch D 124. The following would constitute reasonable excuse: if the mortgagee failed to obtain the title deeds but there was a plausible explanation for his failure to do so (see *Agra Bank v Barry* (1874) LR 7 HL 135; *Barnett v Weston* (1806) 12 Ves 130, 33 ER 50; and *Manners v Mew* (1885) 59 Ch D 725); if the mortgagee received some of the deeds but reasonably believed he was receiving all of them (see *Hunt v Elmes* (1860) 2 De G F & J 578, 45 ER 745; *Ratcliffe v Barnard* (1871) LR 6 Ch 652; and *Dixon v Muckleston* (1872) App 8 Ch 155); if the mortgagee gave the title deeds to a person in a fiduciary relationship to him, but the latter without the scope of his apparent authority fraudulently or negligently parted with the deeds (see *Shropshire Union Railways and Canal Co. v R* (1875) 7 HL 496; and *Carritt v Real and Personal Advance Co.* (1889) 42 Ch D 263).

[53] Except for bills of lading.

[54] For example, negotiable instruments and insurance policies; see Chapter 3 above. Note that it is doubtful whether *Spencer v Clarke* [1878] 9 Ch D 137 was correct in treating an insurance policy as a document of title. See John De Lacy, 'Reflections on the Ambit of the Rule in *Dearle v Hall* and the Priority of Personal Property Assignments', *Anm LR* (1999) 87 at p. 117. Note the only documents of title in respect of goods are bills of lading.

[55] For example, share certificates of corporations; see Chapter 3 above.

[56] For example, possession of the negotiable instruments in the case of a pledge; see Chapter 3 above.

[57] For example, legal mortgage of shares of a corporation is effected by registration of the creditor as owner in the register of members of the corporation and issuance of new certificates in the name of the creditor; see Chapter 3 above.

security.[58] Value means any consideration in money or money's worth. The conditions of '*bona fide*' and 'without notice' have received considerable judicial consideration. To constitute 'bona fide' the subsequent purchaser has to show that it was not guilty of actual fraud.

'Without notice' can be either actual notice or constructive notice. The subsequent legal creditor has actual notice if it has personal knowledge of the earlier equitable security interest. Constructive notice is broad; it covers all circumstances where the subsequent legal creditor was negligent in safeguarding its own security interests;[59] that is, it would have acquired actual knowledge had it made those inquiries and inspections which a reasonable and prudent creditor would have made.

Although the doctrine of constructive notice appears wide and threatening, in the context of personal property the doctrine's impact is minimal, particularly in relation to tangible personal property.[60] This is due to general law's aversion to applying the doctrine to securities attached to tangible personal property. This is based on a number of justifiable factors, such as the mobility of tangible personal property, lack of documents of title, possession raising a presumption of ownership and the need to promote the free flow of trade.[61] Thus in the subsequent disposition of goods by a debtor holding goods on trust for a creditor,[62] or as mortgagor of land where fixtures thereon are supplied on lease, hire-purchase, or conditional sale, the doctrine of constructive notice has no role to play.[63]

[58] The disqualifying condition of 'without notice' is founded upon equity's view that the taking of an interest after notice of an earlier equitable interest is constructive fraud. It makes it grossly unjust to allow the subsequent purchaser to defeat the just rights of others with its own 'iniquitous bargain'. Story, above, note 44, §395, p. 399, commented that equity did not simply perform a remedial role, but also had a role preventive of injustice.

[59] *Wong Chim Ying v Cheng Kam Wing* [1990] 2 HKLR 3; and also *Kingsnorth Finance Co. v Tizard* [1986] 1 WLR 783. These were land law cases, but the principle would similarly apply to personal property.

[60] In contrast, this doctrine poses serious danger to subsequent purchasers of land in Hong Kong, for it has been held such a purchaser has constructive notice of all non-registrable equitable interests in the land if it failed to make inquiries which would have disclosed those interests. Inquiries include inspecting the land and inquiring with the occupants, if any, of their interests in the land. See *Wong Chim Ying v Cheng Kam Wing* [1990] 2 HKLR 3.

[61] See *Gough v Wood & Co.* [1894] 1 QB 713, 720, where Lindley LJ observed that unless this was so, subsequent persons dealing in good faith with the owner in possession would be exposed to very unreasonable risks and honest business with the owner would be seriously impeded. See also R.M. Goode, *Commercial Law* (London: Penguin, 1982), p. 52, where the author expresses the same view.

[62] See Chapter 2 above.

[63] *Gough v Wood & Co.* [1894] 1 QB 713. See also below in this chapter.

However, the courts have not been consistent in upholding general law in respect of the Bills of Sale Ordinance and the Companies Ordinance. They have rejected invitations to extend the doctrine of constructive notice to the Bills of Sale Ordinance – a statute specifically concerning security over tangible personal property. In the English case of *Joseph v Lyons*[64] the court held that in the absence of clear words in the equivalent English Bills of Sale Act, registration of a registrable security under the Act did not impose constructive notice of the security on the whole world.[65] On the other hand, the courts have held that the registration system under the Companies Ordinance does import the doctrine of constructive notice.[66] This is somewhat strange when the Companies Ordinance, like the Bills of Sale Ordinance, is silent on the role of the doctrine as regards registered security interests. As Madam Justice Kwan noted in the Hong Kong case of *ABN Amro Bank NV v Chiyu Banking Corp Ltd and Others*,[67] 'there is no provision to the effect that registration of the particulars of a charge should constitute deemed notice of the existence of the charge … to all persons for all particulars'.[68]

Both decisions have serious implications. The impact of the doctrine of constructive notice on a registrable security granted by a company is discussed later. In relation to the Bills of Sale Ordinance, the exclusion of constructive notice has an unfortunate effect on legal creditors.[69] According to §43 of the Bankruptcy Ordinance (Cap. 6), goods comprised in a bill of sale are deemed to remain in the 'possession, order or disposition' of the debtor – as a result, the goods vest in the trustee in bankruptcy in the event the debtor is made bankrupt by the court.[70] The legal creditor is not allowed to argue that the trustee in bankruptcy has constructive notice of the registered bill of sale, and is therefore bound by the bill of sale. In this regard, the registration system unfairly gives a false sense of security to the legal creditor. Further, it seems unjust that a legal creditor who has diligently complied with an Ordinance notorious for its technicalities and complexities should be deprived of its security in favour of unsecured general creditors who have not in any way been misled by the conduct of the legal creditor.

[64] *Joseph v Lyons* [1884] 15 QBD 280, p. 286, *per* Cotton LJ.
[65] Ibid. This point will be discussed further below in this chapter.
[66] See *Standard Rotary Machine Co. Ltd* (1906) LT 826; *Wilson v Kelland* [1910] 2 Ch 306; and the Hong Kong case of *ABN Amro Bank NV v Chiyu Banking Corp Ltd and Others* [2000] 3 HKC 381. See also Chapter 4 above.
[67] [2000] 3 HKC 381. [68] Ibid., p. 394.
[69] Indeed on all non-possessory types of security.
[70] *Re Ginger* [1897] 2 QB 461; and *Hollingshead v Egan* [1913] AC 564.

In relation to security over intangible personal property, the doctrine of constructive notice operates in the same way as in the case of tangible personal property. The subsequent legal security is postponed to an earlier equitable security if the legal creditor had been negligent in protecting its own security interest.

The English Law Commission has suggested certain limitations on the use of the doctrine of constructive notice in relation to personal property, particularly in a situation where it is necessary to decide whether a purchaser is bona fide[71] and whether that purchaser can take free of an encumbrance which was held by either an unregistered or a registered security holder. The Commission recommended that the general rule should be that an unregistered security interest would not affect a purchaser who did not know of it. However, a registered security interest would normally bind a purchaser, unless the sale (or other disposition not by way of security) was authorised by the security agreement.[72] Therefore the key issue is whether the relevant security interest is registered or not under the proposed notice-filing system. Specifically, in relation to an unregistered fixed charge, the Commission recommended that purchasers should take free of the charge unless they know of it,[73] and for unregistered floating charges, purchasers who acquire the collateral in the ordinary course of transferor's business should take free of the charge even if they know of its existence, but should not take free of the security if they know that the transfer is in breach of the terms of the floating charge.[74] This rule also applies to registered floating charges, because by the nature of floating charges, the charge holder has authorised the chargor company to dispose of its assets (and thus purchasers could take free) in the ordinary course of business prior to crystallisation.[75] However, as far as registered fixed charges are concerned, purchasers would be subject to the charge unless the chargee has authorised the sale or other disposition under the security agreement.[76] However, it should be noted that these recommendations were not implemented in the UK Companies Act 2006.

[71] Hereafter a purchaser also includes a buyer of accounts receivable other than a secured party. See English Law Commission Report No 296, para. 4.18.

[72] Ibid., para. 3.210.

[73] Ibid., para. 3.216(1). See also draft reg. 28(1), 'Company Security Regulations 2006', attached to the same report.

[74] English Law Commission Report No 296, para. 3.216(2). See also draft reg. 28(3), 'Company Security Regulations 2006', attached to the same report.

[75] English Law Commission Report No 296, para. 3.221. See also draft reg. 29(2), 'Company Security Regulations 2006', attached to the same report.

[76] English Law Commission Report No 296, para. 3.218.

Equitable interest and subsequent equitable interest Competing equitable security interests can arise in the following situations:

- equitable fixed charges against equitable fixed charges;
- equitable fixed charges against floating charges, where the chargor is a company; and
- floating charges against floating charges, where the chargor is a company.

Equitable fixed charge against equitable fixed charge Here, on the basis of the first-in-time rule, the first equitable fixed charge will have priority over the subsequent equitable fixed charge. The doctrine of notice, whether actual or constructive, has no relevance because the two securities are equitable securities.

The only circumstance that will postpone the first equitable fixed charge is when the security holder is guilty of fraud or gross negligence that has caused the creation of the second equitable fixed charge.[77]

Floating charge against equitable fixed charge As between a floating charge and an equitable fixed charge, the doctrine of the *bona fide* purchaser for value without notice generally has no relevance, because the first-in-time rule is simply displaced by the nature of the floating charge. Earlier, Chapter 4 considered that a floating charge permitted the chargor to deal with the property freely,[78] including the chargor's power to create subsequent mortgages in the ordinary course of business, until the floating charge crystallises. Consequently, a subsequent equitable fixed charge, being superior in quality, has priority over the floating charge,[79] even if the subsequent chargee had actual notice of the floating charge.[80]

[77] The concepts of 'fraud' and 'gross negligence' have already been discussed in this chapter.

[78] See Chapter 4 above.

[79] The theory of implied authority is favoured by *Gower's Principles of Modern Company Law*, 4th ed. (London: Stevens & Sons, 1979), p. 474; W.J. Gough, *Company Charges*, 2nd ed. (London: Butterworths, 1996), Chapter 9, particularly pp. 194, 214–20; R.M. Goode, *Legal Problems of Credit and Security*, 3rd ed. (London: Sweet & Maxwell, 2003), p. 157. The company is not, however, to be regarded as an agent of the debenture holder. This proposition has support from *Re Castell v Brown Ltd* [1898] 1 Ch 315. On the other hand, R.R. Pennington, *Company Law*, 5th ed. (London: Butterworths, 1985), pp. 480–1, and J.H. Farrar, 'Floating Charges and Priorities', *Conv* 30 (1974), 315 at p. 316, expressed the view that the basis of the company's power to deal with the assets freely is not actual authorisation by the lender but its capacity under its memorandum and articles of association and general law.

[80] *Wilson v Kelland* [1910] 2 Ch 25; and also *Re Castell v Brown Ltd* [1898] 1 Ch 315. In *Wilson v Kelland* it was held that a subsequent fixed chargee's actual notice of the floating

It has been established in several English cases that if the floating chargee attempts to challenge the priority of the subsequent fixed charge it will be estopped from denying that the chargor did not have the power to create subsequent legal and equitable charges.[81]

On this basis, it is arguable that the floating charge is by itself an independent exception to the first-in-time rule. However, to maintain the focus of the discussion it is considered under this heading.

In recent years, banks in Hong Kong[82] and in other common law jurisdictions have commonly inserted in their debenture instruments constituting a floating charge a 'negative pledge' or 'restrictive clause' so as to improve their position vis-à-vis other creditors.[83] Under such a clause, the chargor essentially agrees that it will not, during the subsistence of the charge and without the written consent of the bank, create any charge or other encumbrance[84] upon the secured property to rank in priority to or *pari passu* with the floating charge or enter into any agreement having that effect, and no charge or encumbrance created in breach of the agreement will have priority over or rank *pari passu* with the subsisting floating charge.[85] The clause is, therefore, of narrow application. Such clauses permit the chargor to deal with the property freely in its ordinary course of business, except in relation to creating subsequent security that is superior to the earlier floating charge. This is fair and reasonable.

charge was not actual notice or constructive notice of a negative contained in the floating charge; accordingly it prevailed over the floating chargee.

81 *Re Florence Land and Public Works Company* (1878) 10 Ch D 530, *per* James LJ; and *Wheatley v Silkstone and Haigh Moor Coal Company* [1885] 29 Ch 715.

82 Although it is common to insert a negative pledge in the debenture creating the floating charge in Hong Kong, according to Mr Patrick Ho (formerly credit manager of Belgian Bank), a negative pledge is sometimes found in a separate document and executed by the bank's customer. The negative pledge is also widely used by banks in Singapore; see C.H. Tan, 'The Negative Pledge as a Security Device', *SJLS* (1996), 415 at p. 415. Note that negative pledges when used alone are more common in international lending and where the loan is large; see D.E. Allan, 'Negative Pledge Lending – Dead or Alive? How to Re-invent the Mortgage', *JIBL* 5 (1990), 330.

83 In *ABN Amro Bank NV v Chiyu Banking Corp Ltd and Others* [2000] 3 HKC 381 the debenture used the expression 'restrictive clause'.

84 *Per* Romer J in *Jones v Barnett* [1899] 1 Ch 611, 620, who stated, 'In Wharton's Law Lexicon I find "incumbrance" defined as being "a claim, lien, or liability attached to property ...".'

85 Based on a sample of debentures provided by Baker & McKenzie, Clifford Chance, Deacons, Johnnie Yam, Jacky Lee & Co., and Linklaters.

In spite of the widespread adoption of the negative pledge, there is no Hong Kong or English authority on its precise juridical nature. According to leading texts,[86] a negative pledge clause in a floating charge does not constitute a proprietary security interest, but is merely a personal covenant between the chargor and the chargee. But it certainly has some value – if the floating chargor threatens to breach the negative pledge, the floating chargee can apply to the court for an order restraining the chargor from doing so,[87] or it can crystallise the security into a fixed charge.[88]

However, more importantly, how effective is the negative pledge in preserving the interest of the floating chargee against subsequent equitable fixed charges resulting from the debtor's breach of its negative undertaking? Two schools of thought on this issue can be discerned. The first can be labelled the 'anti-negative pledge school' and the other the 'pro-negative pledge school'. The anti-negative pledge school consists of the courts, which have consistently held that a subsequent fixed charge granted by the floating chargee is a transaction in the ordinary course of business of the floating chargee and the subsequent fixed chargee is not bound by the negative pledge unless the fixed chargee has actual notice of the negative pledge.[89] Consequently, the negative pledge may be ineffective or unreliable in protecting the floating chargee against subsequent security taking priority because such a clause itself is not required to be registered, although both parties have expressly agreed that the subsequent security is unauthorised.[90] Attempts to eject this rule on the basis of common usage[91]

[86] For example, Gough, above, note 79, p. 211; P. Gabriel, *Legal Aspects of Syndicated Loans* (London: Butterworths, 1986), p. 85; G.A. Penn, A.M. Shea and A. Arora, *The Law and Practice of International Banking – Banking Law* (London: Sweet & Maxwell, 1987), vol. 2, p. 113; Goode, above, note 79, p. 16; and Tan, above, note 82, pp. 415–41.

[87] See Allan, above, note 82, pp. 330–3, where he states, 'Breach of the negative pledge covenant is itself a breach of contract which would give rise to an action for damages or to a claim for injunctive relief to restrain that or subsequent breaches.' See also Tan, above, note 82, particularly pp. 431–2; and also R. Tomasic and S. Bottomley, *Corporations Law in Australia* (Sydney: The Federation Press, 1995), para. 17.3.1, citing the case of *Pullen v Abalcheck Pty Ltd* (1990) 8 ACLC 1087.

[88] See Chapter 4 above.

[89] See *Wilson v Kelland* [1910] 2 Ch 306; and *ABN Amro Bank NV v Chiyu Banking Corp Ltd and Others* [2000] 3 HKC 381.

[90] English Law Commission Report No 296, para. 3.177.

[91] Since the negative pledge is now common in floating charges. See Farrar, above, note 79; G.B. Parker and M. Buckley, *Buckley on the Companies Act*, 14th ed. (London: Butterworths, 1981), p. 265; and Meagher, Gummow and Lehane, above, note 43, para. 854.

and constructive notice[92] were rejected by the courts, both in Hong Kong[93] and in England.[94]

The courts give two reasons for this stance. Firstly, registration constitutes only constructive notice of the existence of the charge. Secondly, it is only where a document must necessarily affect the title of third parties, such as a fixed charge, that notice of its existence would constitute constructive notice of the contents of that document. A floating charge is a document which may or may not necessarily affect the title of third parties; registration would not therefore amount to constructive notice of its contents.[95]

The courts' approach is justifiable because a negative pledge is prejudicial to third parties, who 'would not discover the existence of a negative pledge clause'[96] by searching at the Companies Registry alone. This is because, in Hong Kong, the registration of company charges system is a registration of particulars of charges – no document or copy constituting the charge is deposited with the Companies Registry for public inspection. However, this position may change in the new Companies Bill that will rewrite the Hong Kong Companies Ordinance.[97]

The second school of thought is, however, based on the theory of freedom of contract and considers that the agreement of the creditor (the floating chargee) and the debtor (the floating chargor) should be given full effect. Any prejudicial effect this theory might create could be avoided by requiring the negative pledge to be publicised conspicuously at the Companies Registry. Concurring with this argument, the UK, Parliament, in 1989, enacted §415(1) of the UK Companies Act,[98] which required particulars

92 Examination of the samples provided showed that all the debentures constituting the floating charge contained a negative pledge clause, e.g. 'The Borrower shall not, without the prior consent of the lender create or permit to exist any encumbrance on or affecting the Charged Property or any part thereof ranking in priority to or *pari passu* with the charges created pursuant to Clause 3.1' (Deacons's sample); 'No chargor shall create or permit to subsist any security over the charge, nor do anything else prohibited by this agreement, except as permitted by the relevant clause' (Linklaters' sample); 'The Company hereby covenants with the Bank that the Company shall not be at liberty without the consent in writing of the Bank to create any mortgage or charge upon the property and asset or any part or parts thereof comprised in this security to rank in priority to or *pari passu* with the charge created' (Jacky Lee's sample).

93 *ABN Amro Bank NV v Chiyu Banking Corp Ltd and Others* [2000] 3 HKC 381.

94 Ibid. 95 Ibid., at 398, *per* Susan Kwan DJ.

96 A.L. Diamond, *A Review of Security Interests in Property* (London: HMSO, 1989), para. 22.4.5.

97 See above, Chapter 4.

98 Following the recommendation of Diamond, above, note 96, the negative pledges should be mentioned in the particulars of the floating charge registered with the Companies Registry; see para. 16.10.

of the floating charge, including any undertaking by the chargor company not to create other charges ranking in priority to or *pari passu* with the charge, to be delivered to the Companies Registry for registration. Section 416(1) of the same Act further provided that a person taking a charge over a company's property is taken to have notice of any matter requiring registration, including a negative pledge, which is disclosed on the register at the time the charge is created. However, these provisions were not brought into force or re-enacted in the Companies Act 2006. However, a similar mechanism is found in Australia. Section 263(1)(a) of the Australian Corporation Acts requires particulars prohibiting or restricting the floating chargee from creating subsequent charges to be registered with the Companies Registry within forty-five days of the creation of the floating charge.[99] In 1991, the Hong Kong Standing Committee on Company Law Reform[100] also subscribed to this idea. It recommended that the Hong Kong Companies Ordinance should be reformed along the lines of English legislation and it remains to be seen whether this is going to be included in the awaited Companies Bill in 2010.

The English Law Commission,[101] under its proposed notice-filing system, recommended a simplified rule on the respective priority of a charge against another charge or a pledge. The rule should simply depend on the date of registration of the financial statement (or the date of perfection of a pledge), whether the charge was fixed or floating,[102] so rendering the protection devices for floating chargees such as negative pledges and automatic crystallisation clauses unnecessary. However, as previously noted, this reform is unlikely to be enacted in the foreseeable future.

Floating charge against floating charge The general rule is that priority between a floating charge and a subsequent floating charge over the same assets is determined by the first-in-time rule.[103] The first floating charge has priority. This is so even if the subsequent floating charge crystallises before the first floating charge. As the courts have held that the dealing

[99] Also in Scotland, where particulars of a negative pledge have to be registered; see Companies Act 1985, §417(3)(e).

[100] Eighth Report, 1991, pp. 83–6.

[101] See Consultation Paper No 164.

[102] English Law Commission Report No 296, paras. 3.157, 3.177–3.180.

[103] See *Re Household Products Co. Ltd et al and Federal Business Development Bank* (1981) 124 DLR (3d) 325, particularly pp. 331–2, where Hughes J stated, '*qui prior est tempore potior est jure* must prevail in this case over the contention that anyone who appoints a receiver can turn a floating charge into something "crystallised" which gives it priority over another floating charge earlier created'.

power implied in a floating charge does not extend to the grant of a subsequent floating charge over the same assets,[104] a natural consequence is that the act of crystallisation cannot change the nature of the interest held by the subsequent debenture holder so as to give it priority over a predecessor.[105] The reason is that it would be incompatible with the company's bargain with the first floating chargee to put its floating charge behind or on the same footing as a subsequent floating charge by giving a charge of the same character.[106]

The first-in-time rule can, however, be altered by express agreement between the debtor and the first floating chargee.[107] To achieve this, express words such as 'the company may create subsequent mortgages "ranking in priority to" or "*pari passu*" with the first floating charge' are not essential. It is sufficient if the debenture reserves to the floating chargor a power to charge specified classes of assets further, such as 'the company is at liberty to create such mortgages, charges or other encumbrances as the company shall think proper'.[108] In the absence of such reservation, a subsequent floating charge over specific property will not have priority over an earlier general charge.[109] To do otherwise, according to Mr Justice Sargant (as he then was) would be 'contrary to all professional and commercial views on the subject'.[110]

In Hong Kong, the possibility of a subsequent floating charge upsetting the first-in-time rule is rare, because the first-in-time rule is usually

[104] But it remains permissible for the company to grant a subsequent floating charge over part of those assets ranking in priority to or *pari passu* with the earlier floating charge. See *Re Automatic Bottle Makers Ltd* [1926] Ch 412.

[105] *Re Household Products Co. Ltd et al and Federal Business Development Bank* (1981) 124 DLR (3d) 325, p. 332, cited as representing the common law view by H. Picarda, *The Law Relating to Receivers and Managers*, 1st ed. (London: Butterworths, 1984), p. 23; and by Goode, above, note 79, p. 178.

[106] *Benjamin Cope & Sons Ltd* [1914] 1 Ch 800, 807, *per* Sargant J; approved in *Re Automatic Bottle Makers Ltd* [1926] 1 Ch 412, CA.

[107] *Benjamin Cope & Sons Ltd* [1914] 1 Ch 800, p. 806.

[108] *Re Automatic Bottle Makers Ltd* [1926] 1 Ch 412, All ER Rep 618, CA. Here clause 7 of the first debenture constituted a general floating charge which gave the chargor the power to create charges, including a floating charge, over certain assets. A subsequent floating charge over dock warrants, bills of lading, raw materials and stock which came within the specified class of assets was held to be valid and had priority over the first floating charge.

[109] *Cox Moore v Peruvian Corpn Ltd* [1908] Ch 604; and *Re Automatic Bottle Makers Ltd* [1926] Ch 412.

[110] *Benjamin Cope & Sons* [1914] 1 Ch 800, 806, *per* Sargant J.

reinforced by the creditors incorporating a negative pledge clause in the debenture deed.[111]

The doctrine of tacking further advances The doctrine of tacking[112] affects priority between successive secured creditors in the sense that money advanced by an earlier secured creditor after the creation of a later security can rank for repayment ahead of advances secured by the later security.

Sykes observed that a secured creditor's right of tacking can arise by law or by agreement.[113] In respect of the former, the earlier secured creditor's interest must be legal. If the interest is equitable, the creditor has no right to tack. With regard to the second type of tacking, the debtor expressly agrees in writing that the earlier secured creditor may use the security to secure further advances. Here, the security interest can be equitable.[114] At this point, it is worthwhile to mention that Chapter 1 of the present volume accepted Allan's proposition that one of the essential criteria of an efficient credit security legal framework is that it permits the security to secure further advances.[115] Whether this is correct will now be considered.

There have been no reported cases in Hong Kong on the first type of tacking. However, tacking by agreement is commonly inserted in Hong Kong security documents such as debentures. The tacking clause usually states,

> ... the Charges are continuing security and will extend to the ultimate balance of the liabilities ...[116]

[111] Based on samples of debenture provided by Baker & McKenzie, Clifford Chance, Deacons, Johnnie Yam, Jacky Lee & Co. and Linklaters.

[112] The doctrine of tacking is an equitable concept, originating in land law. In Hong Kong, in relation to land, the doctrine is now governed by §45(1) of the Conveyancing and Property Ordinance (Cap. 128). But it is well settled that it also applies to security over personal property; see *West v Williams* [1899] 1 Ch 132. See R.E. Megarry and W.R. Wade, *The Law of Real Property*, 4th ed. (London: Stevens & Sons, 1974), p. 978, which states, 'It may apply both to realty and to personalty'; and also *Snell's Equity*, 29th ed. (London: Sweet & Maxwell, 1990), p. 435: 'It applies to realty and personalty.' Both textbooks referred to *Coote's Law of Mortgages*, 9th ed. (London: Sweet & Maxwell, 1927), vol. 1, p. 1245; and Waldock, above, note 5, p. 406.

[113] E.I. Sykes, *The Law of Securities: An Account of the Law Pertaining to Securities over Real and Personal Property under the Laws of the Australian States*, 2nd ed. (Sydney: Law Book Company, 1973), pp. 324–5; and also G. Rowley, 'Tacking Further Advances', *Conv* 22 (1958), 44 at pp. 44–5.

[114] Sykes, above, note 113. [115] See above, Chapter 1.

[116] Clause 21.1 of sample debenture of Linklaters, Hong Kong. Clause 1 of the debenture further defines 'liabilities' as all present and future monies, debts and liabilities due, owing or incurred by the chargor to the lender.

> ... the security created herein shall be a continuing security and shall be available to secure whatever may be the balance at any time or from time to time due by the Borrower pursuant to this charge, and such continuing security shall not be discharged by the release of any security or securities or additional security.[117]

The practical consequence is that the doctrine prejudices a subsequent intervening secured creditor – under current law such a creation cannot claim priority over the same assets against the earlier secured creditor in respect of further advances made by the earlier creditor. The only limitation to the earlier secured creditor's right of tacking is that it cannot tack further advances in priority to a claim of an intervening secured creditor if it has notice of the second security before it makes its further advances.[118] This limitation has been criticised as being too rigid because it applies even if the earlier secured creditor had a contractual obligation to make further advances to the debtor. In such cases, at common law, once the first chargee has been given notice of the second charge, any further advances by the first chargee would rank behind the second charge.[119]

However, proposing a notice-filing system with a view to achieving a simplified regime in priority on the basis of date of filing (a situation could occur that a filing was made before the charge actually came into existence), the English Law Commission Report No 296 recommended

[117] Clause 29 of sample debenture of Belgian Bank, Hong Kong. Similar tacking provision was found in the English case of *Siebe Gorman v Barclays Bank* [1979] 2 Lloyd's Report 142.

[118] *West v Williams* [1899] 1 Ch 132, *per* Lindley MR; and also *Siebe Gorman v Barclays Bank* [1979] 2 Lloyd's Report 142, where the bank could not rely on a tacking clause to claim its priority over the subsequent assignment of the borrower's book debts against further drawdown of the borrower's overdraft because, inter alia, the bank had notice of the intermediate assignment. Note that in the context of mortgage of land, §45(1) of the Conveyancing Property Ordinance (Cap. 218) gave statutory effect to the doctrine and rendered the notice of the mortgagee irrelevant if certain conditions are satisfied.

[119] *Hopkinson v Rolt* (1861) 9 HL Cas 514. See also English Law Commission Consultation Paper No 164, para. 2.56. Note that in England, the Law Property Act 1925, §94(1), altered the rule. It provides that if the first security holder is under an obligation to make further advances, these may be added to the secured sum even if the security holder has knowledge of the second security. In Hong Kong the rule has also been altered by §45(1) of the Conveyancing and Property Ordinance (Cap. 219). Under that section, the first secured creditor's notice of the second charge would not defeat its right to tack in two situations, namely (i) where the further advance or re-advance together with the outstanding advance does not exceed the maximum amount secured under the original mortgage, and (ii) where the original mortgage is made in favour of a licensed bank, or restricted licensed bank or a deposit-taking company, and the mortgage is expressed to secure all money which may from time to time be owing to the prior mortgagee. However, §45(1) applies only to security over land. It does not apply to personal property.

that the priority of an earlier charge still apply to all advances (including future ones) made under the charge, regardless of whether those advances were made after the earlier chargee had notice of a subsequent charge, or whether or not those advances were made under an obligation.[120] Therefore it seems that the English Law Commission has made an attempt to weaken the position of the doctrine of constructive notice in respect of the priority of charges for further advances. Having strengthened the position of an earlier chargee in respect of further advances, it further pointed out that it would always be possible for a second potential creditor to reach a subordination agreement with the earlier creditor. However, the new rule would not apply to the battle between an earlier chargee and an execution creditor who is an unsecured creditor.[121] But these reforms were not implemented in the UK Companies Act 2006.

Weaknesses of the present registration system Unfairness to a subsequent creditor is caused by weaknesses in the publicity system for security transactions in Hong Kong.[122] Briefly, for the present purpose, they are:

- The registration system under the Companies Ordinance does not require charge documents to be deposited with the relevant registry, the particulars registered with the Companies Registry are inadequate, and the Certificate of Registration of the charge only shows the amount secured at the date of registration of the charge.[123] But this may change when the Companies Ordinance rewrite process is finalised, as a full copy of the original debenture document may need to be registered in addition to relevant particulars.
- In respect of security in the form of bills of sale, security documents deposited with the High Court Registry are not easily accessible.[124] Consequently, it is difficult for a subsequent creditor to ascertain whether the security gives the earlier secured creditor the right to tack

[120] English Law Commission Report No 296, paras. 3.151–3.155; and also draft reg. 24(1)–(4) and the corresponding explanatory notes of Company Security Regulations 2006 attached to the same report.

[121] See draft reg. 24(11), Company Security Regulations 2006, attached to the English Law Commission Report No 296. Generally, advances made without any obligation to do so after the chargee has notice of the interests of an execution creditor will not have priority over the interests of the execution creditor.

[122] The main aspects of the weaknesses have already been considered in Chapters 2, 3 and 4.

[123] See Chapter 4 above.

[124] See Chapter 2 above.

further advances. The subsequent creditor may inquire with the earlier secured creditor, but the latter is not under any obligation to reply.

With regard to security over intangible property, such as choses in action, where perfection and publicity are governed by the rule in *Dearle v Hall*, the prejudicial effect of the doctrine is equally serious.[125]

In light of these difficulties it appears that Allan's criterion in Chapter 1 – that an efficient credit security legal framework should permit the security to create further advances – is doubtful.

However, the current majority view is in favour of the criterion. For example, the New Zealand Personal Property Security Act 1999 allows the parties to agree that the security may extend to future advances and, provided that it was expressly agreed at the outset, the security interest has the same priority in respect of all advances, including future advances.[126] The majority view rests on cost and expediency. In respect of the former, if the earlier secured creditor has no right to tack further advances, subsequent advances would be expensive. Every subsequent advance would require a new security to be created and registered with the Companies Registry. In respect of expediency, the English Law Commission commented that without this right, further advances of credit would become extremely cumbersome, if not impossible. This is because the debtor would have to obtain the consent of the subsequent creditor, of whom the first secured creditor had notice.[127] Accordingly it opined that the right to tack further advances should be allowed, if further advances are contemplated by the first security document. It further expressed the view that the difficulties discussed above can be solved by requiring that the right to tack further advances be clearly stated in the particulars that have to be registered with the relevant registration authority.[128]

Exceptions to the first-in-time rule under statute

The Bills of Sale Ordinance, Companies Ordinance, Patents Ordinance and Trade Marks Ordinance affect the first-in-time rule in very special circumstances and in different ways.[129]

125 This is discussed further below in this chapter.

126 See New Zealand Personal Property Security Act §71(1)(2) and §72. Saskatchewan Personal Property Security Act, §35(5), and the United States UCC Revised Article 9, §9-323, also permit tacking of future advances.

127 English Law Commission Consultation Paper No 164, para. 4.154.

128 Ibid.

129 The Sale of Goods Ordinance and the Factors Ordinance affect the first-in-time rule to a very limited extent, particularly §9 of the Factors Ordinance (Cap. 48) and §27(1)(2) of

Bills of Sale Ordinance

The Bills of Sale Ordinance excludes the basic rule by making the date of registration of the bill of sale the date for determining priority. Section 9(2) of the Ordinance provides that if several bills of sale are granted over the same personal chattels and they are all duly registered, priority is ranked according to the date of registration; that is, the date of perfection.

The nature of the security interest, legal or equitable, is not relevant. The statutory rule of priority has three advantages. Firstly, the rule is simple – it avoids the complexities inherent in the first-in-time rule. Secondly, it encourages diligence amongst the creditors. Thirdly, it encourages the speedy publication of the security.

However, on further examination of the actual operation of the statutory rule, the supposed advantages are weakened significantly in three situations:

- where there is competition between an unregistered absolute bill of sale and a bill of sale in the form of security,
- where there is competition between a registered inferior bill of sale in the form of security and superior security and
- where there is a subsequent bona fide purchaser for value without notice.

Competition between an unregistered absolute bill of sale and a bill of sale in the form of security As between an earlier unregistered absolute bill of sale and a duly registered bill of sale in the nature of a security, the former will prevail. This is because the secured creditor is not within the class of persons defined by §7(b) of the Bills of Sale Ordinance,[130] against whom an unregistered bill of sale is void.[131]

The basis of the exception is that since ownership is transferred to the buyer, the seller–debtor cannot create a valid subsequent mortgage. It is submitted that this justification is unsatisfactory. On the one hand, the system requires absolute bills of sale to be registered, yet on the other hand, it does not render an unregistered absolute bill of sale void against

the Sale of Goods Ordinance (Cap. 26), which give validity to certain transactions, such as a pledge, by the person who has possession of the goods, but is not the owner, with a third party. This book does not include them because they are more relevant to the sale of goods.

130 For details of §7(b) see Appendix A of the Ordinance.

131 According to Waldock, above, note 5, at p. 122; and E.F. Cousins and I. Clarke, *The Law of Mortgages*, 2nd ed. (London: Sweet & Maxwell, 2001), pp. 162–3.

duly registered competing security claims. From the perspective of a subsequent diligent creditor this is unfair. If the register had been searched, so suggesting that it was safe to grant a loan on the security of a bill of sale, the creditor could later discover that its security was postponed to an absolute bill of sale, which did not appear on the register.

Competition between a registered inferior bill of sale in the form of security and superior security The second exception arises when there is a competition between a registered bill of sale, which is inferior in quality (such as an equitable mortgage), and a subsequent superior non-registrable security (such as a pledge). In the absence of actual notice, the pledgee's security prevails over the earlier equitable mortgage on the basis of 'where the equities are equal the legal title must prevail'. This is so, even if the equitable mortgage is duly registered. This exception is traced to the English case of *Joseph v Lyons*,[132] where Lindley LJ held that 'the defendant [i.e. the pledgee] is entitled to recover in the present action … the defendant has the legal title, and he has not had either express or even constructive notice of the plaintiff's equitable title'.[133]

When counsel for the equitable mortgagee invited the court to impose constructive notice on the pledgee by virtue of the registration, Lindley LJ stated that 'the modern doctrine as to constructive notice has been pushed too far', and he refused to extend it.[134]

It is submitted that this second exception puts the pledgee in a very strong position. Only in two special circumstances can the pledgee's security be postponed:

- where the pledgee, before the pledge is made, is informed of the existence of the earlier equitable mortgage from a reliable source, and it failed to search the register in order to inform itself of its contents;[135] or

[132] (1884) 15 QBD 280. [133] Ibid., at 287.

[134] Ibid., also Cotton LJ at 286. The intention was to maintain commercial certainty; for example see *Manchester Trust v Furness* [1895] 2 QB 539, though this is not a case concerned with the Bills of Sale Act. Lindley LJ said, 'in commercial transactions possession is everything, and there is no time to investigate title and if we were to extend the doctrine of constructive notice to commercial transactions we should be doing infinite mischief and paralyzing the trade of the country'. However, the English case law has not been consistent in the doctrine of constructive notice; for example, constructive notice was applied which converted a contractual right into a proprietary interest; see *De Mattos v Gibson* (1859) 4 DE G & J 276; and *Lord Strathcona Steamship Co. v Dominion Coal Co.* [1926] AC 108. But there have been criticisms of these cases. They are discussed in N. Palmer and E. McKendrick (eds.), *Interests in Goods* (London: LLP, 1998), pp. 495–504.

[135] *De Mattos v Gibson* (1859) 4 DE G & J 276.

- where the earlier duly registered bill of sale is a legal mortgage.[136]

As between the legal mortgage and a pledge, the latter is inferior, because the pledgee does not acquire any legal title in the goods, but only a 'special property'.[137] This fine distinction is a pitfall for potential creditors. Unless the earlier creditor understands the distinctions between bills of sale that create a legal mortgage, an equitable mortgage or a charge, the creditor will not know whether its security will have priority over possible subsequent claims. The English Law Commission recognised this untenable situation and recommended that under its proposed notice-filing system a duly registered security interest (depending on the date of registration), legal or equitable, should have priority over a subsequent pledge on which date it is perfected.[138] Needless to say, reform of the Hong Kong law, which has substantially the same defects, is highly unlikely.

Subsequent bona fide purchaser for value without notice A duly registered bill of sale that creates a security, whether legal or equitable, has no priority over any subsequent purchaser who acquires personal chattels in the ordinary course of the debtor's business without actual notice of the security.[139] It has been held that any express term in the bill of sale prohibiting a subsequent disposition of the personal chattels does not matter.[140] It seems strange, if not ironic, that while it is generally accepted[141] that a non-corporate debtor is incapable of creating a floating charge because of the Bills of Sale Ordinance, such an individual is given the right of disposal of an asset that is associated with a floating charge. In addition, it also ignores the fact that bills of sale by way of security are fixed security,

136 A legal mortgage of personal chattels can be created by way of assignment of the legal title with a proviso, express or implied, for reassignment on redemption, and possession is irrelevant to the mortgagee's title. Cousins and Clarke, above, note 131, p. 41.

137 *Donald v Suckling* (1866) LR 1 QB 585; and *The Odessa* (1916) 1 AC 145, 158–9, *per* Lord Mersey: 'the so called "special property" … is in very truth no property at all. The expression "special property" seems to exclude the notion of that general property which is the badge of ownership'.

138 See the English Law Commission Consultation Paper No 164, para. 4.145; and the English Law Commission Report No 296, paras. 3.157 and 3.180. See also draft reg. 24(5) of Company Security Regulations 2006 attached to the same report.

139 Section 2 of the Bills of Sale Ordinance; see its Appendix A for details. Cases on this effect of §2 are *National Mercantile Bank Limited v Hampson* (1880) 5 QBD 177; and *Walker v Clay* (1880) LT 369.

140 *National Mercantile Bank Limited v Hampson* (1880) 5 QBD 177.

141 See Chapter 2 above.

which under general law does not give the debtor the right to dispose of the secured goods freely without the consent of the secured creditor.

The Companies Ordinance

The Companies Ordinance does not exclude the rule of first in time of creation and the associated exceptions.[142] But, through the importation of the doctrine of constructive notice,[143] it may postpone security interests which might otherwise obtain priority under both rules.

For instance, company A creates a first equitable fixed charge in favour of B over A's existing tangible personal property. The charge is duly registered. A subsequently creates a legal mortgage of the same property in favour of C and the mortgage is duly registered. B has priority, although C has the legal title, for C has constructive notice of B's interest.

The Companies Ordinance's preservation of the first-in-time rule of priority and the five-week registration period also weakens the registration system in two situations. The first is this:

A creates a legal mortgage in favour of B.

A subsequently creates an equitable mortgage in favour of C over the same property.

Both securities are duly registered within the five-week period. But C's mortgage is registered earlier than B's legal mortgage. B's legal mortgage has priority. This is so even if C had searched the register before C accepted the charge and C had been more diligent than B in perfecting its charge.

B is given priority on the ground that its security is first in time of creation and B is not guilty of any inequities as B is given five weeks to perfect his security. Registration therefore does not determine priority of duly

[142] *ABN Amro Bank NV Chiyu Banking Corp Ltd and Others* [2000] 3 HKC 381. Other Commonwealth country cases which share the same view are the Canadian cases of *Robin Hood Flour Mills v Fuller Bakeries Ltd, The Queen (garnishee) and Bank of Nova Scotia (Intervenor)* (1963) 42 DLR (2d) 534; *Bank of Montreal v Union Gas Co. of Canada and Revelstoke Companies Ltd* (1979) 94 DLR (3d) 962, though they were concerned with the registration of Assignment of Book Debts Act. Note D.W. Lee, 'Perfection by Registration', *Can Bar Rev* 47 (1969), 420 at pp. 432–3: 'as between consecutive assignees, the first to give notice of the assignment to the account holder will take priority, irrespective of the order of registration, assuming the first to give notice was without knowledge of the competing assignment'.

[143] See Chapter 4 above. Gough, above, note 79, pp. 834–6, criticised the extension of the doctrine by the courts to regulate company charges as unfortunate, for it creates confusion and an inefficient means of regulating priorities.

registered competing securities. It only affects validity of registrable securities.

The second situation is this:

A creates a first equitable fixed charge in favour of B.
A subsequently creates a second equitable fixed charge in favour of C.
Both are registered within the five-week period. The first fixed charge will have priority being first in time of creation. Again, the fact that C may have searched the register before it took the charge and duly registered the charge before B's registration will not upset B's priority.

The United Kingdom Department of Trade and Industry (DTI) in its consultation paper called this the 'five-week invisibility problem'.[144] Diamond criticised the prejudicial effect of the period.[145] He commented, 'Inspection of the register showing that there is no charge means nothing, because there may already be in existence valid charges which may subsequently be registered.' The English Law Commission agreed. It stated, 'However, registration itself is not a priority point: by this we mean that a chargee cannot ensure priority over another chargee of the same asset simply by registering his charge first.'[146]

The DTI, however, thought the invisibility problem period 'greater in theory than in practice'.[147] It suggested that shortening the period to ten days could reduce the problem.[148] The Hong Kong Standing Committee on Company Law reform suggested that the five weeks be reduced to twenty-one days.[149] However, the English Law Commission recommended abolition under its proposed notice-filing system. Under this system, subject to special exceptions, the date of registration normally determines priority of all registrable security.[150] The recommendation, it is submitted, would strongly promote diligence amongst creditors and efficiency of the registration system. However, the pre-existing system was retained in the UK in the Companies Act 2006, save that the registration period was reduced

[144] United Kingdom Department of Trade and Industry consultation paper, Modern Company Law – For a Competitive Economy: Registration of Company Charges, URN 00/1213 (October 2000), para. 3.79, p. 39.

[145] *A Review of Security Interests in Property* (London: HMSO, 1989), para. 26.1.

[146] English Law Commission Consultation Paper No 164, para. 3.25.

[147] Ibid., para. 3.80, p. 39. [148] Ibid.

[149] Eighth Report (1991), Hong Kong Standing Committee on Company Law Reform, p. 81.

[150] English Law Commission Report No 296, para. 1.33 and draft reg. 24 of Company Security Regulations 2006, attached to the same report.

to twenty-one days.[151] The same change is now proposed for inclusion in the rewritten Companies Ordinance in Hong Kong.[152]

The Patents Ordinance

The Patents Ordinance has a direct impact on the first-in-time rule of priority. According to the Ordinance, priority of securities over patents is determined by the date of registration.[153] Unregistered security is ineffective against registered security, except where the subsequent duly registered secured creditor had actual notice of the earlier unregistered security at the time of creation of the subsequent security.

The Patents Ordinance rules of priority, therefore, conflict with the Companies Ordinance (or any proposed notice-filing system). However, the English Law Commission still recommended that all charges created by companies over patents[154] should be required to be registered with the Central Registry under the proposed notice-filing system, whether or not the charge is also registered in the relevant specialist register.[155] The specialist register should continue to operate separately under its proposed notice-filing system, and those specialist rules relating to priority should apply in place of the general rule of priority from date of filing under their proposed system.[156]

The Trade Marks Ordinance

The Trade Marks Ordinance requires security over trademarks to be registered. The secured creditor's failure to register the security does not render it void. But the Ordinance is vague on the issue of priority and the doctrine of constructive notice.[157] Section 31 simply states that equities relating to trademarks may be enforced in the same manner as any other personal property. Whether registration imposes constructive notice on the whole world is not clear.[158] As a result the situation is complex.

151 Companies Act 2006, §870 (1)(a).

152 See Consultation Conclusions on Company Names, Directors' Duties, Corporate Directorships and Registration of Charges, 10 December 2008, available at www.fstb.gov.hk/fsb/co_rewrite/eng/pub-press/doc/cdrc_conclusion_e.pdf.

153 Patents Ordinance (Cap. 514), §52(1).

154 This is limited to companies registered in England and Wales, and assets also cover registered aircraft and ships and other intellectual property rights. See English Law Commission Report No 296, para. 3.231.

155 English Law Commission Report No 296, para. 3.41.

156 English Law Commission Report No 296, paras. 3.233–3.235.

157 English Law Commission Consultation Paper No 164, para. 2.55, commented that the question of constructive notice is not clear.

158 Contrast with the position in the UK where the Trade Marks Act 1994, §25(3), provides that a later transaction will have priority over an earlier one if the party to the later

It is proposed, firstly, that the rule of first in time of creation,[159] and the exceptions under general law, should apply,[160] and secondly, that if the security provider is a company, registration of the security should impose constructive notice on the subsequent creditor. Thus the subsequent secured creditor will take subject to an earlier registered security. On the other hand, if a non-corporate debtor granted the security, only the general exceptions should apply.[161]

The English Law Commission made the same recommendations in respect of charges over trademarks and other intellectual property rights created by companies registered in England and Wales to be registered at the Company Security Register under the proposed notice-filing system, as in the case of charges over patents.[162] Again, this reform was not implemented in the UK Companies Act 2006.

6.3.2 *Rule of priority in* Dearle v Hall *in Hong Kong*

According to the rule in *Dearle v Hall*, priority is determined according to the time the secured creditor (hereafter referred to as the 'assignee') serves notice on the person who has the legal title or control over the intangible personal property (hereafter referred to as the 'debtor').[163]

The facts of *Dearle v Hall* are relatively simple. Briefly, the issue before the court was whether or not a subsequent purchaser of the annuity of a beneficiary under a will had better claim to the annuity vis-à-vis two earlier assignees. The Rolls Court held that the subsequent purchaser was entitled to succeed in its claim against the two earlier assignees, because the subsequent purchaser of the annuity had perfected his title by giving notice to the debtor, but the two earlier purchasers had not.

In Hong Kong, the rule in *Dearle v Hall* was applied in *ABN Amro Bank NV v Chiyu Banking Corp Ltd and Others*[164] where the court held that a subsequent charge over a company's fixed deposit with the subsequent chargee bank had priority over an earlier fixed charge because the earlier fixed chargee did not serve notice on the subsequent chargee bank.[165] The

transaction is ignorant of the earlier one. It seems that the Act does not exclude the doctrine of constructive notice in priority issues.

159 The rule in *Dearle v Hall* is not applicable because the trademark owner is also the debtor.

160 See above in this chapter. 161 See above in this chapter.

162 English Law Commission Report No 296, para. 3.41.

163 See Chapter 3 above. The reasons for the rule in *Dearle v Hall* and its origin were discussed in that chapter.

164 [2000] 3 HKC 381.

165 The fixed charge was originally a floating charge but was converted to a fixed charge due to the activation of an automatic crystallisation clause.

subsequent chargee had satisfied the requirement of notice because it was also the debtor, therefore there was no need to give notice to itself.

As with the first-in-time rule of creation, the rule in *Dearle v Hall* is also subject to exceptions. They can be classified under three headings – the doctrine of the bona fide purchaser for value without notice,[166] the doctrine of tacking[167] and the Companies Ordinance.

Doctrine of the bona fide purchaser for value without notice

If a subsequent assignee has diligently served notice first on the debtor, but it acquired the chose in action with actual notice or constructive notice of an earlier unnotified assignment, its priority is postponed to the earlier assignment.[168] If the debtor pays the money to the second assignee, the latter will hold the money as constructive trustee for the earlier assignee.[169] The debtor is discharged from its obligation. Harman J in *Rhodes v Allied Dunbar Pension Services*[170] explained that this exception was necessary to prevent people jumping in and taking advantage of a technical failure to serve notice on the debtor.[171]

The doctrine of constructive notice needs some examination, though it embodies the same concept of negligence discussed earlier.[172] It was first applied in the English case of *Spencer v Clarke*.[173] There Hall VC held that a subsequent equitable assignee of a life insurance policy could not claim priority over an earlier unnotified assignment of the same policy, although it had served notice on the insurance company as it had constructive notice of the earlier assignment. The notice was imposed on the subsequent assignee on the ground that had it made proper inquiry why the assignor had not been able to deliver the insurance policy to it, it would have discovered the earlier assignment. Hall VC's decision has been criticised on the ground that he wrongly relied on the dictum of Kindersley VC in the land law case of *Rice v Rice*.[174] De Lacy further reinforced this criticism on the grounds that land and choses in action possessed distinct juridical and physical natures. Therefore the doctrine does not work well in cases involving choses in action.[175]

166 See below in this chapter. 167 See below in this chapter.

168 *Lloyds v Banks* (1868) 3 Ch App 488; *Spencer v Clarke* (1879) 9 Ch D 137; *Mutual Life Assurance Society v Langley* (1886) 32 Ch D 460; *Re Weniger's Policy* [1910] 2 Ch 291.

169 *Martin v National Surety Co.* (1937) 81 L Ed 822.

170 [1987] 1 WLR 1703, 1708. 171 Ibid. 172 See above in this chapter.

173 [1878] 9 Ch D 137. 174 (1853) 2 Drew 73.

175 De Lacy, above, note 54, at p. 117.

In land law it was settled that deposit of the document of title could create legal or equitable encumbrances over the land. Consequently, if the mortgagee who has a right to the title deeds fails to acquire them without reasonable excuse, the mortgagee's interest will be defeated by any prior encumbrancer who has possession of the title deeds.[176] However, in contrast, insurance policy contracts are not documents of title and they do not enjoy the same advantages as a document of title.[177]

There is, however, difficulty with this argument. It should be noted that although an insurance policy was not strictly a document of title, it was a settled practice by the time of *Spencer* that an equitable mortgage of a life insurance could be effected by depositing the insurance policy with the creditor.[178] Hall VC thus expected the subsequent mortgagee to be aware of the practice and it should have queried the assignee's failure to deliver the policy.

When this practice of creating an equitable mortgage is understood, it becomes clear that Kindersley VC's broad dictum is applicable to the circumstances of *Spencer*. As His Lordship stated, if there are two competing equitable interests, the better equity prevails even if created later. In examining the merits of the equities, the court has to pay attention to the following matters: the nature and condition of their respective equitable interests, the circumstances and manner of their acquisition, and the whole conduct of the parties in relation to each other. When examining these points the court must apply the broad principles of right and justice which equity applies universally in deciding upon contested rights. The court should not be hampered by any technical rule or any rule of partial application.[179]

In Rice a vendor of land handed the title deeds to the purchaser and a receipt for the purchase money was endorsed on the conveyance although the purchase price was unpaid. The purchaser deposited the title deeds with a mortgagee for a loan. Kindersley VC held that the equitable mortgage was postponed because the vendor had been guilty of

[176] *Worthington v Morgan* (1849) 16 Sim 547, 60 ER 987; *Colyer v Finch* (1856) 5 HL Cas 905, 10 ER 1159; and *Clarke v Palmer* (1882) 21 Ch D 124.

[177] Especially when a contract of insurance may exist without a 'policy' written agreement. See M.A. Clarke, *The Law of Insurance Contracts*, 2nd ed. (London: Lloyd's of London Press, 1994), p. 3, para. 1–1A; see also R. Colinaux, *The Law of Insurance*, 4th ed. (London: Sweet & Maxwell, 1979), p. 18, para. 1-27.

[178] See *Ord v White* (1840) 3 Beav 356, 49 ER 140; *Maugham v Ridley* (1863) 8 LT (NS) 309; and *Le Feure v Sullivan* (1855) 10 Moore PC, 14 ER 88. In all these cases the mortgage was effected by deposit of the insurance policy.

[179] *Rice v Rice* (1853) 2 Drew 73, 78.

misrepresentation that the land was free from encumbrances, thereby inducing the mortgagee to grant a loan on it.

The decision of Hall VC in *Spencer* was not therefore based on any strict notion of land law, but on an application of a broad equitable criterion that found that an omission to follow a settled procedure by the subsequent encumbrancer – that is, custody of the policy – was sufficient to postpone his interest.

Spencer was followed in *Re Weniger's Policy*.[180] There it was held that a subsequent assignment could not effectively tack a further advance made by a subsequent assignee (hereafter referred to as 'B') without being subject to an earlier unnotified assignment (hereafter referred to as 'A') because, by reason of B's failure to make inquiry of the whereabouts of the insurance policy, he had constructive notice of it. At first sight the facts seem to suggest that the decision is harsh to B. A had discharged the loan of the assignor owing to the original lender (hereafter referred to as 'OL') and took possession of the insurance policy as security for a loan which was twice the amount owing to OL, a fact which was not brought to the notice of B. Nevertheless, B could not be regarded as being unfairly prejudiced by the change of events as B's assignment expressly stated that its assignment was subject to OL's assignment, albeit that it was taken over by A. In addition, if it had made inquiry with OL, it would have discovered that the insurance policy was delivered to A. That itself would have prompted B to inquire with A as to the nature of the custody.

The above argument does not necessarily mean that the doctrine of constructive notice is sound. It is only justifiable when there is a document of title to the chose in action, such as a negotiable instrument, or where the right to the chose in action is evidenced by a document, and a deposit of which is capable of creating a security interest. It should not be extended to situations where a chose in action does not fall into any of these categories.[181] De Lacy argued that the non-physical character and lack of document of title would not generally give rise to any suspicion that it may be encumbered.[182] Whether that argument will prevail has yet to be seen. There is no direct authority on this point. However, by analogy to cases involving the Bills of Sale Act,[183] there is authority, such as *Joseph v Lyons*,[184] to support this proposition.

180 [1910] 2 Ch 291.

181 See *Manchester Trust v Furness* [1895] 2 QB 539, p. 545, *per* Lindley LJ. See note 134 above.

182 De Lacy, above, note 54.

183 Equivalent of the Bills of Sale Ordinance.

184 (1884) 15 QBD 280.

In addition to the above, the doctrine of *Dearle v Hall* is impractical and not cost-effective for assignees who carry on the business of factoring debts. To ensure that it has priority, a factor–assignee has to check with every debtor, which may be a large number of persons, as to whether the debtor has received notice of an earlier assignment.

However, the problem would be solved if the English Law Commission's recommendation of a notice-filing system were to be adopted. Under such a system, all assignments of receivables must be registered, failing which they should not be effective against an administrator or liquidator of the debtor company at the onset of insolvency.[185] The registration is subject to four classes of exemption.[186] The factor–assignee could check the register, and upon discovering no registration has been made, all unregistered assignments should be invalid against the factor–assignee.[187] In respect of the priority between competing assignment of receivables by companies (e.g. with subsequent creditors or purchasers) under its proposed notice-filing system, it would depend on the date of registration of the financing statement relating to the assignment stored in the Company Security Register, instead of previously being treated as unregistrable security with the priority rule that notice was first given to the debtor as in *Dearle v Hall*.[188] Unfortunately, this reform is unlikely to be enacted in the foreseeable future, given the failure to include any substantial change to the company charge registration system in the UK Companies Act 2006.

Doctrine of tacking further advances

Where the doctrine of tacking applies,[189] a second assignment of a debt, in respect of which a second notice had been served on the debtor, may be postponed to the further advances of the first assignee. This rule is traced to the English case of *Calisher v Forbes*.[190] There the court held that a first mortgage covered a further advance of £25, though only one notice of the

[185] English Law Commission Report No 296, para. 4.25; and draft reg. 20 of Company Security Regulations 2006, attached to the same report.

[186] English Law Commission Report No 296, para. 4.31. and draft reg. 4(1)(b)–(e) of Company Security Regulations 2006, attached to the same report.

[187] English Law Commission Consultation Paper No 164, para. 4.194.

[188] (1828) 3 Russ 1. See English Law Commission Report No 296, paras. 4.5 and 4.18; also UK Law Commission Consultation Paper No 164, para. 7.43.

[189] The nature and impact of the doctrine of tacking further advances on the first-in-time rule of creation were discussed earlier in this chapter.

[190] [1871] 2 Ch App 109.

first mortgage was given. *Forbes* was followed in *Re Weniger's Policy*,[191] where the court held that notice of further advances must be given to the debtor only if the first security did not expressly cover them.

The doctrine of tacking and the rule in *Forbes* are security hazards to both the subsequent creditor and the debtor. Firstly, unless the first assignee notifies the debtor of the further advance, the potential subsequent creditor's inquiry with the debtor would be futile. It simply cannot advise the subsequent creditor without the information. Secondly, inquiry with the debtor itself personally may be impractical and expensive for creditors of certain types, especially one which carries on the business of debt factoring. It cannot inquire with each and every debtor.[192] Thirdly, the debtor is put in a very precarious position. If it pays money, which is included in a tacking clause in the security document, to a subsequent creditor it is liable to pay the first assignee the affected amount. To avoid the risk the debtor has to go through the security documents, and find out from the first assignee whether there was any further advance and the amount, whenever it receives notice of a second security or inquiry from a potential second creditor. This places an unfair burden on the debtor.

The Companies Ordinance

The doctrine of constructive notice[193] in company law also affects the rule in *Dearle v Hall*. Thus a subsequent legal creditor, who is fixed with constructive notice of an earlier duly registered company equitable fixed security over a chose in action, such as book debts, but where no notice of the equitable security, has been given to the debtor of the chose in action – the legal creditor cannot obtain priority by virtue of its first serving notice on the debtor.[194] This position was postulated in *Palmer's Company Law*[195]

[191] [1910] 2 Ch 291, p. 296, *per* Parker J: 'If the first mortgagee makes a *further advance on a fresh bargain* he must inquire at the office whether notice of another charge has been received, and if not he may complete his security by giving notice of it' (emphasis added).

[192] English Law Commission Consultation Paper No 164, para. 7.43.

[193] See above in this chapter.

[194] Authorities on this are *Spencer v Clarke* [1878] 9 Ch D 137; *Re Weniger's Policy* [1910] 2 Ch 291; *Rhodes v Allied Dunbar Pension Services* [1987] 1 WLR 1703, 1708, *per* Harman J.

[195] *Palmer's Company Law*, 24th ed. (London: Stevens & Sons, 1987–91), para. 13.108: 'As a holder of a valid charge-back, the bank's position as against other chargees should be considered. If the appropriate priority rule is the rule in *Dearle v Hall*, it would presumably not need to notify itself as the account debtor in order to acquire priority against subsequent chargees. *If it knew of an earlier charge, or had constructive notice of it arising*

and cited with approval, though *obiter*, in *ABN Amro Bank NV v Chiyu Banking Corp Ltd and Others.*[196]

6.3.3 *Doctrine of* nemo dat *on quasi-security interests and competing interests in Hong Kong*

For the purpose of this part, unless otherwise stated, the expression

'creditor' means the owner of goods supplied under hire-purchase and leasing and the seller under a conditional sale transaction;
'debtor' means the hirer, lessor and buyer under hire-purchase, leasing, and conditional sale transactions respectively; and
'third party' means a person who has subsequently acquired goods from the debtor by way of security.

In Hong Kong, the first-in-time rule of priority discussed above does not apply to hire-purchase, leasing and conditional sale, because these transactions are strictly not regarded as creating any security interest in the goods. When confronted with competing interests in the goods supplied under any of these transactions, the creditor has to rely on the doctrine of *nemo dat*. If the creditor is successful, it can claim the goods back from the third party.

However, in Hong Kong, the creditor's legal title may be defeated in the following four special situations:

- the debtor is a mercantile agent,
- the debtor is in possession of the goods or documents of title,
- estoppel and
- the goods supplied to the debtor have become fixtures.

Debtor is a mercantile agent

Section 10 of the Factors Ordinance (Cap. 48) affords special protection to a third party who has acquired goods from the debtor without title under a conditional sale transaction. Under that section the third party takes the goods free from the claim of the creditor if it establishes, at the material time, that the debtor was a mercantile agent, the goods or

out of its registration of a company charge, then it should rank behind the earlier charge' (emphasis added).

196 [2000] 3 HKC 381, p. 403, *per* Deputy Judge Susan Kwan.

the documents of title to the goods were handed to the debtor, it (the third party) was a bona fide purchaser for value without notice, and it obtained the security over the goods in the ordinary course of business of the debtor. The expression 'mercantile agent' carries a broad meaning. It means any professional person who has the authority to sell, consign for sale, buy or raise money on goods, except a consumer debtor.[197]

Debtor in possession of goods or documents of title

Section 27(2) of the Sale of Goods Ordinance (Cap. 26) enables a third party who has acquired goods from a conditional debtor to obtain a good title free from the claim of the unpaid creditor if the third party can establish that the transaction between the debtor and creditor is a sale and purchase transaction, the debtor had possession of the goods or documents of title with the consent of the creditor, and it (the third party) acted in good faith without notice of the claim of the creditor.

Because §27(2) requires the debtor to be a buyer, the hire-purchase and leasing transactions are not within the ambit of §27(2). The creditor under these transactions can therefore claim the goods from the third party who has possession of the goods. The conditional creditor, with or without a retention-of-title clause, is vulnerable under §27(2).

Estoppel

Under §23(1) of the Sale of Goods Ordinance, a creditor who supplies goods on credit can be prevented from denying the debtor's authority to sell if the creditor, by words or by conduct, represents that the debtor had such authority.

This statutory estoppel affects the hire-purchase, leasing and conditional sale transactions. However, generally, the court is slow to invoke the rule in the absence of explicit representation by the creditor. In Hong Kong, it has been held that the fact that a finance company has given the hirer possession of the car, and the registration book with the hirer's name, is not sufficient to invoke the statutory estoppel.[198]

[197] Section 2(1) of the Factors Ordinance.

[198] *WOC Finance Co. Ltd v Fullrate Enterprises Ltd* [1982] HKLR 476.

Goods supplied are transformed into fixtures

Where the goods supplied under a hire-purchase, lease or conditional sale, with or without a retention-of-title clause, are transformed into a fixture and the land on which they are affixed is mortgaged, the *nemo dat* doctrine is completely neutralised.

In land law when a personal chattel is attached to the land and it becomes a fixture, the debtor, as owner of the land, can grant a better title in respect of the fixture it has over the fixture when it disposes of the land by sale or mortgage (hereafter referred to as 'transformatory rule').[199] On the basis of this rule the mortgagee of the land takes the fixture free from the claim of another creditor under a hire-purchase, lease or conditional sale arrangement. It does not matter whether the mortgage was created before or after the personal chattel was supplied.

An illustration of this point is the House of Lords case of *Reynolds v Ashby & Son*.[200] There, after factory premises were mortgaged to the mortgagee, the debtor–mortgagor acquired machines on hire-purchase from the creditor. It was expressly provided in the mortgage document that the mortgage included buildings, fixtures, machinery and fittings erected thereon. When the debtor–mortgagor defaulted in payment of the rentals, the creditor terminated the hire and took possession of the machines. The mortgagee commenced action against the creditor, claiming the machines or damages. The House of Lords unanimously held that the mortgagee was entitled to succeed as the machines had become fixtures and passed to the mortgagee.

It is submitted that the decision in the *Reynolds* case is harsh in two respects. Firstly, it gives a false sense of security value to the creditor's interest. Unless the prior mortgagee is guilty of some fraud that has caused the creditor to supply the personal chattels, the general rules of priority will not assist it, because the mortgage, legal or equitable, being first in time, will prevail over its claim (see below). Secondly, and more importantly, it results in a windfall in the form of the added value to the

[199] *Gough v Wood* [1894] 1 QB 713, 719, *per* Lindley LJ. Note that this general principle flows from the common law maxim *quicquid plantatur solo, solo cedit* – whatever is affixed to the soil belongs to the soil; see *Gebrueder Buehler AG v Peter Chi Man Kwong and Two Others* [1988] 2 MLJ 69 CA, 72, *per* Wee Chong Jin CJ.

[200] [1904] AC 466; see also the New Zealand case of *Trust Bank Central Ltd v Southdown Properties Ltd* (1991) 1 NZ Conv C 190, 851, where the seller of goods sold to the buyer under a retention-of-title clause lost its title to the mortgagee of the house when the goods supplied were affixed to the house and became fixtures.

mortgagee of the land which the mortgagee had not expected or even given consideration to at the time it advanced the mortgage monies.

Reynolds is a case where the fixture was supplied after the mortgage of the land was made. However, in cases where the mortgage was created after the fixture was supplied, it is submitted that the above criticisms appear weak. The reasons are:

- When the creditor attaches personal chattels to the land it represents to the public that the personal chattels are part and parcel of the land and, therefore, belong to the debtor, the owner of the land. It is arguable that this is tantamount to constructive fraud if a third party acts on the representation to its detriment.[201]
- Third parties, including subsequent mortgagees dealing with the debtor, are not expected to verify the true ownership of the personal chattels for there is generally no document of title to personal chattels[202] and possession itself is evidence of ownership.
- There is no general registration for all types of credit arrangement affecting personal chattels to verify their status,[203] and an occupier's potential equitable interest in the land itself has no relevance to the personal chattels.[204]
- The subsequent mortgage is deemed to include fixtures.

In Hong Kong, it is common for the debtor, especially under hire-purchase and leasing agreements, to undertake expressly that they will not encumber the personal chattels while the hire-purchase or lease is still subsisting.[205] However, it has been consistently held that these terms are only enforceable by the creditor against the debtor when the personal chattels have become fixtures; such stipulations do not prevent the mortgagee of the land from claiming the fixtures under general principles.[206]

In Hong Kong, there are two narrow grounds upon which the creditor may try to rely to defeat the claim of the subsequent mortgagee. There is, firstly, the principle of implied authority, and secondly, the doctrine of the bona fide purchaser of a legal estate for value without notice.

[201] See Story, above, note 44. [202] Except a bill of lading.

[203] Except for the narrow registration system under the Bills of Sale Ordinance. See Chapter 2 above, also Chapter 4.

[204] See *Kingsnorth Finance Co. v Tizard* [1986] 1 WLR 783, which was concerned with the non-registrable interest of occupants in real property.

[205] See Chapter 5 above.

[206] See *Holland v Hodgson* [1861–73] All ER Rep 237, HL; *Gough v Wood & Co.* [1894] 1 QB 713; *Ellis v Glover & Hobson, Limited* [1908] 1 KB 388; and *Gebrueder Buehler AG v Peter Chi Man Kwong and Two Others* [1988] 2 MLJ 69.

However, the principle of implied authority is, at best, unsettled. It first appeared in *Gough v Wood & Co.*[207] There the creditor exercised its rights under a hire-purchase agreement by removing a boiler from the debtor's premises. The plaintiff, who was the subsequent legal mortgagee of the premises, instituted proceedings against the creditor for damages for removing the boiler. The Court of Appeal unanimously held that the boiler was a fixture, but the creditor was entitled to remove the fixture free from the claim of the mortgagee before the mortgagee entered into possession of the premises. The decision rested on the basis that the mortgagee, by allowing the debtor–mortgagor to remain in possession of the premises, impliedly authorised the debtor–mortgagor to allow the creditor to remove the boiler.

The court was divided on what should be the grounds to justify implied authority. Lindley LJ, representing the majority view,[208] gave commercial expedition as the reason.[209] He thought that unless this is so, persons dealing bona fide with mortgagors in possession would be exposed to very unreasonable risks, and honest business with them would be seriously impeded. It is somewhat ironic that commercial expediency, which had been consistently used against creditors, should now be applied for their benefit. It is perhaps because of this dubious reasoning that Kay LJ chose to differ. He thought that reasons of commercial expediency would subject the bona fide purchaser or mortgagee to a danger which had not existed.[210] Accordingly, Kay LJ simply based the debtor–mortgagor's implied authority strictly on the facts of the case.

It is submitted that both the implied authority principle and the majority's commercial expediency rationale are flawed. In respect of the latter, quite apart from Kay LJ's criticism, surely the general public interest should not be extended to include that of the creditor who, arguably, was responsible for its own downfall. As mentioned earlier, by giving possession of the goods to the debtor–mortgagor, the creditor had represented to the world that the debtor–mortgagor was the owner and that it was free to deal with them.

The implied authority principle was criticised by Farwell LJ, Cozens-Hardy MR concurring, in the subsequent Court of Appeal case of *Ellis v Glover & Hobson, Ltd.*[211] In their view, possession of the premises upon which the fixture is attached cannot, by itself, confer any implied authority on the debtor–mortgagor to dispose of the fixture or allow the

[207] [1894] 1 QB 713. [208] [1894] 1 QB 713, p. 720. [209] Ibid., Smith LJ concurring.
[210] [1894] 1 QB 722, p. 722. [211] [1908] 1 KB 388.

removal of the fixture, for three reasons. Firstly, a mortgagee is entitled, in accordance with ordinary usages, to leave the debtor–mortgagor in possession of the premises, and no one can be heard to say that they have been induced by such possession to believe that the debtor–mortgagor was the unencumbered owner of the fixture. Secondly, there was no holding out by the mortgagee, whether expressly or by conduct, to the creditor of the fixture that the debtor–mortgagor had the authority to dispose of the fixture. Thirdly, the mortgagee is under no duty to give notice of its mortgage to the creditor of the fixture – it follows that it is not under a duty to inquire whether or not the goods attached to the land belong to the debtor–mortgagor or whether they are supplied under a reservation of title agreement.

His Lordship further reinforced the conservative approach by stating that the court should be cautious in depriving the mortgagee of rights given by the law in the absence of clear exceptional circumstances.[212]

Owing to the problem in *Gough*, the judges distinguished it.[213] They were certainly right that the decisive nature of the businesses in *Gough*, *Reynolds* and *Ellis* were distinguishable being a nursery, a manufacturing business and a laundry respectively, but the distinctions were artificial rather than substantial. Perhaps an important distinguishing factor that has been overlooked, but might provide a more convincing and equitable solution, was the time of the supply and the time of the mortgage. In *Ellis* and *Reynolds* the fixtures were supplied after the mortgage. In *Gough* the fixture was supplied before the mortgage.[214]

In view of this it is submitted that the law in relation to the implied authority of the debtor–mortgagor is unsettled and unsatisfactory.

The creditor of fixtures can defeat the claim of the subsequent mortgagee if it succeeds in establishing that the latter is not a bona fide purchaser

212 Ibid., p. 400.

213 An attempt was made to resuscitate it by the Singapore Court of Appeal in *Gebrueder Buehler AG v Peter Chi Man Kwong and Two Others* [1988] 2 MLJ 69, where the facts were similar to *Ellis*. The machinery, which had become a fixture, was installed after the mortgage. However, the single judgment of the Singapore Court of Appeal approved the minority judgment of Fletcher Moulton LJ in *Ellis*. But a careful analysis of the Singapore Court of Appeal's judgment suggests that its approval is merely *obiter*, for on the facts of the case the implied authority of the mortgagor was not in issue. The receiver of the mortgagee had already taken possession of the factory premises and the machinery and was therefore entitled the machinery.

214 Applying Lindley LJ's observation (or called the New Jersey doctrine in America) a more equitable solution would have been achieved, i.e. the suppliers in *Ellis* and the *Reynolds* case would be entitled to priority.

of a legal estate for value without notice. Thus in *Re Samuel Allen & Sons Limited*[215] it was held that a subsequent equitable mortgage of the land upon which a fixture was annexed was subject to the creditor's prior equitable interest in the fixture, although the equitable mortgagee had no actual or constructive notice of the latter's equity. In contrast, in *Hobson v Gorringe*,[216] the subsequent mortgagee took a gas engine fixture free from the creditor's equitable interest because it was a legal mortgagee for value without notice. As Smith LJ said,

> In our opinion the engine became a fixture, i.e., part of the soil – subject to this right of Hobson which was given him by contract. But this right was not an easement created by deed, nor was it conferred by a covenant running with the land. The right, therefore, to remove the fixture imposed no legal obligation on any grantee from King of the land. Neither could the right be enforced in equity against any purchaser of the land without notice of the right, and the defendant Gorringe is such a purchaser.[217]

The equitable relief is not, therefore, a boon to the creditor. Only in situations where the mortgagee's interest is equitable can the creditor hope to preserve its priority in the fixture. Also, the broad concept of constructive notice has not helped to bolster the creditor's claim. Indeed in all those cases where the creditor's prior claim was postponed to that of the subsequent mortgagee, no grounds could be found to impose constructive notice on the mortgagee.[218]

The dilemma of the supplier of personal chattels in Hong Kong[219] on credit is further compounded by the difficult rules for ascertaining when personal chattels, attached to land, become fixtures. According to Hong Kong's land law, whether or not personal chattels have become fixtures depends on the intention of the creditor and debtor.[220] The intention is

215 [1907] 1 Ch 575. See also *Re Morrison, Jones & Taylor Limited* [1914] 1 Ch 51, where the Court of Appeal held that a subsequent floating charge under a debenture was subject to the prior equitable interest of the supplier.

216 [1897] 1 Ch 182, [1895–9] All ER Rep 1231, CA.

217 Ibid., p. 192, and p. 1236.

218 See *Hobson v Gorringe* [1897] 1 Ch 182, [1895–9] All ER 1231; *Gebrueder Buehler AG v Peter Chi Man Kwong and Two Others* [1988] 2 MLJ 69.

219 See *Gough v Wood* [1894] 1 QB 713, 719, *per* Lindley LJ and see also the Singapore case of *Gebrueder Buehler AG v Peter Chi Man Kwong and 2 Others* [1988] 2 MLJ 69, CA, 72, *per* Wee Chong Jin.

220 For Hong Kong see *Irene Loong v Pun Tsun Hang and American Engineering Corp., Fed. Inc. and Far East Import & Export Ltd* [1959] HKDCLR 192; for England see *Dixon v Fisher* (1843) 5 Sess Cas 775, 793, *per* Lord Cockburn; *Elitestone Ltd v Morris and Another* [1997] 2 All ER 513, 519, HL, *per* Lord Lloyd of Berwick; for Malaysia see *Goh Chong Hin and Another v The Consolidated Malay Rubber Estates Ltd* [1924] 5 FMSLR 86; and see

in turn determined by two criteria,[221] namely the degree of annexation of the personal chattel (hereafter referred to as the first criterion) and the object and purpose of annexation (hereafter referred to as the second criterion).[222] These criteria are objective. The declaratory intention of the parties is generally regarded as not relevant to these criteria, for 'no man can make his property real or personal by merely thinking it so'.[223]

The rationale for the exclusion of the declaratory intention is based on commercial expediency; that is, to promote the free flow of commerce and trade. To include it would require every person dealing in good faith with every occupier of premises thoroughly to investigate the title of every

also *The Shell Co. of the Federation of Malaya Ltd v Commissioner of the Federal Capital of Kuala Lumpur* [1964] MLJ 302; for Singapore see *Gebrueder Buehler AG v Peter Chi Man Kwong and Two Others* [1988] 2 MLJ 69.

221 The interest of the commercial supplier of chattels on conditional sale, hire-purchase or lease was certainly not within the contemplation of the evolutionary process of the two criteria and the exceptions to the general rule, such as trade fixtures. See *Cheshire and Burn's Modern Law of Real Property*, 15th ed. (London: Butterworths, 1994), pp. 145–6, although these forms of arrangement, particularly the conditional sale, were already well developed as credit finance instruments in the mid-nineteenth century. See *Bateman v Gren and King* [1868] IR 2 Ch 607; also The Cork Report on Insolvency Law and Practice (1982) Cmnd 8558, para. 1559; and B. Collier, *Romalpa Clauses: Reservation of Title in Sale of Goods Transactions* (Sydney: Law Book Company, 1989), p. 2.

222 For Hong Kong see *Irene Loong v Pun Tsun Hang and American Engineering Corp., Fed. Inc. and Far East Import & Export Ltd* [1959] HKDCLR 192; *Penta Continental Land Investment Co. Ltd v Chung Kwok Restaurant Ltd and Tai Shing Company Ltd* [1967] HKDCLR 22; *Orient Leasing (Hong Kong) Ltd v NP Etches and Others* [1985] HKLR 292. These criteria are adopted in other Commonwealth jurisdictions – e.g. for Australia see *Reid v Smith* [1906] 3 CLR 656; for Malaysia see *Goh Chong Hin and Another v The Consolidated Malay Rubber Estates Ltd* [1924] 5 FMSLR 86; *The Shell Co. of the Federation of Malaya Ltd v Commissioner of the Federal Capital of Kuala Lumpur* [1964] MLJ 302. Note that the second criterion is not two considerations, but really only one. See *Spyer v Phillipson* [1931] 2 Ch 183, 194, *per* Luxmoore J.

223 *Dixon v Fisher* (1843) 5 Ch D 775, 793, *per* Lord Cockburn. See also *Hobson v Gorringe* [1897] 1 Ch 182, 193, where A.L. Smith LJ stated that whether an object was a chattel or a fixture depended not upon circumstances of a chance agreement that might or might not exist between an owner of a chattel and a hirer thereof, but rather upon circumstances which showed the degree of annexation and the object of such annexation which were patent for all to see; see also *Reynolds v Ashby & Son* [1904] AC 466. The irrelevance of the subjective intention was reaffirmed in the House of Lords case of *Elitestone Ltd v Morris and Another* [1997] 2 All ER 513, HL, particularly the judgment of Lord Lloyd of Berwick, at 519. Note that it is, however, submitted that this is only true where the rights of third parties are involved, such as the mortgagee or subsequent purchaser of the land, but not as between the supplier and the acquirer of the personal chattels, for a party to the contract can be estopped from denying that an object is what he specifically represents it to be. For estoppel by representation see *Cheshire & Fifoot's Law of Contract*, 10th ed. (London: Butterworths, 1981), pp. 272–3; and also *Chitty on Contracts*, 26th ed. (London: Sweet & Maxwell, 1989), vol. 1, para. 218, pp. 160–1.

object on the premises. This would not only be inconvenient but would also paralyse or at least impede honest business dealings with them.[224] In addition it may also unfairly expose the innocent purchaser of the premises to unreasonable risks, for it may allow the purported creditor to recover the goods from it.[225]

The first criterion by itself appears to afford a reasonable degree of certainty to the creditor who wants security over personal chattels supplied, because they would be regarded as fixtures if they could not be severed from the land without causing serious injury to the land.[226] However, the courts today prefer the second criterion to the first.[227]

This appears to suggest that the courts favour personal chattels attached to land being regarded as fixtures.

The first criterion concentrates on the relationship between the personal chattels and the use which is made of the land to which the goods are annexed.[228] If the goods are useful and are a necessary or at least a useful adjunct to the land, considering the purposes to which the object is devoted,[229] they will be treated as fixtures. Thus valuable tapestries affixed by a tenant for life to the walls were regarded as merely personal chattels for they were intended for personal enjoyment and were not intended to form part of the house.[230] On the other hand, in the following cases personal chattels were held to be fixtures: looms attached to a building that enhanced the value of the building although they could be removed with little difficulty and little injury to the building,[231] a house placed on piers for the better enjoyment of the land,[232] a cocoa processing plant installed in a factory to enhance its usefulness as a factory for manufacturing cocoa products,[233] and an air-conditioning unit installed to improve the use of a dance-hall although it was relatively easy to remove.[234]

224 See *Gough v Wood & Co.* [1894] 713, CA, 720, *per* Lindley LJ. 225 Ibid.

226 See *Elwes v Maw* (1802) 3 East 38, 102 ER 510, where the first criterion was strictly applied.

227 See J.G. Riddall, *Introduction to Land Law*, 4th ed. (London: Butterworths, 1988), p. 51; see also *Leigh v Taylor* [1902] AC 157, 162, *per* Lord Macnaghten: 'its relative importance is probably not what it was in ruder or simpler times'. See also *Hellawell v Eastwood* (1851) 6 Exch 295, 155 ER 554, where the second criterion appears to have been first mentioned.

228 Ibid. 229 Ibid. 230 See *Leigh v Taylor* [1902] AC 157.

231 *Holland v Hodgson* [1861–73] All ER Rep 237.

232 *Reid v Smith* [1906] 3 CLR 656.

233 *Gebrueder Buehler A.G. v Peter Chi Man Kwong and Two Others* [1988] 2 MLJ 69, CA.@@@@

234 *Irene Loong v Pun Tsun Hang and American Engineering Corp., Fed. Inc. and Far East Import & Export Ltd* [1959] HKDCLR 192.

It is submitted that the second criterion does not afford any higher degree of certainty to the creditor of personal chattels than the first criterion. The creditor must constantly remember that it is only a general criterion. It is not absolute, nor does it have a life of its own. Each case has to turn on its own special facts. As the Earl of Halsbury LC in *Leigh v Taylor* stated, 'you must apply yourself to the facts of each particular case; and I am content here to apply myself to the facts of this case'.[235]

This, therefore, opens the door for the courts to consider all kinds of factors which may not seem necessarily important to the unsuspecting creditor or debtor, but may appear crucial to the court. Where appropriate, as may be dictated by the facts of the case, the second criterion may be disregarded altogether. This can be seen from the House of Lords case of *Elitestone Ltd v Morris and Another*.[236] There the court had to consider whether a bungalow which rested on concrete foundation blocks fixed to the land was a chattel or a fixture. At first instance, it was held that the bungalow was a fixture. On appeal by the plaintiffs, the Court of Appeal came to the opposite conclusion – it held that the bungalow was a chattel. On further appeal to the House of Lords by the defendants, Their Lordships unanimously agreed with the court of first instance and held that the bungalow was a fixture. The House of Lords in coming to this conclusion adopted a wide approach – that is, a chattel is a fixture if it can only be removed by its complete demolition.[237]

At first sight this wide approach appears to favour the creditor of personal chattels, such as machinery. This is because if the machinery can be dismantled and reassembled elsewhere and used just as effectively, it remains a personal chattel and will not pass to the debtor or the mortgagee. But a careful analysis of the relevant parts of the speeches of Lord Lloyd of Berwick and Lord Clyde, the majority, suggests that this may not be the case. The factors taken into consideration by them were only evidential elements. Their speeches further suggest that in appropriate cases, such as machinery, the court may place strong emphasis on the more pertinent question whether such goods attached to the building or land have been so fixed for the better enjoyment of the objects as goods, or whether they have been fixed with a view to effecting a permanent improvement of the freehold. This approach, as

235 [1902] AC 157, p. 158. 236 [1997] 2 ALL ER 513, HL.

237 The current authors agree that this is a United States concept; see A.G. Guest, 'Accession and Confusion in the Law of Hire-Purchase', *MLR* 27 (1964), 505 particularly at p. 511.

shown in earlier cases,[238] may not necessarily work to the advantage of the creditor.

In addition, it is submitted that it would not avail a creditor if serious injury were caused to the land, even if the goods were intact after removal and could be enjoyed elsewhere. Despite these judgments, they cannot be regarded as a complete jettisoning of the first criterion; that is, the degree of annexation of the personal chattel.

The English Law Commission noted the problem created by the transformatory rule but recommended no special provisions for the registration of priority of charges over fixtures. However, it did recommend, by following §8(6) of the Agricultural Credits Act 1928, that a registered charge over growing crops (whether planted or natural) should have priority over a conflicting interest in the land.[239] However, Article 9 of the United States Uniform Commercial Code (Revised) appears to afford a fair solution to the problem.[240] A perfected[241] security interest[242] in fixtures has priority over a conflicting interest of an encumbrancer or owner of the real property when the security interest is a purchase-money security interest,[243] the interest of the encumbrancer or owner arises before the personal chattels become fixtures, and the security interest is perfected by a fixture filing[244] before the personal chattels become fixtures or within twenty days thereafter.[245]

[238] For example, see the Hong Kong cases of *Irene Loong v Pun Tsun Hang and American Engineering Corp., Fed. Inc. and Far East Import & Export Ltd* [1959] HKDCLR 192; *Orient Leasing (Hong Kong) Ltd v NP Etches and Others* [1985] HKLR 292; the Malaysian case of *Sungei Way Leasing Sdn Bhd v Lian Seng Properties Sdn Bhd and Others (Bank Bumiputra Malaysia Bhd and Another, interveners)* [1989] 2 MLJ 123; and the English case of *Melluish (Inspector of Taxes) v BMI (No 3) Ltd* [1996] AC 454.

[239] English Law Commission Report No 296, paras. 3.225–3.228. The New Zealand Personal Property Securities Act (1999) failed to address the problem; see S. Baas, 'Fixtures under the Personal Property Securities Act: What New Zealand Doesn't Know It's Missing', *NZULR* 19 (2001), 403.

[240] See §9-313 of the Code.

[241] A security is perfected when the security interest has attached to the property. See *Uniform Commercial Code – Official Text with Comments*, 8th ed. (Longwood: Gould Publications, Inc. 2000), p. 569.

[242] The Uniform Commercial Code defined 'security interest' very broadly to include traditional security devices and quasi-security devices.

[243] A purchase-money security interest (PMSI) is one taken by the person who sells the collateral or by the person who advances money so the debtor can buy the collateral; J.F. Beatty and S.S. Samuelson, *Business Law – For a New Century*, 2nd ed. (Australia: West Legal Studies in Business, Thomson Learning, 2001), p. 608. See §16 of the New Zealand Personal Property Security Act, which gives a wider definition to include leases of more than one year, but does not include transactions of sale and lease back to the seller.

[244] That is, filing in the office where the real-estate mortgages are filed or recorded.

[245] Section 9-334, Uniform Commercial Code.

The English Law Commission, however, recommended radical reforms in respect of personal chattels that are not fixtures, and they have significant impact on the *nemo dat* rule. Some of the recommendations[246] have already been discussed earlier.[247]

The other recommendation is that quasi-securities should be treated as purchase-money security interests (PMSIs).[248] Generally, under the PMSI principle, the secured creditor takes priority over a conflicting perfected security interest over the same goods (even one registered earlier).[249] The Law Commission recommended that PMSI, on subsequent registration and notice to earlier secured creditors, especially where the security extends to after-acquired assets, should be given in order to preserve the priority.[250] One view of their consideration is that notice should be given to earlier creditors, irrespective of the nature of the assets.[251] The other view is that registration should be required in all cases. The Law Commission recommended and favoured the second view.[252] It is submitted that the second view is attractive in that it avoids the complications of determining whether or not an asset is an inventory. However, the English Law Commission Report No 296 took an entirely different stance. It noted that 'most of the complexity in the rules of priority was caused by the provisions for purchase-money security interests. These were aimed principally at title-retention devices.' It thought that the whole regime of title-retention devices caused a great deal of controversy and was now under consideration in its future reports; the priority issue on PMSI was therefore omitted.[253]

246 See Chapters 4 and 5 above. 247 See Chapters 4 and 5 above.

248 English Law Commission Consultation Paper No 164, para. 10.24 provided an explanation on PMSI: 'security over property acquired by the debtor with the funds provided by the secured party (as opposed to security granted over an existing item of the debtor's property). The whole purpose of the loan is to enable the secured property to be acquired.' See also a similar definition in draft reg. 4(1) of the English Law Commission Consultation Paper No 176.

249 For reasons for this 'super-priority', see English Law Commission Consultation Paper No 164, paras. 4.155–4.157. See also English Law Commission Consultation Paper No 176, paras. 3.204–3.205.

250 English Law Commission Consultation Paper No 176, para. 3.214; and Consultation Paper No 164, para. 4.162. However, Report No 296 was silent on this point.

251 Under Article 9, §9-324(a) and (b) of the Uniform Form Commercial Code (Revised), and §§73–4 of the New Zealand Personal Property Security Act, notice has to be given to the earlier creditor if the assets are an inventory and registration for other assets.

252 English Law Commission Consultation Paper No 176, paras. 3.213–3.214.

253 English Law Commission Report No 296, paras. 1.29, 3.146.

The Law Commission did not adequately explain the binding effect of PMSIs on subsequent buyers. But according to the system in the United States, the subsequent buyer takes free from PMSI if the PMSI goods are consumer goods, the buyer is a consumer, the buyer has no actual knowledge of the PMSI, and the PMSI holder has not filed a financing statement.[254] This rule, if adopted, would weaken the *nemo dat* rule even further than it is now.[255] But any radical reform along these lines either in England or Hong Kong appears to be unlikely in the foreseeable future.

6.5 Priority of Security Interests in China

6.5.1 Rule of first in time of creation and registration in China in respect of security interests (other than quasi-security interests)

Examination of jurisprudence in China shows that, in contrast to Hong Kong, the rule of first in time of creation has no place at all in Chinese security law. This has been discussed earlier in this chapter. Rather, the rule of first in time of registration largely governs the priority sequence.[256] Article 199 of the Property Law highlights the importance of registration:

> Where the same property is mortgaged to two or more creditors, the proceeds from the auction or sale of the mortgaged property shall be paid according to the following rules:
>
> (1) Where a mortgage contract has been registered [whether it is effective on the date of registration or execution of the mortgage], the payment shall be made according to the chronological order of registration. In the case of same registration date, payment shall be made according to the proportion of the obligations.
> (2) The registered mortgage has priority over the unregistered mortgage.
> (3) Where a mortgage contract has not been registered, payment shall be made according to the proportion to his obligation.

This is the most important priority rule in competing mortgagees, which also underpins the importance of registration and its authorities

254 See Article 9, §307. See Beatty and Samuelson, above, note 243, pp. 613–14.

255 Currently the buyer-in-possession exception under §27(2) of the Sale of Goods Ordinance applies only to conditional sale. PMSI would apply to hire-purchase and finance lease also.

256 Please refer to Articles 44 and 45 of the Security Law relating to the information to be produced to the relevant registration department.

under the Security Law (1995), the Judicial Interpretation of the Security Law (2001) and the Property Law (2007). The common law and equitable exceptions discussed above in this chapter have no place in China, because legal and equitable interests in personal property are unknown in China's civil law.

However, at the same time there are exceptions to the general rule itself. Accordingly, this part focuses on the registration system exception.

6.5.2 *Exceptions to the rule of 'first in time' of registration*

There are three exceptions to the rule of priority of date of registration, namely, bad faith of the duly registered mortgagee, pledge and re-pledge of movable property.

Bad faith

The Security Law is not explicit in relation to the postponing effect of the bad faith of a subsequent duly registered mortgagee vis-à-vis an earlier unregistered mortgage over the same goods. The better view is that the superior claim of a creditor who has acquired a mortgage following the formalities of the law and in good faith cannot be subordinated to the claim of a subsequent purchaser.

The Judicial Interpretation of the Security Law dealt with the 'bad faith' issue. Article 69 provides,

> If a debtor has several ordinary creditors and, when discharging his obligations, conspires in bad faith with one such creditor to mortgage all or part of his assets to the said creditor, thereby losing his capacity to perform his other obligations and prejudicing the lawful rights and interests of the other creditors, the injured creditors may petition the People's Court to nullify such mortgage.

From this provision, we may observe that the 'bad faith' exception has a strict application standard: (1) there must be several creditors, (2) the debtor must mortgage all or part of his assets to one creditor in bad faith, (3) the mortgage is created when the debtor is discharging his unsecured obligations to one of his creditors and (4) the mortgage renders the debtor incapable of repaying his other unsecured creditors. Obviously, the key to determining the validity of such a mortgage lies in ascertaining whether debtor and creditor conspired in bad faith.

By accepting that bad faith is an exception, a substantive problem is created in China – no statutory definition of 'good faith' or 'bad faith' exists in either the Security Law or its Judicial Interpretation, or in the Property

Law. This is somewhat strange, with the expression 'good faith' widely used in various laws, regulations and judicial interpretations. However, academic texts and monographs provide some useful guidelines as to what 'good faith' or 'bad faith' might mean in the context of security over personal property. Shibing Cao, a judge from the Supreme Court and a member of the Judicial Interpretation drafting team, considers that 'bad faith' in this case means that 'the creditor knows that the debtor has several creditors and the debtor is unable to pay due debts, but still concludes a mortgage contract with him'.[257] In this view, 'bad faith' requires two constituent factors: (1) the debtor cannot discharge his debts; (2) the creditor understands this situation and has knowledge of the competing creditors. In such a situation, if the debtor and the creditor agree to create a mortgage over all of the debtor's property, 'bad faith' will be inferred from such an act and requires no further evidence.[258]

Pledge

This exception arises where there is a competition between two different types of security device over the same property: an earlier pledge (either over tangible or intangible property) and a duly registered subsequent mortgage. From general principles, it can be argued that in such a situation the pledge has priority. Besides being 'first in time' of creation, the pledge is effective upon actual delivery and thus no registration is required. Consequently, the pledgee has better title by reason of its possession of the movable property (or its document of title). However, Chinese law makes a peculiar provision on this issue. Article 79 of the Judicial Interpretation of the Security Law provides, 'If the same property is encumbered by both a statutorily registered mortgage and a pledge, the mortgagee ranks before the pledge in receiving payment.' Therefore China's law has adopted a policy on the priority between a mortgage and a pledge, namely that in any circumstances, a statutorily registered mortgage has priority over all pledges.

According to Article 42 of the Security Law (1995), the 'statutory registered mortgage' includes registration of such a security over:

- leasehold land to which there are no attachments;
- urban real property or the buildings of enterprises in townships or villages such as factory buildings;

[257] Shibing Cao, *Solutions and Prospects on Questions Related to Chinese Security Mechanism: Analysis Based on Security Law and its Judicial Interpretations* (Beijing: China Fa Zhi Press, 2001), p. 247.

[258] Ibid.

- forest land;
- aircraft, vessels or vehicles; and
- the equipment or other movables of enterprises.

The Property Law has extended the scope of 'statutory registered mortgage' in Article 187 under which the mortgage contract over the real property stipulated in Article 180 shall be registered to become effective.[259] This includes mortgages over:

- buildings and other things firmly fixed to the land;
- land use rights in relation to a building lot;
- land use rights in relation to development land contracted by a mortgagor by way of bidding, auction or negotiation; and
- buildings under construction.

According to the Security Law, these duly registered mortgages enjoy priority over pledges even if a pledge is created prior to the mortgage. Obviously, there is no reasonable jurisprudential theory to support this peculiar arrangement. An insider's explanation indicates that the provision is due to practical considerations.[260] The rationale behind the provision is one of certainty. The registration time of a mortgage can always be ascertained because a simple review of the register will reflect the date of registration. On the other hand, the date for creation of a pledge cannot be determined with certainty. In instances where the pledgee conspires with the third party to falsify the sequence of pledge and precedent mortgage, the mortgagee will be at a disadvantage.[261] This arrangement reflects the immediate concern of Chinese lawmakers with the protection of creditor's rights under any security arrangements.

Re-pledge of movable property

The Property Law now expressly allows pledged property in the possession of a pledgee to be re-pledged, subject to the consent of the pledgor. Article 217 provides that if, 'During the term of the pledge, the pledgee, without the consent of the pledgor, pledges the relevant property to a third

[259] However, it is unclear whether the registrable *personal* property stipulated in Article 180 falls within the meaning of 'statutory registered mortgage', as the registration of this property is not compulsory but on a voluntary basis. These mortgage contracts, then, already become effective on the date of execution and the purpose of registration is to defend against the claims of third parties of good faith, according to Articles 188 and 189 of the Property Law.

[260] Shibing Cao, above, note 257. [261] Ibid.

party, he shall bear civil liability for any loss or damage to the pledged property.'

Competing interests between an earlier pledgee (who is also the pledgor) and the later pledge may arise. The priority issue is resolved by Article 94 of the Judicial Interpretation of the Security Law:

> Where during the term of the pledge, with the pledgor's consent, the pledgee pledges the relevant property to a third party in his possession to secure his own debt, such pledge shall not exceed the scope of obligation secured by the original pledge, and the exceeding portion, if any, shall not be paid with priority. Re-pledge has priority over the original pledge.
>
> During the term of pledge, where the pledgee grants security in relation to the pledged property to a third party to secure the pledgee's debt without the pledgor's consent, the security shall be invalid. The pledgee shall bear liability for damage caused by the re-pledge.

Thus by reading the two articles together, whether the re-pledge is valid is subject to the consent of the original pledgor. At the same time, the re-pledge is subject to limitations: (1) the re-pledge is to secure the pledgor's own debt, and (2) a re-pledge is limited to the scope of obligation secured by the original pledge for the purpose of priority on payment. A proper re-pledge generally should take precedence over the original pledge for priority on payment. The later pledgee should be paid first, favouring the later party in time of creation. Article 94 implies that possession of movable pledged property is of vital importance in ascertaining the priority of competing interests as between successive pledges of the same movable.

6.6 Position of subsequent buyer of secured assets

In Hong Kong, the rules governing the position of the subsequent buyer of secured assets are very complex. The buyer's position is similar to that of the subsequent secured creditor discussed above. Thus whether the buyer takes free from an earlier security interest depends on a number of factors, such as the nature of the security device (possessory, non-possessory or quasi-security), the juridical nature of the assets, whether or not it had actual or constructive notice and whether special legislation applies. The position of the buyer also generally follows the same path as the subsequent secured creditor.

In China, the position of the buyer of secured assets is governed by the *nemo dat* rule in Article 106 of the Property Law (discussed above in this chapter). If the buyer satisfies the good-faith requirements, he obtains the relevant property rights under the unauthorised transfer. If the buyer does not satisfy the good-faith requirement but possesses the secured asset, the rightful owner of it has the right to recover and request the return of the secured asset.[262] Besides, the priority position of subsequent creditors is relatively simple. The priority of a subsequent secured creditor is governed by the first-in-time rule of registration (for registered mortgages) or by the respective proportions of the claims (for unregistered mortgages).

The English Law Commission made several radical recommendations. The basic rule is that, providing value is given from the debtor, a subsequent buyer of tangible personal property[263] takes free from an unperfected security interest unless the buyer had knowledge of the existence of it.[264] The Law Commission recommended that knowledge should be actual.[265] Therefore it is likely that a buyer or lessee would take free of a security interest perfected by registration under the proposed notice-filing system, as registration is generally regarded as giving constructive notice, unless the buyer or lessee knows that the sale or lease is in violation of the security agreement.[266] A buyer or lessee, without knowledge of a perfected security interest, might also take free goods that are uniquely identifiable on the condition that the unique number was omitted from the filing.[267] The Law Commission was generally not, however, prepared to afford the subsequent buyer of intangible property, particularly receivables, the same privilege.[268] One possible privilege was that a purchaser for value who takes financial collateral[269] in its own name without knowledge

[262] See also Article 34 of the Property Law, which allows the right to request the return of such property.

[263] For example, stock in trade and capital equipment.

[264] English Law Commission Consultation Paper No 176, paras. 3.255–3.256. See also draft reg. 20(4) in the same paper.

[265] English Law Commission Consultation Paper No 176, para. 3.255.

[266] English Law Commission Consultation Paper No 176, para. 3.260, and draft reg 31(2)–(3) in the same paper.

[267] For example, vehicles or goods with serial numbers; see English Law Commission Consultation Paper No 176, para. 3.263, and draft reg. 31(7)–(8) in the same report.

[268] English Law Commission Consultation Paper No 164, para. 4.194.

[269] The term 'financial collateral' is used for the purpose of the Financial Collateral Arrangements (No 2) Regulations 2003 (FCAR) SI 2003 No 3226, which implemented the European Directive on Financial Collateral Arrangements. Financial collateral is explicitly excluded from registration to render the arrangement enforceable; see FCAR reg. 4(1).

that the disposition is in breach of a previous charge agreement should take free of the earlier charge.[270]

6.7 Conclusion

The above dicussion shows that the rule of first in time of creation and the rule in *Dearle v Hall* in Hong Kong suffer from several weaknesses.

Firstly, they are complicated in their practical application. This is due to the highly technical and complex exceptions which include exceptions under common law, equity and various statutes. As a result, whether or not an exception applies is determined by several factors – namely the juridical nature of the security interests (legal or equitable, vis-à-vis the first creditor and the second creditor), the conduct of the parties, the doctrine of tacking and whether any special statutes, such as the Bills of Sale Ordinance, Companies Ordinance, Patents Ordinance and Trade Mark Ordinance, apply. Thus even if a creditor in Hong Kong wishes to act diligently to obtain priority, the complexities inherent in the rules make it difficult for a creditor to be absolutely certain that it would obtain the priority it expects at the outset.

Secondly, the registration systems under the Bills of Sale Ordinance and the Companies Ordinance, particularly, do not provide certainty to the priority system. Insofar as priority is concerned, each performs a different function. Priority of registrable security under the Bills of Sale Ordinance is ranked according to the date of registration. This rule, it is submitted, is more effective. However, in the case of registrable security under the Companies Ordinance, priority is determined according to the date of creation of the security. It thus seems strange that security over the same types of assets should be determined by different rules. As the Companies Ordinance preserves the general rules of priority, the registration system is unreliable. A search at the Companies Registry by a diligent creditor is no guarantee that there may not be an earlier unregistered secured creditor who might later on obtain priority by registration. In this regard, the critical comment of the English Law Commission in respect of the similar English registration system applies equally to Hong Kong. The Commission stated,

> A registration should ensure that those who do register are secure in their priority (for example, there should be no hidden problems as with the 21-day [equivalent of Hong Kong five-week] invisibility problems). In

[270] See the recommendation in para. 5.102, English Law Commission Report No 296.

> addition, the position of third party purchasers should be clear and they should not need to concern themselves with creditors who have not chosen to register what are registrable securities. As we have seen, the current registration scheme clearly fails to fulfil these aims: we think this is a particularly significant weakness.[271]

Despite this trenchant criticism, the UK has not substantially reformed its system of company charges and it is highly likely that Hong Kong will not reform its system either. Complacency and a failure of reforming zeal are apparent in both jurisdictions despite the obvious deficiencies exposed here.

Thirdly, the rules governing competing claims between the creditors of fixtures under a hire-purchase, lease and conditional sale, and the mortgagee of land upon which the fixtures are attached, is unsatisfactory. The law is harsh to the creditor. The law confers an unexpected windfall on the mortgagee at the expense of the creditor. The imbalance is a consequence of dislocation between the substantive rules and the practical difficulties arising from the constantly changing nature of goods. Above all else, the general law has never adequately explained how a creditor's rights could be so drastically altered by an attachment of goods, effected by bolts and screws, to land.[272]

Fourthly, the doctrine of constructive notice plays an inconsistent role. Whether or not the doctrine of constructive notice of a prior security applies is arbitrary. The law is that the doctrine does not apply in relation to the registration system under the Bills of Sale Ordinance, but it does apply to the registration system under the Companies Ordinance. No satisfactory explanation has thus far been given for this inconsistency. In other registration systems, such as for patents and trademarks, it is uncertain whether the doctrine of constructive notice applies or not.

Where the registration system does or does not import the doctrine is largely an issue of whether the subsequent creditor was negligent in taking the appropriate steps to safeguard its security interest. This again is unpredictable, as it varies with the circumstances of each case. Where the title to personal property, both tangible and intangible, is evidenced by some form of document of title, it is more likely that the doctrine will apply than where there are no such documents. Where personal property, especially goods, are bought and sold in the ordinary course of trade, commercial expediency may dictate that the doctrine should be excluded.

[271] English Law Commission Consultation Paper No 164, para. 3.28.

[272] *Holt v Henley* (1913) USSCR 58 L Ed 767, 772, *per* Holmes J.

Thus when and what steps a creditor should take to avoid the ramifications of the doctrine is uncertain, except in the most obvious cases.

Fifthly, the rule in *Dearle v Hall* appears to apply harshly towards the earlier assignee or creditor who has failed to give notice; it loses priority to a subsequent assignee who has duly served notice on the debtor. This is so even though the default did not in any way mislead a subsequent assignee who has not made any inquiry of the debtor. This rule has been criticised as altering a fundamental rule of equity, which is that equity does not deprive a person of an interest unless it has been guilty of inequities *vis-à-vis* a third party. It was thus stated, 'A rule that requires notice but excuses inquiry is not consistent of equity.'[273] Consequently, as Lord Macnaghten said, the rule 'has on the whole produced at least as much injustice as it has prevented'.[274]

In contrast to Hong Kong, the priority rules of China seem simple and effective and to promote diligence by creditors. This is attributable to three factors.

Firstly, the absence of legal and equitable security interests means that the competing superiority of different types of security, as seen in Hong Kong, does not arise in China.

Secondly, the rules of the priority and registration systems do not make any distinction between security granted by companies and by individuals.

Thirdly, priority of mortgages is determined primarily by the date of registration of the mortgage. Owing to the wide use of the mortgage, the rule of first in time of creation and the *nemo dat* rule are subsumed by it. As a result, problems which might have arisen in the same way as in Hong Kong are rarely seen in China.

Although the Chinese Security Law has not provided any statutory definition of 'bad faith' in the priority battle which renders Article 69 of the Judicial Interpretation of the Security Law difficult to apply, these problems do not in practice pose serious hurdles to a creditor, debtor, third party or practitioner. The lack of judicial discussion on the matter seems to be a confirmation of this proposition.

[273] See the United States of America case of *Salem Trust Co. v Manufacturers' Finance Co. et al.* (11 April 1922) No 1515, Circuit Court of Appeals, First Circuit, 280F.803; 1922 US App Lexis 1871, *per* Bingham, Circuit Judge, p. 8. Note that because of this unjustifiable rule, some American states, prior to the enactment of the Uniform Commercial Code, did not apply the rule in *Dearle v Hall*, but applied the first-in-time rule.

[274] *Ward v Duncombe* (1893) AC 369, p. 392.

This chapter therefore concludes that the rules for determining priority of competing claims in Hong Kong have not satisfied the priority criteria established in Chapter 1 because the rules are highly technical, complex and inconsistent. As a result, they are unable to guarantee a secured creditor that its security over personal property, both tangible and intangible, will enjoy the priority it expects after it has complied with the rules relevant to creation and priority. In relation to China, although there are some weaknesses identified, this chapter concludes that its rules have satisfied the priority criteria established in Chapter 1. Generally, the rules are simple and comprehensible, particularly the rule of priority in relation to the date of registration of mortgages.

Chapter 7

Enforcement, and creditor's remedies

7.1 Introduction

The issue of enforcement and remedies arises when the debtor defaults in repayment of the debt or otherwise fails to perform contractual obligations. In Hong Kong and China, the nature of the available remedy determines the enforcement process. Thus a creditor, at the outset, has to consider the types of remedy available in relation to the type of security device created over the encumbered personal property.

In both jurisdictions, remedies can be divided into two categories, namely personal and proprietary. The first is the right of the creditor to sue the debtor or a third party, if there is a personal guarantee/indemnity, for the debt, by way of a personal action. The second is a remedy against the secured property itself. This chapter will not discuss personal remedies as the focus of this book is concerned with secured property. It will, however, discuss the ancillary rights of the creditor to sue the debtor for any deficiency after the creditor has fully exhausted the appropriate proprietary remedy.

In Hong Kong, the proprietary remedies of a legal mortgagee *strictu sensu*, an equitable mortgagee, a chargee and a pledgee ('traditional security holder') comprise the following: (a) taking possession (if the creditor does not have possession), (b) appointment of receiver, (c) foreclosure and (d) sale.[1] The general law defines the circumstances under which these remedies may arise and the procedure governing their exercise. However, in some cases they can be affected by special legislation, such as the Bills of Sale Ordinance.

In contrast, in China, the pledgee and mortgagee ('traditional security holder') are afforded two forms of remedy only, namely taking possession

[1] E.L.G. Tyler, *Fisher & Lightwood's Law of Mortgage*, 10th ed. (London: Butterworths, 1988), p. 281; and see also English Law Commission Consultation Paper No 164, para. B 12.

and conversion, or sale or auction, called 'foreclosure'.[2] Foreclosure in the strict common law sense does not exist in China, because the Security Law (1995) provides that the creditor cannot appropriate the things given by way of pledge or mortgage. Any stipulation to the contrary is null and void.[3] In the case of a pledge, the secured property is already in the possession of the pledgee from the time that the pledge contract was concluded. Taking possession is regarded as both a constituent element of the pledge contract and a form of remedy in case of the other party's default. In the mortgage scenario, however, it is not clear whether mortgagee is entitled to take possession of the secured property in question, as we will see from the later discussion in this chapter.

In Hong Kong, the remedies of the creditor under hire-purchase, lease and conditional sale ('quasi-security holder') are primarily governed by the agreement between the parties. The remedies are mainly the taking of possession of the secured property and thereafter the proceeds of sale of the goods. In China, the remedies of quasi-security holders are similar to those in Hong Kong. However, rather than being regarded as forms of security, they are provided in the Contract Law (1999) and are generally contractual remedies stipulated in that statute.

The objective of this chapter is to determine whether the remedies in Hong Kong and China have satisfied the four criteria of enforcement, namely that the creditor's remedies must be certain, enforcement must be expeditious, the cost must be inexpensive and the amount of money that the creditor is entitled to recover under the security arrangement must be certain.

7.2 Remedies of the traditional security holder in Hong Kong

For the purpose of this part, unless otherwise stated, the expression

'creditor' means the traditional security holder, and
'debtor' means the traditional security provider.

7.2.1 Taking possession

In Hong Kong, the secured creditor's right of seizure and taking possession has to be considered separately in respect of tangible and intangible

[2] In China 'foreclosure' is actually a 'sale' by private treaty or by public auction.
[3] For example, Article 40 and Article 66 of the Security Law.

personal property, because the circumstances under which the right arises are different for each type of property.

Tangible property

In relation to tangible property, the nature of the security device and the agreement, if any, made between the creditor and the debtor determine whether or not the creditor has the right to take possession. If the creditor is a legal mortgagee, the general law is clear – the creditor has the right to seize and take possession of the property, because legal title is vested in the creditor.[4] As Sykes and Walker stated, 'there is no need for the insertion of a clause purporting to give such power'.[5]

However, in practice, the right is postponed so as to enable the debtor to use the property for the purpose of its business.[6] The right is only exercisable upon occurrence of special events that have been agreed between the parties in advance. These events usually consist of the debtor's default in instalment payments or breach of any covenant that jeopardises the property.

On the other hand, if the security device is an equitable mortgage *strictu sensu*, the law is not entirely clear because there are two opposing views. The orthodox view is that the equitable mortgagee–creditor has no right of possession, unless there is a special agreement, or a receiver has been appointed, or a court order entitling the creditor to possession has been granted.[7] In contrast, the liberal view considers that the equitable mortgagee has such a right. But the underlying reasons differ. For instance,

[4] *Four-Maids Ltd v Dudley Marshall (Properties) Ltd* [1957] Ch 317, 320, *per* Harman J; and see also English Law Commission Consultation Paper No 164, para. B 20, for a similar view.

[5] E.I. Sykes and S. Walker, *The Law of Securities*, 5th ed. (Sydney: The Law Book Company Limited, 1993), p. 607.

[6] This has led to English Law Commission Consultation Paper No 164, para. B 20, which commented that the legal mortgagee's powers of taking possession immediately 'bear little relation to modern practice'.

[7] *Coote's Law of Mortgages*, 9th ed. (London: Sweet & Maxwell, 1927), vol. 2, p. 823; C.H.M. Waldock, *Law of Mortgages*, 2nd ed. (London: Sweet & Maxwell, 1950), p. 55; Tyler, above, note 1, p. 332; E.F. Cousins and I. Clarke, *The Law of Mortgages*, 2nd ed. (London: Sweet & Maxwell, 2001), p. 339; and Sykes and Walker, above, note 5, pp. 615–16. Also see H.R.W. Wade, 'An Equitable Mortgagee's Right to Possession', *LQR* 71 (1955), 204. The rationale as stated by Waldock in his text *Law of Mortgages*, p. 55, was because the equitable mortgagee had no right to eject the mortgagor as the mortgagee merely had an equitable title. Wade gave another reason, which is that if the land was let before date of the equitable mortgage, the equitable mortgagee could not collect rent from the tenant without the court's assistance.

Wade thought that the Judicature Act 1875, which fused the procedural aspect of common law and equity, gave the equitable mortgagee such a right.[8] Sykes and Walker supported the liberal view,[9] but from another perspective. They strongly argued that on the basis of the maxim 'equity regards that as done that ought to be done',[10] the equitable mortgagee is entitled to the same rights and remedies as the legal mortgagee. However, they appeared to retreat a little when they suggested that an equitable mortgagee had what they called a 'passive right of possession'; that is, if the mortgagee is able to take possession peaceably, then it could not be ejected either by the mortgagor or by any third party. This, it is submitted, is incorrect as a matter of principle. Surely, if a mortgagee could not be ejected it should have a right at the outset to take possession. In Hong Kong there is no authority on the matter.

If the orthodox view is adopted in Hong Kong, it means that an equitable mortgagee–creditor, who wishes to 'nurse' the security – in the absence of an express power to take possession of the goods – has to adopt the cumbersome and more expensive process of applying to the court for an order of seizure and possession, or for the appointment of a receiver.

If the security is an equitable charge, it is settled that the equitable chargee–creditor has no right to take possession of the property under general law.[11]

However, in Hong Kong, the problem of whether the creditor (equitable mortgagee or chargee) has power to seize and take possession of the property is theoretical. In practice, fixed and floating charges over goods granted by company debtors usually confer such a power on the creditor.[12]

8 Wade, above, note 7. See also E.H. Burn, *Cheshire and Burn's Modern Law of Real Property*, 14th ed. (London: Butterworths, 1988), p. 686.

9 Sykes and Walker, above, note 5, pp. 615–16, cf. pp. 161–3.

10 Established in *Walsh v Lonsdale* (1882) 21 Ch D 9.

11 In *Garfitt v Allen* (1887) 37 Ch D 48, where legacies of the beneficiary were charged on certain real estates, North J said, 'The persons entitled to the annuity or legacies are in the position of persons having a charge on real estate; they have no legal estate. They are in the position of equitable mortgagees; they could not have taken possession of the land; they could have enforced their charge by (amongst other things) getting into the appointment of a receiver if they had thought fit to do so.' See also English Law Commission Consultation Paper No 164, para. B 20, which expresses the same view.

12 Sample charge documents of Baker & McKenzie, Clifford Chance, Deacons, Johnnie Yam, and Jacky Lee & Co. and Linklaters.

In the case of bills of sale granted by non-corporate debtors, the creditor of the bill of sale has an implied power under the Bills of Sale Ordinance.[13] These two factors could be the reason for the absence of reported cases on this matter in Hong Kong.

However, the creditor of a bill of sale has to comply with the strict conditions of §14 of the Bills of Sale Ordinance before it can exercise the implied power of seizure and sale of goods constituting personal chattels. The conditions are:

- the debtor has defaulted in repayment of the loan;
- the debtor has defaulted in any obligation to maintain the goods in good condition or to insure the goods;
- the debtor has been adjudicated bankrupt;
- the goods have been detained for rent, rates or taxes;
- the debtor has fraudulently removed or suffered the goods or any of them to be removed from the premises;
- the debtor has not, without reasonable excuse, upon demand in writing by the creditor, produced to the creditor receipts for rent, rates and taxes; or
- execution has been levied against the goods of the debtor.

There is special protection for the debtor. The creditor may only remove the chattels after the expiry of five days from the date of seizure of the chattels.[14] During this period the debtor – that is, the grantor of the bill of sale – may apply to the court to restrain the creditor from removing or selling the goods. The court may make the restraining order if the reasons for the creditor's seizure no longer exist, such as the debtor tenders payment,[15] or if the liability of the debtor has not actually accrued.[16]

If the above protection is lost, the debtor can look to the equity of redemption. The debtor could at any time redeem the goods by tendering the monies due and owing and all costs lawfully incurred by the creditor in enforcing the security.[17] The Bills of Sale Ordinance has not destroyed that equitable right. But this right is lost if the property is sold or foreclosed.

[13] See Chapter 2 above.

[14] § 17 of the Bills of Sale Ordinance (Cap. 20).

[15] *Ex parte Cotton* (1883) 11 QBD 301. [16] *Ex parte Wickens* [1898] 1 QB 543.

[17] *Johnson v Diprose* [1893] 1 QB 512.

Intangible property

In relation to intangible personal property, legal and equitable, if notice of the security has already been served on the original debtor,[18] the creditor, according to the rule in *Dearle v Hall*,[19] has possession at the outset. If it has not served such notice, the creditor must do so on the original debtor,[20] to effect possession.

The above demonstrates that the substantive rules governing the creditor's right to take possession are complex and uncertain. Whether the creditor has such right depends on several factors – namely, whether the security device a legal mortgage, a charge or a pledge. Is the secured personal property tangible or intangible? Is the security a bill of sale? In most cases, the problem is solved by incorporating an express right of possession in the security agreement. However, this simply shows that the general law is lagging behind actual commercial practice.

The enforcement process to take possession of the secured personal property is expeditious and inexpensive. If the aid of the court is required, the judicial enforcement process is reasonably fast.[21] However, besides fees, which are minimal,[22] the costs of litigation are generally expensive.[23] But this should be discounted, as in a vast majority of cases the aid of the court is not necessary.

Accordingly, the right of possession can be regarded as having satisfied the enforcement criteria established in Chapter 1, namely that the remedy must be expeditious and inexpensive. The criterion that the amount the creditor is entitled to recover must be certain is not relevant here. However, as the substantive right to take possession has not satisfied the enforcement criterion that the creditor's remedies must be certain, the rules governing this remedy must be regarded as inefficient.

[18] That is, the person who has the title or control of the intangible personal property, such as debts or book debts.

[19] See Chapter 3 above. [20] See note 18 above for definition.

[21] The waiting time in the District Court is approximately 120 days from the receipt of application to fix the date for the hearing. See www.info.gov.hk/jud/guide2cs/.

[22] See High Court Fees Rules, LN 25/2001 and District Court Civil Procedure (Fees) Rules, LN 26/2001.

[23] It is difficult to ascertain with accuracy the cost of litigation, particularly lawyer's fees, in Hong Kong. However, there is sufficient literature to show that litigation is expensive in Hong Kong. See M.B. Suleik, 'The Financial Executive', *BusinessWorld* 1–3 (20 September 2001), 1, where the author observed that the costs of litigation were so high in Hong Kong that often victims do not bring lawsuits even though the wrongdoer has clearly violated the law. See also 'High Legal Cost Sparks Reform Call', *Sunday Morning Post*, 3 October 1999, p. 2.

7.2.2 *Appointment of a receiver*

If the debtor is a corporation, the power to appoint a receiver is commonly contained in the debtor's debenture creating a fixed charge and floating charge.[24] The debenture usually contains the following clause:

> If default in payment of any moneys hereby secured has occurred then the Bank may, without notice, by writing under the hand of the Managing Director of the Bank or any other officer of the Bank for the time being in Hong Kong appoint such person or persons as it thinks fit to be a Receiver or Receivers of the property and assets comprised in this security.[25]

If the debtor is a non-corporate debtor and the security device is governed by the Bills of Sale Ordinance and the Ordinance does not give the creditor such a power. This statutory limitation creates an anomaly between the Bills of Sale Ordinance and the Companies Ordinance. If the debtor were a corporation and had granted the creditor a security, which is registrable as a bill of sale (had the debtor been a corporation), the Companies Ordinance would not prohibit the creditor from obtaining an express power to appoint a receiver.

In the absence of an express power to appoint a receiver, the creditor has to apply to the Court of First Instance under §21(L) of the High Court Ordinance for an order appointing a receiver. The court will grant the order if it is satisfied that the security is in jeopardy. In Hong Kong, court-appointed receiverships are rare. This is because the procedure is expensive, and the creditor is exposed to the risk of damages if the claim is unsuccessful.[26] In Hong Kong, in the case of a corporate debtor, the creditor usually appoints a receiver under an express power.

The primary function of the receiver is to realise the company debtor's assets comprised in the security, distribute the proceeds of sale to the secured creditor in satisfaction of its claims, and return any surplus or unrealised assets to the company debtor, which may continue with its business or, if it is insolvent, go into liquidation.

[24] For example, see the charge documents of Baker & McKenzie, Clifford Chance, Deacons, Johnnie Yam, Jacky Lee & Co. and Linklaters, which contain such power.

[25] This clause can be found in all the sample debentures of Baker & McKenzie, Clifford Chance, Deacons, Johnnie Yam, Jackie Lee & Co. and Linklaters.

[26] See S. Fennell, 'Court-Appointed Receiverships – A Missed Opportunity?', *TILP* 14 (1998), 208. The observation was made in the context of England, but it is submitted it should also apply in Hong Kong.

To enable the receiver to discharge that function effectively, the standard debenture in Hong Kong usually confers upon the receiver extensive powers. They typically include the following:

- to take possession of the charged asset;
- to manage and carry on any business of the chargor;
- to sell, transfer, assign, exchange, hire out, lend or otherwise dispose of or realise the charged assets;
- to hive down the assets of the chargor;[27]
- to borrow or raise money either unsecured or on the security of the charged assets;
- to grant leases, tenancies, licences and rights of user, grant renewals and accept surrenders of leases, tenancies, licences or rights of user;
- to insure the charged assets; and
- to bring, prosecute, enforce, defend and abandon actions, suits, and proceedings in relation to the charged assets.

According to general law, the receiver is the agent of the creditor (chargee). However, to avoid being liable for the acts and omissions of the receiver, standard debentures in Hong Kong expressly provide that the receiver is the agent of the debtor (chargor), and the debtor alone is responsible for the receiver's contracts, engagements, acts, omissions, defaults and losses and for liabilities incurred by the receiver.[28] This does not, however, alter the general law that the receiver exercises its powers as agent of the creditor. In *Emsworth Ltd v Howard William Burdett*,[29] a company had agreed to build Burdett a yacht. After Burdett paid part of the purchase price, debenture holders of the company appointed a receiver in respect of the company business. The receiver sold the business to Emsworth. Burdett claimed that since no notice was given of the transfer of the business, Emsworth was liable for the liabilities of the company.[30]

[27] This involves the incorporation of a new company and the transfer of the chargor assets to the new company. The new company is then sold off as a going concern; as the assets are free from encumbrances the new company can obtain a higher value.

[28] Clause 15.4 of sample debenture of Linklaters, Hong Kong. Also clause 8(c) of sample debenture provided by Deacons, Hong Kong. Such clauses are valid; see *Standard Chartered Bank Ltd v Walker* [1982] 3 All ER 938, [1982] 1 WLR 1410.

[29] [1978] HKLR 506.

[30] Section 3 of the Fraudulent Transfers of Business Ordinance provides, 'Whenever any business or any portion of any business is transferred, with or without the goodwill or any portion thereof, the transferee ... shall become liable for all the liabilities arising out of the carrying of the business by the transferor, unless due notice in accordance with this section has been given and has become complete at the date of the transfer.'

The Court of Appeal held that Emsworth was not liable, as the receiver was appointed by the debenture holders to enforce their security. The receiver was not acting on behalf of the company, which had no power to prevent the sale, for the deeming clause of the debentures deemed the receiver the agent of the company in respect of liability for the acts and defaults of the receiver and manager only.

However, a deeming clause, such as the one in *Emsworth Ltd*, will not relieve the creditor of liability for the consequences of the acts or defaults of the receiver, if the acts or defaults were a result of the creditor's direct interference with the receiver's discharge of its functions and duties.[31]

The appointment of a receiver under a debenture is not, generally, a popular remedy in Hong Kong. This is because it is not, generally, an effective remedy, for various reasons. Firstly, it is only a short-term solution to give the debtor a breathing space to rearrange its financial or management affairs, or to wait for the right market conditions to dispose of the mortgaged property. Secondly, the cost of receivership is generally high,[32] and those costs are charged to the debtor's account. Thus, unless the debtor's business can generate sufficient income to meet the costs, it is not economically worthwhile to appoint a receiver. Thirdly, the appointment process is cumbersome. If the creditor wishes to appoint a receiver, it must ensure that the special procedure prescribed by the Companies Ordinance (Cap. 32) is complied with. The creditor has to lodge notice of appointment of receiver with the Registrar of Companies within seven days of the date of the appointment.[33] The receiver has to give notice of its appointment to the company debtor.[34] The company debtor then has to notify the appointment of the receiver in all documents where the name of the company appears, such as the company's invoices, orders for goods or business letters.[35] This special procedure is intended to protect the public that are dealing with the company.

Currently, the powers and authority of the receiver are either expressly or impliedly conferred by the debenture or court order, as the case may

31 See *Standard Chartered Bank v Walker* [1982] 3 All ER 938, [1982] 1 WLR 1410.

32 There are no statistics on the fees charged by receivers. But by analogy to fees charged by liquidators, they are high. The high fees have been criticised by the Hong Kong courts – for example, see *Re Peregrine Investments Holdings Ltd and Others* [1999] 3 HKC 91, CA, where the liquidators' fee amounted to HK$93 million; and also *Re Rhine Holding Ltd (in liquidation)* [2000] 3 HKC 543, where there were no valuable assets, the fees were HK$9.3 million.

33 Companies Ordinance (Cap. 32), §87(1).

34 Ibid., §300A(1)(a).

35 Ibid., §299(1).

be. As a result, the extent and nature of the receiver's powers are not well defined or easily understood by either the creditor or the debtor.

On the basis of the above, it is clear that the creditor's remedy of appointing a receiver is generally clear and has satisfied the enforcement criterion that the creditor's remedies must be certain.[36] The criterion that the amount of money which the creditor is entitled to recover under the security arrangement must be certain is not relevant here. However, the remedy of appointing a receiver is cumbersome and uneconomical in many cases where the costs outweigh the economic benefit, particularly where the loans are large and the value of the assets is low. It is therefore submitted that the remedy of appointing a receiver has not satisfied the other two enforcement criteria of inexpensiveness and expeditiousness. Thus the creditor's remedy of appointing a receiver must be regarded as inefficient.

7.2.3 Foreclosure

Foreclosure is a process whereby the debtor's right to redeem the secured property is declared by the court to be extinguished and the creditor is left as the absolute owner of the property. This is one of the remedies of the equitable mortgagee and equitable chargee.[37] In relation to personal chattels, the Bills of Sale Ordinance is silent. Presumably this general right of the creditor is unaffected.

There are, however, three weaknesses in foreclosure from the viewpoint of the creditor. Firstly, the balance of the debt, if any, is extinguished because the creditor's assumption of the ownership of the property is taken as full satisfaction of the balance of the debt. Secondly, foreclosure is an expensive and slow remedy, as it requires a court order.[38] Thirdly, if the tangible personal property is not commercially useful to the creditors, foreclosure is not of practical utility. Consequently, creditors in Hong Kong do not resort to foreclosure in respect of tangible personal property.[39]

[36] See Chapter 1 above. [37] Sykes and Walker, above, note 5, p. 616.

[38] The waiting time in the Court of First Instance is approximately 180 days from receipt of the application to fix the date of the hearing; see www.info.gov.hk/jud/guide2cs/.

[39] Foreclosure is also not a popular remedy in England in respect of personal property; see A.P. Bell, *Modern Law of Personal Property in England and Ireland* (London: Butterworths, 1989), p. 186. The same also seems to apply in Australia, where Sykes and Walker, above, note 5, p. 609, note that foreclosure only had theoretical significance.

Thus, on the basis of the above, except for the enforcement criterion relating to certainty of remedies of the creditor, foreclosure has not satisfied the enforcement criteria of expeditiousness or inexpensiveness. Further, it is not a practical remedy. Thus foreclosure must be regarded as an inefficient remedy. The criterion that the amount of money recoverable by the creditor under the security arrangement must be certain is not relevant here.

7.2.4 Sale

Sale is the most popular remedy in respect of tangible personal property in Hong Kong. It has been described as the central remedy of the secured creditor of personal property.[40] It is not widely used in respect of intangible personal property, except in shares of companies and quotas, such as textile export quotas. The discussion following will consider the remedy of sale under the headings of pledge, and mortgage and charge.

Pledge

In Hong Kong, a pledgee–creditor of tangible personal property has an implied power of sale.[41] However, there are two restrictions on the creditor's right to exercise its power. Firstly, the pledgor–debtor must have defaulted in the repayment of the loan. Secondly, the pledgee–creditor must have given notice to the pledgor–debtor of its intention to sell the property.[42] The pledgor–debtor may, however, redeem the property at any time before the sale by paying the monies due and owing and all proper costs and expenses incurred by the creditor in exercising the power of sale.[43] There is no special legislation governing the procedure in effecting the sale, except where the pledge is governed by the Pawnbrokers Ordinance (Cap. 166),[44] which is outside the parameters of this book.

Mortgage and charge

In Hong Kong, whether or not a mortgagee–creditor has an implied power of sale is not entirely clear in respect of tangible personal property.

[40] English Law Commission Consultation Paper No 164, para. B 46; and Consultation Paper No 176, para. 5.62.

[41] In Hong Kong it is implied by general law; see *Deverges v Sandeman, Clark & Co.* [1902] 1 Ch 579; and see also the English Law Commission Consultation Paper No 164, para. B 34. Note that in China it is contained in Article 63 of the Security Law.

[42] *Re Morritt, ex parte Official Receiver* (1886) 18 QBD 222, p. 232, *per* Cotton LJ.

[43] Ibid. [44] Basically it is a consumer protection ordinance.

According to *Fisher & Lightwood's Law of Mortgage*,[45] the mortgagee, legal or equitable, of tangible personal property has an implied power of sale if possession of the property has been delivered to it. On the other hand, Sykes and Walker seem to imply that a legal mortgagee 'always has the power to sell the legal title',[46] whether or not it has possession of the property. The authors thought that the prerequisite of possession propounded in the early case of *Re Morritt, ex parte Official Receiver*,[47] on which *Fisher & Lightwood's Law of Mortgage* relied as authority, was wrong. They do not, however, cite any authorities to support their argument.[48] On the other hand, Fry J in his dissenting judgment in *Morritt* doubted if such an implied power existed. If Sykes and Walker are correct, it would seem that an equitable mortgagee does not have an implied power of sale. This would put this view at odds with their earlier argument,[49] that the equitable mortgagee should enjoy the same remedy of taking possession as the legal mortgagee on the grounds of 'equity regards that as done that ought to be done'. Bell took a stricter view and opined that the mortgagee, legal or equitable, has no such power, as there is no authority to suggest otherwise.[50]

It is submitted that the uncertainty of the law in this area is untenable for two reasons. Firstly, the reason a pledgee has an implied power of sale but the mortgagee of tangible personal property has no such implied power (assuming the above majority view is correct) has never been explained. Vaughan Williams LJ criticised this artificial distinction in *Deverges v Sandeman, Clark & Co.*[51] He said,[52]

> I wish at once to say that I do not think that the circumstances which will give rise to an implication of a power of sale in favour of a mortgagee of a chattel, or even of stock or shares, can differ in favour of the mortgagee from those which are necessary to give a right of sale to a pledgee. In both cases the creditor holding security is allowed, as against the debtor in default, to enlarge his interest or estate.

In England, this issue is academic insofar as the mortgage, legal or equitable, of personal property is by deed, because §101 of the Law

45 Tyler, above, note 1, p. 378. 46 Sykes and Walker, above, note 5, p. 609.
47 (1886) 18 QBD 222, CA.
48 English Law Commission Consultation Paper No 164, para. B 34, seems to support Sykes and Walker, but was uncertain in respect of equitable mortgages.
49 See above in this chapter.
50 He argued that if such power existed, there was no necessity for the statutory power under the Conveyancing Act 1881; see Bell, above, note 39, p. 186.
51 [1902] 1 Ch 579. 52 Ibid., 588.

of Property Act 1925 implies a power of sale into such mortgages. In Hong Kong, the Conveyancing and Property Ordinance, which implies a power of sale into all mortgages by deed, only applies to land. The problem is therefore real in Hong Kong in respect of tangible personal property.

Secondly, the distinction between the legal mortgage and the equitable mortgage for the purpose of determining whether the power of sale exists is also artificial. Both are security devices and on the basis of equity's maxim 'equity regards that as done which ought to be done' the equitable mortgagee should be entitled to the same remedy.

However, the uncertainty of the law has not caused serious difficulties in practice, as might be thought at first sight, for the following reasons:

- In corporate commercial lending, the debenture usually confers an express power of sale on the creditor.[53]
- In non-corporate commercial lending, the Bills of Sale Ordinance implies a power of sale in every bill of sale by way of security. The circumstances under which the power of sale is exercisable and its limitations have already been discussed earlier.[54]
- In the absence of an express power or statutorily implied power, a creditor may apply to the court for an order of sale under Order 29, rule 4, of the High Court Rules. This rule gives the court the power to make an interim order for the sale of personal property, which is of perishable nature, or likely to deteriorate if kept, or if for any other reason it is desirable to dispose of the property.[55] The secured property will, under the supervision of the court,[56] be sold free from the debtor's equity of redemption. But this process is expensive.

[53] On the basis of samples of Baker & McKenzie, Clifford Chance, Deacons, Johnnie Yam, Jacky Lee & Co. and Linklaters.

[54] See above in this chapter.

[55] See the English case of *On Demand Information plc and Another (in administrative receivership) v Michael Gerson (Finance) plc and Another* [2003] 1 AC 368, where the court, under the equivalent RSC Order 29, rule 4, granted an order of sale pending the court's determination of whether it had jurisdiction to grant relief against forfeiture. The court subsequently held that it did.

[56] Order 75, rule 23, of the Rules of High Court (Cap. 4A) lays down the procedure for effecting the sale of property under an order of the court. It is noted that while the Civil Justice Reforms 2008 in Hong Kong took effect from 2 April 2009, Order 75 remained largely unchanged. In England, the courts in some cases are sometimes inclined to make such an order even where there is an express power of sale outside court; see English Law Commission Consultation Paper No 164, para. B 35; and see also R.M. Goode, *Commercial Law*, 2nd ed. (London: Penguin, 1995), pp. 691–2.

If the sale is effected under an express power, the property can be sold by public auction or by private treaty.[57]

In the case of secured intangible personal property comprising shares and stocks, insurance policies, and other things in action, it is clear that the secured creditor, legal or equitable, has an implied power of sale.[58] In the English case of *Stubbs v Slatter*,[59] clients of a stockbroker had deposited certain share certificates ('the shares') together with duly executed blank transfers with the stockbroker as security for its running account with the stockbroker. When the clients defaulted in payment of monies owed to the stockbroker under the account, the stockbroker, after repeated demands, sold the shares. The clients sued the stockbroker, *inter alia*, for damages for wrongful conversion on the ground that the stockbroker had no power to sell the shares. The Court of Appeal unanimously rejected the ground and held that the equitable mortgagee had an implied power to sell the shares after reasonable notice had been given to the mortgagor.[60] A similar conclusion was arrived at in the earlier Court of Appeal case of *Deverges v Sandeman, Clark & Co.*,[61] where the security took the form of a legal mortgage. An important point in that case was the court's decision that a month's notice, or even less, may be regarded as reasonable.

The court has not provided a clear rationale for the special treatment of the realisation of security over shares, stocks and other things in action. In *Deverges*,[62] however, the submission of one of the counsel suggested that the reason was one of commercial convenience – that is, commercial persons, owing to pressing matters of business, have no time for a formal mortgage granting an express power, or to apply to the court for a decree of sale or foreclosure. Thus they should be given security that was readily realisable to recover their capital. If this is good reason for shares and stocks, it is difficult to understand why it should not also be good reason that such power should also be implied in security over tangible personal property, *a fortiori*, when the goods are easily perishable.

When and how the creditor exercises the power of sale is governed by the general rules governing the power of sale of land.[63] On the basis of

57 *Bourne v Wall* (1891) 64 LT 530.

58 Tyler, above, note 1, p. 378, citing *Wilson v Tooker* (1714) 5 Broc PC 193, 2 ER 622; *Lockwood v Ever* (1742) 2 Atk 303, 26 ER 585; *Kemp v Westbrook* (1749) 1 Ves Sen 278, 27 ER 1030; *Re Morritt, ex parte Official Receiver* (1886) 18 QBD 222, CA.

59 [1910] 1 Ch 632.

60 Ibid., *per* Cozens Hardy MR; the other justices, Buckley LJ and Joyce J, concurred.

61 [1902] 1 Ch 579.

62 Ibid. at pp. 584–5.

63 See *The China and South Sea Bank Ltd v Tan Soon-gin, George alias George Tan* [1990] 1 HKLR 546, PC, a case involving the sale of shares by the mortgagee. There rules governing

authorities in Hong Kong and England, the rules governing the creditor's power of sale can be summarised as follows:

- The mortgagee–creditor is not a trustee of the power of sale for the mortgagor–debtor. The power is given to the mortgagee–creditor for its own benefit to enable it to better realise the debt.[64]
- The mortgagee–creditor and the receiver are not under any form of duty to exercise the power of sale. They may exercise the power of sale as and when they choose, or not at all.[65]
- When a mortgagee–creditor or receiver exercises a power of sale, it owes the mortgagor, subsequent encumbrances and surety a duty to act in good faith without corruption or collusion with the purchaser and a duty to take such precautions as a reasonable man of business would take to obtain the full market value of the property.[66]

In *The China and South Sea Bank Ltd v Tan Soon-gin, George alias George Tan*,[67] the court observed that the general rules were aimed at balancing the interests of the creditor and the debtor. There, the guarantor who was also the controller of the debtor company claimed in its defence that the bank/creditor had breached its duty of care owing to the guarantor when it did not sell the mortgaged shares until the shares became worthless. The Judicial Committee of the Privy Council, differing from the Hong Kong Court of Appeal, held that the bank/creditor had not breached its duty of care because it was not under a duty to exercise its power of sale over the mortgaged securities at any particular time. To hold otherwise would have subjected the bank/creditor to overly onerous duties and liabilities.

One final point must be made on the power of sale. There has been some judicial and academic debate over whether the duty to obtain the

the power of sale of a mortgagee of land were considered and applied. In the Hong Kong case of *UTG Investment (Far East) Ltd v Petra Bank and Another* [1995] 2 HKC 157, the Court of Appeal held that the equity of redemption, which applied to mortgages of real property, also applied to mortgages of choses in action.

64 *The China and South Sea Bank Ltd v Tan Soon-gin, George alias George Tan* [1990] 1 HKLR 546, PC.

65 Ibid.

66 *Tse Kwong Lam v Wong Chit Sen and Others* [1983] 1 WLR 1349, PC; *The China and South Sea Bank Ltd v Tan Soon-gin, George alias George Tan* [1990] 1 HKLR 546; and *Downsview Nominees Ltd and Another v First City Corporation Ltd and Another* [1993] 2 WLR 86. Note that the Crowther Report, para. 5.618, proposed that the sale must be commercially reasonable in time, price and manner. It is submitted the proposal does not impose any greater burden than the duties under general law.

67 [1990] 1 HKLR 546.

full market value of the property arises from the tort of negligence or from equity.[68] More recently, however, the courts have regarded the debate as frivolous, although on balance the duty rests in equity. They thought, for practical purposes, that it does not really matter whether it is one or the other, for the court will in any case award damages to the mortgagor–debtor if there is a breach.[69]

If the mortgage is a bill of sale within the Bills of Sale Ordinance, special rules apply. The creditor can only sell the goods after the expiry of five days from the date of seizure of the goods.[70] During this period the debtor may apply to the court for relief. The court may, if satisfied that the debtor is able to satisfy the debt by tendering payment or for other sufficient reasons, restrain the debtor from selling the goods.[71]

The remedy of sale is not generally applicable to book debts and other debts, although unrealised book debts or other debts can be sold for less than the amount they represent. In cases of security over unrealised book debts or other debts, the proceeds are collected to settle the debt.[72] In practice, where a bank has taken a security[73] over its customer's account, such as a fixed time deposit, to secure advances provided by the same bank, the bank enforces the security by merging the debtor–customer's credits and debits to take account of the debts owed. This is effected by the bank exercising the right of set-off or combining accounts,[74] or on the grounds that the bank has a better claim over the collateral.

[68] See E.L.G. Tyler, 'Enforcing Mortgage Securities', *ALJ* 55 (1981), 559; P. Davies and N. Palmer, 'Guaranteeing Concern for Guarantors', *Conv* (1981), 329; S. Robinson, 'Mortgages – Care and Protection 1', *Conv* (1981), 339; S. Robinson, 'Mortgage Protection Provisions – 2', *Conv* (1981), 412; L. Bently, 'Mortgagee's Duties on Sale – No Place for Tort?', *Conv* (1990), 431; R.J. Wickins and C.A. Ong, 'Duties of Mortgagees and Receivers: Common Law or Equity?', *HKLJ* 24 (1994), 89; and P. Devonshire, 'The Mortgagee's Power of Sale: A Defining Moment?', *NZBLQ* 7 (2001), 104. See also English Law Commission Consultation Paper No 164, para. B 41, where the Law Commission expressed the view that the duty was equitable.

[69] In *Medforth v Blake* [1999] All ER 97, 111, Scott VC said, 'I do not, for my part, think it matters one jot whether the duty is expressed as a common law duty or as a duty in equity. The result is the same.'

[70] Section 17 of the Bills of Sale Ordinance. [71] Ibid., §14.

[72] See *ABN Amro Bank NV v Chiyu Banking Corp Ltd and Others* [2000] 3 HKC 381.

[73] Under §15A of the Law Amendment and Reform (Consolidation) Ordinance of Hong Kong, a customer can charge its credit balance to the same bank. For detailed discussion on this see Chapter 3 above.

[74] 'Set-off' and 'combination of accounts' mean the same thing in banking law and practice. See B.C.S. Chan, *Hong Kong Banking Law and Practice* (Hong Kong: Hong Kong Institute of Bankers, 2000), p. 54.

The creditor's power of sale basically suffers from the same weaknesses as the creditor's right to take possession discussed above. Whilst the law is clear on the purpose of the power of sale and the duties of the creditor when it exercises it, the law is uncertain as to whether or not the security device obtained by the creditor gives it the power of sale in the first place. This is because whether the creditor enjoys the power of sale depends upon several factors – namely the juridical nature of the security device and the personal property. Further, the situations where a creditor does or does not automatically enjoy a power of sale are highly artificial. As in the case of the right to take possession, the law on power of sale is equally out of step with commercial reality, where the power of sale is usually provided by express agreement between the creditor and debtor. However, if the creditor has the power of sale, the exercise of the power is usually expeditious and inexpensive and the amount of money which the creditor is entitled to recover under the security arrangement is usually certain. In the vast majority of the cases, the aid of the court is not necessary.

But as the law governing the creditor's power of sale has not in theory satisfied the enforcement criterion relating to the certainty of remedies, the power of sale has to be regarded as inefficient.

7.3 Remedies of the quasi-security holder in Hong Kong

For the purposes of this part, unless otherwise stated, the expression

'creditor' means the quasi-security holder under the hire-purchase, leasing and conditional sale transactions, and

'debtor' means the hirer, lessee and conditional buyer under the hire-purchase, leasing and conditional sale transactions, respectively.

7.3.1 Right to take possession and power of sale of the creditor under conditional sale

If the retention-of-title clause under a conditional sale of goods is effective and the debtor has defaulted in repayment of the debt, the creditor, as legal owner, is entitled to recover the goods or the proceeds representing the goods from the debtor, or third parties, who took with notice of the clause, are so entitled. When the creditor has recovered the goods, it is entitled to sell the goods.

However, in practice, these remedies are not always easy to exercise because, as discussed above in Chapter 5, the validity of the retention-of-title clause is often challenged by competing claimants, such as the secured creditors and general creditors of the debtor, in the event of insolvency of the debtor. Thus it may be only after lengthy and expensive litigation where the court determines that the retention-of-title clause is valid that the creditor may exercise the remedies of taking possession and sale of the goods.

The creditor's right of sale suffers from two other uncertainties. Firstly, if the goods are sold and there is a surplus, is the creditor entitled to keep the surplus? It was originally contended that the creditor was entitled to the surplus, as the creditor was the owner of the goods. However, it is also suggested that this would be unjust, as the creditor unfairly obtains a 'windfall'. Therefore the creditor could be made accountable to the buyer on the grounds of unjust enrichment. The issue is still open, as the court in the case of *Clough Mill Ltd v Martin*,[75] which initiated the debate, held that the retention-of-title clause created a charge.[76] The English Law Commission in its Consultation Paper No 164 thought that the state of current law relating to a transaction involving a quasi-security was that 'there is no obligation to account for any surplus from the sale of the repossessed goods'.[77] This is in sharp contrast with traditional security, where the creditor must account to the debtor for any surplus above the amount of the secured sum including costs, charges and expenses that have been properly incurred by the creditor.[78] The Law Commission was critical of the difference. It commented,[79]

> quasi-securities are treated differently from securities in that the former are not subject to the same rules on default. Under a mortgage, for example, any surplus achievable on resale would have to be returned to the debtor; under a quasi-security such as a resale and lease-back it would be retained by the lender. Despite both transactions being designed to achieve the same purpose – acting to secure repayment or the performance of an obligation – they are treated in different ways by the law.

This illustrates the tension generated by the current law's emphasis on form over substance. The Law Commission recommended that creditors who are quasi-security holders should account for the surplus, if any, when goods are sold.[80] The second uncertainty arises when there is a deficiency

[75] [1985] 1 WLR 111, CA.

[76] Ibid., at pp. 119–20, where Robert Goff LJ stated, *obiter*, that a reservation-of-title clause could constitute an equitable charge.

[77] English Law Commission Consultation Paper No 164, para. B 49.

[78] Ibid., para. B 49. [79] Ibid., para. 7.9. [80] Ibid., paras. B 47–B 50.

after the sale: is the creditor entitled to sue for the deficiency? There is no authority on this point whilst commentators are divided.[81] However, the Law Commission also pointed out a practical factor by which lenders are not concerned with recovering more than the capital and interest that is due to them, plus any expenses they have incurred. They would be content for any surplus to be returned to the debtor, even by way of well-drawn agreements with the debtor.[82]

In view of the above, it is submitted, except in very clear, straightforward situations, the rules governing the remedies of possession and sale of the creditor have not satisfied four enforcement criteria, namely certainty of remedies, expedition, inexpensiveness and certainty of amount of monies that are recoverable by the creditor under the security arrangement.

7.3.2 Right to take possession and power of sale of creditor under hire-purchase and leasing

In Hong Kong, when the debtor under a hire-purchase or leasing agreement defaults in payment of the inslatment payments, the creditor terminates the bailment, takes possession of the goods and sells the goods. Unlike conditional sale, these remedies are rarely disputed, because they are usually determined by the contract of hire-purchase and leasing,[83] and the goods rarely lose their identity.[84] There is no special legislation governing the exercise of these remedies in Hong Kong. The right of the creditor to exercise the remedies is therefore settled, effective and does not give rise to substantive problems.

However, there is one problem concerning an ancillary remedy of the creditor; that is, the amount of money the creditor is entitled to recover from the debtor after the goods are sold and where there is a deficiency.

To understand how the law deals with the problem one must begin with the question of what precisely is the amount of money the creditor is entitled to under the hire-purchase or leasing agreement in the event of default by the debtor. There is no deficiency unless the amount to which the creditor is lawfully entitled is less than the realised value of the goods.

Hire-purchase and leasing agreements usually give the creditor the right to forfeit the deposit paid by the debtor and the right to a minimum

[81] Chapter 5 above.

[82] English Law Commission Consultation Paper No 176, paras. 2.110, 5.160.

[83] This has been discussed in Chapter 5 above.

[84] Except where it becomes a fixture; see Chapter 6 above.

payment when the hire-purchase or lease is terminated prematurely.[85] That appears simple. However, cases in Hong Kong and other common law jurisdictions show that the law relating to the validity of these rights is highly complex.

One issue that can be discerned clearly from these cases is that the courts do not easily allow the creditor to exercise such rights under the hire-purchase and leasing agreements without first scrutinising the agreements closely. For this purpose, the courts, in respect of the right to minimum payment, resort to the rule against penalty in contract law. As this topic is sufficiently discussed in major textbooks,[86] no discussion on the nature of the rule is offered here. Reference will, however, be made to the identification in the English Law Commission's Working Paper No 61 of the areas where the rule is and is not relevant.[87]

According to the Law Commission, the rule against penalty applies to cases where the hire-purchase and leasing[88] agreements are terminated as a result of a breach of the agreements by the debtor (hereinafter referred to as situation A). The creditor can effect the termination or it can be automatically terminated according to the terms of the contract.[89]

The rule does not apply to two situations. Firstly, where the debtor voluntarily terminates the agreement under a power conferred on it by the agreement (hereinafter referred to as situation B1).[90] Secondly, where the

[85] See Chapter 5 above.

[86] For general discussion on the rule against penalty, see J. Beatson, *Anson's Law of Contract*, 27th ed. (Oxford: Oxford University Press, 1998), pp. 587–92; G.H. Treitel, *Law of Contract*, 10th ed. (London: Sweet & Maxwell, 1999), pp. 929–32; and B. Ho, *Hong Kong Contract Law*, 2nd ed. (Hong Kong: Butterworths Asia, 1994), pp. 469–73.

[87] Working Paper No 61, *Penalty Clauses and Forfeiture of Monies Paid* (London: HMSO, 1975), para. 19, pp. 340–79, referring to the cases of *Associated Distributors Ltd v Hall* [1938] 1 All ER 511; *Cooden Engineering Co. Ltd v Stanford* [1953] 1 QB 86, CA; *Campbell Discount Co. Ltd v Bridge* [1962] AC 600, HL; *Financing Ltd v Baldock* [1963] 1 All ER 443; *Anglo-Auto Finance Co. Ltd v James* [1963] 3 All ER 566; *United Dominions Trust (Commercial) Ltd v Ennis* [1967] 2 All ER 345. For academics sharing this view see Ho, above, note 86, p. 183; and J. Ziegel, 'The Minimum Payment Clause Muddle', *CLJ* (1964), 108.

[88] The view is that the rule also applies to both hire-purchase and leasing in Hong Kong. See I.A. Tokley, *Hong Kong Banking Law and Practice* (Hong Kong: Butterworths Asia, 1998), paras. 804–1002.

[89] The authorities are: *Elsey & Co. Ltd v Hyde* (unreported, 1926), reference in C.G. Jones and R. Proudfoot, *Notes on Hire-Purchase Law*, 2nd ed. (London: Butterworth & Co., 1930), p. 124; *Chester & Cole Ltd v Wright* (1930), reference in ibid., p. 124; *Associated Distributors Ltd v Hall* [1938] 1 All ER 511.

[90] Cases supporting this proposition include *Associated Distributors Ltd v Hall* [1938] 1 All ER 511; *Re Apex Supply Co. Ltd* [1941] 3 All ER 473; *Campbell Discount Co. Ltd v Bridge* [1961] 1 QB 445.

agreement is terminated on the occurrence of agreed events, which do not involve the exercise of an option to terminate or a breach of contract (hereinafter referred to as situation B2).[91]

In Hong Kong, there is no authority on what constitutes 'agreed events' in situation B2.[92] There are, however, English authorities that the 'agreed events' may include death, bankruptcy or winding-up, as in the case of a company debtor. In *Re Apex*,[93] the hire-purchase agreement allowed the creditor to take possession of the hired machinery if the debtor, inter alia, went into liquidation, compulsorily or voluntarily. The hire-purchase agreement further provided that when the agreement was terminated, the debtor was liable to pay a minimum sum to the finance company. The debtor went into liquidation and the liquidator alleged that the minimum-payment clause was a penalty. The court rejected the allegation. Simons J held that the question of penalty against liquidated damages did not arise, as there was a contract for the payment of a certain sum in a certain event, and that event having happened, that sum was payable.[94] *Re Apex* seems now beyond doubt in light of *Export Credits Guarantee Dept v Universal Oil Products*.[95] There Waller LJ at the Court of Appeal observed, *obiter*, that where the contract provides for a sum of money payable on the happening of an event, no question of a penalty arises and the court will not grant any relief.

The English authorities give two reasons for excluding the rule against penalties from situations B1 and B2. Firstly, the debtor had freely elected to terminate the agreement.[96] Consequently, there was no breach of contract to attract the rule against penalty. Secondly, it has never been the function of the courts to relieve a party from a contract on the mere ground that it proves to be onerous or imprudent.[97] The exclusion was applied in the English cases of *Associated Distributors Ltd v Hall*[98] and *Re Apex Supply Co. Ltd*.[99] Essentially, in each of these cases the debtor was given an

[91] *Re Apex Supply Co. Ltd* [1941] 3 All ER 473; and also *Export Credits Guarantee Dept v Universal Oil Products* [1983] 2 All ER 205, where Waller LJ approved *Re Apex Supply Co. Ltd*.

[92] Tokley, above, note 88, para. 952. [93] [1941] 3 All ER 473.

[94] Ibid., p. 481. [95] [1983] 2 All ER 205.

[96] *Associated Distributors Ltd v Hall* [1938] 1 All ER 511, 513, *per* Slesser LJ.

[97] *Export Credits Guarantee Department v Universal Oil Products Co.* [1983] 2 All ER 205. Note the view of Goode, above note 56, p. 387, that the matter was still open as the House of Lords in *Bridge v Campbell Discount Co. Ltd* has to be reconsidered in view of *Export Credits Department*.

[98] [1938] 1 All ER 511.

[99] [1941] 3 All ER 473; and also *Bridge v Campbell Discount Co. Ltd* [1962] AC 600. Principles were laid down in the *Hall* and *Re Apex Supply Co. Ltd* cases. In *Bridge*, the House of Lords

option to terminate the hire but subject to paying the finance company a minimum payment. In both cases the court held that the debtor was liable to pay the minimum payment when it exercised the option. The question whether the agreed minimum payment was a penalty did not arise. In *Associated Distributors Ltd*, Slesser LJ stated the position of the law as follows:[100]

> This is a case where the hirer has elected to terminate the hiring. He has exercised an option ... It follows in this case that no question of penalty or liquidated damage arises at all, and, therefore, that the money for which the hirer has made himself liable must be paid, and cannot be impeached on any principle of law.

The approaches in *Associated Distributors Ltd* and *Re Apex Supply Co. Ltd* were affirmed by Lord Roskill in the subsequent House of Lords case of *Export Credits Guarantee Department v Universal Oil Products Co.*[101] In rejecting the defendant/debtor's claim that the stipulated liability under a recourse agreement was a penalty, Lord Roskill said,[102]

> My Lords, the reason why the defendants' submissions failed in the courts below can be simply stated. The clause was not a penalty clause because it provided for payment of money on the happening of a specified event other than a breach of a contractual duty owed by the contemplated payer to the contemplated payee ...[103]

Although *Export Credits Guarantee Department* was not a hire-purchase case, the observation of Lord Roskill has broad application.[104]

The current state of dividing up the circumstances into situations A, B1 and B2 and confining the rule of penalty to situation A has been criticised as artificial, especially in respect of situation B1. This is because both, in substance, are the same.[105] Thus, in *Bridge v Campbell Discount*

disagreed with the Court of Appeal and held that the hirer breached the agreement and therefore the rule against penalty, and consequently the minimum-payment clause was a penalty. However, it is submitted that this decision did not abrogate basic principles as the House of Lords' decision was based on interpretation rather than substance.

[100] [1938] 1 All ER 511, p. 513. The other justices, Scott and Clauson LJJ, concurred.

[101] [1983] 2 All ER 205. [102] [1983] 2 All ER 205.

[103] The High Court of Australia in *AMEV-UDC Finance Ltd v Austin and Another* [1986] 68 ALR 185 approved the English court's approach.

[104] However, in Hong Kong, if the hirer were a consumer, the court may under the Unconscionable Contracts Ordinance (1994) examine the minimum-payment clause (§3). If the minimum-payment clause is unconscionable, the court may refuse to enforce the clause or may revise it (§5). The full impact of the Ordinance will not be discussed further as this book is strictly confined to non-consumer security arrangements.

[105] *Cooden Engineering Co. Ltd v Stanford* [1953] 1 QB 86, CA, *per* Hodgson LJ.

Co. Ltd,[106] Lord Denning commented that the law on this point was untenable and ridiculous. He said, 'Let no one mistake the injustice of this. It means that equity commits itself to this absurd paradox: it will grant relief to a man who breaks his contract but will penalise the man who keeps it.' He further thought that equity was not sterile and should play a more robust role in granting relief not only against penalties for breach of contract, but also against penalties for non-performance of a condition.[107] Goode agreed and commented,

> the rule against penalties as developed by the cases, is not strong on logic but does indicate a feeling on the part of the courts that a hire-purchase agreement should be taken at face value and should not be treated as merely another form of conditional sale.[108]

However, in view of the Privy Council's observation in the Hong Kong case of *Philips Hong Kong Ltd v The Attorney General of Hong Kong*,[109] it appears that Lord Denning's dictum is unlikely to be adopted in Hong Kong. In *Philips*, Lord Woolf mentioned the paradox and Lord Denning's criticism, but did not develop it further. The Australian case of *AMEV-UDC Finance v Austin and Another*[110] was less equivocal on the matter. Mason and Wilson JJ, whilst expressing sympathy with Lord Denning, were unwilling to alter the law for two reasons. Firstly, the doctrine of penalties had pursued such a tortuous path in the course of its long development that it was a risky enterprise to construct an argument on the basis of the old decisions. Secondly, the law was now so well settled that it would be inconsistent with modern authority for equity to provide its relief by imposing on the obligor a liability to pay damages which flows not from the obligor's breach of contract, but from the obligee's act in exercising his contractual right to terminate for non-fundamental breach.[111]

106 [1962] AC 600, [1962] 1 All ER 385, 399. Harman LJ at the Court of Appeal, at 458, said, 'it is unsatisfactory if the man who honestly admits to the finance company that he cannot go on may have to pay a penalty, but that if he waits for the finance company to exercise their rights and in the meanwhile breaks the contract, he may be able to escape paying it on the ground that penalty for breach of contract is not enforceable in law'.

107 Ibid., at 458.

108 Goode, above, note 56, at p. 768.

109 [1993] 1 HKLR 269 (PC).

110 [1986] 68 ALR 185, pp. 196–200.

111 Mason and Wilson JJ's dicta were strongly approved by Lord Woolf in *Philips Hong Kong Ltd v The Attorney General of Hong Kong* [1933] 1 HKLR 269, 279 (PC). Mason and Wilson JJ's views were approved in the Australian case of *Esanda Finance Corporation Ltd v Plessnig and Another* [1989] 63 ALJR 238, (1989) 166 CLR 131. Similar conservative views are also found in *Elsey v JG Insurance Agencies Ltd* (1978) 83 DLR 15; and *Robophone Facilities v Blank* [1966] 1 WLR 1428, which favoured the freedom of contract and certainty in commercial law.

However, the English Law Commission in Working Paper No 61[112] took the view that the court should have the power to deal with such clauses in the same way whether or not they come into operation by breach. It was suggested that statutory reforms in this respect should be made to cover all forms of contract.[113]

Where the rule against penalty applies, the three characteristics of a penalty established in the ordinary contract case of *Dunlop Pneumatic Tyre Ltd v New Garage & Motor Ltd*[114] have to be considered. They are: (i) when the sum stipulated is extravagant and unconscionable in amount in comparison with the greatest loss that could conceivably be proved to have followed from the breach; (ii) when the breach consists only in not paying a sum of money, and the sum stipulated is a sum greater than the sum which ought to have been paid; and (iii) when a single lump sum is payable by way of compensation, on the occurrence of one or more or all of several events, some of which may occasion serious and others but trifling damage.[115]

The three characteristics are applied on the basis that the objective of a minimum-payment clause in the hire-purchase agreement is to protect the creditor against any loss in value through depreciation of the goods repossessed or returned to it. On this basis the following principles can be established in the context of hire-purchase and leasing:

- Where the minimum-payment clause does not take into consideration the actual realisable value of the goods recovered or a discount for accelerated payment, it is likely to be struck down as a penalty. As Goode said, 'a clause designed to ensure that upon such termination the owner recovers the full price is likely to be struck down as a penalty, on the

[112] Working Paper No 61, p. 382.

[113] It is submitted that, in light of the Unconscionable Contracts Ordinance, the Hong Kong courts have wide discretion to intervene in cases of consumer hire-purchase agreements, where the minimum sum to be awarded may be unconscionable, and where the rule against penalty does not apply. The current trend in Hong Kong is to give the provisions a broad interpretation. For example, see *Midland Realty (Shatin) Limited v Lau Pui King* (DCC J 26284/98, unreported), where an agency contract freely signed by the defendant – an associate professor, a member of the PRC National People's Congress and a Justice of the Peace – was held to be unconscionable; and *Hang Seng Credit Card Limited and Others v Tsang Nga Lee and Others* [2000] HKC 210, where a term allowing the banks to recover full costs from the credit cardholders was held to be unconscionable. See also C.A. Ong and R.J. Wickins, 'Unshackling Equity's Foot: The Unconscionable Contracts Ordinance', *HKLJ* 25 (1995), 321, where the authors suggested that the Ordinance should be given the widest interpretation to protect the interests of consumers.

[114] [1915] AC 79, HL.

[115] Ibid., p. 389, *per* Lord Dunedin.

ground that it seeks to impose on the defaulting hirer a liability greater than that which he would have incurred if he had not broken the agreement but simply exercised his contractual power of termination'.[116] An English case illustrating this point is *Bridge v Campbell Discount Co. Ltd.*[117] There Lord Radcliffe held that the minimum-payment clause was a penalty on the grounds that it disregarded two considerations essential to any measurement of the creditor's loss. Firstly, the price included a significant interest element, which the creditor did not, in the result, forgo so long as the compensation was paid immediately. Secondly, the vehicle came back into the creditor's possession with a realisable value that, in many circumstances, may exceed the one-third balance of the price which the creditor has not got in. *Bridge* was followed in the Hong Kong case of *Wayfoong Credit Limited v Ho Fai.*[118] There a clause provided that upon termination of the hire-purchase agreement, the debtor had to pay the creditor a sum comprising (a) all overdue rentals, (b) all sums expended in repossession of the vehicle, (c) the estimated cost of putting the vehicle into good repair and (d) compensation for depreciation. The court held that the clause was a penalty.

- Where a minimum sum is payable irrespective of whether the creditor is in breach of a condition or a simple term,[119] which entitles the creditor to terminate the contract by virtue of the right under the agreement, it is likely to be a penalty. This type of agreement falls squarely within the criteria of *Dunlop Pneumatic Tyre Ltd.* In *Financing Ltd v Baldock,*[120] the Court of Appeal held that a clause which required the debtor to pay a minimum sum equivalent to two-thirds of the total hiring cost or the amount of all instalments and other monies, whichever is the greater, in the event 'the hiring be terminated by the hirer', was arbitrary[121] and a penalty.[122] However, it is submitted that there is a difficulty posed by *Baldock* to the creditor. It can be circumvented by including a deeming

[116] Goode, above, note 56, pp. 767–8. [117] [1962] 1 All ER 385.

[118] [1975] DCLR 130.

[119] Lord Denning in *Financings Ltd v Baldock* [1963] 2 QB 104, 113, described it as 'the failure of not going to the root of the contract, and only giving a right to terminate by virtue of an express stipulation in the contract'. In other words, it is what is termed a 'warranty' under the general law of contract, a breach of which does not entitle the owner to repudiate the contract under general law.

[120] [1963] 2 QB 104. [121] Ibid., p. 1218.

[122] This case was followed in *Wayfoong Credit Limited v Ho Fai* [1975] DCLR 130, where on the same grounds the District Court in its varied judgment awarded the owner only the two months' rental in arrears.

provision in the agreement that any default in payment is a breach of condition,[123] thereby excluding the rule against penalty.

- Where the minimum-payment clause confers on the creditor an absolute discretion whether or not to make a reduction in the hire charges in the case of early settlement, it is penal and unenforceable.[124]
- Provisions for the recovery of the estimated cost of putting the goods into good repair may be a penalty if they are unreasonable.[125]

It is submitted that the above are only broad principles, and there is no hard and fast rule. There is no single formula for measuring the damage as any true pre-estimate – the courts have to look at the substance and not merely the form of words used.[126]

When a minimum sum is held to be a penalty, the court will have to assess the appropriate amount payable by the debtor. On this issue, once again the law is far from clear in Hong Kong. The English method of assessment is essentially based on the formula Lord Denning laid down in *Bridge v Campbell Discount Co. Ltd.*[127] In that case, he said that the court has to consider three matters:

- the instalments paid,
- the fair market value of the goods and
- the rebate to be given for interest charges due to early repayment of the capital.

In *Yeoman Credit Ltd v Waragowski*,[128] the Court of Appeal shared similar views with Lord Denning. There, the Court of Appeal held that when there was a repudiatory breach, the amount of damages recoverable

[123] It is noted that there were attempts in Australia to water down the effect of the principle in *Financing Ltd v Baldock*. For example, in *Esanda Finance Corporation Ltd v Plessnig and Another* [1989] 63 ALJR 238, (1989) 166 CLR 131, the Australian High Court held that the owner was entitled to recover the loss according to the formula stipulated in the agreement, although the defaults in payment for three months did not amount to a repudiatory breach. Only Brennan J mentioned the case of *Financing Ltd v Baldock*, at 107, and agreed with Gibbs CJ's view in *AMEV-UDC Finance Ltd v Austin*, that it was not authority that the owner is entitled to claim only rental in arrears if the hirer was guilty of a non-repudiatory breach. Their Honours thought that *Baldock* decided that the owner's claim was restricted to rental in arrears when it terminated the agreement.

[124] *Chartered Finance (Hong Kong) Ltd v Helen Fashions Garment Co. Ltd and Another* [1978] DCLR 20.

[125] *Wayfoong Finance Ltd v Ng Chung and Another* [1975] DCLR 70.

[126] *Dunlop Pneumatic Tyre Ltd v New Garage & Motor Ltd* [1915] AC 79, p. 85, *per* Lord Radcliffe.

[127] [1962] 1 All ER 385, 401. [128] [1961] 3 All ER 145.

by the creditor was based on the hire-purchase price less the following items: (1) the sums already paid or payable by the debtor at the date of the breach; (2) the market value of the goods repossessed or the proceeds, if the goods were sold; (3) the amount payable on the exercise of the option to purchase; (4) a discount in respect of accelerated payment of the capital; and (5) cost of repossession.

However, the English method of assessment has not been well received in Hong Kong. In *Wayfoong Credit Limited v Ho Fai*,[129] Power DJ adopted a different method of assessment: the cash price of the goods less (1) initial payment, (2) instalments of rental paid and (3) the sum that the goods might reasonably be expected to realise when repossessed, plus (a) interest at the prevailing commercial rate per annum on the reducing balance and (b) the cost of repossession.

It seems that the difference between the English methodology and the Hong Kong courts' approach is that the latter will produce a much lower figure than under the English method of calculation,[130] and thus favour the debtor.

Another problem related to the method of assessment in Hong Kong is that the courts have difficulty determining the appropriate rate of interest and the exact amount of the rebate. In moneylending transactions, there is the bank's prime lending rate and the commercial lending rate (which is a few points above the prime lending rate), and there is also the statutory maximum rate of 60 per cent per annum under §24 of the Money Lenders Ordinance (Cap. 163). In *Wayfoong Credit Limited v Ho Fai*[131] Power DJ thought that 11.5 per cent per annum, which was then the prevailing commercial lending rate for home finance, was reasonable for commercial transactions. It is interesting to note the interplay between the economics of quasi-security and mortgage, yet the courts have not been willing to fully treat the quasi-security as a chattel mortgage.

On the rebate issue, there is no settled single judicial formula for calculating the exact quantum of the rebate. There appear to be two acceptable formulae in Hong Kong. The first is the sliding-scale calculation, and the second is the direct-ratio rule or commonly called 'rule of 78'. Under the sliding-scale calculation, interest or hire charges are separated from the capital repayment. The percentage of interest is then charged on each balance of the capital repayment for each month. The interest

[129] [1975] DCLR 130.
[130] Consumer Council Report on Hire-Purchase in Hong Kong (1977), p. 25.
[131] [1975] DCLR 130, pp. 138–9.

payments thus diminish with each month – the amount of interest would be the largest in the first month and smallest in the last month. Power DJ approved this formula in his original judgment in *Wayfoong Credit Limited v Ho Fai*.[132] The problem with this method is that it treats the hire-purchase agreement as a loan and mortgage of chattels,[133] which, as mentioned earlier, the law, as a general rule, does not.

Under the rule of 78 or direct-ratio rebate formula, the charges are spread in the ratio which the number of instalments remaining to be paid bears to the total number of instalments in the agreement. In a twelve-month agreement, a rebate on the charges is calculated as follows: 12/78 of the charge is treated as earned in the first month, 11/78 in the second month, 10/78 in the third month and down to 1/78 in the final month.[134] For a thirty-six-month agreement the sum of the series is 666 (i.e. 36 + 35 + 34 + 33 etc.). Allowance is made for the number of instalments paid. For example, in the case of a thirty-six-month agreement, where six instalments are paid, the allowance will be 36 + 35 + 34 + 33 + 32 + 31 = 201. To arrive at the fraction, subtract 201 from 666 = 465. 465/666 = 69 per cent. The final rebate will be 69/100 multiplied by the total hire charges = amount of rebate. In *Chartered Finance (Hong Kong) Ltd v Helen Fashions Garment Co. Ltd and Another*,[135] Jones DJ held that rule of 78 was a more suitable and equitable formula. Accordingly it would be a genuine pre-estimate of the loss of the creditor.

To fully appreciate the effect of the different formulae discussed above, a case study was developed to apply the sliding-scale and rule of 78 formulae.[136] For the purpose of the study, the relevant terms of the hire-purchase agreement were:

- annual rate of interest: 6.50 per cent,
- hiring period: thirty-six months,
- hire rent per month: HK$1926.00,
- commencing: 6 May 2001,
- price of car: HK$123,000.00,

132 Ibid., at 135. 133 Ho, above, note 86, p. 186.

134 The figure is arrived at by adding consecutive descending numbers from 12 to 1, i.e. 12 + 11 + 10 + 9 + 8 + 7 + 6 + 5 + 4 + 3 + 2 + 1 = 78. It is a figure used by specialists in finance for the purpose of calculating the returns of an investor.

135 [1978] DCLR 20.

136 The authors would like to thank their colleague, Mr Thomas Leung, assistant professor, the Hong Kong Polytechnic University, for allowing them to use his hire-purchase agreement for the case study.

less: initial payment: HK$65,000.00,
balance of cash price: HK$58,000.00,
add: hire charges: HK$11,335.00,
hire-purchase price: HK$69,336.00.

The following assumption is made:

- After paying six instalment payments, the hirer/debtor defaults.
- The six instalment payments totalled HK$11,556.00 (i.e. 6 × HK$1926.00).
- There is a depreciation of 25 per cent of the value of the car and the car was sold for HK$92,000.00.
- The total outstanding amount owing by the hirer/debtor at the date of repossession is HK$57,444.00 (i.e. HK$69,000.00 – HK$11,556.00).

What is the amount of rebate?

If the sliding-scale formula is applied the amount owing by the hirer/debtor is HK$47,334.15. The rebate amount would be HK$10,109.85 (i.e. HK$57,444.00 –HK$47,334.15). The figure is arrived at in Table A below:

Table A

Loan HK$	**Interest HK$**	**Repayment HK$**	**Balance HK$**
58000.00	314.1667	1777.642167	56222.36
56222.36	304.5378	1777.642167	54444.72
54444.72	294.9089	1777.642167	52667.07
52667.07	285.28	1777.642167	50889.43
50889.43	275.6511	1777.642167	49111.79
49111.79	266.0222	1777.642167	**47334.15**

If the rule of 78 formula is applied, the amount owing and payable by the hirer/debtor is HK$49,958.16 (i.e. HK$69,336.00 – 69/100 × HK$11,336.00 = 7821.84 + HK$11,556.00 (six months' payment). There is a rebate of HK$7,821.84.

Finance companies in Hong Kong generally use the rule of 78 formula.[137] The reason is obvious, on the basis of the above case study: the rule of 78 formula favours the creditor. Indeed, it undermines Power DJ's pro-debtor formula.

137 The United Kingdom Report on Consumer Credit (1971) Cmnd 4596, vol. 1, recommended this when customers effect early settlement under a hire-purchase

The courts' inconsistent treatment of the economic rights of the creditor has rendered the remedies of the creditor uncertain.

Relief from forfeiture

The above discussion assumes that the finance company has lawfully and effectively terminated the hire-purchase agreement. However, can the court relieve the hirer from forfeiture of the agreement?

There is no decided authority in Hong Kong on this point. Examination of English authorities shows that a tortous route has been taken to answer that question.[138] Today it is settled, on the basis of the House of Lords case of *On Demand Information plc (in administrative receivership) and Another v Michael Gerson (Finance) plc and Another*:[139] the court has jurisdiction to grant relief against forfeiture of hire-purchase and

agreement. This was stipulated in sample agreements from Belgian Bank (Hong Kong) and Dah Sing Finance Ltd, but was absent in the sample from Wing Lung Finance Limited.

138 In the nineteenth century the courts took a strict view: that the courts would not relieve the hirer against forfeiture caused by default in punctual payments unless the proviso was a penalty; see *Halsbury's Laws of England* (London: Butterworths, 1907), para. 1125; and see also E.J. Prince, 'Equitable Relief in the Law of Hire-Purchase', *MLR* 20 (1957), 620, who supported this view. Relief against forfeiture was thought to be strictly available only for real property but not for chattels. However, since the beginning of the twentieth century the courts have adopted a more robust and expansive approach; see *Shiloh Spinners Ltd v Harding* [1973] AC 691, 722, HL, where Lord Wilberforce stated that if the object of the transaction and forfeiture proviso was to secure the payment of money, equity could relieve the forfeiture on the terms that the payments were made with interest, if appropriate, and also costs. That case was considered in the Hong Kong case of *Golden Eagle Ltd v Golden Achievement Ltd* [1997] 1 HKC 173 (PC), particularly at 183, *per* Lord Hoffmann; and see also *Halsbury's Laws of England*, 4th ed., reissue (London: Butterworths, 1992), vol. 16, para. 897, which showed the change in the court's approach. See also A.L. Diamond, 'Equitable Relief for Hire-Purchaser of Goods', *MLR* 19 (1956), 498; and M. Pawloski, 'The Scope of Equity's Jurisprudence to Relieve against Forfeiture of Interests in Property Other than Land', *JBL* (1994), 372, where the authors argued that relief against forfeiture should apply and that it should not be restricted to forfeiture of interests in land only. For detailed exposition of the case law see *On Demand Information plc (in administrative receivership) and Another v Michael Gerson (Finance) plc and Another* [2000] 4 All ER 734, CA, at the Court of Appeal stage, particularly the decision of Robert Walker LJ. Note that in *Golden Eagle Ltd* the Privy Council refused to grant relief against the seller's forfeiture of the deposit because the sale and purchase of the land agreement was clear on the seller's right. Accordingly, the agreement was not a mortgage and the proviso was not a penalty.

139 [2002] 2 All ER 949, UKHL.

leasing agreements.[140] The decision was based on the ground that the hire-purchase and leasing agreements, which gave the debtor indefinite possession so long as the hire payments were paid, created, in favour of the debtor, a proprietary interest in the chattel.[141] Such agreements with a forfeiture provision satisfied the criteria established in the earlier House of Lords case of *Shiloh Spinners Ltd v Harding*[142] to grant relief. The criteria were stated as follows:

- the primary object of the bargain must be to secure a stated result,
- the result must be one which can be effectively attained when the matter comes before the court and
- the forfeiture provision was added by way of security for the production of that result.

However, in *On Demand Information*, the court refused the debtor relief against forfeiture of the lease because the parties could not be restored to their original positions. The leased equipment had already been disposed of by court order when the application for relief came on for hearing. The debtor was not, however, denied the rights to which it would have been entitled under the lease agreement had the relief been granted. This is because it was agreed between the creditor and the debtor that the order of sale granted was not to prejudice the parties' rights. Accordingly, the debtor, as provided in the lease agreement, was entitled to claim a rebate of 95 per cent from the proceeds of the sale of the leased equipment. *On Demand Information* was a special case. It is submitted that, if not for the without-prejudice term of the order for sale, the relief is lost when the debtor's rights come to an end. This is another feature of equity's relief of right of redemption.

The decision in *On Demand Information* has other significant impacts on quasi-security. Firstly, it may significantly weaken certainty in commercial transactions.[143] The power of sale of the creditor is an important instrument to mitigate its losses in goods which are usually of perishable nature or of precarious value. The delay that may be caused by the

[140] Indeed all the three judicial levels, the High Court, the Court of Appeal and the House of Lords, agreed that the court had power to grant relief from forfeiture in hire-purchase and leasing agreements.

[141] See *On Demand Information plc (in administrative receivership) and Another v Michael Gerson (Finance) plc and Another* [2002] 2 All ER 949 HL, p. 957, *per* Lord Millet.

[142] [1973] 1 All ER 90, HL.

[143] Sir Roy Goode, QC, strongly relied on this point against relief; see *On Demand Information plc (in administrative receivership) and Another v Michael Gerson (Finance) plc and Another* [2000] 4 All ER 734, CA, paras. (c)–(d).

lessee–debtor's application may subject the creditor to the risk that the goods may be worthless, should the application for relief be subsequently rejected. One solution to this dilemma is to adopt the method in *On Demand Information*, which is to apply to the court for a 'without-prejudice' order for sale. But this involves an expensive legal process. Unless the value of the goods outweighs the costs, it is not worthwhile for the creditor to pursue this course of action. Secondly, the court has given effect to the substance of the transaction; that is, it is a credit security transaction.[144] In doing so, the court appears to contradict the earlier observation in *Armour and Another v Thyssen Edelstahlwerke AG*,[145] where the Law Lords unanimously held that a conditional sale agreement that effectively retained title in the goods did not create a security interest in those goods. Thus there appears to be an anomaly in the law between hire-purchase and leasing, both of which are species of conditional sale. On the other hand, if *On Demand Information* is a departure from *Armour*, then *On Demand Information* has opened a Pandora's box in this area of commercial law, which has already been discussed in Chapter 5 and was found to be highly volatile. Lastly, it weakens the effectiveness of forfeiture in ensuring prompt and regular payment of rental by the debtor.[146]

In relation to the cost of enforcing the creditor's right of possession, this can be regarded as minimal.[147] In a vast majority of cases, the court's assistance was not required to enforce the creditor's right of possession. When the repossessed goods are subsequently sold by an auctioneer, the commission is paid according to the prevailing rate, which is currently about 1 to 2 per cent of the sale price.

The above discussion demonstrates that the creditor's right to take possession and to sell the goods is generally expeditious and inexpensive. The rules also appear to be generally certain and clear. However, there are two difficulties, which at first glance appear to have weakened these efficient remedies. Firstly, the amount the creditor is entitled to recover in the event of a deficiency is uncertain. Secondly, the House of Lords recognition of

[144] This was basically the opposite argument of Dr Fidelis Oditah, counsel for the lessee; see *On Demand Information plc (in administrative receivership) and Another v Michael Gerson (Finance) plc and Another* [2000] 4 All ER 734, CA, 743, para. (e).

[145] [1991] 2 AC 339.

[146] See *On Demand Information plc (in administrative receivership) and Another v Michael Gerson (Finance) plc and Another* [2000] 4 All ER 734, CA, 751, *per* Robert Walker LJ.

[147] If the subject matter is a vehicle and it has been towed away by the creditor, the current tow charges are between HK$500 and HK$600.

relief against forfeiture may impair the effectiveness of these remedies. However, it is arguable that, in practice, these difficulties are exceptional issues rather than fundamental causes of concern.

Accordingly, the remedies of the right to take possession and to sell can be regarded as having satisfied all the enforcement criteria, namely certainty of creditor's remedies, expedition, expense, and certainty of the quantum the creditor is entitled to recover under the security arrangement.

7.4 Remedies of the traditional security holder (other than the quasi-security holder) in China

For the purposes of this part, unless otherwise stated, the expression

'creditor' means the traditional security holder under a mortgage and pledge, and
'debtor' means the mortgagor and pledgor.

This section examines the remedies of taking possession and foreclosure by way of conversion, auction or sale in China.[148]

7.4.1 Taking possession

Pledge

By virtue of the nature of a pledge,[149] a pledgee enjoys the right of possession[150] during the currency of the pledge contract. Where the pledgee is not repaid at the expiry of the agreement, he may retain the pledged property and can also exercise other rights over the whole of the pledged property.[151] However, after receiving payment from the pledgor, the pledgee is obliged return the pledged item. In the case of a pledge of intangible rights, the concept of 'possession' is either evidenced by delivery of a document of title or by the registration of the

148 Another special remedy includes the creditor's right to collect 'fruits' (natural or statutory derivatives) from the secured property stipulated in Article 197 of the Property Law (mortgage) (formerly Article 47 of the Security Law) and Article 213 (pledge) which is applicable to tangible and intangible property by virtue of Article 229.

149 Article 208 of the Property Law, formerly Article 63 of the Security Law.

150 In case of pledges, it can be classified as physical (direct) and constructive (indirect) possession. The latter case allows the pledgee to appoint a third party to keep the pledged property. The pledgee's right will not be lost by the fact that the pledged property is not temporarily under his direct control or management, Article 69 of the Security Law.

151 Article 95 of the Judicial Interpretation of the Security Law.

pledge with the relevant authorities to protect the pledgee against the pledgor's transfer or use of the pledged rights.[152]

Mortgage

The traditional view is that the mortgagee's right of possession is implied by the Security Law.[153] This is because when default occurs and the creditor desires to foreclose, he must necessarily take the mortgaged property into his hands; his right to do this is implied from the provision which gives him the right to sell.

However, this may not necessarily be an accurate representation of the position in China. Article 195 of the Property Law (formerly Article 53 of the Security Law, with some changes) provides:

> When the mortgagor fails to pay its/his due debts or any circumstance for realizing the mortgagee's right as stipulated by the parties occurs, the mortgagee may, by concluding an agreement with the mortgagor, convert the property under mortgage into money or seek preferred payments from the money incurred from the auction or sale of the property under mortgage.[154]

The provision does not specify whether the mortgagee is entitled to take possession of the secured property. Thus it appears from the wording of this provision that the mortgagee is not automatically entitled to possession. Taking into consideration the fact that the mortgaged property is in the mortgagor's possession,[155] and that any conversion or sale or auction of the secured property has to be agreed upon by the mortgagee and mortgagor, it is submitted that there is no compelling reason why the mortgagor should part with possession to the mortgagee, unless this is voluntarily agreed either in the mortgage contract or subsequently.

Thus, similar to Hong Kong, the mortgagee–creditor's right of possession to encumber personal property is not clear in China.

Theoretically, if the mortgage agreement expressly confers such power on the mortgagee, it can be exercised without the assistance of the court.[156] However, creditors in China usually apply to the court for an order of

[152] See Articles 224–8 of the Property Law.

[153] There are no statutory provisions implied in the Security Law (1995), the Judicial Interpretation of the Security Law (2000) and the Property Law (2007).

[154] Please refer to provisions of the Auction Law of the People's Republic of China (amended in 2004).

[155] Article 179 of the Property Law, formerly Article 33 of the Security Law.

[156] Article 195 of the Property Law, formerly Article 53 of the Security Law.

possession even if an express power to take possession is contained in the mortgage contract. This is for two reasons.[157] Firstly, debtors often do not voluntarily deliver possession of the goods to the creditor. Secondly, the creditor will wish to take advantage of the right to sue the debtor for any deficiency after the goods are repossessed and sold by virtue of a court order. This issue is discussed later in this chapter.

But the judicial process has two weaknesses. Firstly, the cost of litigation is generally high.[158] Secondly, the judicial process is very slow and cumbersome.[159]

In light of the above, the remedy of taking possession has not satisfied the enforcement criterion that the creditor's remedies must be certain. The criterion that the amount of money the creditor is entitled to recover is not relevant here. Further, the remedy has not satisfied the enforcement criteria that the creditor's remedies must be expeditious and inexpensive, because in many cases the creditor has to resort to the slow and expensive judicial process in order to effectively enforce the remedy. This is compounded by the fact that Chinese procedural rules usually require that the debtor be sued in his local court, which may be geographically far away from the creditor's place of business. Even if judgment is obtained from a local court, actual enforcement of the court order afterwards often proves difficult or impossible due to 'local protectionism' or even outright corruption in the judicial system. These are severe practical limitations on the effectiveness of remedies in China and have been identified and discussed in detail elsewhere.[160] On these grounds, it is submitted that the creditor's remedy of taking possession is not efficient.

7.4.2 Foreclosure by way of conversion, auction or sale

As in Hong Kong, the creditor's right of conversion, auction or sale in China is the most popular remedy in respect of tangible personal property. This section examines the pledgee–creditor and mortgagee–creditor's

[157] Shibing Cao, *Solutions and Prospects of China's Security Problems* (Beijing: China Fa-Zhi Press, 2001), pp. 249–50.

[158] This is discussed further below in this chapter.

[159] Also discussed further below in this chapter.

[160] For an extensive discussion of the local protectionism, corruption and other problems in China's judicial system, see Benjamin L. Liebman, 'China's Courts: Restricted Reform', *Columbia Journal of Asian Law* 21(1) (2007), 2; and J. Pien, 'Creditor Rights and Enforcement of International Commercial Arbitral Awards in China', *Columbia Journal of Transnational Law* 45 (2007), 586.

power of conversion, auction and sale under the pledge and the mortgage respectively, as the means of realising the creditor's rights. The powers of mortgagees or pledgees are derived from the similar set of rules under the Security Law, the Judicial Interpretation of the Security Law and the Property Law.

The extent to which the creditor's rights can now be realised should be considered carefully. In case the secured creditor has security both over property and in the form of a personal guarantee, Article 176 of the Property Law provides that for the purpose of realising the creditor's rights (mortgagee or pledgee)[161] and where the agreement has not expressly so provided, the creditor may then enforce his rights of realisation against both the secured property and/or request the guarantor (if any) to undertake surety ship liability. In other words, the current law provides for both personal claims and proprietary claims in the common law sense. Under the Security Law, a guarantor was responsible only for obligations not secured by the property.[162]

Pledge

Both the Security Law (including its Judicial Interpretations) and the Property Law are laws of general application. Under Article 219 of the Property Law,[163] the creditor may, through agreement with the debtor, exercise the power of conversion, auction or sale either after the debtor has failed to pay the debt when it falls due[164] or after the occurrence of events that can trigger the realisation of the pledge ('realisation events'). Clearly, the Property Law provides more protection to the creditor than the former Article 71 of the Security Law, which only allowed the power to be exercised when the debt fell due. In other words, the power of conversion, auction or sale can now be exercised prior to the due date of the debt. However, the Security Law is silent on whether notice of the creditor's intention to exercise the power of sale has to be given to the debtor. Some influential monographs hold that it is not necessary that the creditor give notice to the debtor before exercising his power of sale.[165]

161 Such right of realisation arises when the debtor has failed to pay the debt when it falls due or after the events regarding the realisation of the security interest have been triggered ('realisation events').

162 Article 28 of the Security Law.

163 Formerly Article 71 of the Security Law.

164 Where the debtor performs his obligation at its maturity, or where the pledgor pays, prior to maturity, the debt secured, the pledgee shall return the pledged property, pursuant to Article 219 of the Property Law.

165 Shibing Cao, above, note 157, p. 287.

This view is based on two arguments. Firstly, there is no provision in the Security Law which requires the creditor to give prior notice; secondly, the debtor should be aware that if default is made, the secured property will be appropriated to repay the secured debt.[166] Cao argues that even if it is not required to give prior notice under the current law, it might be advisable for the debtor to insert a clause into the contract of pledge, stating that notice will first be served on the debtor so as to give the debtor a last opportunity to prevent the appropriation and sale of the secured property.

When the creditor exercises its power of sale, Article 219 of the Property Law, paragraphs 2 and 3, must be followed. It states:

> Where the pledgee has not been paid at the maturity of the obligation or the events relating to the realisation of the pledge agreed between them have occurred ['realisation events'], the pledgee may conclude an agreement with the pledgor that the pledged property be converted into money in order to pay the debt, or he may auction or sell the said property according to law.[167]
>
> Market prices shall be used as reference in conversion or sale of the pledged property.

From this provision, it is clear that the pledgee has three options. Firstly, he may enter into private agreement with the debtor, converting the security property into money. Conversion means the cancellation of the entitlements of the creditor, repayment and transfer of the ownership of the secured property to the creditor.[168] When the debt falls due, instead of further demanding the debt owed, the creditor has the right to become the owner of the secured property. In practice, the creditor may choose to purchase it from the debtor at a newly negotiated price. Secondly, he may conclude a sale contract with a third party, which is regulated by the Contract Law (1999),[169] in order to satisfy the debt. Thirdly, the pledgee may opt to auction the property through a competitive bidding process. If so, the rules and procedure are governed by

[166] Ibid.

[167] According to Article 95 of the Judicial Interpretation of the Security Law, the creditor should enjoy an implied right of retaining the pledged property before he exercises the power of conversion, auction or sale. However, once the debt has been satisfied, the creditor shall return the pledged property.

[168] Ping Jiang, *Property Law of the People's Republic of China: Explained* (Beijing: China University of Political Science and Law Press, 2007), pp. 282–3.

[169] Chapter 9 (sales contracts) of the Contract Law (1999).

the Auction Law.[170] However, whichever method is chosen, Article 221 of the Property Law (formerly paragraph 3 of Article 71 of the Security Law) further provides that where the money obtained from the pledged property, or where the proceeds from auction or sale, exceed the debt secured, the balance shall be paid to the pledgor. Where the money or the proceeds do not cover the whole debt secured, the deficit remains payable by the debtor.

Traditionally, the exercise of the creditor's rights has been regarded as a matter of choice; that is, he can choose to exercise any of these rights at any time after either of the conditions in Article 219 of the Property Law has been satisfied. However, the new Article 220 has provided extra protection for the debtor when the creditor does not enforce his rights of pledge in a timely manner when the debt falls due. The article provides two new protections once the debt has fallen due. Firstly, from that moment and upon the debtor's request to the creditor to enforce his rights, the creditor shall compensate any loss arising from delay.[171] Secondly, if the creditor does not exercise his right in due time, the debtor may request the People's Court to conduct the auction or sale of the pledged property. Academics think that the debtor can only approach the People's Court for protection when an unreasonable delay in the pledgee's taking action has occurred.[172] Aside from these simple provisions, the Security Law, its related Judicial Interpretations and the Property Law give no further detailed guidance as to how the creditor and the debtor should exercise the pledge remedies. Compared with the equivalent provisions in Hong Kong, the enforcement and remedy provisions in the Security Law seem rudimentary and lack sophistication.

In China, intangible personal property such as shares in companies are commonly pledged.[173] Similarly to tangible personal property, pledged intangible personal property shall be converted into money, sold or auctioned in case of default. The creditor's exercise of these powers and the debtor's protections are the same as those discussed above in relation to

[170] The Auction Law of the People's Republic of China was enacted by the Standing Committee of Chinese People's Congress in 1996, effective on 1 January, 1997, and was amended in 2004.

[171] See also Article 95 of the Judicial Interpretation of the Security Law. Protection is only limited to loss due to depreciation of the pledged property arising from the pledgee's delay in exercising his right.

[172] Ping Jiang, above, note 168, p. 283.

[173] See Chapter 3 above.

tangible property.[174] In relation to both types of personal property, any stipulation in the contract indicating that ownership of the pledged property be transferred to the pledgee if the obligation is not discharged at its maturity is invalid.[175]

Diya Mortgage

In China, similar to pledges, *Diya* mortgage realisation by way of foreclosure can be undertaken by way of conversion, auction or sale.[176] Article 195 of the Property Law (formerly Article 53 of the Security Law) provides that the mortgagee,

> who is not paid at the maturity of the obligation or after the events regarding the realisation of the mortgage agreed between the parties have been triggered ['realisation events'[177]], may, through agreement[178] with the mortgagor, be paid out of the proceeds from the conversion of the mortgaged property or from the auction[179] or sale of the mortgaged property; other creditors may request the People's Court to cancel such agreement within one year after they know or should have known *the cause of cancellation* if the interest of such creditors are adversely affected.[180]
>
> If the mortgagee and mortgagor fail to reach an agreement as to the way in which the mortgage is to be realised, the mortgagee may request the People's Court for auction or sale.

174 Article 229 of the Property Law, formerly Article 81 of the Security Law, expressly provides that the pledge of rights is also governed by all the rules of the pledge of tangible property.

175 Articles 211 and 229 of the Property Law, formerly Articles 66 and 81 of the Security Law.

176 Article 195 of the Property Law, formerly paragraph 1 of Article 53 of the Security Law.

177 Note that in relation to charges over tangible property stipulated in Article 181 of the Property Law, Article 196 provides the events ('crystallisation events') in which the charged property is to be determined: (1) the claim is not paid at the maturity of the obligation, (2) the chargor becomes insolvent or dissolved, (3) events regarding the realisation of the charge agreed between the parties have been triggered, and (4) other circumstances which may seriously affect the realisation of the charge.

178 According to Article 74 of the Judicial Interpretation of the Security Law, where there is no agreement on the order of payment it is presumed to be in the following order: (1) expenses to realise the mortgage right, (2) interest of the principal obligation and, (3) principal obligation.

179 See the Auction Law of the People's Republic of China (amended in 2004).

180 The interest of other creditors is formerly recognised under Article 57 of the Judicial Interpretation of the Security Law. Article 195 of the Property Law now affirms such right of cancellation upon request of the People's Court by other creditors whose interests are adversely affected during the realisation of the mortgagee's interest. See also Articles 74 and 75 of the Contract Law (1999).

> Market price should be taken as reference when converting the mortgaged property into money or selling the mortgaged property.[181]

Conversion means the transfer ownership of the secured property to the creditor at a price agreed between the creditor and the debtor. In practice, when debt falls due, instead of demanding the debt owed, the creditor can choose to purchase the secured property at a mutually agreeable price. However, in distinction to common law foreclosure, such a transfer of secured property is not taken as a settlement of the debt. Where the agreed transfer price is lower than the secured debt, the balance remains payable by the mortgagor. On the other hand, if the transfer price is higher than the debt, the creditor shall pay the surplus to the morgagor.[182]

The Property Law has also made some important changes to the enforcement of the creditor's right of mortgage realisation. Article 195 (paragraph 2) stipulates that where the mortgagee and mortgagor fail to reach an agreement as to the way in which the mortgage is to be realised, the mortgagee may request the People's Court to order auction or sale, as opposed to Article 53 of the Security Law where the mortgagee was required file a litigation suit with the People's Court. This indicates that the mortgagee will no longer need to file a full litigation action with the People's Court, which should make realisation of the mortgage easier.[183] However, Article 202 has reduced the limitation period for applying to the court for realisation of a mortgage. The mortgagee previously had two years in addition to the statutory limitation.[184] The extended limitation period has now been reduced. Article 202 now provides that the mortgagee can only enforce his rights within the statutory limitation period.

The purpose of the power of auction or sale is to realise the mortgaged property. The Chinese security law confers on the creditor two types of power of sale, namely extrajudicial sale (without court order) and judicial sale (with court order). It should be noted that under Chinese security law, these two powers are parallel remedies available for mortgagee/

[181] Ping Jiang, above, note 168, p. 254, suggested that where there are subsequent mortgages created over the same property, the market price should not be taken during the realisation of the mortgaged property because this would affect the interests of other mortgagees.

[182] Article 198 of the Property Law, formerly paragraph 2 of Article 53 of the Security Law.

[183] Jinnan Li and Gulong Ren, 'Impact of the New Property Rights Law on Banking Practices in the PRC', King & Wood PRC Lawyers Banking Newsletter, 2007, p. 2.

[184] Article 12 of the Judicial Interpretation of the Security Law, read together with Articles 135 and 137 of General Principles of Civil Law (1986).

creditor, and that the exercise of extrajudicial sale is not a precondition to judicial sale. The creditor is entitled to choose either of them as long as the debtor is in default.

Extrajudicial sale If the creditor decides to dispose of the mortgaged property (such as in the case of pledge) through extrajudicial sale, it could either enter into a private sale agreement (i.e. foreclosure by way of sale) with the third party governed by Chapter 9 (sales contract) of the Contract Law (1999), or sell it at an auction (i.e. foreclosure by way of auction) as governed by the Auction Law (1999, amended in 2004). However, unlike in Hong Kong, there are several procedural steps to comply with additional to those contained in the Contract Law and the Auction Law, namely:

- extrajudicial sale can only be effected after the date on which the term of the mortgage is exceeded;[185]
- where there is no agreement between the creditor and the debtor, the proceeds from the sale must be applied in the following order: costs and expenses of the sale, interest on the principal debt, principal debt.[186]

It is noteworthy that the relevant Chinese law provisions, in contrast to the common law in Hong Kong, do not specify any procedure to protect the debtor against collusion between the creditor and the purchaser in the sale and purchase of the property, or to provide for the fair treatment of the debtor. However, if the creditor and the debtor cannot agree upon the value of the secured property, the creditor must apply to the court for an order of sale. Therefore this obvious deficiency should not cause significant problems theoretically.

Judicial sale If the creditor and the debtor cannot reach an agreement as to the conversion, sale or auction of the secured property, the creditor has recourse to the court. From the creditor's perspective, there are two advantages. Firstly, the defaulting debtor seldom delivers the mortgaged property to the creditor voluntarily. Consequently, the creditor has to apply to the court for an order of possession. Secondly, the creditor sees it

[185] For example, the mortgagee is not paid at the maturity of the obligation or after the events regarding the realisation of the mortgage ('realisation events') agreed between them have been triggered, pursuant to Article 195 of the Property Law.

[186] Article 74 of the Judicial Interpretation of the Security Law.

as convenient and cost-effective to apply for a judicial order of sale at the same time since private negotiation often cannot lead to agreement on the value of the mortgaged property.[187]

Prior to the enactment of the Property Law, it was usual that the mortgagee/creditor did not apply to the court for an order of foreclosure, but had to commence a general lawsuit. Article 53 of the Security Law provided that 'if the mortgagee/creditor and the mortgagor/creditor fail to reach an agreement, the mortgagee may bring a lawsuit in a People's Court'. Obviously, a lawsuit in its general sense in Article 53 of the Security Law is different in nature from the judicial sale assumed by common law lawyers. The difference lies in the fact that the phrase 'lawsuit' implies a prolonged and complicated process, involving multiple procedural steps such as the commencement of suit, discovery, response, a court hearing and reply, appeals and retrial pursuant to the Civil Procedure Law (1991), rather than a summary procedure to obtain the possession and sale of an encumbered property.

However, with the enactment of the Property Law, the position appears to be different, though the operative effect has yet to be seen. Article 195 of the Property Law (formerly Article 53 of the Security Law) provides, 'If the mortgagee and mortgagor fail to reach an agreement as to the way in which the mortgage is to be realised, the mortgagee may request the People's Court for auction or sale.' The meaning of 'request' and its effect are yet unknown. However, some authors consider that the realisation of the mortgage under Article 195 should become procedurally less complicated.[188] It has already been suggested that judicial foreclosure is used in order to facilitate the creditor's realisation of mortgage rights.[189] If the common judicial foreclosure regime is applicable under Article 195, the process involved is simplified. It is usually sufficient for the creditor merely to set out the particulars of the relevant mortgage contract and its registration. If the court accepts the truth of the information, the court will ascertain the amount due to the creditor and order that same amount to be paid to the mortgagee. However, the preceding judicial sale regime under the Security Law was generally perceived as slow and expensive,[190] but the situation may now improve under the Property Law,

[187] Jun Wang and Zhenyu Liu, 'On Improving the Realisation of Mortgage Rights', *Economists* (*Jingjishi*) 8 (2004), 63 at pp. 63–5.

[188] Jinnan Li and Gulong Ren, above, note 183.

[189] Jianyuan Cui, 'Studies on Perfection of Mortgage Rights', *Application of Law* (*Falüshiyong*) 6 (2004), 20.

[190] Shibing Cao, above, note 157, p. 251.

which came into effect on 1 October 2007, though it is too soon to be sure that this will be so.

Once the court has decided the case in the creditor's favour and ordered judicial sale of the encumbered property, various execution procedures need to be followed. Prior to 2005, the relevant procedure was contained in the Provisions on Various Issues Concerning People's Court's Implementation Work promulgated by the Supreme Court of China in 1998. However, these provisions were considered to be incomplete and inadequate. Currently, the Provisions on Sale and Auction of Properties in Civil Enforcement Proceedings by the People's Court, promulgated by the Supreme Court of China and effective from 1 January 2005, contain the rules governing the judicial sale of secured property.[191] According to these provisions, an auction is the basic method of judicial sale.[192] In some exceptional circumstances, sale by private treaty may be allowed.[193]

Consequently, the creditor's remedy of sale in China are now generally well defined by the Security Law, its Judicial Interpretations and the Property Law. The remedy therefore satisfies the criterion of certainty of the creditor's remedies. However, the remedy suffers from serious practical difficulties. Firstly, the process of judicial sale has been slow and expensive in the past but there is the possibility of improvement following the promulgation of the Property Law. Secondly, the process of judicial sale is impractical for intangible property, as a high degree of uncertainty exists regarding the price the creditor may obtain at the actual date of auction.

Thus the creditor's remedy of sale has failed to satisfy the other three enforcement criteria, namely that the remedy must be expeditious and inexpensive and that the amount which the creditor is entitled to recover must be certain. Accordingly the remedy of sale must be regarded as inefficient.

7.5 Conclusion

The above examination shows that each of the remedies of the creditor in Hong Kong and China has particular strengths and weaknesses.

[191] Jinshan Zhao, 'Understanding and Application of Provisions on Sale and Auction of Properties in Civil Enforcement Proceedings by the People's Court', *People's Administration of Justice* (*Renminsifa*) 2 (2005), 26.

[192] Article 2 of the Provisions on Sale and Auction of Properties in Civil Enforcement Proceedings by the People's Court (2005).

[193] Ibid., Article 34.

However, the weaknesses are more practically significant in China than in Hong Kong.

In Hong Kong, the traditional and quasi-security creditor's remedies of taking possession and sale are in practice generally effective. There are, however, some weaknesses. Firstly, in the absence of an express agreement, whether or not a traditional secured creditor has a right of possession or sale is determined by various complex and technical rules. Although this weakness has only theoretical significance in the vast majority of cases, it does illustrate that the substantive law is outdated. Secondly, there are substantive difficulties in respect of the quasi-security creditor's ancillary remedies following the sale of the repossessed goods. In respect of hire-purchase and leasing, the amount of money the creditor may recover is in some cases subject to the tedious rule against penalty and rebate, although this is not serious in practice. In relation to conditional sale, whether or not the creditor may keep the surplus or sue for the deficiency is also uncertain.

The other remedies of the traditional security holder, namely the power to appoint a receiver and foreclosure, are generally not useful. The former is cumbersome and uneconomical in many cases, particularly where the costs outweigh the economic benefit to the creditor. The latter, because of the nature of personal property, particularly tangibles, is impractical for commercial creditors.

In relation to China, there are several weaknesses. Firstly, unless the traditional and quasi-security transactions come within the parameters of the Security Law it is uncertain whether or not the creditor is entitled to any of the statutory remedies. Secondly, the creditor's main remedies of taking possession and sale are slow, expensive, and cumbersome.[194] Thirdly, some of the remedies, such as the quasi-security creditor's remedy of cancellation, are too pro-debtor and are outdated. They make no distinction between commercial and consumer debtors. The former does not need the special protection which is afforded to the latter. Fourthly, the efficiency of the remedies of taking possession and judicial sale is further weakened by an inefficient judicial infrastructure. There is undue delay by the courts in assisting creditors to enforce their remedies.

[194] However, judicial foreclosure in the common law sense might appear after the enactment of the Property Law, pursuant to Article 195 of the Property Law, as opposed to Article 53 of the Security Law.

This chapter concludes that due to the creditor's remedies, the enforcement processes, taken as a whole, in Hong Kong and China have not satisfied all of the four enforcement criteria of a credit security transaction, thus the creditor's remedies and the enforcement process are regarded as inefficient.

Chapter 8

Conclusion

8.1 Validation of the hypothesis

In Chapter 1, the hypothesis of this book was postulated in the following terms:

> the credit security legal frameworks governing security over personal property in domestic credit security arrangements in Hong Kong and China are not efficient if they fail to promote effectively the functions of (i) reducing the financial risk of the secured creditor, (ii) asset utilisation, (iii) fraud prevention and (iv) cost minimisation through four functional mechanisms, namely (a) creation, (b) perfection, (c) publicity and (d) enforcement of such security.

To test this hypothesis, a set of criteria was also established. In Chapters 2–7 these criteria were applied to the creation, perfection, publicity and enforcement of various types of traditional and quasi-security device in respect of tangible and intangible personal property in Hong Kong and China.

On the basis of these findings, we conclude that the hypothesis has been established in both jurisdictions. In other words, the existing credit security legal frameworks governing security over personal property in Hong Kong and China are inefficient.

To substantiate this conclusion, the following discussion collates the findings and highlights the strengths and weaknesses of the existing credit security legal frameworks of Hong Kong and China as they relate to the four functional mechanisms of creation, perfection, publicity and enforcement of security.

We then make recommendations for reform of the existing law and practice in both Hong Kong and China.

8.2 Collation of findings

8.2.1 Creation of credit security

With respect to the creation of both traditional and quasi-credit securities, seven criteria were considered against the rules governing the creation of security in Hong Kong and China. The criteria were as follows:

(1) the process of creating secured transactions must be simple, comprehensible, expeditious and inexpensive;
(2) the process must enable the security to be created over clearly defined and identifiable assets with a minimum of formality;
(3) the security device must leave the debtor in possession of the asset;
(4) the security must be capable of identifying and protecting the legitimate interests of all parties to the transaction;
(5) the debtor should be able to deal freely with the secured assets, though subject to the security interests of the creditor;
(6) the security must be able to secure future advances; and
(7) the security should be capable of attaching to after-acquired or future assets.

We consider that our analysis conducted in Chapters 2–7 has demonstrated that Hong Kong's credit security legal framework is able to satisfy criteria (3), (4), (5), (6) and (7). Apart from the pledge, the other security devices leave possession of the secured assets with the debtor. This allows the debtor to use the assets in the ordinary course of its business. However, the fact that the pledge does not satisfy criterion (3) does not necessarily suggest that the framework is inefficient. As was shown in Chapter 2, this is due to the pledge being mainly used to secure short-term loans. This is especially so where the perfection processes, for example, registration of other non-possessory security devices, are less convenient.

Hong Kong's credit security legal framework performed poorly in relation to criteria (1) and (2). With respect to (1), the rules governing the creation of security over personal property are neither simple nor comprehensible, and neither creditors, debtors nor third parties can easily understand the consequences of creation. There are two reasons for this failure:

- a plethora of security devices with diverse terminology and
- a multiplicity of highly technical rules governing creation.

These are discussed below.

A plethora of security devices exhibiting terminological complexity

In Chapters 2–6 we identified nine species of security device that can be created over personal property in Hong Kong: (i) legal mortgage,

(ii) equitable mortgage, (iii) equitable charge (fixed charge and floating charge), (iv) pledge, (v) hypothecation, (vi) trust receipt, (vii) hire-purchase, (viii) lease and (ix) conditional sale.

This multiplicity of security devices has the potential to create significant confusion for the creditor, debtor or third party. Quite often, if a dispute arises between the creditor and a third-party claimant, the label that was used to describe the instrument by the parties may not reflect the view of the court when it rules on the correct designation in law. Examples of this phenomenon were discussed in Chapters 2, 4 and 5. In Chapter 2 we demonstrated that the courts regarded security instruments described as 'hypothecation' in some cases as 'charges' and in other cases as 'trust receipts'. There were also cases in which the courts regarded 'charges' and 'trust receipts' as 'bills of sale' and others when the courts did not, although the distinction between them was very fine.

In Chapter 4, a similar characterisation problem was noted in relation to fixed and floating charges created by corporate debtors. A charge labelled as a 'fixed charge' by the creditor and debtor, when tested in court, could be designated a 'floating charge'.

In Chapter 5, it was shown that the characterisation problem was particularly critical in respect of conditional sale with retention-of-title clauses. The rules for determining when a retention-of-title clause is a 'charge' and when it is not are complex and confusing, and the adjudicative result in the event of litigation was shown to be unpredictable.

The different labels affixed by the courts and the parties to transactions are not simply a problem of semantics; they have serious legal implications for the priority of claims of successive creditors. For instance, a 'fixed charge' that is subsequently regarded as a 'floating charge' means that the creditor's security will be ranked after a number of preferential claims, and might be postponed to subsequent but superior securities, such as a fixed charge. A retention-of-title clause regarded by the court as a charge, against the legitimate expectation of the creditor, can result in the security being regarded as null and void for default of registration with the relevant authority.

Among the factors that contribute to this characterisation problem are complexity and confusion, which are traceable to conflicting approaches adopted by the courts. Sometimes form has been emphasised rather than the substance of the transaction; on other occasions, the court adopts the opposite approach and ignores the language used by, and the intent of, the parties and concentrates on the substance of the transaction to define the legal nature of the security. In some cases, particularly in relation to quasi-security, the courts have regarded retention-of-title clauses as having created a charge, whereas in other cases these have been regarded as pure sale-and-purchase transactions.

The different juridical rulings with respect to the application of these eight security devices are unnecessary and unjustifiable. A single common thread runs through all of them, which is to provide the creditor with security over specifically identified assets or the general assets of the debtor or a third-party security provider.

A multiplicity of technical rules governing creation

In Chapters 2–6 we explained that the process of creating each type of security device is governed by different rules – those of common law, equity and legislation. It is not always easy for lawyers, let alone laypeople, to determine which set of rules applies at the outset. This is because the applicable rule(s) can be determined by a number of complex factors, such as the juridical nature of the personal property, the concerned security provider or the security device. For instance, if the property is equitable, rules of equity determine the nature of the security device and also define the process of creating the security. If the security provider is a non-corporate body, the applicable law is general law (which defines the nature of the security) but also the provisions of the Bills of Sale Ordinance (which regulates the form the security should adopt to be valid).

The rules of equity have an impact in situations in which the creditor and debtor decide to use an equitable security device, irrespective of whether the property is legal or equitable. In contrast, if the property is legal, and if the parties decide to use a legal security device, the rules of common law govern the process of creation. The complexity is further exacerbated when special legislation superimposes additional requirements or replaces general law. Chapter 2 shows that this has occurred where security is granted over personal chattels granted by non-corporate debtors.

In relation to the quasi-security devices, Chapter 5 has shown that whether a retention-of-title clause is effective depends on a number of factors. These include the legal skill of the draftsman, the formulae used, the nature of the goods, the ultimate fate of the goods, and the approach of the courts to the matter. It is clear that some of these factors are beyond the control of the creditor and the debtor.

Does it matter which rules apply? Does it matter if a mistake is made? The answers to these questions are both positive and negative.

These rules do not really matter if the intention to create a security is clearly shown and if no special legislation invalidating that intention intrudes. In these circumstances, the creditor will not be denied a security. Thus, even if an assignment by way of a legal mortgage fails to comply with §9 of the Law Amendment and Reform (Consolidation) Ordinance (LARCO), it will nonetheless take effect as an equitable assignment by way of an equitable mortgage. An ineffective retention-of-title clause can still take effect as a charge. A security that fails to take effect as a legal mortgage might still take effect as an equitable mortgage.

However, the rules (and mistakes regarding them) do matter if other circumstances pertain, and the creditor can be left with an inferior security or no security at all. Chapter 6 has shown that a legal security, even if created after an earlier equitable security, has priority over the equitable security. However, if the legal mortgage were to be treated as an equitable mortgage, it could lose priority to an earlier equitable mortgage. A fixed charge has priority over an earlier floating charge, but not if the fixed charge was treated as a floating charge.

The Bills of Sale Ordinance is a good illustration of this situation of 'no security at all'. If the security holder of personal chattels makes an error and overlooks the Ordinance (by failing to comply with the registration requirement or the statutory security form), the bill of sale will be invalid. This appears draconian, especially in situations in which no intervening interests over the same property are affected.

To resume the discussion of the criteria, criterion (2) above has two parts. The first states that the assets capable of forming the subject matter over which security is to be given must be clearly identifiable. The second states that the security must be capable of being created with minimum formality.

With regard to the first part, the credit security legal framework of Hong Kong fails in two situations:

- In relation to security granted over personal chattels by non-corporate debtors, Chapter 2 has shown that the definition of 'personal chattels' (with its exceptions) is unduly complicated; it is beyond the reasonable understanding of laypeople.
- Chapter 4 has shown that there is an anomaly between two forms of intangible property, namely book debts and the credit balances of a company debtor with a bank. The latter are not regarded as book debts

and, accordingly, fixed charges over them are not registrable; rather, they can only be subject to a floating charge. Both situations create difficulty and uncertainty for creditors when they have to determine whether or not the Bills of Sale Ordinance and the registration provisions of the Companies Ordinance govern security arrangements with non-corporate and corporate debtors respectively.

With regard to the second part of criterion (2), in relation to 'minimum formality', Chapter 2 has shown that some arrangements are subject to minimum formality and some are not. A registrable bill of sale must comply with the statutory Form 2; failure to comply with the requirements of the form can render the bill of sale invalid against both the debtor and the claims of other creditors. In contrast, quasi-security devices are not subject to any substantial formality. For example, a retention-of-title clause can be effected with the use of just four sentences in contractual documents.

One factor in favour of the Hong Kong 'system' is that it is inexpensive to create security. However, this appears to be outweighed by the other significant weaknesses previously discussed.

Therefore, because criteria (2) and (3) are not satisfied, the credit security legal framework in Hong Kong in relation to the creation of security is inefficient.

In contrast, the credit security legal framework of China appears to have satisfied five of the seven criteria, namely (1)–(5). This is attributable to several factors The credit security legal framework adopts a simple and streamlined approach in creating a security interest over personal property. The same set of credit security rules applies to both corporate and non-corporate debtors, as the same security devices – the pledge and chattel mortgage – are available and thus, identical rules of creation apply. This promotes simplicity in the applicable legal rules.

Whilst there are essentially two types of security device – the pledge and chattel mortgage[1] – in recent years, two issues have emerged in the credit security arena to complicate the picture. The first has been the introduction of a new security concept, the 'floating' Diya mortgage.[2]

[1] There exist three other available security devices: lien, deposit and trust receipt. However, as mentioned in Chapter 2 above, a lien does not require the parties' intention to 'create' such a security device over the property. Deposit is in nature a 'cash' guarantee, and trust receipt is not mentioned in either the Security Law or the Property Law, but is a common practice in the banking industry. Therefore they are not included in our discussion of the principal security devices.

[2] See Chapter 2 above.

This creation of English law does not easily fit into the strict parameters of civil law. However, the problematic issues arising from this development are not serious as yet, due to the short time since its introduction in the Property Law 2007; the new device is at an embryonic stage of development. Undoubtedly, the legislature will have to amend the law to address the potential difficulties posed by this new form of security. The other problematic issue concerns the pledge and the chattel mortgage – which do not seem to work well in respect of intangible property, such as shares and intellectual property rights. However, the difficulties lie in inadequate remedies which cause the perceived weakness, rather than in the creation and perfection process.

The creation process is primarily governed by legislation – the Security Law 1995 and the Property Law 2007. These apply to corporate and non-corporate debtors equally with the same effects and consequences, so again promoting simplicity and a uniform set of creation rules.

Property in China is divided into immovable property and movable property. Movable property can be conveniently classified as tangible and intangible property. All movable property, both tangible and intangible, can form the subject matter of a pledge or a Diya mortgage. The legal framework is thus free from the problem of the characterisation of property experienced in Hong Kong.

Pledges and Diya mortgages are subject to an *ad valorem* Registration charge. However, the amount is minimal.

Whilst there is a degree of formality involved in the creation of a pledge or chattel mortgage, this formality requirement does not contain hidden risks or surprises for the creditor, debtor or third party and is not overly burdensome.

However, the rules of creation can only partially satisfy criteria (6) and (7). In respect of (6), except for 'floating' Diya mortgage pursuant to Article 181 of the Property Law, the widely used floating Diya mortgage cannot secure future advances, which is a significant weakness. Further, in respect of (7), only the pledge extends to after-acquired property, unless otherwise stipulated in the contract.[3]

Therefore, the rules of creation in China cannot be regarded as having wholly satisfied the criteria of creation of credit security. Accordingly they must be regarded as inefficient, although the problems are less fundamental than those encountered in Hong Kong.

[3] Article 213 of the Property Law.

8.2.2 *Perfection of credit security*

In respect of perfection, two criteria were tested against the rules governing the perfection process in Hong Kong and China, namely whether the perfection process was simple, comprehensible, expeditious and inexpensive, and also whether the rules regulating the priority of competing claims against the secured asset provided a fair and just ordering of those claims.

The application of the first criterion was discussed in Chapters 2–5. The application of the second criterion was discussed in Chapter 6.

We believe that we have shown that in Hong Kong, the rules governing the perfection process have satisfied only part of the first criterion, in that the perfection process is expeditious and inexpensive.

However, the rules have not satisfied the other criterion of simplicity and comprehensibility. This is due to the multiplicity of perfection rules. In some cases creation and perfection co-exist simultaneously, such as in hire-purchase, leasing and conditional sale. In other cases, which are more numerous, a further step is required of the creditor to perfect the security. This is the position in respect of bills of sale by way of security, assignments of intangible property by way of security, and fixed and floating charges over company assets. In the first and third situations, the creditor has to take the additional step of registering the security with the relevant authority. In default, the security is invalid against creditors or a liquidator, as the case may be. In the second situation, the creditor has to serve notice on the original debtor. Default in undertaking these additional steps diminishes the creditor's priority over any subsequent secured creditor claiming the same intangible property.

Unfortunately, it is also clear that Hong Kong's credit security legal framework has not satisfied the prioritisation criterion either. Chapter 6 demonstrated that the rules governing competing security interests are highly complex and do not guarantee that the creditor undertaking the apparently correct procedures will produce the priority anticipated. This problem is due to several factors.

There is no single common rule to determine competing security claims. In Chapter 6 two basic rules of priority were identified – the first-in-time rule and the rule in *Dearle v Hall*. According to the first-in-time rule, the priority of competing security interests over tangible personal property is determined by the date of creation of the security. According to the rule in *Dearle v Hall*, priority of competing security interests over intangible personal property is generally determined according to the date on which the notice of the security was served on the original debtor. The first-in-time rule is not generally difficult to establish for secured transactions over tangible property, because they are usually in written form and so dated. However, in respect of the rule in *Dearle v Hall*, there are some difficulties in relation to the contents of the notice to be given to the original debtor. In Chapter 3 it was shown that the courts apply an objective test to determine whether a 'notice' constitutes sufficient notice. The weakness of this test is that it depends on the circumstances of each case, which can vary, so resulting in different outcomes. Consequently, the outcome of the application of the test is unpredictable.

The two basic rules of priority are subject to several exceptions. Chapter 6 showed that the exceptions could be divided into general law and statutory rules. Under general law, the exceptions are creatures of equity, such as the generalisation that subsequent legal security interests will prevail over earlier equitable security interests. But this general exception is itself subject to several qualifications. The most important of these is the doctrine of constructive notice. A subsequent superior secured creditor, who would otherwise obtain priority over an earlier inferior secured creditor, is subordinated in priority if it had constructive notice of the latter. Again, the test for determining whether constructive notice is imposed is objective, but unreliable. The statutory exception is the registration system under the Companies Ordinance. It imports the doctrine of 'constructive notice' as a result of its registration procedure. Chapter 6 considered that the registration of a charge constitutes constructive notice of the existence of the charge to the whole world, but this is not notice as to the contents of the charge. This makes the position of third parties dealing with the debtor uncertain, especially with respect to automatic crystallisation and negative pledge clauses that may be contained in the charge document.

Anomalies between registration systems have a serious impact on the first-in-time rule and on the rule in *Dearle v Hall*. The registration systems under the Bills of Sale Ordinance, Companies Ordinance, Patents Ordinance and Trade Marks Ordinance treat the two basic rules differently. The registration system for bills of sale excludes altogether the first-in-time rule and the doctrine of constructive notice. Priority is determined according to the date of registration. In contrast, the registration system of charges under the Companies Ordinance preserves the two basic rules. All duly registered charges are determined according to the date of creation of the charge. An unsuspecting subsequent creditor, who has acquired a superior security interest, might think that that security would prevail, but it could be defeated by the doctrine of constructive notice if the earlier inferior security had been registered earlier. Thus, in practice and in effect, the doctrine of constructive notice has indirectly displaced the first-in-time rule of creation with the date of registration of the charge. It is also strange and potentially confusing to a creditor that the courts should exclude the doctrine of constructive notice from the registration system of bills of sale, but include it in the registration system for charges under the Companies Ordinance – even though the Bills of Sale Ordinance and the Companies Ordinance are silent as to the effect of the doctrine, and even though the assets affected might be identical. The courts have not, to date, offered any compelling reasons for this difference in treatment. In respect of security over patents, the Patents Ordinance prescribed the date of registration with the Patents Registry as determining priority. In contrast, the law of trademarks appears to allow the general rules of priority to apply in determining priority of all competing registered securities. The state of the law is thus complex and confusing.

The five-week period is also a cause of great uncertainty as it is arguably too long. This proposition has now been accepted and it will likely be shortened as part of the forthcoming reform of the Companies Ordinance. A secured creditor who has duly registered its security cannot be certain that an earlier secured creditor, whose five-week period has not expired, might not register its security subsequently and thereby obtain priority.

Two far more sinister factors that seem to wreak havoc on both rules of priority are the accepted concept of automatic crystallisation and the doctrine of tacking. Chapter 4 considered that an automatic crystallisation converts a floating charge into a fixed charge automatically when certain agreed events occur. Chapter 6 considered that the doctrine of tacking permits the first secured creditor to tack further advances. Both automatic crystallisation clauses and the right of tacking prejudice subsequent creditors who attempt to create subsequent security interests that ordinarily would have priority over earlier weaker security, such as a floating charge or other equitable security. The reason is that such creditors have no means of knowing whether there exist such automatic crystallisation clauses or rights to tack, except by calling for the instrument and meticulously examining it.

There is no rule governing priority of competing claims between the security interests of creditors of fixtures on hire-purchase, lease and conditional sale, and those of mortgagees of land on which the fixtures are attached. The general rule is that the mortgagee's security covers the fixtures, whether or not the mortgage was created before or after the fixtures became attached to the land.

Lastly, the Bills of Sale Ordinance works unfairly against the creditor in that it does not distinguish between the effects of 'attachment' and 'perfection'.[4] A bill of sale which includes attachment by way of security is nonetheless invalid against the creditor if it contravenes certain provisions of the Ordinance, such as the registration provisions. In contrast, a similar contravention whereby an attached security is granted by a company would be valid against the debtor under the Companies Ordinance.

For all these reasons it is submitted that the Hong Kong legal framework is inefficient as regards perfection of credit security over personal property.

In contrast, whilst China's credit security legal framework appears not to have satisfied the criterion of the creation process by being simple, comprehensible, expeditious and inexpensive, it does partially satisfy the criterion relating to the assets being easily defined with minimum formality. With respect to the former, Chapters 2 and 3 have shown that the registration system of China is based on the nature of assets. This is in contrast to the Hong Kong registration system, where registration is based on the identity of the owner, namely ownership by companies at the Companies Registry, and ownership by individuals at the Registry of the High Court. In China, the problem of identifying the correct registration agency responsible for each particular type of asset and the geographic location of the local administrative offices concerned causes unnecessary delay and confusion, so increasing the costs of registration considerably.

The legal framework partially satisfies the second criterion, relating to the creation of security over easily identifiable property with minimal formality. Firstly, the priority of competing security interests created by *Diya* mortgages is determined by one single and straightforward rule, namely the date of registration with the relevant registration authority. Article 199 of the Property Law makes it very clear that where two or more mortgages are created over the same property, the mortgage registered first has priority over one subsequently registered. Further, a registered mortgage has priority over an unregistered one. Where all mortgages are unregistered they are paid *pari passu*. This simplicity contrasts sharply with the Hong Kong situation and highlights the need for

[4] 'Attachment' is an expression used in the United States Uniform Commercial Code, Article 9. Basically, it means that the security becomes enforceable against the debtor when value is given, that the debtor has rights to the assets and that the rules governing creation are complied with. See Consultation Paper No 164, para. 11.21.

Hong Kong to consider reform of its complex and confusing priority allocation system. Secondly, China makes it compulsory that (except for the 'floating' *Diya* mortgage pursuant to Article 181 of the Property Law) any transfer of the mortgaged property by the debtor requires notification to both the mortgagee and the transferee by the mortgagor.[5] Furthermore, the mortgagor's transfer of mortgaged property without the mortgagee's consent is invalid, unless the transferee pays the outstanding debt so as to eliminate the mortgagee's right to security,[6] subject to the 'bona fide purchaser' rule.[7] This has the effect of alleviating the potential problem of competing claims.

However, as is the case in Hong Kong, China's registration system does not address the competing claims of creditors of fixtures in relation to hire-purchase, leasing, and conditional sale agreements, or mortgagees of the land upon which fixtures are attached.

As the credit security legal framework of China has satisfied only one criterion, and then only in part, it is submitted that the system of perfecting secured transactions in China is inefficient, although less seriously so than in Hong Kong.

8.2.3 Publicity of security interests

In respect of the publicity requirement, Chapters 2–5 considered four criteria against the rules governing the publicity of security interests in Hong Kong and China.

The criteria chosen were:

(1) there must be publication of security transactions, and that publicity must be inexpensive to file and easy to search;
(2) the publicity process relating to secured transactions must be simple, comprehensible, expeditious and inexpensive;
(3) the publicly available information must provide an accurate description of the nature of the security, the status of the affected assets and the level of financial exposure of those assets;
(4) access to the information must be expeditious and inexpensive.

The discussion in Chapters 2–5 shows that the rules in Hong Kong governing the publicity of security have, as a whole, failed to satisfy these criteria, except for the inexpensiveness of the publicity and the

[5] Article 49 of the Security Law. [6] Article 191 of the Property Law.
[7] Article 106 of the Property Law.

search process. This failure is caused by two factors. Firstly, the general rule is that no publicity of any security interest is required. Secondly, there are highly complex exceptions to the general rule, including the rules in *Dearle v Hall*, §9 of LARCO and the Bills of Sale Ordinance, the Companies Ordinance, the Patents Ordinance, and the Trade Marks Ordinance.

The rule in *Dearle v Hall* and §9 of LARCO apply only to equitable security of intangible property and to choses in action in the possession or control of the debtor, respectively. Both require notice to be served on the debtor. However, the discussions in Chapters 3, 4 and 6 have shown that they suffer from three defects, namely that the law is uncertain as to the content of the notice, that the debtor is under no obligation to respond to any enquiry as to the status of the relevant intangible personal property, and that there is no standard form in which the information about security interests should be kept – the quality of information thus varies from one original debtor to another.

The Bills of Sale Ordinance, the Companies Ordinance, the Patents Ordinance and the Trade Marks Ordinance promote publicity through their registration systems. But they suffer from several defects.

In respect of the Bills of Sale Ordinance, deficiencies include a lack of qualified officials, failure of the register to record particulars accurately, a poor filing system and delay in providing copies of security documents deposited with the High Court Registry.

In respect of the Companies Ordinance, the information is well kept and easily accessible because particulars of company charges are electronically recorded and accessed through computer terminals. However, a major defect of the system is that it does not publicise all charges, which may affect the financial status and assets of the company, as well as private agreements that might prejudice subsequent creditors. In respect of the former, such charges comprise non-registrable fixed charges over the company's shares in another company and receivables other than book debts. With regard to the latter, the register does not record or publicise automatic crystallisation clauses or negative pledges.

In respect of the Patents Ordinance and the Trade Marks Ordinance, it is uncertain as to whether they import the use of the doctrine of constructive notice or not.

A shared weakness in the registration systems of the Bills of Sale Ordinance and the Companies Ordinance is that their application is restricted. Firstly, trust receipts and quasi-security devices (that is, hire-purchase, lease and conditional sale) are not registrable under either registration system. Secondly, the registration system under the Bills of Sale Ordinance does not apply to security over non-personal property within the definition of the Ordinance. Thus security granted by non-corporate debtors over valuable intangible personal assets (such as credit balances and choses in action) are excluded. Thirdly, the registration system under the Companies Ordinance does not apply to fixed security over a number of assets, including debts (other than book debts) and credit balances at a bank.

As a result of these lacunae, significant information crucial to creditors and third parties is not accessible. This may adversely affect their decision-making processes especially with regard to deciding whether to lend to or deal with the debtor. Creditors or third parties who nonetheless deal with the debtor are subject to the risk that the debtor might be over-extended financially or not be creditworthy or the asset offered as security might already be encumbered.

The common strength of the two registration systems is that the costs of accessing the information are minimal. However, this advantage is outweighed by the defects discussed above.

Therefore we conclude that the rules governing the publicity of credit security devices in Hong Kong are inefficient.

In contrast, the rules in China generally satisfy the first and second criteria, partially satisfy the third but fail to satisfy the fourth. The positive aspects are attributable to the consistency observed in China's policy of publicising security interests. Except for the pledge and trust receipt, all chattel mortgages created by both non-corporate and corporate debtors are publicised through the relevant administrative departments based on the nature and location of the mortgaged property. However, regional inconsistencies in relation to the extent of detail required to be registered may exist which seriously affect the quality of available information.

The third criterion is only partially satisfied because the Security Law requires equipment owned by enterprises and other movable property to be registered with the SAIC office at the location where such property is situated, not where the enterprise is registered and against the asset itself rather than against the name of the firm. This creates a great risk for lenders since the secured property may be moved to another place after registration is completed. When a new potential lender consults the mortgaged property register in the new location of the property, he may be misled into believing that it is free from encumbrances, whilst in fact an encumbrance over the property has actually been registered elsewhere.

The fourth criterion is not satisfied, as China's search procedure appears simple only in theory. In practice, property is registered according to its type, and each province and municipality has its own cohort of registration departments. This results in a lengthy and cumbersome process for accessing information. Furthermore, as data held by some registration departments are not computerised, searching is slow and cumbersome unless the complete mortgage file number is known. Even if the available information is identified, it may well be misleading for the reasons mentioned in relation to the third criterion.

These defects seriously undermine what would otherwise be an efficient registration system, and also render meaningless the minimal registry search cost. Further, as in Hong Kong, the practice in China with regard to goods supplied on lease with an option to purchase, or subject to a lease, is that they are not registrable, and special terms in the security document (such as security over after-acquired and future property) are not transparent.

Due to the importance of the third and fourth criteria, and also because they are either completely or only partially unsatisfied, China's credit security framework has to be considered inefficient in respect of the publicity criterion.

8.2.4 Enforcement of credit security

In respect of enforcement, four criteria were tested, namely:

(1) the creditor's remedies must be certain,
(2) enforcement of the creditor's remedies must be expeditious,
(3) enforcing the remedies must be inexpensive and
(4) the quantum that a creditor is entitled to recover under the security transaction must be certain.

Chapter 7 showed that Hong Kong's legal framework for credit security generally accorded with the success criteria for enforcement, and that the system is therefore efficient. The strength is attributable to three factors. Firstly, Hong Kong's legal framework offers a multiplicity of remedies to the creditor to enforce the security against the assets, and they are cumulative.[8] These combined characteristics allow creditors to pursue the most appropriate remedy in the prevailing economic circumstances without fear that the exercise of one remedy might deprive it of any of the

[8] See Chapter 7 above.

others. This is important especially when the first action adopted might subsequently prove to be inappropriate or ineffective. This is an advantage that creditors in China do not enjoy.

The creditor in Hong Kong can therefore take possession and sell the secured property, and sue the debtor for the balance, if any, in an action for a debt; or it can sue the debtor for the debt and enforce the security later. The only limitation to this cumulative remedy concept is the remedy of foreclosure. When a property is foreclosed, all actions against the debtor for any difference between the value of the assets and the outstanding balance are barred. This limitation is not serious in Hong Kong, because the remedy of foreclosure is rarely exercised in respect of secured tangible or intangible personal property. However, this is evidence of the ineffectiveness of the foreclosure remedy.

Secondly, the more popular remedies of taking possession, seizure and sale are generally cost-effective and expeditious. This is because these remedies are usually explicitly contained in the security document, and the aid of the courts is seldom needed. Furthermore, even if that aid is necessary, the judicial process is reasonably expeditious because the judicial infrastructure is efficient.

Thirdly, the substantive rules governing the rights of the creditor to exercise the remedies are generally clear. But there are some uncertainties concerning the substantive aspects of some remedies. For instance, the equitable secured creditor's rights of possession and sale in respect of tangible personal property in the absence of express agreement are unsettled. There is also uncertainty on the juridical nature of the duty of care of the creditor when it exercises the power of sale. Although, as was argued in Chapter 7, these uncertainties have only theoretical significance (and, in practice, they do not appear to hamper the effectiveness of the remedies), they do have some bearing on the substantive structure of the legal framework. At the very least, the structure appears weak. Thus it is submitted that the Hong Kong rules of enforcement, although strong, have not satisfied the criteria as a whole.

In contrast, China's credit security legal framework only satisfies the first criterion, that the creditor's remedies must be certain. Enforcement in China does not satisfy the other three requirements – that enforcement must be inexpensive and expeditious, and that the amount that the creditor is entitled to recover under the security arrangement must be clear. These are several causes of these weaknesses.

In case of debtor's default, the creditor's remedy in China is generally well defined by the Security Law, its Judicial Interpretations and the

Property Law. Both the pledgee and the mortgagee have three options: (1) conversion, which involves the creditor entering into a private agreement with the debtor, converting the security property into money, (2) to conclude a sale contract with a third party, and (3) to realise the security through auction or a competitive bidding process (with or without the assistance of the court).

Despite the rather straightforward remedies of the creditor in law, as illustrated in Chapter 7, in practice the process often proves lengthy, cumbersome and sometimes wholly ineffective. Firstly, it is not clear under Chinese law whether the mortgagee has the right to take possession of the property in case of default. If the mortgagee does not take possession, the subsequent negotiation with either the debtor or the third party on the realisation of the property may be difficult. Even if the right to take possession is stipulated in the mortgage contract, debtors often do not voluntarily deliver possession of the property to the creditor; further, it should be noted that it is not possible to appoint a receiver in China. In cases where agreement is not reached between the debtor and creditor, the creditor must resort to court action because the creditor will want to take advantage of the right to sue the debtor for any deficiency after the goods are repossessed and sold as a result of a court order. If the judicial process is involved, not only will the litigation costs be high, but the process will also be slow and cumbersome and have an unpredictable result as to the precise amount of monies entitled to be recovered by the creditor. Therefore the realisation process does not satisfy the second, third and fourth criteria. Further, the practical difficulties of issuing proceedings in the distant home court of the debtor, obtaining an order for enforcement of another court's judgment and executing the enforcement order all present considerable difficulties to the judgment creditor.

Despite these procedural problems, the Property Law adopts a progressive stance by enabling the creditor to apply for an order of foreclosure, instead of a lawsuit in the general sense.[9] The difference lies in the fact that the term 'lawsuit' implies a full civil action involving a prolonged and complex procedure, whereas the new provision provides a summary process. Implementation of this procedure is new and its effectiveness is, as yet, unknown. This is a useful reform to expedite the creditor's remedies and may reduce the cost and uncertainties of enforcement.

[9] See Chapter 7 above.

Consequently, we consider that China's credit security legal framework in respect of remedies is inefficient.

8.3 Suggestions for reform in Hong Kong and China

Although it is clear that the credit security legal frameworks of both Hong Kong and China are inefficient, they do possess some redeeming features upon which future reforms can be built. For instance, the greatest strength in China's legal framework lies in its simple and streamlined approach in defining the rules for creating and perfecting credit security. For Hong Kong, its strength lies in its expeditious and cost-effective cumulative remedies.

In considering the possible direction of future reform in Hong Kong and China, this book has considered five models in the Western economies. The models are commonly called the 'notice-filing system' of security over personal property. Some of the models are already in operation, for example the notice-filing system of Article 9 of the Uniform Commercial Code (UCC) of the United States of America,[10] the Personal Property Security Acts of the ten Canadian provinces[11] and three territories,[12] and the Personal Property Securities Act 1999 of New Zealand.[13] The proposed models are the notice-filing systems of the Australian Law Reform Commission[14] and the English Law Commission.[15] The actual notice-filing systems of the Canadian provinces and territories and New Zealand, and the proposed notice-filing systems of Australia and the United Kingdom, are all modelled on the notice-filing system of Article 9 of the UCC. These four jurisdictions have modified Article 9 to suit their domestic idiosyncrasies.

Essentially a notice-filing system contains the following features:

- There is a unitary approach to transactions secured by personal property. Expressions such as 'mortgagor and mortgagee', 'pledgor and

[10] It was introduced in 1952, and revised in July 2001. The UCC Revised Article 9 has been adopted by all states.

[11] Namely Alberta, British Columbia, Manitoba, New Brunswick, Newfoundland and Labrador, Nova Scotia, Prince Edward Island, Saskatchewan.

[12] Namely Northwest Territories, Nunavut and Yukon Territory.

[13] As amended by the Personal Property Securities Amendment Act 2000 and the Personal Property Securities Act 2001.

[14] See ALRC Report No 64, Personal Property Securities (1993) Chapter 4, 'Policy Goals and Directions for Reform', and particularly Chapter 5, 'Scope of the Regime'.

[15] That is, Consultation Paper No 164, Parts IV and VII.

pledgee', 'owner and hirer', 'lessor and lessee', 'conditional sale seller and buyer', and 'trustor and trustee' are not used. These persons are called 'debtor' and 'secured party'.[16]

- There is a functional definition of a secured transaction. Any transaction is regarded as security if, in substance, it secures the payment or performance of an obligation.
- A security is enforceable against the debtor when the security interest 'attaches' to the collateral. Basically, a security interest attaches if there is a formal agreement between the debtor and the secured party, if the secured party has given value and if the debtor has rights in the collateral.
- A security is valid and enforceable against third parties if a financing statement is filed with the relevant registry.[17] The financing statement describes the nature of the security, the assets affected, the period of the security, the debtor and the secured party, and so on.
- The general rule is that priority of competing interests is determined according to the date of filing of the financing statement.
- This is the exemption from the notice-filing requirement of certain types of secured transaction (such as the pledge and security) that arise by operation of law.
- Certain types of subsequent transaction affecting the secured assets, such as sale of consumer goods in the debtor's ordinary course of business, are free from the claim of the secured party (notwithstanding that the security is duly registered).
- The rights and remedies of the debtor and secured party are clearly defined.

After careful consideration, we adopt the recommendations contained in the English Consultation Paper No 164, Registration of Security Interests: Company Charges and Property Other than Land, as a working basis upon which to formulate suggestions for reform of the credit security legal frameworks of Hong Kong and China. There are three reasons for this. Firstly, these recommendations are, to a great extent, a synthesis of the models (actual or proposed) of the jurisdictions noted above. Secondly, the proposed notice-filing system aims to provide a simple and comprehensive credit security legal framework governing security over personal property that is user-friendly, easily accessible, cost-effective

[16] For example, see §16, Part 2 of the New Zealand Personal Property Securities Act, as amended.

[17] The exception being that the secured party has possession of the collateral.

and imbued with operational certainty. This fits well with the essential objectives of the book in respect of Hong Kong and China. Thirdly, with respect to Hong Kong only, the existing credit security laws, as discussed in Chapter 1,[18] are rooted in the English credit security laws of the nineteenth century, a large part of which continues to operate in England today. Thus it is logical and sensible to focus on the recommendations of the English Law Commission. However, some of the special strengths of other models and recommendations will also be considered in some of the suggestions offered below.

With regard to the following suggested reforms, it should be borne in mind that, owing to constraints inherent in this book (with respect to space and the parameters of the book), the suggestions are broadly based, and, owing to the civilian-based legal system in China, specific variations are proposed where appropriate.

With these caveats, our suggestions for reform are set out below.

We consider that securities granted by corporate and non-corporate debtors in Hong Kong should be governed by a common set of new credit security laws.

The uniform approach in China has shown that this practice is functional and has greatly reduced the complexity of the law. The English Consultation Paper No 164 has made the same recommendation. It stated that the 'scheme provisionally proposed for company securities should be extended to security interests created by non-corporate debtors'.[19]

We believe that in Hong Kong, the two major registration systems under the Bills of Sale Ordinance and the Companies Ordinance should be abolished and replaced with a new notice-filing system that is applicable to corporate and non-corporate debtors.[20] In China, a centralised registration system should be introduced, with the name of the entity or person granting the security being the registered entity rather than effecting registration against the property itself.

Any efficient notice filing system must embody the following features:[21]

- a central registry for registration;
- registration effected by filing a 'financing statement' with the central registry (a suggested format for such a financing statement is discussed below);

[18] See Chapter 1 above. [19] Consultation Paper No 164, para. 1.

[20] See Consultation paper No 164, Part IV: 'Notice Filing for Company Charges'.

[21] Ibid.

- allowance for the statement to be filed before[22] or after the security transaction is entered into;
- legislation clearly defining the rules relating to the priority of filed security interests, with the basic rule being that priority is determined by the date of registration of the filing, but subject to some narrow exceptions, such as 'purchase-money interests',[23] further advances granted under tacking provisions,[24] proceeds from the sale of secured assets,[25] and innocent buyer of goods for value in the ordinary course of business of the debtor[26] and without actual notice of the debtor's breach of its obligations under the security agreement;[27]
- registration and search at the central registry to be operated electronically;[28]
- the register to adopt a simple, expeditious and inexpensive system of registration and access to information; and

[22] Currently the two registration systems under the Bills of Sale Ordinance and the Companies Ordinance do not permit advance registration. This creates a problem for potential creditors. During the period it takes to negotiate and set up the security there is no way in which the creditor can ensure that the borrower will not create charges that will rank ahead of its earlier charge. See Consultation Paper No 164, para. 3.29.

[23] Basically, 'purchase-money interest' means a loan provided by another creditor to the debtor to purchase additional property where the loan is secured by that property; see Crowther Report para. 5.2.12, Diamond Report para. 11.5.9 and Consultation Paper No 164, para. 4.15.

[24] Provided further advances are agreed in the security agreement and are covered by the financing statements. See Consultation Paper No 164, para. 4.154.

[25] Provided the security extends to the proceeds and the proceeds are identifiable and traceable; see Consultation Paper No 164, paras. 4.166–4.172.

[26] Ibid., paras. 4.173–4.197, pp. 112–19. Consultation Paper No 164 appears to recommend that, except for readily identifiable assets, a subsequent bona fide buyer of goods without actual notice should take free from a floating charge and a fixed charge where the goods are purchased in the ordinary course of business of the company. This, together with the recommendation that a floating charge denies the company authority to create subsequent interests having priority (see ibid., para. 4.1.3), virtually brings an end to the floating charge. This raises the question of why, then, does the Consultation Paper recommend the retention of the floating charge in the first place? The confusion is further compounded when it is implicitly suggested that the practice of inserting an automatic crystallisation clause could continue but that such a clause should be included in the financing statement and that it would be necessary to register the activation of the provision when the floating charge is crystallised (see ibid., para. 4.1.4). Consultation Paper No 164 cannot on the one hand recommend its retention and on the other, by various designs, reduce it to insignificance in practice.

[27] For example, vehicles or goods with serial numbers which can be recorded in the financing statement. See para. 4.186 of Consultation Paper No 164.

[28] Ibid., para. 4.11.

- possible access to the main register via remote terminals, whether public or private.

In China, the current multiplicity of registration agencies should be reduced so that the person or company granting the security should be the registered entity against which a public search could be made, rather than the existing system whereby security is registered against the asset class encumbered in the place where the asset is located. This would ensure certainty and improve efficiency and the value of the security to the creditor.

In Hong Kong, the specialist registers, such as of land,[29] patents, ships, and trademarks, wherein details of ownership of, or charges over, particular assets have to be recorded, should continue to operate separately.[30]

This would avoid conflict that might arise between the new notice-filing system and the specialist registers. Charges over 'specialist' assets should not be registrable in the Central Registry.[31] However, the English Law Commission recommended that the special registry should forward appropriate information to the Companies Registry without the need for further substantial data input.[32]

The specialist registers should also operate a simple, expeditious and inexpensive system of registration and accessibility to the information.

In Hong Kong and in China, for the purpose of determining what arrangements are registrable under the new notice-filing system, the registration framework should embody the following three principles:

- a broad definition of 'security interests' should be adopted;[33]
- the expression should be defined in such a way that encompasses all arrangements which, in substance, secure the payment or performance of an obligation; and[34]
- all security interests should be made registrable unless the security interests are exempted.[35]

[29] The Land Registration Ordinance operates a separate registration system for registrable interests affecting land.

[30] Consultation Paper No 164, paras. 4.199–4.212.

[31] Ibid.

[32] Ibid., paras. 4.09–4.10.

[33] Ibid., para. 7.20.

[34] Ibid., para. 7.19. The functional approach would therefore include quasi-securities discussed in Chapter 4; and see also ibid., para. 7.76.

[35] Ibid., para. 5.123. The exemptions proposed by the Consultation Paper include charges over property for which there is a specialist asset register (i.e. ships, patents, trademarks

This suggestion is also relevant to China because the credit security legal framework does not recognise the lease with option to purchase, lease and conditional sale as credit security transactions.

Charges granted by overseas companies over property in Hong Kong should be registrable only when companies actually register their place of business in Hong Kong.

This will ensure legal certainty and facilitate commercial lending.[36] In respect of security created by overseas companies over property that is outside Hong Kong, the security should be registrable only when the property is brought into Hong Kong.[37]

The floating charge should be abolished in Hong Kong and replaced with the form of statutory floating lien as found in the Personal Property Security Acts of the Canadian provinces and territories.

Whether the floating charge in Hong Kong should be retained in a notice-filing system requires some consideration as the matter has received considerable attention in other common law jurisdictions. The floating charge has no place in Article 9 of the UCC[38] and the New Zealand Personal Property Securities Act 1999. The Canadian statutes abolished it and operate a statutory fixed charge (hereafter called 'statutory floating lien') that permits the debtor to deal with the assets in the ordinary course of its business. Under the statutes, a registered statutory floating lien takes priority from the date of registration.[39] The Australian Law Reform Commission[40] recommended that the floating charge should be retained,[41] and suggested that a registered floating charge should take priority from the date of registration. The English Consultation Paper No 164 discussed the matter at some

and copyrights); charges over shares and investment securities where the secured party has possession of the certificate or has control by being registered as owner; charges over bank accounts which are under the control of the chargee; and charges on goods and on insurance policies on goods, where the goods are abroad or at sea, or are imported goods before they are delivered to a buyer or deposited in a warehouse factory or store. Ibid. Also exempted from the proposed scheme are possessory securities such as the pledge and trust receipt. Ibid., paras. 4.15–4.17.

[36] Ibid., paras. 5.19–5.93. The uncertainty was discussed in Chapter 6 above.

[37] Consultation Paper No 164, para. 5.94.

[38] The closest analogue is a floating lien under §9-204, which is a fixed security that permits subordination.

[39] See *Canadian Imperial Bank of Commerce v Otto Timm Enterprises Ltd* (1995) 130 DLR (4th ed.) 91, a case concerned with the Personal Property Security Act of Ontario.

[40] See Report No 64, Personal Property Securities (1993), Chapter 8, para. 8.37.

[41] Ibid., para. 8.37, states, 'Their present operation should be preserved, to avoid disruption to commerce, for good reasons.'

length.[42] The Commission was clear on the following points: the floating charge should be retained, but should not allow the debtor to create a subsequent security ranking *pari passu* or having priority over the floating charge;[43] and where there is an automatic crystallisation clause in a floating charge and where a floating charge has crystallised pursuant to an automatic crystallisation clause, the secured party should be required to register that fact.[44] However, these recommendations seem to leave open the issue of whether a registered floating charge should take priority from the date of registration.

In respect of Hong Kong, the likely reasons for retaining the floating charge (discussed in Chapter 4) are that it is widely used in Hong Kong and that to abolish it might be too drastic a step for the commercial community.[45] This worry may be overstated. Hong Kong is a small jurisdiction and, besides, its economy has undergone a drastic restructuring from a manufacturing and trading-based economy to a service-based economy in which the types of tangible personal property that commonly form the subject of a floating charge might become increasingly less significant.[46] Accordingly, we suggest that the floating charge be abolished in Hong Kong and replaced with the form of statutory floating lien of the Personal Property Security Acts of the Canadian provinces and territories. However, as previously discussed in Chapter 4, it seems unlikely that our recommendation will be followed in the proposed new Hong Kong Companies Ordinance despite the obvious deficiencies in the current system of corporate security.

China is in the process of gradually introducing the concept of a charge over rotating assets into business and banking practice. The reason for this is to extend the variety of assets that can be used as security, thereby alleviating the financing constraints faced by many small and medium-sized enterprises. Given the present comparative advantages China has

42 See paras. 4.126–4.130.

43 Consultation Paper 164, paras. 4.135–4.136, offers two alternatives. The first is what has been stated in the text above. The other is 'simply that a floating charge does not give the company the authority to create subsequent interests having priority to the floating charge'. The reasons for this book's adoption of the first alternative is that the second alternative will result in no difference between a floating charge and a fixed charge in practice.

44 Consultation Paper No 164, paras. 4.143–4.144.

45 This also was noted in England; see Consultation Paper No 164, para. 4.127; and in Australia see ALRC Report 64, para. 8.37.

46 See Hong Kong Chief Executive's Policy Address (2003), para. 1.7, 'Enhancing core industries'. The core industries are financial services, logistics, tourism and producer services.

in an export-oriented manufacturing economy, and that China has a *de facto* notice-filing system for mortgages, reform of the existing arrangements is unnecessary. The Chinese system needs to expand the asset base that is capable of being offered as security so as to promote the grant of low-cost secured loans by banks especially to small and medium-sized enterprises, so promoting further economic development.

Should our proposal as regards Hong Kong not be adopted, and if the floating charge is preserved, the financing statement should clearly state whether the charge is fixed or floating (or both),[47] and the recommendations of Consultation Paper No 164 should be adopted in relation to the position of the floating charge under the proposed notice-filing system.

The English Law Commission appears to suggest that whether a charge is fixed or floating should be left to the determination of the court.[48] The Australian Report No 64 also appears to adopt this view. We respectfully disagree as this would only perpetuate legal uncertainty and increase the burden of the courts, while achieving nothing in relation to the predictability of the identification of whether a charge is fixed or floating. Rather, it is proposed that the nature of the charge as described in the financing statement (and as recorded in the register) should be deemed to be that which was intended by the parties. This would remove the uncertainty and difficulty that revolves around the question of the designation of fixed and floating charges. This position draws support from the concept in the United States of 'estoppel',[49] which estops the secured party from denying the accuracy of the financing statement in relation to the extent of the coverage of the security.[50]

We further suggest that in Hong Kong, non-corporate bodies should be permitted to create both fixed and floating charges (or a 'floating lien' as suggested above) in the same way that companies are permitted to do.[51] China already adopts this position.

To simplify the charge registration system, the private registers at the registered offices of companies in Hong Kong should be abolished if the list of registrable securities, as proposed above, is widened.

[47] See Consultation Paper No 164, para. 4.142.

[48] See Consultation paper No 164, para. 4.140.

[49] UCC Revised Article 9, §9-338.

[50] Consultation Paper No 164, paras. 4.44–4.46. Indeed, para. 4.44 raised the question whether this concept should be adopted in the proposed notice-filing system.

[51] Consultation Paper No 164, para. 9.13, states, 'The law of security should be neutral between business forms.' Although it was not expressly stated that the Bills of Sale Act should be repealed, the recommendations contained in the paper necessarily mean the end of the Act.

Continuation of the records kept privately by the companies will not serve any useful purpose.[52] This suggestion is supported by current practice in China, which does not require any registration in the company's private records. This arrangement has not prejudiced third parties dealing with companies in China.

Subject to the exceptions suggested below, the quasi-security devices of hire-purchase, leasing and conditional sale in Hong Kong should continue to operate and enjoy priority over earlier securities. However, these arrangements should be regarded as 'securities' under the broad definition of 'security interests' and should be registrable under the new notice-filing system.[53]

This suggestion applies equally to the lease with option to purchase, lease and conditional sale in China.

Trust receipts in Hong Kong and China should be made registrable under the notice-filing system if, after fifteen days, the debtor continues to have possession of the goods.[54]

A trust receipt would be imperfect if it is not so registered. However, a registered trust receipt should not be enforceable against a subsequent bona fide purchaser of goods in the ordinary course of business of the debtor, except by a subsequent security provider who is expected to enquire at the relevant registry. This exception is in line with our proposals set out below.

In light of the above suggestions, an ideal financing statement in Hong Kong should contain the following information:[55]

- the names and addresses of the parties, including the companies' registration numbers if the parties are corporations;
- a general description of the type of property subject to the security, including, where appropriate, an indication that its proceeds are also subject to the security;
- an indication of the period of validity of the security agreement;
- an indication of whether the charge is fixed or floating (or both);
- an indication of whether the charge also secures after-acquired and future property;

[52] Indeed this was discussed above in Chapter 4, and in note 312 of that chapter, which showed that creditors in Hong Kong do not search the private register.

[53] See Consultation Paper No 164, para. 7.22.

[54] See the criticisms in Chapter 2 above.

[55] They are substantially based on the recommendation contained in Consultation Paper No 164, para. 421, and the general views expressed in Part IV, 'Notice-Filing for Company Charges'.

- an indication of whether future advances can be tacked on to the charge;[56]
- where applicable, any unique serial number identifying the secured asset; and
- confirmation that the chargor's interest in the property is charged.

It is proposed that this formulation is also appropriate for China to adopt, subject to such necessary modification as is necessary to meet local conditions. This would make the information filed with the relevant registration agency more easily comprehensible, remove the need to file original documents (which can be voluminous), and so improve administrative efficiency.

In Hong Kong, the principle that the certificate of registration issued by the Registrar of Companies is conclusive that the requirements as to registration have been satisfied should be abolished.

Under the proposed new notice-filing system, particulars of the financing statement can be challenged, but errors or omissions should not be allowed to invalidate the filing. However, the secured creditor could be estopped in relation to 'seriously misleading' information;[57] that is, the secured creditor cannot claim a greater security interest than it has indicated in the financing statement.[58] In addition, the secured creditor should be liable for any loss or damage suffered by another person who has relied on inaccurate information.[59] From the conclusion reached on this issue by the Hong Kong Financial Services and Treasury Bureau in 2008, this reform will be incorporated in the proposed new Companies Ordinance, although, as previously mentioned, a comprehensive notice-filing system will not be adopted.

The doctrine of constructive notice in Hong Kong and China should be abolished except in very special circumstances. Subsequent 'innocent' buyers (not a security provider) of consumer goods and goods acquired in the ordinary course of the business of the creditor should take free from any prior security interests (fixed or floating), except where the subsequent purchaser has actual knowledge of the charge or where the goods are uniquely identifiable.[60]

[56] Consultation Paper No 164, para. 4.154.

[57] Ibid., para. 4.40.

[58] Ibid., para. 4.44. The Consultation Paper expressed the view that the absence of a conclusive certificate is unlikely to deter lenders as it would not expose the lender to any greater risk than is now the case under the present conclusive certificate; see para. 4.50.

[59] Ibid.

[60] Ibid., see para. 4.186. For example, motor vehicles and goods which have a serial number and are easily identifiable.

This recommendation is made to ensure the free flow of trade and commerce. The uniquely identifiable exception, which would safeguard finance companies against the potential risk of losing their security in motor vehicles, are quasi-security interests under the hire-purchase, leasing and conditional sale arrangements to a subsequent consumer purchaser. This provision is different to the position in England,[61] where a separate complex statutory system governs the rights of subsequent purchasers.[62] Our proposal would be easier to implement in Hong Kong and China where, at present, quasi-securities are unregulated. Indeed, the proposed new notice-filing system and exception would afford greater protection to third parties dealing with the debtor, particularly in Hong Kong.[63]

We recommend that the doctrine of constructive notice should apply if the subsequent purchaser is a commercial credit provider as it has the resources, finance and knowledge to conduct the appropriate inquiry. Without this limitation, the proposed notice-filing system would work against the creditor to a significant degree. It must be remembered that one of the criteria of an efficient credit security legal framework is that it must, as far as possible, balance the interests of three parties: the creditor, debtor and any third party.

The doctrine of constructive notice should also apply to registered securities in respect of receivables. The English Law Commission recommended that all subsequent purchasers acquiring receivables should be expected to check the register and be bound by earlier charges.[64]

Consequently, we therefore propose that an unregistered (but registrable) security should be void against a subsequent purchaser unless the purchaser had actual knowledge of the security.

This suggestion reaffirms the rule in common law (but not the general law of China) that a person should not be allowed to take advantage of the technical error of another of which it has actual knowledge. In China, actual knowledge is not a bar to taking encumbered property free of the mortgage where it has not been registered correctly. On the other hand, a subsequent purchaser of receivables represented by a negotiable instrument takes free from a registered security if the subsequent purchaser

61 The problem is discussed in some length in Consultation Paper No 164, paras. 7.55–7.66.

62 Namely the Consumer Credit Act 1974 and the Hire Purchase Act 1964.

63 See Chapter 5 above, where an innocent third-party purchaser of a motor vehicle under a hire-purchase agreement was held subject to the claim of the finance company although the debtor possessed the registration book etc.

64 Consultation Paper No 164, para. 4.190.

takes possession of the negotiable instruments. Commercial transactions would be hampered if this were not the case.[65]

The transformation rules of converting personal chattels supplied under hire-purchase, leasing or conditional sale[66] to fixtures, which favours the mortgagee of land in Hong Kong and China, should be abolished.[67]

It is recommended that the creditor of goods who believes that the goods have become fixtures should register the security interest in the fixture with the Land Registry in Hong Kong or the relevant land registration department in China.[68] Broadly, a subsequent mortgagee of the land will take free from the interest in the land unless the interest in the fixture is registered. However, to be consistent with our other proposals, a subsequent mortgagee should take free from the interest in the fixture if the goods are consumer goods, even if the interest is registered – provided it has no actual notice of the debtor's breach of its obligation.

The law should provide that the creditor should account for the surplus and clearly define the rights and duties in respect of the surplus,[69] and define a mechanism that enables a fair and just calculation of the amount that the creditor is entitled to recover from the debtor (for this purpose, no distinction is made between lawful and unlawful termination of quasi-security contracts).

As was seen in Chapter 5, in Hong Kong, there are two major problems with quasi-security – the creditor is generally not accountable to the debtor for any surplus, and there is uncertainty regarding the amount that the creditor is entitled to recover. The latter is prevalent in hire-purchase and leasing.

This proposal will also help to define the amount of deficiency,[70] if any, to which the debtor would be liable.

[65] Ibid., para. 4.95.

[66] The Consultation Paper raised the question whether persons acquiring ownership or possession of goods in the ordinary course under a hire purchase agreement, lease and conditional sale should take free from the owner's security interest. This book has reservations on this, as it may greatly prejudice the supplier, as many of the goods supplied may not be uniquely identifiable except for vehicles and industrial machinery.

[67] Consultation Paper No 164, paras. B70–B72, made this point and referred to the Uniform Commercial Code and Saskatchewan Personal Property Security Act 1993, but did not appear to recommend any rules of conversion for adoption. The New Zealand Personal Property Security Act (1999) does not contain adequate protection for the suppliers of fixtures. See S. Baas, 'Fixtures under the Personal Property Securities Act: What New Zealand Doesn't Know It's Missing', NZULR19 (2001), 403.

[68] See Australian Law Reform Commission, Personal Property Security, para. 5.45; and see also Article 9-334 of the Uniform Commercial Code of the United States.

[69] Consultation Paper No 164, paras. B47–B50. [70] Ibid.

In the case of retention of title, if the security interests in goods have lost their identity in a final product or mass, the security interest should continue in the product or mass. The priority of the security interest should be limited to the value of the goods on the day on which the goods became part of the product or mass.[71] If there is more than one continuing security interest, each security interest should be entitled to share in the product or mass according to the ratio of their respective values.[72]

These suggestions should also apply to China, in the event that the lease with option to purchase, lease and conditional sale are treated as security transactions.

Purchase-money security interests (PMSIs)[73] should, as a general rule, have priority over other earlier or subsequent non-PMSIs in Hong Kong and China.

In implementing this recommendation, as in the United States[74] and New Zealand,[75] special exceptions (such as inventory and non-inventory goods) must be made in order to strike a balance between competing interests in PMSI assets.

Any codified law in Hong Kong and new legislation in China should include provisions that all registrable credit security that has attached to the collateral is always valid against the debtor.[76]

In Hong Kong, this will resolve the anomaly between the Bills of Sale Ordinance and the Companies Ordinance (see above). In China, it will clarify the rights and obligations between the parties.

In Hong Kong, the rules governing security over personal property should be clarified, streamlined and codified, particularly the rules relating to creation, perfection, publicity and enforcement of the security.[77]

[71] See New Zealand Personal Property Security Act (1999), §82. [72] Ibid., §84.

[73] Basically it means 'a security interest taken in collateral by a seller to the extent that it secures the obligation to pay all or part of the collateral's purchase price'; see §16, Personal Property Securities Act of New Zealand.

[74] For example, a PMSI in collateral other than an inventory takes priority over a conflicting security interest if the PMSI is perfected at the time the debtor receives the collateral or within ten days of the buyer's receiving it; see UCC Article 9-312(4).

[75] See §73 of the Personal Property Security Act, basically the same as Article 9 of the UCC.

[76] Basically, this means that the security becomes enforceable against the debtor when value is given, that the debtor has rights to the assets and that the rules governing creation are complied with. See Consultation Paper No 164, para. 11.21.

[77] This was one of the major recommendations made by Consultation Paper No 164, Part XI, 'Restating the Law of Security', para. 11.40, and Appendix B, 'A Restatement of the Law of Security'.

In general, the same rules should apply to traditional security (both legal and equitable) and quasi-security interests.[78]

This will make the law more comprehensible and user-friendly. However, based on the experience of China, codified law can become outdated quite quickly. Thus any future codified law in Hong Kong might have to be monitored and revised to take into account rapidly evolving commercial practices. Of course, similar considerations also apply to China.

The proposed Hong Kong codification implies that, in all credit security arrangements, the following should appear in writing: (i) the power to take possession, (ii) the power of sale and (iii) the power to appoint a receiver.

Although it was observed in Chapter 7[79] that the power to appoint a receiver was slow and expensive, it should be retained because it is useful in some cases, particularly if the security over personal property is part of a larger corporate security lending arrangement.

In China, a computerised, centralised notice-filing system against the personal or corporate name of the debtor should replace the current system of multiple registration agencies based on the nature of property.

The proposed centralised notice-filing system should integrate the existing registrations at provincial and municipal level into a national database. This would significantly resolve the current problems of poor accessibility of information and administrative cost.

In China, any new legislation should include the right of a secured creditor to appoint a receiver, and to stipulate the rights of the receiver.

The concept of the receiver is currently unknown in China, but receivership constitutes a useful remedy for secured creditors in that it not only ensures efficient preservation of secured assets and minimises the risks associated with a debtor's or corporate management's misconduct, but also reduces the burden on the courts, which could in turn reduce lengthy and costly judicial processes.

In China, at present the 'floating' Diya mortgage security device is only available to 'enterprises, individual industrial and commercial households or agricultural production operators', and the type of asset that can be subject to this security includes only 'manufacturing facilities, raw materials, semi-manufactured goods and products, present and future'.[80] In the future, China should consider extending the eligibility of the parties

[78] Consultation Paper No 164, para. 11.40. [79] See Chapter 7 above.
[80] See Chapter 2 above.

capable of creating 'floating' Diya mortgages to individuals, and the type of chargeable assets to include other property (such as book debts[81]).

It must be noted that currently individuals are excluded from being able to create a 'floating' Diya mortgage because of the undeveloped nature of the personal credit and security system in China. At present there is no personal bankruptcy law in China, there are no databases on consumer creditworthiness, and information in relation to enterprise credit and government credit is both rudimentary and problematic. To precipitately allow individuals to create floating securities (in the common law sense) over their present and future property would be too drastic a change and may impose unnecessary risks on creditors. Therefore we consider this a proposal that might be considered in the medium term, once the necessary credit infrastructure has been established.

There must also be reform of the judicial infrastructure of China to make it more effective and efficient. Without this reform, improvements in the substantive law and relevant procedures will be futile. Clearly, this would be a very substantial change and progress has to date been limited.

8.4 Conclusion

The book concludes that its radical suggestions for reform in Hong Kong and China, if adopted, would create a more rational, effective and comprehensible legal framework governing credit security over personal property in both jurisdictions. Such reforms would ensure that Hong Kong remains the pre-eminent regional commercial centre for decades to come and would allow Hong Kong to keep pace with the rapid economic and legal reforms, including credit security laws,[82] of its immediate

[81] Though currently the book debt is not allowed to be created as a floating charge by way of mortgage under Article 181 of Property Law, Chinese law seems to allow the pledge of rights over present and future book debt. This position can be shown from the user guidelines promulgated by the People's Bank of China in its Credit Reference Centre (a nationwide, internet-based bulletin system for the sole purpose of registration and publicity of accounts receivable), of which it is provided that the pledgor can choose to describe the pledged book debt in either a specific, a stylistic or a broad manner.

[82] In 1995, the National People's Congress enacted its first national Security Law, which came into force on 1 October 1995. Under the Act, five types of security interest can be created, namely guarantee, mortgage of real property and certain movable property, pledge of movable property or rights, lien, and deposit. See V. Bath, 'Taking Security in Asia – China', ABLR 18 (1997), 32 at p. 34. In 2007, the newly promulgated Property

neighbour, mainland China. For China itself, the proposed reforms of the credit security system are relatively modest save for the reorganisation of the registration administrative system and the urgent need to strengthen the judicial system more generally. China has the advantage that its substantive credit security laws are embryonic, and so change is somewhat easier to achieve than in Hong Kong, where the long-established, but substantially compromised, system will be much harder to reform. This is especially so given the conservatism and complacency exhibited by the Financial Services and Treasury Bureau's recent pronouncements on company charges in Hong Kong.

Lawyers and businesspeople in Hong Kong will find such a framework efficient and user-friendly. For foreign businesses, such a system will have the added advantage of being familiar to many of them.[83]

With regard to China, the reforms suggested would significantly modernise and strengthen its current credit security legal framework, and this would undoubtedly enhance the flow of capital to small and medium-sized enterprises and so enhance the development of its private commercial sector, which is an essential and dynamic part of China's ongoing economic transformation.

Law provided a more sophisticated legal framework for security interests over personal property.

83 The major trading partners of Hong Kong include the United States, Canada, the United Kingdom, Europe and Australia (see www.cedb.gov.hk/citb/ehtml/home.html), some which will already have a notice-filing system in operation or may have one in operation in the near future.

INDEX